Theory of Computation

K. R. Chowdhary

Theory of Computation

Automata, Formal Languages, Computation and Complexity

Springer

K. R. Chowdhary
Department of Computer Science
JNV University
Jodhpur, Rajasthan, India

ISBN 978-981-97-6236-1 ISBN 978-981-97-6234-7 (eBook)
https://doi.org/10.1007/978-981-97-6234-7

This Springer imprint is published by the registered company Springer Nature Singapore Pte Ltd.
The registered company address is: 152 Beach Road, #21-01/04 Gateway East, Singapore 189721, Singapore

To my wife
Suman
and children
Gudia, Chutku, Ranjan

Preface

Computer science[1] is a field of science as well as engineering, with many areas, like—data structures, operating systems, networking, artificial intelligence, and computer languages. The subject of theory of computation (TOC) attempts to establish a theory to account for all these domains. In contrast to the technical and applied areas of computer science, theoretical computer science is strongly aimed at fundamental questions about the existence of algorithmic solutions, physical limits of computing, and methodologies of algorithm design.

Let us first attempt to answer the question—"What is computer science?" Usually, it is difficult to provide an exact and complete definition of a scientific discipline. A commonly accepted definition is: computer science is the science of algorithmic processing, representation, storage and transmission of information. This definition presents information and algorithm as the main objects that are investigated in computer science.

Second question regarding the substance of computer science (CS) is—to which scientific discipline does computer science belong? The answer is that CS cannot be uniquely assumed to belong to any discipline. The CS includes aspects of mathematics, and natural sciences as well as Engineering. Similar to philosophy and mathematics, computer science investigates general categories such as: determinism,[2] non-determinism[3] randomness, information, truth, untruth, complexity of solution,[4]

[1] Prior to immersing yourself in the contents of this book, it is strongly advised to read the preface. Doing so will provide you with a comprehensive overview of the course and facilitate a more organized approach to your study. This initial step not only enhances your overall understanding but also contributes to time-saving efficiencies throughout your learning journey.

[2] Deterministic finite automata (FA), deterministic Pushdown Automata (PDA), deterministic Turing Machine (TM).

[3] (Nondeterministic—FA, PDA, TM).

[4] Complexity theory.

languages,[5] proofs, communication, approximation, algorithms,[6] simulations,[7] etc., and the attributes to the understanding of these categories.

The study of the subject of theory of computation provides an insight into the characteristics of computations in these categories. Such insight can be aimed to: (i) predict the complexity of desired computations, (ii) choosing the appropriate approach to solution, and (iii) developing tools that facilitate the design of computation. Study of computations can reveal that there are problems that cannot be solved, as well as that there are problems which require arbitrarily large amount of time, say millions of years, and may require infinitely large memory. These revelations, though sound unfriendly, can act as useful warnings against such problems.

Significance of Theory

Every theory increases our understanding of the subject and systematizes our knowledge about the subject. Theory also leads to advancement of practicals, which is the second advantage, and is of immediate use to us.

The theory of computation, which we will study, will be of immediate use in writing of programs, to construct compilers, assemblers, operating systems, etc., as well as understanding of existing high-level languages and construction of new languages.

These theories are more of intuitive, logical, and abstract, but have strong relations with physical computers, and are deciding factors for the type of computers.

A computer scientist has an intuitive grasp of notion of computable in the form of an *algorithm* or *program.* To be precise, for a computer scientist, the most obvious way to define something as computable is to represent it in the form of an algorithm or a program written in a typical programming language. Such a suggestion is not valid for a *meta-computer scientist*[8] because for that the solution should be sufficiently simple so that it can be verified with the help of mathematical proofs.

Background and Motivation

I taught this course of Theory of Computation at M B M. Engineering College to Bachelor of Engineering (BE) students majoring in Computer Science & Engineering (CSE), and to Information Technology (IT), for the academic years 2001–2013. Additionally, I taught the same course at the Indian Institute of Technology, Jodhpur

[5] Regular, Context-free, context-sensitive, and unrestricted languages.

[6] Turing machine.

[7] of TMs.

[8] Meta: Knowledge about some knowledge.

(IITJ), during the sessions 2010–12 and 2015–17, to B.Tech. CSE, and at JIET (Jodhpur Institute of Engineering & Technology) to B.Tech. CSE during 2018–2020.

Furthermore, I delivered an advanced course on the Theory of Formal Languages to Master of Engineering (ME) students in CSE at M B M Engineering College from 2005 to 2022. Since the course of TOC was taught in parallel to two or sometimes to three different classes having different levels, effectively, if considered sequentially, it was taught for almost 30 years.

Over the years, while teaching this course I improved over my class notes, exercises, and the solutions, and typeset all these in latex. During these years, I felt the need for a book that connects the theory of computation intimately to various CS courses taught at undergraduate and masters that should provide thorough guidance to students, be self-taught mostly, and should provide codes for theoretical models of computation, like Finite Automata, Pushdown Automata, etc.

The feeling of the need of such a book motivated me to reorganize my class notes, type set them properly, and present in the form of a book, and this book is the end result of that.

The Scope, Organization, and Approach

The objective of this course is twofold: to introduce CS students to the rich heritage of models and abstractions that have arisen over the years; and to develop the capacity to form abstractions of their own and reason in terms of them.

The book is essential in the present perspective, as computer science and computing has emerged as vast field, therefore, there is need of course that unifies it, in respect of hardware of machine that computes, languages that code problems, implementation of languages, nature of structures in languages, what are the nature of problems one can solve on computers and what cannot be.

The topics covered in this book have been organized in six parts:

- Preliminaries (one chapter).
- Finite Automata and Regular Languages (four chapters).
- Context-Free Grammars, Languages, and Pushdown Automata (three chapters).
- Turing Computations and Chomsky Hierarchy (three chapters).
- Decidability and Undecidability (one chapter).
- Complexity of Computations (two chapters).

The course explains the CS theory in a compact form and is theory about: algorithms, data structures, speech processing, compilers, translators, high languages, natural language processing, computation, complexity of computation, computer architecture, parallel processing, computer networks, solvability and unsolvability, problem reductions, information security and encryption. Hence, the course of Theory of Computer should preferably be taught before these courses.

In addition to the lectures, I have included at every chapter end, the self-review questions, categorized exercises—concept-based, analysis-based, proof-based, multiple-choice-based (MCQ), and advanced knowledge assessment for homework. Solving these by the student, either by way of teacher's assignment or by self-assignment are aimed to provide in depth understanding of this course. Some of the exercises come with hints and solutions—those with solutions are annotated with stars.

The text employs straightforward English, offering logical explanations and self-contained content. To enhance students' comprehension of computing models, such as Finite Automata and Pushdown Automata, the inclusion of program codes is a notable feature. Demonstrations of language acceptability are provided through the execution of these codes, allowing students to grasp the practical workings of the concepts.

The Target Audience

A keen learner having knowledge of high school level mathematics and basic computer science will be able to grasp most of this material. The content places a strong emphasis on intuitive concepts and logical reasoning.

Nevertheless, a foundational grasp of courses such as computer architecture, data structures and algorithms, discrete mathematical structures, and proficiency in a programming language like C will significantly enhance the learning experience.

This course is tailored for undergraduate programs, including BE (Bachelor of Engineering)/B.Tech. (Bachelor of Technology) majoring in Computer Science & Engineering (CSE), Artificial Intelligence, Machine Learning, and Data Science. Certain sections, such as Parsers (if Compiler is covered separately) and specific parts of the chapter on Decidability, Undecidability, and Unsolvability, may be skipped for these majors.

Furthermore, the book is highly recommended for individuals who have completed a Bachelor's program in a non-CS major and are currently pursuing M.Tech. (Master of Technology)/M.Eng. (Master of Engineering)/MS/M.Sc. (Master of Science) majoring in Computer Science/CSE, M.Sc. in Mathematics, and M.Sc. in IT. It also serves as a valuable resource for practitioners, professionals, and scientists in the fields of Computer Science and Information Technology.

Jodhpur, India K. R. Chowdhary

Acknowledgments

I express my heartfelt appreciation to the esteemed institutions listed below, where I had the privilege of teaching the Theory of Computation course and where this manuscript took its shape:

- M B M Engineering College, where I served as Associate Professor and later as Professor. I delivered this course to BE (Bachelor of Engineering) majoring in CSE (Computer Science & Engineering) and BE (Information Technology) students, and the Theory of Formal Languages course to Master of Engineering in CSE,
- Indian Institute of Technology, Jodhpur (IITJ), which provided me the opportunity to impart this course to their B.Tech. program in CSE,
- Jodhpur Institute of Engineering and Technology (JIET), where I served as Professor/Director. Here, I had the privilege of teaching this course to B.Tech. (CSE) students.

This diverse teaching experience exposed me to a wide demographic of students, each with varying levels of intellectual competence and language proficiency. It presented a unique opportunity to tailor the teaching material to cater to the diverse needs of such a varied student body—a fundamental purpose that any educational book aspires to achieve.

I extend my deep gratitude to the former heads of the CSE department at IITJ, Prof. Gaurav Harit and Prof. Venkat Raman Badarla, for offering me the opportunity to teach the Theory of Computation course at IITJ. The substantial part of this book took shape during my teaching this course for four academic sessions from 2010 to 2017.

I am sincerely thankful to all my students of Theory of Computation from MBM, IITJ, and JIET. Special mentions go to Archit Agarwal, Arnav Jindal, Sonu Mehta, Ashish Kumar, Pratibha Choudhary, Anupama Bhati, Kiran Yadav and the many others who enriched the learning experience through thoughtful and engaging questions.

I owe an immeasurable debt of gratitude to my wife, Suman, for her unwavering love, support, and remarkable patience, especially during the final stages of this project. My love extends to our children—Gudia, Chutku, and Ranjan.

My heartfelt thanks also go to my teachers, colleagues, and friends who have played a pivotal role in shaping my academic and research journey. I express my profound gratitude to the late Prof. Alam Singh and Prof. V. S. Bansal for their steadfast support and inspiration.

I extend my gratitude to the anonymous reviewers whose insightful feedback contributed to the approval of this manuscript. Additionally, would also like to acknowledge Swati Meherishi, Divya Meiyazhagan, Ritika Manhas, and the entire team at Springer Nature, New Delhi, for their prompt handling of my queries and invaluable assistance throughout the publication process.

I welcome suggestions and criticisms from readers, and encourage them to reach out to me via email at kr.chowdhary@acm.org. Your insights are invaluable and greatly appreciated.

Jodhpur, India
November 2023

Prof. Dr. K. R. Chowdhary

Contents

About the Author

Prof. K. R. Chowdhary currently teaches at JNV University, Jodhpur. He received his Bachelor's degree in Electronics & Communication Engineering with Honors division and later his Ph.D. from the same institution, in the area of Natural Language Processing.

His career has traversed diverse landscapes, encompassing pivotal roles in both research and education. His professional trajectory includes contributions in Research & Developments at Bhabha Atomic Research Centre in Mumbai and imparting knowledge and expertise as a faculty member at the IIT Jodhpur. The major part of his career was spent as Associate Professor and then Professor at MBM Engineering College, Faculty of Engineering in JNV University, in the Department of Computer Science & Engineering, where he was responsible for curricula development at undergraduate and post graduate courses of CS.

He served as Head (Chair) of the Department of CS for over ten years, and was responsible for academic and infrastructural development in this department. He also held the position of Director at Jodhpur Institute of Engineering & Technology (JIET) during 2014–2020, where apart from the academic management, he was responsible for curriculum development for B.Tech. undergraduate courses of AI and Data Science.

Professor Chowdhary is Senior Member of IEEE and ACM, and Fellow of Institution of Engineers (India), and Featured Reviewer of Computing Reviews. He has authored the book of Fundamentals of Artificial Intelligence, published by Springer Nature, New Delhi, and Fundamentals of Discrete Mathematical Structures, published by PHI (India).

His research interests encompass a wide spectrum of topics, including automata theory, formal languages, complexity theory, distributed processing, artificial intelligence, machine learning, natural language, and speech processing.

Acronyms

2DFA	Two-Way DFA
AT	Automata Theory
CFG	Context-Free Grammar
CFL	Context-Free Language
CNF	Chomsky Normal Form
COMPOSITS	Class of All the Composite Numbers
CPU	Central Processing Unit
CS	Computer Science
CSL	Context-Sensitive Language
CSP	Constraint Satisfaction Problem
CTT	Church-Turing Thesis
DCFG	Deterministic CFG
DCFL	Deterministic Context-Free Language
DFA	Deterministic Finite Automata
DPDA	Deterministic Pushdown Automata
DSPACE	Class of Languages Decided by Space Bounded Deterministic TM
DTIME	Computation Time for Deterministic TM
DTM	Deterministic Turing Machine
EXP	Deterministic Exponential Complexity Class
FA	Finite Automata
GNF	Greibach Normal Form
GNFA	Generalized NFA
IA	Inherently Ambiguous
iff	if and only if
IPG	Incremental Parser Generator
L	Deterministic log space class
LALR	Look-Ahead LR
LBA	Linear-bounded Automata
LL	Left-to-Right, Leftmost Derivation
LL(k)	Left-to-Right Leftmost Derivation, k-Symbols Look-Ahead
LR	Left-to-Right, Rightmost Derivation

LR(k)	Left-to-Right, Rightmost Derivation, k-Symbols Look-Ahead
MN	Myhill-Nerode Theorem
NDCFL	Nondeterministic Context-Free Language
NDTM	Nondeterministic Turing Machine
NEXP	Nondeterministic Exponential Complexity Class
NFA	Nondeterministic Finite Automata
NL	Nondeterministic Log Space Class
NP	Nondeterministic Polynomial Time Complexity
NPC	NP-Complete Problem
NPDA	Nondeterministic Pushdown Automata
NP-Hard	NP-Hard Problem
NSPACE	Class of Languages Decided in Polynomial Space by Nondeterministic TM
NTIME	Computation Time for Nondeterministic TM
NTM	Nondeterministic Turing Machine
OP	Operator Precedence
P	Polynomial Time Complexity
PC	Program Counter
PDA	Pushdown Automata
PRIMES	Class of All the Prime Numbers
PSPACE	Class of Languages Decided in Polynomial Space by Deterministic TM
RAM	Random Access Machine
RASP	Random Access Stored Program
Regex	Regular Expression
RHS	Right Hand Side
RISC	Reduced Instruction Set Computing
SAT	Satisfiability Problem
TM	Turing Machine
WFF	Well-Formed Formula
Yacc	Yet Another Compiler Compiler

List of Figures

List of Tables

List of Algorithms

Part I
Preliminaries

Chap. 1 introduces with essential mathematics topics as prerequisite for theory of automata, formal languages, computation, and complexity. The topics are presented with logical dependence and have been kept brief and simple, such that the reader feels excited to venture into the actual contents of theory presented in the remaining chapters.

If you already have a background in discrete mathematical structures, you may choose to skip Chap. 1. However, it's worth noting that there are specific topics covered here that aren't typically included in a discrete mathematics course. Thus, a review of Chap. 1 may still prove valuable.

When teaching this course, you can integrate the material from Chap. 1 as you move through the relevant chapters (Chaps. 2–14). For example, topics like Russell's Paradox and Cantor's diagonal argument can be introduced just before delving into the chapters on undecidability and unsolvability. Similarly, discussions on set theory and string operations can be incorporated before Chap. 2, and so forth.

The chapter begins by outlining the learning objectives, providing a clear overview of what you'll gain from the topics covered within it. It concludes with a summary, self-review questions, and categorized exercises, including concept-based, analysis-based, proof-based, and advanced knowledge assessment problems. Special attention is given to problems marked with a star (*), as their solutions are provided in the end part of this book.

Chapter 1
Mathematical Preliminaries

Abstract The course of Automata, formal languages, computation and complexity is backbone of computer science; the mathematical preliminaries are the essential base and prerequisite for understanding of this course. This first chapter covers: Set operations, countable and uncountable sets, types of proofs, concept of solvability and unsolvability, computable and non-computable functions. Considering that many problems in computer science can be transformed into graphs—the platform from which solution can be more easily obtained using the graph algorithms, the chapter provides the coverage to essential part of graph theory. There is an analogy between models of computing machines and algebraic systems, and operations in algebra are isomorphic to those in these models, this has motivated to cover algebraic system in this chapter. Knowing that closure operation on strings is analogous to operations on languages, the operations on strings are presented, as well as the countable and uncountable languages. The chapter ends with self-review questions, followed with large number of classified exercises, and the references.

Keywords Sets · Set operations · Proof · Relation · Function · Graph theory · Group · Semigroup · Homomorphism · Isomorphism · Strings · Languages · Languages representation · Languages operation · Countable languages · Uncountable languages · Languages representation · Graph theory · Directed and undirected graphs

1.1 Introduction

Any *scientific theory* is primarily concerned with representing the real-world entities in the form of abstract mathematics. The representation should facilitate the discovery of mathematical relationships in the form of equations or laws. For example, in the case of classical dynamics, the real-world entities include the distance, speed, force, and acceleration. The distance is usually represented as a function of time, and speed as derivative of distance function. The basic mathematical relations governing them are Newton's laws of motion, and the laws of gravitation.

K. R. Chowdhary, *Theory of Computation*,
https://doi.org/10.1007/978-981-97-6234-7_1

To each theory, there is corresponding *meta-theory*, which is concerned with analyzing theory itself, i.e., precisely defining the concepts used in the theory and in discovering the limitations of the theory. The meta-theory for the theory of computer science is *mathematics*, which formalizes the notion of sets, proofs, and theorems, and attempt to discover their limitations. Typically, a theory is concerned with establishing useful positive results, whereas the meta-theory consists largely of results often of a negative nature, which define and delimit the subject matter of the theory.

Two major goals of meta-computer science are

1. To define the term computable precisely.
2. Given such a definition, to discover what (if any) are the theoretical limitations of computability, thus delimiting the subject matter and scope of the computer science.

Our theory of computation is divided into three parts: 1. the theory of automata, which is concerned with very elementary machines, that are capable to say only Yes/No, and accept the languages, called *regular languages*; 2. theory of Formal languages, which is concerned with computer languages, and human languages and their grammars and the machines which recognize these languages; and 3. theory of computation, the last theory, is about how to model the computations, analyze their difficulty levels (complexity), and memory requirements for these languages for carrying out the computations.

The set theory is foundation of this subject, because the computer languages are nothing but infinitely large number of statements, made of symbols from the alphabet of the corresponding language, with proper syntax. We can join the sentences to build complex sentences (concatenation), and join two languages to build union of these, complement of a language is set of all the sentences that are not in that language, and so on. These and other operation on the languages we represent using sets. Like, sets, the languages can be finite (say, possible set of instructions to ATM—the automated teller machine) or infinite (e.g., the language whose words are all prime numbers).

This chapter presents the essential mathematics needed for understanding the remaining chapters of this book. In the following discussion, we shall try to relate that mathematics with some of the topics covered in the remaining chapters of this book.

Like in Sets, mapping of *data* and *operations* can be done from one system to other, for example, we can map every positive integer x to $\log x$ using the functional operation of logarithm, we can map a high-level language statement to a sequence of assembly language statements through the device, called compiler, thus compiler can be treated as a function, and so on.

Because various domain knowledge of computer science can be represented using mathematics, and there are statements which are true always, the mathematical proofs of these statements can be carried out using proof methods, called contradiction, induction, and deduction.

The sets can be finite (say alphabet of a language) or infinite, e.g., the set of all natural numbers ($\mathbb{N}$).[1] But, the set of all real numbers ($\mathbb{R}$) is also infinite. The infinite set $\mathbb{N}$ is countable, while of $\mathbb{R}$ is not, since in the latter there is no concept of next x, for x as real number. These two infinite sets are useful in proving many theorems in our this subject, including the proof of unsolvability. Similarly, if any problem which can be mapped to Russell's paradox is unsolvable.

Using the sets we can define relations on them—the basic relations are reflexive, symmetric, and transitive. Using these we can define *equivalence* and *partial ordering* relations. Now, if we find that certain regular language has n equivalence classes, then a finite automaton that recognizes that language will have no less that n number of states. In other words, we cannot simplify the corresponding finite automaton to less than n states—an important result.

The mathematical functions are relations on sets. If a relation (mapping) is invertible, the corresponding function too is invertible. A cryptographic function is considered best if it cannot be inverted whatever the computation effort we put for it. Our banking transactions are secured due to this fact! Apart from treating the functions as mapping of sets' elements, e.g., $f : x \to x^2$, where every integer x maps to its square value, the functions have other important property. If we can compute $f(x)$ given x, then the function is *computable*. The computation process is a method (algorithm) to be carried out by computer. If $f(x)$ cannot be computed for all the values of x, then it is called *partially computable function*. If a function cannot be computed then it called *non-computable*.

The other thing we shall discuss in this chapter is graphs—they can represent the relations pictorially, can represent the steps in computation (transitions), or can represent computing machines where a path of edges represent the sequence of steps of a computation, or sequence of steps of a language translation (like in a parse-tree), and so on.

The algebraic theory of machines, which we shall introduce, is used to describe the computing machines and their standard operations and relations on them. The set of data, and the operations on them can be transformed from on algebraic system to another while keeping the result of computation as same. For this there are transformations, of homomorphism and isomorphism.

From the above discussions, it becomes clear that some type of mathematics is very important in operations of languages (human and of the machine), representation of computation and its analysis, like counting the steps of computation, can be modeled using graphs, and many principles of set theory are useful in understanding, representation, and analysis of computation, and this is the reason we must have foundational knowledge of that special mathematics which is backbone of this course.

Learning outcomes of this chapter:

1. Proof and theorems. [Knowledge], [Application]
2. Set theory and languages. [Synthesis]

[1] We include the 0 in the definition of $\mathbb{N} = \{0, 1, 2, 3, ...\}$, as zero is essential in mathematics.

3. Functions and relations. [Synthesis], [Application]
4. Cantor's theorem. [Synthesis], [Application]
5. Graph theory. [Knowledge]
6. Algebraic theory of Machines. [Knowledge]
7. Concept of Algorithm. [Knowledge]

1.2 Set Theory

Often in day-to-day use, we refer to group of discrete objects as a Class, or *Set*. For example, a set of computer science (CS) students, a set of CS teachers, sets of books on "Theory of Computation" in the library, etc. In all these cases, each one is a Set, and comprises finite number of discrete objects or elements. All the discrete objects in a set are called *elements* or *members* of that Set. In general, we represent the Set by upper case letters A, B, C, etc. in English alphabet, and the elements or its members by small letters like a, b, c, etc. Therefore, a set can be represented as $A = \{a, b, c\}$, and $a \in A$, $b \in A$, where a, b are members of set A; "$\in$" is symbol for *membership*. The order of elements in the set is not important. Thus, two sets having same elements but in different order are same. The size of a set A is denoted by $|A|$, and known as *cardinality* or *order* of the set A.

When number of elements in a set is large and it is not convenient to list them exhaustively, we prefer to represent them by specifying their common properties, e.g.,

$$S = \{0, 2, 4, 6, 8, 10\}$$

can also be represented as

$$S = \{x \mid 0 \leq x \leq 10 \text{ and } x \text{ is even}\},$$

where $0 \in S$, $2 \in S$, and $3 \notin S$ ($\notin$ is symbol for "not a member").

A set with no elements is called *null set*, and represented by {} or ϕ. Given two sets P and Q we say P is subset of Q if P contains only the elements from Q. This is represented by $P \subseteq Q$, we call "P is subset of Q". If $P = \{a, b, c, d\}$ and $Q = \{a, b, c\}$, then $Q \subseteq P$, and also $Q \subset P$ (called proper subset).

A set with finite number of elements is called *finite set*, while a set with infinite number of elements is called *infinite set*. Following are infinite sets:

$\mathbb{N}$ is Set of *non-negative integers* or *natural numbers*, $\mathbb{N} = \{0, 1, 2, 3, ...\}$ (note that "0" $\in \mathbb{N}$).
$\mathbb{Z}$ is Set of *integers*, $\mathbb{Z} = \{..., -3, -2, -1, 0, 1, 2, 3, ...\}$.
$\mathbb{Z}^+$ is Set of *positive integers*, $\mathbb{Z}^+ = \{1, 2, 3, ...\}$.
$\mathbb{Q}$ is Set of *rational numbers*, $\mathbb{Q} = \{a/b \mid a, b \in \mathbb{Z},\ \text{and } b \neq 0\}$.
$\mathbb{Q}^+$ is Set of *positive rational numbers*, $\mathbb{Q}^+ = \{r \mid r \in \mathbb{Q} \text{ and } r > 0\}$.

$\mathbb{R}$ is Set of *real numbers*.
$\mathbb{R}^+$ is Set of *positive real numbers*.
$\mathbb{C}$ is Set of *complex numbers*.

The sets play important role in languages and machines. A language is in fact a set of valid sentences, a sentence is a set made of subset of alphabet (symbols in a language), and for every language there is a machine that recognizes that language, hence there are set of machines. The finite languages and machines can be mapped to other finite sets, while infinite languages and machines can be mapped to infinite size sets of integers or real number depending on whether they are countable or uncountable. A program, when encoded, can be considered as a large integer, and similarly when a machine is encoded, it can be thought as a large integer. Thus, programs and machines can be thought as large integers. Hence, they (machines and programs) can be analyzed and studied, in many ways, similar to large integer numbers.

1.2.1 Operations on Sets

The sets can be combined to yield new sets. The popular operations on sets for combining them are *union, intersections*, *difference*, and *symmetric difference.* In addition, there are operations of *compliment* and *inversion*, which are performed on a single set to yield a new set [8].

Union and Intersection

The operation of union is represented by symbol "∪" and intersection by "∩". Let P be the set of students who play basketball and Q be the set of students who play football. Then, set of students who play either football or basketball is $P \cup Q$ and those play both the games are $P \cap Q$. Let $P = \{a, b, c, d, f, g, h\}$, and $Q = \{c, d, h, j, k, l\}$. Then, $P \cup Q = \{a, b, c, d, f, g, h, j, k, l\}$, and $P \cap Q = \{c, d, h\}$. Therefore, *Union* of sets P and Q consists of all the elements x such that $x \in P$ or $x \in Q$. Formally, the union operation of two sets P and Q is expressed by

$$P \cup Q = \{x \mid x \in P \text{ or } x \in Q\}.$$

Similarly, the *Intersection* of sets P and Q consists of all the elements x such that $x \in P$ and $x \in Q$, expressed by

$$P \cap Q = \{x \mid x \in P \text{ and } x \in Q\}.$$

Following examples also demonstrate the use of ∪ and ∩ operations on two sets.

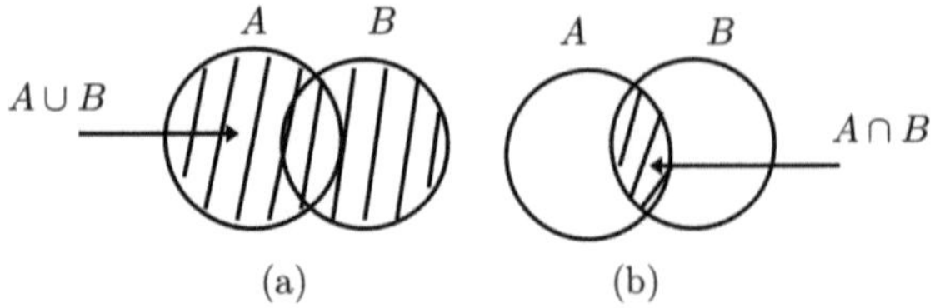

Fig. 1.1 **a** Union of sets A and B. **b** Intersection of sets A and B

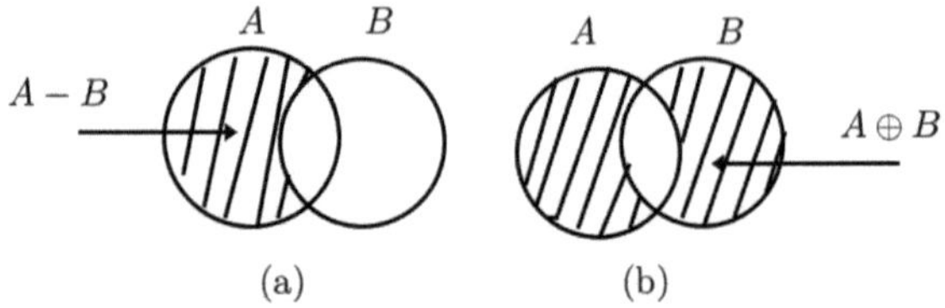

Fig. 1.2 **a** Difference of sets A and B. **b** Symmetric difference of sets A and B

$$\{a, b, c\} \cap \{d, e, f\} = \{\} = \phi,$$
$$\{a, b, c\} \cup \phi = \{a, b, c\},$$
$$\{a, b, c\} \cap \phi = \phi,$$
$$\phi \cap \phi = \phi,$$
$$\phi \cup \phi = \phi.$$

The shaded parts in Fig. 1.1a and b, respectively, represent the set union and intersection.

In the above, the symbols ϕ and $\{\}$ stand for *null* or *empty* set, i.e., a set with no elements.

Difference and Symmetric Difference

If there are sets A and B, then the *difference set* $A - B$ or $A \backslash B$ is a set comprising elements in set A but not in set B. Thus, given $A = \{a, b, c, d, e\}$, and $B = \{b, c, g, h\}$, $A - B = \{a, d, e\}$. Similarly, $B - A = \{g, h\}$. Obviously, $A - B \neq B - A$. Formally,

$$A - B = \{x \mid x \in A \wedge x \notin B\}. \tag{1.1}$$

The Set Difference operation is often known as the *relative complement*, as we are taking the complement of B relative to A rather than with respect to the universe U.

The *symmetric difference* of sets A and B is

$$A \oplus B = \{x \mid (x \in A \wedge x \notin B) \cup (x \in B \wedge x \notin A)\}. \tag{1.2}$$

The shaded part in Fig. 1.2a and b, respectively, indicates the difference and symmetric difference of sets A and B. Naturally, $A \oplus B$ and $B \oplus A$ are same.

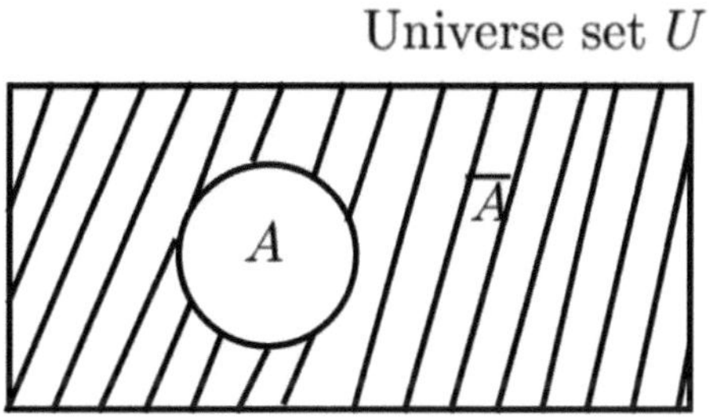

Fig. 1.3 A set and its complement set

Complement of a Set

Complement of a Set is set of elements not in that set. To define element not in a set, we need to give the concept of *Universe set*. Thus, if Universe set is $U = \{a, b, c, d, e, f, g, h\}$, and set $A = \{a, b, c\}$, then complement of A, expressed as $\overline{A} = \{d, e, f, g, h\}$. Figure 1.3 shows the relationship between Set A, its complement $\overline{A}$, and Universe Set U.

1.2.2 Properties of Sets

The sets have following properties, however their proofs are left to the reader; one can refer to more fundamental materials in Ref. [3].

(a) Associative properties:

$$A \cup (B \cup C) = (A \cup B) \cup C$$

$$A \cap (B \cap C) = (A \cap B) \cap C.$$

(b) Idempotent properties:

$$A \cup A = A$$

$$A \cap A = A.$$

(c) Commutative properties:

$$A \cup B = B \cup A$$

$$A \cap B = B \cap A.$$

(d) Distributive properties:

$$A \cup (B \cap C) = (A \cup B) \cap (A \cup C)$$

$$A \cap (B \cup C) = (A \cap B) \cup (A \cap C).$$

(e) Double complement property:

$$(A')' = A.$$

(f) Identity properties:

$$A \cup \phi = A$$

$$A \cap U = A.$$

(g) Complement properties:

$$A \cup A' = U$$

$$A \cap A' = \phi.$$

(h) De Morgan's laws:

$$(A \cup B)' = A' \cap B'$$

$$(A \cap B)' = A' \cup B'.$$

In the above, ϕ is empty set, and U is universe set.

1.2.3 Ordered Pairs and Cartesian Products

Our initial description of a set is, given a set A, exactly one of the following statements is true: (i) $x \in A$, (ii) $x \notin A$. Thus, set is simply a collection of elements, and no other condition is required. While retaining that concept, we now consider two-element sets in which *order* is imposed.

Definition 1.1 (*Ordered pair*) An ordered pair (a, b) is a set whose elements are a and b, where a is first component and b is second component. Further,

$$(a, b) = (c, d)$$

if and only if $a = c$ and $b = d$. □

For an analogy in geometry (in Cartesian coordinates), a may be taken as distance in x-axis and b may be taken as distance in y-axis in two-dimensional geometry. In the ordered pair (a, b), the a and b may be same element, e.g., $(1, 1)$, in that case also its application in geometry can be justified. Now we define a Cartesian product using this ordered set.

Definition 1.2 (*Cartesian product*) The Cartesian product $A \times B$ of sets A and B is the set of ordered pairs, (x, y), where $x \in A$ and $y \in B$. Thus,

$$A \times B = \{(x, y) \mid x \in A \text{ and } y \in B\}.$$

In the above sets A and B can be same also. □

Let A, B be sets, $A = \{a, b, c\}$, and $B = \{1, 2\}$. The *Cartesian product*, denoted by $A \times B$, is set

$$A \times B = \{(a, 1), (a, 2), (b, 1), (b, 2), (c, 1), (c, 2)\}.$$

The term "Cartesian product" is evidently, due to its analogy with totality of points in Cartesian geometry.

1.2.4 Countable Sets

How to count objects? What can be the basic (the most primitive idea of counting)?. We can represent set of all natural numbers using a *generating rule*, where we have initial set 0, which is *empty set*. Using this we can generate its successor set 0^+ and call it 1, having its members from its predecessor set 0, and one more element, which is predecessor set itself. Similarly, 2 is successor of 1, and so on. Using this rule we may go on generating successors, to arbitrarily large numbers [3].

$$\begin{aligned}
&0 = \{\} = \phi \\
&0^+ = 1 = \{\} \cup \{\phi\} = \{\phi\} \\
&1^+ = 2 = \{\phi\} \cup \{\{\phi\}\} = \{\phi, \{\phi\}\} \\
&2^+ = 3 = \{\phi, \{\phi\}\} \cup \{\{\phi, \{\phi\}\}\} = \{\phi, \{\phi\}, \{\phi, \{\phi\}\}
\end{aligned}$$

and so on. In general,

$$n^+ = \{\text{elements in set } n, \ \text{set } n \text{ as an element}\}.$$

Naturally, we have applied the rule of induction to generate the sets 0, 1, 2, 3, ..., i, ..., where $|i|$ is cardinality[2] of the ith set. Let us call the set of these elements as set $\mathbb{N} = \{0, 1, 2, 3, ..., i, ...\}$. The above definition of **N** can be reorganized as follows:

(i) $0 \in \mathbb{N}$,
(ii) if $n \in \mathbb{N}$ then $n^+ \in \mathbb{N}$,
(iii) nothing else is member of $\mathbb{N}$ except (i) and (ii) above.

Because, for every $n \in \mathbb{N}$ there is a unique successor element $n^+ \in \mathbb{N}$, the elements of $\mathbb{N}$ are countable. Also, since for every $n \in \mathbb{N}$, there is always a never terminating next element $n^+ \in \mathbb{N}$, the set $\mathbb{N}$ is infinite. Since every number $n \in \mathbb{N}$ has a successive, the set $\mathbb{N}$ is countable, and this counting goes to infinity. Thus, $\mathbb{N}$ is *countably infinite* set.

Consider a set $A = \{a, b, c\}$. We note that the elements of A have *bijection* with the elements of set $3 \in \mathbb{N}$, where $3 = \{\phi, \{\phi\}, \{\phi, \{\phi\}\}\}$. This shows that if $n \in \mathbb{N}$, then n is finite, however the $\mathbb{N}$ itself is infinite.

Definition 1.3 (*Finite set*) Any set S having bijection with set $n \in \mathbb{N}$ is a *finite set.* □

Definition 1.4 (*Infinite set*) Any set S having bijection with set $\mathbb{N}$ is an infinite and countable set (also called countably infinite set). □

For example, $S = \{1, 3, 5, 7, ...\}$ is countably infinite set, because for every $i \in \mathbb{N}$, there is $2i + 1 \in S$. That means every element in $\mathbb{N}$ maps to one unique element of S. Also, for every $j \in S$, there is $(j - 1)/2 \in \mathbb{N}$. When these two conditions are combined, there is one-to-one mapping between set S and its image in $\mathbb{N}$.

We now discuss the basic countable and uncountable sets. We begin with the definition of countable.

Definition 1.5 (*Countable*) A set S is said to be countable if there exists an injection $f : S \to \mathbb{N}$. Equivalently, S is countable if these exists a surjection $g : \mathbb{N} \to S$. □

It is obvious that a finite set is countable. We now consider infinite countable sets.

Example 1.1 The set $\mathbb{Z}$ is countable. Consider the injection, $f : \mathbb{Z} \to \mathbb{N}$, where

$$f(x) = \begin{cases} 2^x : x \geq 0 \\ 3^{|x|} : x < 0 \end{cases}$$

We will later discuss about the uncountable sets. Here, we discuss about the proof techniques.

[2] Cardinality of a set is number of elements in that. For example, $\{1, 3, 4\}$ has cardinality 3, $\{\}$ has cardinality zero, and $\{\{\}\}$ has cardinality 1.

1.3 Theorems and Proofs

The only way to determine the true or falsity of a mathematical statement is through mathematical proof. Proving some statements requires general reasoning and hence is straightforward. For example, to show that predicate statement $\forall x\ P(x)$ is false, it suffices to show that a simpler statement $\neg\forall x\ P(x)$ or its equivalent $\exists x\ \neg P(x)$ is true.

Definition 1.6 A *proof* is a convincing and logical argument about a statement, that the given statement is true. □

In mathematics an argument must be convincing in an absolute sense, so that it can be proved, or its proof can be analyzed. However, in everyday life or standard law, the proof is of lower level. In law the weight of evidence may compel the jury to accept the innocence or guilt of the suspect. But the evidence plays no role in mathematical proof. A mathematical proof demands a total absence of doubt.

Definition 1.7 A *theorem* is a mathematical statement proved true. □

Definition 1.8 Some statements, which help us to prove other related statements, are called *Lemmas*. □

Definition 1.9 The related statements concluded from the theorems are called *Corollaries* of the theorems. □

Various proof methods are: *Contradiction, Deduction*, and *Induction*.

1.3.1 Proof by Contradiction

To prove a statement or its part is to get an intuitive feeling of why it should be true. For example, consider some objects or object types and verify that they actually possess some property. After doing this, try to find an object that fails to meet that property. We shall call this as *counter-example*. If the statement is actually true, you will not be able to find a counter-example. Seeing that it is impossible to find a counter-example, it establishes that the statement is true. However, if we succeed in finding a counter-example, the statement is false. We call this as *proof by contradiction*. It is important to note that if we fail to produce a contradiction statement, it does not necessarily mean that the statement is true. May be in remote future someone later provide a contradiction statement for that.

Consider the statement "All natural numbers are divisible by 2", which is false. This is expressed in predicate form as $\forall x$ divisibleby$(x, 2)$. If we negate this statement, it becomes

$$\neg\forall x \text{ divisibleby}(x, 2) = \exists x\ \neg\text{divisibleby}(x, 2). \tag{1.3}$$

This is because, in a universally quantified predicate, when it is negated, the quantifier is changed from universal to existential, and negation sign goes inside. This is equivalent to the statement, "there exists some natural numbers that are not divisible by 2". Now it suffices to find one natural number not divisible by 2 (say $x = 3$), to show that the second part of the statement (1.3) is true. Hence, the original statement is false. However, it is always not so straight forward to find such counter-examples for the proof.

It is always not possible to produce an algorithm that enumerates all possible interpretations of some predicate expression. This happens if the expression has quantifiers, or an expression with n variables; for a large n it requires providing 2^n interpretations, which is exponential.

Example 1.2 Prove using method of contradiction that $\sqrt{2}$ is irrational number.[3]

Proof To arrive at the contradiction later, first we assume that $\sqrt{2}$ is rational. Hence, let us assume that

$$\sqrt{2} = \frac{m}{n},$$

where m and n are both integers. If both m and n are divisible by any integer greater than 1, then divide both of them by that. This is not going to change the value of the ratio. Now at least one of m or n must be odd, else, both the numerator and denominator will again be divided to simplify it. The above expression is equal to

$$\begin{aligned} 2 &= \frac{m^2}{n^2} \\ 2n^2 &= m^2. \end{aligned}$$

This shows that m^2 is even, and hence m is also even. For some integer k, we can rewrite the above expression as

$$\begin{aligned} 2n^2 &= (2k)^2 \\ &= 4k^2 \\ \text{or } n^2 &= 2k^2. \end{aligned}$$

This shows that n^2 is also even, and hence n is also even. That is, both m and n are even. This is in contradiction to earlier assumption that at least one of m and n is odd. Therefore, the assumption ($\sqrt{2}$ is rational) is wrong. This proves by contradiction that $\sqrt{2}$ is irrational. □

---

[3] It cannot be written as an equivalent number in the form of ratio of two integers.

To prove a statement through contradiction, we need to carefully read the statement, break it in its own words in parts, and consider each part separately. For example, consider the statement "P if and only if Q", which is often written as "P iff Q", where both P and Q are mathematical statements. This notation is shorthand for a two part statement, the first part is "P only if Q", i.e., if P then Q or $P \Rightarrow Q$. The second part is "P if Q", i.e., if Q then P, or $Q \Rightarrow P$. This statement, written as $P \Leftrightarrow Q$, is combination of $P \Rightarrow Q$ and $Q \Rightarrow P$, and is called *multipart* statement. Other way of writing multipart statement is $P \equiv Q$. The statement $P \Leftrightarrow Q$ can be proved if we are able to show that every member of P is member of Q (i.e., $P \subseteq Q$), and every member of Q is also member of P (i.e., $Q \subseteq P$).

1.3.2 Proof by Deductions

Consider that we have to prove the statement $\forall x(P(x) \rightarrow Q(x))$, which means, for all possible vales of x, whenever $P(x)$ holds (true), the $Q(x)$ is also true, for fix and arbitrary x. In other words, we have to deduce the statement $Q(x)$. This is *proof by deduction*.

Deductive proof: Initial statement(s) or hypothesis (say s_0), which implies

$$\begin{aligned} s_0 &\Rightarrow s_1 \\ &\Rightarrow s_2 \\ &\dots \\ &\Rightarrow s_n, \end{aligned}$$

where s_n is conclusion.

A deductive proof consists of a sequence of statements whose truth leads from some initial statement, called hypothesis, to a conclusion statement. Each step in the proof must commence based on some logical principle. This principle may be either from the given facts, or from some of the previous statements in the proof, or from both.

In plane geometry, at school level you must have studied the deductive proofs, where you show the truth of a statement by deductive sequence of steps and reasons. These formal proofs are important in establishing the truth or falsity of a statement. Following example explains a proof by deduction.

Theorem 1.1 *If it is given that $x \geq 4$, then prove that $2^x \geq x^2$.*

Proof In this theorem, $x \geq 4$ is hypothesis with parameter x. The hypothesis is false for $x = 1, 2, 3$ and true for $x = 4, 5, 6, \dots$ and so on. Similarly, the conclusion $2^x \geq x^2$ is false for $x = 1, 2, 3$ and true for $4, 5, 6, \dots$.

In addition, after x has grown larger than 4, the value 2^x doubles every time x increases by 1. Whereas x^2 grows for the same by a ratio of

$$\frac{(x+1)^2}{x^2} \Rightarrow \left(\frac{x+1}{x}\right)^2.$$

For $x \geq 4$, the term $((x+1)/x)^2$ cannot be greater than $(1.25)^2 = 1.5625$. Because $1.5625 < 2$, therefore $2^x \geq x^2$. This proves the theorem through deduction —a logical sequence of steps. □

1.3.3 Proof by Induction

Many theorems state that a statement $P(n)$ is true for all positive integers n, where $P(n)$ is a propositional function. Mathematical induction is a technique for proving a theorem of this kind. In other words, mathematical induction is used to prove propositions (i.e., *statements*) of the form $\forall n\ P(n)$ (read as "for all n, n has property P"), where *Universe of discourse* is the set of all positive integers. The latter is a Universal Set comprising all the positive integers.

A proof by mathematical induction, that $P(n)$ is true for every n, consists of two steps:

1. *Basis step:* The proposition $P(0)$ is shown to be true.
2. *Induction step:* $P(n) \rightarrow P(n+1)$, i.e., show that if P holds for n then it also holds for $n+1$.

Therefore, we can conclude $\forall n\ P(n)$, i.e., P holds for every n. The $P(n)$ is called *inductive hypothesis*.

When we have completed both steps of a proof by mathematical induction, we have proved that $P(n)$ is true for all positive integers n; that is, we have shown that $\forall n\ P(n)$ (read as "for all n, $P(n)$ holds") is true. When expressed as a rule of interference, this proof technique can be stated as

$$[P(0) \wedge (P(n) \rightarrow P(n+1))] \rightarrow \forall n\ P(n). \tag{1.4}$$

The first thing is to show that $P(0)$ is true. This amounts to showing that particular statement obtained when n is replaced by 0 in $P(n)$, then that statement is true. Next, we must show that $P(n) \rightarrow P(n+1)$ is true for every n. To prove that this implication is true for every n, we need to show that $P(n+1)$ is true when $P(n)$ is true (i.e., "true → true" is "true"). This can be accomplished by assuming that $P(n)$ is true and then showing that under this hypothesis the $P(n+1)$ must also be true, for a general value n.

Example 1.3 Using mathematical induction prove that sum of first n odd positive integers is n^2.

Let us list the first n odd integers and their sums.

$$\begin{aligned} 1 &= 1^2 \\ 1+3 &= 2^2 \\ 1+3+5 &= 3^2 \\ 1+3+5+7 &= 4^2 \\ 1+3+5+7+9 &= 5^2. \end{aligned}$$

In similar way, we get

$$1+3+5+\cdots+(2n-1)=n^2, \tag{1.5}$$

and

$$1+3+5+\cdots+(2n-1)+[(2n-1)+2]=(n+1)^2. \tag{1.6}$$

Now, assuming the correctness of the general form in (1.5), we substitute its result in (1.6),

$$1+3+5+\cdots+(2n-1)+[(2n-1)+2]=n^2+[2n+1]=(n+1)^2.$$

This shows that we have assumed the validity of $P(n)$ and substituted its result into $P(n+1)$, and the $P(n+1)$ has been also calculated using different approach,[4] to be equal to $(n+1)^2$. It is important to note that expression for $(n+1)^2$ was first obtained through symmetry, and later using expression for n^2 followed with deduction, to arrive at $(n+1)^2$. Both results are same, which is a proof through induction. □

The proofs have important role in computer science and it is something that every computer scientist must understand. For example, *formal proofs* are often used to verify correctness of a program. Because it is not possible to test a program for every possible input, only a formal proof-based test approach can assure its correctness.

On the other hand, testing a program for certain sample input (*basis* step of induction), checking it for some iteration/recursion steps (hypothesis), and verifying its correctness for rest of the steps based on the hypothesis are nothing but proof by *mathematical induction*.

An approach using sequence of fixed number of program steps is a process of *deduction-based proof*, and iteration or recursion is an example of mathematical induction-based proof. Understanding the working of iteration of a program appears essentially the same as the process of theorem proving using mathematical induction.

[4] $a^2+2a+1=(a+1)^2$.

The theory of automata also helps in establishing both the deductive proof (a sequence of justified steps) and inductive proof (recursive steps), in parameterized statements.

1.4 Russell's Paradox and Cantor's Diagonal Argument

In the start of twentieth century, a great interest arose to formalize the mathematics. In particular, the famous mathematician David Hilbert sought to show that "any mathematical statement is either provably true or provably false, and such a system is logically consistent". The mathematician Kurt Gödel showed through his Incompleteness Theorem that Hilbert's goal is unattainable. The Incompleteness Theorem stated that every logical system is either incomplete or inconsistent. At that time, Alonzo Church and Alan M. Turing were developing the foundations of theoretical computer science. So many of the new ideas appeared in theoretical computer science. In the following, we introduce the Russell's paradox—a classical set theoretic paradox and the Cantor's diagonal argument, also called Cantor's theorem. The later shows that $\mathbb{R}$ (set of all real numbers) is uncountable. The diagonalization technique employed by Cantor appears frequently in computability and complexity theory.

Definition 1.10 (*Russell's Paradox*) Let $R = \{A \mid A \text{ is set}, A \notin A\}$. So R is set of sets which do not contain themselves. Russell's paradox asks if there is $R \in R$? If $R \notin R$, then R should contain itself, i.e., R contains sets which do not contain themselves. This is clearly a contradiction. Similarly, if $R \in R$, then R contains itself, contradicting the fact that it only contains sets satisfying $A \notin A$. So $R \in R$ implies that $R \notin R$. We obtain $R \in R$ if and only if $R \notin R$. □

The mathematical foundations, such as modern set theory, type theory, and category theory, all have axioms to prohibit a Russell's paradox scenario.

We now discuss the basics of countable and uncountable sets.

In elementary set theory, Cantor's theorem states that for any set A, the set of all the subsets of A (the power set of A, i.e., $\mathscr{P}(A)$) has strictly greater cardinality than set A itself. For finite sets, Cantor's theorem can be seen to be true by much simpler proof, because in addition to subsets of A with just one member, there are others as well, and since $n < 2^n$ for all natural numbers $n \in \mathbb{N}$. But theorem is true for infinite sets as well. In practice, the power set of a countably infinite set is uncountably infinite [6].

Theorem 1.2 *There is no bijection (see Sect. 1.5.1) from any non-null set A to its* Power set $\mathscr{P}(A)$.

Proof To establish Cantor's theorem it is enough to show that given any set A, no function f from A to $\mathscr{P}(A)$ (power set of A) can be *surjective* (*onto*). In other words, to show the existence of at least one subset of A that is not an element of the image of A under f. Such subset $B \in \mathscr{P}(A)$ is given by the following construction.

$$B = \{x \in A \mid x \notin f(x)\}. \quad (1.7)$$

This means, by definition, that for all $x \in A$, there is $x \in B$ if and only if $x \notin f(x)$.

For all x, the sets B and $f(x)$ cannot be the same because B was constructed from the elements of A whose images (under f) did not include themselves.

More specifically, consider any $x \in A$, then there is $x \in f(x)$ or $x \notin f(x)$. In the former case, $f(x)$ cannot be equal to B because $x \in f(x)$ by assumption, and $x \notin B$ by construction of B (Eq. 1.7). In the other case (i.e., $x \notin f(x)$), the $f(x)$ cannot be equal to B because $x \notin f(x)$ by assumption and $x \in B$ by the construction of B. Thus, there is no x such that $f(x) = B$.

In other words, B is not in the image of f. This is because B is in the power set of A, and the power set of A has greater cardinality than the set A itself.

This proves the theorem. □

Theorem 1.3 *The set* $2^{\mathbb{N}}$ *is uncountable.*

Proof Let us consider the contrary, i.e., the set $2^{\mathbb{N}}$ is countable. Accordingly, let $f : \mathbb{N} \rightarrow 2^{\mathbb{N}}$ be a bijection. As f is bijection, every element of $2^{\mathbb{N}}$ is mapped. We shall show the contradiction by constructing an element in $2^{\mathbb{N}}$ that is not mapped by f.

We try to define a set S, where $S \in 2^{\mathbb{N}}$ such that $i \in S$ if and only if $i \notin f(i)$. If $i \in f(i)$, then $i \notin S$, so $f(i) \neq S$. By similar argument, if $i \notin f(i)$, then $i \in S$, so $f(i) \neq i$. Therefore, such a S is not mapped by any element of $\mathbb{N}$. As our choice of f was arbitrary, no such bijection can exist. Therefore, $2^{\mathbb{N}}$ is not countable. □

Note that we have used Russell's paradox in proving that $2^{\mathbb{N}}$ is not countable. We will use the similar case to show that $\mathbb{R}$ is uncountable; to be more precise, we will show only that [0, 1] is not countable.

Let us consider the countably infinite set $\mathbb{N}$, and set $\mathbb{R}$ of real numbers. Is there a bijection between these two infinite sets? Since both of them are extending to infinity, we may convince ourselves as Yes. But, it is contrary. The following theorem proves this.

Theorem 1.4 Diagonalization Theorem *There is no bijection between two sets* $\mathbb{N}$ *and* $\mathbb{R}$ *(i.e., set* $\mathbb{R}$ *is not countable).*

Proof We will try to prove it by contradiction, where, first, we assume that there is a bijection, then we arrive at a contradiction.

Let us assume that bijective mapping from $\mathbb{N}$ to $\mathbb{R}$ be $f : \mathbb{N} \rightarrow \mathbb{R}$. We consider only the elements of a subset of $\mathbb{R}$ in the interval (0, 1], and let all positive real numbers be represented by binary fractional numbers, shown in Table 1.1.

The entry b_{ij} is binary 0 or 1 value in the table. Since the mapping has been assumed to be bijective, the list $\mathbb{R}$ should be exhaustive. Let us consider an entry $x \in \mathbb{R}$ of this table equal to complement of the diagonal, i.e., $x = \neg b_{00} \neg b_{11} \neg b_{22} \neg b_{33} \ldots \neg b_{ii} \ldots$. This entry is not equal to first row of $\mathbb{R}$ since its first column b_{00} mismatches with $\neg b_{00}$ of x, it is also not equal to second row since its second column mismatches, and so on, for any row and any column.

Table 1.1 $f : \mathbb{N} \rightarrow \mathbb{R}$ (hypothesized)

$\mathbb{N}$	$\mathbb{R}$
0	$0.b_{00}b_{01}b_{02}b_{03}\ldots$
1	$0.b_{10}b_{11}b_{12}b_{13}\ldots$
2	$0.b_{20}b_{21}b_{22}b_{23}\ldots$
...	...
i	$0.b_{i0}b_{i1}b_{i2}b_{i3}\ldots$

It is clear that, x mismatches with all the entries given in the exhaustive list of real numbers (0, 1], which we assumed to have 1–1 correspondence with the elements of $\mathbb{N}$. The latter is countably infinite. The x will neither fit in any ith row, nor at end anywhere, as $\mathbb{N}$ is ordered and infinite set. Certainly, the fractional number x is a new binary number which does not map to any $i \in \mathbb{N}$. This is in contradiction to our assumption, hence there is no bijection from $\mathbb{N}$ to $\mathbb{R}$.

The set $\mathbb{R}$ is not countable, and is called *uncountably infinite* [5].

The above proof is called *Cantor's diagonalization argument*, and the language, $L_d = \{x \mid x \text{ is complement of the diagonal}\}$, is called *diagonal language*. □

In the next section, we will return back to Sets under the title "Relations and Functions". In fact, when two sets' (or one set to itself) elements are mapped, it is called a *relation* between sets, which turns out to be a subset of Cartesian product of two sets, and a function is nothing but mapping between elements of two sets.

1.5 Set Relations

The mathematics deals with statements about *objects* and the *relation* between them. It is obvious that "less than" is a relation between objects of a certain kind, e.g., between numbers 5 and 7, but does not hold between 8 and 7 or between 7 and itself. We are interested to express relation between objects using the language of sets—think of a relation being a set itself. For example, relation "less than" on set $A = \{1, 2, 3, 4\}$ is $\{(1, 2), (1, 3), (1, 4), (2, 3), (2, 4), (3, 4)\}$, where each element of the *relation set* is a pair (a, b), such that $a < b$. These pairs are called *ordered pairs* or the *ordered set*.

A *Cartesian product* for the sets $A = \{a, b, c\}$, and $B = \{1, 2, 3\}$, we may define as

$$\begin{aligned} A \times B &= \{a, b, c\} \times \{1, 2, 3\} \\ &= \{(a, 1), (a, 2), (a, 3), (b, 1), (b, 2), (b, 3), (c, 1), (c, 2), (c, 3)\}, \end{aligned}$$

which is an ordered set, where, such that in every element $(a, b) \in A \times B$, there is $a \in A$ and $b \in B$.

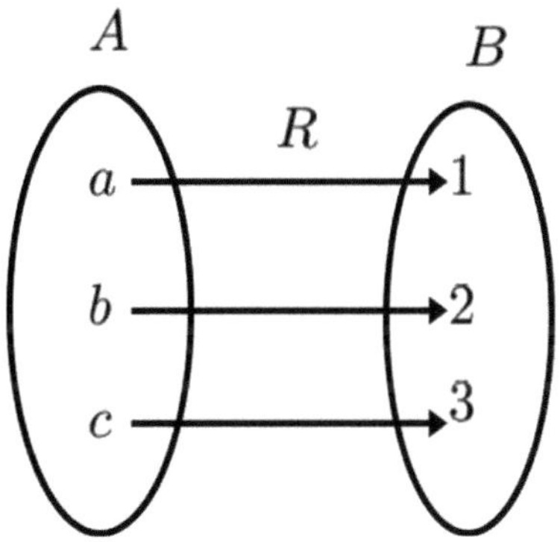

Fig. 1.4 A relation between two sets A and B

The above can be expressed in more compact form as

$$A \times B = \{(p, q) \mid p \in A \text{ and } q \in B\}.$$

A *binary relation* on two sets A and B is subset of $A \times B$, for example, $R = \{(a, 1), (b, 2), (c, 3)\}$ is a binary relation on the sets A and B. The set A is called *domain* of the relation, and set B is called *range* of the relation. The mapping or the relation from set A to set B can be expressed as a binary matrix, e.g.,

$$R_{A\times B} = \begin{bmatrix} 1\,0\,0 \\ 0\,1\,0 \\ 0\,0\,1 \end{bmatrix},$$

where set A elements are rows in the matrix and the set B elements are columns. Hence, first row is $(a, 1), (a, 2), (a, 3)$. Since only the pair $(a, 1)$ is present in the relation from first row, the first element of first row is marked true (i.e., 1), and others are false. In second row, second element $(b, 2)$ is true, while in the third row, the third element, $(c, 3)$, is true; accordingly they are marked true, and others are marked false.

The above relation R can also be represented as a mapping from set A to B, as shown in Fig. 1.4.

Given the sets A and B above, a subset of $A \times B$ is say, $R = \{(a, 1), (a, 3), (b, 2), (c, 1), (c, 3)\}$, then R is a relation between A and B. Using R we can define R^{-1}, which is *inverse* of relation R (not complement!). The R^{-1} is relation between set B and set A, and expressed as $R^{-1} = \{(1, a), (3, a), (2, b), (1, c), (3, c)\}$.

Example 1.4 Let $R = \{(x, y) \mid y = x^2, \text{ and } x, y \in \mathbb{N}\}$. Then $R^{-1} = \{(y, x) \mid y = x^2, \text{ and } x, y \in \mathbb{N}\}$. □

Consider there is a set $C = \{w, x, y, z\}$, and sets A and B are $A = \{a, b, c\}$, and $B = \{1, 2, 3\}$. A relation between sets A and B can be $R = \{(a, 1), (b, 2), (c, 3)\}$, and let there be a new relation S between B and C expressed as $S = \{(1, w), (2, y), (3, z)\}$. With this we can define a composition relation $R \circ S$ as

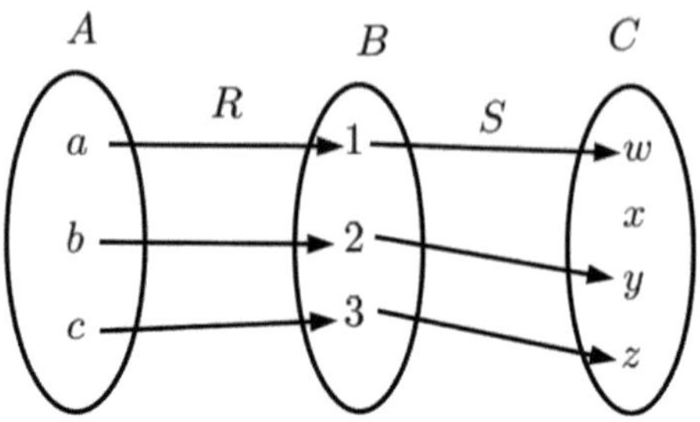

Fig. 1.5 A composition operation on sets: $T = R \circ S$

$$\begin{aligned} T = R \circ S &= \{(a, 1), (b, 2), (c, 3)\} \circ \{(1, w), (2, y), (3, z)\} \\ &= \{(a, w), (b, y), (c, z)\}. \end{aligned}$$

The above operation of composition is demonstrated through mapping in Fig. 1.5.

1.5.1 Properties of Relations

Consider a set $A = 1, 2, 3, 4$, and a relation R on this set as

$$R = \{(1, 1), (2, 2), (3, 3), (4, 4)\}.$$

This relation can also be represented using a binary matrix whose rows and columns are 1–4 as the relation is from set A to A itself.

$$R_{A \times A} = \begin{bmatrix} 1\,0\,0\,0 \\ 0\,1\,0\,0 \\ 0\,0\,1\,0 \\ 0\,0\,0\,1 \end{bmatrix}.$$

This relation is called *reflexive relation*.

For following definitions, we consider that A is a set, $A = \{a, b, c, ...\}$, and R is some relation on set A.

Definition 1.11 A relation R on a set A is *reflexive* if $(a, a) \in R$ for every $a \in A$. However, a relation where no single (a, a) is in R is called *irreflexive relation*. □

Definition 1.12 If for every $(a, b) \in R$ there is also $(b, a) \in R$, then the relation is called *symmetric relation*. □

The relation of "a is spouse of b" is symmetric relation.

Definition 1.13 If $(a, b) \in R$, then $(b, a) \in R$ only when $a = b$, the relation R is called *antisymmetric relation.* □

Definition 1.14 The relation R is *asymmetric relation* if, whenever $(a, b) \in R$ then the condition of $(b, a) \notin R$ holds true. The relations of "$>$" and "$<$" are asymmetric relations. □

Definition 1.15 If for every $(a, b) \in R$ and $(b, c) \in R$, and there is also $(a, c) \in R$ is called *transitive relation.* □

The relation of "less than", "less than or equal", and similarly "$>$" and "$\geq$" are transitive relations. Similarly, the "$\subseteq$" and "$\supseteq$" are also transitive relations.

1.5.2 Equivalence Relation

The *equivalence relations* are of particular importance in computer science. Intuitively, an equivalence relation compares which elements in a set A share common property. The goal is to then to partition A into equivalence classes such that all the elements in a part are all equivalent to each other. This allows us to select an arbitrary distinct representatives from each equivalence class and consider only that representative.

Definition 1.16 A relation which is reflexive, symmetric, and transitive is called *equivalence relation.* □

This idea of partitioning is useful quite often. The integer modulo n, denoted by $\mathbb{Z}/n\mathbb{Z}$, is a canonical example. Big-Theta (θ is used to indicate complexity) is another important equivalence relation. The equivalence relations allow us to prove powerful theorems, for example, Cauchy's theorem from Group Theory, as well as it is useful to construct a procedure to minimize finite-state automata using Myhill–Nerode theorem (Chap. 4).

Consider the relation of "congruent modulo 4" on natural numbers.[5] Based on this relation two numbers 5 and 9 are equivalent because when divided by 4, their remainder is 1. Thus, this relation divides $\mathbb{N}$ into four sets: $\{0, 4, 8, ..\}$, $\{1, 5, 9, ...\}$, $\{2, 6, 10, ...\}$, and $\{3, 7, 11, ...\}$. All numbers in the first set are equivalent since they have remainder 0 when divided by 4. Similarly, all the numbers in second set are equivalent to each other, and same applies for third and 4th sets. Since "congruent modulo" partitions the set, it is also called *partition relation* [3].

Definition 1.17 (*Congruent relations*) Let $n \geq 1$ be an integer. The congruence relation modulu n is a binary relation on $\mathbb{Z}$ given by $a \equiv b(mod\ n)$ (read as a is congruent to b modulo n) if and only if n divides $b - a$. □

[5] We will be using $\mathbb{N} = \{0, 1, 2, 3, ...\}$ as set of natural numbers.

Note that $a - a$ is divisible by n, hence reflexive; if $a - b$ is divisible by n then so is $b - a$, hence symmetric, and if $a - b$ is divisible by n, and $b - c$ is divisible by n, thus $a - c$ is also divisible by n, as $a - b + b - c = a - c$. Thus, transitive. Hence, congruent to modulo n is an equivalence relation.

Definition 1.18 A relation which is reflexive, antisymmetric, and transitive is called *partial ordering relation.* □

The relations of "$\leq$", "$\geq$", "$\subseteq$", and "$\supseteq$" are all partial ordering relations.

1.5.3 Power Sets and Characteristic Sequences

Power set of a set S is set of all its subsets. If S is set then we denote power set of S as 2^S or $(\mathscr{P}(S))$. This is because, the subsets count of S is $2^{|S|}$. Hence $2^{|S|} = \{R | R \subseteq S\}$. If $S = \{a, b, c\}$ then power set $2^S = \{\phi, \{a\}, \{b\}, \{c\}, \{a, b\}, \{b, c\}, \{a, c\}, \{a, b, c\}\}$.

The power set can also be represented by bit-vectors. If we indicate the presence of member in subset by 1 and its absence by 0 then above power set $\mathscr{P}(S)$ can be represented by $\{000, 100, 010, 001, 110, 011, 101, 111\}$, where bit-vector 111 stands for subset $\{a, b, c\}$, and 100 stands for subset $\{a\}$. We will call *bit-vector* as *characteristic sequence* of the power set. For a set S, all the bit-vectors are of length $|S|$ and characteristic sequence's count is $2^{|S|}$.

1.6 Functions

A function is a mathematical object, which expresses how items at its input (domain) can be turned into output (range). Thus, $f : D \rightarrow R$ shows that elements in domain D are mapped to range R; where f is name of function, $f : D \rightarrow R$ is called *signature*, which indicates the operation performed on the elements of D. For example,

$$+ \ : \text{Int} \times \text{Int} \rightarrow \text{Int}$$

denotes the signature of "integer addition", domain is "Int $\times$ Int", range is Int (for integer), and f is addition operation [5]. Note that "$\times$" is called "product", which we have taken as operation of addition, and it is not necessarily be a multiplication operation.

Let $S = \{a, b, c\}$ and we have signature,

$$\subseteq \ : S_1 \times S_2 \rightarrow \{T, F\},$$

where $S_1, S_2 \subseteq S$. That is, if $S_1 \subseteq S_2$ then it maps to range element T else to F.

1.6.1 Some Properties of Functions

Definition 1.19 (*Total function*) The functions defined over their entire domain are called total functions. □

For example, $f : x \rightarrow 2x$, for $x \in \mathbb{N}$, where $\mathbb{N} = \{0, 1, 2, 3, \dots\}$, is a total function.

Definition 1.20 (*Partial function*) A partial function is one, which is defined for some domain points. □

For example, $f : x \rightarrow 2/x$, for $x \in \mathbb{N}$, is *partial function*, because it is undefined for $x = 0$.

A partial function can be used to model the iteration, which may go into infinite loop for some values of input. For example,

$$f(x) = \begin{cases} 1, & \text{if } x = 0; \\ f(x) & \text{otherwise,} \end{cases}$$

which terminates for $x = 0$ and loops for all other values.

Definition 1.21 (*One to One*) A function $f : D \rightarrow R$ is *one-to-one* or *1-1* if every y, for $y \in image(f)$, is mapping of exactly one distinct $a \in D$. In other words, $f(a) = f(b) \Rightarrow a = b$ for all $a, b \in D$. □

Another example of injection is *pred:* $\mathbb{N} \rightarrow \mathbb{N}$, where f is $pred$ (predecessor). For example, $pred(5) = 4$, $pred(2) = 1$, etc. The $pred$ is Partial Function because $pred(0)$ is undefined.

Definition 1.22 (*Onto*) A function $g : D \rightarrow R$ is onto function if image$(g) = R$. Thus for each element $a' \in R$, there is an element $a \in D$ such that $a' = g(a)$. The onto functions is also called *Surjection.* □

Definition 1.23 (*Bijection*) If a function $h : D \rightarrow R$ is both one-to-one and onto, then h is called a one-to-one correspondence or bijection. If D is finite then h is called a permutation. □

Example 1.5 If f is a permutation on set $\{1, 2, 3, ..., n\}$, then it can be represented in the form:

$$\begin{pmatrix} 1 & 2 & \dots & n \\ f(1) & f(2) & \dots & f(n) \end{pmatrix}.$$

If we consider that $n = 4$, and $f(a) = d$, $f(b) = c$, $f(c) = b$, and $f(d) = a$, then we denote the function f as permutation:

$$\begin{pmatrix} a & b & c & d \\ d & c & b & a \end{pmatrix}.$$

Let there be other function g with first row as argument and second row as value of function:

$$\begin{pmatrix} a & b & c & d \\ b & d & a & c \end{pmatrix}.$$

Given f and g, we can find the composition $f \circ g$ as follows. Assume that we have to compute $(f \circ g)(a)$. Since $g(a) = b$, and $f(b) = c$, we find $(f \circ g)(a)$ by going from a down to b in g and then going b down to c in f, so $(f \circ g)(a) = c$. □

Some of the examples of functions are as follows:

$f : x \rightarrow 2x$ is one-to-one.
$f : x \rightarrow x \; mod \; 4$ is many-to-one.
$f : x \rightarrow x$, is one-to-one onto.
The following two are partial functions:

$$f(x) = \begin{cases} \frac{x}{2}, & \text{if } x \text{ is even;} \\ \text{undefined otherwise.} \end{cases}$$

$$f(x) = \begin{cases} x + 1, & \text{if } x \text{ is even;} \\ x - 1 & \text{otherwise.} \end{cases}$$

$pred^{-1} : \mathbb{N} \rightarrow \mathbb{N}$ is total (it is successor function).

For every one-to-one function f, we denote its inverse to be f^{-1}. The f^{-1} is defined at all its image points. Hence, if f is defined at x, we have $f^{-1}(f(x)) = x$.

1.6.2 *Composition of Mappings*

Consider the sets as $A = \{3, 4, 5\}$, $B = \{2, 3, 7\}$, and $C = \{1, 9, 14\}$. Given these we define the function $f : A \rightarrow B$, and $g : B \rightarrow C$, as

$$f = \{(3, 2), (4, 3), (5, 7)\}$$

and

$$g = \{(2, 1), (3, 9), (7, 14)\}.$$

Having given these,

$$g(f(3)) = f(2) = 1,$$

$$g(f(4)) = g(3) = 9,$$

$$g(f(5)) = g(7) = 14.$$

Thus, the substitution of the mappings f into the mapping g has resulted new mappings, called *composite* of functions g and f, and denoted by $g \circ f$, which is equal to

$$\{(3, 1), (4, 9), (5, 14)\}.$$

Note that in the composition $g \circ f$, the value of f is computed first, and that is used as an argument to the function g.

1.6.3 Computable Functions

A computable process maps inputs to output, which can be easily modeled using functions. For example, given two matrices, a computational process may compute the multiplication of these and may produce an output. All the functions whose mappings can be obtained through mechanical means are called *computable functions*, or *effectively computable functions*, or *algorithmically computable functions*.

Following functions are computable:

- each function with finite domain;
- each constant function $f : \mathbb{N}^k \rightarrow \mathbb{N}$, e.g., $f(n_1, n_2, \ldots, n_k) = n$;
- addition function, $f : \mathbb{N}^2 \rightarrow \mathbb{N}$, e.g., $f(n_1, n_2) = n_1 + n_2$;
- function which gives prime factors of a number;
- GCD of a number.

Each computable function has finite procedure giving explicit, unambiguous instructions on how to compute it. This procedure has to be encoded using finite alphabet, so there are only countably many computable functions. For example, procedure may be encoded using alphabet $\{0, 1\}$.

Definition 1.24 (*Language computability*) A language is computable (synonymous to recursive or decidable) if there is a computable function f such that $f(w) = 1$ if the word w is in the language, and $f(w) = 0$ if the word is not in the language. □

Definition 1.25 (*Computably enumerable language*) A language is computably enumerable (synonymous to recursively enumerable, or semi-decidable), if there is a computable function f such that $f(w)$ is defined if and only if word w is in the language. □

1.6.4 Non-computable Functions

There exist *non-computable functions* also. These are the functions, which are mathematically well defined but their mappings cannot be obtained mechanically, i.e., through machines. Following are non-computable functions:

- Most subsets of natural numbers are not computable.
- The halting-problem function, which correctly labels the program-input pairs as halting or on-halting, is easy to describe but not computable.
- The tiling function, which given any finite set of polynomial tiles, outputs the size k of largest $k \times k$ square that can be tiled by them, or 0 if they tile the entire plane.

1.7 Graph Theory

The Graph Theory is a subject whose deceptive simplicity makes its vast applicability. The Graph Theory provides simple mathematical structures known as graphs to model the relations of various objects. There are numerous applications of graphs, which includes, e.g., efficient storage of chemicals (graph coloring), optimal assignments (maximal matching), distribution network as a graph (flows), efficient storage of data (tree-based data structures), and machine learning. The directed graphs are used for visual representation of finite automata machines, pushdown automata, linear bounded automata, and Turing machine. In these, many elementary notions come from graph theory, such as path finding and walks.

In complexity theory, many combinatorial optimization problems of interest are graph theoretic in nature. Accordingly, we discuss the basic notions of graph theory.

The graphs are kind of simplest *geometric* objects; a graph is also the visual part of combinatorics[6]; and the part most accessible to geometrically minded mathematicians.

1.7.1 Undirected Graphs

Figure 1.6 shows the example of a typical graph, where $v_1, ..., v_6$ are vertices, which are expressed as a set $V = \{v_1, ..., v_6\}$, and $e_1, ..., e_8$ are edges, which are represented as a set $E = \{e_1, ..., e_8\}$. The set of edges are usually represented as set of pairs of vertices; hence, $E = \{(v_1, v_2), (v_2, v_3), (v_1, v_4), (v_3, v_4), (v_3, v_6), (v_2, v_6), (v_3, v_5), (v_5, v_6)\}$. Since there is no direction shown in the edges, an edge between two vertices can be represented as (v_i, v_j) or (v_j, v_i). The entire Graph is $G = (V, E)$. An edge sequence e_1, e_2, e_7 or $(v_1, v_2), (v_2, v_3), (v_3, v_5)$ is called a *path* in a graph.

A formal definition of a graph is as follows.

Definition 1.26 A (finite) *graph G* consists of a finite set of objects v_i, called its vertices, and set of pairs $e_k = (v_i, v_j)$, called its edges. □

[6] Combinatorics is an area of mathematics and computer science which is primarily concerned with counting for certain properties of finite structures. The methods of combinatorics can be used to estimates about how many operations a computer algorithm will require to carry out the given task.

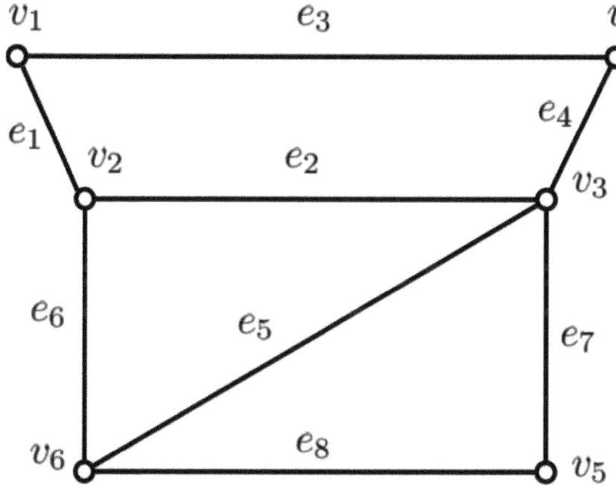

Fig. 1.6 A typical graph

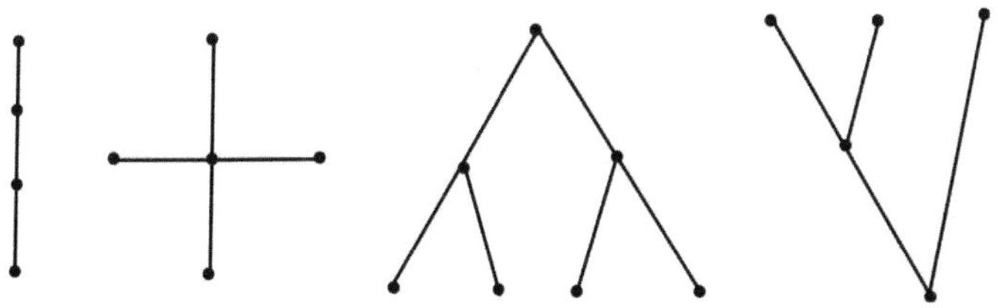

Fig. 1.7 Four trees

Fig. 1.8 Plane and non-plane views of a graph

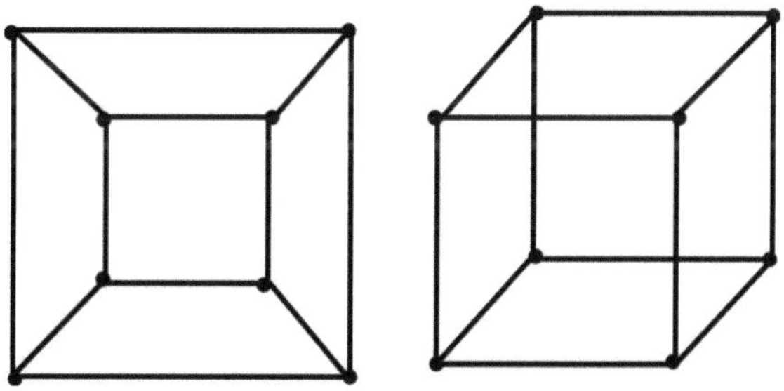

A graph G is *cconnected* if every pair of vertices occur in some path.

A *tree* is a connected graph containing no simple closed path (i.e., there is no loop). Some examples of trees are shown in Fig. 1.7. Each edge in a tree leads to a new vertex, else a path with loop will be created. Hence, a tree cannot be drawn crossing the edges previously drawn. If a tree has V as set of vertices, and E set of edges, then a relation $|E| = |V| - 1$ holds always. This relation is also called *Euler's characteristic* of every tree.

Figure 1.8 shows the plane and non-plane view of a graph, however the graph is actually planer.

Fig. 1.9 A directed graph

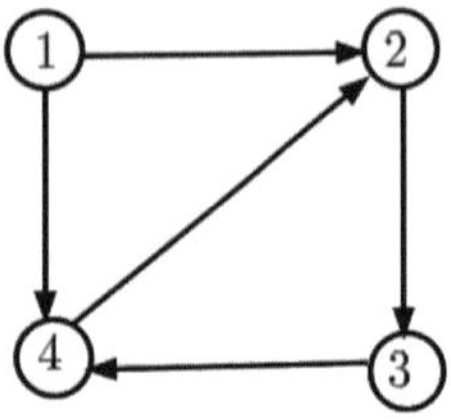

Definition 1.27 A *Planar Graph* is one whose vertices are points of $\mathbb{R}^2$ and whose edges are polynomial paths, which meet only where they have common end points. □

To capture the idea of a planar graph being a picture of another graph, the idea of isomorphism is important.

Definition 1.28 Two graphs G and G' are *isomorphic* if there is one-to-one correspondence $v_i \leftrightarrow v'_i$ between the vertices v_i of G and vertices v'_i of G', such that (v_i, v_j) is an edge of G iff (v'_i, v'_j) is an edge of G'. □

The graphs in Fig. 1.8 are isomorphic graphs.

1.7.2 Directed Graphs

A directed graph (*digraph*) $G = (V, E)$ consists of a set of vertices $V = \{v_1, v_2, ..., v_n\}$, and a set of edges,

$$E = \{(v_i, v_j) \mid \text{ there is an edge with arrow from } v_i \text{ to } v_j\},$$

where arrow of the edge is called "head" and other end of the edge is called "tail" of the edge. Figure 1.9 shows a directed graph, where $V = \{1, 2, 3, 4\}$, and $E = \{(1, 2), (2, 3), (3, 4), (4, 2)\}$. A path in a graph is sequence of vertices, e.g., $1 \to 2 \to 3 \to 4 \to 2$ (Fig. 1.9), and length of the path is number of edges in the path. A path is *simple path* if all the vertices in the path, except the first and last, are distinct.

A simple cycle is a path of length at least one that begins and ends at the same vertex. In Fig. 1.9 $1 \to 2 \to 3 \to 4$ is simple path, while $2 \to 3 \to 4 \to 2$ is a simple path as well as a simple cycle. If edges of a directed graph are labeled, then it is called *labeled digraph.*

1.7.3 Non-planar Graphs

A graph in which no edge cross its any other edge is called *planar* graph. The graphs shown in Fig. 1.10 are non-planar graphs.

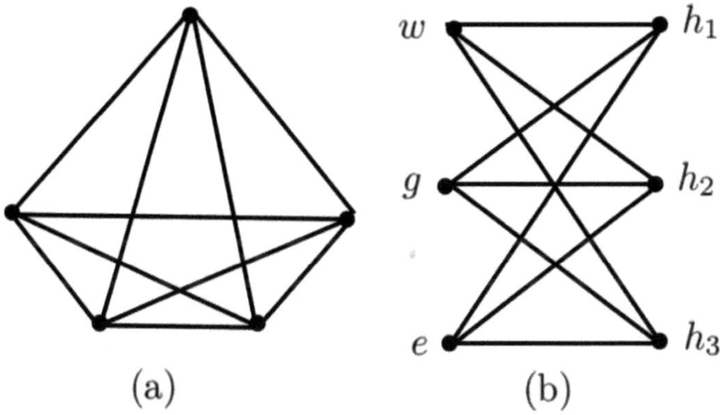

Fig. 1.10 Non-planar graphs

The Graph in Fig. 1.10a is called K_5, the complete graph of five vertices, where along with five vertices it has ten edges that connect five vertices; these edges connect all pairs of distinct vertices. The graph in Fig. 1.10b is called $K_{3,3}$, which is also called *complete bipartite graph* on two sets of three vertices. The $K_{3,3}$ contain an edge from each vertex in the first set of three vertices to each vertex in the second set of three. This graph is also called *utility graph*, i.e., it supplies 3-utilities (say gas, water, and electricity) to 3-different houses from three different sources.

1.8 Algebraic Theory of Machines

Algebra (and algebraic geometry) has big role in cryptography, with *elliptic curve groups*, and (number-theoretic) lattices are the basis for nearly all modern cryptographic work. Analyzing any problem with a lot of symmetry is facilitated using group theory. Under group theory there are *syntactic monoids* for formal languages and *trace* and *history monoids* have applications in parallel/concurrent computing. Apart from these, there are *semi-ring frameworks* for graph processing and semiring-based parsing.

Algebraic Combinatorics and Graph Theory

Cayley's Theorem from group theory states that every group is subgroup of some *symmetry group*, i.e., every group is a *permutation group*. This motivates us to study the algebraic combinatorics. Group actions are used to study symmetries, or *automorphisms* of mathematical objects. Informally, a group action is a dynamical process on an object, which partitions its members into sets which we call orbits. The study of the structure and quantity of these orbits yields important combinatorial results. In general, finding the full automorphism group of an object (such as a graph) is a non-trivial exercise.

Consider graph homomorphisms. In particular, a proper coloring of a graph is a graph homomorphism. If the graph X has chromatic number c, then there exists a graph homomorphism $\theta : X \rightarrow K_c$. So, there is a direct connection to complexity theory here, as graph coloring is NP-Hard problem. The constraint satisfaction problems (CSPs) are generalizations of this, where we study homomorphisms of relational structures of finite rank. The CSPs arise frequently in artificial intelligence. Algebraic techniques (granted, not senior level algebra techniques) arise in the study of CSPs. The Dichotomy Conjecture states that every CSP is either in P or NP-Complete. Following two areas of this text makes use of algebraic theory.

Automata Theory

The set of regular languages forms a *Kleene semi-ring* over the operations of set union (addition) and concatenation (multiplication). The notion of the derivative also comes up, due to Brzozowski's Derivatives (Chap. 5). We can leverage this fact to design a linear-algebraic algorithm (see the Brzozowski Algebraic Method, Chap. 5) to convert a finite automaton to a regular expression.

Complexity Theory

Groups are mathematical structures capturing the notion of symmetry (reversible processes, or operations that can be undone). Algebraically, semigroups are the generalization of the concept of group. Semigroups can capture irreversibility as well, not just symmetry like groups, i.e., there can be operations that cannot be undone. The only requirement is that the passage of time should be preserved by the associativity of the operation [3, 4, 7, 9].

The Graph Isomorphism problem makes connection of algebra to computer science. Group actions and representation theory are used for study of problems like Graph Isomorphism and Group Isomorphism. Regarding the Group Isomorphism problem, it is undecidable in the general case. For finite groups, the best bound is something like $n \log(n)$. This is easy to obtain, simply by showing that every finite group has a generating set with at most $\log 2(n)$ generators. For Abelian groups, Group Isomorphism has an $O(n)$ time solution. For solvable groups, the $n \log(n)$ bound has been relatively untouched. The following part briefly introduces the building blocks of Algebraic Group Theory.

1.8.1 Semigroup

Definition 1.29 (*Semigroup and Monoid*) A semigroup is a pair $(S, *)$, where S is a set and "$*$" is a binary associative operation from $S * S$ to S. A monoid $(S, *, 1)$ is a semigroup admitting an identity element 1, in multiplication such that $s * 1 = 1 * s = s$, for every $s \in S$. □

Let S be a non-empty set on which there is defined a binary operation, denoted by $*$. For $a, b \in S$, the outcome of operation between a and b is denoted by $a * b$. Then S is called *semigroup* provided following applies:

(a) for all $a, b \in S$, there is $a * b \in S$ (closure property) and
(b) for all $a, b \in S$, there is $(a * b) * c = a * (b * c)$ (associative property).

A group is a *monoid* such that for every $s \in S$, there exists an element $s^{-1} \in S$ and $s * s^{-1} = 1$.

Definition 1.30 (*Subsemigroup and generators*) A subsemigroup T of S is a subset $T \subseteq S$, which is closed under multiplication, i.e., $T^2 \subseteq T$. A subgroup of S is a subsemigroup of a group. □

A *finite semigroup* can be described by its *multiplication table*. The *trivial semigroup* consisting of the singleton set $\{e\}$ is of course a monoid and group. In the sequel, we will not make a difference between semigroup and monoid.

The semigroups are algebraic aspect of automata: The input symbols of an automaton can be considered as transformations of state set, as functions. Therefore, we can use the precise mathematical tools available in algebra for studying the phenomena being described as an automaton. Philosophically, this aspect also gives us a very nice level of abstraction for computational structures: we can consider processes and memory as the very same resource, since they are not distinguished in the semigroup.

1.8.2 Groups

A group is structure that satisfies the following axioms:

$$a(bc) = (ab)c \quad (\textit{associative laws})$$
$$a.a^{-1} = a \quad (\textit{identity})$$
$$a.a^{-1} = \mathbf{1} \quad (\textit{inverse})$$

The above axioms are nothing but *field*, but having nonzero element. However, in the absence of other field axioms, they have vastly greater scope. In fact, the identity **1** need not to be number 1.

Definition 1.31 (*Abelian group*) A group G such that $ab = ba$ for each a and each b in G is an *Abelian* (named after mathematician Nils Henrik Abel) or *commutative* group. If there exist x and y in G such that $xy \neq yx$, the group is called *non-Abelian* or *noncommutative*. □

The "+" notation is only used for Abelian groups. If any other notation is used, it will be specifically specified as whether or not the group is Abelian.

The group operation, which combines the group elements a and b into the element written as ab, could be addition on $\mathbb{Z}$, in which case the combination of a and b would be written as $a + b$, the inverse of a is written as $-a$, and the identity element is 0. The associativity in this case is $a + (b + c) = (a + b) + c$, which holds true in $\mathbb{Z}$. Thus we can say that $\mathbb{Z}$ is group under the "+" operation. The same is there of any *vector space* under the operation of vector sum (with zero vector as the identity element).

As another example, where we can reverse to the "product" notation, is collection of *invertible functions* on any set, under the operation of function composition (i.e., function of a function). If $f, g, h, \ldots$ are functions, we take fg to be a function defined by $fg(x) = f(g(x))$, hence it is easy to see that

$$f(gh)(x) = (fg)h(x) = f(g(h(x))),$$

thus this "product of" functions is associative. The identity element **1** is the identity function defined by $\mathbf{1}(x) = y$, from this it is easy to follow that $f \cdot \mathbf{1} = f$. Finally, the *inverse function* f^{-1} of function f is its inverse function, defined by the condition that

$$f(x) = y, \text{ iff } f^{-1}(y) = x.$$

From above it is easy to see that $f \cdot f^{-1} = \mathbf{1}$.

There are groups called *commutative groups* such as $\mathbb{Z}$ under addition. The most important groups, such as these which arise from general polynomials equations, are, however, not commutative. Hence, group axioms had to omit the statement of commutativity. However, in matehmatics, there exists noncommutative multiplication.[7] The reason that a noncommutative multiplication is difficult is that it is quite close to the operation of *Turing machine* (TM) (see Chap. 9). If elements of a group are denoted by $a, b, c, d, e, \ldots$, then their products are "words", like, cat, dog, etc. Since the order of letters changed, the "word" maintains it integrity. However, it can be disturbed to some extent by insertion of adjacent inverse letters, like in

$$\text{dog} = \text{dott}^{-1}g.$$

The above (disturbance) can be demonstrated through the operations of a TM. A TM can be simulated as a *group* by a finite set of equations between words that allows replacement of certain strings of symbols by other strings. The idea can be realized by encoding the initial configuration of a TM that consists of input, position of reading head, and initial state. By certain string, the encoding of subsequent configurations is obtained by replacing substrings.

Power Elements

Suppose G is group and $x \in G$. As in elementary arithmetic, we set

$$x^2 = x \cdot x$$
$$x^3 = x^2 \cdot x = (x \cdot x) \cdot x.$$

This we define as follows.

[7] The order of letters or the numbers cannot be used.

Table 1.2 Group $G = \{a, e\}$

$\cdot$	e	a
e	e	a
a	a	a

Definition 1.32 (*Power elements of a group*) If G is group with identity element as e, then for each $x \in G$, we set

$$x^0 = e,$$

and for each non-negative integer k, we set

$$x^{k+1} = x^k \cdot x. \qquad \square$$

Then x^n is defined for all non-negative integers n, and for all $x \in G$. The x^n is nth power of the element x.

Order of a Group

The groups can be divided into two categories: those which have infinitely many elements and those comprising only the finite number of elements.

Definition 1.33 A group with finite number of elements is *finite group*, and the number of elements in this group is called *order* of the group. A group with infinitely many elements is called *infinite group* and its order is *infinite order*. $\square$

Example 1.6 Let $G = \{e, a\}$ be a two-element group, $a \neq e$, and let "." be the binary operation on G defined by Table 1.2.

Obviously, the G together with "." constitutes a group. Now if $\mathbb{Z}$ is the additive group of integers, then we define an operation:

$$H = \mathbb{Z} \times G; \tag{1.8}$$

hence, $H = \{(n, x) \mid n \in \mathbb{Z} \text{ and } x \in G\}$ and H has infinitely many elements. For $(m, x) \in H$ and $(n, y) \in H$, we can define $*$ on H by

$$(m, x) * (n, y) = (m + n, xy), \tag{1.9}$$

where $+$ is the operation of addition of integers in $\mathbb{Z}$ and "." (juxtaposition) is the operation on G defined by Table 1.2. Note that following holds in this case:

1. $*$ is a binary operation on H;
2. $(0, e) \in H$ is called *left neutral* element; and
3. for each $(m, x) \in H$, the element $(-m, x^{-1})$ is *left inverse* of H. Note that for each $x \in G$, there is $x^{-1} = x$.

Table 1.3 $(P, *)$

$*$	a	b	c
a	a	b	c
b	b	c	a
c	c	a	b

Hence, the system consisting of H and $*$ is a group. It can be easily checked that $(0, e)$ and $(0, a)$ both elements are finite order. In fact these are the only elements in H of finite order. □

1.8.3 Homomorphism

We are concerned with mappings that preserve algebraic structures. Such mappings are called *homomorphism* (Greek: *homo* = same, *morph* = form). We have following definitions.

Definition 1.34 (*Homomorphism*) Let S and T be semigroups and let $f : (S, *) \rightarrow (T, *')$ be a mapping such that

$$f(x * y) = f(x) *' f(y) \tag{1.10}$$

for all $x, y \in S$. Then f is called Homomorphism from S to T, and it is one-to-one function (injection), but not onto (surjection). Also, $f(x), f(y) \in T$. □

Example 1.7 Let function $f : \mathbb{R} \rightarrow \mathbb{R}^+$ be given by $x \rightarrow e^x$. This is a bijection, as we have a well-defined inverse function: the natural logarithm. We can easily verify the condition of homomorphism for this, as,

$$f(x + y) = e^{x+y} = e^x e^y. \tag{1.11}$$

□

1.8.4 Isomorphism

Let $(P, *)$ and $(Q, *')$ be two algebraic systems, shown in Tables 1.3 and 1.4 along with their elements and operations.

Definition 1.35 (*Isomorphism*) Given these algebraic systems, we can define *isomorphism* formally as follows: An algebraic system Q is isomorphic to the algebraic system P if there is *one-to-one* and *onto* functional relationship from P to Q. And,

Table 1.4 $(Q, *')$

$*'$	l	m	n
l	l	m	n
m	m	n	l
n	n	l	m

for all $a, b \in P$, image of product in P, i.e., $f(a * b)$ is equal to product of images in Q, i.e., $f(a) *' f(b)$, expressed by

$$f(a * b) = f(a) *' f(b). \tag{1.12}$$

□

Since both the systems P and Q are abstract, one can always change the algebraic system P into Q without affecting the results. Hence, the two systems are in fact the same when they are isomorphic to each other.

Example 1.8 Prove that for an isomorphism f from $(P, *)$ to $(Q, *')$, the inverse functional relationship f^{-1} holds from Q to P.

Let $a, b \in P$, and $a', b' \in Q$ such that $f(a) = a'$ and $f(b) = b'$. Since f is one-to-one and onto, therefore, $f^{-1}(a') = a$, and $f^{-1}(b') = b$. The proof for f^{-1} from Q to P can be obtained as follows:

$$\begin{aligned} f^{-1}(a' *' b') &= f^{-1}(f(a) *' f(b)) \\ &= f^{-1} f(a * b) \\ &= a * b \\ &= f^{-1}(a') * f^{-1}(b'), \end{aligned}$$

which proves that f^{-1} is an isomorphism and it exists from Q to P. □

Example 1.9 Let G be a group, then the identity map $id : G \to G$ is an isomorphism. □

There are several problems related to group isomorphisms. For example,

- Given any two groups, how many isomorphisms exists between them?
- Given two groups, to find out if they are isomorphic?

In some cases it is easy to decide if two groups are isomorphic or not. However, the general case of isomorphic is undecidable, i.e., no algorithm exists that can say if given two groups are isomorphic or not.

1.9 Operations on Strings

The ability to represent the information is crucial for its processing and communication. Human beings created spoken languages to personally communicate with few people, then developed writing ability to reach a larger number of people.

All the computer programs and algorithms have one objective—ultimately manipulation of symbols stored in computer's memory. These symbols may be representative of numerical information or string. Therefore, the mathematical study of the theory of computation must begin with understanding the mathematics of strings of symbols.

1.9.1 String Representation

Alphabets is a finite set of symbols, like $\{a, b, c, \ldots, z\}$ or for binary alphabet, the set $\{0, 1\}$. A *string* is a finite sequence of symbols from some alphabet. For constructing a string, we simply pack the symbols without any commas or other separators. For example, a book is a set of collection of strings[8] over $\{a, b, c, \ldots, z\}$ and 1011011 is string over $\{0, 1\}$. A string may have no symbols at all, in that case, it is called *null string* or *empty string*, denoted by ε. The letters at the end of English alphabet, i.e., u, v, w, x, y, z, and the Greek letters denote strings. For example, $w = abcd$, $v = pqabcd$, $\alpha = abc$, etc. In another representation, for an alphabet set Σ, the representation Σ^* is set of all the strings of arbitrary lengths, including empty string, which can be constructed using Σ.

The length of a string is its length as a sequence. Thus, the length of *abcdg* is 5. The length of a string w is represented by $|w|$; therefore $|abcd| = 4$ and $|\varepsilon| = 0$. Alternatively, by *natural isomorphism*, a string $w \in \Sigma^*$ can be considered a function $w : \{1, 2, \ldots, |w|\} \rightarrow \Sigma^*$. The value of $w(i)$ (for $1 \leq i \leq |w|$) is the symbol in the ith position of w. For example, if $w = keystroke$, then $w(8) = k$. We call these as different occurrence of the symbol. Individual symbols are represented by σ.

Two strings over the same alphabet can be combined to form a third string by the operation of *concatenation*, represented by the symbol "$\circ$". Since the original strings are from an alphabet set, the resultant string will also be from the same alphabet set. Concatenation of strings x and y written as $x \circ y$ is simply written as xy. Therefore, we have representation:

[8] The lower case letters $a, b, c \ldots$ at the beginning of English alphabet will be treated as symbols in strings, and the $\ldots, u, v, w, x, y, z$ toward the end of English alphabet will be used for names of strings, as standard notation in this book, unless otherwise it is explicitly specified.

$$w = x \circ y \text{ iff } |w| = |x| + |y|, w(i) = x(i),$$
$$\text{for } i = 1, \ldots, |x|, \text{ and}$$
$$w(|x| + j) = y(j), \text{ for } j = 1, \ldots, |y|. \tag{1.13}$$

For the empty string and another string $w \in \Sigma^*$, $\varepsilon \circ w = w \circ \varepsilon = w$. Since the process of concatenation is associative, we have $(xy)z = x(yz)$ for any strings x, y, and z. A string v is a substring of another string w, if there are strings x and y such that $w = xvy$. Since x and y both can be empty strings, the v is a substring of itself, and, therefore, every string is a substring of itself. In the similar way, we can conclude that, an empty string is a substring of every string. If $w = xy$ is a string made of two strings then x is called prefix string of w, and y is called suffix string of w.

1.9.2 String Manipulations

A string may have several occurrences of same substring, for example, substring *ab* in *abcdabbcabad* occurs three times. There is compact representation possible for such strings. For each string w and each natural number i, the string w^i is defined as

$$\text{(i) } w^0 = \varepsilon$$
$$\text{(ii) } w^{i+1} = w^i \circ w, \text{ for } i \geq 0.$$

Therefore, $w^1 = w$, and $(ab)^3 = ababab$.

Above is an example of *mathematical induction*. Here, for $i = 0$, $w^i = w^0 = \varepsilon$ is the *basis step*. For *induction step*, assume that w^i is true, we verify that w^{i+1} is true, by tracing back to the basis step form w^{i+1}.

For $(ab)^2$, with $i = 1$, we have

$$\begin{aligned}(ab)^2 &= (ab)^{i+1} \\ &= (ab)^1 \circ (ab)\end{aligned}$$

According to the definition, with $i = 0$,

$$
\begin{aligned}
(ab)^1 &= (ab)^0 \circ (ab) \\
&= \varepsilon \circ (ab) \\
&= ab.
\end{aligned}
$$

By substituting both these results in Eq. (1.13), we get

$$
\begin{aligned}
(ab)^{i+1} &= (ab)^1 \circ (ab) \\
&= (ab) \circ (ab) \\
&= abab.
\end{aligned}
$$

Other operation on strings is *reversal* of a string w, denoted by w^R, is a string spelled in backward direction. For example, computer^R = retupmoc. A formal definition for reversal of a string can be given as follows.

Definition 1.36 (*String reversal*)

(i) For $|w| = 0$, $w^R = w = \varepsilon$.
(ii) For $|w| = n + 1 > 0$, and $w = ua$, for $a \in \Sigma$, and $u \in \Sigma^*$, we have $w^R = (ua)^R = au^R$. □

We illustrate in the following that a proof by induction can depend on definition by induction. It can be easily verified that for any strings w and x, it holds that $(wx)^R = x^R w^R$. For example, (keyboard)^R = (board)^R(key)^R = draobyek.

Theorem 1.5 *Prove by methods of induction that reverse of string uv, i.e.,* $(uv)^R = v^R u^R$.

Proof The proof by induction for reversal of a string is given as follows.

Basis step: Let $|v| = 0$. Thus $v = \varepsilon$, and let $u \in \Sigma^*$. The reversal of string holds for $v = \varepsilon$ (null string) concatenated with another string u as follows.

$$
\begin{aligned}
(uv)^R &= (u\varepsilon)^R \\
&= u^R \\
&= \varepsilon u^R \\
&= \varepsilon^R v^R \\
&= v^R u^R.
\end{aligned}
$$

Induction step: Assuming that, if $|v| = k$, and $v \in \Sigma^*$, it holds that

$$(uv)^R = v^R u^R. \tag{1.14}$$

We need to prove that $(uv)^R = v^R u^R$ for $|v| = k + 1$. Let $v = wa$, for some $w \in \Sigma^*$, $a \in \Sigma$, and $|w| = k$.

$$\begin{aligned}(uv)^R &= (u(wa))^R\\ &= ((uw)a)^R, \text{ by the rule of association,}\\ &= a(uw)^R, \text{ by definition of reversal of a string,}\\ &= a^R w^R u^R, \text{ by induction hypothesis above,}\\ &= (wa)^R u^R, \text{ by definition of reversal of string,}\\ &= v^R u^R, \text{ since } v = wa.\end{aligned}$$

□

For an alphabet Σ, let $x \in \Sigma^*$ and $a \in \Sigma$. We define $|x|_a$ as the number of occurrences of a in x. Hence, $|(abbab)|_a = 2$, and $|(11bb0|_0 = 1$. For all $x \in \Sigma^*$, we have

$$|x| = \sum_{\sigma \in \Sigma} |x|_\sigma, \tag{1.15}$$

where σ is variable for every symbol present in string x. Many times, we need a fixed order of text out of a large text of words over a given alphabet. The most convenient way is to consider the *canonical order*. Let $\Sigma = \{a_1, a_2, \dots, a_n\}$, for $n \geq 1$, be an alphabet set and $a_1 < a_2 < \cdots < a_n$ be a linear order of elements in Σ. We define the canonical order over Σ^* for all $u, v \in \Sigma^*$ by

$$\begin{aligned}u < v \Leftrightarrow &(|u| < |v|) \vee (|u| = |v| \wedge u = x \cdot u_i \cdot u' \wedge v = x \cdot v_i \cdot v',\\ &\text{for some } x, u', v' \in \Sigma' \text{and } u_i < v_i).\end{aligned} \tag{1.16}$$

In the above, u_i and v_i are ith characters in strings u and v, respectively. □

1.10 Strings and Languages

A language, whether a natural language such as English or a programming language such as *C* or *Java*, can be considered to be a set of sentences, that is, finite strings of elements of some basic vocabulary. The definition of a language introduced here is based on this notion and is, consequently, general enough to include both natural and programming languages. The *syntactic specification* of a language with finitely many sentences can be given, at least, in principle, by listing the sentences. This is not possible for languages with infinitely many sentences. The main problem of formal language theory is to develop finite representations for infinite languages.

Let us shift our attention from individual strings in previous section to *finite* and *infinite* strings. The simple models of computing machines can be described in terms of regularities in the strings. Therefore, it is important to understand the general rules of combining and describing the strings.

Definition 1.37 For an alphabet set Σ, every set of strings over Σ is language over Σ. □

Since it is possible to construct an arbitrarily large number of sets of strings over $\Sigma (|\Sigma| \neq 0)$, there can be arbitrarily large number of languages over a finite alphabet. All possible strings over Σ are represented by Σ^*, called *Kleene star* of Σ. As per the above definition, any subset of Σ^* is also a language over Σ. Accordingly, ε, Σ and Σ^* all are languages over Σ.

Definition 1.38 All the finite set of strings over Σ are finite languages over Σ. □

For example, $\{abc, abcd, a, bc\}$ is a finite language over $= \{a, b, c, \dots, z\}$. Whereas $\{a, ab, abb, abbb, \dots\}$ is an infinite language. An infinite language will have infinite number of strings of infinite length, in addition to finite length strings.

Most languages of interest for teaching and learning the theory of formal languages are infinite, and listing all those strings may not be feasible. The Languages that might be considered are, for example,

1. $L_1 = \{1, 11, 111, 1111, \dots\}$,
2. $L_2 = \{w \in \{0, 1\}^* \mid w \text{ has an equal number of 0 and 1}s\}$, and
3. $L_3 = \{w \in \Sigma^* \mid w = w^R\}$.

In general, we specify an infinite language by a statement like

$$L = \{w \in \Sigma^* \mid w \text{ possesses the property } P\}. \tag{1.17}$$

1.10.1 Concatenation of Languages

For the sake of understanding and to give formal treatment to the topic, there is no loss of generality if a string is treated as a sentence of the language.

The complement L^c of the language L with respect to Σ is the language $\Sigma^* - L$. Following are some examples of languages, which may not have any practical use, but in computer theory they have.

$L = \phi$ is the empty language.

$L = \{\varepsilon\}$ is the language that contains only the empty word.

If L_1 and L_2 be the languages over alphabet set Σ, then

$$\begin{aligned} L_1 \circ L_2 &= L_1 L_2 \\ &= \{w \mid w = xy, x \in L_1 \text{ and } y \in L_2\} \end{aligned}$$

is *concatenation* of L_1 and L_2. Given L as a language over alphabet set Σ, some of the languages we can construct over this alphabet are

$$\begin{aligned} L_0 &= L_\varepsilon, \\ L^{i+1} &= L^i \circ L, \text{ for all } i \in \mathbb{N}. \end{aligned}$$

1.10.2 Kleene star Operation

Following are the Kleene star operations on Languages.

$$L^* = \{x \mid \exists k \in \mathbb{N}, \text{ and } x \in L^k\}$$

or

$$L^* = \bigcup_{i \in \mathbb{N}} L^i$$

$$L^+ = \bigcup_{i \in \mathbb{N} - \{0\}} L^i = L^i \circ L^*.$$

Here L^* is called *Kleene star* of L.

Note that as per the above definition, $o^* = \{\varepsilon\}$. This is also because we must have a basic element in the recursive definition of concatenation. In our case, ε is identity element for the string.

Some examples of concatenation are as follows:

- $\{a, b\}^*$ is all possible strings over a and b, including the null string.
- $\{a\}^*$ is all possible strings over a, including ε-string.
- $\{a, b\}^*$: When $k = 1$, it is a, b, when $k = 2$, it is aa, ab, ba, bb, hence for k, it is k length strings made of a and b.

Following sets are examples of languages over the alphabet set $\Sigma = \{a, b\}$.

$$L_1 = \phi$$
$$L_2 = \{\varepsilon\}$$
$$L_3 = \{\varepsilon, ab, ab, abab\}$$
$$L_4 = \Sigma^* = \{\varepsilon, a, b, aa, \dots\}$$
$$L_5 = \Sigma^+ = \{a, b, aa, ab, \dots\}$$
$$L_6 = \{a\}^* = \{\varepsilon, a, aa, aaa, \dots\}$$
$$L_7 = \{a^p | p \text{ is prime }\}$$
$$L_8 = \{a^i b^i c^i \mid i \in \mathbb{N}\}$$
$$L_9 = \Sigma$$
$$L_{10} = \Sigma^3 = \{aaa, aab, aba, abb, baa, bab, bba, bbb\}.$$

We note that $L_1, L_2, L_3, L_9, L_{10}$ are finite languages, and $L_4 \dots L_8$ are infinite languages.

Theorem 1.6 *Show that Kleene star operation on any finite set of alphabet produce countably infinite number of strings.*

Proof If Σ is a finite set, then Σ^* is an infinite set. It can be easily shown that Σ^* is an infinite set. To construct a bijection, $f : \mathbb{N} \to \Sigma^*$, let $\Sigma = \{a_1, \dots, a_n\}$, where $a_1, \dots, a_n$ are distinct elements. The members of Σ^* can be enumerated in the following way:

(i) For $k \geq 0$, all the strings of length k are enumerated before all the strings of length $k + 1$.
(ii) The n^k strings of length k are enumerated lexicographically, i.e., $a_{i_1}, \dots, a_{i_k}$ precedes $a_{j_1} \dots a_{j_k}$ in every string; for some $m, 0 \leq m \leq k - 1$, there is $a_{i_m} = a_{j_m}$ and $a_{i_{m+1}} < a_{j_{m+1}}$. For example, if $\Sigma = \{a, b\}$, the order would be ε, a, b, aa, ab, ba, bb, aaa, aab, aba, abb, baa, bbb, $\dots\}$.

Since the elements of Σ^* can be mapped to the elements of $\mathbb{N}$, the Σ^* is countably infinite. □

In the above theorem, the ordering used is called *lexicographic ordering*, which is slightly different from the dictionary ordering. If Σ is Roman alphabet, $\Sigma = \{a_1, \dots, a_{26}\} = \{a, \dots, z\}$, then lexicographic order of equal length strings is the order used in the dictionaries, but the ordering described above in (i) and (ii) for all strings in Σ^* lists all shorter strings before the longer strings are listed.

We note that the *languages* are *sets*, hence they can be combined using operations of sets, like *union, intersection*, and *difference*.

Though languages are sets, certain operations are meaningful only when the sets are treated as languages. For example, if L_1, L_2 are languages over Σ, i.e., $L_1, L_2 \subseteq \Sigma^*$, then the concatenation of languages L_1 and L_2 is $L_1 \circ L_2 = L_1 L_2$, where $L_1 \circ L_2 = \{w \in \Sigma^* \mid w = x \circ y, \text{ for } x \in L_1 \text{ and } y \in L_2\}$. For example, if $\Sigma = \{0, 1\}$, a language may be defined as,

$$L_1 = \{w \in \Sigma^* \mid w \text{ has even number of } 1\,s\},$$

$$L_2 = \{w \in \Sigma^* \mid w \text{ has odd number of } 1\,s\},$$

then

$$L = L_1 \circ L_2 = \{w \in \Sigma^* \mid w \text{ has odd number of } 1\,s\}.$$

Another language operation used for languages but not found in sets are *Kleene star*. The Kleene star of a language L is denoted by L^*, which is set of all the strings obtained by concatenating zero or more number of strings of the language L with itself. Therefore,

$$\begin{aligned} L^* = \{w \in \Sigma^* \mid w = \varepsilon \circ w_1 \circ w_2 \circ \ldots w_k, \\ \text{for } k \geq 0 \text{ and } w_0, \ldots, w_k \in L\}. \end{aligned} \tag{1.18}$$

Considering that, $L = \{0, 11, 10\}$, the result of $11 \circ 10 \circ 10 \circ 0 \circ 11 = 111010011 \in L^*$.

It may be noted that the use of Σ^* to denote the set of all strings over Σ is consistent with the notation for the Kleene star of Σ, called *finite language*. For example, if $L = \Sigma$ and we apply definition as above, then Σ^* is set of all strings $w_1 \circ \cdots \circ w_k$, for $k \geq 0$, and some $w_1, \ldots, w_k \in \Sigma$.

For another example, of extreme case, let $\Sigma = \{\} = L$. Therefore, $L^* = \Sigma^*$ is Kleene star, and $w_1 \circ \cdots \circ w_k$ with $k \geq 0$, and $w_1, \ldots, w_k \in L$. Since $|L| = |\Sigma| = 0$, therefore k in the above case is always zero, and concatenation of null strings any number of times results to null string. Hence, sole member of L^* is ε, i.e., the null string.

We write L^+ for the language LL^*. Hence L^+ is a language $\{w \in \Sigma^* | w = w_1 \circ w_2 \circ \cdots \circ w_k,$ for $k \geq 1$ and some $w_1, \ldots, w_k \in L\}$. Note that L^+ can be considered as closure of L under the function of concatenation. That is, L^+ is the smallest language that includes L and all strings that are concatenation of strings in L.

1.10.3 Complement of a Language

Using the Kleene star notation discussed above, we can define a *universe set* as Σ^*, of strings. The complement is defined with respect to the universe set Σ^*. Considering that alphabet of some language L is $\{a, b\}$. The *complement* of language L is defined as,

$$\overline{L} = \{x \mid x \in \Sigma^* - L\} \tag{1.19}$$

that is, x is in Σ^* but not in L.

Definition 1.39 Let Σ is an alphabet set and there be a language L over Σ. Then $\overline{L}$, the complement of L is $\Sigma^* - L$. □

1.10.4 Homomorphism Over Strings

We discussed about general homomorpshim in Sect. 1.8.3. In the context of strings, a homomorpshim is a function that maps strings to strings, and it represents string concatenation. Consider that Σ^* and Γ^* are two sets of strings, and let h is homomorpshim from Σ^* to Γ^*, i.e., $h : \Sigma^* \rightarrow \Gamma^*$. This homomorpshim satisfies two conditions:

- $h(\varepsilon) = \varepsilon$
- For strings $x, y \in \Sigma^*$, where $w = xy$, there is $h(xy) = h(x) \cdot h(y)$. This means, result of concatenating the application of h to x and y individually, is equal to concatenating of x and y, then applied h over that.

In the above, $h(x), h(y) \in \Gamma^*$.

Definition 1.40 (*Inverse homomorphism*) Given a homomorphism h, an *inverse homomorphism* h^{-1} maps a string y to the maximal set of strings from which y has been obtained. An inverse homomorphism over y is expressed by,

$$h^{-1}(y) = \{x \mid h(x) = y\}. \tag{1.20}$$

1.11 Closure Properties of Languages

A mathematical structure can be imposed on a family of languages by introducing operations which yield new languages from given languages. A family of languages $\mathscr{L} = \{L_1, ..., L_n\}$ is closed under the binary operation of θ iff, whenever θ is applied on L_i, L_j, and $L_i \theta L_j \in \mathscr{L}$. If θ is a unary operator (e.g., complementation) then, whenever L_i is closed on θ, there is $L_i \in \mathscr{L}$, for all $L_i \in \mathscr{L}$.

Since languages are sets, the operation θ is set theoretic operation of *union, intersection, difference* and *complement*, as defined below. Assume that Σ is alphabet set of languages, then we can define following operations over languages [3].

$$L_i \cup L_j = \{w \mid w \in L_i \text{ and } w \in L_j\}$$
$$L_i \cap L_j = \{w \mid w \in L_i \text{ and } w \in L_j\}$$
$$L_i - L_j = \{w \mid w \in L_i \text{ and } w \notin L_j\}$$
$$\overline{L_i} = \{w \mid w \in \Sigma^* - L_i\}$$

The other operation on languages is *concatenation*, defined as,

$$L_i \circ L_j = \{u \cdot v \mid u \in L_i \land v \in L_j\}$$

The concatenation of languages is associative because the concatenation of words is associative. Therefore, we may define, L_i, $i \geq 1$, to be the language obtained by concatenating i copies of L. Further, L^0 is language $\{\varepsilon\}$, which is empty value.

The *concatenation* closure (or iteration) of a language L, in symbols L^*, is defined to be the union of all powers of L:

$$L^* = \bigcup_{i=0}^{\infty} L^i, \tag{1.21}$$

thus $\varepsilon \in L^*$.

A ε-free concatenation closure of L in symbolic form is L^+, it is union of all the positive powers of L:

$$L^+ = \bigcup_{i=0}^{\infty} L^i. \tag{1.22}$$

Clearly, L^+ is equal to L^* or $L^* - \varepsilon$ depending on whether $\varepsilon \in L$ or $\varepsilon \notin L$.

1.12 Representation of Languages

One of the central issues of theory of computation is representation of languages. For any finite language (a set), its representation is possible by exhaustively listing all its possible strings of it, one by one. However, if the language is not finite then it becomes impossible to exhaustively list all the strings in that.

How many languages are there? The integers are countable, as they can be ordered, but they are infinite (members of set $\mathbb{N}$). Hence, the integers are countably infinite. On the other hand, the real numbers are not countable, as they cannot be ordered, because there is no concept of next number in the real numbers. For example, in the sequence 1.0, 1.5, 2.0, 2.5, ..., 10.0, what is next number after the real 1.5? It is not 2.0, in fact there are infinite real numbers between 1.5 and 2.0! Thus, real numbers, though infinite, they are not countable, hence, they are called uncountably infinite. Note that the concept of countable comes from the concept of existence of next number.

We ask the question, how many languages are there?

(1) Languages are finite or infinite?
(2) If the languages are infinite, are they countable or uncountable?

In the following we conclude the answers for above questions.

1.12.1 Uncountably Infinite Languages

Considering the alphabet set of languages as $\{0, 1\}$,[9] each language L over Σ can be represented by an infinite *characteristic sequence*, which tells which among the infinite number of strings over $\Sigma = \{0, 1\}$ are present in L, and which are absent. The concept of characteristic function (earlier mentioned in Sect. 1.5.3) is as follows:

Consider that all strings over $\Sigma = \{0, 1\}$ in lexicographic order are:

$$L_{\Sigma^*} = \{\varepsilon, 0, 1, 00, 01, 10, 11, 000, ..., 111, 0000, 0001, ...\} \tag{1.23}$$

Say, a language, $L = \{\varepsilon, 0, 1, 00, 11, 000, ...\}$, which is subset of L_{Σ^*}, is represented by the characteristic sequence, 11110011.... That is, if $x \in L_{\Sigma^*}$ at position i is also present in language L at position i, then the ith position of characteristic sequence is 1, else it is 0. We note that in L first four strings $\varepsilon, 0, 1, 00$ are present, hence first four characters are 1111 in the characteristic sequence. If we assume a decimal point preceding to this characteristic sequence, it becomes 0.11110011..., which is a number in the interval $[0, 1]$ of real numbers. Since all the real numbers in $[0, 1]$ are uncountable and infinite (uncountably infinite), the number of characteristic sequences (vectors) are also uncountably infinite. Since, each characteristic sequence represents a unique language, the number of languages over $\{0, 1\}$ are *uncountably* infinite. This result, i.e., "number of languages for the alphabet set $\{0, 1\}$ are uncountably infinite", we shall be using at many places in this text.

1.12.2 Countably Infinite Algorithms

A language is recognized by a program (an algorithm), like, "*main*(){*bla..bla..bla*}", and each such program can be encoded as a large integer when we substitute each symbol in this program by its ASCII code. Therefore, each and every program is a big integer number, of possibly many thousand digits. Since the integers (member of $\mathbb{N}$)[10] are countable, the programs or algorithms are also countable. In fact many of

---

[9] All the other alphabets can always be encoded into strings made of 0 and 1s.

[10] Since a program P, when encoded, is a large integer, hence the program $P \in \mathbb{N}$.

these programs are not for language recognition, since, as they are for examination result processing, accounts and financial processing, reservations in trains and flights, and so on.

By other argument, a program (algorithm) is nothing but a Turing machine (as we will study later), and each Turing Machine can be encoded as a big integer. Hence, the program and the Turing machine are both big integer numbers, and are countable and infinite.

Since, the programs (algorithms) are countable and infinite (member of $\mathbb{N}$) and number of languages are uncountable and infinite (member of $\mathbb{R}$), there is no one-to-one mapping between programs and languages, and there are far more languages than algorithms. Thus, there are many languages which cannot be and will never be recognized, as there would not be algorithms for recognizing them. This is certain, whatever the power and memories of future computers we build. These language which cannot be recognized, are called *non-Turing Recognizable*, as they do not have algorithms.

Therefore, our first result in the theory of computation is: irrespective of the type of methods we use for representing languages, only countably many languages can be represented, so long as the representations themselves are finite. In fact, there are uncountably many languages in all, and the vast majority of them are inevitably missed under any finite representation scheme.

1.12.3 Algorithmic Problem

Any problem, which is solvable by computer in finite time (finite steps), its solution can be expressed with the help of an algorithm. We treat the word *algorithm* and *program* to be synonymous to each other and what language is used for representing an algorithm is not important. It is assumed that the program computes a correct output for each feasible input. This means that for each input the program does not run indefinitely but halts ultimately when the solution is computed. Given this assumption, a program A performs a mapping,

$$A : \Sigma_1^* \rightarrow \Sigma_2^* \tag{1.24}$$

for some alphabet sets Σ_1 and Σ_2, where input of the program is represented over the alphabet Σ_1, output over the alphabet Σ_2, and the mapping from input to output is deterministic and unambiguous.

For the program A and input x, we denote $A(x)$ as the output produced when A runs with input x. Two programs A and B, if running over the same input $x \in \Sigma_1^*$, are equal if and only if $A(x) = B(x)$, for all the x.

As an example, if A is a C-compiler, and x is a C-program, then the compilation process produces the machine code represented by $A(x)$.

1.13 Summary

The theory of computation attempts to establish a theory to account for all the fields of computer science, like—data structures, languages, compilers and language translators, operating system, databases, networking, etc. The meta-theory for the theory of computer science—mathematics, is concerned with ultimate limits of computation, solvability/unsolvability of problems, i.e., whether there exists algorithms for certain problem, the complexity of those algorithms, models of computations, languages models, and about the machines recognizing certain class of languages.

An important foundation of automata, formal languages, and computation is *Set Theory*—a theory of discrete objects, operations on the collections of these objects, properties of these operations, and types and sizes of these sets. The sets are the basis of counting, and so also the basis of infinite and finite number of objects.

A *proof* is convincing logical argument that a statement is true.

A *theorem* is mathematical statement proved true.

A statement which helps to prove other related statements is called *Lemma*.

The mathematical proofs used in computer science are proof by contradiction, proof by deduction, and proof by Induction.

The sets and counting further become the basis of Russell's Paradox—ultimate unsolvability through logic based proofs, and Cantor's Diagonal Argument—unsolvability of languages problem and many other theorems based on countability and uncountability.

The *Diagonalization* theorem states that a set of infinitely large integers $\mathbb{N}$ does not have a *bijection* with the infinite set of real numbers $\mathbb{R}$.

However, the set of rational numbers $\mathbb{Q}$ have bijective relation with the set of natural numbers $\mathbb{N}$.

The *theory of functions* is closely related to the field of theory computation. A function is an object that turns its inputs to an output.

A function f is invertible if given its output the input can be obtained by doing inverse operations, i.e., f^{-1}.

Functions are classified as *injective*, *surjective*, *bijective*, *partial*, and *total*, depending on the mapping between input and output. A function is computable if it can be completed through a mechanical procedure.

The *Cantors theorem* states that a set (finite and infinite) has no surjection relation with its power set, hence it cannot have a *bijection* with its power set. This conclusion leads to many important theorems.

When a computable process maps input to output, it can be easily modeled using functions, called *computable functions* or algorithmically computable. Other functions, though mathematically well defined, but their mapping cannot be obtained mechanically, are called non-computable functions.

Graph Theory provides mathematical structures known as graphs to model the relations on objects. They are also used for visualization of automata machines.

Algebra has an important role in cryptography. Lattices are the basis for nearly all modern cryptographic works. The algebra has applications in combinatorics, graph theory, automata theory, and complexity theory.

The transformation, like homomorphism, and isomorphism are used for carrying the solutions of problems from one platform to other with the aim to achieve simpler solutions and better ways to analyze these solutions.

The machines can be represented in the form of algebraic structures like, monoid, semigroup, groups and the arithmetic on these structures can map to that performed on the machines. This helps greatly in study of machines, because they can be treated as algebras.

Languages can be defined on an alphabet set, as a sets of strings. Thus languages have all the operations of sets, in addition, the languages have an operation of Kleene star, which is operation of concatenation executed an arbitrary number of times.

Given any alphabet, infinite number of languages can be defined—that are not countable. But, all possible algorithms though infinite, are countable only. With this argument it can be concluded that, there can exist many languages for which no algorithms exists to recognize them.

Self Review Questions

1. Define computer science.
2. Why computer theory is important in the highly practical field of computer science?
3. Define computability.
4. Write formal description for following sets:

   a. Set containing 1, 10, 100, and 1000.
   b. Set containing an empty string.
   c. Set containing only string *abc*.
   d. Set containing natural numbers that are <10.

5. State whether the following as True or False.

   a. $A \in \mathscr{P}(A)$, where $\mathscr{P}$ is power set.
   b. $\{a, b, c\} \notin \{a, b, \{a, b, c\}\}$.
   c. $\{a, b, c\} \subseteq \{a, b, \{a, b, c\}\}$.
   d. $\phi \subseteq A$.
   e. $\{\phi\} \subseteq A$.

6. Define the following terms:
   semigroup, monoid, ring, field, group, commutative group, Abelian group.
7. Give formal definition of concatenation of strings.
8. Is computer closer to science or mathematics? Justify.
9. Explain in your own way the proof by Induction and by Deduction.
10. What is canonical order?

11. How the definitions of strings in this chapter differ from strings in C-language?
12. What basic operations can be performed on Sets?
13. What is string manipulations?
14. Define the string concatenation using recursion.
15. What set operations can be performed on Languages?
16. Given a finite set of alphabets, why there exist an infinite number of languages on that?
17. What is mathematical concept of Algorithm?
18. What operations of sets are not allowed on Languages?

Exercises

A. Concepts based Problems

Note: The $*$ marked exercises are provided with solutions at the end of this book.

1. Define the discipline of computing. What are the areas covered under this? Is it Science or Engineering? Explain with justification.
2. Define and describe Meta Computer Science?
3. Given an alphabet set, describe a language over that.
4. Define *Kleene's star* operation Σ^* on alphabet set Σ, and discuss its significance.
5. Given the languages $L_1 = \{\varepsilon, 0, 1\}$ and $L_2 = \{\varepsilon, 01, 11\}$, find out $L_1 \cap L_2$, $L_1 \cup L_2$, L_1^*, L_2^*, $L_1 \circ L_2$, and $L_1 - L_2$, $L_2 - L_1$.
6. What is meaning of the statement: Countably infinite representation of languages and uncountably infinite existence of languages? What is its theoretical significance?

B. Analysis-based Problems

7. How the *Process* and *Memory* can be treated as same resource, when represented using semigroup?
8. Give a mathematical definition of solvability of a problem.
9. List the first 10 strings of $\{a, b, c\}^*$.

   a. In alphabetical order.
   b. In canonical ordering.
   c. In lexicographic order.

10. Which of the following are functions?

    a. A bijection from $\{\varepsilon\}$ to $\{0\}$.
    b. A partial one-to-one and onto from $\mathbb{N}$ to $\mathbb{N}$.
    c. A partial one-to-one and onto from Int to $\mathbb{N}$.
    d. A bijection from Int to Real.
    e. A bijection from a set to its power set.
    f. A many-to-one from power set to a set.

11. * For the sets $|A| = m$, and $|B| = n$, find the maximum number of functions that can be defined from A to B.
12. * Which of the following functions are computable?

    a. A function, which inverts every bit of an infinite stream of bits.
    b. $S = \{x \mid x \notin x\}$
    c. $f(x) = \begin{cases} x, & \text{if } odd(x); \\ x = x - 1, & \text{otherwise.} \end{cases}$
    d. $f : x \rightarrow \text{succ}(x)$.

13. Can there be an algorithm that can find out whether a given C language program terminates on an input x? Justify your answer for Yes/No.
14. How many strings of length l are in Σ^* if Σ is alphabet of cardinality r?
15. For each of the following cases give the first 10 strings in Σ^* if $\Sigma = \{a, b, c\}$.

    a. Σ^* is given in alphabetical order.
    b. Σ^* is given in canonical order.

16. It is given that $L = \{01, 00, 100\}$. Which of the following strings are in L^*? 01001000100, 000010000, 10000100001, 100000100

C. Proof-based Problems

17. For any arbitrary sets A, B, C, prove the following:

    a. $A - B \subset A$.
    b. $A \cap (B - A) = \phi$.
    c. $A \cup (B - A) = A \cup B$.

18. If $A \subset B$ then prove that $A \cup (B - A) = B$.
19. Show that "congruent modulo" n is an equivalence relation.
20. If a, x, y are elements of a group G, then prove that $ax = ay$, iff $x = y$.
21. If a, b are elements in a group G, then show that $(ab)^{-1} = b^{-1}a^{-1}$.
22. If G is a multiplicative group, such that for each $x \in G$, there is $xx = e$, where e is *neutral element*. Show that G is Abelian group. [Hint: 0 is neutral element for multiplication, such that $x \cdot 0 = 0$.]
23. Prove that every group containing five or less elements is Abelian group.
24. Prove that if G is a group, then every element in G has finite order.
25. Every element x in group G is infinite order if and only if x^{-1} has infinite order.
26. Prove that inverse of one-to-one mapping between set A and set B is one-to-one mapping between B and A.
27. Prove using contradiction that ϕ is subset of every set.
28. * If x is composite integer, then show that there is at least one prime p that divides x, and $p \leq \sqrt{x}$.
29. Write down the formal proofs to show that $\sqrt{3}$ and $\sqrt{6}$ are irrational.
30. Prove that $\sqrt{2} + \sqrt{3}$ is irrational.
31. The sum of two rational numbers is always rational. Is the sum of two irrational numbers also irrational? Prove or disprove.

32. Prove by induction that $|A \times B| = |A| \cdot |B|$ for all sets A and B.
33. Prove that the inverse of a one-to-one correspondence between A and B is one-to-one correspondence between B and A.
34. * If $f : A \rightarrow B$, and $g : B \rightarrow C$, then prove the following:

    a. If f and g are both *bijections* then $g \circ f$ is also *bijections*.
    b. If f and g have inverses then $(g \circ f)^{-1} = f^{-1} \circ g^{-1}$.
    c. If $f \circ g$ is injection then g is injection.
    d. If $f \circ g$ is surjection then f is surjection.

35. Prove that power set of any set $|A| \neq \phi$ has cardinality greater than set A.
36. * Show that rational numbers are countable.
37. Can there be an algorithm, which can find out whether any two arbitrary C-programs P_1 and P_2 will produce same result for same inputs? Justify your answer.
38. Prove that there is a bijection $A \times (B \times C) \rightarrow (A \times B) \times C$.

D. Advanced Knowledge Assessment Problems

39. Set theory is said to be backbone of computer science. Write an essay in about 200–300 words, as how this statement is true, considering the diversity of topics like computer languages, hardware, system and applications software, and theory of computation?
40. What is significance of the topics: Cantors's diagonal argument and Russell's paradox?
41. Give examples of some problems of practical importance in computer science, which can be modeled using Graphs.
42. What is significance of Homomorphism and Isomorphism in data encryption/security?

References

1. Aigner M, Ziegler GM (2003) Proofs from the book, 3rd edn. Springer, July 2003
2. Chowdhary KR (2016) Introduction to theory of computation. http://www.krchowdhary.com/toc/1-intro.pdf. Cited 02 Aug 2020
3. Chowdhary KR (2015) Fundamentals of discrete mathematical structures, 3rd edn. PHI Learning, New Delhi
4. Egri-Nagy A (2005) Algebraic hierarchical decomposition of finite state automaton—a computational approach. PhD thesis, submitted to school of Computer Science, Faculty of Engineering and Information Sciences, University of Hertfordshire, November 2005
5. Ganesh G (2009) Computation engineering-applied automata theory and logic. Springer International Edition
6. Gueron S (2001) A game-like activity for learning Cantor's theorem. Coll Math J 32(2):122–125

7. Kenneth K, John R (1965) Algebraic theory of machines. I. Prime decomposition theorem for finite semigroups and machines. Trans Am Math Soci 116:450–464
8. Landin J (2012) An introduction to algebraic structures. Courier Corporation
9. Wallace DAR (1998) Groups, rings, and fields. Springer International Edition

Part II
Finite Automata and Regular Languages

Part II of the book delves into Chaps. 2 to 5, which encompass topics such as finite automata, regular expressions, variants of finite automata, automata minimization, and regular languages. While these topics may initially seem distinct, they share an underlying equivalence relationship: FA (finite automata) = regular expressions = regular language = NFA (nondeterministic finite automata) = 2DFA (two-way deterministic finite automata). Consequently, the book explores various methods and algorithms for converting between these different forms, including the conversion of finite automata to regular expressions and vice versa, simplifying automata for minimization, and performing set operations on machines, regular expressions, and regular languages.

Distinguishing itself from the others, the sections on finite automata with output, encompassing Mealy and Moore machines, go beyond mere acceptance or rejection of input. Instead, it produces output strings corresponding to input strings, finding applications in fields like speech recognition and modeling natural phenomena.

The remaining three components—finite automata, regular expressions, and regular languages—find wide-ranging applications in language processing, development of lexical analyzers in compiler construction, natural language processing, modeling switching circuits, and practical applications like elevator simulation. Furthermore, finite automata play a crucial role in high-speed text searching.

Notably, these devices exhibit linear complexity, both in space and time. The sets of finite automata machines, regular languages, and regular expressions are all infinite and countable, with a one-to-one mapping to the set of natural numbers, $\mathbb{N}$.

Each of these chapters is accompanied by an extensive collection of related exercises, with solutions provided for some of them to aid in comprehension and practice.

Chapter 2
Finite Automata and Regular Expressions

Abstract The finite automata and regular languages have been used in a wide variety of problems in computing, communication, and control, including formal modeling and verification. Finite automata (FA) are recognizers of the simplest kind of the languages—the regular languages. The sentences of these languages are tokens, which have applications in compilers and natural language processing; many modern language processing have also tokenization as a built-in feature. This chapter presents the theory of FA with emphasis on problem solution. The regular expressions and operation on them are introduced in a self-taught style. The design aspects of FA for some applications are also introduced. Other topics, like compilation of regular expressions to build lexical analyzers, countable sets, decidable properties of FA, and recursive and recursively enumerable languages, have been introduced. The number of worked examples have also been added, along with self-review questions and exercises for practice followed by relevant references at the end.

Keywords Automata theory · Models of FA · Language recognizers · Transition function · Regular expressions · Language generators · Regular languages · Countable sets · Recursive languages · Recursively enumerable languages · FA applications

2.1 Introduction

The theoretical computer science is divided into three key areas, namely, automata theory, computability theory, and complexity theory. The goal of this theory is to ascertain the power of computation and limits of computation. In order to study these aspects, it is necessary to define precisely what constitutes a model of computation, and what constitutes a computational problem. The computation models are automata, while the computational problems are formulated as formal languages. A common theme of study is relation between the model of computation and the computational problem it solves. The Church–Turing thesis (Chap. 9) conjectures that any problem that can be solved through computational means, can be solved by a Turing machine, hence the notion of algorithm is equal to a Turing machine.

K. R. Chowdhary, *Theory of Computation*,
https://doi.org/10.1007/978-981-97-6234-7_2

Fig. 2.1 A machine's model

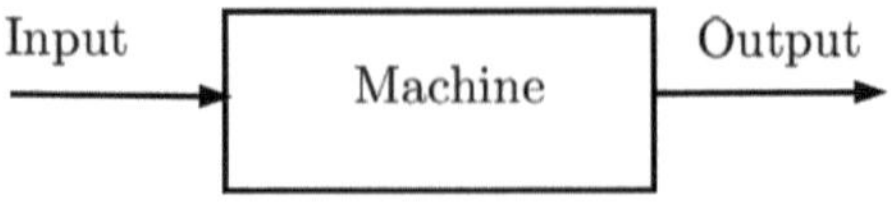

The main concern for us is designing of computer. By making some arbitrary decisions here we shall continue our attention to certain sub-classes of automata. The first decision we make is to use only discrete descriptions; this means that between any two moments there is a finite number of other moments. This design is consequence of our interest in digital computers. It emphasizes discrete mathematics in analysis of the system under investigation: recursive function and symbolic logic [3].

We always exclude an "actual infinity" of elements at each time; and each element can be in only one of a finite number of states, at any time. Thus total sates possible are finite. The stipulation that behavior of automata at time $t + 1$ is determined by the past, leaves unsettled question as to how the remote past influences the present. We will assume that such inferences occur indirectly through states at intermediate time moments, so that to calculate the state of automaton at $t + 1$ it is not necessary to know its state for any time earlier than the preceding moment t. Thus, we assume that for the present to be influenced by an event, which happened in the remote past, a record of that event must have been preserved internally during the intervening time. This postulate corresponds closely to the actual mode of operation of automatic systems.

Keeping the above in mind, the principal goal in this chapter is to model the behavior of a machine that accepts finitely many inputs and produces finitely many outputs (see Fig. 2.1). A machine accepts something from the outside world, processes it, and then produces something for the outside world.

Computer Science is rife with diverse examples of machines, ranging from simple hardware components like combinational circuits to software systems like compilers and text editors, to the very structure of a computer itself. The modern world is full of machines that are by no means *high-tech*, yet display the input/output principle. Some are ridiculously simple, like as a grinder, or mechanical as a car or electromechanical as an elevator. The more complex one could consider the human brain as a machine.

The finite automata have many applications in computer science. Following are some most common applications:

- *Lexical analysis*: Finite automata are extensively used in compilers and programming language processing for lexical analysis, which involves tokenizing the source code into meaningful tokens. Lexical analyzers, also known as scanners, use finite automata to recognize and classify the tokens based on patterns specified by regular expressions. This process is a crucial first step in the compilation process.
- *Regular expressions and pattern matching*: Regular expressions are powerful tools for specifying patterns in strings. Finite automata can be constructed from regular expressions, allowing efficient pattern matching in text processing applications. Finite automata-based pattern matching algorithms enable tasks such as searching

for specific patterns in documents, validating input against a defined pattern, or extracting information from structured data.

- *Network protocols*: Finite automata find applications in the modeling and analysis of network protocols. Network protocols often have specific rules and state transitions, which can be represented and analyzed using finite automata. This helps in protocol verification, testing, and the development of efficient implementations.
- *Circuit design*: Finite automata are used in digital circuit design and sequential circuit analysis. Sequential circuits, such as finite-state machines (FSMs), can be modeled as finite automata. This allows designers to analyze and optimize the behavior of circuits, verify correctness, and ensure proper functioning of the sequential components.
- *DNA sequence analysis*: Finite automata are employed in bioinformatics for DNA sequence analysis. By modeling DNA sequences as input strings, finite automata can be used to search for specific patterns or motifs in genomic data, aiding in gene identification, sequence alignment, and other bioinformatics tasks [4].
- *Protocol analysis and security*: Finite automata are used in the analysis and verification of communication protocols and security protocols. They help identify possible protocol violations, detect security vulnerabilities, and analyze the behavior of complex systems involving multiple interacting entities.

The aim of the following discussion is to take a theoretical from a mathematical standpoint. What all machines seem to have in common is that while processing input they can change their *internal state* from one internal configuration to another as a reaction to that input. The actual physical form of a machine's configuration is not really important. Far more to the point is that, at any point in time, a machine finds itself in a given state. Another characteristic of real-world machines is that they are finite and, as such, can only assume a finite number of states. In modeling a machine's behavior it is important to consider the machine's transitions from one state to another.

Learning Outcomes of this Chapter:

1. Concepts in automata and formal languages. [Knowledge]
2. Finite state machines. [Comprehension], [Application]
3. Regular Expressions. [Knowledge]
4. Recursive languages vs regular expressions. [Synthesis], [Evaluation]
5. Recognition of regular languages. [Application]

2.2 Automata Theory

The automata theory tools, or broad knowledge, comprise the equally broad subject of computation, or what can be computed or processed. Computation is a broad subject because it not only includes much of the artificial world, such as computer hardware circuits and software, but also the natural world, such as brain and nervous system operations and the plant growth processes, and their modelings. In order to facilitate the study of this very broad subject of computation, the automata is introduced.

The automata is like a black box, with inputs, outputs, and states. The states represent the behavior of the internal workings, which are not important. At any moment in time, the automata (also automaton) is in only one of the states. The output of automaton is based on the state of the automaton and its inputs. Thus, automaton is an abstract mathematical concept, or model of the computation or a process of interest. The mathematics which is used to study problems in AT is appropriately called *abstract algebra*, which we have discussed in the first chapter.

The abstract concepts in CS are not easy to grasp at undergraduate. Quite often one's first course in AT is sequential machines theory, which is a real-world foundation. The AT's abstractness lends to versatility. For example, a concept that is expressed in abstract algebra might have originated in computer circuit. Once in algebraic notation, formal mathematics can be applied to it to analyze it, change it to different forms, and possibly find ways to optimize or minimize it. Further, by being in this abstract form, the concept could be translated into (realized or synthesized in) any of several structures such as hardware circuits, software programs, biological systems, or combinations thereof.

Automata Theory Versus Computer Science

Automata theory is an abstract mathematical representation of computational procedures used in modern digital computations. The goal of automata theory is to provide a sound mathematical model for the investigation of these processes. It is a simulation model for the study of computation; usually, the model exists only on paper and is described in the language of mathematics. One of the principal advantages of using a simulation model is that it provides insight into the behavior being simulated. These insights frequently get obscured when we look directly into the process at an operational level. A model satisfies its purpose if it can predict the behavior of the process it is modeling, to the desired degree of detail [2].

Our automata-theoretic models will be designed to grasp the overall structure of computational problems and to eliminate the superfluous detail. Sometimes, a process of designing a model can be instrumental in increasing our understanding of the original process. Thus, our reasons for studying automata theory are twofold:

(a) to create a mathematical model to investigate computational processes, and
(b) to gain insights into the organization of problems for computer-based solution.

The theory of automata consists of the foundation for many branches in computer science. In essence, it is a theory about *sequences* of discrete events occurring one after other and about formalism for describing sets of such sequences, most notably by finite-state transition system (automata) that generates or accepts them. Since automata can model computer programs, digital circuits, and many other discrete event dynamic systems, they can be used for simulation, verification, and synthesis of such systems.

Originally, the theory of finite automata was developed as a mathematical theory for sequential circuits. A sequential circuit maintains a present state from a finite number of possible states. The circuit logic (which is a finite-state control) decides the new state based on the present state of the circuit and the input. Once an input is processed, the circuit will not be able to read it again.

The FA concept is used in the design of *lexical analyzers* in compilers, where various tokens such as $+$, $-$, $=$, *begin*, *end*, *temp* are identified in the input source program. Simulated finite automata can be used for searching the string patterns in any arbitrarily large text. Other applications of FA are string matching, natural language processing, speech processing, and text compression.

2.3 Modeling of Programs and Computation

Finite automata (FA) or *finite-state machine* (finite automaton for singular) is the simplest computing model considered in computer science. In fact, finite automata correspond to special restricted programs that solve design problems without the use of variables. Finite automata works in real time; the input word is read only once, from the left to the right on a tape, and output (i.e., result) is decided immediately after the last symbol of the input has been read. The FA provides a very transparent and simple way for explaining how to model computations. It introduces the basic notion of theoretical computer science such as configurations, computations and computation steps, simulation, determinism, and nondeterminism, and gives a reasonable intuition about the general meaning of these fundamental terms and also some experience in working with them. These concepts would help us later in simplifying the way of explaining the exact meaning of these terms in the framework of general models of algorithmic computations.

FA as CPU

The finite automaton shares its features with the real computer in the sense that it has a Central Processing Unit (CPU) of fixed finite and very limited capacity, called finite control. It always receives the input as a string of symbols, which is delivered to it through an input tape. The FA does not deliver any output, but simply gives an indication as whether the string which has been input to it is accepted or not. It is a restricted model of real computer, because the memory unit of a real computer is absent in the finite automata, and whatever is memory part, is present only in the CPU. Since the input and intermediate results cannot be stored, a finite automaton is severely limited in its capacity to "remember" the things during the computational process. Though a finite automaton is limited in capability due to the absence of memory, it is useful in understanding the working of computers, as well as it has applications in the design of several types of computer algorithms.

Since finite automaton does not have any memory, except the memory where the program is permanently saved and a pointer showing the currently executed row (instruction) of the program, which means that a program may not use any variable. At the first look, this appears unacceptable as how a program computes without variables. The idea is that the content of the pointer, i.e., the number of the actual

Fig. 2.2 FA as program

$$\begin{array}{l}\text{row } q_0 \text{ select, input} = a_1 \text{ goto } q_{i_1}\\ \text{row } q_1 \text{ select, input} = a_2 \text{ goto } q_{i_2}\\ \cdots\ \cdots\ \cdots\cdots\ \cdots\cdots = \cdots\ \cdots\cdots\ \cdots\\ \text{row } q_{n-1} \text{ select, input} = a_k \text{ goto } q_{i_m}\end{array}$$

(executed) program row is the only changing information and the program computes with this pseudo-variable, called *state*.

If $\Sigma = \{a_1, a_2, \ldots, a_k\}$ is the alphabet over which the input is represented, then a finite automata may only use the following instructions, as shown in Fig. 2.2.

The meaning of the *select* is that the program reads the next input symbol and compares it with $a_1, a_2, \ldots, a_k$. If input symbol that has been read is equal to a_j, the program continues next instruction in the row q_{i_j} ($i_j \in \{0, 1, ..., n-1\}$) and automata reads the next symbol. Every row of the program contains exactly one instruction of this type. The rows of the program are $q_0, q_1, q_2, \ldots, q_{n-1}$ and FA always start at *row* q_0. The row number corresponds to state of the FA. If the program consists n rows $\{0, 1, \ldots, n-1\}$, then one could choose a subset $F \subseteq \{q_0, q_1, \ldots, q_{n-1}\}$, where F is an accepting set. After reading the last symbol of the input word, if the program moves to a row $q_i \in F$, the word is accepted by the program, i.e., the program gives the answer "yes" for this entire input sequence. If the final value of row is in $\{q_0, q_1, \ldots, q_{n-1}\} - F$, the program does not accept the input and the answer is "No".

The size of the input string $|w| = l$, may be more than the number of rows. If set of rows is $|Q|$, then if $|w| \geq |Q|$, at least one row is repeated at least once in the process of reading the input.

2.4 Finite Automata Model

The conceptual model of finite-state machine is illustrated in the Fig. 2.3. The strings of symbols are read by the FA through an *input tape*, which has equal size squares on it, and each of them holds one symbol. The principle part of FA is *finite control*, which occupies one of the states at a time out of a number of states. The finite control has *reading head*, which always points to the input tape and can read one symbol at a time. There is no writing head, hence FA can only **read** the input symbols from the input tape.

Before reading the input, the read head remains pointing to the leftmost square on the tape and the finite control is set to the specified initial state called *start state*. Every time a symbol is read from the tape, the finite control moves to a definite next state depending on symbol read and the current state of the finite control, and the read head advances to next square on the input tape. This process continues until the input symbols' string on the tape is exhausted, i.e., end of the input string is reached.

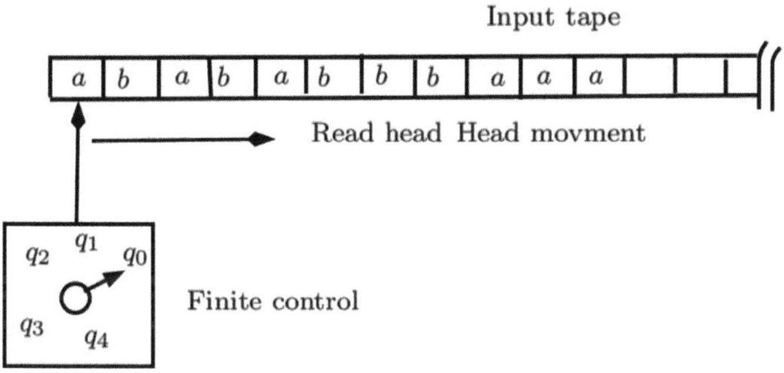

Fig. 2.3 Physical model of FA

Thus, the new or next state is a deterministic function of two parameters: (i) the current state of FA, and (ii) the current input symbol at the read head. Because the next state is definite or deterministic in nature, the automaton is called *Deterministic Finite Automaton* (DFA).[1]

When FA ultimately reaches to the end of the input string, it indicates its approval or disapproval about the acceptance of the input string, through the state in which it finally lands. If it is one of the final states, the input string is accepted otherwise not. In this way, a finite automata ultimately leads to the final state for certain (valid) input strings, and to non-final for other strings. Thus, language accepted by a particular FA is the set of those valid strings that it accepts.

2.4.1 Mathematical Model

Now, we are in a position to formally define a FA, i.e., deterministic FA (DFA), as a 5-tuple. However, we may use both the names FA and DFA interchangingly in our discussions, which means same type of machine unless it is specifically mentioned. We shall represent the FA by symbol M as,

$$M = (Q, \Sigma, \delta, s, F), \tag{2.1}$$

where

Σ is a finite set of *input alphabet* (every symbol present on input tape is from Σ),
Q is *finite* set of states,
δ is *transition function*, which decides new state based on the current state and current input symbol. Therefore,[2]

---

[1] We will be using the term FA to mean deterministic finite automata, and when we shall study the nondeterministic finite automata in the next chapter, we will mention specifically NFA. In fact, a DFA is a special case of an NFA, as we will see later.

$$\delta : Q \times \Sigma \mapsto Q, \tag{2.2}$$

s is *start state* of DFA, $s \in Q$, and
F is set of *final* or *accepting states*, and $F \subseteq Q$

The rules according to which finite automaton M picks up the next state are encoded in the transition function δ (delta). Therefore, if DFA M is in state $q \in Q$ and the symbol read from input tape is $\sigma \in \Sigma$, then the next state is $\delta(q, \sigma) \in Q$, which is uniquely determined state to which M will move.

Given an input string, the DFA will go through different *configurations* when it reads the input symbols one after another. Each configuration (also called ID—*Instantaneous Description*) of DFA is a combination of—*finite control* and *input tape*. In other words, each configuration is an element[3] of $Q \times \Sigma^*$. For a configuration $(q_i, abcd)$, where the current state is q_i and input symbol a, if the DFA moves to new state q_j, then its new configuration will be (q_j, bcd). A binary relation $\vdash_M$ (read as moves) represents this change of configuration of a FA in a single move. Hence,

$$(q_i, abcd) \vdash_M (q_j, bcd), \tag{2.3}$$

where $a, b, c, d \in \Sigma$, and $q_i, q_j \in Q$. Figure 2.4a and b show two different configurations of a DFA.

In general, we can say (q_i, u) yields (q_j, v) in single move specified as $q_i u \vdash q_j v$, where $u, v \in \Sigma^*$. In the process of moving a DFA from one configuration to the next, ultimately v becomes *null* when end of the input string is reached. After this, no further move takes place. Hence, $\vdash_M$ is a mapping from $Q \times \Sigma^*$ to $Q \times \Sigma^*$ expressed as

$$\vdash_M : Q \times \Sigma^* \mapsto Q \times \Sigma^*. \tag{2.4}$$

2.4.2 FA as Language Recognizer

Let us ponder what problems this simple machine can solve. Most problems in mathematics require memory, and the size of memory required is arbitrarily large for an arbitrary size of the problem. One of the problems in this category is of primality testing. As the number to be tested for primality becomes larger and larger, the memory required becomes larger and larger. On the other hand is the problem to test whether a given sequence of binary bits has odd or even parity. This problem will

[2] The symbol '$\mapsto$'stands for "mapsto", and does not allow for reverse mapping. However, instead of this, we shall be mostly using the symbol '$\rightarrow$'(implication) in our discussions, due to its popularity in computer science.

[3] The symbol "*" is called Kleene star of Σ here, which stands for any arbitrary string made of symbols from Σ. The string may be of arbitrary length, including of null string (ε).

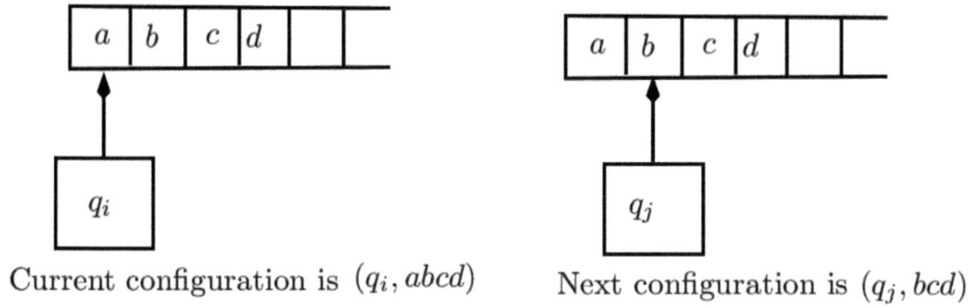

Fig. 2.4 **a** FA with read head at start. **b** FA with read head at intermediate position

Table 2.1 δ functional relationship

Current state q	Next state for Input 0	Next state for Input 1
q_0	q_0	q_1
q_1	q_0	q_2
q_2	q_2	q_1

require finite memory and arbitrary size of the tape to hold input string of binary sequence. The finite automata is considered fit for solving this second category of problems.

Consider that a configuration (q_0, w) results to (q', w') configuration after certain moves have taken place by the FA, which we represent as follows:

$$(q_0, w) \vdash_M \cdots \vdash_M (q', w'). \tag{2.5}$$

This can also be represented by $(q_0, w) \vdash_M^* (q', w')$, where $\vdash_M^*$ is called *transitive closure* of $\vdash_M$, showing that FA moves from configuration (q_0, w) to (q', w') in zero or more number of moves. The string $w \in \Sigma^*$ is accepted by the finite automata if $w' = \varepsilon$ (null string) and $q' \in F$. Thus, the language accepted by the DFA M, is set of all the strings accepted by M, i.e.,

$$L(M) = \{w \mid w \in \Sigma^* \text{ and } (q_0, w) \vdash_M^* (q', \varepsilon) \text{ and } q' \in F\}. \tag{2.6}$$

Example 2.1 Represent the DFA $M = (Q, \Sigma, \delta, s, F)$ using transition graph, and find out the language recognized by this, for the following values of tuples:

$Q = \{q_0, q_1, q_2\}$
$\Sigma = \{0, 1\}$
$s = q_0$
$F = \{q_1\}$
δ is transition Table 2.1.

The intuitive idea of solution is as follows: while the FA is at state q_0 with input '0', it goes back to state q_0, which indicates a loop at the start state q_0, and similar is the

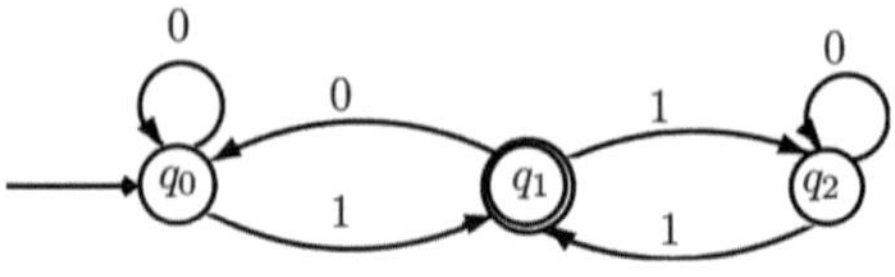

Fig. 2.5 A finite automata

situation at q_2. The transition graph (also called *state diagram*) for M, corresponding to the transition Table 2.1 is shown in Fig. 2.5. The q_0 is the starting state, shown by a circle with incoming arrow, and the final state (q_1) is enclosed in double circles to make it distinct from other states.

Note that, DFA has every possible transition (corresponding to a symbol in Σ) at every state. Hence, the total number of transitions are $|\Sigma| \times |Q|$, which, in this case is $2 \times 3 = 6$.

Given an input of $w = 00110001$, the sequence of configurations to which the machine passes is as follows:

$$\begin{aligned}(q_0, 00110001) &\vdash_M (q_0, 0110001)\\ &\vdash_M (q_0, 110001)\\ &\vdash_M (q_1, 10001)\\ &\vdash_M (q_2, 0001)\\ &\vdash_M (q_2, 001)\\ &\vdash_M (q_2, 01)\\ &\vdash_M (q_2, 1)\\ &\vdash_M (q_1, \varepsilon).\end{aligned}$$

Since $(q_0, 00110001) \vdash_M^* (q_1, \varepsilon)$ and $q_1 \in F$, the string 00110001 is accepted by M. □

2.4.3 *Extended Transition Function*

Let us assume that an input string *abb* causes a FA to go through states q_1, q_2, and q_3 in order, from its initial state q_0. These transitions can be specified by

$\delta(q_0, a) = q_1$
$\delta(q_1, b) = q_2$
$\delta(q_2, b) = q_3$.

From above, we get

$$\delta(\delta(q_0, a), b) = q_2.$$

When part of this q_2 is substituted for q_2 in third equation above, we get

$$\delta(\delta(\delta(q_0, a), b), b) = q_3.$$

This shows a case of multiple applications of transition function δ, equal to n times, where n is the length of the input string. We can rewrite the above expression as

$$\delta^*(q_0, abb) = q_3,$$

where δ^* is called as *extended* transition function, and defined as

$$\delta^* : Q \times \Sigma^* \mapsto Q. \tag{2.7}$$

Also, $\delta^*(q_0, w) \in F$, if w is accepted by the finite automaton.

Definition 2.1 (*Language of FA*) If w is set of all the strings in $L(M)$—the language of FA, then

$$L(M) = \{w \in \Sigma^* \mid \delta^*(q_0, w) \in F\}, \tag{2.8}$$

and the complement of this language of M is a set of strings,

$$\overline{L(M)} = \{w \in \Sigma^* \mid \delta^*(q_0, w) \notin F\}, \tag{2.9}$$

which is set of all the strings in Σ^* but not in $L(M)$. In other words, the finite automata accepting complement of a language is a new finite automata with final and non-final states interchanged. □

Example 2.2 Design a deterministic finite automaton M that accepts the language $L(M) = \{w \in \{a, b\}^* \mid w \text{ does not contain two consecutive } b\text{'s}\}$.

Let the finite automata which recognizes this language be $M = (\Sigma, Q, \delta, s, F)$. The intuitive idea for a FA for this is as follows: The string $w \in L(M)$ should not contain two consecutive bs, but it may contain any number of bs and any number of as. In addition, once the FA receives two consecutive bs at input, it should reach to a state from where it cannot reach to the final state, irrespective of whatever additional sequence it receives.

Figure 2.6 is DFA and Table 2.2 is corresponding transition table. Note that once two consecutive b's are received the DFA enters into state q_2 from where it can never exit. Thus, q_2 is called *dead state*. Since, only condition for non-accepting is bb substring, the other all the strings, without bb as substring, are accepted. Hence, all the remaining states except q_2, are accepting states.

All the strings of language $L(M)$ for the above finite automaton can be described using a regular expression $(a + ba)^*(b + \phi)$, and,

$$L(M) = \{\varepsilon, a, b, ab, ba, bab, \ldots\}.$$

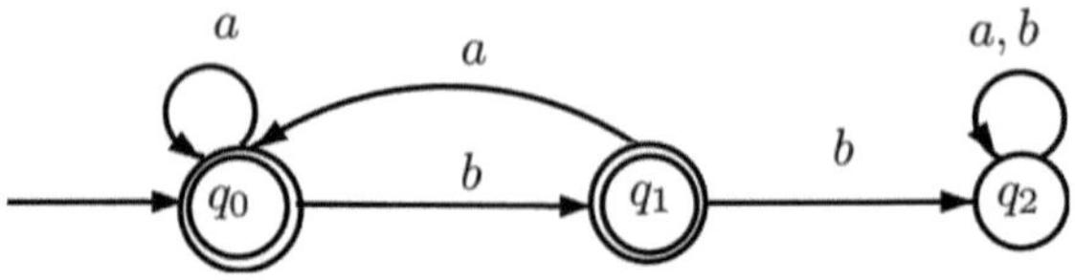

Fig. 2.6 A DFA with two accepting states

Table 2.2 Transition table

Previous state q	Current input a	Current input b
q_0	q_0	q_1
q_1	q_0	q_2
q_2	q_2	q_2

We note that no string with bb as substring can be generated by this regular expression. □

Example 2.3 How many DFAs with two states can be constructed over an alphabet of $\Sigma = \{a, b\}$, with the designated initial state.

For each state, there can be $|\Sigma|$ number of edges coming out, so there are total $|\Sigma| \times |Q|$ possible ways edges can be connected to $|Q|$ states. So total DFAs are $2^{\Sigma Q} = 2^{2\times 2} = 2^4 = 16$, with two states in each. These two states can be in the following possible forms:

1. q_0 start state, and q_1 as final state,
2. reverse of above,
3. both the states as final, and
4. no final state.

Hence, the total possible number of DFAs with two states and $\Sigma| = 2$ can be $4 \times 16 = 64$. □

2.5 Regular Expressions

A regular expression (regex), often called a *pattern*, is an expression that describes a set of strings. They are used to give a concise description of a set, without having to list its all elements. For example, a set containing three strings "Raj", "Rajan", and "Rajam" can be described by the pattern "Raj(ε|an|am)". The vertical bar separates alternatives, and the parentheses are used to define the scope and precedence of operators. In most formalism, if there is any regex that matches a particular set, then there are an infinite number of such expressions. The quantifier $*$ (asterisk) as power to an expression indicates that the expression repeats an indefinite number of times. For example, "ab^*cd" matches all the strings $acd, abcd, abbcd, abbbcd$, etc. A "+" sign is used in place of separator '|'. Thus, the regex $ab + cd + efg$ matches all the strings ab, cd, efg. A sign of concatenation "$\circ$" is used to join the strings. Thus, the regex $ab \circ cde$ matches with the string $abcde$. For the sake of convenience, in this text, a reference to strings ab, cd, efg will mean "ab", "cd", "efg", respectively. Various constructs, like $+$, $*$ and | can be combined to form arbitrarily complex regular expressions very much like one constructs arithmetic expressions from numbers and operators $+$, $-$, $*$, and $/$.

In the design of sequential circuits, the first step is obtaining an unambiguous description of a circuit's behavior. For a certain class of problems, language of regular expressions greatly simplifies this first step of *synthesis*. In general, the richer the language, the easier it is to write the problem specifications.

The regular expressions have number of applications in computer science; for example, they can be used for designing sequential circuits, and in the *lexical analysis* of programs. The other applications are pattern recognition and pattern matching, text editing, and in bibliographic search systems. Common to all these approaches is that regular expressions must be converted into a finite automaton [5].

As an application of regular expression, Ken Thompson built the notations of regular expressions into the editor QED as a means to match patterns in text files [8]. Later, he added this capability into the *Unix* editor *ed*. The regex was later used in the design of other Unix tools, like: *grep* (global regular expression print), *expr* (expression evaluation), *awk*,[4] *vi* (visual editor), *lex* (lexical analyzer generator), and in the scripting languages *Perl* and *Tcl*.

2.5.1 Operations on Regular Expressions

To begin our study of finite representations, we consider expressions in the form of symbols that describe how language can be built up using the operations. Suppose that we have the language

$$L = \{w \mid w \in \{0,1\}^*, w \text{ has two or three occurrences, of 1, first and second of which are not consecutive}\}.$$

This language can be described using only *singleton* sets and the symbols: $\cup$, $\circ$, and ϕ as below.

$$\{0\}^* \circ \{1\} \circ \{0\}^*\{0\} \circ \{1\} \circ \{0\}^* \circ ((\{1\} \circ \{0\}^*) \cup \phi).$$

It can be easily verified that the language represented by the above expression is precisely the L, and can also be represented in a simplified and compact form $0^*10^*010^*(10^* + \phi)$, called *regular expression*. A regular expression describes a

[4] Scripting and token processing language, after the name of three computer scientists—Aho, Weinberger, and Kernighan, who authored this language.

language exclusively by means of language alphabets and ϕ, and possibly combined with symbols, $\circ$, $\cup$, and $*$.

The regular expressions over the alphabet are defined inductively [10].

Definition 2.2 (*Regular Expression*) Given the Σ as alphabet, a regular expression is defined recursively as follows:

(a) ϕ, ε, and each $a \in \Sigma$ is a regular expression,
(b) If α and β are regular expressions then so are $\alpha \circ \beta$, $\alpha \cup \beta$, α^*, β^*,
(c) Nothing other than (a) and (b) above is a regular expression. □

The step (a) above is called *Basis* step and step (b) is called *Induction step*, hence this definition is called *Inductive definition* of regular expression. Every regular expression represents a language according to the interpretation of symbol $\cup$ and $*$, which are set union and Kleene star respectively, and *juxtaposition* of expressions using concatenation operator '$\circ$'. Formally, a relation exists between the regular expression and the language it represents. This relation is expressed by the function $\mathscr{L}$, such that if α is any regular expression then $\mathscr{L}(\alpha)$ is the language represented by it. In other words, $\mathscr{L}$ is a function from regex strings to the language [5].

Definition 2.3 (*Language over a Regular expression*) Given a regular expression, the language over this can be inductively defined as follows [6]:

1. $\mathscr{L}(\phi) = \phi$, $\mathscr{L}(\varepsilon) = \{\varepsilon\}$, $\mathscr{L}(a) = \{a\}$, for $a \in \Sigma$.
2. If α and β are regular expressions, then
   a. $\alpha\beta$ is regular expression, and corresponding regular language is $\mathscr{L}(\alpha\beta) = \mathscr{L}(\alpha)\mathscr{L}(\beta)$,
   b. $\alpha \cup \beta$ is regular expression and corresponding regular language is $\mathscr{L}(\alpha) \cup \mathscr{L}(\beta)$,
   c. α^* is regular expression, and corresponding regular language is $\mathscr{L}(\alpha^*) = (\mathscr{L}(\alpha))^*$. □

The statement (1) above defines the language $\mathscr{L}$ as ϕ, $\{\varepsilon\}$, and $\{a\}$ for the regular expression ϕ, ε, a, respectively. The expressions (2) define the language for the regular expression obtained by combining the regular expressions. The combination is done using operators of $+$ and $\circ$. The operator of $*$ (Kleene star) is a repeated application of $\circ$. Therefore, every regular expression is mapped into some language; this mapping is *bijective*. This language is called *regular language*. The regular expression $\alpha \cup \beta$ is also represented as $\alpha + \beta$.

Example 2.4 What are the strings in the language represented by the regular expression $((a \cup b)^* a)$?

The language or the set of strings for this regular expression can be obtained using definition (2.3), as follows:

$$\begin{aligned}\mathcal{L}((a \cup b)^*a) &= \mathcal{L}((a \cup b)^*)\mathcal{L}(a)\\ &= (\mathcal{L}(a \cup b)^*)\{a\}\\ &= (\mathcal{L}(a) \cup \mathcal{L}(b))^*\{a\}\\ &= (\{a\} \cup \{b\})^*\{a\}\\ &= \{(a + b)^*\{a\}\\ &= \{a, aa, ba, aaa, aba, baa, bba, \ldots\} \ \square.\end{aligned}$$

Any language that can be represented by a regular expression can also be represented by infinitely many regular expressions. For example, the regular expressions $\alpha \cup (\beta \cup \gamma)$ and $\alpha \cup (\beta \cup \gamma)$ represent the same language. Normally, we omit extra parentheses '('and ')'in regular expressions, and treat $(a \cup b) \cup c$ as a regular expression $a + b + c$.

The regular expressions and the languages they represent can be defined formally and unambiguously.

2.5.2 *Regular Expressions as Recognizers and Generators*

Let us return back to the general scheme for representation of the language L over Σ as

$$L = \{w \in \Sigma^* \mid w \text{ has property } P\}. \tag{2.10}$$

What properties of P should we consider to define the language L? For example, what makes the properties like—"w consists of a certain number of 0s followed by arbitrary number of 1s", or "w has no occurrence of 111", as obvious candidates for regular expression? We emphasize only one property P such that for the strings possessing property P to be admissible as specification for a language, there must be an algorithm for deciding whether it belongs to the language. The algorithm, which is in a position to decide precisely that "the string w is member of L", is called *language recognition device*. Consider that it is required to recognize the following language L, where

$$L = \{w \in \{0, 1\}^* \mid w \text{ does not have 111 as substrings}\}.$$

The idea of recognizing this language is as follows: The device recognizing this language must read the input string character by character and should have a built-in counter, that counts consecutive 1's. Whenever, it reads character 0, it resets the counter to 0 and when reads 1, it increments the count. As soon as the counter is increased, it checks if the counter is 3, if Yes, the device goes into *Reject* State, and prints the message "No", indicating that string is not the member of L. Once it reaches to *Reject* State, it does not exit from that state, and loop on this state for all further inputs. If end of the input is reached, and count has not reached to 3, the string is considered part of the language L and "YES" is printed in the output [11]. In a FA accepting this language, there is one *Reject* State corresponding to input substring "111", and all the other states are accepting states.

An alternative, and a direct method, for specifying a language is to describe how a generic specification in the language is produced. For example, a regular expression such as $(a \cup aa)(a \cup ab \cup abb)^*$ may be viewed as a way of generating members of the language, as follows:

> To produce the members of language L based on the regular expression $(a \cup aa)(a \cup ab \cup abb)^*$, first write a or aa, followed with that a string made of a or ab or abb is written zero or more number of times.

Thus we may call the regular expressions as *language generators* and they are truly *not* the algorithms, because they are not designed to answer questions and are not explicit about what they do. This is because, how one can choose which one of a or ab or abb is to be written next? To generate all the possible outputs, we can enumerate all outputs; every new output generated is checked in the previously generated strings, if it matches to any, it is rejected, else inserted in the list generated so far, so that the list grows bigger and bigger.

These regular expressions are useful means of representing languages all the times. Both the language recognizers and language generators are *finite specification* of languages.

Though the regular expressions are parenthesized expressions, for the convenience and ease of readability the parenthesis are dropped but the meaning remains unchanged. For example, the regular expression $((1)^*1)0 \cup (1(1)^*)$ can be represented by parenthesis-free regular expression $1^*10 + 11^*$. Even after obtaining regular expressions in this form, they can be further simplified using the following rules:

$1^*(1 + \varepsilon) = 1^*$, where ε is null string,
$1^*1^* = 1^*$,
$0^* + 1^* = 1^* + 0^*$,
$(0^*1^*)^* = (0 + 1)^*$.

In the following, we have some examples which explain how we can create regular expressions once the language specifications are given. Note that, these are based on intuitive notion, and the actual algorithmic approach shall be presented in the next few chapters.

Example 2.5 Determine regular expression for the language of strings of 0*s* and 1*s* such that all strings are of even length.

The possible even length strings are 00, 01, 10, and 11. Thus, regular expression from either of these strings is the strings repeated zero or more number of times. Hence, desired regular expression is

$$(00 \cup 01 \cup 10 \cup 11)^* = (00 + 01 + 10 + 11)^*. \quad \square.$$

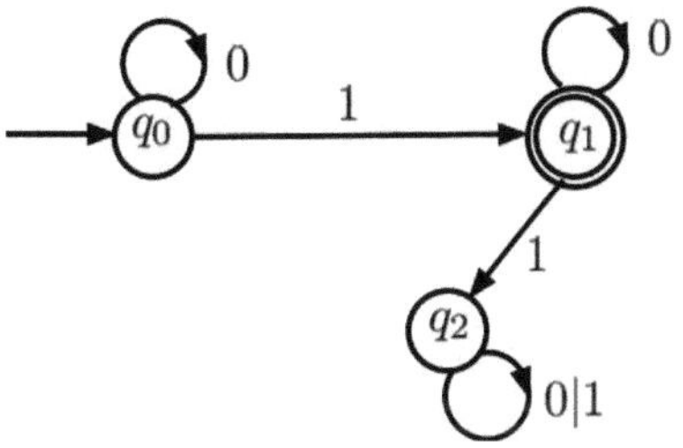

Fig. 2.7 FA for the regular expression 0^*10^*

Example 2.6 Determine the regular expression for the language L in which every string contains at least one occurrence of 1, for $\Sigma = \{0, 1\}$.

The possible regular expressions can be, $(0 + 1)^*1(0 + 1)^*$. □

It should be noted that there are more than one way to obtain the language for the given specifications. Accordingly, $0^*1(0 + 1)^*$ and $(0 + 1)^*10^*$ are also the solutions for the above problem.

Example 2.7 Given a language $L = \{w \mid w \in \{0, 1\}^*$, and w is of odd length$\}$, determine the regular expression.

The answers are: $(0 + 1)(00 + 01 + 10 + 11)^*$ and $(00 + 01 + 10 + 11)^*(0 + 1)$, both of them generate the same strings. □

Example 2.8 Find out the Regular Expression (see Sect. 2.5) for the Finite Automaton shown in Fig. 2.5.

By intuition, we can say that the Regular Expression for FA shown in Fig. 2.5 is $0^*1(00^*1 + 10^*1)^*$. However, in Chap. 5 (Sect. 5.5), we will study, how to construct a regular expression, given a finite automaton. □

Example 2.9 Write a *C* program to implement a FA to recognize the language strings corresponding to regular expression 0^*10^*.

Since there is a first loop for 0's, and after this, there is 1 in the input string, then next there is a loop of 0's. Accordingly, the corresponding finite automaton is as shown in Fig. 2.7.

The *C* program to recognize the language strings of regular expression 0^*10^* is as follows:

```
/* simfa.c */
#include <stdio.h>
int main(){
char ch;
char t[1000]; //tape length
char st; //state symbol
int i=0;  // head position
ch=getchar();
while(ch != '\n'){  // write w on tape, followed with <enter>
```

```
    t[i] = ch;
    i++;
    ch=getchar();
}
t[i]='\0'; // end of w indicator
i=0;
st='0';      // initial state q0
while(t[i] == '0'){   // scan w
      st='0'; // loop in state q0
      i++;
}
if(t[i] == '1'){
      st='1';  // in state q1
      i++;
}
while(t[i]=='0'){ // loop in q1
      st='1';
      i++;
}
if (t[i] == '1'){
       st='2';    // in state q2
       i++;
}
while(t[i] == '0' || t[i] == '1'){
       st='2';  // loop in state q2
       i++;
}
if(st=='1')
       putchar('y'); // accept w
else
       putchar('n');   // reject w
putchar('\n');
return 0;
}
```

The above program will work correctly on *gcc* compiler. The program gives output of '*n*' for languages strings not belonging to regular expression, and output of '*y*' for strings corresponding to the regular expression. Following are the commands:

```
$ gcc simfa.c
$ ./a.out
00000100000
y
$./a.out
000000000000110000000
n
```

The above C program *simfa.c* simulates the finite automaton (Fig. 2.7) whose regular expression is 0*10*. The program simulates the states q_0, q_1, q_2 of FA as states 0, 1, 2, respectively. We note that, in the program, there are loops at states 0, 1, and 2, corresponding to the states $q_0, q_1, and q_2$, respectively. The tape is simulated using a character array $t[1000]$, which is first written using loop at line nos. 9–12 in the program by inputting w from keyboard; the input is terminated by a newline character. The program has been run and tested using *gcc* compiler on the Ubuntu operating system. □

2.6 Applications of Finite Automata

The *regular expression* was first used as a description of finite-state automata by Kleene. He defined regular expressions and regular sets of sequences and proved that:

1. Any set of sequences recognized by a finite-state machine is a regular set of sequences.
2. A finite-state machine can be constructed to recognize any regular set of sequences described by a finite regular expression. Later, it was established that a regular expression characterizing the events recognized by a finite-state machine can be obtained directly from the state diagram.

There are software as well as hardware design-related problems, which can be simplified by automatic conversion of regular expression notation to efficient computer's program implementation or some hardware circuit implementation. Finite automaton is an algorithmic tool. A regular expression can be used for logic design with respect to sequential circuit, as well as for operating system design with respect to process status and transitions.

2.6.1 Design of Sequential Circuits

In the design of sequential circuits, the first step consists of obtaining an unambiguous description of the circuit behavior. For a certain class of problems, the language of regular expressions greatly simplifies this first step of synthesis. In general, the richer the language, the easier it is to write the problem specification. It is possible to obtain state diagrams for sequential circuits from such regular expressions.

A finite automaton can be used in conceptual realization of hardware components like *flip-flops*, *counters*, *adders*, and various *combinational* and *sequential* circuits.

Example 2.10 Design of a 3-bit binary counter.

Consider a 3-bit binary counter (Fig. 2.8), which counts from 000 to 111, going through 8 states q_0 to q_7. An input 1 every time causes the movement of FA to next state and input 0 does not change a state, but loops in the same state. The counting restarts from state q_0, called the start state, which corresponds to count 0 (binary 000), and state q_7 is the last state, corresponding to count 111. □

2.6.2 Lexical Analysis Using Finite Automata

One of the applications of finite automata is to automatically generate lexical processors. Here, a program accepts an input description of the multi-character items or of words allowable in a language, given in terms of a subset of regular expressions. The output of the systems is a lexical processor, which reads a string of characters and combines them into the item as defined by the regular expression. Each output item is identified by a code number together with a pointer to a block of storage containing the characters and the character count in the item.

The processors produced by this program are based on finite-state machines. Each state of a "machine" corresponds to a unique condition in the lexical processing of a character string. At each transition, appropriate actions are taken based on the particular character read.

The functioning of a compiler can be described in the following four logically separable steps:

1. Read the characters of the source language and assemble them into meaningful words or items (lexical analysis);
2. Group the "words" of the language into phrases and sentences for analysis (parsing);
3. Extract the meaning of the source language sentences (modeling);
4. Produce the appropriate object code.

Step 4, in the general case, represents the algorithm for the particular problem and as such is not amenable to general solutions. Step 3, the analysis of the parsed language, again is not amenable to general solutions. Step 2 is much more amenable to generalized solution. Very general systems exist for producing special-purpose processors for parsing language. Such automatically produced parsers are being used in compilers and other computer problem-solving applications.

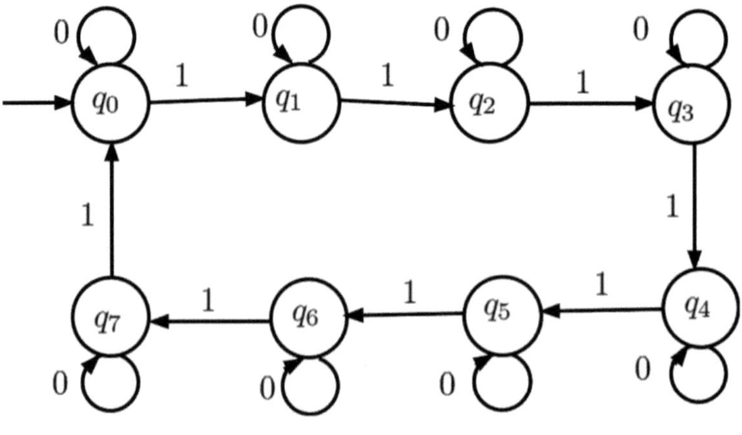

Fig. 2.8 FA for 3-bit binary counter

With some exceptions, lexical properties have been assigned a very minor role in computer languages, and lexical processing has been incorporated as an incidental part of the syntactic analysis programs. There are some good reasons for separating these functions both logically and programmatically.

- A large portion of compiler's time is consumed in lexical analysis, making it essential that this function be as efficient (fast) as possible.
- The development of effective languages requires attention to the lexical as well as the syntactic properties of the languages. Separating the two functions promotes recognition of this fact, and allows the functions to be investigated independently.
- Separation allows the development of systems for automatic syntactic and lexical analysis. The third point is particularly important since the existence of such systems allows the language developer or compiler writer to experiment with various lexical and/or syntactic schemes without the burden of the immense programming times which would otherwise be required.

2.6.3 Lexical Analyzers

The tokens of a programming language are expressible in the form of regular sets. For example, for the C language, the identifiers are expressible as sequence of letters in upper or lower case, followed by any combination of digits, underscores and letters. Optionally, an underscore may precede all the above characters. Thus, a C identifier can be represented as

$$\{\_\}^*\{\text{letter}\} \circ \{\text{letter} \cup \text{digit} \cup \_\}^*.$$

When expressed as regular expression, the above becomes

$$\_^*(\text{letter}) \circ (\text{letter} + \text{digit} + \_)^*.$$

A somewhat similar but specific regular expression exists for keywords and data units in the programs. Therefore, a FA can be used to recognize different tokens in the programming languages, these tokens are different strings constituting the sequence of symbols used to form identifiers, operators, keywords, data sets, etc. The corresponding programs are called *Lexical Analyzers* and the process involved is called *Lexical Analysis*.

The programs, called *Lexical Analyzer Generators*, receive the input as a sequence of regular expressions describing the various types of tokens in a particular language, and produce a single FA, which recognizes all these tokens. The lexical analyzer generator converts the regular expressions into NFA (nondeterministic FA) with null transitions. This NFA is converted into DFA for implementation purpose. The DFA so constructed has number of final states, where each final state indicates some

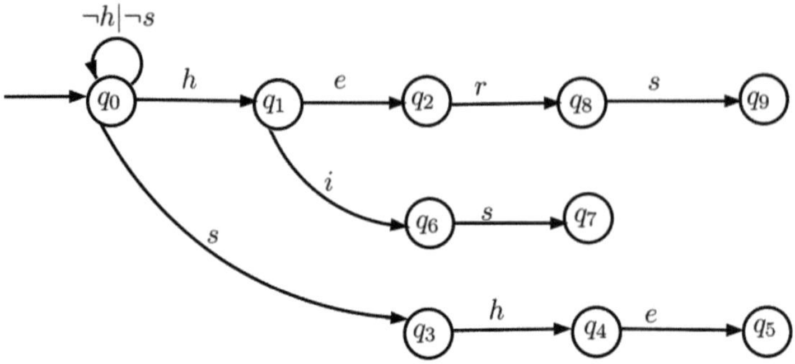

(a) Goto function (δ)

state (s) :	q_1	q_2	q_3	q_4	q_5	q_6	q_7	q_8	q_9
$\lambda(s)$:	q_0	q_0	q_0	q_1	q_2	q_0	q_3	q_0	q_3

(b) Failure function (λ)

state : (s)	Output
q_2	$\{he\}$
q_5	$\{she\}$
q_7	$\{his\}$
q_9	$\{hers\}$

(c) Output function.

Fig. 2.9 Pattern matching functions for search

particular token is found. These lexical analyzers are produced directly in the form of object codes or in some form of high-level language code, which is later translated into machine language, when executed, the lexical analyzer recognizes the tokens.

The lexical analyzers are used for completion of first phase of compilation process called Lexical Analysis, which identities the tokens in the input source program. The output of the Lexical Analysis is in form of tokens in some kind of representation, which is passed to next phase of compilation called *syntax analysis* or *parsing*. This phase assembles the tokens together and identities then in the form of statements, and also stores each statement in the form of a tree, called *syntax tree*.

2.6.4 *Efficient String Matching*

In many information retrieval and text-editing applications, there is a requirement of locating quickly some or all occurrences of user-defined patterns of words and phrases in text. This section describes a simple and efficient method to locate all occurrences of any of a finite number of keywords and phrases in an arbitrary text. The approach using finite automata greatly simplifies the search. It consists of two parts, in the first part, we construct from a set of keywords a finite-state machine; in the second part, we apply the text string as input to the pattern matching machine. The machine signals whenever it has found a match for a keyword [1].

One state (usually q_0) is designated as a start state. Fig. 2.9 shows states as q_0 to q_9. The *goto* function λ maps a pair consisting of a state and an input symbol into a state or the messages *fail*. The directed graph in Fig. 2.9a represents the goto function. For example, the edge labeled h from q_0 to q_1 indicates that $\delta(q_0, h) = q_1$. The absence of an arrow indicates fail for the given input symbol. Thus, $\delta(q_1, \sigma) =$ *fail* for all input symbols σ that are not e and i. All pattern matching machines have the property that $\delta(q_0, \sigma) \neq fail$ for all input symbols $\sigma \in \Sigma$. We shall see that this property of *goto* function on state q_0 ensures that one input symbol will be processed by the machine in every machine cycle. In Fig. 2.9, $\neg h$ and $\neg s$ transitions on state q_0 indicate that as long as the symbol is not h and not s, it will keep on looping in state q_0.

The failure function λ maps a state into a state. The failure function is consulted whether the *goto* function reports fail.

Certain states are designed as *output states*, each one of that indicate that a words has been found (Fig. 2.9c). The output function formalizes this concept by associating a set of keywords (possibly empty) with every state.

An *operating cycle* of such a pattern matching machine is defined as follows. Let s be the current state of the machine and let a be the current symbol of the input string x.

1. If $\delta(s, a) = s'$, the machine makes a *goto* transition, enters state s' and the next symbol of string x becomes the current input symbol. If output(s') $\neq$ empty, then the machine emits the set output(s') along with the position of the current input symbol. The operating cycle is now complete.
2. If $\delta(s, a) =$ fail, the machine consults the failure function λ and makes a failure transition. If $\lambda(s) = s'$, the machine repeats the cycle with s' as the current state and a as the current input symbol (see Fig. 2.9b for $s = q_4, q_5, q_7, q_9$). Note that the failure function causes FA to ultimately return to state q_0.

An interesting question from automata theory is: Given a regular expression R of length m and an input string of length n, how quickly can one determine whether x is in the language denoted by R? One method for solving this problem is to first construct from R a nondeterministic finite automation M and then to simulate the behavior of M on input x. This gives a solution with complexity $O(mn)$, which is linear in time.

Another approach along these lines is to construct from R a nondeterministic finite automation M, then to convert M into a deterministic finite automation M' and then to simulate the behavior of M' on x. The only difficulty with this method is that M' can have of the order of 2^r states, where r is the number of states in nondeterministic FA (NFA) (see Chap. 3 for details). The simulation of M' on the other hand is linear in n of course, however, the overall complexity is $O(2^r n)$. In this process, we have not accounted for the complexity of conversion from NFA to DFA, which again is discussed in Chap. 3.

2.7 Automata Concepts Through Games

Concepts of *deterministic finite automaton* can used to create puzzle games based on automata theory. The puzzle games can be designed in such a way that it becomes difficult to solve them without understanding the fundamental concepts of automata, such as "accept", "reject", and "determinism". The game outputs a history of each player's actions, which we refer to as the play log. We analyze the correct-answer rate and play logs to gauge the understanding of individuals. To clarify questions, we analyze not only the individual's correct-answer rate (to the questions) but also their process, which is available from the play logs. We can analyze questionnaires given to the players after playing the game. We can also measure the play time to evaluate how much time they devoted to the game [7].

The games can be modeled using directed graphs or finite automata with edge transitions. Let S be a set of sequences that are classified into two types: *acceptable* and *unacceptable*. An automaton A recognizes S if A accepts the acceptable sequences in S and rejects the unacceptable sequences in S. The "questions" are puzzles with state transition diagrams, like in [9]. A sequence of materials is called a *recipe*; thus, a recipe can be thought of as an input sequence to the machine (automaton). In the finite-state games with finite-size inputs, one can input all the meaningful permutations of inputs, and can check what all inputs are accepted. This becomes brute-force approach. Such permutation sequences can be generated and recorded as logs, to be analyzed later. A similar approach can also be used for testing software, where branching at states simulate *if–then* conditions, and the loops simulate the *program loops*.

2.8 Summary

Finite automata can be used to model any physical phenomena in the world. If the state of an object or system changes with time, then this change can be broken up into intermediate states, and there is a transition through all of those intermediate to reach the final or specified state.

The automata theory is a subject to study the process of these transitions from one state to the next state. The automaton is foundation for many branches of computer science as well as for the switching circuits.

A finite automaton (FA) can be used to model a computer language recognizer device, for the set of regular languages.

Physically, a FA model consists of an infinite tape to hold an arbitrary size of input string, a read head to read the tape symbols, and a control that goes through a finite set of states. While changing the states, a FA moves through sequence of configurations. A configuration is a combination of the current state and the part of the input string yet to be read.

In addition to its capability as language recognizer, a finite automaton can be used for pattern matching and for high-speed search. The patterns are called *regular expressions*.

There appears to be three main varieties of automata: *acceptors, generators*, and *transducers*. If Σ be any alphabet, $\varepsilon \in \Sigma^*$, and Q is any set of states, then an *acceptor* is an automaton having a single axiom qw with or without end marker, such that every terminal result is of the form q. An acceptor accepts w if and only if there exists a derivation in the acceptor yielding a terminal result of the form q. A set of words is definable if there exists an acceptor that accepts it.

A *generator* is an automaton having a single axiom of the form q such that every terminal result is a word on symbols of $\Sigma - \{\varepsilon\}$ only. A terminal result of a generator is called *sentence* and the set of all such sentences of a generator is a language. Generators are also called generative grammars, when rules are constructed in such a way that the derivation of a sentence reveals its grammatical structure. The study of languages from this point of view is part of mathematical linguistics; thus linguistics and automata theory have much in common.

Regular expression is the name given to a text pattern. The set of strings, which can be generated using this text pattern, makes a language, called *regular language*. Depending on the text pattern, the corresponding language could be finite or infinite.

There are three basic operations that can be performed on the regular expression: *union*, *concatenation*, and *Kleene star*. The resultant expression obtained due to these operations is again a regular expression. Thus, the regular expressions are said to be closed under these operations.

A finite regular language is called *recursive language*, and an infinite regular language is called *recursively enumerable*. All the regular languages can be enumerated, but a set of all subsets of infinite regular language is not countable. This concludes that there are other languages, which are not countable (i.e., not regular).

Since, the regular expressions are directly related to the regular languages, they are called generators[5] of regular languages, as well as recognizers (acceptors)[6] of these languages.

Self Review Questions

1. Define the finite automata.
2. What is output of an automaton?
3. What is input of an automaton?

---

[5] The regular expressions specify operations of union and concatenation on the symbols of the language alphabet. By performing these operations, one can generate all the strings of the corresponding language. However, the true generators of regular languages are regular grammars, which are covered in this text later.

[6] Truly speaking the regular expressions are not the accepters of regular language, but regular expressions are isomorphic to FA and the latter accept only regular language, that way regular expressions can be taken as the accepters of regular language.

4. Does a FA has memory?
5. What part of computer can be designed using finite automata?
6. What are the applications of finite automata?
7. How a finite-state machine can recognize an infinite language?
8. Explain the significance of expression: $\vdash_M: Q \times \Sigma^* \mapsto Q \times \Sigma^*$.
9. What is time complexity of recognizing a string $|w| = n$ by finite automata?
10. What is space complexity of recognizing a string $|w| = n$ by finite automata?

Exercises

A. Concepts based Problems

Note: The $*$ marked exercises are provided with solutions at the end of this book.

1. Define regular expression and regular language. How they are related? What are the properties of regular languages?
2. * Describe in simple words the languages corresponding to each of the below given regular expressions:

   a. $(1 + 0)^*$
   b. $(01)^*(10)^*$
   c. $(0 + 1)^*(0 + 1)^+$
   d. $((1 + 0)^2)^*(\varepsilon + 1)^*$

3. For the alphabet set $\Sigma = \{a, b\}$, define the languages and corresponding regular expression for each of the following:

   a. All words that contain exactly 3 a's in total.
   b. All words that do not contain the substring bbb.
   c. All strings that do not have substring ab.

4. Describe the application of FA in building lexical analyzers for compilers.
5. Write a program in C to recognize the language accepted by finite automata shown in Fig. 2.10.
6. For a FA with input $|w| = n$, and states $|Q| = m$, what are the space and time complexities of this FA?

B. Analysis-based Problems

7. Give logical justification that the contents of Fig. 2.2 (Sect. 2.3) is a Program.
8. Write regular expressions for following languages, having alphabet set $\Sigma = \{0, 1\}$.

   a. $\{w \mid w$ has 0s and 1s with even number of 0s and ending with $101\}$.
   b. $\{w \mid w$ does not consist 00 and 101 as substrings$\}$.
   c. $\{w \mid w$ has at least one occurrence of 11 as substrings$\}$.

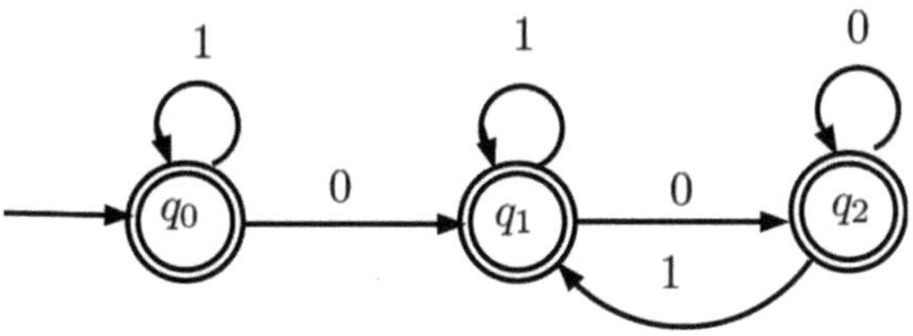

Fig. 2.10 A DFA

9. * Which of the following statements about regular expressions are True? (Note: R, S, T are regular expressions.)

   a. $R(S+T) = RS + RT$
   b. $(R+S)^* = (R^*S^*)^*$
   c. $(R+S)^* = (R^* + S^*)$
   d. $(RS+R)^*RS = (R+S)^*$
   e. $(RS+R)^*R = R(SR+R)^*$
   f. $S(RS+S)^*R = R + S(R+S)^*$
   g. $(R+S)^*S = (R^*S)^*$

10. * Consider the language Σ^*, where $\Sigma = \{a, b\}$. How many words this language has of length 2, of length 3, of length n?
11. For $\Sigma = \{a, b\}$, write the regular expressions for the following sets:

    a. All strings in Σ^* with no more than two as.
    b. All strings in Σ^* with even counts of a or b.
    c. All strings in Σ^* with exactly one count of bbb.
    d. All strings in Σ^* with exactly two b's or exactly two a's.
    e. All strings in Σ^* such that length of each is divisible by 3.

12. Describe the language accepted by the automaton corresponding to the transition diagram given in Fig. 2.10. Also, give its regular expression.
13. Find regular expressions for the following regular sets:

    a. $\{ab, ac, ad\}$
    b. $\{a, ab, abb, abbb, abbbb, \ldots\}$
    c. $\{ad, ae, af, bd, be, bf, cd, ce, cf, \ldots\}$
    d. $\{abcd, abef, cdcd, cdef\}$

14. Show that following pairs of regular expressions define the same languages over the alphabets $\Sigma = \{a, b\}$.

    a. $(a+b)^*$ and $(a^* + b^*)^*$
    b. $a^*(ba^*)^*$ and $(a^*b)^*a^*$
    c. a^* and $(aa)^*(\varepsilon + a)$
    d. $(a+b)^*ab(a+b)^* + b^*a$ and $(a+b)^*$

15. Classify the following languages into clusters so that languages in each cluster are equal to each other.

$(L^* \cup M^*)^*$, $(M^* \circ L^*)$, $(M^* \cup L^*)$, $(L^* \cup M)^*$, $(L^* \cup M)^*$, $L \circ (L \circ M)^*$, $(L \circ M)^* \circ L$, $(L \cup M)^*$.

16. Construct the regular expressions for the following.

    a. Decimal integer number with sign.
    b. Decimal float type number.
    c. Binary fraction number.
    d. Binary integer number.

17. Which of the following strings are generated by the regular expression $(111 + 010)^*011^*$.

    a. 111010011
    b. 010000000
    c. 111111111111
    d. 1111110100100101110000011101011111

18. For a given set of states Q, and input alphabet Σ, find out the expression for the maximum number of unique FAs that can be constructed?
19. * Derive expressions for count of FA that can be constructed using the following number of states: 3, 4, and 5. Thus, derive a general expression for count of finite automata, using n number of states. Note that, there can be only one start state, and final states can be one or more, or may not be present.
20. For $\Sigma = \{a, b\}$, find the finite automata for each of the following regular expressions:

    a. $aa^*bb^*cc^*$
    b. $(aba^*ba^*b)^*$
    c. a^*b^*
    d. $(a + b)^*$

21. Construct a DFA that accepts the following language:

$$L = \{w \mid w \in \Sigma^*, w \text{ contains substring } 0101\}.$$

22. Design a finite automaton as controller for a swing door with a front pad and rear pad. There are two states corresponding to door *open* and *closed*, and four possible inputs: *front*, *rear*, *neither*, and *both*.

C. Proof-based Problems

23. Show that for a DFA, for every $q \in Q, a \in \Sigma, \delta(q, a) = q$, there is $\delta^*(q, x) = q$, for every $x \in \Sigma^*$.
24. * Show that there cannot be a DFA of less than four states which can recognize the language,

$$\{w \in \{a, b\}^* \mid w \text{ contains even number of } a\text{'s and } b\text{'s}\}.$$

25. For $x, y \in \Sigma^*$, prove that for any DFA $\delta(q, xy) = \delta(\delta(q, x), y)$.
26. a. Show that every finite language is regular.
    b. Show that a language of finite length strings is regular.
    c. How you will show that language accepted by a FA is empty?
    d. How you will show that language accepted by a FA is infinite?
27. Prove that there exist many languages that are not regular.

D. Multiple choice Questions

28. Which of the following regular expression generates the same language the regular expression $0^*(10^*)^*$?
    (A)$(0 + 1)^*10(0 + 1)^*$ (B)$(1^*0)^*1^*$
    (C)$0 + (0 + 10)^*$ (D)$(0^*10^*)^*$
29. * Consider the deterministic finite-state automaton M in Fig. 2.11.
    Let A be the subset of binary strings of the language accepted by FA shown in Fig. 2.11. What is the size of set A if for every $w \in A$, its 1st, 4th, and 7th bits are 1?
    (A) 2 (B) 4 (C) 5 (D) 7
30. Consider the regular expression $R = (111 + 11111)^*$. What is the minimum number of states in any DFA that accepts the language of this regular expression?
    (A) 3 (B) 5 (C) 8 (D) 9
31. The languages accepted by the finite automaton shown in Fig. 2.12 can be expressed by the following regular expression:
    (A) $b^*ab^*ab^*ab^*$ $(B)b^*a(a + b)^*$ $(C)(a + b)^*$ $(D)b^*ab^*ab^*$
32. Which one of the following languages over the alphabet {0, 1} is described by the regular expressions: $(0 + 1)^*0(0 + 1)^*0(0 + 1)^*$?
    (A) All strings containing at least two 0*s*
    (B) All strings containing the substring 00
    (C) All strings containing at most two 0*s*
    (D) All strings that begin and end with either 0 or 1.
33. * The DFA shown in Fig. 2.13 accepts the set of all strings over {0, 1} that,
    (A) end with 00 (B) contain the substring 00.
    (C) begin either with 0 or 1 (D) end with0
34. Let $L = \{w \in (0 + 1)^* \mid w$ has even number of $1's\}$. Which one of the following regular expressions represents L?
    (A) $0^*(10^*1^*)^*0^*$ (B) $0^*1(10^*1)^*10^*$
    (C) $(0^*10^*1)^*$ (D) $0^*(10^*10^*)^*$
35. * The regular expression 1^*1^* is equal to which of the following? (select one or more choices):
    (A) $(1 + \varepsilon)^*$ (B) $\varepsilon 1^*$
    (C) 1^* (D) $(11)^*$.

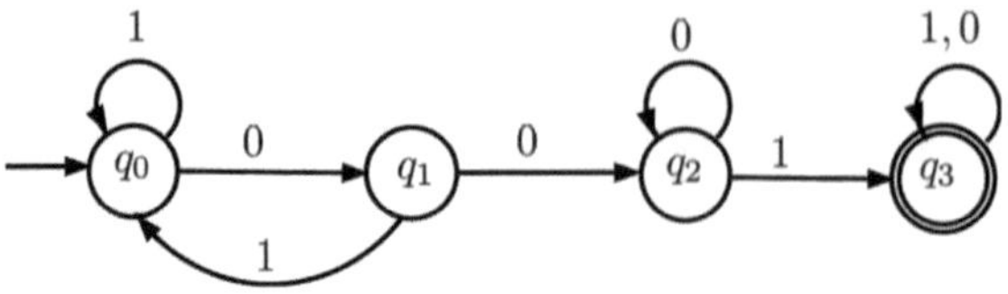

Fig. 2.11 FA for $\Sigma = \{0, 1\}$

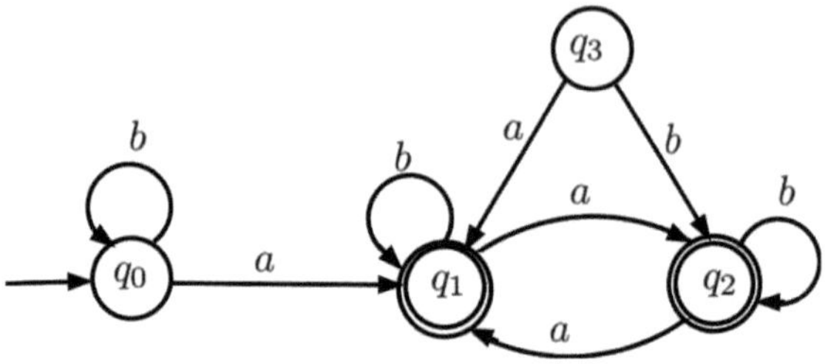

Fig. 2.12 A FA for $\Sigma = \{a, b\}$

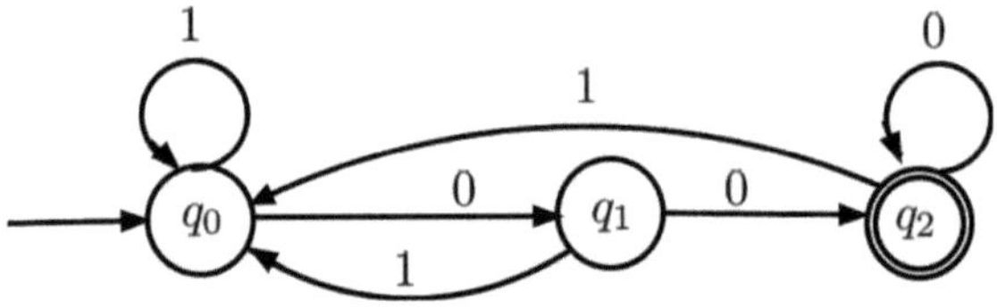

Fig. 2.13 A FA for $\Sigma = \{0, 1\}$

E. Advanced Knowledge Assessment Problems

36. Show that the entire set of finite automata machines are countable and infinite. Countable here means that this set has a one-to-one correspondence with the set of natural numbers $\mathbb{N}$.
37. Show that in the above problem, if "finite automata machines" is replaced by "regular expressions", then also it holds true.
38. Prove that, when set of all FA and the set of all regular expressions map to $\mathbb{N}$, then they map to each other.

References

1. Aho AV, Corasick MJ (1975) Efficient string matching: an aid to bibliographic search. Commun ACM 18(6):333–340
2. Barnes BH (1972) A programmer's view of automata. ACM Comput Surv 4(4):221–239
3. Burks AW, Wang H (1957) The logic of automata-Part I. J ACM 4(2):193–218
4. Chowdhary KR, Bansal VS (2010) Bioinformatics and computational technologies. In: UGC national conference on bioinformatics and computational technologies (2009: Department of Computer Science & Engineering, MBM Engineering College). Scientific Publishers
5. Ernst L (1980) Constructing a finite automaton for a given regular expression. In: ACM SIGACT New, Fall, pp 81–97
6. Ott G, Feinstein N (1961) Design of sequential machines from their regular expressions. J ACM 585–600

7. Isayama D, Ishiyama M, Relator R, Yamazaki K (2016) Computer science education for primary and lower secondary school students: teaching the concept of automata. ACM Trans Comput Educ (TOCE) 17(1):1–28
8. Thompson K (1968) Regular expression search algorithm. Commun ACM 11(6):419–422
9. Chowdhary KR (2020) State space search. In: Fundamentals of artificial intelligence. Springer, New Delhi. https://doi.org/10.1007/978-81-322-3972-7_8
10. Chowdhary KR (2016) Regular expressions. http://www.krchowdhary.com/toc/2-reg-exp.pdf. Cited 02 Aug 2020
11. Nelson RJ (1965) Basic concepts of automata theory. In ACM 20th national conference, August 1965, pp 138–161

Chapter 3
Variants of Finite Automata

Abstract There are not much of reasons to deal with nondeterminism in mathematics. However, it works with values, sets, and functions. Corresponding to these, nondeterminism exists in the Turing machine and in finite automata (nondeterministic FA). Using the latter, we can build nondeterministic models of computation. Unlike a deterministic FA, a nondeterministic FA can have many transitions (in parallel) for an input symbol, or there may not be any transition at some states, or there may be transitions without any input. Given any regular expression we can build a nondeterministic FA as a first step, then convert this NFA into DFA, and then minimize the DFA. Another variant of FA is two-way FA, unlike FA it has head movement in both directions—left and right, which makes it more like a Turing machine, but the tape head can read only. Yet another interesting coverage in this chapter is finite-state transducers (FSTs)—they produce output sequences corresponding to input sequences in contrast to finite automata which produce yes/no output for an input sequence. The FST can be in the form of a Mealy machine or a Moore machine. The FSTs have applications in human speech processing and phonological and morphological analysis in Natural language Processing. The chapter ends with self-assessment review questions, a number of practice exercises, and solved exercises at the end.

Keywords Nondeterministic FA · Equivalence of DFA and NFA · Conversion of NFA to DFA · Complement of NFA · Complement of DFA · Two-way FA · Finite-state transducers · FSTs · Moore machine · Mealy machine · Mealy-to-Moore · Moore-to-Mealy

3.1 Introduction

Mathematics never saw much of a reason to deal with something called nondeterminism. It works with values, functions, sets, and relations. In computing science, however, nondeterminism has been an issue from the very beginning, if only in the form of *nondeterministic Turing machines* or *nondeterministic finite-state machines*. Nondeterminism arises in a natural way when discussing concurrency, and models

K. R. Chowdhary, *Theory of Computation*,
https://doi.org/10.1007/978-981-97-6234-7_3

of concurrency, which typically also model nondeterminism. In hardware, it is a race problem. There are also numerous variants of process languages and algebra, event structures, and state transition systems, which concern nondeterminism.

In terms of modeling, nondeterminism may be considered a purely operational notion. However, one of the main reasons for considering nondeterminism in computer science is the need for abstraction, allowing one to disregard irrelevant aspects of actual computations. Typically, we prefer to work with models that do not include all the details of the physical environment of computations such as timing, temperature, representation on hardware, and the like. Since we do not want to model all these complex dependencies, we may instead represent them by nondeterministic choices. The nondeterminism of concurrent systems usually arises as an abstraction of time. Similarly, nondeterminism is also a means of increasing the level of abstraction when describing sequential programs, and as a way of indicating a "don't care" attitude as to which among a number of computational paths will actually be utilized in a particular evaluation [10].

Definition 3.1 (*Bounded and Unbounded Nondeterminism*) Bounded nondeterminism refers to the case where every terminating computation has only a finite number of possible results; unbounded—to the one where the set of the possible results may be infinite. □

A two-way DFA (2DFA) provides freedom to read head to move in both directions.[1] Thus, a two-way finite automaton (2DFA) is a generalized version of one-tape FA, where it can revisit the characters already processed. Though, a 2DFA has more flexible access to memory and appears to be more powerful than a DFA, however, its has no higher problem-solving capability than a simple DFA, and a 2DFA can always be reduced to a simple DFA [9].

This chapter also introduces a kind of FA called transducers. In the beginning, we describe two different machines, the *Moore machine* and *Mealy machine*; at first the output is associated with each state, while in the second the output is associated with transitions or edges of the transition graph. We will also show that these two different-looking machines are in fact equal. The final section of this chapter introduces with application of these transducers.

Learning outcomes of this chapter:

1. Nondeterministic finite automata. [Knowledge]
2. Nondeterminism in computation. [Synthesis]
3. Equivalence of NFA and DFA. [Analysis], [Proof]
4. Deducing NFA to equivalent DFA. [Application]
5. Mealy and Moore machines. [Knowledge], [Application]
6. Equivalence of Mealy and Moore machines. [Analysis], [Proof]
7. Converting Moore machine to Mealy machine. [Synthesize]
8. Converting Mealy machine to Moore machine. [Synthesize]
9. Sequential transducers. [Apply]

---

[1] We often call the two-way DFA two-tape automation, as its head can move from a central position to left as well as right. These two dimensions are nothing but two tapes.

3.2 Nondeterministic Finite Automata Model

The Finite Automata (FA) introduced in the previous chapter are models of determinable computation. That is, in every configuration it is determined without any ambiguity as to what will happen in the next computation step. Hence, a program or deterministic finite automata (DFA) can always determine unambiguously the computation over an input string.

In contrast, a nondeterministic computation allows in each configuration a choice from finitely many actions. This has the consequence that a nondeterministic program can have many different computations on the same input. The only requirement is that one of them should ultimately yield the correct result. This corresponds to an artificial rule: a nondeterministic program always chooses a correct computation. A choice from several possibilities is called nondeterministic decision. The acceptability criteria of NFA (Nondeterministic Finite Automata) is as follows: with an alphabet set Σ, a string $w \in \Sigma^*$ leads to a sequence of configurations, where one of the configurations is an accepting configuration [2].

Although an NFA being a model of a nondeterministic program does not seem to be useful for practical purposes, the study of nondeterminism will certainly contribute to our understanding of nondeterministic computations.

Like DFA, an NFA is also a five-tuple represented by

$$M = (Q, \Sigma, \delta, s, F) \tag{3.1}$$

where
Q is a finite set of states,
Σ is a finite set of alphabets,
δ is a set of transitions,
s is the start state, and
F is a set of final or accepting states.

Since the next state after a transition in an NFA is a state-set instead of a single state, and there can be 2^Q state sets for Q states, a state in an NFA is a member of 2^Q states. Its transition function is defined as

$$\delta : Q \times \Sigma \mapsto 2^Q. \tag{3.2}$$

Due to the same reason the final states are also members of 2^Q or $F \in 2^Q$, and $F \subseteq Q$. An NFA (Fig. 3.1) consists of infinite tape holding a string $w \in \Sigma^*$, and a read head, which can move to one direction only and reads the symbols on tape, square by square. The finite control of NFA in Fig. 3.1 indicates that in a particular configuration, the machine has taken a move into two states together, i.e., q_1 and q_2, accordingly the next state is a set shown as $\{q_1, q_2\}$.

In an NFA the next state in a move is always a set, which is a subset of Q, of size greater or equal to one, but can be a null set also. Hence, DFA is a special

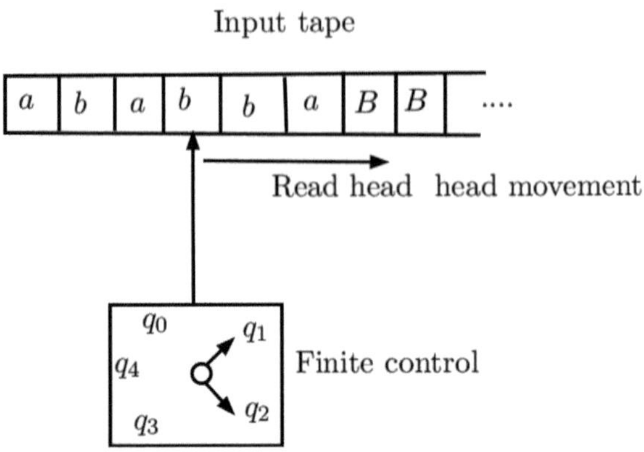

Fig. 3.1 Nondeterminictic finite automaton

case of NFA, where the next state is always a single state. The NFA is considered a generalized case of DFA. Thus, in NFA we may have,

$$\delta(q, a) = \{q_i, q_j, q_k\} \subseteq Q. \tag{3.3}$$

Example 3.1 Figure 3.2 shows the transition diagram of an NFA. When an input symbol $a \in \Sigma$ is read at state q_0, and the next state is $\delta(q_0, a) = \{q_1, q_2, q_0\}$, where all the three states are equally likely. This is because after reaching state q_1 the NFA can move to state q_2 without an input, and from there it can come to state q_0 again by ε-transition.

An NFA accepts a string w if it leads to a sequence of moves where at least one sequence has the end element a final state. The string is rejected if there is not a single sequence of moves that can lead to a final state.

Equation (3.3) indicates that the next state is a set of states in which there can be maximum $|Q|$ states. For example, if there are three states $Q = \{q_0, q_1, q_2\}$ in an NFA, then the total number of next states can be 8 and a subset can have a maximum of three states. The possible sets of states in this case can be: $\{\}$, $\{q_0\}$, $\{q_1\}$, $\{q_2\}$, $\{q_1, q_2\}$, $\{q_2, q_3\}$, $\{q_1, q_3\}$, $\{q_1, q_2, q_3\}$.

A distinguishing feature of an NFA is: that it can cause a transition without any input, that is, a null (ε) input can also cause a transition. Hence, the input symbol in NFA is a member of $\Sigma \cup \{\varepsilon\}$. The general transition function δ for the NFA can therefore be defined as

$$\delta : Q \times \Sigma \cup \{\varepsilon\} \mapsto 2^Q \tag{3.4}$$

Fig. 3.2 Transition diagram for an NFA

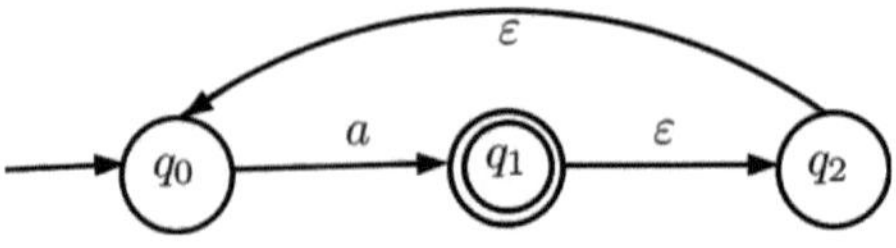

The extended transition function δ^* for an NFA can be defined in the same lines of DFA,

$$\delta^*(q_i, w) = Q_j, \tag{3.5}$$

where $Q_j \subseteq Q$, $w \in \Sigma^*$, and Q_j one of the set of states in which NFA may exist when it had started at state q_i and has completely read the string w. Thus, the language accepted by an NFA is

$$L(M) = \{w \in \Sigma^* \mid (q_0, w) \vdash^* (Q', \varepsilon)\}, \tag{3.6}$$

where $Q' = \{..., q_f, ...\} \in 2^Q$, $q_f \in F$. Alternatively, we can say that a string w is accepted if $\delta^*(q_0, w) \cap F \neq \phi$, where q_0 is start state.

The nondeterministic automata are not true models of real computers but are simply useful notational generalizations of finite automata. They are useful because they greatly simplify the description of finite automata. We will show later that an NFA is equivalent to DFA and at the same time, it appears in much simplified form. When an NFA has more than one possible next state, it can be viewed as more than one DFA working in parallel.

3.3 Properties of NFA

We will show that, there are some qualities of NFA, and that is why at the initial state, a system is constructed as an NFA, and then later it is converted into a DFA. Subsequently, the DFA needs to be simplified through minimization to reduce its complexity, i.e., reduction in the number of states.

3.3.1 NFA is Simpler

Designing an NFA is simpler than a DFA, and at the same time, an NFA is far less complex than a DFA. Consider the language

$$L = \{w \mid w \in (ab + aba)^*\}$$

with alphabet set $\Sigma = \{a, b\}$. We note that regular expression and the corresponding language appear to be simple. However, the corresponding deterministic finite automaton, shown in Fig. 3.3, is complex. More is the number of states and transitions in an FA, it is considered as more complex because that will increase the complexity of the corresponding logic.

It can be shown that it is not possible to obtain a DFA of less than five states for regular expression $(ab + aba)^*$.

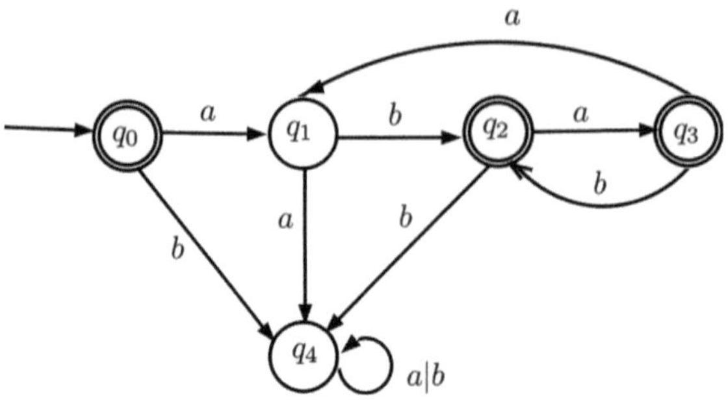

Fig. 3.3 DFA for language $(ab + aba)^*$

The language strings generated by the regular expression $(ab + aba)^*$ are also recognized by an NFA shown in Fig. 3.4. However, there also exist paths in NFA using which the same string cannot be recognized. For example, for string aba, the path q_0, q_1, q_2, q_0 recognizes it. But q_0, q_1, q_0, q_1 does not. The requirement for recognition of a string by NFA is that there should be some path(s) available for a walk-through that ultimately leads to a final state when the complete string is read.

For an NFA, unlike the DFA, it is not necessary that all transitions corresponding to inputs are available at each state. For example in Fig. 3.4, at state q_0 as well as at q_2 the input b is not accepted. Hence $\delta^*(q_0, abb) = \phi$, as there is no state available after receiving the string abb. Such configurations are called *dead configurations*. We note that, in spite of dead configurations, the NFA in Fig. 3.4 is much simpler than the DFA shown in Fig. 3.3.

Equally simpler NFA is shown in Fig. 3.5, which can also recognize the language of the regular expression $(ab + aba)^*$. This NFA includes a null transition at state q_2, i.e., a transition occurring in the absence of any input.

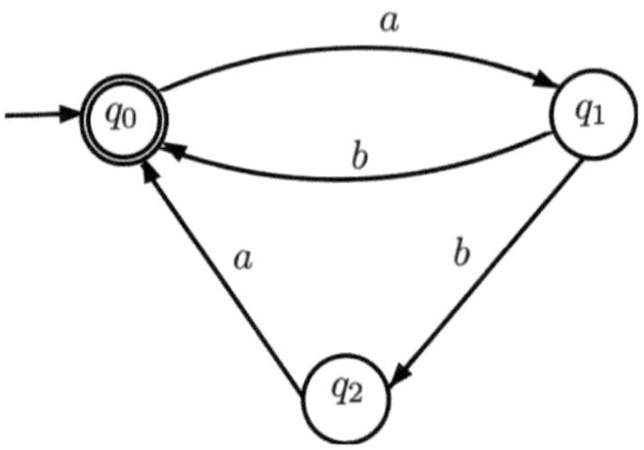

Fig. 3.4 NFA-I for language $(ab + aba)^*$

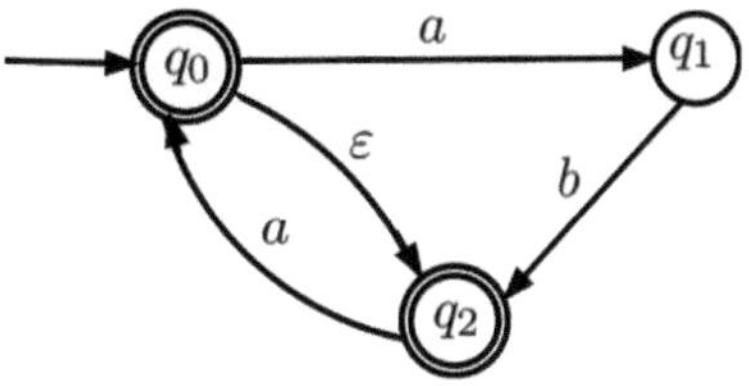

Fig. 3.5 NFA-II for language $(ab + aba)^*$

3.3.2 *Cloning of DFAs in NFA*

Computers are deterministic machines and their final states are predictable if their initial state and input are known. However, for an NFA as a computing model, every next state is a set (often of more than one) of states, thus NFA is not predictable. This drawback of NFA is a blessing as it helps in faster problem-solving by carrying many states together.

Any problem solution requires the exploration of a number of states. All these states put together are called *state space*. To solve a problem, we exhaustively search this state space to find out if it leads to the final state. In the process of searching, we may sometimes reach a state where it is not possible to reach a solution. In that case, we backtrack to some previous state and again search in the state space. This *backtrack* might repeat a number of times depending on the size of state space and nature of the problem being solved [3].

In an NFA, while searching the state space, we carry on a number of states together, and one or more of them may lead to the final state, and hence to the solution. Since backtracking is not required in an NFA, it may lead to a faster and more efficient solution.

Example 3.2 For the NFA shown in Fig. 3.6, find out whether the string $w = aab$ is accepted by this NFA.

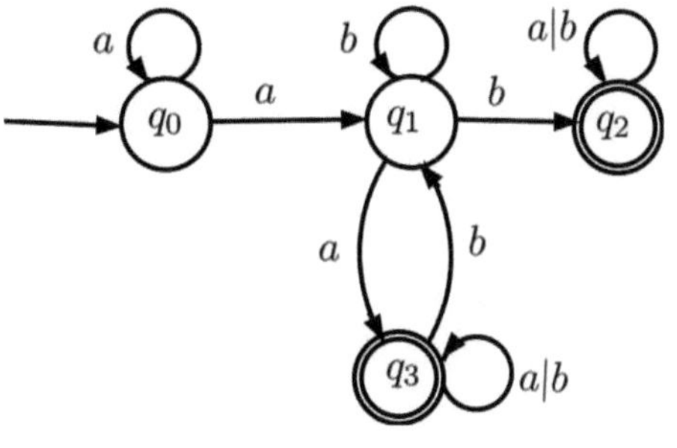

Fig. 3.6 An NFA

Table 3.1 Transition table for automata in Fig. 3.6

Current state	Input a	Input b
q_0	$\{q_0, q_1\}$	ϕ
q_1	$\{q_3\}$	$\{q_1, q_2\}$
q_2	$\{q_2\}$	$\{q_2\}$
q_3	$\{q_3\}$	$\{q_1, q_3\}$

We show the sequence of configurations through which this NFA moves when it reads the input aab.

$$\begin{aligned}(q_0, aab) &\vdash (\{q_0, q_1\}, ab)\\ &\vdash (q_0, ab) \cup (q_1, ab)\\ &\vdash (\{q_0, q_1\}, b) \cup (q_3, b)\\ &\vdash (q_0, b) \cup (q_1, b) \cup (q_3, b)\\ &\vdash (\phi, \varepsilon) \cup (\{q_1, q_2\}, \varepsilon) \cup \{\{q_1, q_3\}, \varepsilon\}\\ &\vdash (q_1, q_2, q_3), \varepsilon)\end{aligned}$$

Note that, we have excluded ϕ state in the final step, as there is no state ϕ in this NFA.

Figure 3.7 and Table 3.1 shows the transitions in NFA of Fig. 3.6, and gives the impression of more than one DFAs are running in parallel. For example, when input is a at state q_0, two "clone" states are produced for automaton, one transition goes to state q_0 and the other goes to state q_1. At the next state, when a is input, it clones two further automata—one with state q_0 and the other with state q_1. The maximum possible number of cloning at any time can be equal to the number of states Q.

We note that the NFA reaches to a states set $\{q_1, q_2, q_3\} \in 2^Q$ when the input string aab is fully read. Since q_2 and q_3 both are final states, aab is accepted. □

Definition 3.2 (*Deterministic FA*) An automaton $M = (Q, \Sigma, \delta, s, F)$ is deterministic if $|s| = 1$ and all the edges originating from any state carry different labels, i.e., $|\delta(q, a)| \leq 1$ for $\forall q \in Q$, $\forall a \in \Sigma$, and $\varepsilon \notin \Sigma$. Otherwise, it is nondeterministic. □

3.3.3 *Complementss of NFA and DFA*

Consider the language, for $\Sigma = \{0, 1\}$ as

$$L = \{x \in \Sigma^* \mid \text{third symbol from end of } x \text{ is } 0\}.$$

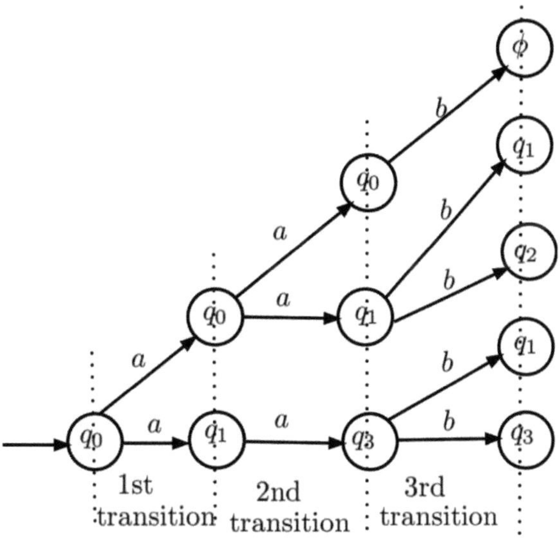

Fig. 3.7 Transitions of NFA of Fig. 3.6, for input *aab*

The NFA for L is shown in Fig. 3.8a. The complement of L can be given by

$$\overline{L} = \overline{L(M)} = \{x \in \Sigma^* \mid \text{ third symbol from end of } x \text{ is } 1\}.$$

Using the approach of complementing the DFA, we get the complement NFA as shown in Fig. 3.8b, where the third symbol from the end of the string is changed from 0 to 1, and the final and non-final states are exchanged. Note that this new NFA has

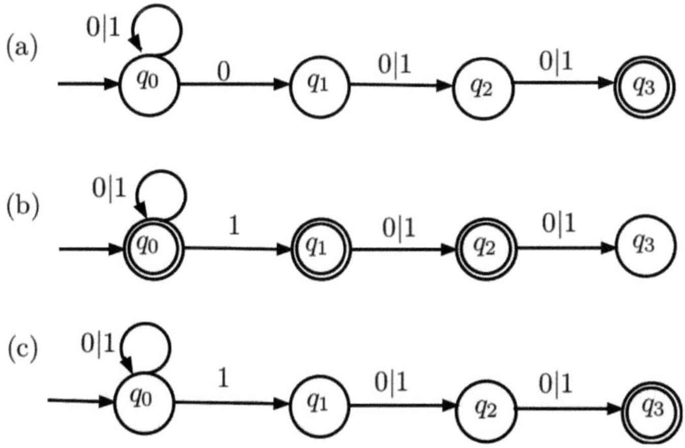

Fig. 3.8 **a** An NFA. **b** Its incorrect complement. **c** Correct complement

nothing to do with a complement of an NFA, as its language is not $\overline{L}$. The correct NFA for $\overline{L}$ is shown in Fig. 3.8c.

The logic behind not getting straight forward complement of an NFA is, in one sense, the NFA itself is nondeterministic, hence its complement cannot be obtained the way it is done for DFA. Another reason is that, for a given DFA there can be many possible NFAs, and when they are complemented the language accepted by these can be different, and all of them cannot match with the language of corresponding complemented DFA. The NFA has its significance, because there are straight forward algorithms for obtaining NFA for any given regular expression, and there are efficient algorithms to convert an NFA into DFA, and algorithms available to minimize any given DFA to make it run efficiently in terms of time and space. These topics are covered in detail in Chaps. 4 and 5.

3.4 Equivalence of NFA and DFA

For a language L, if an NFA recognizes it then there also exists an equivalent DFA that recognizes it. In fact, in this DFA only certain sequences of transitions of NFA are to be selected for the given input to reach to final state, and other sequences of states exist, in NFA, but are not accounted for final walk-through. Therefore, the class of languages accepted by a DFA is a subset of the class of languages accepted by an NFA. It will be shown that these classes are in fact equal. An NFA though makes available a much more generality than DFA, but is in no way more powerful than the corresponding DFA. An NFA can always be converted into a DFA that recognizes the same language that is recognized by the original NFA.

Any two finite automata M_1 and M_2 are equivalent if the languages accepted by them are equivalent, i.e., $L(M_1) = L(M_2)$. This criterion is used in the following theorem that proves that for every NFA there exists an equivalent DFA.

Theorem 3.1 *For every NFA there exists an equivalent DFA.*

Proof Let $M_N = (Q, \Sigma, \delta, s, F)$ be an NFA, and we intend to show that there exists a DFA $M_D = (Q', \Sigma, \delta', s', F')$ equivalent to M_N. Both the automata have the same alphabet sets. To prove this we need to represent tuples of M_D in terms of the tuples of M_N.

We know that after each symbol is read, an NFA occupies a set of states out of 2^Q. If each set is considered as a single state for an equivalent DFA, the maximum number of states in M_D will be $Q' = 2^Q$. Accordingly, we denote an element of Q' by $\{\ldots, q_i, \ldots\}$, where $q_i \in Q$.

The definition of transition function δ' in M_D is a bit complex. A move in an equivalent M_D on reading an input symbol $a \in \Sigma$ simulates a transition in M_N, possibly associated with a number of *null* (ε) transitions in M_N. For any state $q_i \in Q$, we define $\mathscr{C}(q_i)$ as *ε-closure* of q_i as a set of all the states of M_N that are reachable from state q_i with ε-input, including the state q_i itself. Hence,

$$\mathscr{C}(q_i) = \{q_i\} \cup \{q_j \in Q \mid \delta(q_i, \varepsilon) = q_j\}. \tag{3.7}$$

In other words, $\mathscr{C}(q_i)$ is ε-*closure* of the set $\{q_i\}$ under the relation,

$$\{(q_j, q_k) \mid \text{ there is a transition of the form } \delta(q_j, \varepsilon) = q_k;\\ q_j \in \mathscr{C}(q_i), \text{ and } q_k \notin \mathscr{C}(q_i)\}.$$

The set $\mathscr{C}(q_i)$ is computed using Algorithm 3.1.

Algorithm 3.1 ε-*Closure*

for $i := 1$ to n **do**
  $C(q_i) := \{q_i\}$
end for
while there is transition $\delta(q_j, \varepsilon) = q_k$; $q_j \in C(q_i)$ and $q_k \notin C(q_i)$ **do**
  $C(q_i) := C(q_i) \cup \{q_k\}$
  Drop stand alone state q_k along with ε-transition edge from q_i to q_k
end while

The loop will ultimately terminate, as there can only be a finite number of relations possible in the while loop condition, which can hold true. Whenever some input causes more than one transition from any state q_i to say, state q_j and q_k, it forms two clone FA running in parallel, we can represent these two states as union state $\{q_j, q_k\}$, which is subset of Q. Thus, now there is only one transition from q_i to $\{q_j, q_k\}$. The number of union states can be at the worst all possible subsets of Q, which is 2^Q.

Based on the above, different tuples of the equivalent deterministic finite automata M_D can now be defined as

$$Q' = 2^Q$$
$$s' = \mathscr{C}(s), \text{ (ε-closure of s)}$$
$$F' = \{D\}.$$

In the above, every element D of F' is defined as follows: if $q_f \in F$, then $D = \{\dots, q_f, \dots\} \in F'$. In addition, for each $a \in \Sigma$ and for each $D \in F'$ the δ' can be generalized as follows:

$$\delta'(D, a) = \bigcup \{\{q_j\} \mid \delta(q_j, a) = q_k; q_j \in D \text{ and } q_k \in Q\}, \tag{3.8}$$

where $\{q_j\} = \mathscr{C}(q_j)$, is set of all the states reachable from q_j through ε-transitions. Hence, the $\delta'(D, a)$ is a state of M_D corresponding to the set of all the states of M_N to which M_N can move by reading an input a followed by possibly any number of ε-transitions. The set of these Ds form the final states in equivalent DFA.

Since we have defined all the tuples for a DFA in terms of the tuples of NFA, it can be concluded that there exists an equivalent DFA consisting of these tuples, for every NFA. □

Theorem 3.2 *Prove that, Theorem 3.1 gives a correct equivalent DFA for an NFA.*

Proof We can arrive at the required proof through the method of *induction* for an input string of arbitrary length.

Basis step: With input $a \in \Sigma$, a transition in NFA M_N from state q_0 to q_i corresponds to a transition in equivalent DFA M_D from state $\{q_0\}$ to state $\{\dots, q_i, \dots\}$. The remaining states in $\{\dots, q_i, \dots\}$ are ε-transitions from q_i to itself.

Induction Hypothesis: A walk-through in M_N with input string $v \in \Sigma^*$, for $|v| = n$, from state q_0 to state q_j implies a walk-through from state $\{q_0\}$ to state $Q_j = \{\dots, q_j, \dots\}$ in M_D.

Induction step: Consider an input $w = va$ to the NFA M_N, which causes a sequence of transitions from q_0 to q_k. Correspondingly, there must then be a sequence of edges form $\{q_0\}$ to $\{\dots, q_j, \dots\}$ for input v, followed by an edge or sequence of edges from $\{\dots, q_j, \dots\}$ to $\{\dots, q_k, \dots\}$ in M_D.

As per Theorem 3.1 of conversion from NFA to DFA, there will be a labeled walk v from $\{q_0\}$ to Q_j. In addition, there will be an edge from Q_j to some state in 2^Q, whose one of the labels is a. Thus, this walk-through holds for all the strings of length $n + 1$ also. Similarly, whenever $\delta^*(q_0, w) = \{\dots, q_f, \dots\}$ and $q_f \in F$, then the $\delta^*(q_0, w)$ moves to final state in DFA. This proves the theorem. □

The following corollaries can be constructed using Theorem 3.2.

Corollary 3.1 *A language is regular if and only if some finite automaton recognizes it.*

Corollary 3.2 *A language is regular if and only if some nondeterministic finite automaton recognizes it.*

An equivalent DFA for a given NFA can be obtained using the Algorithm 'refnfadfalgo, called *subset construction method*. Let G_N and G_D respectively represent the transition graph for existing NFA and an equivalent DFA being created. The construction of equivalent DFA is obtained using Theorem 3.1.

This algorithm adds an edge to $\mathscr{C}(q_i)$ in every pass through the while loop. The transition graph thus formed for the DFA M_D can have at most $2^{|Q|} \times |\Sigma|$ number of edges, hence the loop should eventually terminate.

In later chapters, we will study how the equivalent states can be merged together using the subset construction method, to obtain a minimized DFA.

The following example demonstrates the conversion of an NFA to DFA, using Algorithm 3.2.

Algorithm 3.2 Subset construction: NFA to DFA (Input: NFA, Output; DFA)

Start creating a transition graph G_D with a vertex $\mathscr{C}(q_0) = \{q_0\}$. Let this be the start vertex.
For every state q_i, such that $\delta(q_i, \varepsilon) = q_j$, obtain $\mathscr{C}(q_i) = \mathscr{C}(q_i) \cup \{q_j\}$, i.e., $\mathscr{C}(q_i)$ is union of all the states reachable from q_i with ε-transitions.
Drop the corresponding ε-edge, and q_j
while there remains an un-traversed edge in NFA **do**
    Pick up a vertex $\{\dots, q_i, \dots\}$ in G_D that has no outgoing edge for label $a \in \Sigma$.
    Find $\delta'(\{\dots, q_i, \dots\}, a) = \{..., q_j, ...\}$
    Connect $\{\dots, q_i, \dots\}$ and $\{..., q_j, ...\}$ through an edge labeled as a
end while
Mark the states $\{\dots, q_j, \dots\}$ of G_D as member of F', where $q_j \in F$.

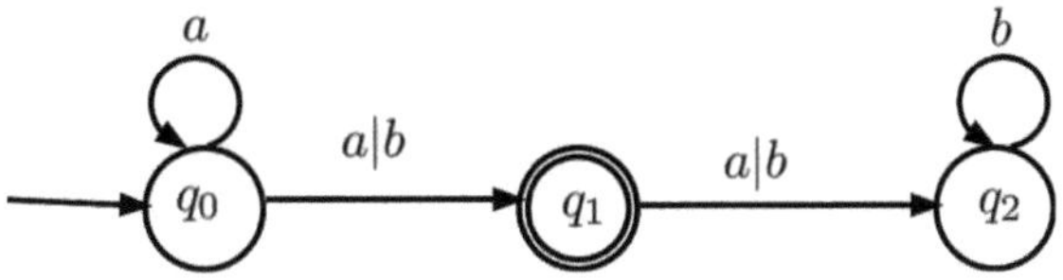

Fig. 3.9 An NFA

Example 3.3 Given the NFA in Fig. 3.9 find an equivalent DFA.

In this NFA there is no ε-transition; however, it is NFA because there are two different transitions for the same input symbol, resulting two different states, for example, due to "a" at state q_0. We will merge these two states to make a union state—a subset of Q.

Let the transition function for *NFA* be δ, for equivalent DFA as δ', and the start state of equivalent DFA be $\{q_0\}$. Using the Algorithm 3.2 we have

$$\delta'(\{q_0\}, a) = \{q_0, q_1\}$$
$$\delta'(\{q_0\}, b) = \{q_1\}.$$

In the remaining solution, we obtain the next state for every state generated, for each input a and b.

$$\begin{aligned}
\delta'(\{q_0, q_1\}, a) &= \delta(q_0, a) \cup \delta(q_1, a)\\
&= \{q_0, q_1\} \cup \{q_2\}\\
&= \{q_0, q_1, q_2\}.\\
\delta'(\{q_0, q_1\}, b) &= \delta(q_0, b) \cup \delta(q_1, b)\\
&= \{q_1\} \cup \{q_2\}\\
&= \{q_1, q_2\}.
\end{aligned}$$

Proceeding in the similar way we compute the other states and finally obtain the equivalent DFA shown in Fig. 3.10.

$$\delta'(\{q_1\}, a) = \{q_2\}$$
$$\delta'(\{q_1\}, b) = \{q_2\}.$$

$$\begin{aligned}\delta'(\{q_0, q_1, q_2\}, a) &= \delta(q_0, a) \cup \delta(q_1, a) \cup \delta(q_2, a)\\ &= \{q_0, q_1\} \cup \{q_2\} \cup \phi\\ &= \{q_0, q_1, q_2\}.\\ \delta'(\{q_0, q_1, q_2\}, b) &= \delta(q_0, b) \cup \delta(q_1, b) \cup \delta(q_2, b)\\ &= \{q_1\} \cup \{q_2\} \cup \{q_2\}\\ &= \{q_1, q_2\}.\end{aligned}$$

$$\begin{aligned}\delta'(\{q_1, q_2\}, a) &= \delta(q_1, a) \cup \delta(q_2, a)\\ &= \{q_2\} \cup \phi\\ &= \{q_2\}.\\ \delta'(\{q_1, q_2\}, b) &= \delta(q_1, b) \cup \delta(q_2, b)\\ &= \{q_2\} \cup \{q_2\}\\ &= \{q_2\}.\end{aligned}$$

$$\delta'(\{q_2\}, a) = \delta(q_2, a) = \phi$$
$$\delta'(\{q_2\}, b) = \delta(q_2, b) = \{q_2\}.$$

We note that the number of states in the equivalent DFA is six, as the empty state has been dropped. The maximum states in 3-state DFA can be $2^{\{q_0, q_1, q_2\}} = 8$.

A state-set label in the equivalent *DFA* is a final state if one of the states $q_i \in F$ in this set. These final states in the resultant DFA have been labeled accordingly as shown in Fig. 3.10. □

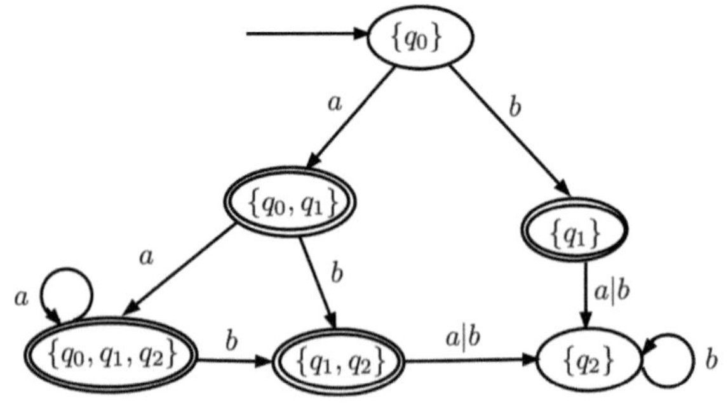

Fig. 3.10 Equivalent DFA for the NFA in Fig. 3.9

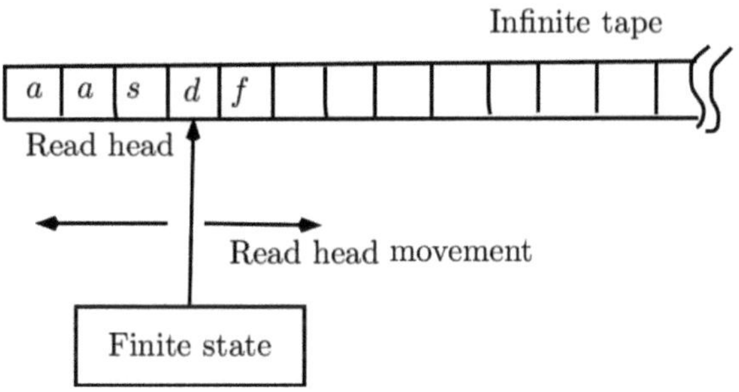

Fig. 3.11 Two-way DFA

3.5 Two-way Finite Automata

A two-tape automaton is an ordinary automaton having an additional structure to determine which tape is to be used. Except for the left and right moves of the read head, the process of state transitions remains the same as in the standard DFA. Intuitively, such devices should be able to accept more than one regular set, since they can revisit certain parts of the input tape (Fig. 3.11).

A 2DFA can read the input back and forth with no limit on how many times. Are 2DFA unrealistic? 2DFA is in fact a model that it solves problems that are solvable by a computer using finite memory. In most real-life computing tasks performed by a computer, the input saved in RAM (random access memory) can be read in both directions. So, 2DFA is indeed a meaningful and arguably more realistic model of computer than 1DFA.

How does DFA compare to 2DFA? Clearly, DFA is a restricted version of 2DFA. Therefore, 2DFA should solve any problems that are solvable by DFA. Are there problems that can be solved by 2DFA but cannot be solved by DFA? In fact, a 2DFA can always be simulated by a DFA. That is, whatever problems can be solved by 2DFA can also be solved by DFA. In addition, a 2DFA is closer to *Turing Machine*, to be discussed in later chapters, where the head is *read/write* and can move forward as well as backward and can write also apart from reading. For every 2DFA there is an equivalent DFA that recognizes the same language as the DFA.

The mathematical model of 2DFA is also a 5-tuple, $M = (\Sigma, Q, q_0, \delta, F)$, where Σ, Q, q_0, F has the same meaning as in the standard DFA, and δ is a mapping:

$$\delta : Q \times \Sigma \mapsto Q \times \{L, R, S\} \tag{3.9}$$

The above equation indicates that after a state transition, the head may move to the left (L), may remain stationary (S), or may move to the right (R). With current state p and input a, if it moves to state q, then $\delta(p, a) = (q, L)$, or $\delta(p, a) = (q, S)$, or $\delta(p, a) = (q, R)$. If a 2DFA tries back off the left end of the tape, it stops operating without accepting the input.

The 2DFA has a nondeterministic version, called 2NFA, with transition function as

$$\delta : Q \times \Sigma \mapsto 2^{Q\times\{L,R,S\}}. \tag{3.10}$$

An *ID* (*Instantaneous Description*) in 2DFA is a member of $\Sigma^* \times Q \times \Sigma^*$, where first Σ^* is substring before the read head, and second Σ^* is substring from read head position to end of the input string. For example, a configuration (u, q, v) indicates that currently, the machine is in state q, the string to the left of the read head is $u \in \Sigma^*$ and the head pointing to the first symbol of string $v \in \Sigma^*$. If the input string has been completely read, then the configuration should be (u, q, ε). As it reads the input symbols, the machines move from one ID to another, e.g.,

$$(u_1, q_1, v_1) \vdash_M (u_2, q_2, v_2) \tag{3.11}$$

such that $\delta(q_1, \sigma) = (q_2, m)$, where $\sigma \in \Sigma$ and $u_1, v_1, u_2, v_2 \in \Sigma^*$ and the move $m \in \{L, R, S\}$. Fig. 3.12a and b, respectively, indicate the movement of the read head to left and to right, after it has read the input symbol.

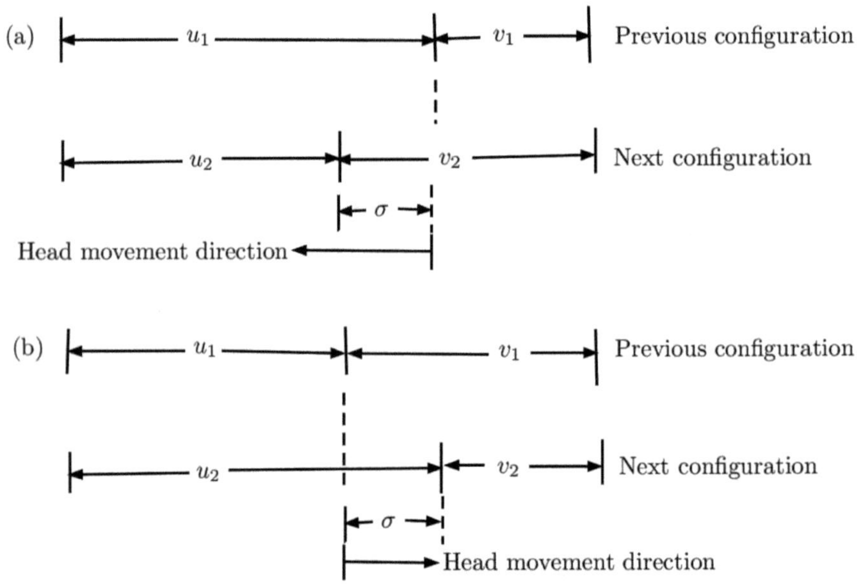

Fig. 3.12 **a** Read head moved left after reading input. **b** Read head moves right after reading input

Formally, these transitions are represented as follows:

Fig. 3.12a:
For $m = L$
$u_1 = u_2\sigma$, and
$v_2 = \sigma v_1$.
Fig. 3.12b:
For $m = R$
$u_1\sigma = u_2$ and
$\sigma v_2 = v_1$.

Note that $u_2\sigma$ and σv_1 are concatenations of σ with u_2 and v_1, respectively.

When Head is stationary (i.e., $m = s$), following holds: $u_1 = u_2$, $v_1 = v_2$, and $\sigma =$ null.

The *derive-operator* $\vdash_M^*$ is both *reflexive* and *transitive closure*. The 2DFA accepts a string w if the following configuration sequence holds true and $q_f \in F$:

$$(\varepsilon, q_0, w) \vdash_M^* (w, q_f, \varepsilon). \tag{3.12}$$

The following transitive relations are important for 2DFA.

(1) $q_i v \vdash^* q_j v$
(2) $uq_i v \vdash^* uq_j v$

If (1) holds, then M starts on the leftmost symbol of v, processes v, then returns back to the same place. Thus, if (a) holds then (b) also holds, i.e.,

$$q_i v \vdash^* q_j v \Rightarrow uq_i v \vdash^* uq_j v.$$

Let us consider that if (b) holds then (a) holds or not? Arguing in a counter way, we can suggest that in (b), the machine read head may move left over u in part or fully, and after processing it, the read head may return at the same *ID* $uq_j v$ without touching v at all. Thus (b) may indicate a case of *nil* processing of v. Whereas (a) shows that v has been processed and the final *ID* is the same as it was earlier. Thus, given (b) we cannot conclude (a), hence,

$$uq_i v \vdash^* uq_j v \not\Rightarrow q_i v \vdash^* q_j v.$$

Definition 3.3 (*Language of 2DFA*) The language $L(M)$ for 2DFA is a set of strings w given as, $L(M) = \{w \mid (\varepsilon, q_0, w) \vdash_M^* (w, q_f, \varepsilon)$ and $q_f \in F\}$. □

Example 3.4 Consider a 2DFA $M = (\Sigma, Q, q_0, \delta, F)$. The read head moves to the right as long as it reads 0. The FA remains in state q_0 after every such transition. On encountering 1 it changes to state q_1 and the head moves to the left. Subsequently, it moves to the left side each time 1 is read and remains in the state q_1 until it reads 0 at which it moves to the right and the process repeats. The q_0 is both the start and final state.

Table 3.2 Transition table for 2DFA

Current state	Input 0	Input 1
q_0	(q_0, R)	(q_1, L)
q_1	(q_0, R)	(q_1, L)

Find out whether, the strings $w_1 = 0000$ and $w_2 = 0101$ are accepted by the M. Also, find out the language accepted by the machine.

For this, various tuples of this FA can be constructed as follows.

$$\Sigma = \{0, 1\}$$
$$Q = \{q_0, q_1\}, F = \{q_0\}, s = q_0.$$

The transition function for this FA is as given in Table 3.2, as well as the transition diagram in Fig. 3.13.

Let us first find out the final *ID* of the machine when w_1 and w_2 are applied to it.

(a) For w_1 (i.e., 0101) input:

$$\begin{aligned}(\varepsilon, q_0, 0101) &\vdash_M (0, q_0, 101)\\ &\vdash_M (\varepsilon, q_1, 0101)\\ &\vdash_M (0, q_0, 101)\\ &\vdash_M (\varepsilon, q_1, 0101).\end{aligned}$$

Since there is a loop, as the *ID* $(\varepsilon, q_1, 0101)$ is repeated, the read head can never reach the end of the input. Hence $0101 \notin L(M)$.

(b) For w_2 (i.e., 00000) input:

$$\begin{aligned}(\varepsilon, q_0, 0000) &\vdash_M (0, q_0, 000)\\ &\vdash_M (00, q_0, 00)\\ &\vdash_M (000, q_0, 0)\\ &\vdash_M (0000, q_0, \varepsilon).\end{aligned}$$

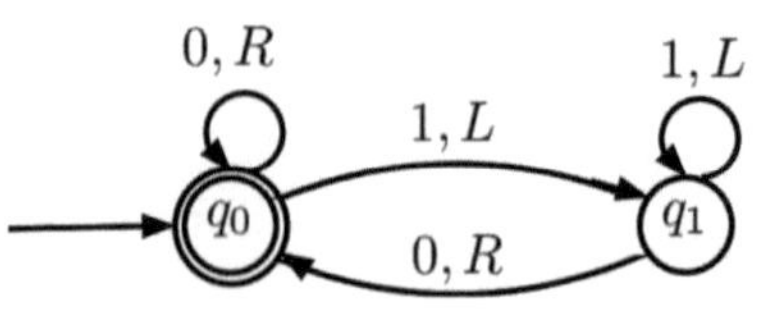

Fig. 3.13 Transition diagram of 2DFA

Since last state is q_0, hence $w_2 \in L(M)$. In fact, the only language accepted by this 2DFA is one having strings with all 0s. □

Unlike the DFA, a 2DFA needs only one *accept* state and one reject state. We can think of halting immediately when it enters one of these states, although formally it keeps running but remains in the *accept* or *reject* state. The machine does need not to read the entire input before accepting it. Indeed, it need not even accept or reject at all but may loop indefinitely without ever entering an accept or reject state.

However, there is an interesting result about the conversion of 2NFA into a 2DFA. It is an open problem whether every 2NFA can be converted into a 2DFA with only a polynomial increase in the number of states [8].

3.6 Finite Automata with Output

The finite automata receives input as a sequence of symbols on the input tape and the output is in the form of yes/no (accepted/rejected). When compared with the real computers, this turns out to be a limitation as there is no alphabet-numeric sequence produced at the output. Many times, there is a requirement of a sequence of symbols in the output, instead of a yes/no answer. For example, in computers, input is in the form of programs and data, and the output is alphanumeric strings. As another example, in speech processing the input may be phonetic symbols and output in text form as English language sentences. The output produced in these cases may appear immediately after the input is processed, or it may be stored in memory and sent to the output device later at one stretch. The machines having these properties are called finite automata with output or *finite-state transducers* (FSTs) [4]. Note that, in contrast to FA which defines formal languages by defining the set of accepted strings, the FST defines relations between sets of strings. FSTs are also used in the lexical analysis phase of compilers to associate the semantic values with the discovered tokens.

The *Moore machine* is a finite-state automaton, where outputs are determined by the present state alone and do not depend directly on input. Most digital/electronic systems designed as clocked sequential systems are the restricted form of Moore machine, where the state changes are decided by the global clock signal. Typically, the current state is stored in flip-flops, and a global clock signal is connected to the "clock" input of the flop-flop. A typical electronic Moore machine includes a combinational logic chain to decode the current state into the output. The instant a current state changes, it ripples through a chain, and almost instantaneously the output changes. Thus, in effect, a Moore machine duplicates a finite automaton.

Mealy machine is a finite-state machine (to be precise, a finite-state transducer) that generates an output based on its current state and input. This means that the state diagram (transition diagram) will include both an input and output symbol for each transition edge [5].

3.6.1 Moore Machine

A Moore machine is defined as a six-tuple,

$$M_o = (Q, \Sigma, \delta, s, \Gamma, \lambda), \tag{3.13}$$

where the first four tuples: Q, Σ, δ, s are the same as in the FA. That is,

Q : Set of states,
Σ : Input alphabet set,
Γ : Output alphabet set,
$\delta : Q \times \Sigma \rightarrow Q$, the transition function,
s : start state,
$\lambda : Q \rightarrow \Gamma$, mapping function from states to output.

If the states of M_o are $q_0, q_1, q_2, \ldots$, then output sequence is $\lambda(q_0), \lambda(q_1), \lambda(q_2)$, ..., respectively. Thus, every input string creates an output string corresponding to the states through which the machine transits; $|\Gamma| \leq |Q|$, since every state has some output symbol, and there can be the same output for two different states.

A Moore machine does not define a language on its input alphabets. Thus, there is no concept of the final state in the Moore machine. However, since it has a finite number of states, it is a finite automaton. Processing of an input string gets terminated when the last input alphabet is received and the last output alphabet is printed. However, it is possible to turn a Moore machine into a language recognizer, i.e., produces a yes/no answer.

Let us consider that there is a Moore machine with states q_0, q_1, q_2, q_3, and the corresponding outputs are a, b, c, d, respectively, the q_0 is a start state. Suppose that input sequence 101 causes the Moore machine to switch to states q_1, q_2, q_3, respectively, starting from the q_0. Since each output symbol is associated with a state and during the input sequence 101 the machine has seen the states q_0, q_1, q_2, and q_3, the output will also correspond to these four states. Hence, the output corresponding to input 101 is $abcd$, which is one character longer than the length of input (see Fig. 3.14). We assume that the output sequence produced is stored on output tape.

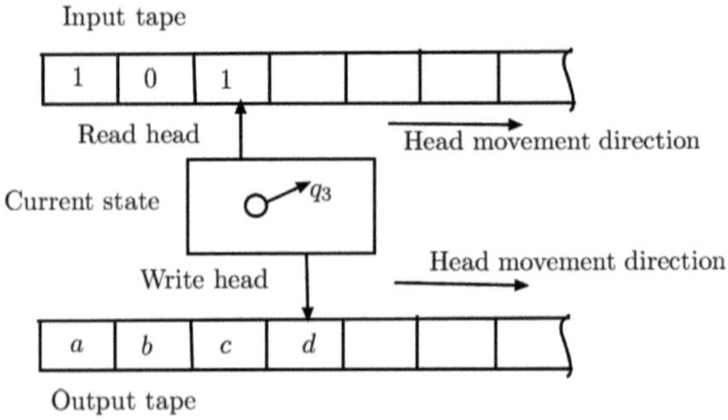

Fig. 3.14 Physical model of a Moore machine

Table 3.3 Transition table for Fig. 3.15

Current state (q_i)	Output $\lambda(q_i)$	Next state for Input a	Next state for Input b
q_0	1	q_1	q_3
q_1	0	q_3	q_1
q_2	0	q_0	q_3
q_3	1	q_3	q_2

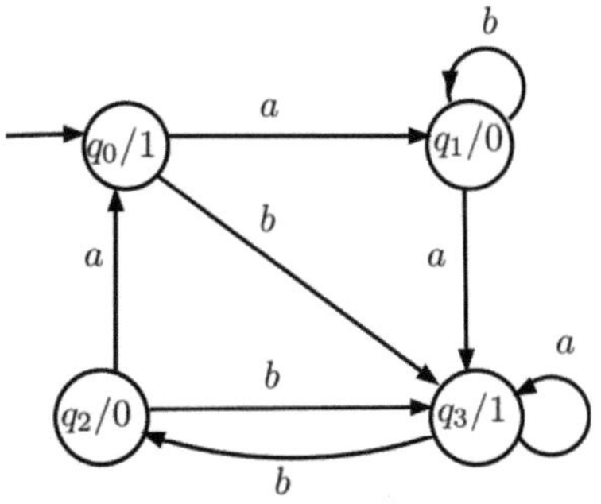

Fig. 3.15 Transition diagram of a Moore machine

Example 3.5 Construct a Moore machine, whose details are as follows:

$$M_0 = (Q, \Sigma, \delta, s, \Gamma, \lambda),$$
$$Q = \{q_0, q_1, q_2, q_3\},$$
$$\Sigma = \{a, b\},$$
$$s = q_0,$$
$$\Gamma = \{0, 1\}.$$

The transition function δ and the mapping function $\lambda : Q \rightarrow \Gamma$ are given in Table 3.3. The transition diagram for Moore machines can be obtained as shown in Fig. 3.15, where q_i in $\lambda(q_i)$ is the current state of the Moore machine.

The output associated with each state is shown in the state itself. The slash ("/") sign separates the state name and the output. If the input is *abab* the corresponding outputs can be found out as follows. The initial state is q_0, and the transition sequence of states produced are

$$\delta(q_0, a) = q_1$$
$$\delta(q_1, b) = q_1$$
$$\delta(q_1, a) = q_3$$
$$\delta(q_3, b) = q_2.$$

Hence, for the input sequence *abab* the output string is 10010. We note that Moore machine gives an output string of length $n + 1$ for an input string of length n. One extra character in the output is due to the start state, which Moore machine was occupying before the first input had arrived. □

From the Exercise 3.19 we note that based on the criteria of accepting an input string the new automaton becomes a finite automaton, and it accepts all the languages strings having one or more occurrences of substring 111 in the input, and the input terminates with 111. Thus q_3 becomes the accepting state. Hence, it demonstrates that Moore's machine can be used as a language recognizer.

3.6.2 *Mealy Machine*

The Mealy Machine is represented by

$$M_e = (Q, \Sigma, \delta, s, \Gamma, \lambda), \tag{3.14}$$

where Q, Σ, δ, s and Γ are same as that in the Moore Machine, and $\lambda : Q \times \Sigma \to \Gamma$ is output function, i.e., $\lambda(q, a)$ is output associated with the transition edge from state q with input a for $q \in Q$ and $a \in \Sigma$.

Consider that the input sequence is $w = abcd$ and suppose the Mealy machine goes through the sequence of transition states q_0, q_1, q_2, q_3 due to this input. The output sequence corresponding to this is denoted by $\lambda(q_0, a)\lambda(q_1, b)\lambda(q_2, c)\lambda(q_3, d)$. The q_0 is start state, and other states are given by $\delta(q_0, a) = q_1$, $\delta(q_1, b) = q_2$, $\delta(q_2, c) = q_3$, and $\delta(q_3, d) = q_4$. Note that, for the input string $|abcd| = 4$, the output string also has length 4. Thus, in Mealy Machine length of input and output strings are equal.

In Moore Machine, we noted that for an input ε (null string) there is finite output produced, even though there is no transition. However, for the Mealy machine, for ε input, there is no output produced. In addition, like the Moore Machine, the Mealy Machine also does not define a language, since it does not have any final state.

Example 3.6 Construct a Mealy Machine to invert an arbitrary binary string made of alphabet $\Sigma = \{0, 1\}$.

Figure 3.16 shows the required Mealy machine. The output of the Mealy machine associated with the transition edge is shown with 1 and 0 corresponding to the input of 0 and 1, respectively. Various tuples of this Mealy Machine are as follows.

$$\Sigma = \{0.1\}, \Gamma = \{0, 1\}$$
$$Q = \{q_0\}, s = q_0,$$

δ and λ are given in Table 3.4.

Note that the job performed by this simple machine is to complement the binary bits of the input string with 1's complement. □

Table 3.4 Transition table for Mealy machine (Fig. 3.16)

Current state	Next state/output for Input = 0	Next state/output for Input = 1
q_0	$q_0/1$	$q_1/0$

Example 3.7 Construct a Mealy Machine, which increments any given binary input string by 1 and prints the incremented string at output.

For the input string 1010 ($D_3 D_2 D_1 D_0$), the output will be:

$$\begin{array}{cccc} D_3 & D_2 & D_1 & D_0 \\ 1 & 0 & 1 & 0 \\ & & + & 1 \\ \hline 1 & 0 & 1 & 1 \end{array}$$

which is the case of non-carry.

For input of 10111, the output is

$$\begin{array}{ccccc} 1 & 0 & 1 & 1 & 1 \\ & & & + & 1 \\ \hline 1 & 1 & 0 & 0 & 0 \end{array}$$

which is the case of carry. As long as there is carry generated, the output toggles with respect to the input.

The input string enters into the automaton (least significant bit (LSB) first), and at the output also the LSB appears first.

From above we note that there are two alternatives from the start state: one leads to a carry-state (q_1), and the other no-carry state (q_2). While in the no-carry state, irrespective of the value of the input (0 or 1), the remaining output is a replica of the input, and the machine remains in the same (no-carry) state. Hence, no-carry is a dead state, once entered into it there is no exit.

Various tuples of this machine are: $\Sigma = \{0, 1\}$, $\Gamma = \{0, 1\}$, $Q = \{q_0, q_1, q_2\}$, and $s = q_0$. The Mealy machine for this is shown in Fig. 3.17, and the Transition table is Table 3.5. □

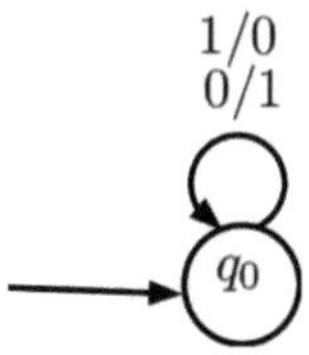

Fig. 3.16 Mealy machine to complement a binary string

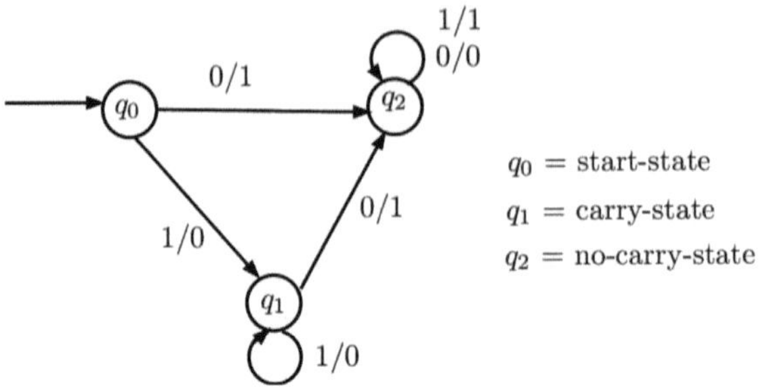

Fig. 3.17 Mealy machine to increment a binary string

Table 3.5 Mealy machine transition table for Fig. 3.17

Current state	Next state/output (for Input = 0)	Next state/output (for Input = 1)
q_0	$q_2/1$	$q_1/0$
q_1	$q_2/1$	$q_1/0$
q_2	$q_2/0$	$q_2/1$

3.7 Equivalence of Moore and Mealy Machines

Let, for a Moore machine M_o there is an equivalent Mealy machine M_e. Hence, for an input w, the output of these machines are $M_o(w)$ and $M_e(w)$, respectively. These two machines will be equivalent if $M_o(w) = aM_e(w)$, where a is the output of the Moore machine at state q_0, without any input. In fact, they cannot give identical output, because $|M_o(w)| > |M_e(w)|$.

3.7.1 *Mealy Machine to Moore Machine*

If the output due to the start state of the Moore machine is ignored it is possible to construct the Mealy machine that produces the same output as that of a Moore Machine. Alternatively, if the output of the Moore machine at q_0 is prefixed with the output of the Mealy machine and the output produced in each transition in the Mealy machine is the same as that of the output produced in the Moore machine for input w, then $M_o(w) = aM_e(w)$. Here we assume that Q, Σ, s, Γ are identical in the two machines, and the δ and λ produce the same next state and outputs, respectively, in both the states.

Theorem 3.3 *For every Moore machine, there exists an equivalent Mealy machine.*

Proof Let $M_o = (Q, \Sigma, \delta_o, s, \lambda_o, \Gamma)$ be a Moore machine, and there is a Mealy machine M_e, which we want to prove to be equivalent to M_o.

Let $M_e = (Q, \Sigma, \delta_e, s, \lambda_e, \Gamma)$. These two machines will be equivalent if they pass through the same sequence of states for the same input, and produce the same output.

This becomes possible, if we can define the output of an equivalent Mealy machine as $\lambda_e(q_i, a)$ when the output of the Moore machine is $\lambda_0(\delta(q_i, a))$, and both these are equal.

For Moore machine, if there is a transition $\delta_o(q_i, a) = q_j$, and $\lambda_o(q_j) = b$, the corresponding equivalent Mealy machine should have the transition,

$$\delta_e(q_i, a) = q_j, \lambda_e(q_i, a) = b.$$

In other words, the transformation of M_o into M_e is equivalent to the transformation shown in Fig. 3.18. An important point to be noted is, that a Mealy machine produces the output on the edge of transition, while the equivalent Moore machine produces the output when the transition has taken place, and it has gone to the next state. □

3.7.2 *Moore Machine to Mealy Machine*

Theorem 3.4 *For every Mealy machine M_e, there exists an equivalent Moore machine M_o.*

Proof To find an equivalent Moore machine for a given Mealy machine, applying the reverse approach to what is used in Theorem 3.3, may not work always. This is because, for a Mealy Machine when there are different output symbols on the incoming edges of a state, they will conflict when moved into the next state of an equivalent Moore machine. Figure 3.19a shows this situation.

Therefore, to get a Moore machine for this kind of Mealy machine, we create two states—one q_i' and other q_i'', as shown in Fig. 3.19b. The two different outputs existing on input arcs are moved into two different states and the output symbol from the corresponding input arcs is removed. All the outgoing transitions of original q_i shall remain common for q_i' and q_i''. Note that we have changed only one state while converting the Mealy machine to the Moore machine, the other states will also be modified in a similar manner.

In fact, the number of states in an equivalent Moore machine for any given state in the Mealy machine will depend on how many incoming arcs have different outputs. This results in a Moore machine M_o whose output for a given string w would be the same as that for the original Mealy machine.

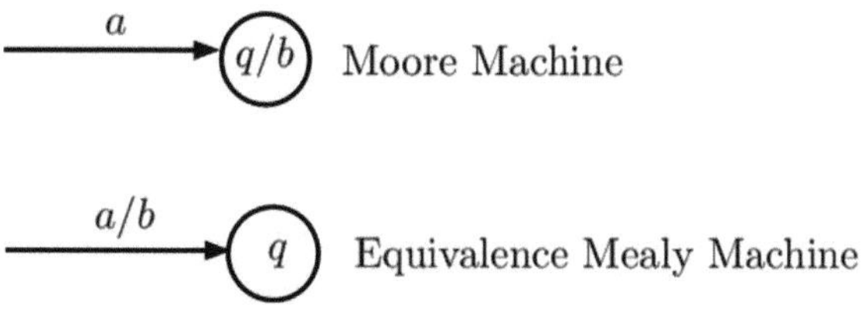

Fig. 3.18 Single state Mealy and Moore machine

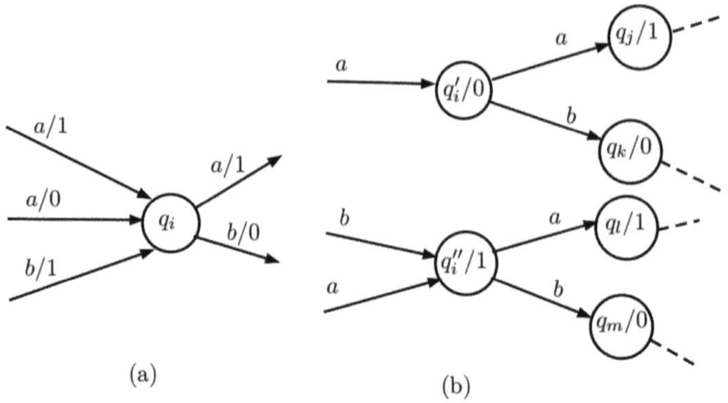

Fig. 3.19 **a** Mealy machine state q_i. **b** Corresponding equivalent Moore machine with two states

Formally, we can say that, if $M_e = (Q, \Sigma, \delta_e, s, \lambda_e, \Gamma)$ is a Mealy machine, then there is an equivalent Moore machine M_o specified as follows:

$$M_o = (Q \times \Gamma, \Sigma, \delta_o, [s, b], \lambda_o, \Gamma), \tag{3.15}$$

where

- b is any arbitrary value in Γ (It is due to the output of the start state in Moore machine),
- $Q \times \Gamma$ indicates that states in M_o are pairs $[q, b]$ where $q \in Q$, and $b \in \Gamma$, and in general, the number of states in the equivalent Moore machine will be more than in the original Mealy machine, $Q \times \Gamma$ is the worst-case number of states,
- $\delta_o([q, b], a) = [\delta_e(q, a), \lambda_e(q, a)]$, where b is output of some state in M_o, which made transition from state q with input a,
- $\lambda_o([q, b]) = b$, due to start state in Moore machine.

In conclusion, we say that if Mealy machine M_e goes through the states $q_0, q_1, \dots,$ q_n, with input sequence $a_1, a_2, \dots, a_n$ (q_0 being the start state), and produces output $b_1, b_2, \dots, b_n$, then corresponding equivalent Moore machine M_o goes through the states $[q_0, b_0], [q_1, b_1], \dots, [q_n, b_n]$. The output b_0 associated with start state q_0 in M_o has no corresponding output in the M_e, as this output is arbitrary and is not generated due to the input string. This proves that for every Mealy machine, there exists an equivalent Moore machine. □

By Theorems 3.3 and 3.4 we prove that $M_e \equiv M_o$.

Example 3.8 Given the Moore machine in Fig. 3.20a, find out an equivalent Mealy machine.

Applying Theorem 3.3, for the Moore machine given in Fig. 3.20a, the equivalent Mealy machine is derived as shown in Fig. 3.20b. Note the difference of symbols at the edges of both machines and inside a state in the Moore machine. The symbol

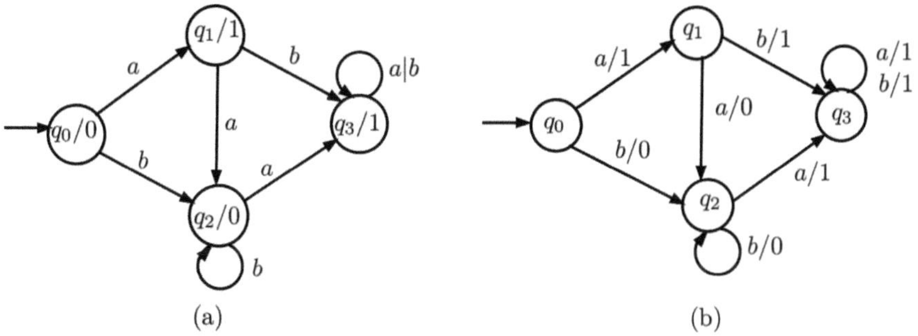

Fig. 3.20 **a** Moore machine. **b** Equivalent Mealy machine

"/" inside a state of a Moore machine stands or the mapping between that state and its output; the same symbol on the edge of the Mealy machine indicates the mapping, e.g., $(q_i, a) \rightarrow b$, shown as a/b, where a is input symbol and b is output symbol produced on the edge. However, the symbol "|", on Moore machine, e.g., $a|b$ indicates that the input can be a or b. □

3.8 Finite-State Transducers

A finite-state transducer or simply a transducer, is a finite-state automaton whose edges comprise pairs of labels representing paths of words taken from a finite set of alphabets. The first component of each pair on the edge of the transition diagram is the input label, while the second is the output label. The transducers may or may not have accepting states. The relation defined by a transducer is the set of pairs of words, which are labels of an accepting path in the transducer. We assume that the relations defined by these transducers are functions. The Moore machine and the Mealy machine are both transducers. However, the Mealy machine is commonly used for the representation of transducers.

The transducers are used in many applications, ranging from lexical analyzers to language and speech processing, to design the controllability systems in air-crafts, to model coding schemes (compression schemes, convolution coding schemes, coding schemes for constrained channels, etc.). The transducers are also used in program analysis. The determinization of a transducer is the construction of another transducer that defines the same function and has a deterministic (or right resolving) input automaton. Such transducers allow a sequential encoding and thus are called *sequential transducers* [6].

Very large finite-state transducers can be used in various domains of natural language processing. In some applications, such as speech processing, the size of these machines exceeds millions of states. Reducing the size of these graphs without losing their recognition properties is then crucial. The solution exists for DFA, where any DFA admits an equivalent one with the minimum number of states and classical algorithms can be used to compute the minimal automaton from a given one, in an efficient way. However, for transducers, it is challenging and involves work. Due to their complexity caused by a large number of states, the speech recognition systems are complex and slow [7].

Transducers Over Finite Words

Let A and B denote the finite set of alphabets. A *free monoid*[2] denoted as A^* is the set of finite words or sequences of letters of A. The symbol ε is an empty word. A transducer over the monoid $A^* \times B^*$ is composed of set Q of states, a set $E \subseteq Q \times A^* \times B^*$ of edges, and two sets I, $F \subseteq Q$ of initial and final states. An edge $e = (p, u, v, q)$ from state p to q is denoted by

$$p \xrightarrow{u/v} q$$

Thus, a transducer is the same object as an automaton, except that the labels of the edges are pairs of words instead of letters. A path in a transducer $\mathscr{T}$ is specified as a sequence,

$$p_0 \xrightarrow{u_0/v_0} p_1 \xrightarrow{u_1/v_1} p_2 \dots \xrightarrow{u_n/v_n} p_n. \tag{3.16}$$

In short, the above path is denoted by

$$p_0 \xrightarrow{u/v} p_n. \tag{3.17}$$

In the above, $u = u_0u_1u_2 \dots u_n$, and $v = v_0v_1v_2 \dots v_n$. A path is successful if it leaves the initial state and ends in a final state. The set recognized by the transducer is the set of labels of its successful paths, which is actually a relation $R \subset A^* \times B^*$.

A transducer computes a function if, for any word $u \in A^*$, there exists at most one word $v \in B^*$ such that $(u, v) \in R$. We call it the function realized by the transducer. Thus, a transducer can be seen as a machine computing non-deterministically output words from input.

A transducer is finite if its set of states and its set of transitions are finite.

Example 3.9 A finite-state transducer.

The automaton or finite-state transducer in Fig. 3.21 recognizes the relation $(a^2, b^2)^* \cup (a^2, c^2)^* \cup (a, c)$ over the alphabet sets $A = \{a\}$ and $B = \{b, c\}$. This relation is actually the function which maps a^n to b^n if n is even and c^n if n is odd [1, 1, 7]. □

---

[2] In Algebraic systems, a semigroup is a set that is closed under associative binary operation. A monoid is a semigroup with an identity element.

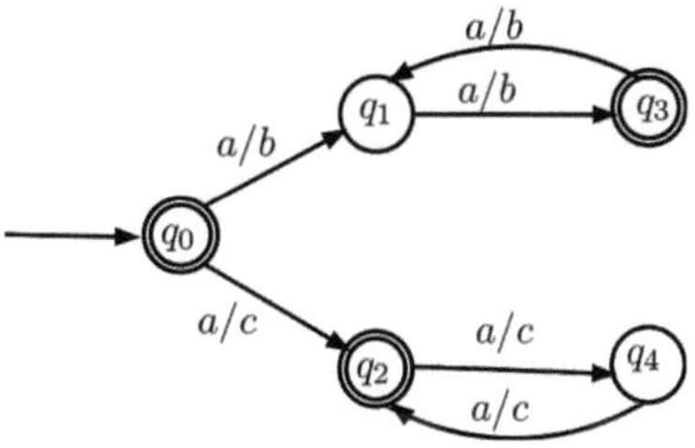

Fig. 3.21 Transducer for relation $(a^2, b^2)^* \cup (a^2, c^2)^*(a, c)$

3.9 Summary

NFA

Nondeterminism arises when discussing concurrency. The models of concurrency typically also model nondeterminism. There are also numerous variants of processes' languages and algebra, and event structures, state transition systems, which concern nondeterminism.

Nondeterminism is a means of increasing the level of abstraction when describing sequential programs, and as a way of indicating a "don't care" attitude as to which among a number of computational paths will actually be utilized in a particular evaluation.

An NFA, like DFA, has input tape, finite control, and read head. In a deterministic FA, there is always a definite next state for the current: "state × input symbol" pair. However, an NFA may have one or more next states or even an empty next state for such a pair. The next state in an NFA is a set, which is a subset of 2^Q, for Q states in the NFA.

A sequence of configurations and moves in an NFA is defined as

$$(\{q_i\}, w) \vdash^* (\{q_j, \ldots, q_k\}, \varepsilon). \tag{3.18}$$

If at least one of the states q_j, ..., q_k is in final state F, then w is accepted by the corresponding NFA at state q_i.

Alternatively, w is accepted by an NFA if,

$$\delta^*(q_0, w) \cap F \neq \phi. \tag{3.19}$$

If one or more paths exist in an NFA from start state to final state for a given input w, the string is accepted. However, along with this, there may be paths from the start state for input w, which do not lead to the final state. The number of paths leading to the final state corresponds to the number of DFAs running in parallel for the given clones of DFA. Thus, an NFA appears to behave like a number of DFAs running in parallel.

However, the power of this NFA (capability to compute) is in no way more than that of its equivalent DFA.

An NFA is simpler than a DFA. If an NFA has n number of states, the corresponding equivalent DFA may have as many as 2^n numbers of states, and n states in a DFA, its NFA may have only $\log n$ states. A DFA can be simplified by merging equivalent states and removing unreachable states.

For every NFA, there exists an equivalent DFA, which can be obtained as follows: each of the state members of 2^Q states are represented as a new single state, Q_i, Q_j, etc. The state sets having final state as an element, are designated as new final states. If a transition exists in the original NFA from $q_i \in Q_i$ to $q_j \in Q_j$ through an edge $a \in \Sigma$, then a transition is created in equivalent DFA from set Q_i to state Q_j with edge $a \in \Sigma$.

2DFA

A two-way finite automaton is an extension of an ordinary finite automaton and can read the symbols by moving in both directions on the tape. But it is in no way more powerful than ordinary FA, as it can solve only those problems that can be solved by a standard single-tape FA. For each transition, a 2-way finite automaton moves to a new state, and the read head may take a right move or remain stationary, or may take a left move. When compared with a Turing machine, a 2-way DFA is more close to the Turing machine than a 1-way DFA.

FA with Output

The finite automaton with output provides an output for each input, like an ordinary finite automaton. However, it is different, because now the output is in the form of a sequence of symbols, instead of yes/no.

This "FA with output" is closer to conventional computers. For example, a finite automaton with output (we will call it now sequential transducer) for *text-to-speech* (TTS) translation will provide output as phone sequence for text input to it or may provide output as text string for speech input in *speech recognition system*. Because of its property to produce a stream at the output instead of yes/no, it is also called *transducer*.

The output in a sequential transducer may be associated with: (a) each state, or (b) with each transition. In the first case, it is called *Moore machine*, while in the second it is *Mealy machine*. Since there is an output sequence in both machines there is no concept of final state.

In addition to transition function δ in finite-state machines, each of the above machines has an additional function λ for output. In Moore's machine, the output function,

$$\lambda_o = Q \to \Gamma, \tag{3.20}$$

states that output is associated with each state. In Mealy machine, the function,

$$\lambda_e = Q \times \Sigma \to \Gamma \tag{3.21}$$

says that output is associated with each transition.

For a given input string w, if δ causes the same and equal number of transitions in some Moore and Mealy machines, and the output sequence associated with transitions in them are same, then the two machines are equivalent to each other. However, in the Moore machine, we need to ignore the output associated with the start state since there is no corresponding transition in the Mealy machine.

The finite-state machines are also used in many areas of computational linguistics. Their use can be justified by both linguistic and computational arguments. Linguistically, finite automata are convenient since they allow one to describe easily most of the relevant local phenomena encountered in the empirical study of languages. The transducers often lead to a compact representation of lexical rules, or idioms and cliches, that appears natural to linguists.

Self Review Questions

1. Every NFA has one equivalent minimized DFA (True/False).
2. Every DFA has one equivalent NFA (True/False).
3. Explain the Algorithm 3.2 in Sect. 3.4 in your own words.
4. How will you complement a DFA?
5. Is DFA also an NFA (True/False)?
6. Why does the NFA carry its significance as a language-recognizing device, in spite of not being a model of real computation?
7. Can there be more than one start state in an NFA?
8. Which of the following can be modeled using the Mealy machine?
   a. Sequential circuits
   b. Combinational circuits
   c. Shift registers
   d. Counters
   e. Accumulator
   f. Serial adder
   g. Parallel adder
9. Why there are no final states in Moore and Mealy machines?
10. How does the 2DFA resemble more closely to a real computer than the 1DFA?
11. If states in a Mealy machine are Q and output symbols' set is Γ, what can be the worst-case number of states in an equivalent Moore machine?
12. Why Moore and Mealy's machines are called Transducers?
13. Do the Moore and Mealy machines remember the history of inputs?
14. Answer the following questions as True or False.
    a. Finite-state machines are widely used in phonology and morphology.
    b. A finite-state transducer (FST) is essentially an FSA (finite-state automaton) that works with two or more tapes.

Table 3.6 δ_1 transition table

Current state	Input a	Input b
q_0	$\{q_0, q_1\}$	q_0
q_1	q_2	q_2
q_2	q_3	ϕ
q_3	q_3	q_3

Table 3.7 δ_2 transition table

Current state	Input a	Input b
q_0	$\{q_0, q_3\}$	q_1
q_1	q_2	$\{q_1, q_2\}$
q_2	q_3	q_0
q_3	ϕ	q_0

c. It is useful to talk of an FST as reading one of its tapes and writing to the others.

15. What is the time complexity of sequential transducers?
16. What may be the typical number of states in a transducer used for speech recognition application?
17. Why an NFA is often simpler than a DFA for any given problem?

Exercises

A. Concepts based Problems

Note: The $*$ marked exercises are provided with solutions at the end of this book.

1. * Construct an NFA that accepts the strings based on the regular expression $(01 + 001 + 010)^*$.
2. Draw the transition diagrams for the NFAs M_1, M_2, and convert these into equivalent DFAs. The δ_1 and δ_2 are given in Tables 3.6 and 3.7, respectively.

   a. $M_1 = \{\{q_0, q_1, q_2, q_3\}, \{a, b\}, \delta_1, q_0, \{q_3\}\}$
   b. $M_2 = \{\{q_0, q_1, q_2, q_3\}, \{a, b\}, \delta_2, \{q_1, q_3\}\}$

3. If an NFA has Q states and alphabet Σ, what can be the worst-case maximum number of edges in the equivalent DFA?
4. Give short answers for the followings:

   a. What is a clone DFA in an NFA?

Fig. 3.22 An NFA

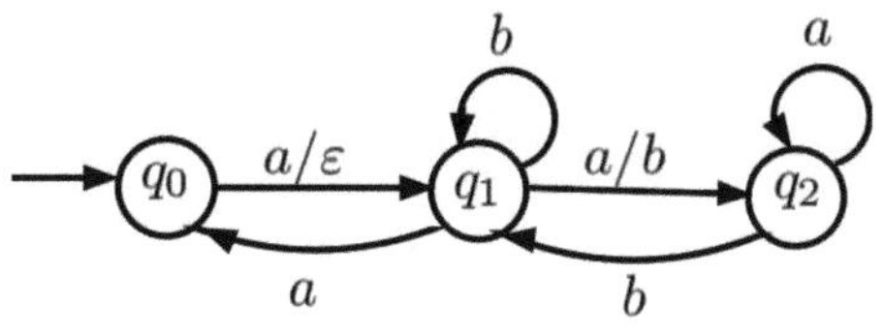

b. What is the meaning of *closure* of state in an NFA?
c. Why the NFA in Fig. 3.8b in Sect. 3.3.3 is not the complement of the NFA in Fig. 3.8a?

5. * For each of the following regular expressions draw the transition diagrams for corresponding NFAs.

a. $(0+1)^*01011(0+1)^*$
b. $(0+1)^*(011+0101)(0+1)^*$

6. Construct the DFA or NFA for each of the following four expressions.

a. 0^*10^*
b. $(001)^*1(001)^*$
c. $0^*(1 \cup \Sigma)^*0$
d. $(0 \cup 1)(0 \cup 1)(0 \cup 1)^*$

7. * Construct an NFA-ε for the language consisting of zero or more a's followed by zero or more b's followed by zero or more c's.
8. Construct equivalent DFA for Fig. 3.4 in Sect. 3.3.1 and compare with Fig. 3.3 in Sect. 3.3.1.
9. Construct equivalent DFA for Fig. 3.5 in Sect. 3.3.1. How it compares with Fig. 3.3 in Sect. 3.3.1?
10. Convert the NFA shown in Fig. 3.22 into the equivalent DFA.
11. For the NFAs shown in Fig. 3.23a–c construct the equivalent DFA for each.
12. Convert the NFAs shown in Fig. 3.24 to equivalent DFAs, and find out their regular expressions.
13. * Consider an NFA having four states corresponding to regular expression: $(01+011+0111)^*$. Obtain an equivalent DFA using subset construction method.
14. Construct the Transition Tables for the Mealy machines shown in Fig. 3.25a and b.
15. Convert the Mealy Machines in Fig. 3.25a and b into equivalent Moore Machines.

B. Analysis-based Problems

16. * A DFA can be inverted by changing final states to non-final states and vice-versa. How you will invert an NFA?
17. Construct a Moore machine that duplicates the finite automaton shown in Fig. 3.26, i.e., accepts the same strings accepted by this FA.

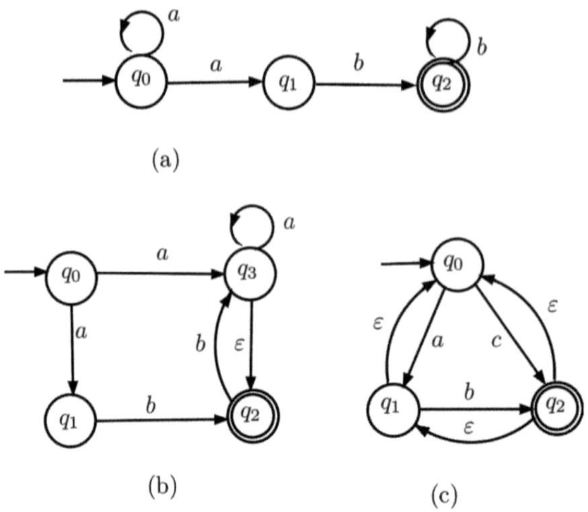

Fig. 3.23 NFA: (a) With a duplicate transition, (b) With duplicate and null transitions, (c) Having absence of certain transitions

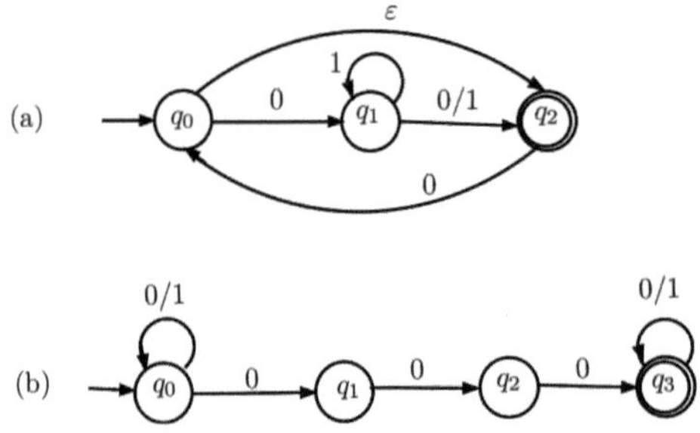

Fig. 3.24 NFA: (a) With a null transition, (b) Having absence of transitions from some states

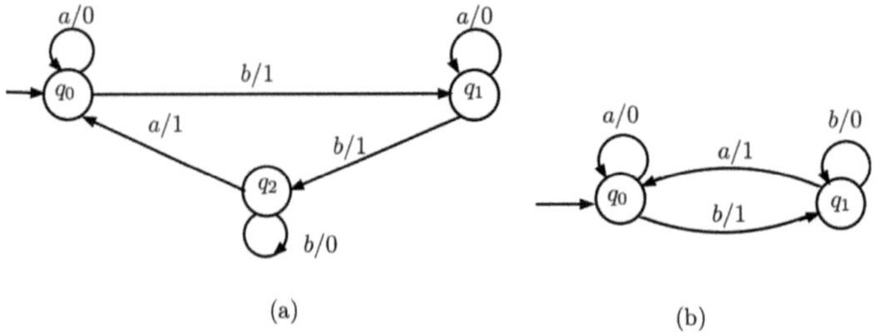

Fig. 3.25 Mealy machines

18. Convert the Finite Automaton in Fig. 3.26 into Mealy Machine (Note: Consider that acceptance of a substring in Mealy machine corresponds to an output of 1 and nonacceptance to output of 0).

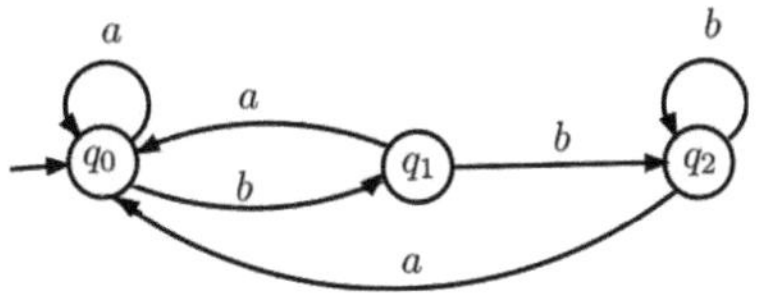

Fig. 3.26 A finite-state automaton

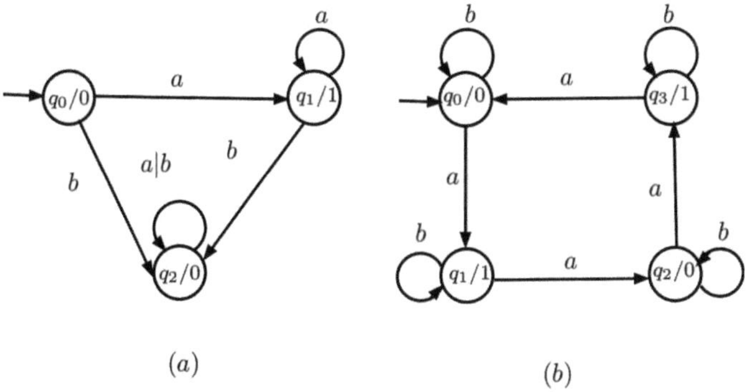

Fig. 3.27 Moore machines

19. * Construct a Moore Machine that can count the number of occurrences of substring 111 in the input string. The input alphabet is $\Sigma = \{0, 1\}$.
20. Given the transition diagrams of the Moore machines in Fig. 3.27a and b, find out the equivalent Mealy machines.
21. Let $Z_5 = \{\bar{0}, \bar{1}, \bar{2}, \bar{3}, \bar{4}\}$ be a set of integers modulo 5 where sum of two integers is found by adding the numbers and finding the remainders of this sum when divided by 5. Thus, $\bar{2} + \bar{3} = \bar{0}$ and $\bar{1} + \bar{2} = \bar{3}$. Construct a Moore Machine that gives a sum of initial strings of elements of Z_5. Hence, for an input of $\bar{1}\ \bar{2}\ \bar{0}\ \bar{3}\ \bar{4}$ the output will be $\bar{0}\ \bar{1}\ \bar{3}\ \bar{3}\ \bar{1}\ \bar{0}$.

C. Proof-based Problems

22. Prove that a two-way finite automaton accepts a regular set.
23. Prove that for every NFA, there exists an equivalent DFA (Note: The proof is Theorem 3.1) (see Sect. 3.4).
24. Find out the ε-closures of NFAs shown in Figs. 3.22, 3.23b, and c.
25. Prove through logical arguments that Mealy and Moore's machines are equivalent.

D. Multiple choice Questions

26. * Consider the NFA M shown in Fig. 3.28. Let the language accepted by M be L. Let L' be the language accepted by an NFA M' obtained by interchanging the accepting and non-accepting states of M. Which of the following statements is

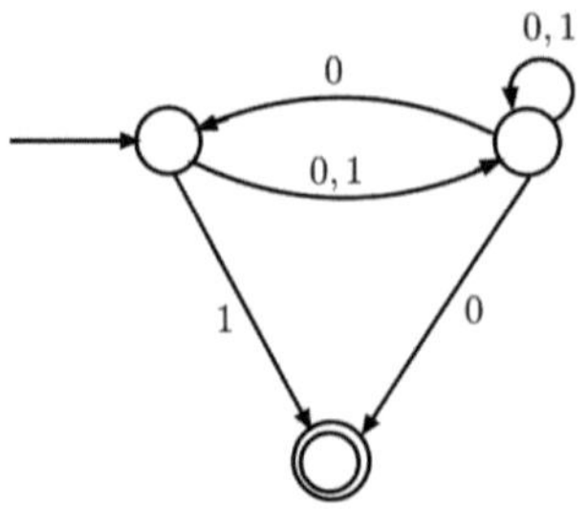

Fig. 3.28 NFA M with a dead state

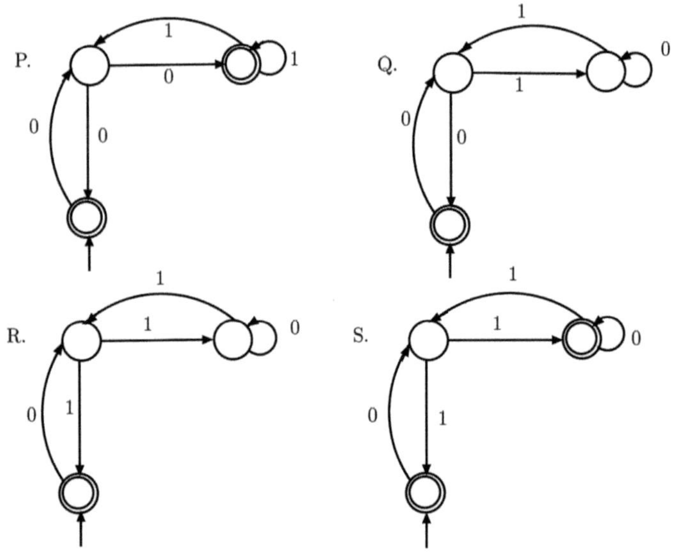

Fig. 3.29 NFAs P, Q, R, S

true?
(A) $L' = \{0, 1\}^* - L$ (B) $L' = \{0, 1\}^*$ (C) $L' \subseteq L$ (D) $L_1 = L$

27. Map the NFA (P to S), shown in Fig. 3.29, with the regular expressions (A to D):

   A. $\varepsilon + 0(01^*1 + 00)^*01^*$
   B. $\varepsilon + 0(10^*1 + 10)^*10^*$
   C. $\varepsilon + 0(10^*1 + 00)^*0$
   D. $\varepsilon + 0(10^*1 + 10)^*1$.

E. Advanced Knowledge Assessment Problems

28. Construct a transducer to correct the misspelled following given words: "Book", "Computer", "Bnad". The transducer comprises input tape with these words, and produces correctly spelled words on the output tape. There are intermediate tapes also. How you will make a choice of the most likely correct word for a misspelled word?
29. Give a logical explanation, of how the Moore/Mealy machine can be used for speech recognition.
30. Can nondeterminism be used to model practical problems? Give a few examples to justify your argument.

References

1. Béal M, Carton E (2001) Determinization of transducers over finite and infinite words. Theor Comput Sci 289(2002):225–251
2. Chowdhary KR (2016) Nondeterministic finite automata. http://www.krchowdhary.com/toc/4-nfa.pdf. Cited 02 Aug 2020
3. Floyd RW (1967) Nondeterministic algorithms. J ACM 14(4):636–644
4. Huffman DA (1954) Synthesis of sequential switching circuits. J Franklin Inst 257(3–4):161–190 and 275–303
5. Mealy GH (1955) A method of synthesizing sequential circuits. Bell Syst Tech J 34(5):1045–1079
6. Mohri M (1997) Finite-state transducers in language and speech processing. In: Computational linguistics, vol 23, Issue 2. Association for Computational Linguistics
7. Mohri M et al (2000) Minimization algorithm for sequential transducers. Theor Comput Sci 234:177–201
8. Rabin MO, Scott D (1959) Finite automata and their decision problems. IBM J Res Dev 3:114–125
9. Shepherdson JC (1959) The Reduction of two-way automata to one-way automata. IBM J Res Dev 3:198–200
10. Walick M, Meldal S (1997) Algebraic approaches to nondeterminism: an overview. ACM Compu Surv 29(1):30–81

Chapter 4
Minimization of Finite Automata

Abstract Minimization of a finite automaton, i.e., reducing its total number of states is important—an automata with fever states is more efficient, it requires less memory and less time in recognition of input strings. The basic approach used is often to eliminate states that cannot be reached from start state and to merge the states whose behavior is indistinguishable with each other. The chapter presents approach of NFA homomorphism to merge the indistinguishable states, followed with solved examples and discusses the limitations of this approach. Number of theorems and lemmas have been presented that act as ground work for minimization of finite automata, followed with the famous Myhill–Nerode theorem and its applications. A formalism is presented based on distinguishability, followed with number of worked out exercises and list of other exercises for practice.

Keywords Nondeterministic FA · Minimization of FA · NFA homomorphism · Distinguishability · Indistinguishability · Dead states · Unreachable states · Reachable states · Accessibility relation · Equivalence relation · Myhill–Nerode theorem

4.1 Introduction

Deterministic and nondeterministic finite automata are abstract models of machines used for capturing behavior of systems. Because both these approaches have different time and space complexities, each has some advantage over the other. Each Deterministic Finite Automaton (DFA) defines a unique language. However the reverse is not true. For any given regular language, there may be more than one representation of finite automata having varying number of states. Higher is number of states in a finite automaton, higher is the memory requirements, as well as higher complexity in its implementation. Therefore, it is desirable that a DFA has minimum possible number of states.

A regular expression is usually converted into an FA, in most cases it is deterministic finite automaton. This is usually achieved by first constructing a nondeterministic automaton that accepts the language denoted by the expression, then applying the

K. R. Chowdhary, *Theory of Computation*,
https://doi.org/10.1007/978-981-97-6234-7_4

subset construction process[1] to obtain equivalent DFA, followed with possibly reducing the resulting deterministic automaton. A closer look at the algorithms involved in this process reveal that as far as its computational complexity is concerned, the construction of a nondeterministic automaton takes $O(n)$ time, where n is number of nodes. The running time of NFA via backtracking takes $O(2^n)$ time in the worst case, where n is number of states in the NFA. Luckily, there are smarter algorithms that take $O(m \cdot n)$ time though they do not support backtracking, here m is length of input and n is number of states. However, the running time of a n-state DFA is $O(n)$.

If we can construct a nondeterministic automaton with $|Q| = n$ states corresponding to a given regular expression, then the equivalent deterministic automaton may have as many as 2^n states. The reducing of an m-state deterministic automaton is of time complexity $O(m \ \log m))$ [1]. The complete process, of first converting an NFA into a DFA and then reducing the DFA, may therefore be of time complexity:

$$\begin{aligned} m \log m &= 2^n \log 2^n \\ &= n \cdot 2^n \end{aligned}$$

which is $O(n \cdot 2^n)$, as n exponential term. Note that reduction of states is a process of merging the states, e.g., like *merge-sort*, where for a data size of n the merge-sort takes $n \log n$ time. However, the complexity further depends on the size of the alphabets [2].

However, suppose that in the first step we obtain a nondeterministic FA with $2n$ states (instead of n states), the complexity of the complete process can be as bad as $O(2n * 2^{2n})$, which is almost square of the previous complexity. Thus, it is very important to construct a nondeterministic automaton as small as possible for any given regular expression. Consequently, the state minimization problem of an NFA is *computationally hard* (PSPACE-complete). The worst-case complexity for the same problem for DFA is $O(|Q| \times |\Sigma| \log |Q|)$. The minimization (or optimization) of a deterministic finite automaton refers to detecting those states whose absence in the DFA does not affect the language acceptability of the automaton. Hence, these states can be eliminated. A reduced automaton should consume lesser memory and complexity of the algorithm implementing the automaton should be minimum possible [3, 4].

Learning Outcomes of this Chapter

1. Homomorphism and Isomorphisms in FA. [Apply]
2. Minimization of FA. [Apply], [Comprehend]
3. Equivalence Relations. [Knowledge]
4. Myhill–Nerode Theorem. [Proof], [Apply], [Comprehend]
5. Partition Algorithm on Finite Automata. [Comprehend], [Apply]
6. Partition Algorithm on Regular Languages. [Comprehend], [Apply]

---

[1] For n states, all possible subsets can be as many as 2^n.

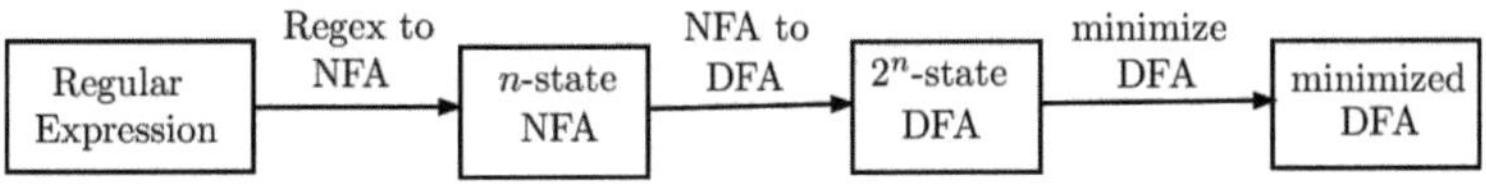

Fig. 4.1 Regular expression to NFA, and NFA to DFA

In the following, we study certain theorems and some basic principles to build a base for minimization of FA, followed with applications and worked examples of minimization [5].

4.2 From Regular Expression to DFA

The NFAs are simple to implement, given a regular expression. We have shown this in Chap. 2 that to recognize a language we need to obtain an equivalent DFA for the given NFA. Figure 4.1 shows the journey from NFA to DFA. If length of a Regular Expression is l, the construction time for an NFA is $O(l)$. Let this NFA has n-states. It will take $O(n)$ time to accept or reject an input string $|w| = m$ in a nondeterministic way, of length m, i.e., linear time, which is independent of number of states. However, for recognizing the same input, it will take $O(2^n)$ time as worst case, through backtracking.

To be of any practical use, an NFA needs to be converted into DFA. To convert an n-state NFA into DFA, the DFA may have at the worst-case 2^n states, thus the time complexity of conversion is $O(2^n)$ in worst case. This new DFA will take $O(m)$ time to accept an input string of length $|w| = m$. Minimization of a DFA of n states has worst-case time complexity of $O(n^2)$. Hence, to minimize a DFA of 2^n states, it will take $O((2^n)^2)$, which is $O(2^{2n})$. Thus, for finite automata with large numbers of states, these algorithms are grossly inefficient.

4.3 Formalism for Minimization

In the following, we define some important properties about finite automata that are helpful in minimization of the FA.

Definition 4.1 (*Unreachable States*) There exists states in an FA that are not reachable for any input sequence. In general, if q_0 is start state then state q' is an unreachable state if there does not exist any string $w \in \Sigma^*$ such that $\delta^*(q_0, w) = q'$. □

The unreachable concept is useful for minimization of automata, since these states cannot be reached through any input string they do not play any role for the FA. Hence, these states can be removed without affecting the language-recognizing capacity of the automaton.

Definition 4.2 (*Dead States*) A dead state is non-final state from which transition terminates to itself on every input. That is, for every $a \in \Sigma, q$ is dead state if $\delta(q, a) = q$, and $q \notin F$. □

A dead state cannot be removed, it indicates that if some input x has led the automaton into dead states, then whatever may be the input after that, it will not be accepted.

Definition 4.3 (*Reachability Relation*) A state $q' \in Q$ of an automaton M is accessible if there exists some string $w \in \Sigma^*$ such that when w is completely read, M is in state q'. For q_0 as start state, the reachability relation is $(q_0, w) \vdash^* (q', \varepsilon)$. □

The state q' is not required to be a final state, it is simply reachable for some string w when FA started at state q_0.

Definition 4.4 (*Indistinguishable States*) Two states p and q are called indistinguishable if, for all $q \in \Sigma^*$,

$$\delta^*(p, w) \in F \Rightarrow \delta^*(q, w) \in F$$

and

$$\delta^*(p, w) \notin F \Rightarrow \delta^*(q, w) \notin F.$$

On the other hand, if there exists some $w \in \Sigma^*$ for which $\delta^*(p, w) \in F$ and $\delta^*(q, w) \notin F$ or vice versa, then p and q are distinguishable. □

It is simple to understand that if p and q are not indistinguishable, then they are distinguishable states.

Note that, one method of reducing the states in a DFA is finding and combining indistinguishable states.

Definition 4.5 (*Equivalence Relation on States*) Two states p and q are equivalent (represented as $p \approx q$) with respect to the acceptability of string $w \in \Sigma^*$ by them, if they are related by the following relations:

Reflexivity: $p \approx p$,
Symmetry: $p \approx q$ implies $q \approx p$.
Transitivity: $p \approx q$ and $q \approx r$ implies $p \approx r$.

We denote the corresponding set of equivalence classes under these relations by $Q/\approx$. □

Definition 4.6 (*k-equivalent*) Any two states p, q are k-equivalent if

$$\delta^*(p, u) \in F \Leftrightarrow \delta^*(q, v) \in F$$

for all $u, v \in \Sigma^*$ with $|u|, |v| \leq k$. This relation is written as $p \approx_k q$. The states p and q are equivalent ($p \approx q$) if $p \approx_k q$ for all k.

We denote the corresponding set of equivalence classes under these relations by $Q/\approx_k$. □

It is not difficult to verify that $p \approx_k q$ and $p \approx q$ are *equivalence relations*.

4.4 Minimization of Finite Automata

In the following, we discuss the minimization of finite automata based on the principle of state indistinguishability, where indistinguishable (equivalent) states are merged together step by step, and when we are left with all the states as distinguishable, the automata is minimum. To carry out this, we make use of definitions of sate-equivalence and other definitions we have discussed in the previous section. Additionally, we need to remove the unreachable and dead states. Thus, minimization of a DFA refers to following major steps:

i. *Identify and eliminate unreachable states.*
ii. *Identify indistinguishable states and merge them.*

Thus, first step in minimization of a DFA is to find all the *reachable states*. Let the set of all these states be S_R. Then $Q - S_R$ is set of all *non-reachable* states. The reachable states can be determined as a closure of $\{s_0\}$, where s_0 is start state under the relation:

$$R = \{(p, q) \mid \delta^*(p, w) = q,\ \forall p, p \in \{s_0\}, q \in Q \text{ and } \exists\, w \in \Sigma^*\}. \tag{4.1}$$

The set of all the reachable states S_R can be computed through Algorithm 4.1.

Algorithm 4.1 Finding Reachable States

1: $S_R = \{s_0\}$
2: **while** $\exists p, \delta(p, a) = q, a \in \Sigma, p \in S_R, q \notin S_R$ **do**
3: $S_R = S_R \cup \{q\}$
4: **end while**

Definition 4.7 (*Accepting State*) A sequence w is accepted by a state $q \in Q$ of finite automaton M, if starting with state q and when end of w is reached, the resulting state is an accepting state. That is, $\delta^*(q, w) \in F$. □

Theorem 4.1 *Suppose that M is a DFA without unreachable states, then M is minimum if and only if all pairs of states are distinguishable.*

Proof *Part-I*: M is minimum if all pairs of states are *distinguishable*.

This implication is easy, for if M has two indistinguishable states, one of them can be eliminated, and the transitions into this state can be changed to go to the other. This will not affect the accepted language. (Formal proof omitted.)

If no indistinguishable states exist, no state can be eliminated. Hence, the FA is already minimum.

Part-II: If M is minimum then all pairs of states are *distinguishable*.

We want to show this by contradiction, i.e., let us assume that it is not minimum, but all states in M are pair-wise distinguishable. Let M has k states. Consider any other FA M' with k' states and $k' < k$. We need to prove that $L(M) \neq L(M')$.

Let q_0 be start state of M. For each state q of M, choose an arbitrary string w_q such that $\delta^*(q_0, w_q) = q$. We note that such w_q exists for each q follows from the assumption that all states are reachable. Since $k' < k$, there are two states $p \neq q$ of M such that in M' we have $\delta^{*'}(q_0, w_p) = \delta^{*'}(q_0, w_q)$. The start states are equal in both the automata. Since p, q are distinguishable in M, there is a string v such that $\delta^*(p, v) \in F$, but $\delta^*(q, v) \notin F$ (or vice versa). This means that M accepts $w_p v$ but not $w_q v$. But in M', we have $\delta^{*'}(q_0, w_p v) = \delta^{*'}(q_0, w_q v)$, so M' either accepts both $w_p v$, $w_q v$ or rejects both. Therefore $L(M) \neq L(M')$, as claimed. This proves the theorem. □

The idea of combining indistinguishable states requires to repeatedly combine indistinguishable states, i.e., if p is indistinguishable with q, combine it with q. Similarly, if r is indistinguishable with q then combine it with q, and so on. But suppose that p, q are indistinguishable, and q and r are indistinguishable. We want to combine p with q, and we also want to combine q with r. Then, it would be better to consider that p and r are also indistinguishable. In fact, they are. This property is formalized in the following lemma.

Lemma 4.1 *State Indistinguishability is an equivalence relation.*

Proof Consider that p, q, r are the states in a finite automaton. We write $p \approx q$ if p is indistinguishable from q. We need to check the following three conditions for indistinguishability:

Reflexivity: $p \approx p$.
Symmetry: $p \approx q$ implies $q \approx p$.
Transitivity: $p \approx q$ and $q \approx r$ implies $p \approx r$.

All conditions are trivially true, directly from the definition of the indistinguishability relation. □

Definition 4.8 (*Equivalent Strings*) For a given DFA, $M_D = (\Sigma, Q, q_0, \delta, F)$, two strings $x, y \in \Sigma^*$ are called equivalent with respect to M_D, if x and y both drive M_D from state q_0 to the same state q', i.e.:

$$\delta^*(q_0, x) = q',$$

and

$$\delta^*(q_0, y) = q'.$$

This relation is represented by $x \approx_{M_D} y$. □

All the strings which drive M_D into same state are equivalent, and are related by the equivalence relation $\approx_L$, and those that are related by $\approx_L$ are elements of same set or partition.

As in the case of $\approx_L$, the $\approx_{M_D}$ is also an equivalence relation, and divides the states Q of M_D into equivalence classes.

Theorem 4.2 *Two states q_j and q_k are indistinguishable iff the regular expressions R_j and R_k denoting the set of sequences accepted by q_j and q_k, respectively, are equal.*

Proof If q_j and q_k are indistinguishable then finite automaton M that started in q_j and q_k produce identical sequences of transitions for any input $w \in \Sigma^*$. In particular, the sets of sequences ending in final state must be identical, i.e., $R_j = R_k$.

Now suppose that $R_j = R_k$ but q_j and q_k are distinguishable. Then there must exist a state q' producing different output sequences. Consider the first position in which the output sequences differ. Clearly, the initial portion of q' up to and including that position is accepted in one case and rejected in another, contradicting $R_j = R_k$.

It is clear that, if a sequence q' takes M (which accepts R) from some q_λ to q_j, then the regular expression R_j is simply the derivative of R with respect to q'. If we take the first q' that takes M from q_λ to q_j, then with each state we can associate a unique derivative with respect to that first q'. This proves the theorem. □

Example 4.1 Minimize the DFA shown in Fig. 4.2a.

Let the original DFA be $M = (Q, \Sigma, \delta, q_0, F)$ and the DFA after minimization be $M' = (Q', \Sigma, \delta', s_0, F')$. There are no unreachable states. The states q_1 and q_2 are indistinguishable because the input string $w = 0^*1$ leads to final state both from q_1 and q_2, as per Theorem 4.2. The sets of indistinguishable states (equivalence classes) are

Fig. 4.2 **a** Original finite automaton. **b** Minimized FA

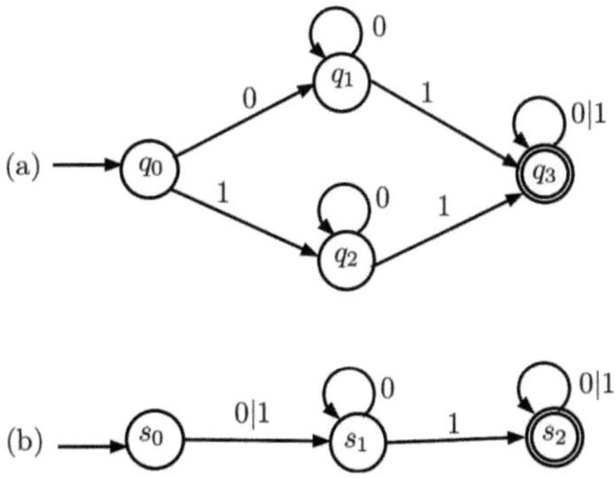

$$s_0 = \{q_0\},$$
$$s_1 = \{q_1, q_2\},$$
$$s_2 = \{q_3\}.$$

Since there is a transition $\delta(q_0, 0) = q_1$ in M, there should be a corresponding transition $\delta'(s_0, 0) = s_1$ in M'. Similarly, there is a transition $\delta'(s_0, 1) = s_1$ corresponding to $\delta(q_0, 1) = q_2$. The other transitions in M are as follows:

$$\delta(q_1, 0) = q_1, \text{ and}$$
$$\delta(q_2, 0) = q_2.$$

Similarly, there is single transition $\delta'(s_1, 0) = s_1$ in M. For the transitions,

$$\delta(q_1, 1) = q_3, \text{ and}$$
$$\delta(q_2, 1) = q_3,$$

in M, the corresponding transition in M' is $\delta'(s_1, 1) = s_2$. Since q_3 in M is accepting state, the corresponding state s_2 in M' is accepting state. Based on above, the reduced and equivalent DFA M' is shown Fig. 4.2b. □

Theorem 4.3 *For any DFA $M_D = (\Sigma, Q, q_0, \delta, F)$, with corresponding language $L = L(M_D)$, and $x, y \in \Sigma^*$, if $x \approx_{M_D} y$, then $x \approx_L y$.*

Proof Let, for $M_D = (\Sigma, Q, q_0, \delta, F)$, an input $x \in \Sigma^*$ causes transitions such that $\delta^*(q_0, x) = q'$. Note that for $y, z \in \Sigma^*$, $xz \in L(M_D)$ if and only if $\delta^*(q', z) \in F$. It is given that, $x \approx_{M_D} y$, then as per the definition of $\approx_{M_D}$, $\delta^*(q_0, x) = \delta^*(q_0, y) = q'$. Therefore, $x \approx_{M_D} y$ implies that, "$xz \in L(M_D)$, if and only if, $yz \in L(M_D)$". The later statement is nothing but $x \approx_{L(M_D)} y$. □

In the following example, we minimize the DFA using Theorem 4.2, which merges indistinguishable states based on the criteria of acceptability of identical strings.

Example 4.2 Minimize the DFA shown in Fig. 4.3a.

We note that state q_6 has no role in the automaton because it is unreachable state. Thus, removing q_6 along with its all incoming as well as outgoing transitions will not affect language recognition of the capability automaton.

The behavior of states q_1 and q_5 is indistinguishable as per Theorem 4.2 in Sect. 4.4, as they accept the same regular expression (01)*, i.e., all strings of this regular expression when applied to these states, they are accepted. Thus, if all the transitions reaching to q_1 are diverted to q_5 or vice versa, the behavior of the finite automaton remains unchanged. Hence, q_1 and q_5 are equal and are merged into a

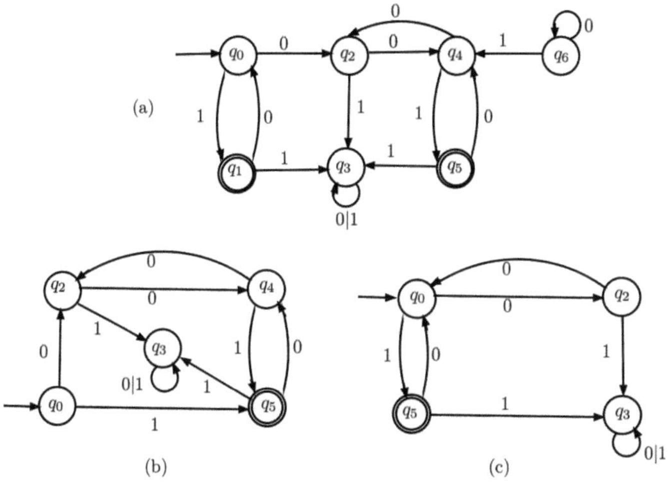

Fig. 4.3 **a** DFA to be reduced. **b** Reduced FA. **c** Minimized FA

single state q_5. Similarly, the states q_0 and q_4 are indistinguishable because they accept the same regular expression $1(01)^*$. In Fig. 4.3b, we show q_1 removed and transitions coming to it and going from it are shifted to q_5, as follows:

$q_0 \to q_1$ transition is shown connected from q_0 to q_5, with edge 1;
$q_1 \to q_3$ already exists as $q_5 \to q_3$, connected with edge 1;
$q_1 \to q_0$ with edge 0 moves to $q_5 \to q_0$ with edge 0. This is shown in Fig. 4.3b as q_0, q_4 are indistinguishable, and $q_5 \to q_4$ with edge 0 already exists.

Since states q_0 and q_4 are indistinguishable, q_4 is merged into q_0 and we get the final minimized automaton as shown in Fig. 4.3c, where now exists four states compared to earlier seven states. It can be verified that minimized FA accepts the same regular language as the original FA. □

There are also software tools which can be used for minimizing finite automata. The distinguishing feature of *ReFam*—a software tool for minimizing nondeterministic finite automata is that it is primarily aimed at nondeterministic finite automata minimization, and provides several exact and heuristic minimization methods and uses parallel techniques to speed up the most time-consuming parts of the implemented algorithms [6]. In [4], basic minimization problem is studied: Given a DFA (deterministic FA), find a minimum equivalent nondeterministic FA (NFA). This paper shows that the natural decision problem associated with it is PSPACE-complete.

4.5 NFA Homomorphism

To understand homomorphism, we must know the concept of *equivalence relation* ($\approx$). An equivalence relation is one which is *reflexive*, *symmetric*, and *transitive*.

An approach for obtaining equivalent for an NFA $M = (Q, \Sigma, q_0, \delta, F)$ is to obtain a *homomorphism* for it.

Definition 4.9 (*NFA Homomorphism*) An *NFA homomorphism* h of an NFA M yields a matching (or equivalence) of states p, q of M, such that $p, q \in Q$ are h-equivalent iff $h(p) = h(q)$. □

In short, a homomorphism yields a state-equivalence [3].

The converse of above also holds. That is, a state-equivalence yields to a homomorphism. For this purpose, we consider a partitioning of the states of the NFA M, and write $p \approx q$ (p and q are equivalent) if p, q are in the same class $q/\approx \{p \in Q \mid p \approx q\}$ (i.e., they are equivalent).

Definition 4.10 (*Quotient Automaton*) The quotient automaton $M/\approx$ of M is defined by

$$M/\approx \; = (Q/\approx, \Sigma, q_0/\approx, \delta/\approx, F/\approx), \tag{4.2}$$

with

- $Q/\approx$ is set of all $\approx$ classes $q/\approx$ for $q \in Q$ (set of equivalence classes).
- $q_0/\approx$ is equivalence class of $M/\approx$.
- The state transition function $\delta/\approx$ is defined on

$$\delta/\approx(q_i/\approx, a) = q_j/\approx. \tag{4.3}$$

  The $q_i/\approx, q_j/\approx$ are also represented by $[q_i]$, $[q_j]$, respectively, for $q_i \in [q_i]$ and $q_j \in [q_j]$.
- The triple $(P, a, R) \in \delta/\approx$ iff there are state $p \in P, r \in R$ with $(p, a, r) \in \delta$, for $\approx$-classes P, R.
- $p \in F/\approx$ iff there exists $p \in P$ with $p \in F$.

If all the above holds, then $h : q \mapsto q/\approx$ is a *homomorphism* from M to $M/\approx$. □

A quotient automaton recognizes *superset* of a given automaton. Following example demonstrates the application of NFA homomorphism.

Example 4.3 Obtain the NFA homomorphism for the automaton shown in Fig. 4.4a.

To get homomorphism of DFA in Fig. 4.4a, we follow Definition 4.9, and find that $h(q_0) = h(q_5) = A$, $h(q_1) = h(q_4) = B$, and $h(q_2) = h(q_3) = C$.

Note that we draw a 1-transition from A to B, which is the equivalent (homomorphic automaton) from q_0 to q_1 (but not from q_5 to q_1) of the initial automaton. This is because the definition requires only the existence of a member in each class

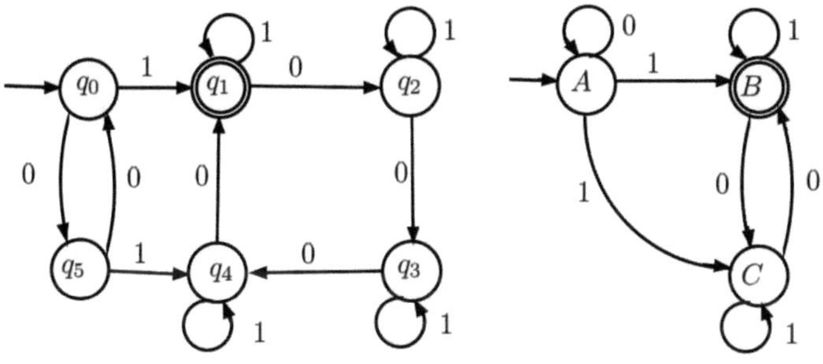

(a) Original DFA (b) Reduced FA(NFA)

Fig. 4.4 Finite automaton and reduced FA

that is linked with each other over such a transition. We conclude that what language is accepted by the initial automaton is also accepted by the reduced, but not the reverse. For example, the original automaton accepts $w = (00)^*1$, but the equivalent automaton accepts 0^*1. □

From the above example, we observe that if an automaton M_2 results from an automaton M_1 by mapping the states then $L(M_1) \subseteq L(M_2)$. If we could find a way to merge the states correctly so that the resulting automaton recognizes exactly the same language as the initial ($L(M_1) = L(M_2)$), then we would have improved the initial automaton by reducing the number of states without affecting its functionality.

In addition, the best possible merging of states would lead to an equivalent automaton with the minimum number of states. This is what we call the minimization problem of the NFA. Note that we are returning the minimum of NFA instead of DFA, as NFA is more general, and what apply to it will also apply to DFA.

Example 4.4 For the language $L = \Sigma^*0\Sigma$, over the alphabet $\Sigma = \{0, 1\}$, find out the minimal and non-minimal automaton.

The minimal NFA (M) and the minimal DFA which recognizes the same language L are shown in Fig. 4.5a and b, respectively. □

4.6 State Minimization Based on Equivalence Classes

Given a language L, and a pair of strings x and y, a *distinguishing extension* is a string z such that exactly one of the two strings xz or yz belongs to L. Based on this, a relation $\approx_L$ is defined on strings as follows [7].

Definition 4.11 (*Distinguishing Strings*) Let $M = (Q, \Sigma, \delta, s, F)$ be a finite automaton. The string $w \in \Sigma^*$ is a distinguishing string for states $p, q \in Q$ if exactly one of the states $\delta^*(p, w), \delta^*(q, w)$ is in F. □

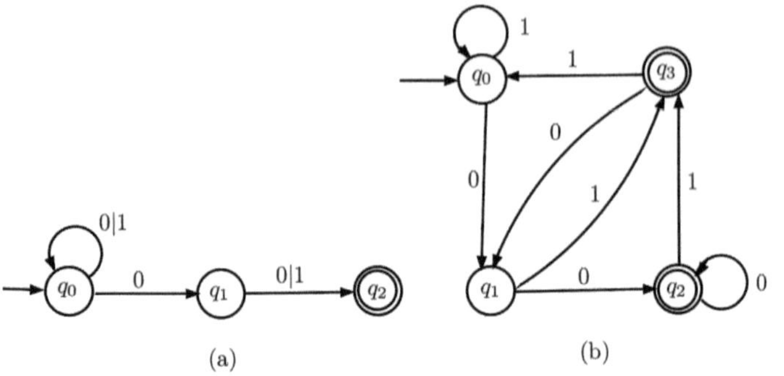

Fig. 4.5 **a** Minimal NFA M for $\Sigma^*0\Sigma$. **b** Minimal DFA M' for $\Sigma^*0\Sigma$

Fig. 4.6 Distinguishable states

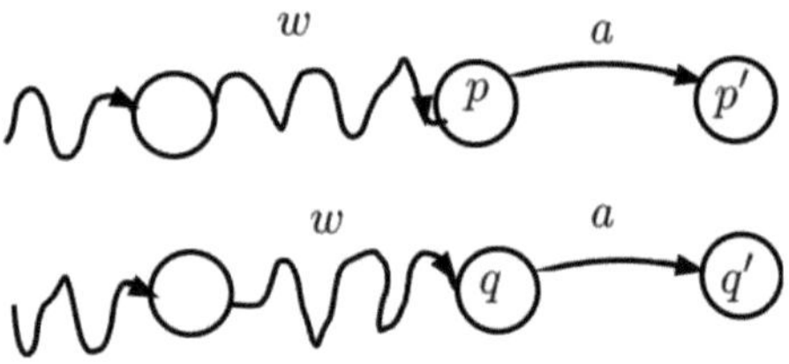

Intuitively, a distinguishing string w for states p and q in an automaton M is a string mapped to an accepting state from exactly one of p and q. In other words, the existence of a distinguishing string for a pair of states $p, q \in Q$ shows that states p and q are not equivalent.

Lemma 4.2 *Let $\delta(p, a) = p'$ and $\delta(q, a) = q'$, for any $a \in \Sigma$. Then, if p' and q' are distinguishable then so are p and q.*

Proof This is simple, for if p and q are distinguished by some string w, then p', q' are distinguished by string wa.

Figure 4.6 shows this scenario. □

Definition 4.12 (*Right Invariant*) An *equivalence relation* E on strings is *right invariant* iff concatenating a string z onto two equivalent strings x and y produces two strings (xz and yz) that are also equivalent, i.e., for all x, y, and z, there is $x \; E \; y \Rightarrow xz \; E \; yz$.[2] □

The definition states that an equivalent relation has the right-invariant property if two equivalent strings (x and y) that are in the language are still equivalent if a third string (z) is appended to the right of both of them.

Definition 4.13 (*Equivalence Relation for Languages*) Let L be a language over Σ. Two words $x, y \in \Sigma^*$ are called L-equivalent, written as $x \approx_L y$, if and only if there

[2] We will be writing $x \; E \; y$ as $x \approx y$, and $xz \; E \; yz$ as $xz \approx yz$.

is no distinguishing extension $z \in \Sigma^*$, such that $xz \in L$ and $yz \notin L$. In other words, if $\approx_L y$, then $xz \in L \Leftrightarrow yz \in L$.

This relation is also called as *Canonical Equivalent Relation* $\approx_L$ on Σ^*. □

For $x, y \in \Sigma^*$, there is $x \approx_L y$ if and only if there is no distinguishing extension z for x and y. The idea behind the distinguishing extension is that, a given automaton M cannot distinguish between strings x and y. It can be easily shown that $\approx_L$ is an equivalence relation on strings for M, and thus it divides the set of all finite length strings, $w \in \Sigma^*$, into equivalent classes.

From above we note that since L is a regular language there exists a DFA $M = (Q, \Sigma, \delta, s, F)$ that accepts L. We know that $\approx_M$ is a right-invariant relation of finite index, hence

$$L = \bigcup_{x:\delta(q_0,x)\in F} [x], \tag{4.4}$$

where $x \in \Sigma^*$.

Theorem 4.4 *A language L is accepted by a DFA iff L is the union of some equivalence classes of right-invariant equivalence relation of finite index.*

Proof Part-(I). Suppose that a language L is accepted by a DFA $M = (Q, \Sigma, \delta, q_0, F)$. Define an equivalence relation $\approx$ so that two strings x and y are equivalent iff the DFA M, starting at q_0, would transition to same state when it reads x or y, i.e.:

$$x \approx_L y \text{ iff } \delta^*(q_0, x) = \delta^*(q_0, y).$$

Let $C(q_i)$ represent the equivalence class $\{w \mid \delta^*(q_0, w) = q_i\}$, which is the set of strings that transit the DFA to state q_i. It is straight forward to verify that all the members of $C(q_i)$ are in fact equivalent to each other. The equivalence relation $\approx_L$ is finite index, because the set of equivalence classes is finite. Note that size of this set is $|\{C(q_i) \mid q_i \in Q\}|$, which is finite, and equal to $|Q|$.

A string $w \in L$ iff w transitions the DFA to accepting state, L is union of all the equivalence classes of accepting states, which is

$$L = \bigcup_{q_i \in F} C(q_i). \tag{4.5}$$

Now we need to show that L is right invariant. To show this, consider Fig. 4.7. If $x \approx y$, then as per this figure,

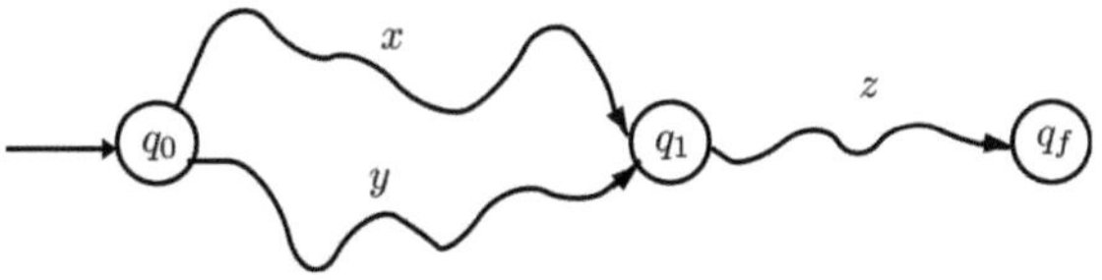

Fig. 4.7 A case of right-invariant equivalence

$$\begin{aligned}\delta^*(q_0, xz) &= \delta^*(\delta^*(q_0, x), z)\\ &= \delta^*(\delta^*(q_0, y), z)\\ &= \delta^*(q_0, yz).\end{aligned}$$

Part-(II). Let us consider that "$[w]$" represent the equivalence class to which w belongs. Consider a right-invariant equivalence relation E (i.e., $\approx$ on Σ^*) for the DFA $M = (Q, \Sigma, \delta, q_0, F)$, and let E be of finite index. Consider that set of equivalent classes is finite and equal to $|Q|$, and there is $F \subseteq Q$, a subset of equivalence classes whose union is L. Let the start state q_0 is equivalence class $[\varepsilon]$, and we define the transition function as $\delta([x], a) = [xa]$, where $x \in \Sigma^*$ and $a \in \Sigma$.

Note that this new transition is well defined: if x and y are in the same equivalence class, then $[xa] = [ya]$ because the equivalence relation E is right invariant [8].

To show that DFA M recognizes the language L, we will prove by induction that after reading a string w, the DFA goes into state $[w]$, i.e., to show that $\delta^*(q_0, w) = [w]$.

- Base case. If $w = \varepsilon$, then $\delta(q_0, \varepsilon) = q_0 = [\varepsilon]$.
- Induction case. If $w = xa$, where $x \in \Sigma^*$, and $a \in \Sigma$, then

$$\begin{aligned}\delta^*(q_0, xa) &= \delta(\delta^*(q_0, x), a)\\ &= \delta([x], a)\\ &= [xa].\end{aligned}$$

This proves "only if" part of the theorem. Hence the proof. □

Theorem 4.5 *Let L be a regular language, and let R be the equivalence relation,*

$x\ R\ y$ *iff, for all* $z \in \Sigma^*$, *there is* $xz \in L \Leftrightarrow yz \in L$,

then R is of finite index, and DFA constructed using Theorem 4.4 is minimal.

Proof Let E be an equivalence relation satisfying Theorem 4.4. Then, the equivalence relation R must be either equal to E, or it must be consolidation of E, i.e., each equivalence class of R must either be an equivalence of E or it must be formed by consolidating several equivalence classes of E into a single equivalence of R.

Consider the contrary case that there are two strings x and y that are equivalent under E but not under R. Then, there must exist a string z such that $xz \in L \not\Leftrightarrow yz \in L$. But, x and y are equivalent under E. This is because E is right invariant, else otherwise Theorem 4.4 will not hold true. Since E has finite index, so does R, and it is minimal [8]. □

Lemma 4.3 *Let L be a language accepted by DFA M, and x and y be the distinguishable strings with respect to L. Then, terminating states reached with input x are different from those reached when y is input.*

Proof Suppose by contradiction that the DFA M reaches to same state q instead of two different states on input x and input y. Now, let z be the strings, such that $xz \in L$ and $yz \notin L$. Let the state reached by xz is q'. Note that q' is reached when input z is provided at state q of M. But, on input yz the automaton must reach the state q', because M reaches to q with input y and then goes to q' by z. This means M either accepts both xz and yz or rejects both. In either case, M is incorrect and we reach to contradiction. This proves the lemma. □

Lemma 4.4 *If L is a language, and let there be a set of k distinguishable strings with respect to L, then every DFA for L has at least k states.*

Proof Let $M = (Q, \Sigma, \delta, q_0, F)$ be the DFA for L, and let $\{x_1, x_2, ..., x_k\}$ be the set of distinguishable strings with respect to L, and let each string transits the DFA to some state: x_1 to q_1, x_2 to q_2, ..., x_k to q_k. Since every x_i and x_j are distinguishable (for $i \neq j$), so q_i and q_j are also distinguishable, for $q_i \neq q_j$ (by Lemma 4.3). So, there are k different states q_1, ..., q_k in M, hence M has at least k states. □

We introduce a new characterization of regular languages that leads to insight into the border between regular and non-regular languages. This insight we shall draw from ideas we had discussed in the above section. A good characterization should clarify what type of languages can be regular and what are not.

Just as a FA can divide Σ^* into categories, we can think of a language L as doing the same. Any two strings x and y belong to the same category with respect to L, which we say that x is indistinguishable from y, if and only if either both xz and yz are in L or xz and yz both are not in L, for all the z. We see this in the following example.

Example 4.5 Equivalence classes.

In Fig. 4.8, consider the set of strings x which are related by the equivalence relation of "$|x|$ mode 3". The relation divides all strings in three blocks based on whether x mode 3 is 0, 1, or 2. They terminate respectively on the states by the same name 0, 1, and 2. We note the following in respect of x:

Fig. 4.8 Three equivalence classes

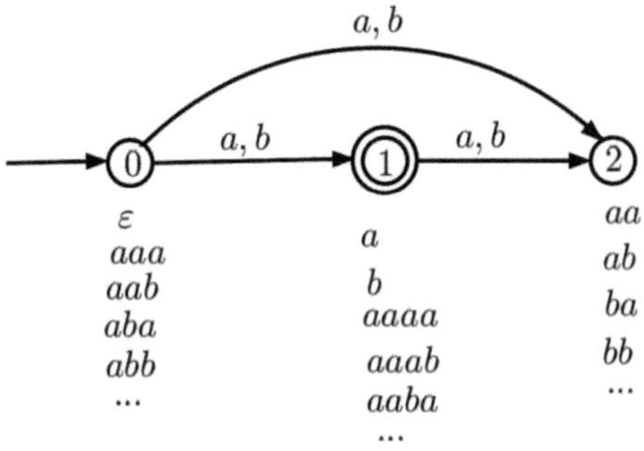

- the strings $x = \varepsilon$ and $y = aab$ are indistinguishable with respect to L, because for $z = \varepsilon$, there is $xz = \varepsilon \notin F$ and $yz = aab \notin F$.
  Also, for $z = a$, there is $xz = a \in F$ and $yz = aaba \in F$.
- Similar situations exist for strings that have "length mode 3" as 1 and 2.
- The strings aaa and $aaaa$ are *not* indistinguishable with respect to L. □

4.7 Myhill–Nerode Theorem

We say two strings x and y are indistinguishable with respect to L and write it as $x \approx_L y$ if they are not distinguishable. That is, $x \approx_L y$ means that, for every string z, the string xz belongs to L if and only if yz also belongs. As per the definition of equivalence relation, the relation $\approx_L$ is an equivalence relation over the strings in Σ^*.

The equivalence relation is over a set, which is partitioned into subsets (i.e., blocks), called *equivalence classes*. An equivalence class in Σ^* with respect to $\approx_L$ is a set of strings that are all indistinguishable with each other and that are all distinguishable from other strings that are not in that set. All the strings that are equivalence to string x are denoted by $[x]$, naturally $x \in [x]$.

A simple way of stating Lemma 4.4 is that every DFA for L must have at least as many states as the number of equivalence classes in Σ^* with respect to $\approx_L$. The converse is also true—there is always a DFA that has precisely as many states as the number of equivalence classes [9].

Theorem 4.6 (Myhill–Nerode) *Let $L \subseteq \Sigma^*$ be a regular language, then following statements are equivalent [10].*

1. *There is a DFA that accepts the L.*
2. *There is a right-invariant equivalence relation $\approx$ of finite index, such that L is equal to the union of some of the equivalence classes of $\approx$.*
3. *$\approx_L$ is finite index.*

Proof The proof we are going to provide uses the implication (1) $\Rightarrow$ (2) $\Rightarrow$ (3) $\Rightarrow$ (1).
(1) $\Rightarrow$ (2). Since L is a regular language, there exists a DFA $M = (Q, \Sigma, \delta, q_0, F)$ that accepts L. In this case, $\approx_M$ is a right-invariant relation of finite index. For this, L is union of equivalence classes, represented by

$$L = \bigcup_{x:\delta(q_0,x)\in F} [x], \tag{4.6}$$

where $x \in \Sigma^*$. Equation (4.6) is nothing but part (2) above. This proves (1) $\Rightarrow$ (2).

(2) $\Rightarrow$ (3). Let us assume that L is union of some equivalence classes of right-invariant relation $\approx$ of finite index. Now, if the partition imposed by $\approx$ is a refinement of the partition imposed by $\approx_L$, then $\approx_L$ must be of finite index since it has fever equivalence classes than $\approx$. We will see that $\approx$ is truly a refinement of $\approx_L$.

Since $\approx$ is right invariant, we have for every pair $x, y \in \Sigma^*$ such that $x \approx y$, then it must hold that $\forall z, xz \approx yz$. In addition, since L is union of some equivalence classes of $\approx$, so if $x \approx y$, then $x \in L \leftrightarrow y \in L$. By combining these two implications we get

$$x \approx y \Rightarrow \forall z, xz \approx yz \Rightarrow \forall z, xz \in L \leftrightarrow yz \in L \Rightarrow x \approx_L y. \tag{4.7}$$

This shows that $x \approx y \Rightarrow x \approx_L y$, which gives the conclusion that $\approx$ is refinement of $\approx_L$.[3]

(3) $\Rightarrow$ (1). To show that if $\approx_L$ is of finite index then L is regular, it suffices to construct a DFA M for an arbitrary $\approx_L$ that accepts L. For constructing such a DFA we will make use of equivalence classes $\approx_L$ as states of this DFA. Let $x_1, ..., x_k$ represent k different equivalence classes of $\approx_L$. Having defined this, we define the DFA $M = (Q, \Sigma, \delta, q_0, F)$ as follows:

- $Q = \{[x_1], ..., [x_k]\}$;
- Σ = the alphabet of L;
- $q_0 = [\varepsilon]$, where ε is empty string; and
- $F = \{[x] \mid x \in L\}$.

It is clear that δ is well defined, and $\delta(q_0, x) \in F$ iff $x \in L$. This proves the theorem. □

4.8 Partitioning State Space

Not only the Myhill–Nerode (MN) theorem provide an informative characterization of recognizable languages, but it also suggests an algorithm for minimization of DFAs. Before we proceed to algorithm, we wish to make a few definitions that will be helpful in understanding of DFA minimization algorithm.

Definition 4.14 (*Partition/Block*) Let A be a set. A finite partition of A is a set $B = \{A_1, ..., A_k\}$ of mutually disjoint non-empty sets $A_1, ..., A_k$, such that

- $A_i \subseteq A$, for $1 \leq i \leq k$.
- $A_i \cap A_j = \phi$, for $i \neq j$.
- The union of the sets in the partition is equal to whole set A. Formally,

$$A = \bigcup_{i=1}^{k} A_i. \tag{4.8}$$

[3] Consider that $A = \{a, b, c\}$, and $B = \{a, b\}$. Naturally, $A \Rightarrow B$ here, and also we must agree that $A \supseteq B$

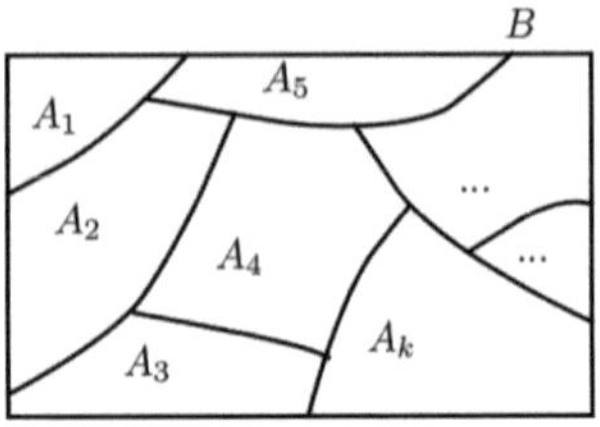

Fig. 4.9 Blocks of set B

The components A_1, ..., A_k are called the *blocks* or *parts* of B. If $a \in A$, then we denote it by $[a]_B$, which represents the unique block of B to which a belongs. When set B is implied, we use only the notation $[a]$. □

Figure 4.9 shows blocks A_1, ..., A_k of partition B.

In Theorem 4.6 in Sect. 4.7, we showed that if L is regular, and index of $\approx_L$ is finite, then it is necessary and sufficient condition for a DFA to have finite number of states to recognize the language L.

Let $M = (Q, \Sigma, \delta, q_0, F)$ be the DFA that recognizes regular language L. Further $[q]$, where $q \in Q$ be the set of strings $\{x \mid x \in \Sigma^*$ and $\delta(q_0, x) = q\}$. We observe that $\{[q] \mid q \in Q\}$ partitions Σ^*, such that for every $q \in Q$, and $x, y \in [q]$, it holds that $x \approx_L y$ and the partition imposed by $\approx$ is refinement over the partition imposed by $\approx_L$. The significance of refinement here means that if number of states of automaton M exceeds the number of equivalence classes $\approx_L$, then the automaton can be reduced in size without altering the language that it recognizes.

A first attempt to minimize M could be to find for each equivalence class B_i[4] in the partition of Σ^* that follows from $\approx_L$. This is a subset Q' of Q such that

$$B_i = \bigcup_{q' \in Q'} [q']. \tag{4.9}$$

As next step, merge the states of Q' into single state. However, the problem with this approach is that, to be sure that two states p and q can be merged we must examine $\delta(p, w)$ and $\delta(q, w)$ for every string in $\{w : |w| \leq |Q|$ and $w \in \Sigma^*\}$. Fortunately, the string w will be finite, and will not more than $n - 1$, where n is number of states in the original automata.

4.9 Partition-Refine Algorithm

Definition 4.15 Partition refinement is a technique for representing a partition of a set that allows the partition to be refined by splitting its sets into a larger number of smaller sets. □

[4] All the elements in a block/equivalence class are equivalence.

At the begin, the partition-refine methods assume that all the accepting states are merged into one set, while all the non-final states into other set, and then *refine* this initial partition until it is stable. By stable we mean that if states p and q both belong to block B of the partition, then for all $\sigma \in \Sigma$, state p goes to block B' if and only if q goes to B' [1].

If the refinement process is allowed to continue long enough, then the partition will eventually become a set of singletons. In that case, it is stable and termination is guaranteed. The minimization algorithm that results from above can be described as follows.

There exists w such that only one of the two states $\delta(p, w)$ and $\delta(q, w)$ is in F and other is not.

4.9.1 Minimization Algorithm

To fix an appropriate w, we proceed step-wise on its length. In first step, we take $w = \varepsilon$ and separate all final and non-final states $(F, Q - F)$.

In the next step, we declare two (not yet separated) states p and q as non-equivalent, if for some $a \in \Sigma$, $\delta(p, a)$ and $\delta(q, a)$ have been confirmed to be non-equivalent.

According to this concept, we *refine* the earlier classification $(F, Q - F)$ as long as this is possible. Formally, the partition $Q - F$ has to be split into two with respect to F if, "there exists $p, q \in Q - F$ and an alphabet a, with $\delta(p, a) \in F$ and $\delta(q, a) \notin F$, then the partition $Q - F$ is split into $\{p \in Q - F \mid \delta(p, a) \in F\}$ and $\{q \in Q - F \mid \delta(p, a) \notin F\}$".

For every following step and a currently available partition $(B_1, B_2, \ldots, B_k)$, the task is generally describable as follows.

B_i is split into two partitions with respect to B_j and $a \in \Sigma$, if there exists $p, q \in B_i$, such that

$$\delta(p, a) \in B_j, \text{ but } \delta(q, a) \notin B_j.$$

This partitioning splits B_i into two partitions:

$$(*)\{p \in B_i \mid \delta(p, a) \in B_j\} \text{ and } \{q \in B_i \mid \delta(q, a) \notin B_j\}. \tag{4.10}$$

This partitioning process is represented by the *Partition-Refine* Algorithm 4.2.

Algorithm 4.2 Partition Refine

```
1: Initialization: B_1 = F, B_2 = Q − F
2: while ∃ B_i, B_j, and a ∈ Σ with (*) do
3:    partition B_i with respect to B_j
4: end while
```

One could easily modify Algorithm 4.1 that finds the reachable states (Sect. 4.4) to generate a string for each reachable state q of the automaton M, such that q distinguishes it from every state $q_j \notin [q]_{L(M)}$ as follows: with every state q we associate a string $w_q \in \Sigma^*$. At the begin, when the algorithm first enters the *refine Partition*, all the associated strings are empty. Every time a block B_i is found to be unstable with respect to some input symbol a and is consequently partitioned into smaller blocks, the symbol that forced the split is appended to w_q for all q that belonged to B_i. Eventually, the algorithm terminates by outputting a DFA $M' = (Q', \Sigma, \delta', q_0, F')$. The states of M' are equivalence classes of $\approx_{L(M)}$. It holds for every pair of states $[q_i], [q_j] \in Q'$, such that w_q $(q \in [q_i] \cup [q_j])$ is a distinguishing string for $[q_i], [q_j]$.

To find indistinguishable states pair, we form unordered pair p, q of all the distinguishable states and mark each pair. At the end of this process if any of the pair remains unmarked, it is pair of indistinguishable states. These are then merged.

If P and P' are the partition sets of set Q, then we say P' is refinement of P if $P' \supseteq P$.

Example 4.6 Let $Q = \{1, 2, 3, 4, 5, 6, 7, 8, 9, 10\}$, $P' = \{\{1, 2, 3\}, \{4, 5, 6\}, \{7, 8, 9\}, \{10\}, \}$, and $P = \{\{1, 2, 3\}, \{4, 5, 6\}, \{7, 8, 9, 10\}\}$. Then $|P'| \geq |P|$, and P' is called as refinement over P. □

We summarize the above-discussed method as follows: Since every final state is distinguishable from every non-final state, initially we mark all final sates' set as one block B_i and all non-final states' set as other block, say B_j. Note that every state in B_i is distinguishable from every state in B_j. States from every pair like this, which are distinguishable, we back-propagate for some input, and mark them also as distinguishable, as per Lemma 4.2 in Sect. 4.2. This step is *partition refinement*. We then repeat this process for every pair of distinguishable states, until no further state can be marked as distinguishable. At the end, the state pairs which are not marked (are not distinguishable), hence they are merged together as equivalence classes. For example, if q_i, q_j are not distinguishable, then $\{q_i, q_j\}$ becomes an equivalence class in the minimized automata. And, if $\{q_i, q_j\}$ are not distinguishable and $\{q_j, q_k\}$ are also not distinguishable, then they are merged and $\{q_i, q_j, q_k\}$ is a single state in the minimized automata.

This algorithm can be implemented in the form of a *table-filling algorithm*. The algorithm partitions the state space and refinement of partitions is created in the process. Using Myhill–Nerode theorem, the states which cannot be marked as distinguishable (hence, they are indistinguishable) are ultimately merged into single states.

4.9.2 *Complexity of Partition-Refine*

There can be at most $|Q| - 1$ steps, or so many loop iterations. In every iteration, there are $|\delta(q, a)|$ maximum possible computations, for all $q \in Q$ and for all $a \in \Sigma$. This is $|Q| \times |\Sigma|$. Hence, the worst-case complexity of this is second-order polynomial $O(|\Sigma| \cdot |Q|^2)$. For n states, since $|\Sigma| = k$ is constant, this complexity is $O(kn^2)$ or simply $O(n^2)$ [1].

Does it necessarily mean that reduced Turing machine M' is minimum? Possibly, there could be a completely different automaton, with a new topology but with fewer states, that accepts the same language as M. But, this is impossible, because any automaton whose all states are pair-wise distinguishable must be minimum.

The average-case complexity of partition-refine can be computed as follows. If we look at the partition-refine Algorithm 4.2, where a partition of two blocks (final and non-final state sets) is created at start. In every next step, one of the blocks is split into two or not, depending on the criteria of distinguishability of state pair chosen. Like this, for n states, there are $\log n$ splits possible on the average. But, every time we do comparison of chosen state with all the $n - 1$ states. This makes average-case time complexity of $O(n \log n)$. This running time is applicable when the blocks are always partitioned equally.

4.10 Table-filling Algorithm

Assume that DFA $M = (Q, \Sigma, \delta, q_0, F)$ is represented by a directed graph. First of all remove all the states that cannot be reached from q_0, as well as the corresponding transitions. Use the DFS (depth first search) to mark all the reachable states. The unreachable states, if any, are then removed. For this we use Algorithm 4.1 in Sect. 4.4.

The table-filling algorithm makes use of a table of rows and columns as state pairs (p, q) to mark the distinguishable state pairs. The additional condition is that there should not be a junction of row-column, i.e., cell, where $p = q$. The logic, which is heart of the algorithm, is as follows: the set $Q - F$ and F are disjoint, thus pairs of the states $(Q - F) \times F$ are distinguishable, hence marked as "$\times$" at their junction in the table. For the junction of pairs of states (p, q) and (r, s) in the table, where $\delta(p, a) = r$ and $\delta(q, a) = s$, if r is already distinguishable from s, then p is marked distinguishable from q (see Lemma 4.2 in Sect. 4.6). Therefore, junction of the state pair (p, q) is marked with "$\times$". The steps of this algorithm are given in Algorithm 4.3.

The following example demonstrates the use of table-filling algorithm to minimize a DFA.

Example 4.7 Minimize the DFA shown in Fig. 4.10.

Applying the table-filling algorithm the DFA shown in Fig. 4.10 can be minimized through following steps.

Step 1. The only unreachable state q_3 is removed first of all.
Step 2. Figure 4.11 shows the marking of the pairs of final and non-final states by setting a cross (X) in the table column. This shows the distinguishable state pairs. The table is constructed such that no row state crosses an identical column state.

Algorithm 4.3 Table-Filling

1: Remove unreachable states
2: *Initialization step*. For $p \in F$ and $q \in Q - F$ put a cross-mark "×" in the table at the junction (p, q). This shows that p and q are distinguishable in the minimum machine M'.
3: *Iteration Step*. Follow the iteration by applying input $a \in \Sigma$ to each state (p, q). If there is $\delta(p, a) = r$, and $\delta(q, a) = s$, and if (r, s) were earlier marked as distinguishable, mark position (p, q) also as distinguishable by symbol "×".
4: *Equivalent classes*. Group the table states into equivalent classes: Each unmarked pair of states in a (row, column) of table is an equivalent class. Group them where transitivity holds between them.
5: *Final state*. If a group state is $\{q_i, ..., q_f, ..., q_k\}$, where $q_f \in F$ in original automata, then mark the state $\{q_i, ..., q_f, ..., q_k\}$ as final state.

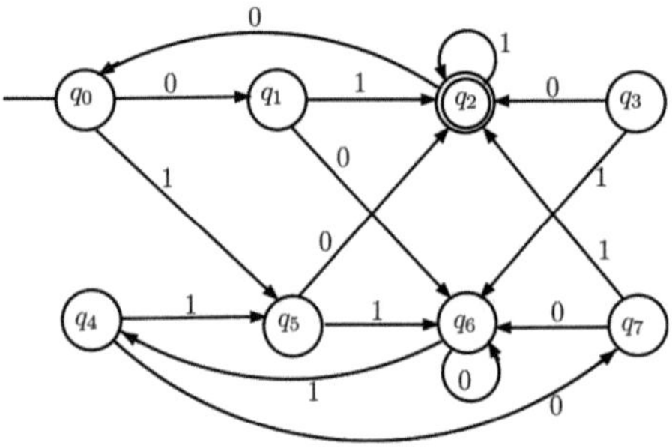

Fig. 4.10 A deterministic finite automaton

Fig. 4.11 Marking pairs as Final and Non-Final States-I

q_1						
q_2	×	×				
q_4			×			
q_5			×			
q_6			×			
q_7			×			
	q_0	q_1	q_2	q_4	q_5	q_6

Step 3. Figure 4.12 shows that in the first iteration we examine all unmarked pairs (i.e., X). For example, for the pair q_0, q_1, we have $\delta(q_0, 1) = q_5$ and $\delta(q_1, 1) = q_2$, and the pair q_2, q_5 is already marked distinguishable, so we mark q_0, q_1 as distinguishable pair. Similarly, we make other state pairs.
Step 4. Figure 4.13 shows that in the next iteration we examine the remaining pairs. For example, we will mark pair q_0, q_6 because $\delta(q_0, 1) = q_5$ and $\delta(q_6, 1) = q_4$, since the pair q_4, q_5 is already marked. In the table obtained no further marking is possible, which means we have now the *stable partition*.
Step 5. We now group the states into equivalent classes. Since q_0, q_4 are equivalent (not distinguishable) and q_1, q_7 are equivalent, the groups are $\{q_0, q_4\}$, $\{q_1, q_7\}$, $\{q_2\}$,

q_1	×					
q_2	×	×				
q_4		×	×			
q_5	×	×	×	×		
q_6		×	×		×	
q_7	×		×	×	×	×
	q_0	q_1	q_2	q_4	q_5	q_6

Fig. 4.12 Marking distinguishable state pairs-II

q_1	×					
q_2	×	×				
q_4		×	×			
q_5	×	×	×	×		
q_6	×	×	×	×	×	
q_7	×		×	×	×	×
	q_0	q_1	q_2	q_4	q_5	q_6

Fig. 4.13 Final marked table of distinguishable states

$\{q_5\}$, $\{q_6\}$. The minimal automaton obtained is shown in Fig. 4.14. It is important to note that, if q_i, q_j are not distinguishable and q_j, q_k are also not distinguishable, the group formed will be $\{q_i, q_j, q_k\}$, similarly, for bigger size groups. □

NFA Minimization

In the beginning of this chapter, we discussed some methods for NFA minimization, however, they are not completely foolproof. While the method of partitioning works for DFA, it does not work for NFA. However, the exhaustive search may minimize an NFA, there is no polynomial-time algorithm to minimize general NFAs unless

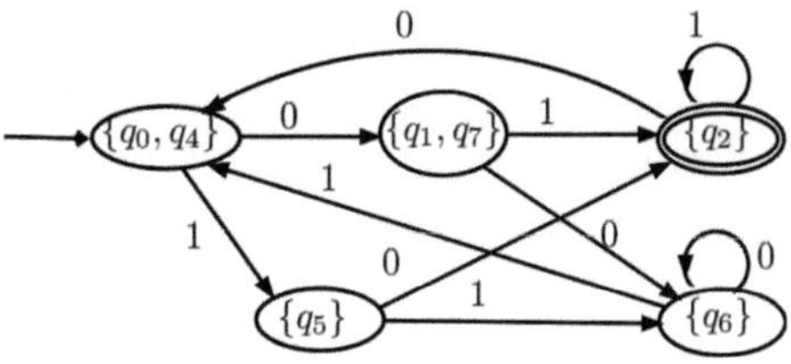

Fig. 4.14 Minimized finite automaton of Fig. 4.10

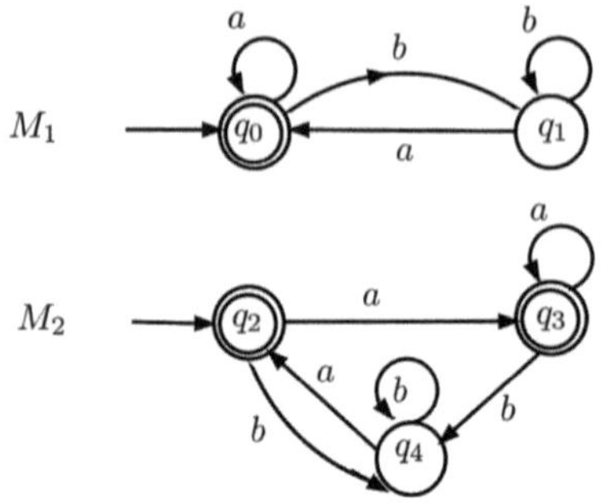

Fig. 4.15 Finite automata M_1 and M_2

P = PSPACE[5]—an solved conjecture in computational complexity theory—widely believed to be false.

4.11 Equivalences of Regular Expressions

The partition-refine algorithm can be used to determine whether the given two regular expressions are equivalent. The partition-refine algorithm can be used for testing equivalence of finite automata) of up to several thousand states [1]. For this, first we need to convert each regular expression into DFA. Consider a DFA whose states are union of states of the DFA obtained from regular expressions. Note that we assume that the names of the states in the two automata are distinct, so that the transition function δ is simply the combination of the transition functions for the two automata. This DFA has two start states. We can assume any one out of these as the start state of the new DFA. Once the algorithm is completed, if the start states of the two DFAs are still not distinguishable, then these DFAs accept the same language, and thus they are equivalent for $w \in \Sigma^*$, we can conclude that the regular expressions are also equivalent.

The following example demonstrates this process.

Example 4.8 Find out whether the automaton M_1 and M_2, shown in Fig. 4.15, are equal.

Consider that Fig. 4.15 represents a single DFA with states q_0 to q_4, where q_0 is taken as start state, and $\Sigma = \{a, b\}$. There is no unreachable state. Applying the table-filling algorithm's step-2, we get the table as shown in Fig. 4.16. The marking of "$\times$" in a row-column junction indicates that corresponding states are distinguishable. The numbers of markings in step-3 are nil.

Further, we note from table above that states q_2 and q_3 are indistinguishable, apart from other states which are also indistinguishable. This is also supported by $\delta^*(q_2, w) = \delta^*(q_3, w)$. Also, q_1 and q_4 are indistinguishable, because $\delta^*(q_1, w) =$

[5] See Chap. 13.

Fig. 4.16 Distinguishable state pairs in the DFAs of Fig. 4.15

q_1	×			
q_2		×		
q_3		×		
q_4	×		×	×
	q_0	q_1	q_2	q_3

$\delta^*(q_4, w)$, provided that q_0 and q_2 are indistinguishable, which are in fact so. It shows that two states q_0 and q_2 are equivalent.

Also, we note that if indistinguishable states q_2 and q_3 are merged together, the DFA M_1 and M_2 are identical.

Hence, we conclude that DFAs M_1 and M_2 accept the same language, i.e., the corresponding two regular languages are equivalent. □

Since the method to compare equivalence of two finite automata is same, i.e., table-filling algorithm, the complexity of this method is also $n \log n$.

4.12 Summary

Every NFA has an equivalent DFA. An NFA is actually simpler than DFA. If an NFA has n number of states, the corresponding equivalent DFA may have maximum 2^n states, out of which some states may be unreachable. Therefore, removal of these states results to reduction of the DFA.

A finite automaton is often realized in the form of a program or some finite sequential circuit. The complexity of the program increases with number of states. Minimization or reduction of a FA is reducing in number of these states, while its functionality (acceptability of languages) remains the same.

Some states in a DFA are *indistinguishable* from other states because any string input at these states results to identical transitions and same ending state when string is fully consumed. These states can be merged together to simplify the automaton. As a result, the behavior of the automaton remains unchanged.

Indistinguishability is a relation, which is *reflexive*, *symmetric*, and *transitive*. Hence, indistinguishability is an *equivalence relation*. Each pair of states in a class of indistinguishable states is related by indistinguishability relation. The classes built as per this relation are distinguishable with respect to other classes, and form a set of classes in new minimized FA. If $Q_i = [q_i]$ and $Q_j = [q_j]$ are two equivalence classes, and there is a transition $\delta(q_i, a) = q_j$, then a transition $\delta(Q_i, a) = Q_j$ should be created in the new equivalent automaton. If $Q_0 = [q_0]$ is equivalence class, then Q_0 becomes the start state and $Q_f = [q_f]$ is final state in equivalent automaton if $q_f \in F$ is final state in the original automaton.

Often, an approach to design of a DFA is to first represent the solution in the form of an NFA, then convert this NFA into DFA, and then optimize (minimize) the DFA.

The first step in minimization is removal of all the unreachable states and empty (null) states, along with all the associated transitions with them. The next step is merging of similar looking states. If any two states p and q have identical transitions for any input $x \in \Sigma^*$ to these states, then these states are called indistinguishable states, and can be merged. In this process, one state, say p, is removed and all the transitions leading to p are diverted to state q. And outgoing transitions of state p are ignored.

To establish whether any two states p, q are equivalent, we need to verify that $\delta^*(p, w) = \delta^*(q, w)$, for all $w \in \Sigma^*$. This is a time-consuming process, as one need to test all the possible strings w, which may be infinitely large in number.

For $L \subseteq \Sigma^*$, the equivalence means *right congruence*, i.e., $\approx_L$, which has the following two properties:

1. if $x \approx_L y$ and $x \in L$, then $y \in L$;
2. if $x \approx_L y$ then $xz \approx_L yz$, for all $z \in \Sigma^*$.

Partition refinement is a technique for representing a partition of a set that allows the partition to be refined by splitting its sets into a larger number of smaller sets.

The partition will eventually become a set of singletons. In that case, it is stable and termination is guaranteed.

A better approach is called *table-filling algorithm*, where, in the beginning, a pair of states $p \in F$ and $q \notin F$ are marked distinguishable, then the states r, s are marked distinguishable such that $\delta(r, a) = p$ and $\delta(s, a) = q$ for all $a \in \Sigma$. This process is iterated until no further such r, s are left. Thus row (p), column (q) junctions which remains unmarked is the indistinguishable pair of states.

The table-filling algorithm has also an application to define if any given two FA are equal. This is based on the indistinguishability of their starting state.

If it is found that numbers of equivalence relations $x \approx_L y$ for a language are infinite, the language is non-regular

For a general representation of equivalence class as $[x],\ x \in \Sigma^*$ the language L for a DFA is expressed as union of all the equivalent states, i.e.,

$$L = \bigcup_{x:\ \delta(q_0, x) \in F} [x].$$

As per the Myhill–Nerode (MN) theorem there is a unique DFA with minimum number of states for every regular language, and the theorem can be used for minimization of DFA.

Self Review Questions

1. Define the following terms:

   a. Homomorphism.
   b. Equivalence relation.

2. Define the following terms:

   a. Indistinguishable States.
   b. Reachable States.
   c. Unreachable States.
   d. Dead States.
   e. Reachability Relation.

3. For a given regular expression there can be more than one DFA that recognize the corresponding language (True/False).
4. What is the maximum number of states in an equivalent DFA for an NFA of 4 states?
5. Is it possible to determine minimum number of the states in the NFA if an equivalent DFA has n states?
6. Two states in a DFA are indistinguishable from each other if their behavior is indistinguishable from each other for a specific input string (True/false).
7. Define the k-equivalence relation between two states of a DFA.
8. Does the k-equivalence relation between two states holds for $w \leq k$ or for $w \geq k$?
9. If p and q are two indistinguishable states in a finite automaton, then one of them can be removed including its incoming and outgoing edges, without effecting its language recognition capability of the FA (True/False).
10. Myhill–Nerode theorem can be used for minimization of finite automaton (True/False).

Exercises

A. Concepts based Problems

Note: The $*$ marked exercises are provided with solutions at the end of this book.

1. What is NFA homomorphism? Explain.
2. Explain in your own words, how you will determine whether any given two DFAs are equal?
3. * What is difference between NFA homomorphism and DFA homomorphism?
4. Give an example that shows that merely merging the states is not enough to obtain a minimized automaton.

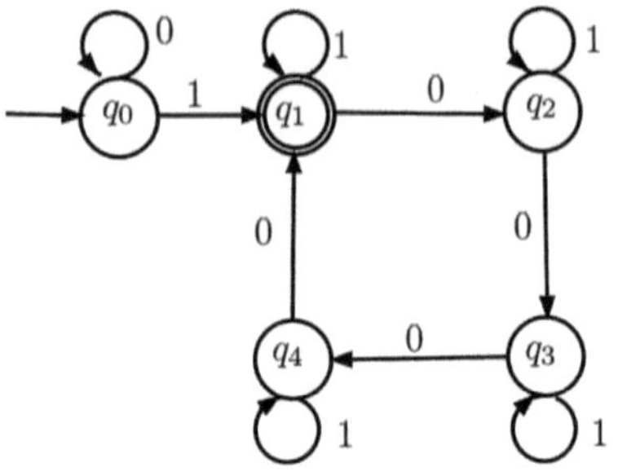

Fig. 4.17 Finite automaton to be reduced

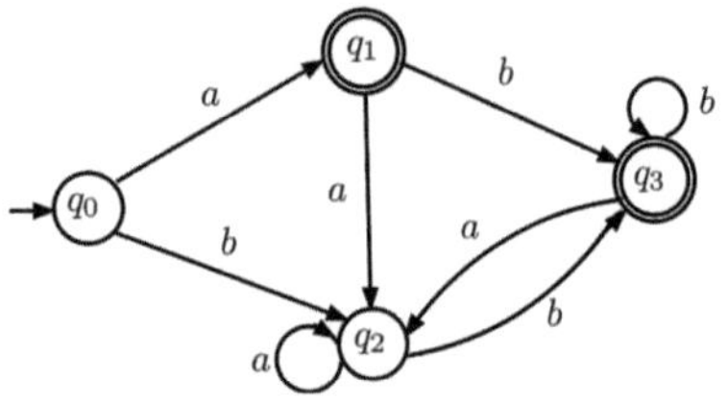

Fig. 4.18 Finite automaton-I

5. Write your own version of algorithm for minimization of a DFA using partition-refine algorithm.
6. What is count of number of equivalence classes in the language $\{a^n b^n \mid n \geq 0\}$?
7. * Find the minimal automaton through merging of states for the automaton shown in Fig. 4.17.
8. Make use of MN theorem to find the minimal automaton for each of the following regular expressions:

   a. $aa^*(b + c)$.
   b. $a(b + c)^*bb^*$.
   c. $(abc)^*(b + c)$.

9. Draw the transition graph for the DFA for following regular languages and minimize each.

   a. $L = \{0^n \mid n \geq 1,$ and n is odd$\}$.
   b. $L = \{0^m 1^n \mid m$ and n are greater than or equal to $2\}$.

10. Minimize the number of states in the automaton shown in Figs. 4.18, 4.19, 4.20, and 4.21.

B. Analysis-based Problems

11. When an NFA can always be converted to DFA and DFA is minimized, why it is important to construct a smallest possible NFA given the regular expression?
12. * Is it possible that you get two different homomorphisms for a given DFA?
13. * Write a C program for minimization of 5-state DFA, with $\Sigma = \{a, b\}$.
14. If a given DFA has $|Q| = n$ states, what is the complexity of constructing an equivalent homomorphic FA? Suggest the steps for this algorithm.

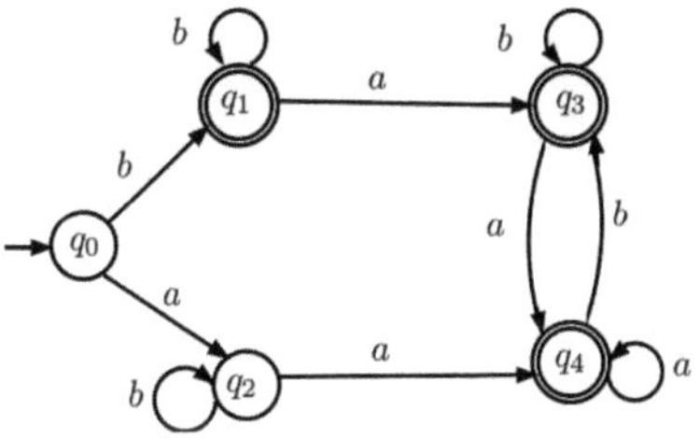

Fig. 4.19 Finite automaton-II

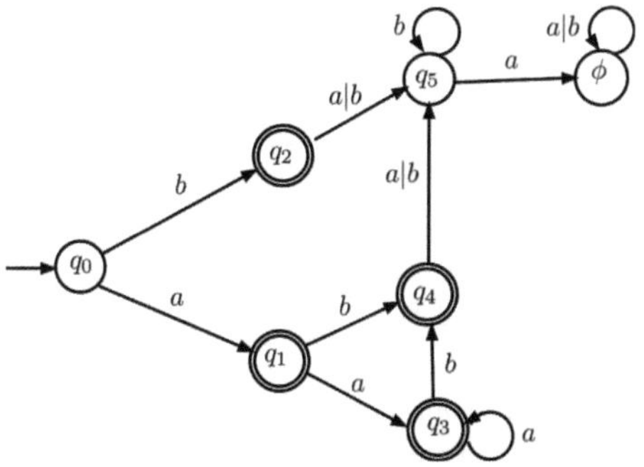

Fig. 4.20 Finite automaton-III

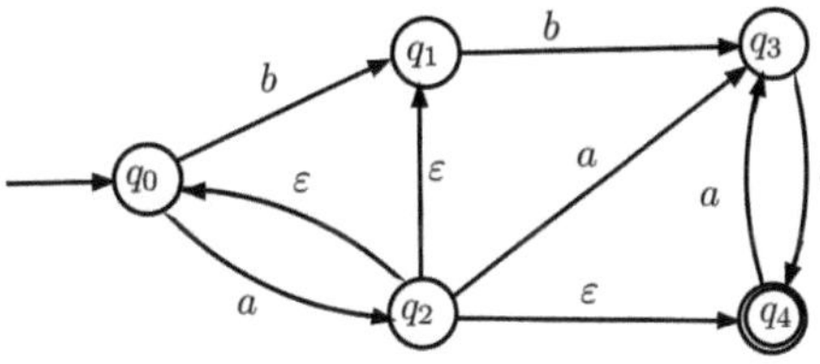

Fig. 4.21 An NFA with many null transitions

15. * For the alphabet $\Sigma = \{a, b\}$, find out the equivalent classes for $L = \Sigma^* a \Sigma$.
16. Derive the time and space complexity of table-filling algorithm given on Algorithm 4.3.
17. * How will you determine if a given DFA is minimum?
18. * Find out the minimum DFA using table-filling (partition) method for the DFA shown in Fig. 4.5b in Sect. 4.5.
19. Let x and y be strings and L be any language. We say that x and y are distinguishable by L if some string z exists whereby exactly one of the strings xz or yz is a member of L. Otherwise, for every string z, we have $xz \in L$ whenever $yz \in L$ and we say that x and y are indistinguishable by L, i.e., $x \approx_L y$. Show that $\approx_L$ is an equivalence relation.
20. * Find the equivalent reduced automaton for the one shown in Fig. 4.22, using table-filling algorithm.

Fig. 4.22 Deterministic finite automaton

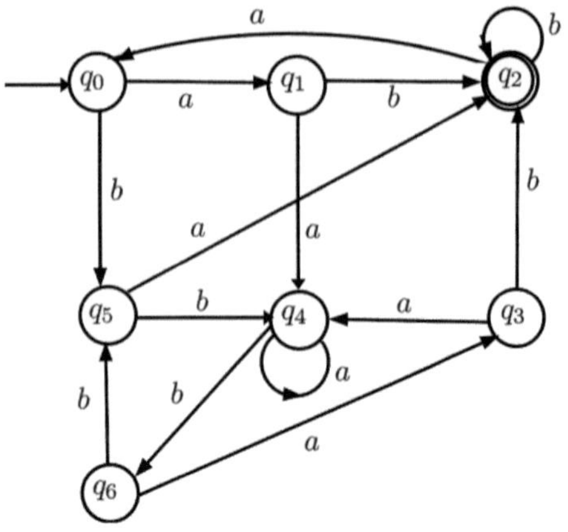

C. Proof-based Problems

21. Prove that *distinguishability* is not an equivalence relation.
22. How you will show that any given two regular expressions are equal?
23. Show, using the Myhill–Nerode theorem, whether the following languages over the alphabet $\Sigma = \{a, b\}$ are regular or not:

    a. $\{w \in \Sigma^* \mid \#_a(w) = \#_b(w)\}$.
    b. $\{w \in \Sigma^* \mid \#_a(w)\ mod\ 3 = \#_b(w)\ mod\ 3\}$.

24. * What conclusions you draw from the following implications? Are these implications valid?

$$\delta^*(p, u) \in F \Rightarrow \delta^*(q, u) \in F, \text{ therefore}$$
$$\delta^*(p, v) \notin F \Rightarrow \delta^*(q, v) \notin F.$$

25. * Show using concept of finite index of regular languages:

    a. $\{a^n b^n \mid n \geq 0\}$ is not regular language,
    b. $\{w \mid w \in (a + b)^* b(a + b)\}$ is regular language.

D. Multiple choice Questions

26. The minimized version of the FA shown in Fig. 4.23 has following number of states:
    (A) 1, (B) 2, (C) 3, (D) 4.
27. If the refined partition is P' and the original partition is P, which relation is true for them?
    (A) $|P| \leq |P'|$, (B) $|P| \geq |P'|$, (C) None of these.

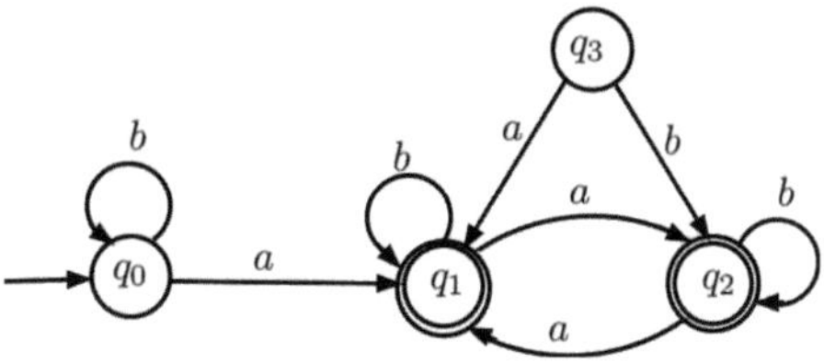

Fig. 4.23 FA with $\Sigma = \{a, b\}$

E. Advanced Knowledge Assessment Problems

28. Prove that Myhill–Nerode theorem gives a truly minimized finite automata.
29. Construct an algorithm to minimize a DFA with given some additional constraints.
30. Minimize a DFA with multiple acceptance criteria: consider a DFA that accepts multiple languages or patterns, while considering all acceptance criteria.
31. Minimize a DFA with dynamic changes: Consider a DFA that may undergo dynamic changes (e.g., states and transitions are added or removed), and implement an algorithm to dynamically update the minimized DFA.

References

1. Hopcroft J (1971). An $n \log n$ algorithm for minimizing states in a finite automaton. In: Theory of machines and computations (Proceedings of international symposium, Technion, Haifa, 1971). Academic Press, New York, pp 189–196. MR 0403320. See also preliminary version, Technical Report STAN-CS-71-190, Stanford University, Computer Science Department, January 1971
2. Watt SM (2013) Regular language homomorphisms and transition complexity: dealing with large alphabets. http://citeseerx.ist.psu.edu/viewdoc/summary?doi=10.1.1.408.9018
3. Kameda T, Weiner P (1970) On the state minimization of nondeterministic finite automata. IEEE Trans Comput C-19(7):617–627, July 1970
4. Tiang T, Ravikumar B (1993) Minimal NFA problems are hard. SIAM J Comp 22:1117–1141, December 1993
5. Chowdhary KR (2016) Minimization of finite automata. http://www.krchowdhary.com/toc/5-minimize.pdf. Cited 02 Aug 2020
6. Tsygamov AV (2012). ReFam: a software tool for minimizing nondeterministic finite automata. In: 14th international symposium on symbolic and numeric algorithms for scientific computing, pp 187–191. https://doi.org/10.1109/SYNASC.2012.49
7. Hogberg J, Larsson L (2020) DFA minimisation using the Myhill-Nerode theorem. https://athena.nitc.ac.in/~kmurali/Courses/18TOC/myhill-nerode.pdf. Cited 31 Jan 2022
8. Myhill-Nerode Handout. www.cs.cmu.edu/~emc/flac09/nerode.pdf. Cited on 05 July 2020
9. Nerode A (1958) Linear automaton transformations. Proc Am Math Soc 9(1958):541–544
10. Khoussainov B, Nerode A (2001) Automata theory and its applications. Birkhauser Springer International Edition

Chapter 5
Regular Languages

Abstract In certain class of problems, including sequential circuits, lexical analyzers, text processing, and pattern recognition, the first step is to obtain the circuit's behavior or the pattern of text in the form of a regular expression. Richer the description in the form of regular expression, easier it is to write the problem specifications. The regular expressions, finite automata, and regular languages are isomorphic to each other, thus a problem can be solved in any one platform and can be transformed into the other. This chapter presents many important closure properties of regular languages, conversion from regular expressions to finite automata and vice versa, the concerning theorems and examples, and many approaches to understand the famous pumping lemma and worked out problems related to pumping lemma, its limitations, and Myhill–Nerode theorem that overcomes that limitation of pumping lemma. In addition, many approaches are presented to deduce a regular expression for a given finite automata. The chapter concludes with self-review questions, practice exercises, and references to important resources.

Keywords Languages closures · Regular expressions · Finite automata · Brozozolwsky's method · Arden's rule · Non-regular languages · Myhill–Nerode theorem · Equivalence classes · Equivalence classes index · Transitive closure · State removal · Generalized NFA · Arden's rule · Pumping lemma · Canonical DFA · Indistinguishable states · Distinguishable states

5.1 Introduction

The regular languages are the most common, well-known, and well-applicable languages both in theory and practice: they are used in design of programming languages, operating systems, compilers, etc. They are the simplest languages in Chomskyhierarchy, and can be described by regular expressions, and the finite automata accept them [11].

In certain class of problems, including the design of sequential circuits, the first step consists of obtaining an unambiguous description of the circuit behavior in the form of regular expression. The language of regular expressions greatly simplifies

K. R. Chowdhary, *Theory of Computation*,
https://doi.org/10.1007/978-981-97-6234-7_5

this first step of synthesis. In general, richer the language the easier it will be to write the problem specification. In this chapter, we will use regular expressions with any number of logical connectives, and discuss methods to obtain state diagrams from these regular expressions.

Regular expressions have applications in computer science: the most important one is probably the lexical analysis of programs. The other are pattern recognition and pattern matching (including the text editing and bibliographic search). Common to all these applications is that the regular expression must be converted into a finite automaton; in most cases, it is to be a deterministic finite automaton (DFA). This is usually achieved by first constructing a nondeterministic finite automaton (NFA), which accepts the language represented by the regular expression. Then we apply the subset construction to it, possibly by reducing the resulting DFA afterward.

We know that class of languages accepted by finite automaton are only those represented by regular expressions, i.e., regular languages. Now our approach will be to show that there is an NFA with ε-transitions, which accepts these languages. We have studied in previous chapters that for every NFA there exists an equivalent DFA. We will also show that for every DFA there exists a regular expression that represents the language of that DFA. The above discussion leads to a cycle like phenomena shown in Fig. 5.1. The diagram indicates that corresponding to a regular expression there is a regular language, and corresponding to a regular language there is an NFA, and corresponding to an NFA there exist a DFA, and finally corresponding to a DFA there exists a regular expression. To prove the above representation of cyclic sequence, we need to show that every regular language corresponds to an NFA with ε-transitions. Since every regular language corresponds to a regular expression, we arrive at a proof that for every regular expression there exists an NFA that recognizes the corresponding Regular Language.

Learning outcomes of this chapter:

1. Closure properties of regular languages. [Knowledge], [Proof].
2. Regex to FA. [Apply].
3. FA to regex. [Apply].
4. Generalized NFA. [Analysis].
5. Pumping Lemma. [Proof], [Apply], [Knowledge].
6. Brozozowsky's method. [Analysis], [Apply].
7. Arden's rule. [Apply].
8. Kleene star properties of regular languages. [Synthesis].

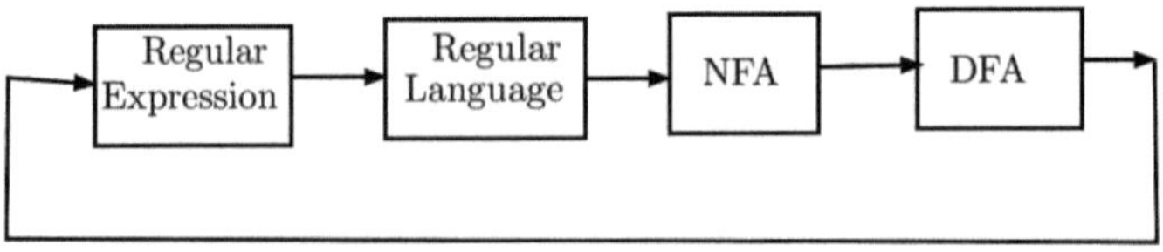

Fig. 5.1 Equivalence of regular expression, regular language NFA, and DFA

5.2 Regular Languages

If $\mathscr{R}$ is a set of Regular Languages over some alphabet set Σ, then we define some relations over these, as follows:

i. $\phi \subseteq \mathscr{R}$,
ii. $\{\varepsilon\} \subseteq \mathscr{R}$,
iii. $\{a\} \subseteq \mathscr{R}$, for all $a \in \Sigma$, and
iv. If $L_1 \subseteq \mathscr{R}$ and $L_2 \subseteq \mathscr{R}$, then $L_1 \cup L_2 \subseteq \mathscr{R}$, $L_1 \circ L_2 \subseteq \mathscr{R}$, $L_1^* \subseteq \mathscr{R}$.

In other words, a language is regular if it is built using only the elementary languages and operations of union, concatenation, and Kleene star over them.

Example 5.1 Show that $(a^*b)^* \cup (b^*a)^* = (a \cup b)^*$.

Since $(a \cup b)^*$ generates all possible strings over a, b, and $(a^*b)^* \cup (b^*a)^* \subseteq (a \cup b)^*$. From the following, we can show the other half of the proof, i.e., $(a \cup b)^* \subseteq (a^*b)^* \cup (b^*a)^*$.

Consider an arbitrary word $w = w_1w_2 \ldots w_n \in (a \cup b)^*$. There can be four different ways in which the subset relations can be specified:

i. Let $w = a^n$, therefore, $w \subseteq (\varepsilon a)^* \subseteq (b^*a)^*$.
ii. Let $w = b^n$, therefore, $w \subseteq (\varepsilon b)^* \subseteq (a^*b)^*$.
iii. When w consists both as and bs, and ends with a:
$w = b \ldots ba \ldots a \in (b^*a)^*$.
iv. When w consists both as and bs, and ends with b:
$w = aa \ldots b \ldots b = a^*b(a^*b)^* \in (a^*b)^*$.

From i. to iv. above, we have $w \in (a^*b)^* \cup (b^*a)^*$. Therefore, $(a \cup b)^* \subseteq (a^*b)^* \cup (b^*a)^*$. Hence, the proof. □

Theorem 5.1 *The class of regular languages are closed under the operation of union, concatenation, and $*$ (Kleene star).*

Proof The theorem states that if L_1 and L_2 are regular languages, then so are $L_1 \cup L_2$, L_1L_2, L_1^*, and L_2^*.

The proof is direct in the definition of regular expressions. Let R_1 and R_2 be regular expressions corresponding to regular languages L_1 and L_2. Therefore, $R_1 \cup R_2$, R_1R_2, R_1^* and R_2^* are regular expressions as per Definition 2.2 in Sect. 2.5.1. The operations on regular sets $R_1 \cup R_2$, R_1R_2, R_1^*, and R_2^* produce the strings which belong to regular languages $\mathscr{L}(R_1 \cup R_2)$, $\mathscr{L}(R_1)\mathscr{L}(R_2)$, $\mathscr{L}(R_1^*)$, $\mathscr{L}(R_2^*)$, respectively. This proves that the regular languages are closed under the operation of union, concatenation, and Kleene star. □

In addition, the regular languages are closed on *intersection*, *complementation*, and *word-reversal*.[1]

[1] Acceptance on word-reversal means, if a FA A accepts string w then there exists a FA B that accepts w^R.

Definition 5.1 (*Reversal of a Language*) The reversal w^R of a string w is defined as follows: $\varepsilon^R = \varepsilon$, and if $w = a_1 a_2 ... a_n$ with $a_i \in \Sigma$, then $w^R = a_n ... a_2 a_1$. The reversal of a language L is $L^R = \{w^R \mid w \in L\}$. □

Definition 5.2 (*Reversal of a DFA*) The reversal of a DFA $M = (Q, \Sigma, \delta, q_0, F)$ is an NFA M' obtained from M by reversing all the transitions and by swapping the role of starting and final states, i.e., $M^R = (Q, \Sigma, \delta^R, F, \{q_0\})$, where $\delta^R(q, a) = \{p \in Q : \delta(p, a) = q\}$. □

Theorem 5.2 *The regular languages are closed on word-reversal.*

Proof Consider that M is a finite automata and it accepts some arbitrary string w, i.e., $w \in L(M)$. What is required to show here is that w^R is accepted by some finite automata M'. For this we will consider that M' is an NFA, which can be converted into DFA using subset construction method. What was start state in M is designated as final state in M', and the final state of M is designated as start state in M', as shown in Fig. 5.2.

It follows that w^R is in $L(M')$. By the same logic we can explain that if w^R is accepted by a DFA M' then there exists a DFA M that accepts w. □

5.2.1 Finite Regular Languages

Creating regular expression for finite language is straightforward. Consider that there is a finite language L (i.e., a language with only finitely many words). To make a regular expression that defines language L, we simply insert plus sign between all these words. If $L = \{a, b, ab, bb, ba\}$ then corresponding regular expression is simply $a + b + ab + bb + ba$.

Theorem 5.3 *Every finite language is regular.*

Proof The word "finite" here means exactly n elements, for $n \in \mathbb{N}$. This suggests proof by *induction*.

The statement to be proved is—"for every $n \geq 0$, every language having exactly n elements corresponds to some regular expression".

Basis Step: Consider $n = 0$, hence there are 0 strings. Therefore, the language with zero number of strings is ϕ, which, according to Definition 2.2 in Sect. 2.5.1, corresponds to a regular expression ϕ.

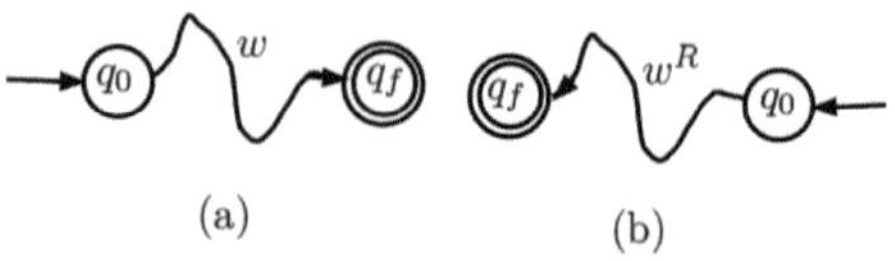

Fig. 5.2 **a** String w is accepted by DFA M. **b** String w^R is accepted by NFA M'

Induction Hypothesis: Let k $(0 < k <= n - 1)$ be an arbitrary integer. Assume that any language with exactly k elements is regular.

Induction step: We want to show that any language L with $k + 1$ number of elements is regular. Let L be such a language. We may express L as a union of two languages L_1 and L_2, where L_1 has k elements and L_2 has one element. By our inductive hypothesis, L_1 corresponds to some regular expression r_1 and let r_2 be a regular expression corresponding to L_2. Hence, as per Definition 2.3 in Sect. 2.5.1 of regular languages, $r_1 + r_2$ is regular expressions corresponding to the languages $L_1 \cup L_2$, which is L, with $k + 1$ number of elements. Similar way, we can construct all the languages of finite number of strings, and all these will be regular. □

Theorem 5.4 *All languages of finite length strings are regular.*

Proof The set of finite length strings can be only a finite set. Hence, for this, the same theorem, Definition 2.3 in Sect. 2.5.1, is applicable, as above. □

5.2.2 *Regular Languages Versus Countable Sets*

The *countable sets* or *enumerable* or *denumerable* sets are those set elements which can be counted. For example, set $\mathbb{N} = \{0, 1, 2, 3, \ldots\}$. Thus any set, whose elements can be paired with the elements of $\mathbb{N}$ (having *bijection*), is countable set. The set $\{2, 3, 1, 5, 7, 9, \ldots\}$, which is exhaustively listed, can be paired with $\mathbb{N}$ as

$$\{(2, 0), (3, 1), (1, 2), (5, 3), (7, 4), \ldots\}.$$

Similarly, the set of all words over $\{a, b\}$ can be enumerated by systematically by pairing with the elements of $\mathbb{N}$, in the increasing order of their length, and those strings which are equal length, the ordered pair is in lexicographic order.

$$\{(\varepsilon, 0), (a, 1), (b, 2), (aa, 3), (ab, 4), \ldots\}.$$

Both the examples above are of regular sets. Hence, we conclude that (these) regular sets can be enumerated. In fact, a set of regular sets is always enumerable. Consequently, the sets of regular expressions are also enumerable.

However, we know from Chap. 1 that "set of subsets of enumerable set is not enumerable". This subset is all possible languages. Thus, given that, all languages are uncountable, and regular languages are countable, we can easily conclude that there are many languages that are *non-regular*.

An alternate argument for the above is as follows: Each regular language corresponds to a regular expression. All the regular expressions can be exhaustively listed, by listing the regular expressions in order of their size, and those of the same size can be listed lexicographically. Thus regular expressions are countable. Hence, the regular languages are also countable. However, we have discussed that all possible languages are not countable as they are exponential power[2] over 2 of Σ^*. This concludes that there are languages other than regular languages.

5.3 Closure Properties of Regular Languages

We discussed in the previous chapters that regular expressions are formed by *union*, *concatenation*, and *Kleene star* operation on regular expressions. In other words, a regular expression is closed under the operations of union, concatenation, and Kleene star. Hence, the *class of regular languages* should also be closed under the operations of union concatenation and Kleene star. To prove this, an approach used here will be similar, i.e., applying the operations of union, concatenation, and Kleene star on class of languages accepted by finite automation [5, 6].

5.3.1 Closure on Union, Concatenation, and Kleene star

Theorem 5.5 *Prove that class of languages accepted by finite automata are closed under the operation of union, concatenation, and Kleene star.*

Proof For each of the three cases to be proved, we consider two automata M_1 and M_2 as

$$M_1 = (Q_1, \Sigma_1, \delta_1, s_1, F_1), \text{ and}$$
$$M_2 = (Q_2, \Sigma_2, \delta_2, s_2, F_2),$$

and construct an automata M, taking each case individually. The simplified diagrams of M_1, M_2 are shown in Fig. 5.3. For any input x, the automata[3] M_1 starts with state s_1, followed with any number of transitions, then ultimately leading to one of the final states in F_1. Thus, for $x \in L(M_1)$, there is $\delta_1^*(s_1, x) \in F_1$. In the similar way, the automata M_2 accepts.

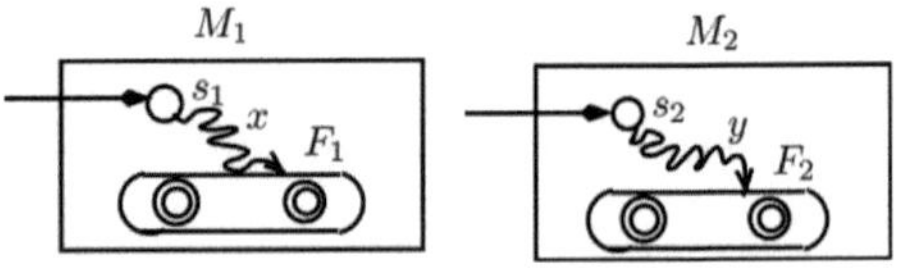

Fig. 5.3 The finite automata M_1 and M_2

[2] The subsets of Σ^* are 2^{Σ^*}, which is exponential order.

[3] The reference, automata in this chapter means Finite Automata, which may be a DFA or an NFA.

(a) *Union of two regular languages*: Let M_1 and M_2 be DFAs accepting the languages $L(M_1)$ and $L(M_2)$, respectively. Therefore, the language accepted by resultant automata M will be $L(M) = L(M_1) \cup L(M_2)$. Let this M be an NFA.

Figure 5.4 shows the automaton $M = (Q, \Sigma, \delta, s, F)$ constructed using automata M_1 and M_2. For an input string w, every path of sequence of states in M will start from s, and then there will be a ε-transition to either to s_1 or s_2. If there is input $x \in L(M_1)$ then there is a transition to s_1, and then rest of the states are traversed in M_1, followed with a transition to F_1, followed with a ε-transition to f. Otherwise, if input is $y \in L(M_2)$ then there is a ε-transition to s_2, then the traversing of path would be through M_2 until the final state in F_2 of M_2 is reached. This is followed with a ε-transition to f. Hence, M accepts the string $\{w\} = \{x\} \cup \{y\}$, if M_1 or M_2 accepts it. Therefore, $L(M) = L(M_1) \cup L(M_2)$.

Let input to the machine M be at state s, and from here it makes a guess to choose a ε-transition to s_1 or s_2. The tuples of M can be defined in terms of the tuples of M_1 and M_2 as follows:

$$
\begin{aligned}
s &= \text{start state},\\
Q &= Q_1 \cup Q_2 \cup \{s, f\},\\
\Sigma &= \Sigma_1 \cup \Sigma_2 \cup \{\varepsilon\},\\
F &= \{f\},\\
\delta &\text{ for any } q \in Q \text{ and } a \in \Sigma \text{ is:}
\end{aligned}
$$

$$
\delta(q, a) = \begin{cases} \delta_1(q, a), \text{ if } q \in Q_1 \text{ and } a \in \Sigma_1,\\ \delta_2(q, a), \text{ if } q \in Q_2 \text{ and } a \in \Sigma_2,\\ \delta(q, a) = \{s_1\} \cup \{s_2\}, \text{ if } q = s \text{ and } a = \varepsilon\\ f, \text{ if } q \in F_1 \cup F_2 \text{ and } a = \varepsilon. \end{cases} \tag{5.1}
$$

Considering that $x \in L(M_1)$ and $y \in L(M_2)$, the language $L(M)$ of finite automaton M can be defined as

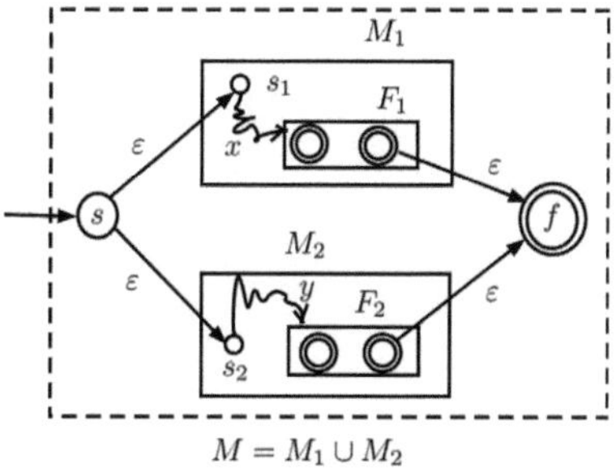

Fig. 5.4 The finite automata $M = M_1 \cup M_2$

$$L(M) = \{\{x\} \cup \{y\} \mid x \in L(M_1) \text{ and } y \in L(M_2)\}. \tag{5.2}$$

If input is $x \in L(M_1)$ at s, it will be nondeterministically decided to process x in M_1. Alternatively, for input $y \in L(M_2)$, the processing will be through M_2.

(b) *Concatenation of two regular languages:* In this case again we consider M_1, M_2 as two finite automata, shown in Fig. 5.3, and construct a combination NFA M shown in Fig. 5.5, such that $L(M) = L(M_1) \circ L(M_2)$.

Let the finite automata M_1, M_2 are defined as earlier, and we define the combination automaton M in terms of M_1 and M_2 as follows:

Let $M = (Q, \Sigma, \delta, s, F)$, such that

$$Q = Q_1 \cup Q_2$$
$$\Sigma = \Sigma_1 \cup \Sigma_2 \cup \{\varepsilon\}.$$

The δ for $q \in Q$ and $a \in \Sigma$ is

$$\delta(q, a) = \begin{cases} \delta_1(q, a), & \text{if } q \in Q_1 \text{ and } a \in \Sigma_1, \\ \delta_2(q, a), & \text{if } q \in Q_2 \text{ and } a \in \Sigma_2, \\ \delta(q, a) = s_2, & \text{if } q \in F_1 \text{ and } a = \varepsilon. \end{cases} \tag{5.3}$$

$s = s_1$, and $F = F_2$.

For any string $w = xy$ applied as input to M, where $x \in L(M_1)$ and $y \in L(M_2)$, there will be a path from s_1 to f_1 labeled by string x, then there will be a ε-transition from f_1 to s_2, then there will be a path from s_2 to f_2 labeled by y. Therefore, $L(M) = \{xy \mid x \in L(M_1) \text{ and } y \in L(M_2)\}$. Hence, $L(M) = L(M_1) \circ L(M_2)$:

(c) *Kleene star on* $L(M_1)$: Let M_1 be a nondeterministic finite automaton. Using this we want to construct an NFA M such that $L(M) = (L(M_1))^*$. For example, for $^* = 3$, there is $L(M) = L(M_1) \circ L(M_1) \circ L(M_1)$. Therefore, Kleene star is a concatenation operation on the language of an FA, with that language itself any number of times. The resultant NFA M obtained after * operation on M_1 is shown in Fig. 5.6.

It should be noted that a separate initial state s has been added in M to cause a ε-transition from s to s_1. Since $\varepsilon \in L(M_1)^*$, a ε transition has been added between

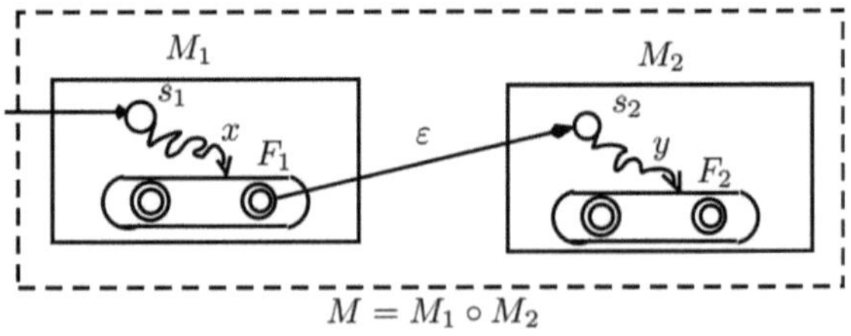

Fig. 5.5 Finite automata $M = M_1 \circ M_2$

Fig. 5.6 Finite automata $M = M_1^*$, constructed using Kleene star operation on M_1

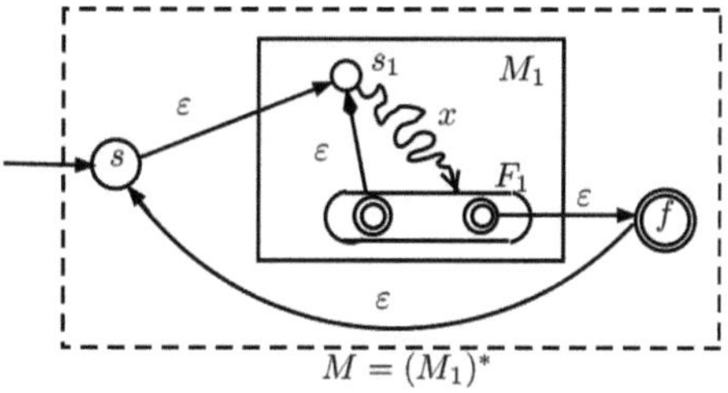

states s and f. The Kleene star has the effect of ε-transitions from all the final states F in M to start state s_1 of M_1.

If the finite automata M_1 is represented by $M_1 = (Q_1, \Sigma_1, \delta_1, s_1, F_1)$ then the finite automata $M = (Q, \Sigma, \delta, s, F)$ can be represented in terms of M_1 as

$$\begin{aligned} s &= \text{ start state}, \\ Q &= Q_1 \cup \{s\}, \\ \Sigma &= \Sigma_1 \cup \{\varepsilon\}, \\ F &= \{f\}, \text{ and} \end{aligned}$$

the transition function δ is

$$\delta(q, a) = \begin{cases} \delta_1(q, a), \text{ if } q \in Q_1 \text{ and } a \in \Sigma_1, \\ s_1, \text{ if } q \in F_1 \text{ and } a = \varepsilon, \\ \{s_1, f\}, \text{ if } q = s \text{ and } a = \varepsilon. \end{cases} \tag{5.4}$$

Therefore, $L(M) = (L(M_1))^*$. This concludes the proof that a class of languages accepted by finite automata are closed under the operation of *union*, *concatenation*, and *Kleene star.* □

In terms of programs, the application of Theorem 5.5 can be interpreted as follows: Consider that P_1 and P_2 are two programs that recognize regular languages L_1 and L_2 (of text strings), respectively. Let the language $\{w\} = \{x \in L_1\} \cup \{y \in L_2\}$ be recognized[4] by program P. The P in turn calls program P_1, which, if accepts $w = x$, then P accepts. Otherwise, P calls P_2, which, if accepts $w = y$, then P accepts.

To recognize $w = x.y$, first x is recognized by P_1 and then y by P_2. The outputs of P_1 and P_2 are ANDed together, if the result is Yes, the $w = x \cdot y$ is accepted, else not.

For $w = \varepsilon, x, x \cdot x, ...$, program P_1 can be designed to accept without any input (i.e., ε), and each input of x calls P_1 from P, and P accepts when P_1 accepts. Similarly, for the input y^*.

---

[4] Until the chapter on Turing machine, we consider that the words "accepts" and "recognize" have the same meanings.

Thus, we can conclude that, we can construct programs P_1, P_2, and P as extensions of the program `simfa.c` in Sect. 2.5.2.

In the following example, we make use of this Theorem 5.5 to construct a FA for a given regular expression.

Example 5.2 Consider a regular expression $r = (ab + aba)^*$, and construct a finite automation which accepts the language $L(r)$.

Let us first consider only part of the regular expression, $ab + aba$, and let $r_1 = ab$ and $r_2 = aba$. Therefore, $r_1 = a \circ b$. Applying the rule of concatenation from Theorem 5.5, the FA which can recognize $L(r_1)$ is given as shown in Fig. 5.7a.

Similarly, the FA which can recognize $L(r_2)$ is shown in Fig. 5.7b. Let $r_3 = r_1 + r_2$. By applying the union operation on the set of languages $L(r_1)$ and $L(r_2)$ (Theorem 5.5), the new language obtained is $L(r_3) = L(r_1) \circ L(r_2) = L(r_1)L(r_2)$. The finite automaton for $L(r_3)$ is shown in Fig. 5.7c. Finally, applying the operation of Kleene star on the language $L(r_3)$ we get $(L(r_3))^* = L(r_3^*)$ (see Definition 2.3 in Sect. 2.5.1). The finite automaton, an NFA, for this is shown in Fig. 5.8. The start state for the NFA M is q_0 and final state is q_{12}.

We have noted that the main part in deriving an FA for a given regular expression is to find sub-expressions in the regular expressions, in the form of $r + s$, $r \circ q$ and r^*. However, parentheses are essential for a complex expression to make precedence explicit. In this way, we can construct an NFA for any given regular expression. This NFA can be converted into DFA using Theorem 3.1 in Sect. 3.4.

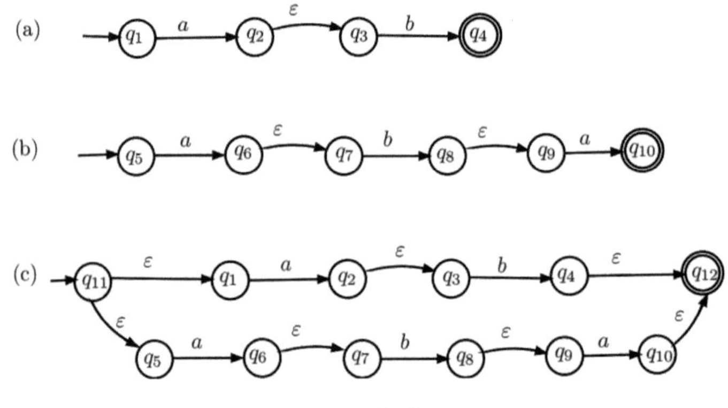

Fig. 5.7 **a** FA for $r_1 = ab$. **b** FA for $r_2 = aba$. **c** FA for $r_3 = r_1 + r_2$

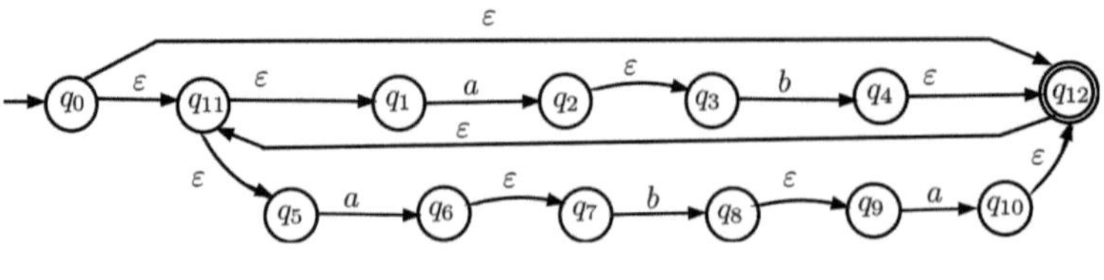

Fig. 5.8 FA for regular expression $(ab + aba)^*$

Apart from this, to understand the associability of various sub-expressions, parsing is required, which is discussed in *context-free languages* and *grammars* in next chapters.

5.3.2 Closure on Complement and Intersection

We know that regular languages are expressible as Sets. The set operations of union and concatenation correspond to language operations. Hence, regular languages have closure properties under these operations. However, the ordinary Sets have no operation like the *Kleene star* operation of Regular Sets. In fact, this can be considered as repeated concatenation operation that exists on sets.

In the following, we explore the closure properties of regular languages corresponding to other operations on sets, like *intersection*, *complementation*, *difference*, and *symmetric difference*.

Theorem 5.6 *The class of languages accepted by finite automata are closed under the operation of (i) complementation and (ii) intersection.*

Proof *I. Complementation)* Let the $M = (Q, \Sigma, \delta, s_0, F)$ be a finite automaton and $L = L(M)$ be the language accepted by this. The complement of M is $\overline{M}$. Let $\overline{M}$ be the FA that accepts the language $\overline{L}$. Obviously $\overline{M}$ should accept language which is not accepted by M and vice versa. Therefore, the final states in $\overline{M}$ are those that are non-final states in M and what are non-final states in $\overline{M}$ are final states in M. In other words, when final states and non-final states are interchanged in M, we get $\overline{M}$. Note that, in this process, the total states remain the same in both the automata. Thus, $\overline{L} = L(\overline{M}) = \Sigma^* - L(M)$ and $\overline{M} = (Q, \Sigma, \delta', s_0, Q - F)$.

Since $\overline{M}$ is a finite automaton, the $\overline{L}$ language accepted by this is regular. This shows that complement of a regular language is also regular. Hence, the regular languages are closed under the operation of complementation.

II. Intersection: Let us assume that intersection of regular languages L_1 and L_2 is language $L = L_1 \cap L_2$. We want to determine whether L is regular. Using De Morgan's theorem we rewrite the expression for intersection of L_1 and L_2 as

$$L_1 \cap L_2 = \overline{(\overline{L_1} \cup \overline{L_2})}. \tag{5.5}$$

This means that the language $L = L_1 \cap L_2$ consists all words that are in $\overline{(\overline{L_1} \cup \overline{L_2})}$. In other words, L consists of those words that are not in $(\overline{L_1} \cup \overline{L_2})$, that is, they are neither in $\overline{L_1}$ nor in $\overline{L_2}$. Since L_1 and L_2 are regular, $\overline{L_1}$ and $\overline{L_2}$ are also regular. In addition, their union $(\overline{L_2} \cup \overline{L_2})$ is regular, and its complement $\overline{(\overline{L_1} \cup \overline{L_2})}$ too is regular. Therefore, the intersection of two regular languages results to a regular language. Hence, the regular languages are closed under the operation of intersection.

Regarding the states of automation recognizing the language $(\overline{\overline{L_1} \cup \overline{L_2}})$, the following proof clarifies it: Let $L_1 = L(M_1)$ and $L_2 = L(M_2)$, where $M_1 = (Q_1, \Sigma_1, \delta_1, s_1, F_1)$ and $M_2 = (Q_2, \Sigma_2, \delta_2, s_2, F_2)$. A combined automation out of M_1 and M_2 can be constructed as $M = (Q, \Sigma, \delta, (s_1, s_2), F)$, where $Q = Q_1 \times Q_2 = \{(q_i, q_j) \mid q_i \in Q_1, q_j \in Q_2\}$. The transition function δ is defined in such a way that M is in state (q_i, q_j) whenever the M_1 is in state q_i and M_2 is in state q_j. Thus, the state transitions in M are defined as

$$\delta((q_i, q_j), a) = (q_k, q_l),$$

if and only if, $\delta_1(q_i, a) = q_k$, and $\delta_2(q_j, a) = q_l$.

Similarly F is defined as the set of all the pairs (q_i, q_j), such that $q_i \in F_1$, and $q_j \in F_2$.

5.4 On Regularity of Languages

For a language to be regular it must be expressible in the form of a regular expression. We have discussed that regular expressions and corresponding languages are closed under the operations of union, concatenation, and Kleene star. Thus, one should be able to identify regularity of a language by observing the structure of the corresponding regular expression, as whether it is constructed using operations of union, concatenation, and Kleene star. But, this is not sufficient to prove that a language is regular.

There are in fact languages that are non-regular. In the following, we discuss the characteristics that are shared by all regular languages but not by non-regular languages. These can be the basis for determining that a language is not regular.

Theorem 5.7 (Kleene's Theorem) *A language is regular if and only if it is accepted by a finite automaton.*

Proof Let the alphabet set be $\Sigma = \phi$, and s be the start state. A finite automaton accepting the regular language over Σ is shown in Fig. 5.9a. The language accepted here is an empty set.

For every finite subset of Σ, if the automaton has no final state, language accepted is again an empty set.

The elements of the non-empty set $\{a_1, a_2, a_3, \ldots, a_n\}$ accepted by an automation are shown in Fig. 5.9b.

If languages L_1 and L_2 are accepted by FA M_1 and M_2, respectively, then there exists an automaton that accepts L_1L_2 (Theorem 5.5 in Sect. 5.3). Using the same theorem we concluded that for $L_1 \cup L_2$ and L_1^* there exists FAs accepting them. Since regular expression can be constructed using the union, concatenation, and Kleene star operations, we can say that, for every regular language there exists an FA, which accepts it.

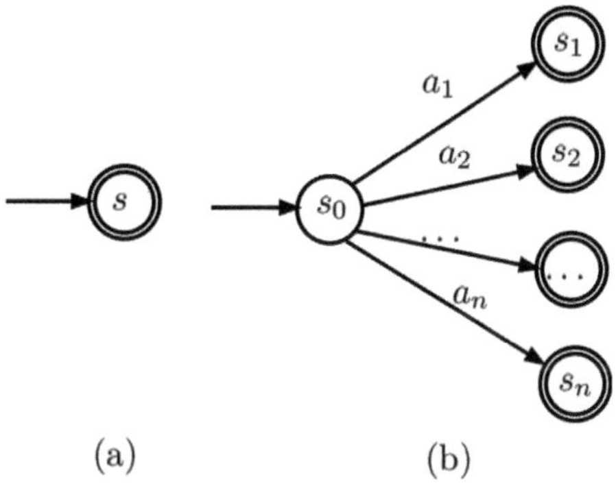

Fig. 5.9 **a** FA with null input. **b** FA with inputs a_1 or a_2 or a_3 ... or a_n

The second part of the proof, that for any finite automaton there exists regular expression, is as follows. We know that given any complex automaton it can be decomposed into elementary finite automata, each of them corresponds to a regular language. These languages are operated on by operators union, concatenation, and kleene star to construct more complex regular expressions corresponding to the entire FA. This proves the theorem. □

5.5 DFA to Regular Expression

The way of representing a regular language using regular expression is fundamentally different from representing it using FA; however, both of these methods turn out to be the same, and they represent the regular languages. We have seen in the beginning of this chapter as how to obtain NFA for any given regular expression. In the following, we will show how to obtain a regular expression for a given DFA. We say DFA here because an NFA can always be converted into a DFA.

The construction of regular expression from finite automata is expensive in time. We may have to construct at the worst n^3 expressions for an n-state automaton; in addition, the length of the expression can grow by a factor of 4 on the average, with each of the n inductive steps if enough simplification is not done on the expressions.

There are fundamentally four basic approaches to convert a DFA into regular expression: (i) transitive closure method, (ii) state removal method, (iii) creating generalized NFA, and (iv) Brozozowski's algebraic method. Each of these methods is discussed in the following.

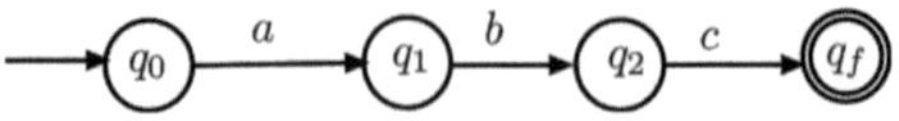

Fig. 5.10 A path in a DFA

5.5.1 Transitive Closure Method

Consider an automaton shown in Fig. 5.10. We know that regular expression for the transition from state q_0 to q_1 is a, from q_1 to q_2 is b, and from q_2 to q_f is c. The regular expression representing the transition from state q_0 to q_f is concatenation of regular expressions a, b, and c, which is abc. Suppose that there exists only one unique path in an automaton M from state q_0 to q_f, then there exists only one regular expression R such that R represents the same string as the DFA M. However, this automaton is trivial only. Let us consider a more general case.

Consider the automaton shown in Fig. 5.11. Since there are multiple paths from q_0 to q_f, we cannot derive a simple regular expression to represent the DFA. However, using the operation of union and concatenation we can build on our previous approach to create a construction that works for all types of DFAs [13].

Suppose a regular expression R_{ij} represents the set of all strings that transits the automaton M from state q_i to q_j. Further, let R_{ij}^k represent the set of all strings that transits the automaton M from q_i to q_j without passing through any intermediate node whose state is higher than state q_k. Note that the beginning and end points of the path are not intermediate nodes. We can construct R_{ij}^k by successively constructing R_{ij}^1, R_{ij}^2, ..., R_{ij}^k. Thus, R_{ij} can be defined by

$$R_{ij}^k = R_{ik}^{k-1}(R_{kk}^{k-1})^* \, R_{kj}^{k-1} + R_{ij}^{k-1}. \tag{5.6}$$

For example, we construct R_{ij} for $k = 1, 2, 3$ and note that every next expression uses the previous expression to build on, as follows:

$$\begin{aligned}
k = 1, \quad R_{ij}^1 &= R_{ik}^0(R_{11}^0)^* \, R_{1j}^0 + R_{ij}^0, \\
k = 2, \quad R_{ij}^2 &= R_{ik}^1(R_{22}^1)^* \, R_{2j}^1 + R_{ij}^1, \\
k = 3, \quad R_{ij}^3 &= R_{ik}^2(R_{33}^2)^* \, R_{3j}^2 + R_{ij}^2.
\end{aligned}$$

To construct the expression R_{ij}^k, we use the following inductive rule: Start at $k = 1$, and finally reach to $k = n$ (number of steps). This successive construction builds regular expression until we have R_{ij}. We can then construct a regular expression

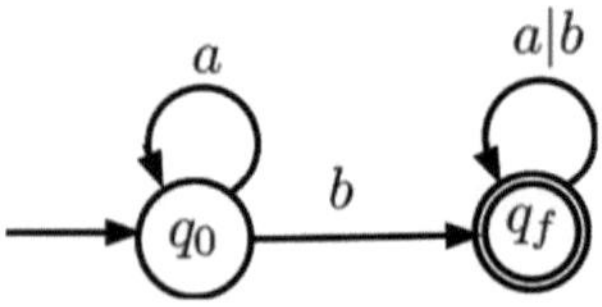

Fig. 5.11 A general DFA

representing the DFA M as union of all R_{0f} where q_0 is the starting state and $q_f \in F$ is final state of M. We note that this approach is of same form as *transitive closure* [4].

The only problem of this approach is that it creates a complex regular expression.

5.5.2 State Removal Method

This approach involves eliminating of its states. It identifies patterns within the graph and removes the states, building up regular expression along each transition. The advantage of this method over the transitive closure-based method is that this method is easier to visualize [10].

Consider that we eliminate some state q_j and there is an arc from state q_i to q_j and an arc from state q_j to q_k. If the language of the automaton is required to remain unchanged, then we should relabel the edges, which will now go from q_i to q_k. These labels will now be strings instead of symbols. These strings may sometimes be infinitely large in numbers and long, hence we label the arcs after elimination of states, by expressions (regular expressions) instead of strings. The language of this new automaton is union of expressions of all the paths from start state to final state of the automaton, and each path's regular expression is concatenation of regular expressions of individual subpaths.

Note that the above approach is consistent with the definition of the language, e.g., if a, b are the labels of two paths from start state to final, the resultant single path will have label $a + b$ or string $\{a\} \cup \{b\}$. When a and b form a single path from start to final state with one intermediate state, then resultant single arc path from start to final state has regular expression label of ab and represents string $\{a\}\{b\}$.

Consider the situation of automaton shown in Fig. 5.12a where state q_j may be removed and automaton may be reduced to the form shown in Fig. 5.12b.

The strategy used for construction of regular expression from a finite automaton is given as follows:

1. For each final state q_f, we apply reduction process to produce equivalent automaton with regular expression labels on the arcs, and eliminate all states except start and final states.
2. If final state is not equal to start state, we may have the automaton after eliminating some states, e.g., like shown in Fig. 5.12b.
3. If the start state is also the accepting state, then after eliminating of states, we are left with only one state, the start state, and the regular expression representing the strings the automaton accepts is r^*, as shown in Fig. 5.13.
4. The required resultant regular expression of the automaton is union of expressions derived in steps (2) and (3).

The regular expression for the accepted strings for the automaton shown in Fig. 5.12a can be described in more than one way, one of them is $r_1^* r_2 (r_3 + r_4 r_1^* r_2)^*$. This expression says that, we can go from start state to itself any number of times,

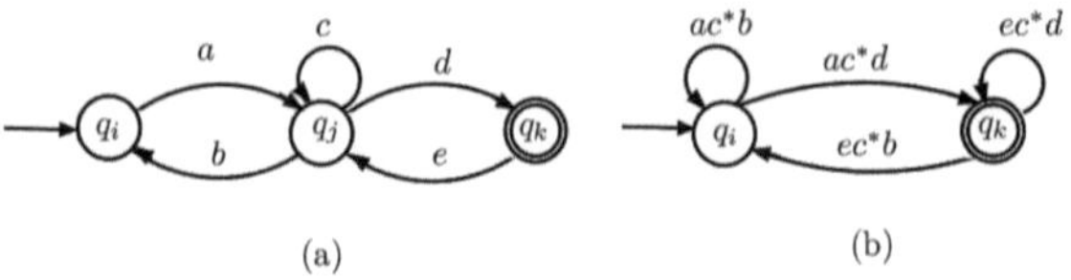

Fig. 5.12 FA with edges labeled with regular expressions

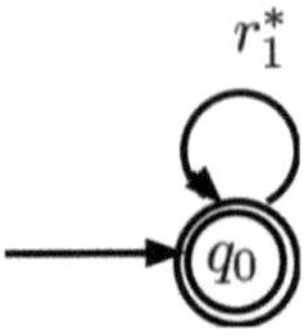

Fig. 5.13 FA with start state as accepting state

then go to final state q_k through r_2, which makes the language as $r_1^*r_2$. Then we may optionally traverse r_3 or $r_4r_1^*r_2$ or their combination any number of times.

In the next section, we follow the steps discussed above to generate the regular expression through a step-by-step process, for any given automaton. The new automaton we obtain after eliminating states is called generalized NFA or GNFA.

5.5.3 *Generalized NFA*

Unlike the NFA, which reads one symbol at a time, a generalized NFA (GNFA) reads block of symbols from the input, and moves along the transition arrows connecting two states when a block of symbols is read. This block of symbols is nothing but a regular expression. The GNFA accepts the input string corresponding to the label if it leads to the final state when the string is completely read [2].

A GNFA is formally defined as

$$G = (Q, \Sigma, \rho, q_0, q_f), \tag{5.7}$$

where

Q is finite set of states,
Σ is alphabet set,
$q_0 \in Q$ is initial state,
$q_f \in F$ is single final state,
$\rho : (Q - \{q_f\}) \times (Q - \{q_0\}) \rightarrow R_\Sigma$.

In the above R_Σ is set of all regular expressions over the alphabet set Σ, and ρ is a function that maps $q_i \times q_k$ to regular expression, i.e., the regular expression connects these two states.

Definition 5.3 (*GNFA*) The GNFA $G = (Q, \Sigma, \rho, q_0, q_f)$ accepts string $w \in \Sigma^*$ iff there exists $x_1, x_2, \ldots, x_f \in \Sigma^*$ and $w = r_0, r_1, \ldots, r_f$ are regular expressions such that $r_0 = q_0, r_i = q_i, ..., r_f = q_f$ and for each $i \in [1, t]$, $x_i \in L(\rho(r_{i-1}, r_i))$. □

An input string is accepted if there is a way to read the input string such that the GNFA is in the accepting (final) state after processing of the entire string. A GNFA has one start state (q_{start}) with no incoming arrows, and one accepting state (q_{final}) with no outgoing arrows.

Lemma 5.1 *If a language is regular, then it can be described by a regular expression.*

Proof Let L be a regular language. Since L is regular, it is accepted by a DFA. We describe a procedure for converting DFA into equivalent regular expressions.

We break this procedure into two parts, using a GNFA. First we show how to convert DFAs into GNFAs, and then GNFAs into regular expressions. The method is called *state removal method* (see Fig. 5.14).

The process of constructing regular expression requires the finite automaton with only one initial and one final state. To achieve this, we eliminate one state at a time from the initial transition diagram. The resulting successive transition graphs are with r arrows, where r is a regular expression.

Converting a DFA into GNFA

1. Add a new start state (q_{start}), with ε-transition from this to q_0.
2. Add a new accept state (q_{accept}), with ε-transition from each of the final state to q_{accept}.
3. If an edge in original DFA has multiple labels, replace the labels with a regular expression formed by the union of these labels.
4. If originally there is no arrow between two states, add a new edge with label ϕ.

Converting a GNFA into Regular Expression

1. We interactively remove states one by one in GNFA such that, after each state is removed, the new GNFA obtained will recognize the same language as the previous one.
2. When states in the GNFA are two, we have achieved the regular expression for the given DFA, represented by the label of the edge connecting these states. □

Removing a state q (not q_{start} or q_{accept}) in the process of construction of GNFA is demonstrated in Fig. 5.15. The new label on the arrow from q_i to q_j becomes regular expression that describes all strings that take GNFA from q_i to q_j either directly or via q (the removed state). Figure 5.15 shows an example of conversion of DFA to an equivalent GNFA.

Fig. 5.14 Conversion of DFA to regular expression

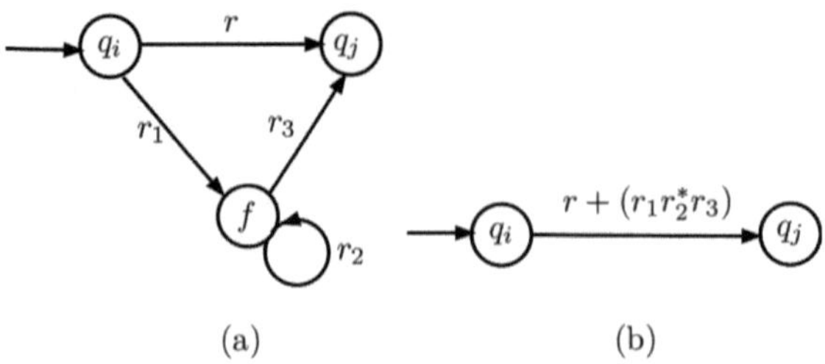

Fig. 5.15 Conversion of DFA to GNFA: **a** DFA. **b** Equivalent GNFA

State Removal Primitives for DFA to GNFA

Obtain Regular expressions for a given finite automata using the approach of GNFA construction (also called state removal method).

In the following, various possible cases are shown for obtaining regular expressions for given finite automata. Each case shows an equivalent automaton for a given regular expression.

Case-I. A finite automaton accepts the expression $r_1 + r_2 + \cdots + r_n$ (Fig. 5.16a). Replace it by the one shown in Fig. 5.16b.

Case-II. If the transition diagram is like the one shown in Fig. 5.17a, replace it by that in Fig. 5.17b.

Case-III. If there are more than one final states, say, f_1, f_2, f_3 (Fig. 5.18a, then replace them with single final state (Fig. 5.18b).

Case-IV. Simplify the transition diagram of three states as in Fig. 5.19a and replace it by Fig. 5.19b.

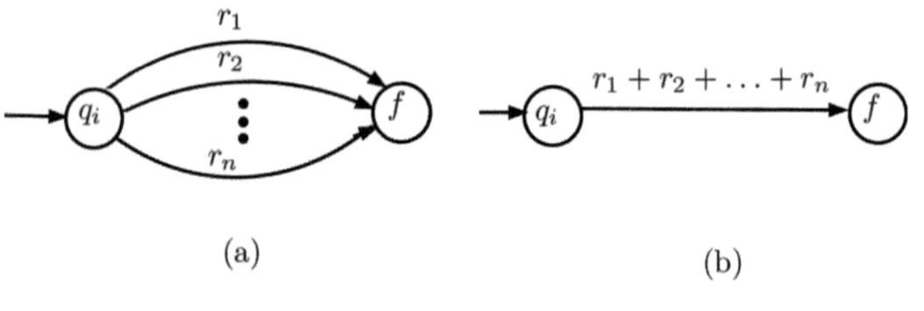

Fig. 5.16 FA to regular expression (Case-I)

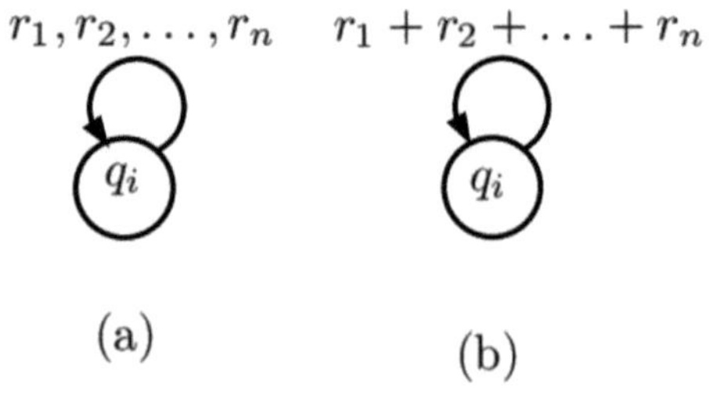

Fig. 5.17 FA to regular expression (Case-II)

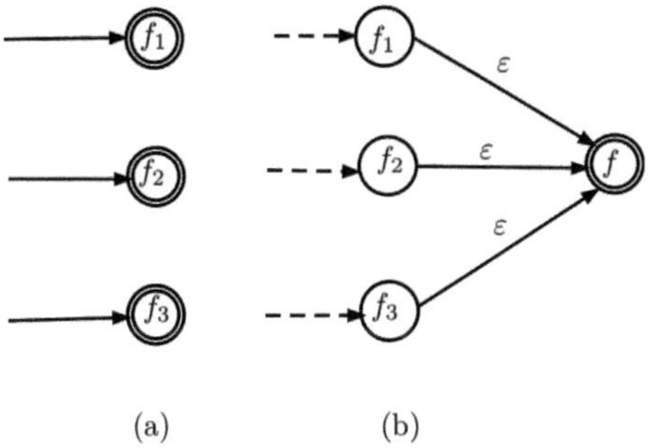

Fig. 5.18 FA to regular expression (Case-III)

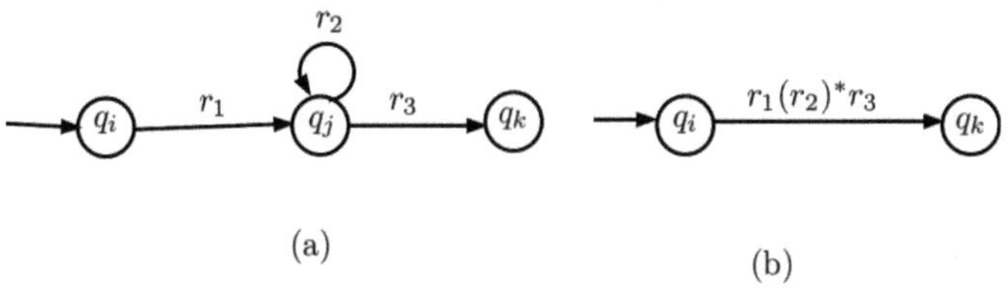

Fig. 5.19 FA to regular expression (Case-IV)

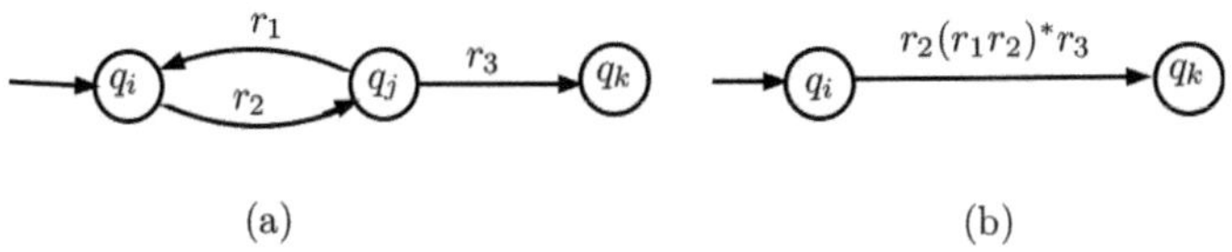

Fig. 5.20 FA to regular expression (Case-V)

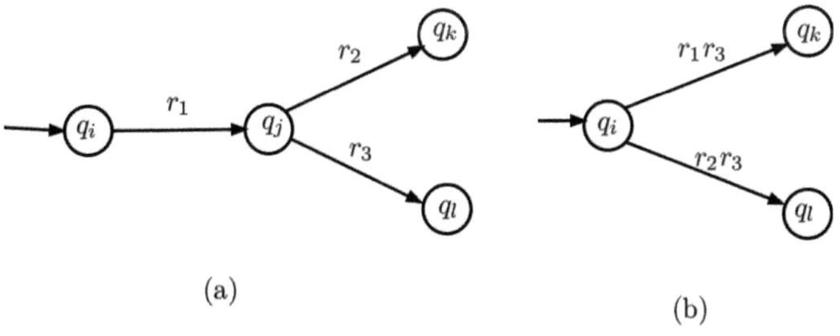

Fig. 5.21 FA to regular expression (Case-VI)

Case-V. Replace the old transition diagram in Fig. 5.20a by shown in Fig. 5.20b.

Case-VI. Replace the old transition diagram in Fig. 5.21a by that in Fig. 5.21b.

In the similar way, using these primitives, any complex automaton can be reduced to GNFA, which ultimately produces the regular expression.

Using the primitives discussed above, in most cases, an DFA can be converted into GNFA and then to regular expression. However, sometimes the above method is too cumbersome, and even may not be a universal solution.

The following section suggests a totally different approach, which is based on representing automaton as a set of algebraic equations and solving these equations for unknown variables.

5.5.4 Brozozowski's Algebraic Method

In order to complete the proof of Kleene's theorem (see Theorem 5.7 in Sect. 5.4), we must show that each finite automaton accepts a regular language. To do this, it suffices to provide an algorithm that converts a finite automaton to corresponding regular expression. If we try to understand Brozozowski's algebraic method, intuitively, the method takes an FA in the form of a transition diagram (a directed graph) and constructs a system of linear equations. These equations are regular expressions, with one regular expression *unknown* for each state in the DFA M, and then we solve this system of equations for R_0 where R_0 is regular expression associated with starting state q_0. These equations are in the form of sum of products, and called the *characteristic equations* of the automaton M, shown as set of Eq. (5.8). A product term is like aR_j, and, if R_j happens to be a final state, ε is also one of the product terms [2, 3].

$$
\begin{aligned}
R_1 &= a_1 R_1 + a_2 R_2 + \cdots .. \\
R_2 &= b_1 R_1 + b_2 R_2 + \cdots .. \\
R_3 &= c_1 R_1 + c_2 R_2 + \varepsilon \\
&\dots \\
R_m &= d_1 R_1 + d_2 R_2 + \varepsilon
\end{aligned}
\tag{5.8}
$$

In the above equations, $R_i = a_i RJ + \cdots + \cdot\cdot$ the a_i are ϕ if there is no transition from R_i to R_j.

These system of equations can be solved using substitution rule, except when an unknown appears on both sides of the equation. This situation occurs when there is a self-loop for state q_i. Arden's theorem is key in solving in these situations, i.e., an expression exists corresponding to a loop [1]. The substitution rules we use are those from high school. Because the set of regular languages forms a *semi-ring* (see Chap. 1), we do not have an inverse for set unions or string concatenations—operations used in construction of regular expressions/languages.

We use these set of equations to isolate R_i on the left side and successively R_i into another equation, and repeat the process until we have found R_0 with no unknown on the right-hand side.

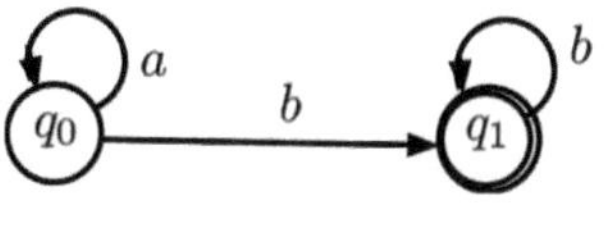

Fig. 5.22 DFA to regular expressions

Note that Brozozowsky's method is solution of linear algebra problems, somewhat similar to Gauss–Seidel method that solves linear set of equations. In addition, we have used Arden's rule to handle loops in the expressions.

Consider the following example where we use the method by Brozozowski as well as Arden's rule[5] to find out the regular expression for a simple DFA.

Example 5.3 Find the regular expression for the DFA shown in Fig. 5.22, using Brozozowski's method.

The system of equations can be represented as follows:

$$\begin{aligned} R_0 &= aR_0 + bR_1 \\ R_1 &= bR_1 + \varepsilon \\ &= b^*\varepsilon \quad \text{(using Arden's rule)} \\ &= b^*. \end{aligned}$$

Now substitute R_1 above, in first equation:

$$\begin{aligned} R_0 &= aR_0 + bb^* \\ &= a^*bb^*. \text{ (again applying Arden's rule)} \end{aligned}$$

Hence, the regular expression for the DFA shown in Fig. 5.22 is a^*bb^*, which we intuitively find as correct. □

Example 5.4 Find the regular expression for the DFA shown in Fig. 5.23, using Brozozowski's method.

The set of equations describe the ways to reach final state q from p. One can scan/generate a 0 and go to state p or one can scan/generate a 1 and go to state q. An expression "$p = 0p$" indicates a loop of 0's at p, and "$p = 1q$" indicates that with input 1 or by scanning 1 we reach from p to q. Combining these we have

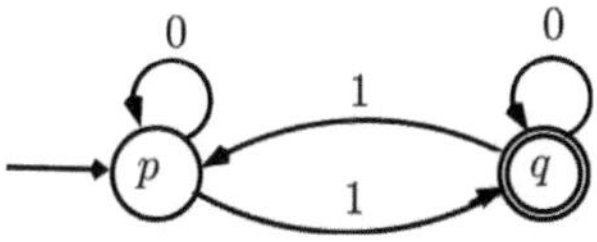

Fig. 5.23 A finite automata accepting odd 1's

[5] Arden's rule states that if there is an expression $R_1 = aR_1 + S$, then it can be replaced by an equivalent expression $R_1 = a^*S$, i.e., when R_1 exists on right-hand side, then drop R_1, replace a by *, and replace + (union) sign by "." (concatenation).

$$p = 0p + 1q. \tag{5.9}$$

From state q, one can scan/generate 1 and go to state p, or scan/generate a 0 and go to state q. In addition, since q is final state, one can do nothing and remains at q, i.e., ε keeps it in final state. This is represented by

$$q = 1p + 0q + \varepsilon. \tag{5.10}$$

Because p is initial state, we construct a regular expression with respect to p, i.e., ways of getting from the initial state p to final state q. We select a state that is not the initial state, to remove. In this case, we remove q. Before we remove q, we use *Arden*'s rule to be removed recursive reference as follows.

$$\begin{aligned} q &= 1p + 0q + \varepsilon \\ &= 0q + (1p + \varepsilon) \\ &= 0^*(1p + \varepsilon) \\ &= 0^*1p + 0^*. \end{aligned}$$

Now, we can rewrite p.

$$\begin{aligned} p &= 0p + 1q \\ &= 0p + 1(0^*1p + 0^*) \\ &= 0p + 10^*1p + 10^* \\ &= (0 + 10^*1)p + 10^*. \end{aligned}$$

Applying Arden's rule again:

$$p = (0 + 10^*1)^*10^*.$$

Hence, regular expression for the FA shown in Fig. 5.23 is $(0 + 10^*1)^*10^*$. □

The transitive closure method is clear and simple, but it will create very long regular expressions some times, while the state removal method (GNFA) is based on manual inspection, but straightforward method. The algebraic approach due to Brozozowski is elegant, generates compact regular expressions, and suited particularly for recursion-based languages.

5.6 Pumping Lemma for Regular Languages

The regular languages have infinitely many strings, which in turn consists of large number of substrings resulting from the Kleene star operations. The name regular indicates the regularity in length. This fact can be used for reasoning about the languages. The approach taken is based on the fact that long strings going through the finite-state machines cannot avoid revisiting the states. Hence, if such strings go from the start state to a final state, one can traverse a loop described by the re-visitation, arbitrary number of times. And the corresponding automaton recognizing these substrings have cycles of states visited, representing Kleene star operations in the regular expressions.

The following theorem is based on the Kleene star operations in regular expressions. When expressed rigorously, this idea forms the basis to show that certain languages are not regular, and take the curious name *Pumping Lemma* [8]. Pumping lemma is a tool to say about non-regularity in certain languages. Algorithms can be designed based on this concept to show whether any given language is not accepted by an FA. To accept such languages, we will see that corresponding FA turns out to be having infinite number of states. Then it is not a finite automaton, and hence the language is not regular.

Lemma 5.2 (Pumping Lemma) *Let Q be the set of states in a finite automata M with $|Q| = n$, L be a regular set such that $w \in L$ and $|w| \geq n$. Having these conditions, w can be considered as made of substrings xyz, where $|xy| \leq n$ (because in x and y there are unique states),*[6] *and $|y| \geq 1$, then for all $k \geq 0$, $xy^kz \in L$.*

Proof Let there be a finite automaton $M = (Q, \Sigma, \delta, q_0, F)$, and $|Q| = n$. Assume that a string $a_1a_2...a_m$, where $|w| \geq n$ is input to this FA. Due to this, the FA goes through the sequence of states $q_0, q_1, q_2, ..., q_m$. Since the number of states in this sequence, i.e., $m + 1$, is more than n (the total number of states in the FA). Hence, according to the *pigeonhole principle* there is at least one state has been visited twice. Let this state be $q_i = q_j$ in the sequence of states traversed, where $0 \leq i < j \leq m$, shown in Fig. 5.24. In the sequence of integers 0 to m, the string $a_{i+1}\ a_{i+2}...a_j$ has length of at least one. Since $0 \leq i$ and $j \leq m$, the length of this string can be maximum m. Let $x = a_1a_2...a_i$, $y = a_{i+1}a_{i+2}...a_j$, and $z = a_{j+1}a_{j+2}...a_m$.

If $q_m \in F$, then the string xyz is accepted by the FA. At the same time, another string xz is also accepted by the FA as follows:

$$\begin{aligned}
\delta^*(q_0, xz) &= \delta^*(\delta^*(q_0, x), z)\\
&= \delta^*(q_i, z)\\
&= \delta^*(q_j, z), \text{ since } q_i = q_j\\
&= q_m.
\end{aligned}$$

[6] Since in x and y path there are unique states, and $|Q| = n$, therefore the unique states in xy are not more than Q. Hence, $|xy| \leq |Q|$.

It can be easily concluded that the finite automaton M (Fig. 5.24) recognizes following strings:

1. $xyz \in L(M)$.
2. $xz \in L(M)$.

The first of above can be expressed as $xyz \in L(M)$ and can be generalized as

$$xy^k z \in L(M), \text{ for } k = 1. \tag{5.11}$$

For $k = 0$, Eq. (5.11) results to string xz. This means that a string $w = xyz$ having a substring y, if y is repeated any number of times, the total string is still be accepted by the FA. In other words, the substring enclosed between parenthesis (i.e., $y = a_{i+1}...a_j$) can be "pumped" any number of times, such that the states corresponding to the path of the substring form a loop in the transition graph, and the resulting string $w = xy^k z$, with $k \geq 0$, is still accepted by the FA. Hence, the name "pumping theorem" or "pumping lemma" is given for this conclusion. □

Since, pumping lemma is often used to prove non-linearity (proves that a language is not regular) of a language—it is called lemma and not theorem.

In general, the pumping lemma describes a property that all languages must have. More precisely it describes property of some strings belonging to regular languages. These strings have some minimum length, called pumping length. The pumping lemma states that there is some way to split $w \in L$ into three substrings, $w = xyz$ such that the middle portion y, which must not be null, can be repeated an arbitrary number of times, including zero times, yields the string w which is still in L. In addition, the pumping lemma guarantees that length of xy will be some minimum.

Example 5.5 The language $L = \{a^n b^n \mid n \geq 0\}$ is not regular. Prove this statement using pumping lemma.

Assume that L is regular and pumping lemma holds true for this. Let us consider some integers n, and let $w = a^n b^n \in L$. Using pumping lemma decompose w into xyz, such that $|xy| \leq n$, and $|y| \geq 1$, for some $k > 0$, and $y = a^k$. We note that there is $xz = a^{n-k} b^n \notin L$. Since it contradicts the assumption, L is not regular. □

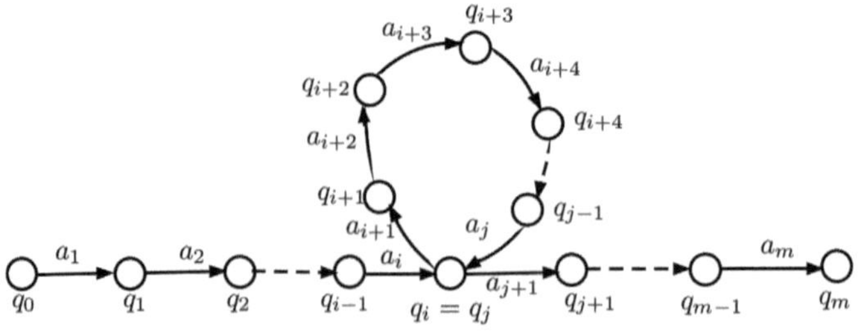

Fig. 5.24 Principle of pumping lemma

Example 5.6 Prove that language $L = \{a^n \mid n \text{ is prime}\}$ is not regular.

Let the finite automaton corresponding to language L be M, and a string w is input to M, where $w = xy^nz$. Let $x = a^p$, $y = a^q$, and $z = a^r$, where $q > 0$ and $p \geq 0$, $r \geq 0$. Now, let us apply the pumping lemma for $w = xy^kz$, for $k \geq 0$.

$$\begin{aligned} w &= xy^kz \\ &= a^p(a^q)^ka^r \\ &= a^p\ a^{kq}\ a^r \\ &= a^{p+kq+r}. \end{aligned}$$

Hence, the value $n = p + kq + r$ should be a prime number with $k \geq 0$.

We prepare a strategy to counter this, and try to show that $p + nq + r$ is not a prime, at least in one instance. Let $k = p + 2q + r + 2$. Then,

$$\begin{aligned} p + kq + r &= p + (p + 2q + r + 2)q + r \\ &= p + pq + 2q^2 + qr + 2q + r \\ &= (p + 2q + r) + q(p + 2q + r) \\ &= (1 + q)(p + 2q + r). \end{aligned}$$

Since it is factorable, $p + kq + r$ cannot be a prime. Since it contradicts the assumption, L is not regular. □

5.7 On Nonregularity of Languages

The regular languages are recognized by finite automata having finite memory in the form of states or at least the memory size is determined in the beginning and anything larger than the size of this memory cannot be stored in it. Thus, the FA cannot distinguish infinitely many strings, i.e., infinitely large number of classes of strings.

Let us think about the string $w = a^nb^n (n \geq 0)$, which is input to a finite automaton. To recognize w, the automaton must first read all a's until the boundary between a and b, and it must remember the count n of a^n, where n may be of arbitrary size. This must be followed by reading all b's. At the end, the automaton must compare and verify that count of b is equal to n. Since arbitrarily large size of n requires arbitrarily large size memory to store it, no finite automata can exist to recognize the language $L(a^nb^n)$. Hence, a^nb^n is not a regular expression.

This fact can also be proved through a different approach given in example below.

Example 5.7 Show that a^nb^n is not a regular expression.

Proof Let us first suppose that $M = (Q, \{a, b\}, \delta, q_o, F)$ be a finite automaton, which recognizes $L(a^n b^n)$. The Q is finite but n can be arbitrarily large. Therefore, according to the *pigeonhole principle*, for two substrings of different lengths a^m and a^n $(m \neq n)$, it is possible that

$$\delta^*(q_0, a^m) = q_i$$

and

$$\delta^*(q_0, a^n) = q_i.$$

Since M accepts $w = a^m b^n$, therefore,

$$\begin{aligned}\delta^*(q_0, a^m b^n) &= \delta^*(\delta^*(q_0, a^m), b^n)\\ &= \delta^*(q_i, b^n)\\ &= q_f \in F.\end{aligned}$$

Similarly,

$$\begin{aligned}\delta^*(q_0, a^n b^n) &= \delta^*(\delta^*(q_0, a^n), b^n)\\ &= \delta^*(q_i, b^n)\\ &= q_f \in F.\end{aligned}$$

This shows that in addition to $a^n b^n$, the M also accepts $a^m b^n$, for $m \neq n$. And for $m \neq n$, there can be infinitely large number of m values for a given n. Hence, it will accept infinitely large number of languages, where $m \neq n$. This is in contradiction to the assumption that M accepts only $a^n b^n$. Therefore, no finite automata can exist which recognizes $a^n b^n$. Hence, $a^n b^n$ is not a regular expression. □

Significance of $a^n b^n$

The expression $a^n b^n$ is not regular, but has its practical significance. Assume that alphabets a and b stand for starting and closing parenthesis, "{" and "}", in languages like C, C++, and Java. Thus, $a^n b^n$ can be viewed as n opening parentheses followed by n closing parentheses. These languages are more powerful because they can recognize parenthesized expressions; in addition, all the high-level programming languages recognize the balancing parentheses (or their equivalent *begin* and *end*), hence they are also more powerful than regular languages.

5.8 Myhill–Nerode Theorem and Its Applications

The pumping lemma holds to prove non-regularity of some languages. That is, for a language to be regular, it should be possible to break the input string w into xy^kz, and still satisfying the property of the given language. If it fails, then we conclude that language is non-regular. In fact, we use the pumping lemma to arrive to this failure. However, arriving to the conclusion of satisfying xy^kz is not important.[7]

The pumping lemma does not have condition to prove that the language is regular. In fact, if pumping lemma fails to prove non-regularity of a language, it does not mean the otherwise, that is, the language is regular. For example, consider the language $\{uu^Rv \mid u, v \in \{0, 1\}^+\}$, where strings over the alphabet $\{0, 1\}$ consist of non-empty even-palindrome followed by another non-empty string. This language is not regular, but can be still pumped for $w = xy^kz$, with $|w| = |uu^Rv| \geq 4$ as follows: If $|u| = 1$ then $|v| \geq 2$ and we can take y to be the first character of v. Otherwise, take y to be the first character in u and note that y^k for $k \geq 2$ starts with the non-empty palindrome yy.

The *Myhill–Nerode* (MN) theorem provides a necessary and sufficient condition for a language to be regular. Following are some definitions, having understood these, we will be equipped to make use of interesting applications of MN theorem [12].

Definition 5.4 (*Equivalence relation for DFAs*) Let M be a DFA. For strings $x, y \in \Sigma^*$, let there be $x \approx_M y$ if and only if the same state in the DFA is reachable from the initial state by reading each of the strings x and y. □

Definition 5.5 (*Equivalence classes index*) An equivalent relation '$\approx$', on a set Σ^* imposes a partition $\Sigma^*/\approx$ on Σ^*, such that elements $[x], [y] \in \Sigma^*$ are in the same part of $\Sigma^*/\approx$ if $[x] \approx [y]$. The parts of Σ^* are called equivalent classes, and we write $[x]\approx$ to denote the equivalence class $\Sigma^*/\approx_x$ to which x belongs. The index of equivalent relation $\approx$ is $|\delta/\approx|$, which is equal to number of unique equivalent classes. □

Definition 5.6 (*Canonical DFA*) $M \approx_L$ is canonical DFA for language L, with finite index $\approx_L$, defined as follows:

The canonical DFA $M_L = (Q_L, \Sigma, q_{0L}, \delta_L, F_L)$ for L is defined as follows:

- $Q_L = \{[x] \mid x \in \Sigma^*\}$, (the finite set of $\approx_L$-classes),
- $q_{0L} = \varepsilon$,
- $\delta_L([x], a) = [xa]$, and
- $F_L = \{[x] \mid x \in L\}$. □

Let us consider the following two languages over the alphabet $\Sigma = \{a, b\}$, as examples.

---

[7] Because it may happen that for some string w, it may be breakable into xy^kz, but that does not mean all the strings are breakable. But, if we fail to break w into xy^kz or the xy^kz does not satisfy the property of the language, then it is a case of contradiction, and one contradiction is enough to show the non-regularity!

- The language $L_1 = \{a^n b^n \mid n \geq 1\}$ consists of strings which have sequence of a's and it is followed with equal number of b's.
- $L_2 = \{w \mid w \in (a+b)^* b(a+b)\}$ is strings of a's and b's with last but one symbol is b.

We start with following basic notation.

Considering language L_1 defined above, let $x = a$ and $y = aa$ are distinguishable with respect to L_1, because if we take $z = b$, then $xz = ab \in L_1$ while $yz = aab \notin L_1$. Similarly, strings $x = aa$ and $y = ab$ are distinguishable with respect to L_2 because $aaa \notin L_2$ while $aba \in L_2$, where $z = a$.

Definition 5.7 (*Distinguishable set of strings*) Let L be a language. A set of strings $\{x_1, x_2, ..., x_k\}$ is distinguishable if for every two strings x_i, x_j out of these, x_i is distinguishable from x_j. □

For example, the set of strings $\{a, aa, aaa\}$ are distinguishable with respect to language $\{a^n b^n \mid n \geq 1\}$.

Consider the set of strings $\{aa, ab, ba, bb\}$, and language $L_2 = \{w \mid w \in (a+b)^* b(a+b)\}$. Let $x = aa$, $y = ab$, and $z = a$. Then, $xz = aaa \notin L_2$ and $yz = aba \in L_2$. Similarly, for $x = ba$, $y = ab$, $z = b$, there is $xz = bab \notin L2$, $yz = abb \in L_2$. We can try any pair in these for strings, we will find that they will be distinguishable for z as a and b. That shows that there can be only four state minimal DFA for L_2.

Theorem 5.8 *Let L be a language over* Σ. *If* Σ^* *has infinitely many equivalence classes with respect to* $\approx_L$, *then L is not regular. Otherwise, L can be recognized by a DFA whose number of states is equal to number of equivalence classes in* Σ^* *with respect to* $\approx_L$.

Proof If there are infinitely many classes, then it follows Lemma 4.4 in Sect. 4.6 and no DFA can recognize L, and hence L is not regular.

Suppose that there is a finite number of equivalence classes in Σ^*. We can define an automaton $M = (Q, \Sigma, \delta, q_0, F)$ for language L as follows that has a state for each equivalence class. The start state is the class $[\varepsilon]$ and every state $[x]$ for $x \in L$ is a final state.

Let us define the transition function as follows. From state $[x]$ after a character $a \in \Sigma$ is read, the automaton moves into state $[xa]$. If states $x \approx_L y$ then the states $[x]$ and $[y]$ are same, so we need to show that $[xa]$ and $[ya]$ are also same. Also, $[xaz]$ and $[yaz]$ are same. In other words, $xaz \in L$ iff $yaz \in L$. This is true because x and y are indistinguishable, and appending az to each makes $yaz \in L$ iff $xaz \in L$. Since we have defined the automaton, with $q_0 = [\varepsilon]$, the δ is defined, F is defined, and it has finite number of states and that are equal to number of equivalence classes (with respect to $\approx_L$). Hence, it proves the theorem. □

Theorem 5.9 (Myhill–Nerode theorem Part-I) *If index of a language L is k, then there is a k-state DFA M such that* $L(M) = L$. *In other words, every language with finite index is regular.*

Proof Let $L \subseteq \Sigma^*$ be a language with index k. Define the following finite automaton $M = (Q, \Sigma, \delta, q_0, F)$ whose states are the L-equivalence classes, and defined as

$$Q = \{[x] \approx_L \mid [x] \subseteq \Sigma^*\},$$
$$\delta \in \delta(p, a) \text{ iff there exists a word } x \in p \text{ such that } xa \in q,$$
$$q_0 = [\varepsilon] \approx_L,$$
$$q \in F \text{ iff there exists a word } x \in q \text{ such that } x \in L.$$

Since for every language L with finite index k there exist a finite automaton of k-state DFA that accepted it, the language L is regular. This proves the part-I of the theorem. □

From the part-I of Myhill–Nerode theorem it follows that for all the states $q \in Q$ either $q \cap L = \phi$ or $q \subseteq L$ (when $|F| \geq 1$). Therefore, for every word $x \in \Sigma^*$, after reading input x, the DFA M ends up in the state $[x] \approx_L$, which accepts if $x \in L$ and rejects if $x \notin L$.

For the $\approx_L$ classes of $[x]$ we write $[x]_L$ or just $[x]$. In the DFA M that recognizes L, we observe that if both x and y lead to the same state, then $x \approx_L y$. This holds because from $\delta(q_0, x) = \delta(q_0, y)$ it implies $\delta(q_0, xz) = \delta(q_0, yz)$ and consequently $xz \in L \Leftrightarrow yz \in L$. This means that there can be at most that many $\approx_L$ classes as there are states [7].

Theorem 5.10 (Myhill–Nerode theorem Part-II) *For every k-state DFA M, index of $L(M)$ is at most k.*

Proof To show this, consider a DFA M and the alphabet of language of DFA as Σ. For two words $x, y \in \Sigma^*$, let $x \approx_M y$ iff after reading input x, the DFA M ends up in the same state as after reading input y. The number of $\approx_M$ equivalence classes is equal to the number of states of M, say k. If $x \approx_M y$, then $x \approx_{L(M)} y$, because input xz and yz always lead to the same state. Hence, there cannot be more $\approx_{L(M)}$ equivalence classes than there are $\approx_M$ equivalence classes. In other words, the index of $L(M)$ is at most k. This proves the part-II of theorem. □

The part-II of this theorem can be used to show that a language is non-regular: it suffices to argue that its index is ∞. This corollary is frequently used to show that a language is non-regular.

Therefore, the part-II can be strengthened to show that if M is reduced (i.e., $M = M/\approx$), then the index of $L(M)$ is always k.

The MN theorem states that a language L over alphabet Σ is regular iff it is union of some of the *equivalent classes* of an equivalent relation $\approx$ on Σ^*, and the relation is right invariant, and has finite index.

Example 5.8 Using MN theorem show that $L = \{ww \mid w \in \{a, b\}^*\}$ is non-regular.

Consider the set of strings $S = \{a^n \mid n \geq 0\}$ as an infinite set over the alphabet $\{a, b\}$. S can be shown to be pair-wise distinguishable with respect to L as follows. Let a^k and a^m be arbitrary strings of S, where k and m are positive integers and $k \neq m$. Select ba^kb string to be appended to a^k and a^m, respectively. As a result we get $a^kba^kb \in L$ but $a^mba^kb \notin L$. Hence a^k and a^m are distinguishable with respect to L.

Since a^k and a^m are arbitrary strings of S, and S satisfies the condition of MN theorem, L is non-regular. □

Remark 5.1 If a DFA M recognizes the language L, then

$$\text{number of } \approx_L \text{ classes} \leq \text{number of } M\text{-states}. \tag{5.12}$$

It follows that if L is regular, then $\approx_L$ has finite *index*, or partition size, i.e., there are only finitely many equivalent classes.

Theorem 5.11 *Language L over alphabet Σ is regular if and only if the set of equivalence classes of $\approx_L$ is finite.*

Proof (Necessity Condition) Let us assume that L is regular and $x, y \in \Sigma^*$ are distinguishable with respect to L. Then there is a string $z \in \Sigma^*$ such that $xz \in L$ and $yz \notin L$ (or vice versa). This means that if x and y are read by a DFA that recognizes L, the DFA reaches to different states. Alternatively, if there are three strings that are distinguished with respect to L, then DFA reaches to three different states after reading these strings.

This idea can be extended to infinite strings. If there are infinitely many different strings, which are distinguished with respect to L, then the corresponding DFA must have infinitely many states, which is not possible, because a DFA can have only finite number of states. From this, we conclude that if there are infinitely large number of stings, which are pair-wise distinguishable with respect to language L, then this language is not regular. Thus, if L is regular then there are only finitely many classes only.

Sufficiency Condition: On the contrary, if number of classes of strings that are pair-wise indistinguishable with respect to a language L are finite, then language L is regular.

To prove this statement, let $[x]$ be a class of strings that are indistinguishable from a string x with respect to L. We will show that a DFA that accepts L can be constructed using these equivalent classes.

Let n be a number of distinct equivalent classes (i.e., index) of $\approx_L$, and let $[x_0], [x_1], \ldots, [x_{n-1}]$ be representations of those distinct equivalent classes. Then we construct the DFA $M = (Q, \Sigma, \delta, q_0, F)$ as follows:

$$Q = \{[x_0], [x_1], \ldots, [x_{n-1}]\},$$
$$s = q_0 = [x_0], \text{ where } [x_0] = [\varepsilon],$$

$$F = \{[x_i] \mid x_i \in L\},$$
$$\delta([x_i], a) = [x_i a] \text{ for all } a \in \Sigma.$$

Now we want to show that this machine is in fact a DFA and it accepts the language L. First, note that for every string x in $[x_i]$, the xa is in exactly one equivalent class, namely, $[x_i a]$. Because, for $x, y \in [x_i]$, if xa and ya are in different classes then x and y are distinguishable with respect to L, making them belong to different $[x_i]$'s.

Next, we want to show that this DFA accepts L. For this, first note that if $x_i \in L$, then every string in $[x_i]$ is also in L. We then show that for every string w, $\delta^*([x_0], w) = [x_k]$, where $[x_k]$ is the equivalence class to which w belongs. Now we proceed for proof based on induction on w.

Basis step: $w = \varepsilon$. $\delta^*([x_0], \varepsilon) = \delta([x_0], \varepsilon)$ by the definition of δ^* for DFA. Then by the definition of δ, we have $(\delta[x_0], \varepsilon) = [x_0]$. Hence $\delta^*([x_0], \varepsilon) = [x_0]$.

Inductive step: Let induction hypothesis is $\delta^*([x_0], x) = [x_k]$, where $x \in [x_k]$. Then for every $a \in \Sigma$, $\delta^*([x_0], xa) = \delta(\delta^*([x_0], x), a)$ by the definition of δ^*. But, $\delta^*([x_0], x) = [x_k]$ by the induction hypothesis. Hence, $\delta(\delta^*([x_0], x), a) = \delta([x_k], a) = [x_k a]$. Hence $\delta^*([x_0], xa) = [x_k a]$.

This proves that for every string $w \in \Sigma^*$, $\delta^*([x_0], w) = [x_k]$, where $w \in [x_k]$. Since $[x_k] \in F$, if a string in $[x_k]$ is in L, this means that DFA accepts L. □

Example 5.9 Using MN theorem show that language $\{a^n b^n \mid n \geq 1\}$ is non-regular.

Through MN theorem we know that $x \approx y$ if this relation is right invariant, i.e., for some $z \in \Sigma^*$, there is $xz \approx yz$, also x is in the class $[x]$, and such classes are finite. Let $x, y \in \{a^1, a^2, ..., a^k\}$. Let us imagine that some $x_i \approx x_j$ for $i \neq j$, then $x_j z \approx x_j z$ is not true, for $z = b^k$, irrespective of value of k. This means $x_i \approx x_j$ holds only when $i = j$. Therefore, there will be infinite number of classes for $x_i \approx x_j$. Hence, as per MN theorem we conclude that this language is non-regular. □

5.9 Regular Expression to DFA Using MN

The Myhill–Nerode (MN) theorem states that L is regular if and only if $\approx_L$ has a finite number of equivalence classes, and in addition, the number of states in the smallest DFA recognizing L is equal to the number of equivalence classes in $\approx_L$. This implies that there is a unique DFA with minimum number of states. The intuition is that, if such a minimal automaton is obtained, then any strings x and y that drive the automaton into the same state will be in the same equivalence class.

Using this approach, the Myhill–Nerode theorem may be used to show that a language L is regular by proving that number of equivalence classes (i.e., *index*) of L is finite. This may be done by exhaustive case analysis in which, beginning from empty string, distinguishing extensions are used until no more can be found [9].

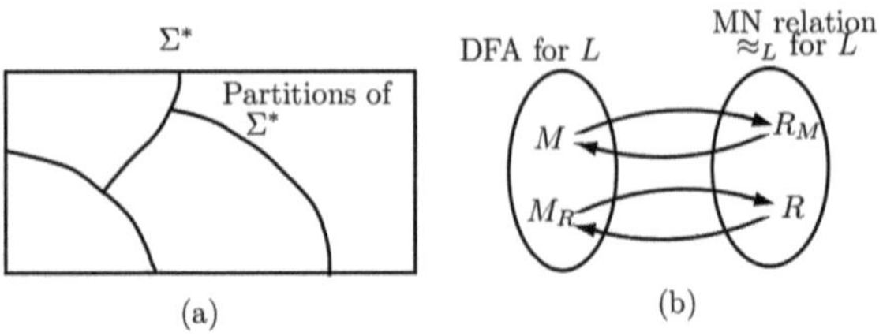

Fig. 5.25 **a** Partitions of Σ^* due to $\approx_L$ relation. **b** DFA for L and MN relation for L have bijection

Theorem 5.12 (Regularity proof) *L is regular iff L is of finite index.*[8]

Proof An MN relation ($\approx$) for L (let us call it R) is an equivalent relation (Fig. 5.25a) on Σ^* satisfying:

1. $\approx_R$ is right invariant, i.e., $x \approx y \Rightarrow xa \approx ya$ for each $a \in \Sigma^*$.
2. $\approx_R$ refines $\approx_L$: for any $x, y \in \Sigma^*$, $x \approx y \Rightarrow x \in L \Leftrightarrow y \in L$.
3. The DFA for L and MN relation for L are in one-to-one correspondence (Fig. 5.25b).

   That is, $M \mapsto R_M$ and $R \mapsto M_R$ are inverses of each other. □

Given the MN relation R, we note that there is a natural one-to-one correspondence (up to isomorphism of automata) between:

- DFA for R with input alphabet Σ and with no inaccessible states.
- Myhill–Nerode relation R on Σ^*.

This is interesting, because it says we can deal with regular sets and finite automata in terms of few simple and purely algebraic properties.

Example 5.10 Describe the equivalence classes of $\approx_L$ for the language $L \subseteq \{a, b\}^*$ comprising the strings in which second last character is b.

We construct the FA for L by intuition as shown in Fig. 5.26a. The minimum string w it accepts is $b(a + b)$. That means, q_0 receives ε input, q_1 should receive b, q_2 should receive ba, and q_3 as bb. Both the q_2 and q_3 should be accepting states, since second last character, when started from q_0, for both of them is b. The remaining edges we construct with the restriction that from each state there are two outgoing edges, one for a and other for b, and the complete automaton should not give any violation of the given rule, and at the same time should accept only the string of language L and no other.
The $\approx_L$ equivalence classes, based of this automaton, are shown in Fig. 5.26b. □

The strings after "." in each block of Fig. 5.26b indicates the iteration using Kleene star operation, e.g., at state q_1 there is loop $(ab)^*$, which is shown by $*$, i.e., Kleene star as ab.

Theorem 5.13 *Prove that index of an equivalence relation is always finite.*

---

[8] Index of a regular language is equal to number of equivalence classes in that language.

Fig. 5.26 **a** FA for $L = \{w \mid w \in \{a, b\}^*$, with second last character as $b\}$. **b** $\approx_L$ for $L = \{w \mid w \in \{a, b\}^*$, with second last character as $b\}$

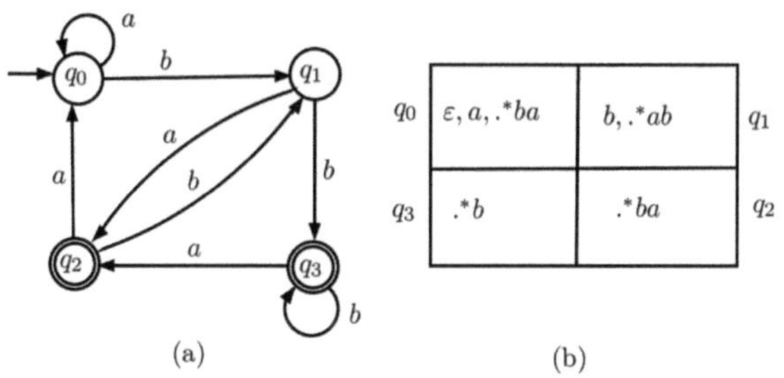

Proof Take any input x. We define a function f_x from the set Q of states to power set $P(Q)$, namely, for any $q \in Q$:

$$f_x(q) = \{q' \mid \text{input } x \text{ transform } q \text{ to } q'\}.$$

Clearly, the number of functions from any set S to its power set $P(S)$ is finite[9]—say there are k such functions. By the definition of $\approx$ ($\approx_D$ or $\approx_L$), we note that for all x and y, the string x is equivalent to y if and only if $f_x = f_y$. Hence, the number of equivalence classes do not exceed to k. Hence, $\approx$ is finite. □

Theorem 5.14 *Prove that for every k-state DFA M, index of L(M) is at most k.*

Proof To prove this, let there is a DFA M over Σ. For $x, y \in \Sigma^*$, let $x \approx_M y$ iff after reading input x, the DFA M ends up in the same state as after reading input y.

As per MN theorem, the number of $\approx_M$ equivalence classes is equal to the number of states of M, say k. If $x \approx_M y$, then $x \approx_{L(M)} y$, because inputs xz and yz always lead to the same state. Hence, there can be no more than $\approx_{L(M)}$ classes as there are $\approx_M$ equivalence classes. That is, index of $L(M)$ is at the most k. In fact, if M is minimized (i.e., $M = M/\approx$), then index of $L(M)$ is exactly k. This proves the theorem. □

Example 5.11 Find $\approx_L$ for the language $L = a(bb)^*$, and construct the finite automaton based on that.

For $w = \varepsilon$, $aw = a \in L$, but $bw = b \notin L$. Then $a, abb, abbbb, \ldots$ are equivalent. Consequently, ε, a, b, ab are pair-wise not equivalent.

To map this automaton to a canonical DFA, we choose the following *isomorphism:*

$$q_0 \mapsto [\varepsilon],$$
$$q_1 \mapsto [a] = [abb],$$
$$q_2 \mapsto [ab] = [abbb],$$
$$q_3 \mapsto [b] = [ba] = [bb].$$

[9] The functions are sets of mappings, and possible mappings can be only finite for P to be finite.

Figure 5.27 shows the automaton accepting language L; q_3 is dead state. Due to loops in the transition diagram, the size of equivalence classes corresponding to states q_1, q_2, and q_3 is infinite. □

5.10 Summary

A language is regular if and only if it is accepted by an FA.

The regular expressions have number of applications: these include lexical analysis in compilers, pattern recognition, and pattern matching.

The regular languages are closed under the operations of: union, concatenation, Kleene star, intersection, and inversion. Based on these rules, given a regular expression one can always find an FA that accepts it.

The GNFA (generalized nondeterministic finite automata) are the FA, which accept string patterns, and have only one start and one accept state. The concept of GNFA is used to obtain the corresponding regular expression for a given FA.

It is also possible to obtain a regular expression, for any given DFA, using *Brozozowski's* algebraic method that is based on solution of a set of simultaneous linear equations, equal to the number of states in FA. A loop on a state can be resolved using *Arden's rule*.

One method to obtain a regular expression for a DFA is using the *transitive closure* method, this is simple, but builds complex regular expressions, to be simplified later.

The Kleene star properties of regular languages can be used to test non-regularity of languages. The pumping lemma is based on the concept of kleene star properties of regular languages, and states that if a language string w is expressed as xy^kz for $k \geq 0$, and we fail to generate a string w, i.e., it does not satisfy the language criteria for some value of k, then the language is not regular.

However, the pumping lemma cannot be used to test regularity of languages.

The pumping lemma holds for some non-regular languages only and does not provide sufficient condition to prove that a language is regular. In fact, if pumping lemma fails to prove non-regularity of a language, it does not mean that the language is regular.

Fig. 5.27 DFA for regular expression $a(bb)^*$

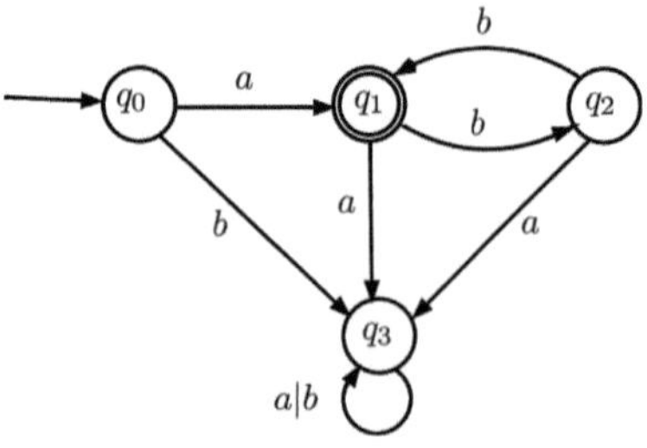

The Myhill–Nerode theorem provides a necessary and sufficient condition for a language to be regular.

The parts I and II of *Myhill–Nerode* theorem are the statements: if index of a language L is k, then there is a k-state DFA M such that $L(M) = L$, i.e., every language with finite index is regular. And other is for every k-state DFA M, index of $L(M)$ is at most k, i.e., has a finite DFA.

On the contrary if it is found that numbers of equivalence relations $x \approx_L y$ for a language are infinite, the language is non-regular.

Self Review Questions

1. What is complement of an automaton?
2. How do you convert regex into FA?
3. How do you convert FA into regex?
4. Pumping lemma can be applied only to infinite languages (True/False).
5. Classify following into regular and non-regular languages:

   a. Set of tokens in high-level languages.
   b. Set of expressions in high-level languages.
   c. The word of English dictionary.

6. A set of all the subsets of an infinite Regular Language is Regular (True/False).
7. Every finite subset of a Regular Language is Regular (True/False).
8. Explain the role of different ε-transitions in Fig. 5.6.
9. Pumping lemma is only sufficient for testing non-regularity of a language (True/False).
10. Can we apply the pumping lemma for finite regular languages?
11. Are the regular languages closed under these operations?

    a. Infinite union.
    b. Infinite concatenation.
    c. Difference.
    d. Symmetric difference.
    e. Complementation.

12. Give any three examples of non-regular languages.
13. Myhill–Nerode theorem can be used to test regularity as well as non-regularity of a language (True/False).
14. How many equivalence classes are there in the language $\{a^n b^n \mid n \geq 0\}$?

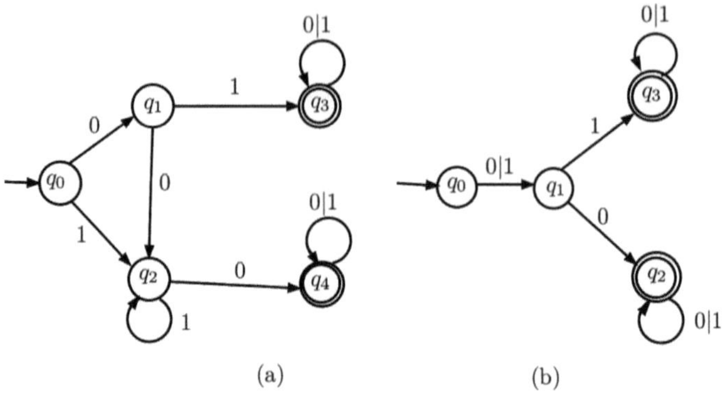

Fig. 5.28 **a** FA-1. **b** FA-2

Exercises

A. Concepts based Problems

Note: The $*$ marked exercises are provided with solutions at the end of this book.

1. Give a brief comparison of different methods used for DFA-to-regular expression conversion.
2. What are the applications of Myhill–Nerode theorem?
3. Find out the regular expressions of the finite automata shown in Fig. 5.28a and b, using state removal method.
4. Find out the regular expressions using Brozozowski's algebraic method for following:

   a. DFAs shown in Fig. 5.29a and b.
   b. DFAs shown in Fig. 5.30a–c.

5. How the Kleene star properties of regular languages are useful?

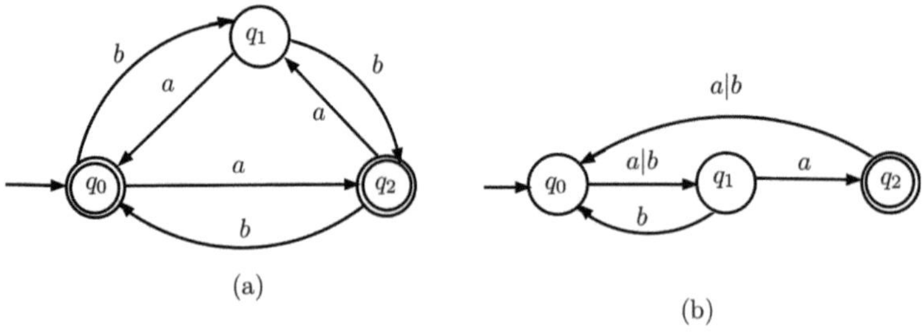

Fig. 5.29 (a) DFA with start state also as accepting state (b) DFA with unique start and accepting states

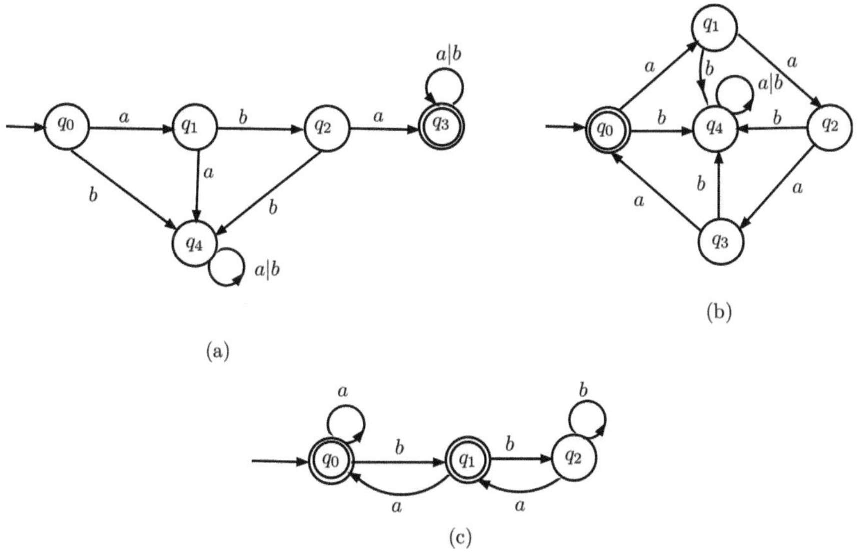

Fig. 5.30 DFA: (a) with two dead states, (b) with no dead state, (c) with more than one accepting states

Fig. 5.31 A finite automaton

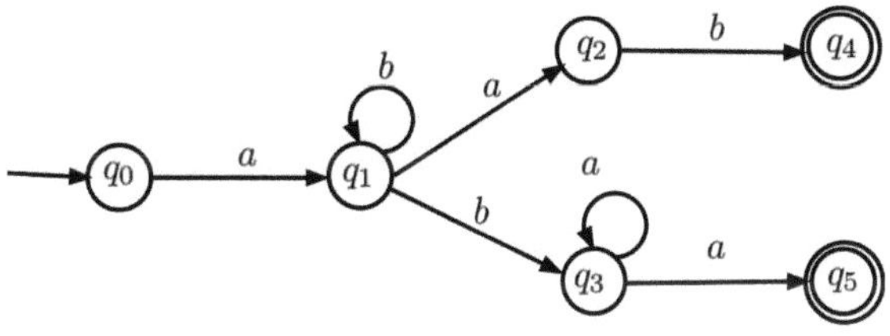

Fig. 5.32 DFA

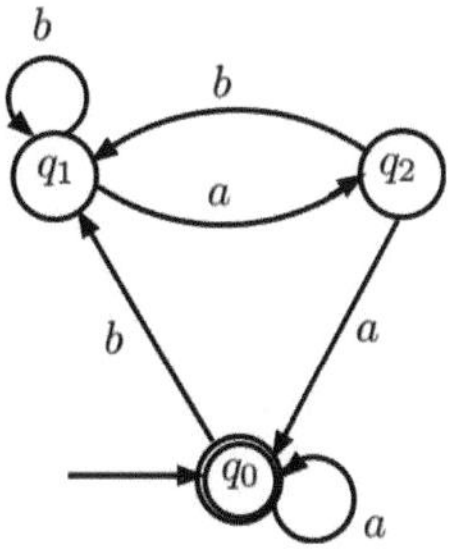

6. * Find the regular expression for the automaton shown in Fig. 5.31 using *state removal method.*
7. * Find the regular expression for DFA shown in Fig. 5.32, using Brozozowski's method.
8. List all the equivalence classes of language $\{w = ab^n c \mid n \geq 0\}$.

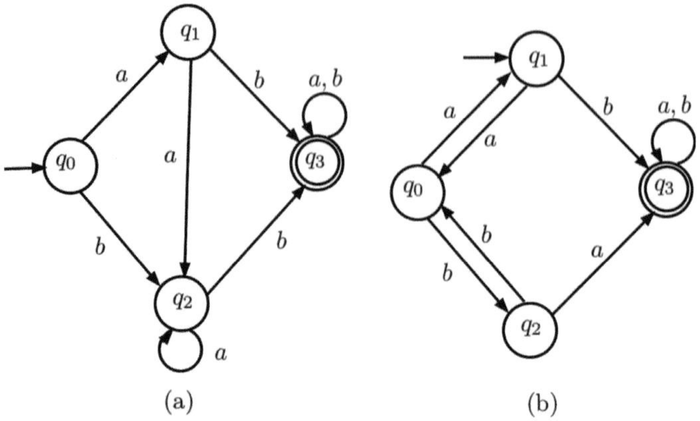

Fig. 5.33 DFA: (a) with accepting state as dead state, (b) with all states having infinite loops

Fig. 5.34 DFA: (a) with three states as final, (b) two states as final, (c) with an unreachable state

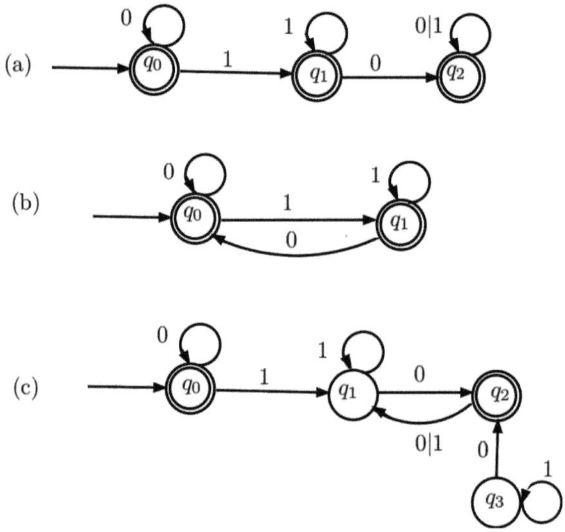

B. Analysis-based Problems

9. Describe the DFA and languages accepted by the DFAs shown in Fig. 5.33a and b.
10. Describe the languages are accepted by the automata shown in Fig. 5.34a–c.
11. What is complexity of union operation of two regular languages?
12. Justify each, whether each of the following statements are True or False.

    a. If L is regular, then $\{xy\}$ is regular, where $x, y \in L$.
    b. If L is regular, then $\{y\}$ is regular, where $y = x^R$ and $x \in L$.
    c. If L is regular, then L_1 is also regular for $L_1 \subseteq L$.

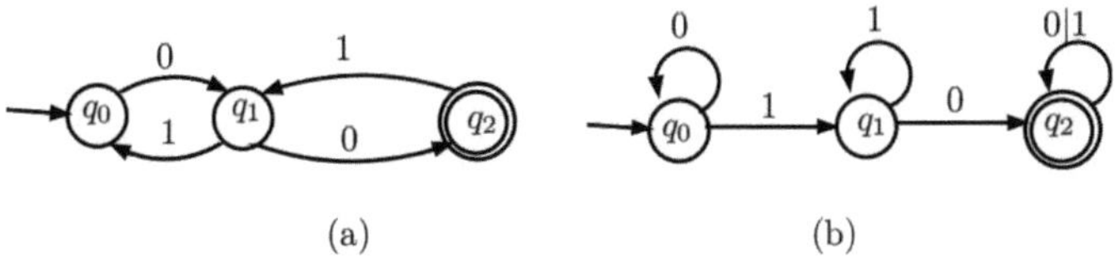

Fig. 5.35 **a** FA-1. **b** FA-2

13. Find out the True and False statements in the following:

    a. If $L_1 \cup L_2$ is regular and L_1 is regular, then L_2 is regular.
    b. If $L_1 \cup L_2$ is regular and L_1 is finite, then L_2 is regular.
    c. If $L_1 \cup L_2$ is regular and $|L_1| = 1$, then L_2 is regular.
    d. If $L_1 \cup L_2$ is regular and L_1 is finite, then L_2 is regular.
    e. If $L_1 L_2$ is regular and L_1 is regular, then L_2 is regular.
    f. If L_1^* is regular, then L_1 is regular.

14. Use pumping lemma/Myhill–Nerode theorem to show that following languages are not regular:

    a. $\{ww^R \mid w \in (a+b)^*\}$.
    b. $\{ww \mid w \in (0+1)^*\}$.
    c. $\{a^n \mid n = 2^k, \text{ for some } k \geq 0\}$.
    d. $\{w \mid w \text{ is a palindrome string}\}$.
    e. $\{a^{n!} \mid n \geq 1\}$.

15. Find out the equivalence classes, index of the language, and DFA, if exists, for each of the following languages, for $\Sigma = \{a, b\}$:

    a. $L_1 = \Sigma^* a \Sigma$.
    b. $L_2 = \{a^n b^n \mid n \geq 0\}$.

16. * For $L = \{a, b\}^* abb \{a, b\}^*$, find out the $\approx_L$-classes.
17. * Given the language L denoted by regular expression $((a^*b + \varepsilon)a)^*$, compute the regular expression that denotes $\overline{L}$.
18. Let L_1 is language accepted by an automata-1 (Fig. 5.35a) and L_2 be the language accepted by the automata-2 (Fig. 5.35b). Construct an NFAs that accepts the following languages:

    a. $L_1 \cup L_2$.
    b. $L_1 L_2$.
    c. L_1^*.

C. Proof-based Problems

19. Given two alphabet sets Σ_1 and Σ_2, and a string homomorphism from Σ_1^* to Σ_2^* under the operation of *string correlation*. If h is this homomorphism then show that

$$h(\varepsilon) = \varepsilon, \text{ and,}$$
$$h(uv) = h(u)h(v), \text{ where } u, v \in \Sigma_1^*.$$

That is, language of concatenation of two strings in Σ_1 is equal to concatenation of languages in Σ_2.

20. If $L_1 \subseteq \Sigma_1^*$ is regular, show that $L_2 = \{h(w) \mid w \in \Sigma_2^*\}$ is regular, where $L_2 \subseteq \Sigma_2^*$, given that $h(w)$ is homomorphic image of L_1 in L_2.
21. Show that if L is regular language then $L^{\mathbb{N}}$ is also regular language, for $\mathbb{N} \geq 0$.
22. If r_1, r_2, and r_3 are three regular expressions show that language corresponding to regular expression $r_1(r_2 + r_3)$ is same as that of $r_1r_2 + r_1r_3$.
23. Let L_1 be a regular language, and $L_2 = \{ww \mid w \in L_1\}$ is language consisting doubled strings of L_1. Is L_2 necessarily regular?
24. * Using pumping lemma, show that $L = \{a^{n^2} \mid n \text{ is integer, and } n \geq 1\}$ is not regular.
25. In case of the following, determine if the set is regular. If not, prove that it is not using pumping lemma.

    a. $\{\{ab\}^n \mid n \geq 1\}$.
    b. $\{a^{2n} \mid n \geq 1\}$.
    c. $\{w \in \{a, b\}^* \mid w$ contains equal number of a's and b's $\}$.

26. Prove that, if words in finite number are added into a regular language, the languages still remain regular.
27. * Show that any language of binary sequences divisible by 3 is regular.
28. Prove that if L is non-regular then LL is also non-regular.
29. * For $\Sigma = \{a, b\}$ and given that $a^n b^n$ is not regular, show that a language $L = \{w \mid w \text{ has equal number of } a's \text{ and } b's\}$ is not regular.
30. Prove that if words in finite number are subtracted from a regular language, it still remains regular.
31. Show that a DFA $M = (Q, \Sigma, \delta, q_0, F)$ accepts an infinite language if and only if it accepts a string w, such that $|w| \geq |Q|$.
32. * Are the class of regular languages closed under the operation of infinite union?
33. Are the class of regular languages closed under the operation of infinite intersection? (Hint: Not closed).
34. Prove that set of palindromes over $\{a, b\}$ is not regular. (Hint: Not closed, since it is not possible to satisfy pumping lemma on $\{ww^R\}$.
35. * Show that the set $R = \{a^n b^n \mid n \geq 0\}$ is non-regular using MN theorem.
36. Prove that if L is non-regular then LL is also non-regular.
37. * Show that $L = \{ww \mid w \in \{0, 1\}^*\}$ is not regular}.

D. Multiple choice Questions

38. Which of the following are regular sets?

I. $\{a^n b^{2m} \mid n \geq 0, m \geq 0\}$.
II. $\{a^n b^m \mid n = 2m\}$.
III. $\{a^n b^m \mid n \neq m\}$.
IV. $\{xcy \mid x, y \in \{a, b\}^*\}$.
(A) I Only, (B) IV Only, (C) I and IV Only, (D) I and II Only

E. Advanced Knowledge Assessment Problems

39. Given two regular languages L_1 and L_2, give an idea to construct a DFA that recognizes both of these languages.
40. Implement Thompson's construction algorithm to convert a regular expression into a nondeterministic finite automaton (NFA).
41. Given a non-regular language, find a regular language that closely approximates it, and discuss the limitations of such approximations.

References

1. Arden DN (1960) Delayed logic and finite state machines. Theory of computing machine design. University of Michigan Press, Ann Arbor, MI, pp 1–35
2. Berry G, Sethi R (1986) From regular expression to deterministic finite automata. Theor Comput Sci 48:117–126, North Holland
3. Brozozowski JA (1964) Derivatives of regular expressions. J ACM 11(4):481–494
4. Chowdhary KR (2015) Fundamentals of discrete mathematical structures, Chapter 10, 2015. PHI Learning Pvt, Ltd
5. Chowdhary KR (2016) Regular languages and their properties. http://www.krchowdhary.com/toc/6-regular-lang.pdf. Cited 03 Aug 2022
6. Ernst L (1980) Constructing a finite automaton for a given regular expression. SIGACT news, Fall, pp 81–87
7. Hogberg J, Larsson L (2020) DFA minimisation using the Myhill-Nerode theorem. https://athena.nitc.ac.in/~kmurali/Courses/18TOC/myhill-nerode.pdf. Cited 31 Jan 2023
8. Jeffrey J (1978) A necessary and sufficient pumping lemma for regular languages. SIGACT News, Summer, pp 48–49
9. Khoussainov B, Nerode A (2001) Automata theory and its applications. Birkhauser Springer International Edition
10. Linz P (2006) An introduction to formal languages and automata. Jones & Bartlett Learning
11. Nagy B (2010) On the union-complexity of regular languages. In: CINTI 2010, 11th international symposium on computational intelligence and informatics, 18–20 November 2010, Budapest, Hungary
12. Nerode A (1958) Linear automaton transformations. Proc Am Math Soc 9(1958):541–544
13. Neumann C (2005) Converting deterministic finite automata to regular expressions. https://www.rose-hulman.edu/Class/csse/csse474/202030/Resources/ConvertDFSMtoRegExp.pdf

Part III
Context-Free Grammars, Languages and Pushdown Automata

This part encompasses three chapters: context-free grammars and languages, minimization and optimization of context-free grammars, often referred to as normalization, and the pushdown automata. These chapters play a pivotal role in the design, implementation, and research, related to programming languages.

Pushdown automata and context-free grammars share a profound connection. Both are adept at recognizing context-free languages, albeit through different means. Pushdown automata achieves this by accepting strings from the language, while context-free grammars generate these language strings. These chapters also delve into the normal forms of context-free grammars and their significance in complexity analysis, proof techniques, and the design of essential tools like translators, such as compilers.

Context-free grammars (CFGs) and languages (CFLs) find wide-ranging applications in syntactical representation, syntax analysis, and the translation of programming languages. Furthermore, they have important applications in various domains such as natural language processing, document analysis, compiler optimization, and code validation and verification. In the present era, CFGs and CFLs are extensively employed in artificial intelligence, automated reasoning, and language modeling, highlighting their enduring relevance and utility.

Pushdown automata (PDA) is a tool that recognizes all the high-level languages, called context-free languages. Though human languages or natural languages, like English (a context-sensitive language), have no well-developed theory like for computer languages, the PDA is also a tool for recognition of these languages. For true conceptualization of PDA, its simulation has been demonstrated through a program that recognizes the language of balanced parenthesis (page no. 297).

PDA is used for parsing of context-free languages. Looking to the sudden surge of research in NLP and related fields, theory of parsers is covered in breadth and depth, which includes basic top-down and bottom-up parsing, more advanced grammars, like *LL(k)* and *LR(k)*, and their parsers. Looking at complexity of modern parsers, the topics like parallel parsing and parallel lexical analysis have also been introduced.

All these chapters are provided with self-review questions, categorized exercises, and solutions to selected problems.

Chapter 6
Context-Free Grammars and Languages

Abstract The largest number of languages we study and are also in practice are context-free languages (CFLs), and the corresponding grammars are the context-free grammars (CFGs). All the high-level computer languages fall in this class. Language processing, e.g., language translation, parsing, ambiguities, and disambiguation, is immensely concerned to the study of context-free languages and grammars. This chapter is concerned with above areas. It starts with regular languages and grammars, their relation to CFLs and CFGs, left- and right-linear grammars. This is followed with closure properties of CFLs and their proofs, derivations/parsing of arithmetic expressions, and parsing of simple natural language sentences. Ambiguities in languages, their types and challenges, and disambiguation methods are presented with their theory and worked examples. The invertible grammar with its significance, and decidable properties of CFLs are also introduced. The chapter concludes with advanced grammar—the operator precedence grammar, summary, self-review questions, and number of exercises at end.

Keywords Context-free languages · Context-free grammars · Regular versus context-free grammars · Parsing · Syntax-trees · Closure properties of CFLs · Sentential forms · Ambiguities · Disambiguations · Inherently ambiguous grammars · Operator precedence grammar

6.1 Introduction

This chapter introduces the Context-Free Grammars (CFG) and the corresponding languages, called Context-Free Languages (CFL). The context-free languages and grammars are more powerful than the regular languages and regular grammars, respectively. The CFGs have applications in describing and recognition of high-level languages, parsing, language translation, generating and recognition of context-free languages, and string processing.

Context-free grammars have been extensively used for describing the syntax of programming languages and natural languages. Parsing algorithms for context-free grammars have important role in the implementation of compilers and interpreters

K. R. Chowdhary, *Theory of Computation*,
https://doi.org/10.1007/978-981-97-6234-7_6

for programming languages, and in programs that understand or translate natural language.

To be specific, some of the applications of CFGs in computer science and related fields are as follows:

- *Programming language syntax*: Context-free grammars are extensively used in defining the syntax of programming languages. Programming language compilers and interpreters utilize CFGs to specify the rules for constructing valid programs. CFGs help in parsing and analyzing the structure of programming language statements and expressions.
- *Compiler construction*: The CFGs play a central role in the construction of compilers. They are used to define the syntax of programming languages, and parser generators such as Yacc (yet another compiler-compiler) use CFGs to automatically generate parsers. These parsers can analyze the input source code according to the language's grammar and produce a parse-tree or an abstract syntax-tree for further processing.
- *Natural language processing*: CFGs are used in natural language processing (NLP) to model the syntax of natural languages. They can describe the structure and syntax of sentences in a language, and enable tasks such as sentence parsing, part-of-speech tagging, syntactic analysis, and grammar checking in applications like machine translation, sentiment analysis, and chatbots.
- *Document analysis*: CFGs find applications in document analysis and understanding. By defining a context-free grammar for a specific type of document (e.g., XML, HTML), it becomes possible to parse and analyze the structure and content of the document. This is useful for tasks such as information extraction, document classification, and data mining.
- *Compiler optimization*: CFGs are used in compiler optimization techniques, such as loop optimization and data flow analysis. CFGs provide a representation of the control flow within a program, allowing optimizations to be applied based on the program's structure. Techniques like loop unrolling, constant propagation, and dead-code elimination leverage CFGs to improve program performance.
- *Syntax checking and validation*: CFGs are utilized in applications that involve checking the correctness and validity of structured data. For instance, XML and JSON (JavaScript Object Notation)[1] documents can be validated against a defined CFG to ensure they conform to the specified structural rules. CFG-based validation is also used in formal verification of software models and specifications.
- *Artificial intelligence and automated reasoning*: CFGs are used in automated reasoning systems, theorem provers, and expert systems. CFGs can model the rules and logic of a domain-specific knowledge base, allowing reasoning engines to analyze and deduce conclusions based on the defined rules.

[1] JSON is ideal for storing temporary data. For example, temporary data can be user-generated data, such as a submitted form on a website. JSON can also be used as a data format for any programming language to provide a high level of interoperability.

Considering natural language, e.g., English, which is understood and spoken by human beings, we become the language processors. Given the sentences, "black cat on the brown table" and "table brown the on cat black", we are able to understand the meaning of first sentence, and not so easily of the second. That way we become the language processor of the English language. Depending on whether it is constructed as per the rules of English grammar or not, we accept or reject an English language sentence. In a certain domain, when we speak a language sentence that is built-up as per the rules of its grammar, we become the language generator.

A language, whether a natural language such as English or a programming language such as *C* or Java, in an abstract sense can be considered as a set of sentences. One criteria for the *syntactic specification* of a language is invariably a finite representation for an infinite class of sentences (here we consider sentence, word, phrase at the same level). In one approach, a finite generative device (grammar) is used to describe a syntactic structure of a language. Another approach is to specify a device or algorithm for recognizing well-formed sentences, where language consists of all the sentences recognized by the device or algorithm. A third possible method for the specification of a language is to specify a set of properties and then consider a language to be a set of words obeying these properties [11].

In the case of regular languages we have studied earlier, the regular expressions are generators of these languages, and the finite automata are recognizer of these languages. Consider a regular expression $a(b + c)^*b$. The algorithm for construction of all the possible strings for this regular expression can be specified in following steps:

1. Write character a.
2. Repeat the following arbitrary number of times: Choose character b or c, write it.
3. Write b.

If this algorithm executes infinitely large number of times and the string produced every time is compared with all the previously constructed strings, if it matches any of them, the current string is discarded otherwise it is retained. The set of all these retained strings is the language generated by this regular expression. To recognize any of such string, we feed this string into the corresponding finite automaton. If it reaches to a final state then the string it recognized by the finite automaton, else not.

Definition 6.1 (*Language recognizer*) A recognizer is an algorithm, which takes an input string and either accepts or rejects it depending on whether or not the string is a sentence of the language. □

Definition 6.2 (*Parser*) A parser is a recognizer, which also outputs the set of all legal derivation-trees of a sentence string. □

The CFGs and CFLs are fundamental to computer science, because they describe structure underlying programming languages. The basic *signature* of a context-free language is *nested parentheses*. For example, nesting occurs in expression, and in many statically scoped structures in computer programs. In contrast, the basic structure of regular languages is "iteration (looping)" according to some ultimate periodicity.

Example 6.1 *C* language production rules for balanced braces.

The productions are

$$\text{Lang-C} \rightarrow main\ ()\ \{braces\}$$
$$braces \rightarrow \{braces\}\ braces \mid \varepsilon$$

□

Learning Outcomes of this Chapter

1. Derivations, derivation-trees. [Synthesis]
2. Context-free grammar. [Knowledge], [Application]
3. Closure properties of CF languages. [Evaluation]
4. Generative grammar. [Analysis]
5. Ambiguous Grammars and Languages. [Evaluate], [Synthesize]
6. Disambiguation of Grammars. [Apply]
7. Language Parsing. [Apply]

6.2 Context-Free Grammars

The context-free languages are powerful and more complex than the regular languages we studied in earlier chapters. The generators of context-free languages are context-free grammars. When compared with regular grammars and languages, the context-free grammars are based on the more complete understanding of the structure of the sentences accepted by the context-free languages.

Using a context-free grammar to help define the syntax of a programming language offers a number of advantages: (i) a grammar provides a clear and precise description of those strings that make up the programming language; (ii) a grammar is particularly useful tool for a language designer who wishes to produce a language whose syntax is clean and free of special-case anomalies; and (iii) if the grammar is carefully designed, it is possible to construct a parser for the language automatically from the grammar. This last process is compilation of compiler or compiler-compiler.

To understand the process of accepting strings of regular languages through an alternative process, i.e., other than FA, let us consider a regular expression $a(b + c)^*b$. Hence, the corresponding language is regular language. We shall show that the language strings of this regular language can also be generated using the following grammar, whose rules, called production rules, are $A \rightarrow aC|B$, which means that A can be substituted by aC or by B.

$$
\begin{aligned}
&1.\ S \rightarrow aA,\\
&2.\ A \rightarrow B \mid C,\\
&3.\ B \rightarrow bB \mid C \mid b,\\
&4.\ C \rightarrow cC \mid B \mid b,
\end{aligned}
$$

where A, B, and C are *nonterminal* symbols; S is special nonterminal symbol, called *start* symbol; and a, b, c are *terminal symbols*.

Using the production rules given above (1–4), we would like to generate a string $abcbcb$. The generation process is as follows:

$$
\begin{aligned}
S &\Rightarrow aA \text{ (rule 1)}\\
&\Rightarrow aB \text{ (rule 2)}\\
&\Rightarrow abB \text{ (rule 3)}\\
&\Rightarrow abC \text{ (rule 3)}\\
&\Rightarrow abcC \text{ (rule 4)}\\
&\Rightarrow abcB \text{ (rule 4)}\\
&\Rightarrow abcbB \text{ (rule 3)}\\
&\Rightarrow abcbC \text{ (rule 3)}\\
&\Rightarrow abcbcC \text{ (rule 4)}\\
&\Rightarrow abcbcb \text{ (rule 4)}
\end{aligned}
$$

Every regular language is CF language also. We know that a language has decided its grammar, and the productions of regular grammar satisfy the condition of productions of CF grammar also.[2] By above statement we say that $a(b+c)^*b$ is context-free language also, since its production rules (Rules 1–4) are subsets of the production rules of CF language. However, by this statement we do not say every regular language is subset of some CF language. For example, a^*b^* is regular, hence it is context free also, but it is not the subset of CF language $\{a^nb^n \mid n \geq 0\}$.

Definition 6.3 (*Phrase-structure Grammar*) If P is a set of productions $\alpha \rightarrow \beta$ such that $\alpha \in V$ is a nonterminal symbol, and β is in $(V \cup \Sigma)^*$, then the rules P are phrase-structure grammar. □

A grammar (also *generative grammar*) is defined as a 4-tuple, defined as follows.

Definition 6.4 (*Generative Grammar*) A generative grammar G is 4-tuple, (V, Σ, S, P), where S is called start symbol, V is set of nonterminal symbols (or variables), Σ is set of terminal symbols, and P is set of production rules (substitution rules). In addition, the condition $V \cap \Sigma = \phi$ holds. □

---

[2] A CFG production rule is $A \rightarrow \alpha$, where A is nonterminal and $\alpha \in (V \cup \Sigma)^*$, where V is set of nonterminals and Σ is set of terminals.

In the above-discussed example, in the substitution rules (1)–(4), the tuples of grammar G are $V = \{A, B, C, S\}$, $\Sigma = \{a, b, c\}$, P is set consisting of rules (1)–(4), and character S is start symbol.

Definition 6.5 (*Regular Grammar*) For a grammar to be regular, the production rules are of the form: $A \rightarrow aB$ or $A \rightarrow a$, where $A, B \in V$ and $a \in \Sigma$. □

Let α be string, called *sentential form*, made of nonterminals and terminals, u is string of terminals, and the uppercase letters S, A, B, C are nonterminals, where S is special nonterminal, called *start symbol*. In addition, for the production rule $A \rightarrow \beta$, the β is either a variable or a terminal followed by variable.

Making use of the production rules of regular grammar, the process of generation of the corresponding regular language can be described using Algorithm 6.1.

Algorithm 6.1 Regular grammar to regular language

```
Let S = α
while there exists a non-terminal symbol A in α do
    search the set P for A → β
    if A → β is not found then
        Declare fail and Exit
    end if
    substitute β for A in current sentence α
    (Let the new α be uβ)
    if u does not match with beginning substring of input w then
        undo the substitution A → β
        goto 3 to try other rule
    end if
end while
Print the generated string.
```

The current string in the algorithm is progressively constructed starting with S, and it is modified through the process of substitutions.

The derivatives of S (with respect to P) are called *sentential forms* and the sentential forms in w_Σ are set of the *sentences* in the *phrase-structure language*. Without restricting the set of phrase-structure languages, we shall assume that for each symbol Y of V there are strings x, z, and t such that $S \Rightarrow xYz$, $Y \Rightarrow t$, and $t \in W_\Sigma$, i.e., every symbol may be used in driving some sentence.

Definition 6.6 (*Context-free Grammar*) A context-free grammar G is a quadruple:

$$G = (V, \Sigma, S, P), \tag{6.1}$$

where

V is a finite set of variables called nonterminal symbols;
Σ is finite set of terminal symbols; V and Σ are disjoint, i.e., $V \cap \Sigma = \phi$;
S is a special variable symbol, called the start symbol;
P is finite set of production rules, where each production is of the form $A \rightarrow \alpha$, where $A \in V$ and α is a string of symbols defined as $\alpha \in (V \cup \Sigma)^*$. □

It may be noted that, first, we designated the language corresponding to $a(b+c)^*b$ as a regular language, and when it was shown to be generated by the CFG, it has been designated as CFL. This is true. In fact, all the regular languages are subset of context-free languages also, that is, every regular language is context free also, but the reverse is not necessarily true.

Explanation and nomenclature of the symbols used is as follows: During the process of generating string *abcbcb* using CFG, the symbols S, A, B, C, a, b, and c have been used. The symbols a, b, c, the final symbols in the generated string, are called *terminal symbols* or *terminals* of the CFG. The symbols S, A, B, C are encountered in the process of generation but they are not the final symbols, which are called *nonterminal* symbols or variables. Since the generation process started with the symbol S, it is called *start symbol* of the CFG, and rules (1) to (4) are called *production rules* of the CFG.

Let us consider an intermediate stage in the substitution process, and look at the current strings, say aaC and $abcbC$. The letter C present in these strings is in two different contexts. In the first case, the substring aa is present before C, which represents context of C. In the second case, the substring $abcb$ represents a different context of C. In both of these cases, C can be substituted by cC as per substitution rule (4), without any consideration for the contexts, i.e., substrings before (or after C). Therefore, the substitution process in CFG is independent of the context. Hence, the name *context-free Grammar* and corresponding language as *context-free Language*. It should be noted that this feature is due to allowing only a single variable and no other symbol on the left side of the production rules [9].

The language $L(G)$, generated by G, is called CFL (context-free language) if G can generate every string in $L(G)$.

Every regular grammar is context-free grammar and hence every regular language is also context-free languages. It is already shown that regular language corresponding to the regular expression $a(b+c)^*b$ can be generated by context-free grammar. Later on it will be shown that language $\{a^n b^n \mid n \geq 0\}$ is context-free language. However, we know that the same is not regular. The languages a^* and b^* are regular languages, and concatenation of regular languages is also regular, hence a^*b^* is also regular.

The Regular Grammars are defined by productions $A \rightarrow aB|a$, whereas context-free grammars are expressed by $A \rightarrow \alpha$, where $\alpha \in (V \cup \Sigma)^*$. Hence, all the productions of regular grammars are contained in the productions of CFGs. Hence, we can say that, regular grammars are context-free grammars.

Fig. 6.1 Every regular language is CFL

Therefore, we see that family of regular languages is proper subset of a family of context-free languages (Fig. 6.1).

It can be easily verified from the above definition that following grammars are context free.

$$
\begin{aligned}
G_1 &= (\{S\}, \{a, b\}, S, \{S \rightarrow aSb, S \rightarrow \varepsilon\}) \\
L(G_1) &= \{a^n b^n \mid n \geq 0\} \\
G_2 &= \{\{S\}, \{a, b\}, S, \{S \rightarrow aSa \mid bSb \mid \varepsilon\}\} \\
L(G_2) &= \{ww^R \mid w \in \{a, b\}^*\}.
\end{aligned}
$$

We note that, in G_1 productions are like $A \rightarrow \alpha$, where $\alpha \in (V \cup \Sigma)^*$ and $\alpha \in aA$. Similar is case with G_2.

Following are the symbols we use during the derivation process of language strings. We will follow these as standard conventions of naming symbols, in the remaining chapters.

- Uppercase English alphabets A, B, C, D, E, S represent variables; these are members of V. The symbol S implicitly represents start symbol.
- Lowercase letters a, b, c, d, e and digits (i.e., 0 ...9) to represent terminals.
- Uppercase letters X, Y, Z to represent variables as well as terminals.
- Lowercase letters u, v, w, x, y, z to represent strings of terminals.
- Greek alphabet α, β, γ represent strings as members of $(V \cup \Sigma)^*$.

6.3 Relation Between FA and Regular Grammars

It was shown in the previous section that regular expressions can be represented by context-free grammars. Also, it should be noted that the approach of representation of regular expression or regular language by CFG is a far simplistic approach, compared to FA.

Let us consider the regular expression $a^*ba^*b(a+b)^*$ and its FA shown in Fig. 6.2a, $M = (\{q_0, q_1, q_2\}, \{a, b\}, q_0, \delta, \{q_2\})$.

It can be easily verified that $w = aababab \in L(M)$.

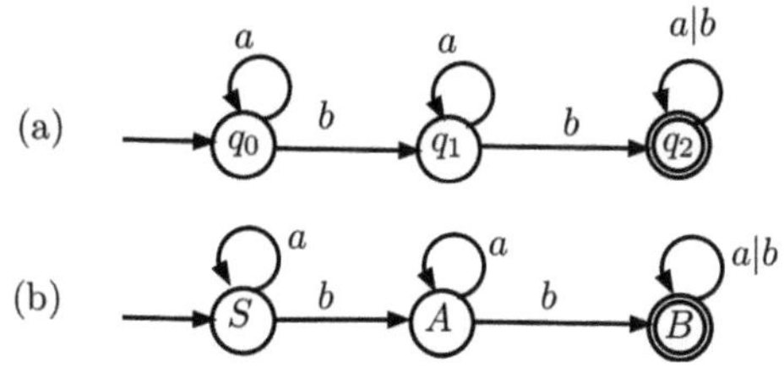

Fig. 6.2 **a** FA for regular expression $a^*ba^*b(a+b)^*$, **b** States in FA expressed by nonterminals of CFG

Let us represent the states in the above FA by variables S, A, B of CFG. The modified FA is shown in Fig. 6.2b. To generate the string *aababab* using this FA, we traverse through the states S, A, B and list the string progressively, as it gets constructed.

$$\begin{aligned} S &\Rightarrow aS \Rightarrow aaS \Rightarrow aabA \Rightarrow aabaA \\ &\Rightarrow aababB \Rightarrow aababaB \Rightarrow aabababB. \end{aligned}$$

Since S generates the final string $aabababB$, we can write $S \Rightarrow^* aabababB$. We terminate this process using the production $B \rightarrow \varepsilon$. Hence, $S \Rightarrow^* aababab$. In fact, this has been achieved through use of production rules. For example, to derive from S to aS, production rule $S \rightarrow aS$ has been used, and to derive from aaS to $aabA$, the production rule $S \rightarrow bA$ has been used. All these productions are listed below.

$$\begin{aligned} &S \rightarrow aS,\ S \rightarrow bA,\ A \rightarrow aA, \\ &A \rightarrow bB,\ B \rightarrow aB,\ B \rightarrow bB,\ B \rightarrow \varepsilon. \end{aligned}$$

These can also be written as

$$\begin{aligned} S &\rightarrow aS \mid bA \\ A &\rightarrow aA \mid bB \\ B &\rightarrow aB \mid bB \mid \varepsilon. \end{aligned}$$

Each *variable* in the production rules of CFG corresponds to a state in the FA. These productions correspond to regular grammars (Definition 6.9, Sect. 6.3). Hence, correspondence exists between various transitions in the states and production rules as follows:

$\delta(S, a) = S$ corresponds to production rule $S \rightarrow aS$;
$\delta(S, b) = A$ corresponds to production rule $S \rightarrow bA$;
$\delta(B, a) = B$ corresponds to production rule $B \rightarrow aB$; and
$\delta(B, b) = B$ corresponds to production rule $B \rightarrow bB$.

In general, we say, $\delta(p, a) = q$ corresponds to $p \rightarrow aq$. Also, for each final state $f \in F$, there is a production $f \rightarrow \varepsilon$. Every FA leads to CFG exactly in a similar way, and therefore a language generated by CFG for a regular expression is exactly the language recognized by the FA.

Definition 6.7 (*Regular Grammar*) A context-free grammar specified as $G = (V, \Sigma, S, P)$ is regular grammar if and only if every production is out of the following forms only.

$$
\begin{aligned}
A &\rightarrow aB \mid a \\
A &\rightarrow \varepsilon,
\end{aligned}
\tag{6.2}
$$

where $A, B \in V$ and $a \in \Sigma$. □

Definition 6.8 (*Right-linear Grammars*) A grammar is called right linear if all its rules are right linear, i.e, of the form $A \rightarrow aB$, where $a \in \Sigma$, or they are terminating, i.e., in the form $A \rightarrow a$. □

Example 6.2 The following regular grammar is a right-linear grammar:

$$
\begin{aligned}
S &\rightarrow 0A \mid 1B \mid \varepsilon \\
A &\rightarrow 1C \mid 0 \\
B &\rightarrow 0C \mid 1 \\
C &\rightarrow 0C \mid 0
\end{aligned}
$$

□

Definition 6.9 (*Left-linear Grammars*) A grammar is called left linear if all its rules are left linear of the form $A \rightarrow Ba$, where $a \in \Sigma$ or they are terminating, i.e., in the form $A \rightarrow a$. □

Every left or right-linear grammar generates a finite-state language, i.e., one corresponding to a regular expression. Also, every finite-state language is generated by a left linear and also by right-linear grammar.

Example 6.3 Following is a left-linear grammar:

$$
\begin{aligned}
S &\rightarrow A0 \mid B1 \mid \varepsilon \\
A &\rightarrow C1 \mid 0 \\
B &\rightarrow C0 \mid 1 \\
C &\rightarrow C0 \mid 0
\end{aligned}
$$

□

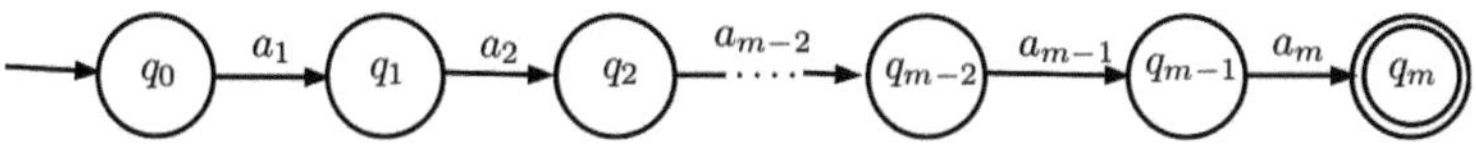

Fig. 6.3 Sequence of transitions for string $a_1a_2...a_m$ to FA

Theorem 6.1 *For any language $L \subseteq \Sigma^*$, L is regular if and only if L is generated using some regular grammar G.*

Proof The proof involves two parts: (I) "L is regular if it is generated by a regular grammar G" and (II) "If language $L = L(G)$ is regular, then G be a regular grammar".

Part-I: Let us assume that G is regular grammar. Given this we want to show that $L(G)$ is regular language, i.e., regular grammar G will generate regular language only. For this, we shall make use of finite automaton, because we know that what language an FA accepts is regular.

The approach is as follows: For every regular grammar we show that for the language generated by this, there exists FA that recognizes it.

Let $M = (Q, \Sigma, q_0, \delta, F)$ be an FA which recognizes L. We define CFG G as follows:

$$
\begin{aligned}
&G = (V, \Sigma, S, P)\\
&V = Q = \{q_0, q_1, ..., q_m\},\\
&S = q_0,\\
&P = \{A \rightarrow aB \mid \delta(A, a) = B\} \cup \{A \rightarrow \varepsilon \mid A \in F\}\\
&\Sigma = \{a_1, a_2, ..., a_m\}, \text{ where, alphabets } a_i \text{ may or may not be unique.}
\end{aligned}
$$

Suppose a string $x = a_1a_2 \ldots a_m$ is recognized by FA M, then there are sequence of transitions of the form shown in Fig. 6.3, and $q_m \in F$. When states in FA represent variables in G, then as per the definition of G, we have the derivation:

$$S = q_0 \Rightarrow a_1q_1 \Rightarrow a_1a_2q_2 \cdots \Rightarrow^* a_1a_2 \ldots a_{m-1}a_mq_m, \tag{6.3}$$

such that $a_1a_2 \ldots a_{m-1}a_m = x$ for $q_m = \varepsilon$.

Similarly, if every x is generated like this, then $x \in L(G)$. And, since L is recognized by FA, L is regular.

Part-II In the second part of the proof, if $L = L(G)$ is regular, it is to be shown that the corresponding grammar G is regular.

Let $G = (V, \Sigma, S, P)$. It is possible to reverse the construction just discussed above in part-I. This means, given the variables set V, define the state set Q for every production $A \rightarrow aB$ such that there is a transition:

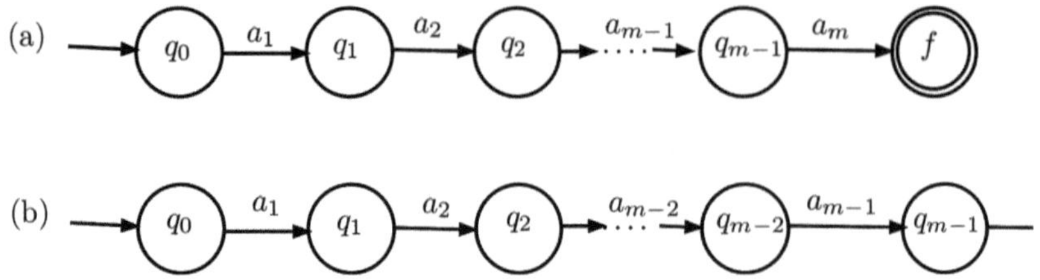

Fig. 6.4 **a** FA to accept $a_1a_2 \dots a_m$, **b** FA to accept $a_1a_2 \dots a_{m-1}$

$$\delta(A, a) = B. \tag{6.4}$$

The problem remains to be solved is how to handle the productions like $A \to a$ and $A \to \varepsilon$? The solution's approach should be such that these productions can be made to lead to final state $f \in F$. Hence, production $A \to a$ can be represented by $\delta(A, a) = f$ and $A \to \varepsilon$ by $\delta(A, \varepsilon) = f$. Assume that there is only one final state $f \in F$. Looking to these transitions the FA $M = (Q, \Sigma, q_0, \delta, F)$ will be an NFA with ε-transitions, which can be defined as follows:

$$\begin{aligned} Q &= V \cup \{f\}, \\ q_0 &= S, \text{ and} \\ F &= \{f\}. \end{aligned}$$

For any $q \in V$ and $a \in \Sigma$, the element of $\delta(q, a) = q'$ includes all those states q' for which, $(q \to aq') \in P$, where P is set of productions in G. Also, if $(q \to a) \in P$, then $\delta(q, a) = f$ and $f \in F$. For any $q \in V, \delta(q, \varepsilon) = f$ if $(q \to \varepsilon) \in P$, otherwise for $q \in V$ and $\delta(q, \varepsilon) = \phi$ if $(q \to \varepsilon) \notin P$.

If $x \in L$ and $L = L(G)$, the derivation for x can be as follows:

$$S \Rightarrow a_1q_1 \Rightarrow a_1a_2q_2 \cdots \Rightarrow a_1a_2 \dots a_{m-1}q_{m-1}.$$

If there is sequence in the FA like one shown in Fig. 6.4a, the last step will be

$$a_1a_2 \dots a_{m-1}q_{m-1} \Rightarrow a_1a_2 \dots a_mq_m.$$

Alternatively, if there is sequence in the FA like one shown in Fig. 6.4b, the last step will be

$$a_1a_2 \dots a_{m-1}q_{m-1} \Rightarrow a_1a_2 \dots a_{m-1}.$$

In every case it follows that $x \in L(M)$.

On the other hand, if $x = q_1q_2 \dots q_m$ is accepted by the FA M, there is a sequence of transitions as specified by Fig. 6.4a or the one given in Fig. 6.4b. Here each transition $\delta(q_{i-1}, a_i) = q_i$ comes from a production $q_{i-1} \rightarrow a_i q_i \in P$, where P is set of production in the grammar G. The last step is either a production $q_{m-1} \rightarrow q_m$, where $q_m \in F$ or $q_m \rightarrow F$ or $q_m \rightarrow \varepsilon$. We conclude that if $L = L(G)$, then FA exists which accepts L, and therefore G is regular. This proves the theorem. □

6.4 Derivation of Sentences

For the CFG defined earlier (see Sect. 6.2), we now give a formal definition of corresponding context-free language. This needs a notation and formal procedure for derivation or generation of language strings. Let A, α, β, γ are symbols, where $A \in V, \alpha, \beta, \gamma \in (V \cup \Sigma)^*$, and $(A \rightarrow \alpha) \in P$. Using this rule, the string $\beta\alpha\gamma$ can be substituted for $\beta A\gamma$, or we say that $\beta A\gamma$ derives $\beta\alpha\gamma$ in grammar G, and expressed by

$$\beta A\gamma \Rightarrow_G \beta\alpha\gamma. \tag{6.5}$$

This is called *direct derivation*. Let us consider the strings, $\alpha_1, \alpha_2, ..., \alpha_n \in (V \cup \Sigma)^*$, and $n \geq 1$, such that α_1 derives α_2, the α_2 derives α_3, ..., and α_{n-1} derives α_n; all expressed by [2]:

$$\alpha_1 \Rightarrow_G \alpha_2 \Rightarrow_G .... \Rightarrow_G \alpha_{n-1} \Rightarrow_G \alpha_n. \tag{6.6}$$

The above process can also be expressed by

$$\alpha_1 \Rightarrow_G^* \alpha_n. \tag{6.7}$$

This states that α_1 derives α_n in CFG G in zero or more number of steps. It should be noted that $\Rightarrow_G^*$ is a *reflexive*, *antisymmetric*, and *transitive* relation. Using above deductions, we can define $L(G)$—the CFL generated by CFG G, as follows:

$$L(G) = \{w \in \Sigma^* \mid S \Rightarrow_G^* w\}. \tag{6.8}$$

If it is implicit that grammar is G, then $\alpha_1 \Rightarrow_G^* \alpha_n$ is written as $\alpha_1 \Rightarrow^* \alpha_n$. Also, in this derivation α_1 derives α_n by application of $(n - 1)$ number of times production rules from P, which may be all unique or some of them may be repeated. If α derives β by application of productions from P, exactly i number of times then it is expressed by

$$\alpha \Rightarrow^i \beta. \tag{6.9}$$

If S derives α in zero or more steps, i.e., $S \Rightarrow^* \alpha$, then the intermediate forms from S to α are called *sentential forms*. Thus, in derivation (6.6), $\alpha_1, \alpha_2, ..., \alpha_{n-1}$ are sentential forms, provided that $\alpha_1 = S$, and $\alpha_n \in \Sigma^*$.

Given any two grammars G_1, G_2, they are treated equal if the languages generated by them are equal, i.e., $L(G_1) = L(G_2)$.

Definition 6.10 (*Leftmost derivation*) A derivation,

$$X \Rightarrow w_1 \Rightarrow w_2 \ldots \Rightarrow w_r = w,$$

generates a tree T of $X \Rightarrow^* w$ satisfying the following: for $0 \le r - 1$, if $w_i = u_i X_i \alpha_i$, $w_{i+1} = u_i \beta_i \alpha_i$, where $u_i \in \Sigma^*$ and $\alpha_i, \beta_i \in (\Sigma \cup V)^*$. Here Σ^* is free semigroup with identity ε, generated by Σ.

Such a derivation is called leftmost derivation. □

Note that, in the leftmost derivation you always expand leftmost nonterminal in the current sentential form.

In the above definition, if positions of u_i and α_i are exchanged, and other part remains the same, derivation is called *rightmost derivation*. The resultant derivations, however, are same.

Definition 6.11 (*Rightmost derivation*) A derivation,

$$X \Rightarrow w_1 \Rightarrow w_2 \ldots \Rightarrow w_r = w,$$

generates a tree T of $X \Rightarrow^* w$ satisfying the following: for $0 \le r - 1$, if $w_i = \alpha_i X_i u_i$, where $u_i \in \Sigma^*$, $X_i \in V$, $\alpha_i \in (\Sigma \cup V)^*$, $w_{i+1} = \alpha_i \beta_i u_i$, $\beta_i \in (V \cup \Sigma)^*$.

Such a derivation is called rightmost derivation. □

Example 6.4 Let us consider the CFG $G = (V, \Sigma, S, P)$, where $V = \{A, B, S\}$, $\Sigma = \{a, b\}$, S is start symbol, and the production rules P are

(1) $S \rightarrow AB$.
(2) $A \rightarrow \varepsilon$.
(3) $A \rightarrow aA$.
(4) $B \rightarrow \varepsilon$.
(5) $B \rightarrow bbB$.

We can find out leftmost and rightmost derivations for string, say, $w = abb$.

Leftmost derivation of *abb*:

$$\begin{aligned} S &\Rightarrow AB, \text{ by } (1) \\ &\Rightarrow aAB \text{ by } (3) \\ &\Rightarrow aB \text{ by } (2) \\ &\Rightarrow abbB \text{ by } (5) \\ &\Rightarrow abb \text{ by } (4). \end{aligned}$$

Rightmost derivation of abb:

$$\begin{aligned} S &\Rightarrow AB, \text{ by } (1) \\ &\Rightarrow AbbB \text{ by } (5) \\ &\Rightarrow Abb \text{ by } (4) \\ &\Rightarrow aAbb \text{ by } (3) \\ &\Rightarrow abb \text{ by } (2). \end{aligned}$$

We note that resultant derivations are same in both. In addition, various production rules applied are also same, only the order of their application is different. □

6.5 Closure Properties of Context-Free Languages

Like closure properties we had studied for regular languages (see Sect. 5.3.1), the context-free languages are also closed on certain set operation. In the following, we prove these properties.

Theorem 6.2 *If L_1 and L_2 are context-free languages then $L_1 \cup L_2$, L_1L_2, and L_1^* are also context-free languages.*

Proof This can be proved almost on the similar lines of regular languages and finite automata discussed earlier. To prove that $L_1 \cup L_2$, L_1L_2, and L^* exist in the form of context-free languages, it is required to define first corresponding CFG for each of these cases.

Let us assume the CFGs corresponding to L_1, L_2 are

$$\begin{aligned} G_1 &= (V_1, \Sigma, S_1, P_1), \\ G_2 &= (V_2, \Sigma, S_2, P_2). \end{aligned}$$

Case-I: (For $L_1 \cup L_2$) Let $G = (V, \Sigma, S, P)$ be union CFG that generates $L_1 \cup L_2$. We can define V and P using G_1 and G_2 as follows:

$$\begin{aligned} V &= V_1 \cup V_2 \cup \{S\}, \\ P &= P_1 \cup P_2 \cup \{S \rightarrow S_1 \mid S_2\}. \end{aligned}$$

If there is a string $x \in L(G_1)$ then S_1 generates x, i.e., $S_1 \Rightarrow_{G_1}^* x$. Similarly, for $y \in L(G_2)$, there is $S_2 \Rightarrow_{G_2}^* y$. In the case of $x \in L(G_1)$, union CFG first uses the production $S \rightarrow S_1$, then continues with the derivation of x in G_1. While in the case of $y \in L(G_2)$, the union CFG first uses the production $S \rightarrow S_2$, then continues with the derivation of y in G_2. Therefore, $L(G_1) \subseteq L(G)$, $L(G_2) \subseteq L(G)$, which can be combined to give $L(G_1) \cup L(G_2) \subseteq L(G)$.

On the other hand, if x is derivable from a production in G, the derivation must start with

$$S \Rightarrow S_1, \text{ or}$$
$$S \Rightarrow S_2.$$

For $S \Rightarrow S_1$, all subsequent productions will be in G_1. Since $V_1 \cap V_2 = \phi$, therefore, $x \in L(G_1)$. Similar is case with $y \in L(G_2)$. Hence, $\{x\} \cup \{y\} \in L(G_1) \cup L(G_2)$, which is $L(G) \subseteq L(G_1) \cup L(G_2)$.

Case-II: (For $L_1 \circ L_2$) Let $G = (V, \Sigma, S, P)$ be a CF grammar, which generates the CF language $L = L_1L_2$. Let G_1, G_2 be the CFGs corresponding to L_1, L_2, respectively. Let $V_1 \cap V_2 = \phi$. Various components of G can be specified as follows:

$$V = V_1 \cup V_2 \cup \{S\},$$
$$P = P_1 \cup P_2 \cup \{S \rightarrow S_1S_2\}.$$

Let $x \in L(G_1)$, $y \in L(G_2)$, and $w = xy \in L(G_1)L(G_2)$. Then $w \in L(G)$ can be derived as follows:

$$S \Rightarrow S_1S_2 \Rightarrow^*_{G_1} xS_2 \Rightarrow^*_{G_2} xy = w,$$

where $S_1S_2 \Rightarrow xS_2$ is derivation in G_1, and $xS_2 \Rightarrow^* xy$ is a derivation in G_2. On the other hand, if x can be derived from S_1S_2 and therefore $w = xy$, where x can be derived from S_1 in G and y can be derived from S_2 in G. Since $V_1 \cap V_2 = \phi$, the above $S_1 \Rightarrow^* x$ derivable from G implies it derivable from G_1. Similarly y derivable from G implies that it is derivable from G_2. Hence $w = xy \in L(G_1)L(G_2)$.

Case-III: (For L_1^*) For this it is required to construct $G = (V, \Sigma, S, P)$, which generates L_1^*. Let $V = V_1 \cup \{S\}$ and $S \notin V_1$.

The language L_1^* will contain strings of the form $w = x_1 \ldots x_n$, where $x_i \in L$. Since $x_1, \ldots, x_n$ can be derived from S_1, for G it is only required to get these strings derived from S. Therefore, a production in G in terms of production of G_1 can be specified as

$$S \rightarrow S_1S \mid \varepsilon.$$

Hence, the production in G can be expressed as

$$P = P_1 \cup \{S \rightarrow S_1S \mid \varepsilon\}.$$

For w to be member of $L(G)$, $w = \varepsilon$ or w can be derived from some string $x_i \in L(G_1)$. In the later case, the only productions in G are those that exist in G_1. Therefore, $w \in L(G_1)^*$. This proves the theorem. □

Example 6.5 Illustration for CFL closed on union, concatenation, and Kleene star operations.

Let L_1 and L_2 are context-free languages defined below:

$$L_1 = \{a^n b^n \mid n \geq 0\},$$
$$L_2 = \{ww^R \mid w \in \{a, b\}^*\}.$$

Both of these are CFLs because these can be generated by the following CF grammars, respectively:

$$S_1 \rightarrow aS_1b \mid \varepsilon,$$
$$S_2 \rightarrow aS_2a \mid bS_2b \mid \varepsilon.$$

The union of L_1, L_2 is $L = \{a^n b^n\} \cup \{ww^R\}$, which can be generated by $S \rightarrow S_1 \mid S_2$.

Similarly, the concatenation $\{a^n b^n\} \circ \{ww^R\}$ can be generated by $S \rightarrow S_1 \circ S_2$, and the Kleene star operation on each language can be generated using productions $S \rightarrow S_1 S \mid \varepsilon$, $S \rightarrow S_2 S \mid \varepsilon$, respectively. □

Theorem 6.3 *Show that CFLs are not closed under the operation of complementation.*

Proof Given that L is a context-free language, there are two approaches to show that $\overline{L}$ is not context free.

Approach I. Let L_1 and L_2 be CFLs. We know from Theorem 6.2 (Sect. 6.5) that CFLs are closed on Union operation. Further, from De Morgan's laws:

$$\overline{L_1 \cup L_2} = \overline{L_1} \cap \overline{L_2}.$$

Let us imagine that $\overline{L_1 \cup L_2}$ is closed on complementation and result is a CFL. In that case $\overline{L_1} \cap \overline{L_2}$ is also CFL, which implies that when it is closed on complement, and it is also closed on intersection. However, from solved Exercise 6.13 (proof-based problems), they are not closed on intersection, hence they are not closed on complementation.

Approach II. Let $L = \{x \mid x$ is not of the form $ww\}$ is a CFL. But, $\overline{L} = \{ww \mid w \in \{a, b\}^*\}$ is not a CFL. This is as follows. If $\overline{L}$ were a CFL, then there is some

$L' = \overline{L} \cap a^*b^*a^*b^* = \{a^ib^ja^ib^j \mid i, j \geq 0\}$ would be a CFL; (which is $L_{CFL} \cap Reg$). But L' is not CFL. Thus $\overline{L}$ is not CFL. This proves the theorem. □

The context-free languages are closed under reversal, homomorphism, and inverse homomorphism, but not on intersection and difference. The first three are left as exercises.

Theorem 6.4 *Union of CFL and regular language is CFL.*

Proof We have studied (see Fig. 6.1, Sect. 6.2) that *regular languages* are also context-free languages. So, when both are CFLs, their union will comprise either one of them or both, which is CFL.

To find out the productions for this union grammar, let us consider that start symbol for CFG is A and that for regular grammar it is B. In the union grammar, we introduce a symbol S and a top-level production as $S \rightarrow A \mid B$, which generates CFL using $S \Rightarrow A \Rightarrow \ldots \Rightarrow u$ for $u \in CFL$, and generates regular language using $S \Rightarrow B \Rightarrow \ldots \Rightarrow v$ for $v \in Reg.L$. □

6.6 Parsing Context-Free Languages

The process of derivation of strings in CFL can be represented using tree structures called *derivation-trees* or *parse-trees*, and the process is called *parsing*. The context-free grammars (also called BNF or "Backus–Naur Form" grammars) have been used extensively for describing the syntax of programming languages. Thus, the parsing algorithms play a large role in implementation of compilers and interpreters for programming languages, and for programs that understand or translate the natural languages. The CFG uses nonterminals which we call as *syntactic classes*. For example, in Natural Language Processing, Noun-Phrase, Verb-Phrase, Verb, and Preposition-Phrase are all syntactic classes. In programming languages, the expression, conjunction operator, disjunction operator, and variable are syntactic classes.

Definition 6.12 (*Parse-tree*) A parse-tree is a rooted tree that represents the syntactic structure of a string according to some context-free grammar. □

Figure 6.5 shows a sample parse-tree for the arithmetic expression $a + b * c$. Note that, when we assemble the terminals of this parse-tree from left to right, we get the ordered expression $a + b * c$.

A parse-tree is an *in-memory* representation of the input, with a structure that conforms to the grammar. Using the parse-tree instead of semantic actions, one can make multiple passes over the data without having to re-parse the input.

Further, a parse-tree is a record of rules (and tokens) that are used to match some input text, whereas a *syntax-tree* records the structure of input and is insensitive to the grammar that produced it. Figure 6.6 shows a sample syntax-tree for the arithmetic expression $a + b * c$.

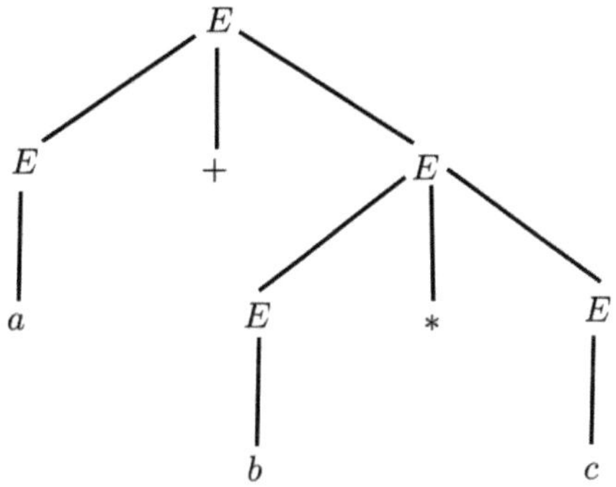

Fig. 6.5 A parsing-tree for the expression $a + b * c$

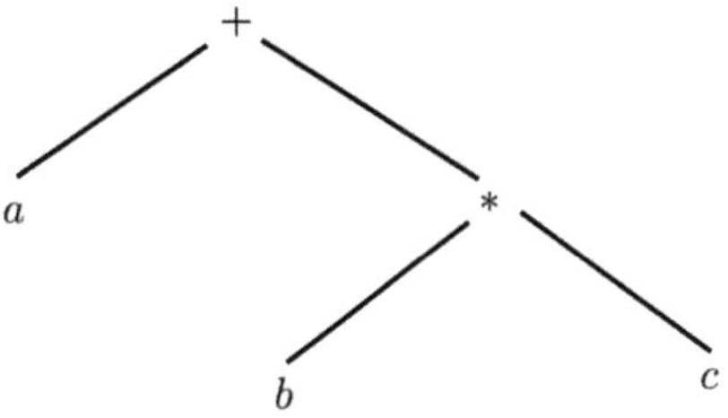

Fig. 6.6 A syntax-tree for the expression $a + b * c$

Example 6.6 Given the grammar $G = (V, \Sigma, P, S)$, where $V = \{S\}$, $\Sigma = \{a, b\}$, and $P = \{S \to aSb, S \to \varepsilon\}$, find out the derivation of strings, as well the language for this grammar.

This grammar has only one variable symbol S, there are two terminal symbols a and b, and two production, $S \to aSb$ and $S \to \varepsilon$. A possible derivation can be

$$S \Rightarrow aSb \Rightarrow aaSbb \Rightarrow aaaSbbb \Rightarrow aaabbb.$$

The above derivation can also be written as

$$S \Rightarrow^* aaabbb.$$

In the above, the sentential form $aaSbb$ has been obtained by applying the production rule $S \to aSb$ on aSb and $aaabbb$ has been obtained by applying the production rule $S \to \varepsilon$ on the sentential form $aaaSbbb$. If we continue the other derivations, it can be easily seen that the language for this CFG is

$$L = L(G) = \{a^n b^n \mid n \geq 0\}. \tag{6.10}$$

It is clear that L is not regular because its grammar is not regular (see Sect. 6.3), hence it can be concluded that some CFL are not regular. □

Example 6.7 Derivation of simple natural language sentences.

Let there be a CFG $G = (NT, \Sigma, S, P)$, where

$NT = \{S, NP, N, VP, V\}$, where NP is for Noun-Phrase, VP is Verb-Phrase, N is Noun, and V is Verb;
$\Sigma = \{man,\ dog,\ bites,\ likes\}$;
$P = \{S \to NP\ \ VP,\ NP \to N,\ VP \to V\ \ NP,\ VP \to\ \ V;$
$N \to man \mid dog, V \to likes \mid bites\}$.

Note: We have used the symbol NT (for nonterminals) since V is used for Verb. We can find out various derivations using this grammar.

The above CFG is description of a limited subset of natural language grammar. In fact, the original motivation for context-free grammars was description of natural languages. The format in this example is structuring of language followed by the linguists, and it is close to the format followed by computer scientists, called BNF (Backus–Naur Form) notation. Let us see generating of some sentences through G.

$$\begin{aligned} S &\Rightarrow NP\ \ VP \\ &\Rightarrow N\ \ VP \\ &\Rightarrow man\ \ VP \\ &\Rightarrow man\ \ V\ \ NP \\ &\Rightarrow man\ \ likes\ \ NP \\ &\Rightarrow man\ \ likes\ \ N \\ &\Rightarrow man\ \ likes\ \ dog \end{aligned} \tag{6.11}$$

Hence, $S \Rightarrow^* man\ likes\ dog$.

Similarly, some other sentences that can be generated through G are

dog likes man
man bites dog
dog bites man
man likes man
man bites man
dog likes dog
dog bites dog

Though some of the sentences in the above are not accepted in a civilized world, but as per context-free grammar G defined above, they are valid. The CFG defined above can generate still more number of sentences. However, it has been left as an exercise for the reader to find out the remaining sentences [3]. □

Fig. 6.7 A sample parse-tree

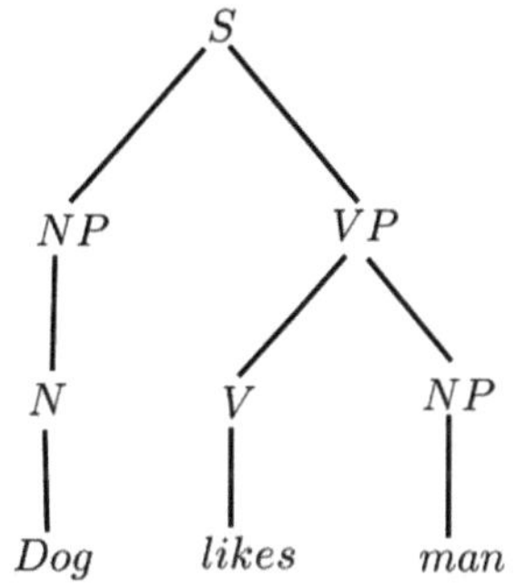

With little insight, we observe that these derivations can also be expressed in the form of a Tree, e.g., in $S \Rightarrow NP \quad VP$, the S is root node of the tree, and NP and VP are the children of that node. The process can be continued further with NP and VP as roots of two subtrees, and so on, until all the children are terminal nodes as shown in Fig. 6.7.

Similarly, the other sentences can be generated by building a tree structure, called parse-tree, for each sentence. The process of generating a sentence is also called parsing. Naturally, for complex sentences, the parse-tree will also be of a complex structure.

Example 6.8 Derivation of mathematical expressions.

If "$E \rightarrow E + E \mid E * E \mid (E) \mid a$" are the production rules in the CFG, then derivation-tree for $a * (a + a)$ can be constructed as shown in Fig. 6.8.

The symbols E and a are for expression and identifier, respectively. Scanning the leaf nodes of above tree from left to right produces the expression $a * (a + a)$. The derivation process in the parse-tree is similar to the conventional derivation of strings

Fig. 6.8 Derivation-tree for $a * (a + a)$

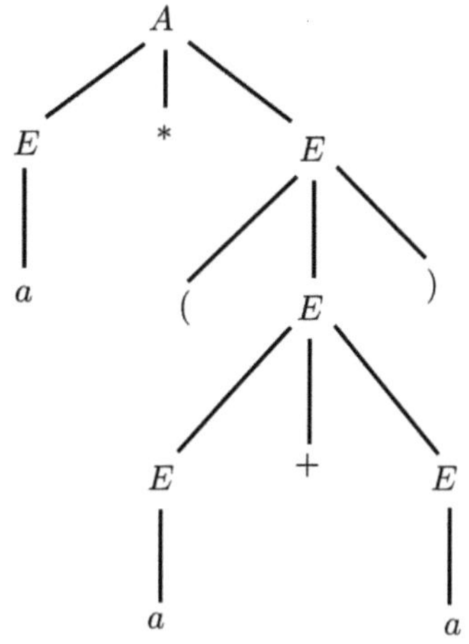

in CFG (see derivations (6.11), Sect. 6.6), but provides a pictorial representation of the parsing process. □

Since we start from start symbol of the grammar as root of a tree and generate the sentence at the bottom of the tree at its children nodes, this parsing is called *top-down parsing*, and corresponding parse-tree is constructed from top to bottom.

Definition 6.13 Let $Q = (V, \Sigma, S, P)$ be a CFG. Consider its two derivations D and D' as follows:

$$D = \alpha_1 \Rightarrow \ldots \alpha_i \Rightarrow \ldots \alpha_n,$$
$$D' = \alpha_1 \Rightarrow \ldots \Rightarrow \alpha_{i'} \ldots \alpha_n,$$

where $\alpha_1 \in V$, $\alpha_n \in \Sigma^*$, and $\alpha_i, \alpha_{i'} \in (V \cup \Sigma)^*$, for $i = 2 \ldots n-1$. We note that D and D' are derivations from single nonterminal symbol. We say a derivation D precedes D', written as $D < D'$, if during the process of derivation the leftmost nonterminal in D is replaced before to that in D'. □

Example 6.9 Consider productions in grammar G as

$$S \rightarrow SS \mid (S) \mid \varepsilon$$

generate some derivations.

The following three derivations generate the same string of balanced parenthesis.

$$D_1 = S \Rightarrow SS \Rightarrow (S)S \Rightarrow ((S))S \Rightarrow (())S \Rightarrow (())(S) \Rightarrow (())()$$
$$D_2 = S \Rightarrow SS \Rightarrow (S)S \Rightarrow ((S))S \Rightarrow ((S))(S) \Rightarrow (())(S) \Rightarrow (())()$$
$$D_3 = S \Rightarrow SS \Rightarrow (S)S \Rightarrow ((S))S \Rightarrow ((S))(S) \Rightarrow ((S))() \Rightarrow (())()$$
$$D_4 = S \Rightarrow SS \Rightarrow S(S) \Rightarrow S() \Rightarrow (S)() \Rightarrow ((S))() \Rightarrow (())()$$

We note that $D_1 < D_2$ and $D_2 < D_3$. The D_4 is *rightmost derivation*, hence substitution starts taking place from rightmost. Thus, the leftmost derivation will always be preceding the rightmost derivation. The parse-tree for all the above derivations D_1, D_2, and D_3 is same, as shown in Fig. 6.9. In the assembled string from terminals, we ignore ε, hence the generated string is "(())()". □

Definition 6.14 Any two derivations D and D' are similar, if they are related by a relation of *reflexive closure*, *symmetric closure*, and *transitive closure* on the relation of "<". Therefore, D and D' have equivalence relation between them. □

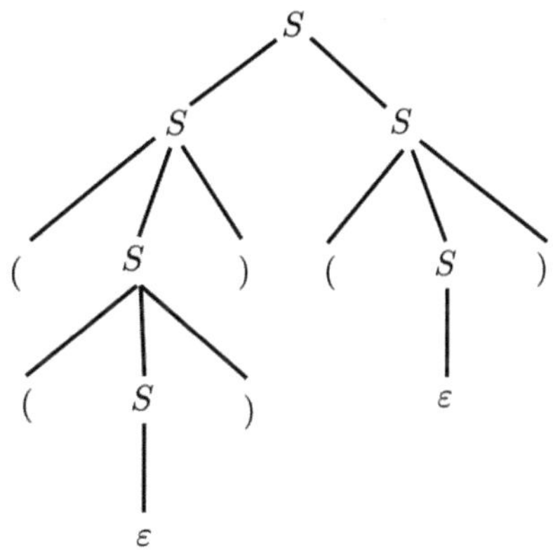

Fig. 6.9 Derivation-tree for balanced parentheses

6.7 Parsing Arithmetic Expressions

When computers are used to perform arithmetic computations, they must follow rigid mechanical procedures so that computation can be automated unambiguously. These rigid criteria are expressed in the syntax of programming languages through the context-free grammar of the corresponding language. The property of being context free also helps in parsing the statements of high-level languages unambiguously. The parsing represents structure of the statements through which various computations are to be performed. For example, following rules can be taken as specifying syntax of various arithmetic expressions:

$$
\begin{aligned}
&< expr > \rightarrow < expr > + < expr >\\
&< expr > \rightarrow < expr > - < expr >\\
&< expr > \rightarrow < expr > * < expr >\\
&< expr > \rightarrow < expr > / < expr >\\
&< expr > \rightarrow (< expr >)\\
&< expr > \rightarrow a
\end{aligned}
\tag{6.12}
$$

This shows that $< expr >$ in the left-hand side of each rule can be substituted by the expression shown on the right-hand side of the "$\rightarrow$" sign. This way we are able to generate the original expression governed by these rules. In addition, the relation between every sub-expression generated and its parent symbol indicates the order of computation and association of various sub-expressions using operators.

Example 6.10 Show that the language $L = \{a^m b^n \mid m \neq n, \text{ and } m, n \geq 0\}$ is context free.

We know that, when $m = n$, the productions in P are

$$S \to aSb,$$
$$S \to \varepsilon.$$

Let us first assume that $m > n$. For this, a grammar similar to $a^n b^n$ can be constructed and the character a can be prefixed one or more times.

$$S \to AE,$$
$$A \to aA \mid a,$$
$$E \to aEb \mid \varepsilon.$$

Similarly, for $m < n$, character b can be appended one or more times to the sentential form:

$$S \to EB,$$
$$B \to bB \mid b.$$

Combining the above two set of productions, we get the productions for the language $\{a^m b^n \mid m \neq n, \text{ and } m, n \geq 0\}$, as follows:

$$S \to AE \mid EB,$$
$$E \to aEb \mid \varepsilon,$$
$$A \to aA \mid a,$$
$$B \to bB \mid b.$$

Since all the productions are of the form $A \to \alpha$, where $\alpha \in (V \cup \Sigma)^*$, the grammar and language are context free. □

6.8 Ambiguous Grammars and Languages

The ambiguous grammars also produce the required strings/sentences, but the derivations are more than one for any given sentence. Since a parse-tree gives the semantics of a sentence that has been produced, these two or more derivations for the same string will have different semantics (i.e., meanings). If such parse-tree is used for translation or more machine code generation, we will get two different machine codes for a given statement/sentence. For example, consider the sentence $a + b * c$, and

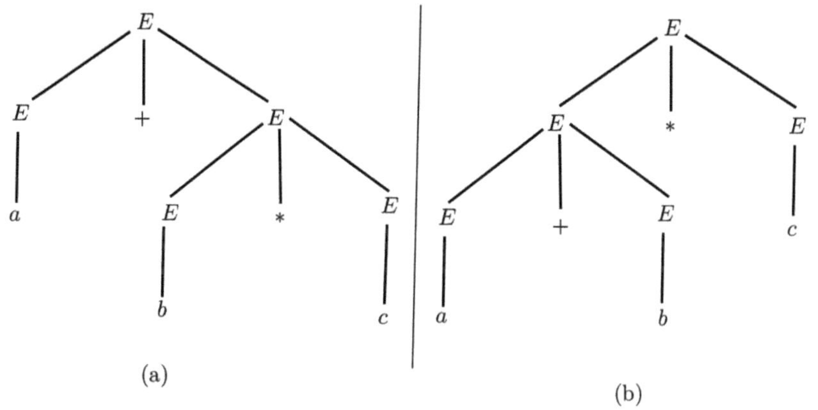

Fig. 6.10 Parse-trees for the expression $a + b * c$

grammar as $E \rightarrow E + E \mid E * E \mid a \mid b \mid c$, we will get two different derivations as follows:

$$\begin{aligned} E \Rightarrow & E + E \Rightarrow a + E \Rightarrow a + E * E \\ \Rightarrow & a + b * E \Rightarrow a + b * c, \end{aligned} \tag{6.13}$$

$$\begin{aligned} E \Rightarrow & E * E \Rightarrow E + E * E \Rightarrow a + E * E \\ \Rightarrow & a + b * E \Rightarrow a + b * c. \end{aligned} \tag{6.14}$$

The parse-trees of above expressions are shown in Fig. 6.10a and b, respectively.

Obviously, the parse-trees above have different meanings: (a) computes $t1 = b * c$ and then $t2 = a + t1$, while (b) computes first $t1 = a + b$, and then $t2 = t1 * c$. When these parse-trees are used to generate machine/assembly code, it will be like this:

```
(a)          (b)
load b       load a
mult c       add  b
stor t1      stor t1
load a       load  c
add t1       mult t1
stor t2      stor t2
```

If a, b, c are 3, 4, 5, respectively, the code (a) when run will produce answer 23, while (b) will produce result 35. By this we can understand that the same expression is differently interpreted by this grammar. And, that is why it is called ambiguous.

One special desirable feature in a grammar for a programming language is freedom from *ambiguity*. A CFG G is said to be ambiguous if and only if some string in $L(G)$

has two distinct leftmost derivations. A CFG G is said to be *inherently ambiguous* if and only if every equivalent CFG is ambiguous. A CFG is said to be *structurally ambiguous* if and only if some string in $L(G)$ has two distinct derivation-trees that are the same except for nonterminal labels [7].

There is extensive interest in ambiguity of natural languages as well as context-free languages. Some of the known results are

1. it is *recursively unsolvable* whether an arbitrary grammar for a language is ambiguous [4];
2. there exists *inherently ambiguous languages*, for example,

$$\{a^i b^j a^i b^k \mid i, j, k \geq 1\} \cup \{a^i b^j a^k b^j \mid i, j, k \geq 1\}. \tag{6.15}$$

   Similarly, the language,

$$L = \{a^i b^i c^j \mid i, j \geq 1\} \cup \{a^i b^j c^j \mid i, j \geq 1\}, \tag{6.16}$$

   is also an inherently ambiguous language [10].
3. No regular language is inherently ambiguous.

The above considerations motivate the study of ambiguity in context-free languages. Given a grammar $G = (\Sigma, V, S, P)$, a word w is said to be ambiguously derivable if there exists at least two derivations of w from S whose associated generation trees are different. A grammar G is said to be ambiguous if there exists an ambiguously derivable word in $L(G)$, and is otherwise unambiguous.

Definition 6.15 (*Unambiguous*) A CFG is unambiguous if for every $w \in L(G)$ there is a unique parse-tree in G with yield w. □

Definition 6.16 (*Inherently Ambiguous*) A language L is said to be inherently ambiguous if there is no unambiguous grammar for L. □

Following are additional terms related to ambiguity:

- The degree of ambiguity of a sentence is the number of its distinct derivation-trees.
- A sentence is unambiguous if its degree of ambiguity is unity.
- A grammar is unambiguous if each of its sentences is unambiguous.
- A grammar has bounded ambiguity if there is a bound on the degree of ambiguity of any sentence of the grammar.
- A grammar is reduced if every nonterminal appears in derivation of some sentence.

If T_1 and T_2 are two distinct generation trees, then their associated leftmost derivations are distinct; the converse also holds. Thus, a word is ambiguously derivable if and only if it has two leftmost derivations. It is well established that there is no decision procedure for determining whether an arbitrary grammar is ambiguous. Also there is no decision procedure (i.e., it is unsolvable) for determining if an arbitrary language is inherently ambiguous. In other words, there is no algorithm for

Fig. 6.11 **a** Parse-tree for the string aba, **b** Different parse-tree for the same string

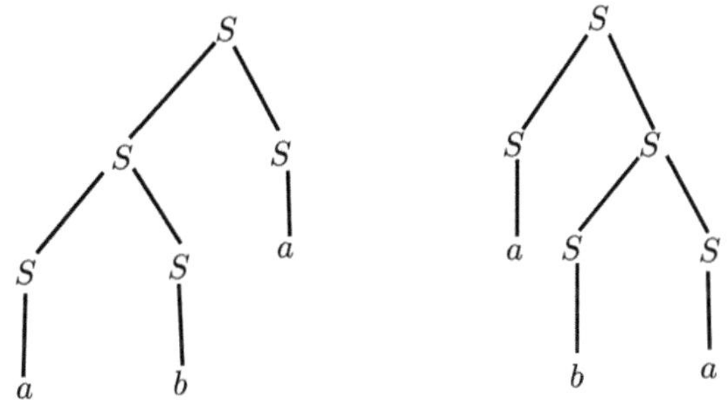

$$\begin{aligned} S &\Rightarrow SS \\ &\Rightarrow SSS \\ &\Rightarrow aSS \\ &\Rightarrow abS \\ &\Rightarrow aba \end{aligned}$$

(a)

$$\begin{aligned} S &\Rightarrow SS \\ &\Rightarrow aS \\ &\Rightarrow aSS \\ &\Rightarrow abS \\ &\Rightarrow aba \end{aligned}$$

(b)

determining of an arbitrary language whether it is generated by some unambiguous grammar.

Given a grammar $G = (V, \Sigma, P, S)$, a sentence w is said to be ambiguously derivable if there exists two derivations of w from S, whose associated generation trees are different, and is otherwise unambiguous.

Example 6.11 Show that grammar with productions

$$S \rightarrow SS \mid a \mid b \tag{6.17}$$

is ambiguous.

Using the grammar (6.17), we construct two different derivation-trees, as shown in Fig. 6.11a, b for the same sentence aba. Hence, as per the definition, we conclude that this grammar is ambiguous. □

In a compiler, the grammar (6.17) will produce two different codes because there are two different parse-trees, or it can assign two different meanings to the same sentence, e.g., *aba* produced by the above parse-trees. This is highly undesirable in most of the applications. The following examples demonstrate the consequences as wrong computations due to two different parse-trees for the same sentence.

Example 6.12 Let us consider the grammar for arithmetic expressions with productions given below.

$$E \rightarrow E + E \mid E * E \mid (E) \mid a \mid b \mid c.$$

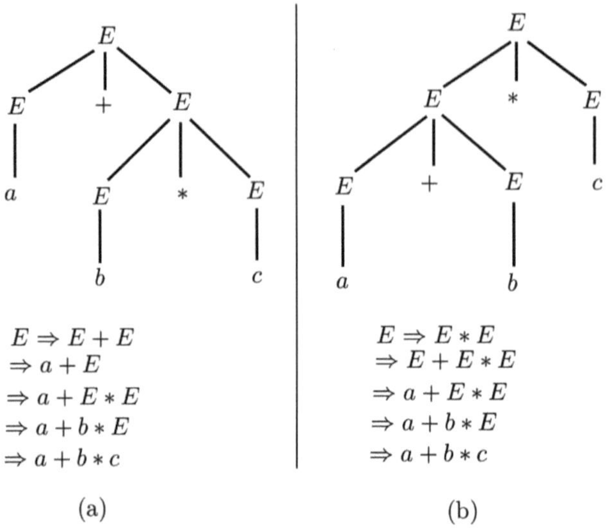

Fig. 6.12 Parse-trees for $a + a * a$

For the sake of simplicity only two operations "+" and "*" have been considered for this purpose as these are sufficient to express the ambiguity presence in the generated expressions. Let us generate the string $a + b * c$. The corresponding derivations and parse-trees are shown in Fig. 6.12a, b.

Consider that values of terminals a, b, c are 4, 5, 6, respectively. Figure 6.12a shows that second and third terms in the expression are to be multiplied and then the result is to be added into the first term, producing the final results as 34. Whereas the parse-tree in Fig. 6.12b shows first and second terms of the expression are to be added together first and then the result of this is to be multiplied with the third term that gives output as 54. Note that parsed sentences by both the parse-trees are same $a + b * c$, but due to different semantics associated with two parse-trees, the compiler will generate different codes, and hence different results when that code is run.

Therefore, this grammar is ambiguous and the corresponding language is ambiguous too. □

In the above example, if the expression to be parsed is $a + (b * c)$, there will be only one parse-tree. However, it is important to note that if we have generated a unique parse-trees for the expressions, e.g., $(a + b) * c$ or $(a * b) + c$, there is no guarantee that all the expressions of that grammar will produce unique parse-trees.

The old language, ALGOL 60, is an ambiguous language. Here is an example for this language.

$$\text{if } E_1 \text{ then } x = y \text{ if } E_2 \text{ then } x = z \text{ else } w = z,$$

where E_1, E_2 represents any Boolean expressions, and $x = y$, $x = z$, and $x = w$ are conditional statements [5].

6.9 Disambiguating Ambiguous Grammars

Ambiguous grammars generate more than one different parse-trees for the same sentence, which in turn represents different meanings. Therefore, it is necessary to remove the ambiguity in the CFGs. One way to remove the scope of ambiguity in, for example, a mathematical expression, is to consider the rule of precedence of operators. Thus, in $a + a * a$, the part $a * a$ needs to be processed before the "+" operator. Hence, in the parse-tree answer $a * a$ is computed first. However, when there are identical operators they are grouped from left to right. For example, $a + a + a$ may be grouped as $((a + a) + a)$ or $(a + (a + a))$. In two cases, the parse-trees are different, but they will evaluate the same result.

Naturally, we are interested to have some algorithm to remove all kinds of ambiguities in a CFG. However, it is *recursively unsolvable* whether an arbitrary grammar for a language is ambiguous. In other words, there cannot be an algorithm to determine if an arbitrary language is generated by some ambiguous grammar or not.

In fact, there are CFLs that have ambiguous CFGs, but removal of ambiguity for such grammar is impossible. It is not always true that ambiguity can be removed from a grammar. However, some ambiguous grammars can always be converted into unambiguous grammar by some changes in it. Sometimes, ambiguous grammars can be made unambiguous by adding some nonterminal symbols through process called disambiguation so that for a given expression there is one parse-tree and one derivation only.

6.9.1 Deterministic Parsing of Ambiguous Grammars

In the following, we discuss using an ambiguous context-free grammar together with disambiguating rules as a method of specifying the syntax of a programming language. The number of common syntactic constructs in programming languages can be specified more naturally and successfully by this method than by using an equivalent unambiguous grammar. These diambiguating rules are based on familiar concepts from operator precedence (OP) grammar.

The usual approach for disambiguation of grammar of Example 6.12 is to rewrite this grammar, such that there is selection of proper tree by defining functions that accept or reject parse-trees of the grammar, so that each string has at most one parse-tree acceptable to all these functions. Each such function is called disambiguation rule. The rule is such that for the grammar in Example 6.12, the '$+$' and '$*$' are to be left associative and '$*$' is to have higher precedence than '$+$'. This grammar accepts only one parse-tree and rejects the other.

However, defining a language in terms of an ambiguous grammar plus a set of disambiguating rules may result to a language that is not context free. But, our concern is mainly to make the language and grammar unambiguous, though, with a cost! Because, it will require additional programming constructs, on the part of the programmer. These constructs, however, will be more economical, and more clear.

The following is the unambiguous grammar after applying the disambiguating rules on the grammar in Example 6.12.

$$\begin{aligned} Expr &\rightarrow Expr + Term \\ &\mid Term \\ Term &\rightarrow Term * Factor \\ &\mid Factor \\ Factor &\rightarrow (Expr) \\ &\mid id \end{aligned} \tag{6.18}$$

This grammar has two or more nonterminals, $Term$ and $Factor$, and two new productions, $Expr \rightarrow Term$ and $Term \rightarrow Factor$. Productions of this form with a single nonterminal on the right side are called *unit productions*. The introduction of nonterminals $Term$ and $Factor$ ensures that signs $+$ and $*$ are left associative, and the unit production enforces the operator precedence. These changes make new grammar larger than the original grammar, particularly, the unit productions contribute to significant amount of the total time consumed in derivation.

Henceforth, we will be referring nonterminals $Expr$, $Term$, $Factor$ by symbols E, T, F, respectively. In the following example, we show and confirm that above method of disambiguation works [1].

Example 6.13 Disambiguate the CFG $G = (V, \Sigma, S, P)$, where

$$\begin{aligned} V &= \{E\} \\ \Sigma &= \{(,), +, *, a, b, c\} \\ S &= \{E\} \end{aligned}$$

and the productions P are

$$
\begin{aligned}
E &\rightarrow E + E,\\
E &\rightarrow E * E,\\
E &\rightarrow (E),\\
E &\rightarrow a \mid b \mid c.
\end{aligned}
$$

This grammar is ambiguous because it generates two difference parse-trees for the expression $a + a * a$. Following modifications can be made in G to disambiguate it. Let us call the new grammar as $G' = (V', \Sigma, S, P')$.

The set of nonterminals (V') are

$$V' = \{E, T, F\},$$

and the set of productions (P') are

$$
\begin{aligned}
E &\rightarrow E + T \mid T,\\
T &\rightarrow T * F \mid F,\\
F &\rightarrow (E) \mid a \mid b \mid c.
\end{aligned}
$$

The Σ and S remain unchanged. The symbols E, T, F stand for *expression, term* and *factor*, respectively.

The parse-tree for $a + b * c$ is shown in Fig. 6.13.

In this rewritten grammar, for any expression containing "+" and "$*$", the parse-tree will situate "$*$" deeper in the tree, i.e., closer to the terminals, in comparison to "+". Thus, in effect, forcing the evaluation of "$*$" before the evaluation of "+".

We note that no other derivation as well as parse-tree is possible for this string. Using this new grammar we can derive $a + b * c$ as follows. The reader can also verify that there is no other sequence possible for this top-down parsing. The modified grammar is unambiguous.

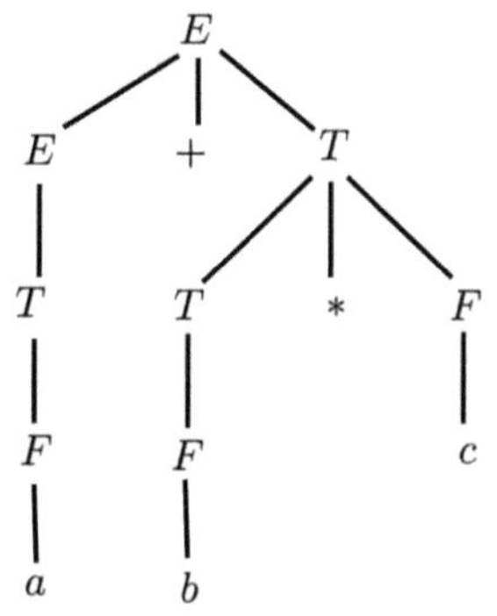

Fig. 6.13 Parse-tree of an unambiguous grammar for string $a + b * c$

$$
\begin{aligned}
E &\Rightarrow E + T \Rightarrow T + T \Rightarrow F + T \Rightarrow a + T \\
&\Rightarrow a + T * F \Rightarrow a + F * F \Rightarrow a + b * F \\
&\Rightarrow a + b * c.
\end{aligned}
$$

Similarly, if $a * b + c$ is expression, the derivation is as follows:

$$
\begin{aligned}
E &\Rightarrow E + T \Rightarrow T + T \Rightarrow T * F + T \Rightarrow F * F + T \\
&\Rightarrow a * F + T \Rightarrow a * b + T \Rightarrow a * b + F \\
&\Rightarrow a * b + c.
\end{aligned}
$$

We note that both the expressions can be unambiguously derived; even if we derive more expressions, there will be only one derivation-tree in each case. Hence, the grammar G' is unambiguous. □

In general, it is impossible to algorithmically decide whether a given context-free grammar is ambiguous. On the worst, there are *inherent ambiguous languages*—languages for which every CFG is ambiguous. For such languages, it is impossible to eliminate ambiguity. In fact, the terminology is *inherently ambiguous language*. An example of inherently ambiguous languages is

$$
L = \{a^i b^i c^j \mid i, j \geq 1\} \cup \{a^i b^j c^j \mid i, j \geq 1\}. \tag{6.19}
$$

It is well known from our discussions earlier that L is context-free language. The intuition for the ambiguity of above is as follows: every grammar for this language must have productions that are aimed to match a's against b's, and b's against c's. In this case, given the string $a^k b^k c^k$, any one of the action may be exercised. The proof that above language is inherently ambiguous context-free language is involved; curious readers may refer to original article [10].

6.9.2 *Canonical Derivation*

Let $G = (V, \Sigma, P, S)$ be a context-free grammar, and let

$$
S = \alpha_0 \Rightarrow_{p_0} \alpha_1 \Rightarrow_{p_1} \dots \Rightarrow_{p_{n-1}} \alpha_n \in \Sigma^*
$$

be a derivation. Here, $p_0, p_1, \dots, p_{n-1} \in P$ are productions. For each i, $0 \leq i \leq n$, $\alpha_i = x_i A_i \gamma_i, \alpha_{i+1} = x_i \beta_i \gamma_i$, where $\beta_i \in (V \cup \Sigma)^*$, $x_i \in \Sigma^*$, $A_i \in V$ (nonterminal), and $p_i = A_i \rightarrow \beta_i$ is in P, then $P = p_0 \dots p_{n-1}$ is said to be a *canonical derivation*. For $n \geq 0$, we may write $S \Rightarrow_P^n \alpha_n$ to indicate number of steps in the derivation sequence as n.

A context-free grammar G is said to be *unambiguous* if each $x \in L(G)$ has exactly one canonical derivation.

6.10 Operator-Precedence Grammars

Floyd's precedence Grammars (FGs) and Floyd's Languages (FLs) are classical subclass of deterministic context-free grammars and languages. In fact, several recently introduced, including XML-like languages are proper subsets of Floyd's languages. Floyd's languages have all the closure properties available for regular languages: reversal, prefixing, suffixing, concatenation, Kleene star, and Boolean operations.

A different argument in favor of FL is that, unlike deterministic languages such as LL(k) and LR(k),[3] parsing does not need to scan the text in a fixed direction, say, from left to right; this freedom is particularly relevant for developing parallel parsing algorithms suitable for current multi-processor architectures [12].

One way to disambiguate the arithmetic expressions is to use operator precedence grammar, a kind of context-free grammar that has the property that no production has either an empty right-hand side or two adjacent nonterminals in its right-hand side. These properties allow precedence relations to be defined between the terminals of the grammar. A parser that exploits these relations is considerably simpler than more general LR(k) ($k \geq 1$) parser.

A *precedence grammar* is an operator grammar for which no more than one of the three relations hold between any ordered pair a, b of terminal symbols. The relations are called *precedence relations* [6].

Definition 6.17 (*Operator precedence grammar*) A context-free grammar G is operator precedence if none of its productions rules P take the form $A \rightarrow xBCy$, where A, B, C are nonterminals and $x, y \in \Sigma^*$. □

The corresponding language is called operator *precedence language*. It can be easily shown through induction that if G is operator precedence grammar then no derivative of any nonterminal, and in particular no sentential form, contains two adjacent nonterminal symbols. That is, a rule,

$$A \rightarrow u_0 A_1 u_1 ... u_{k-1} A_k u_k, k \geq 0, \tag{6.20}$$

is operator form if its r.h.s (right-hand side) does not contain adjacent nonterminals; an operator precedence grammar contains only such rules.

R. Floyd took inspiration from traditional notion of precedence between arithmetic operators in order to define a broad class of languages, such that shape of parse-tree is solely defined by a binary relation between terminals that are consecutive, or become consecutive after a bottom-up reduction step. For example, the Grammar

[3] These are covered in this chapter.

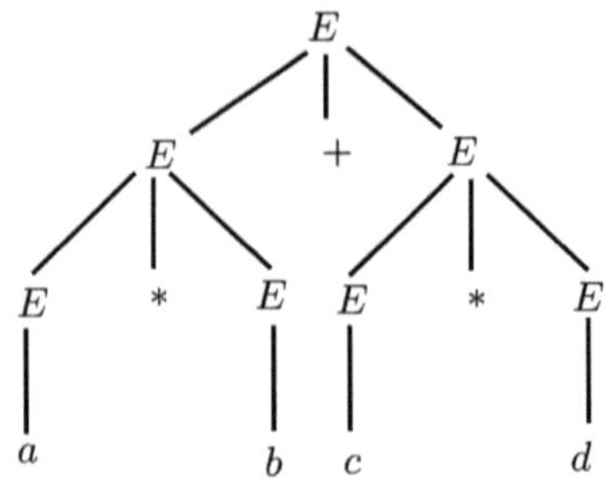

Fig. 6.14 Parse-tree build using operator precedence grammar

$E \rightarrow E * E \mid E + E$ is operator precedence, as the rule is like in expression (6.20). A parse-tree for this grammar is shown in Fig. 6.14.

However, the Grammar $S \rightarrow SS \mid (S) \mid \varepsilon$ is not the operator precedence grammar. Also, $\{S \rightarrow NP\ VP,\ NP \rightarrow N,\ N \rightarrow Shyam \mid Reena \mid school,\ V \rightarrow goes\}$ is not operator precedence grammar.

There are three relations in operator precedence grammar, some or all of which may hold between two terminal symbols $a, b \in \Sigma$:

1. *Equal in precedence*: $a \doteq b$ if there is a production $A \rightarrow xaby$ or $A \rightarrow xaBby$, where $B \in V$.
2. *Takes precedence*: $a > b$ if there is $A \rightarrow xBby$ and a derivation $B \Rightarrow z$ where $B \in V$ and a is the rightmost terminal character of z.
3. *Yields precedence*: $a < b$ if there is a production $A \rightarrow xaBy$ and a derivation $B \Rightarrow z$ where $B \in V$ and b is the leftmost terminal character of z.

For an operator grammar, the operator precedence grammar G, and nonterminal A, the *left* and *right* terminal sets are

$$
\begin{aligned}
L_G(A) =& \{a \in \Sigma \mid A \Rightarrow^* Ba\alpha\},\\
R_G(A) =& \{a \in \Sigma \mid A \Rightarrow^* \alpha aB\},
\end{aligned}
\tag{6.21}
$$

where $B \in V \cup \{\varepsilon\}$.

The operator grammar G, the operator precedence matrix (OPM) $M = OPM(G)$ is a $\Sigma \times \Sigma$ array that to each ordered pair (a, b) associates the set M_{ab} of OP relations between a and b. For two OPMs M_1 and M_2, we define set inclusion and union:

$$
\begin{aligned}
M_1 \subseteq& \text{ if } \forall a, b : M_{1,ab} \subseteq M_{2,ab}\\
M_1 =& M_2 \text{ if } \forall a, b : M_{a,b} = M_{1,ab} \cup M_{2,ab}.
\end{aligned}
$$

Example 6.14 Floyd's grammar for arithmetic expression without and with parentheses.

Table 6.1 Precedence relations matrix for G_1

	a	$+$	$*$
a		$\gtrdot$	$\gtrdot$
$+$	$\lessdot$	$\gtrdot$	$\lessdot$
$*$	$\doteq$		

Table 6.2 Precedence relations matrix for G_2

	a	$+$	$*$	(	)
a		$\gtrdot$	$\gtrdot$		
$+$	$\lessdot$	$\lessdot$	$\lessdot$	$\lessdot$	$\gtrdot$
$*$	$\lessdot$	$\lessdot$	$\gtrdot$	$\lessdot$	$\gtrdot$
(	$\lessdot$	$\lessdot$	$\lessdot$	$\lessdot$	$\doteq$
)		$\gtrdot$	$\gtrdot$		$\gtrdot$

$$G_1 =\{E \rightarrow E + T \mid T, T \rightarrow T \times a \mid a\}$$
$$G_2 =\{E \rightarrow E + T \mid T, T \rightarrow T \times F \mid F, F \rightarrow (E) \mid a\}.$$

Since there is no production in G_1 and G_2 with consecutive nonterminals, the grammars G_1 and G_2 are precedence grammars.

The precedence matrices for G_1 and G_2 are shown in Tables 6.1 and 6.2, respectively. □

Note that the grammar G_2 is extension of G_1, where the matrices of these are conflict free.

Definition 6.18 (*Conflict-free grammar*) A grammar G is an operator precedence or Floyd grammar (FG) if and only if $M = OPM(G)$ is conflict-free matrix, i.e., $\forall a, b : |M_{ab}| \leq 1$. □

Example 6.15 Show that precedence matrices of the language $L_1 = \{a^n b^n \mid n \geq 1\}$ and $L_2 = \{c^n d^n \mid n \geq 1\}$ are conflict free.

The normal forms of the grammars of these languages are, respectively:

$$G_1{}' =\{S_1 \rightarrow A, A \rightarrow aAb \mid ab\}$$
$$G_2{}' =\{S_2 \rightarrow B, B \rightarrow cBd \mid cd\}$$

The precedence matrices M_1 and M_2 of these languages are shown in Tables 6.3 and 6.4, respectively.

We note that these matrices are conflict free. □

Table 6.3 Precedence relations matrix for $G_1{}'$

	a	b	c	d
a	$\lessdot$	$\doteq$		
b	$\gtrdot$			
c				
d				

Table 6.4 Precedence relations matrix for $G_2{}'$

	a	b	c	d
a				
b				
c			$\lessdot$	$\doteq$
d				$\gtrdot$

6.11 Classifying Context-Free Grammars

One way for classification of languages L is according to minimal number of variables in grammars for L. The number of variables in a grammar also provides an intuitive notion of complexity (of description) of grammars and languages and their intrinsic structures. The classification of languages is indicated by these grammars. The intrinsic structure of a grammar G is characterized by the number and by the depth of the *grammatical levels* of this grammar [8].

Definition 6.19 A grammatical level G_0 is designated equal to maximal set of productions of G, whose left-hand side symbols are not mutually exclusive (i.e., they are mutually dependent). □

If classification of languages is denoted by K, then $K(G)$—classes of grammars and $K(L)$—classes of languages are integers. A classification K is called *connected* in an alphabet Σ if for every integer n there is a language $L \subset \Sigma^*$ such that $K(L) = n$. The classifications are according to

i. number of nonterminals,
ii. number of productions rules,
iii. number of grammatical levels,
iv. number of non-elementary levels (i.e., grammatical levels with atleast two variables), and
v. maximal depth of grammatical levels (that is, according to maximal number of variables in grammatical levels) which are connected in any alphabet with at least two symbols.

All these classifications are based on the classification of grammars, and the integer associated to a language L is the minimal of those associated to all grammars for L.

Definition 6.20 Let K be a classification of context-free grammars. Then we extend K to classify context-free languages as

$$K(L) = min\{K(G) \mid L(G) = L\}$$

for every language L. □

A grammatical level of a grammar G is represented by a set of productions of G, whose left-hand side symbols are mutually dependent. We can say that the left-side symbols of productions in a grammatical level are "equally complicated" or are "of the same level" or define "the equally complicated languages".

Definition 6.21 Let $G = (V, \Sigma, S, P)$ be the grammar. For a set $Q \subset V^*$, let

$$G(Q) = \{x \mid T \Rightarrow^* x, x \in \Sigma^*, T \in Q\}.$$

For two variables A and B, there is $A \Rightarrow_G B$ if there are strings x and y such that production $A \rightarrow xBy$ is in P. Let $\Rightarrow_G^*$ be a *transitive reflexive closure* on relation $\Rightarrow_G$. For two variables A, B, put $A \equiv_G B$ if $A \Rightarrow_G^* B$ and $B \Rightarrow_G^* A$. For two productions $p_1 = A \rightarrow \alpha$ and $p_2 = B \rightarrow \beta$ put $p_1 \equiv_{G_1} p_2$ iff $A \equiv_G B$. □

Let G be grammar and G_0 be a grammatical level of G. We denote $Dep(G_0)$ (for depth) as number of distinct variables on the left-hand side of productions in G_0. Also,

$$Dep(G) = max\{Dep(G_0) \mid G_0 \text{ is grammatical level of } G\}.$$

The $Dep(G)/Dep(L)$ is called maximal depth of grammatical levels of G/L, respectively.

For regular language set R, $Dep(R) = 1$, and the language L with $Dep(L) = 1$ is called *sequential*. It is well known that there is a sequential language that is not regular—for example $\{a^n b^n \mid n \geq 1\}$, and there are languages that are not sequential.

6.12 Invertible Grammars

The motivation for studying this class of grammar comes from the theory of *bottom-up parsing*. Crudely speaking, bottom-up parsing consists of successively finding the phrases and reducing them to their parents. Invertible grammars allow reduction decision to be made simpler.

Definition 6.22 (*Invertible Grammar*) A context-free grammar $G = (V, \Sigma, S, P)$ is said to be invertible if no two production rules are the same of right-hand side of the productions, i.e., $A \rightarrow \alpha$ and $B \rightarrow \alpha$ in P implies $A = B$, for $A, B \in V$, and $\alpha \in (\Sigma \cup V)^*$.

Thus invertible grammars have unique right-hand sides of the productions and the reduction phase of the parsing becomes a matter of table lookup. The reason for this name is that P^{-1} is a function exactly when G is invertible.

Next we show that each context-free grammar has an equivalent invertible grammar.

Theorem 6.5 *For each context-free grammar $G = (V, \Sigma, S, P)$, there is an invertible grammar $G' = (V', \Sigma, S, P')$, such that $L(G) = L(G')$. (Note: The proof is trivial, hence left as an exercise.)* □

6.13 Summary

Context-free languages and grammars are more powerful than regular languages and their grammars, they are extensively used for describing the syntax of programming languages and natural languages.

A language recognizer is an algorithm that takes an input string and accepts it or rejects depending on whether or not the string is in the language.

A language is Regular if and only if it is generated by Regular Grammar. The Regular Languages and Regular Grammars are proper subset of context-free Languages and Grammars, respectively. The Regular Grammars are either left linear or right linear, and they are equal to each other.

To recognize a sentence/expression of a context-free language, it needs to be derived (generated) using context-free grammar. Derivation is substitution process that uses rules of grammar.

A derivation can be leftmost derivation, where substitution is done every time for the leftmost nonterminal in a sentential form, or rightmost derivation, where substitution is done every time to rightmost nonterminal symbol.

Context-free languages are closed on *set union*, *concatenation*, and *Kleene star* operations. However, they are not closed on *complementation* and *intersection*.

To show that a sentence/expression is in the given language, it requires to generate it by constructing a parse-tree using the grammar of that language. If we fail to generate it through all the efforts then the sentence is not in the language.

A parse-tree represents the *syntactic structure* of sentence of a language—in case of programming language it represents the syntax of the given statement or expression. In addition, a parse-tree also represents the semantics of the sentence being parsed.

A parse-tree can generate a sentence by starting from the top of the tree (i.e., root) and then generating subtrees by application of production rules of the grammar, until the terminals are reached. This process is called top-down parsing. If the exact given sentence is not generated, it requires to backtrack the generation process.

Other method of parsing is using bottom-up parsing, where a parse-tree is constructed starting from the bottom, i.e., starting from the given sentence's tokens as terminal nodes, and builds up to root of the tree.

If a sentence has two or more different parse-trees, this means the sentence has two or more *semantics*, indicating that the sentence and the corresponding grammar are *ambiguous*. If a sentence has k different parse-trees then the degree of ambiguity of grammar is k. An unambiguous grammar has always only one parse-tree for each sentence.

Some ambiguous grammars can be modified such that they become unambiguous. A grammar for which an equivalent unambiguous grammar cannot be obtained is called *inherently ambiguous*. *Disambiguation* of a grammar requires introduction of some nonterminals and some more production rules in the existing grammar.

It is recursively unsolvable to find out if a given grammar is an ambiguous grammar.

Floyd's precedence grammars and languages (FGs, FLs) are classical subclass of deterministic context-free grammars and languages. One way to disambiguate an arithmetic expression is using the *operator precedence grammar*, as it allows precedence relations to be specified between terminals of the grammar.

Some CFGs have interesting properties of being invertible. A grammar is invertible if productions can be applied and parsing can be carried out with equal ease for top-down and bottom-up. This can be possible if there is unique right-hand side for all the productions, i.e, if there exists $A \rightarrow \alpha$ and $A \rightarrow \beta$, then $\alpha = \beta$.

Every context-free grammar has an equivalent invertible grammar.

Self Review Questions

1. What is difference between parse-tree and syntax-tree?
2. Can a regular language be ambiguous?
3. How to check if a grammar is ambiguous?
4. What is inherently ambiguous grammar?
5. What is degree of ambiguity of a grammar?
6. What is bounded ambiguity?
7. What is reduced grammar?
8. How left-linear grammar is different from right-linear grammar?
9. Which constructs of C language can be called context-free specification of the language?
10. What is difference between leftmost and rightmost derivations?
11. What *constructs* of a high-level language like C cannot be included in CFG's specifications?
12. Why the "goto statement" cannot be implemented in the context-free grammar?
13. How the context-free grammars are classified?

14. What relations are combined in $\Rightarrow^*$ (implication) operation?
15. What is necessary condition for *induced translation*?
16. Given the number of derivations of different sentences from a grammar, is it possible to find out the degree of ambiguity of the grammar?
17. What are the advantages of invertible grammars?
18. What is meaning of depth of a grammar?

Exercises

A. Concepts based Problems

Note: The $*$ marked exercises are provided with solutions at the end of this book.

1. Answer the following terms in brief:

   a. Degree of ambiguity of a sentence.
   b. Degree of ambiguity as 1.
   c. Bounded ambiguity.

2. What is relation between canonical derivation and ambiguity of a language?
3. * Is the following grammar regular? Justify. If yes, find its regular expression.

$$A \rightarrow B0$$
$$B \rightarrow A1$$
$$C \rightarrow 0.$$

4. * Construct the grammar for balancing brackets, i.e., for (), (())), ()()(), ... Why it is important?
5. If $G = (V, \Sigma, S, P)$, and

$$V = \{S, A, B\},$$
$$\Sigma = \{a, b\},$$
$$P = \{S \rightarrow aB \mid bA, A \rightarrow a \mid aS \mid bAA, B \rightarrow b \mid bS \mid aBB\},$$

   derive the string $abbbaaab \in L(G)$ using:

   a. Leftmost derivation.
   b. Rightmost derivation.

6. Define following, and give one example for each:

   a. Inherently ambiguous grammar.
   b. Structurally ambiguous grammar.

7. Give the regular expression for the language generated by following grammar:

$$S \rightarrow abA \mid aB$$

$A \to aaS \mid bA$
$B \to aA \mid b$

8. For each of the following grammars, find out languages generated:

   a. $S \to aSa \mid bSb \mid a \mid b \mid \varepsilon$
   b. $S \to SS \mid aS \mid Sa \mid b$
   c. $S \to aSa \mid B,\ B \to bB \mid a$

9. What are regular grammars for following regular expressions?

   a. ab^*.
   b. ab^*c.
   c. a^*bc^*c.
   d. a^*b^*.

10. "It is recursively unsolvable whether an arbitrary grammar for a language is ambiguous". Explain what this statement means.
11. What are the undecidable and unsolvable problems related to ambiguity of grammars?
12. Give regular expression for the language generated by the grammar $G = (V, \Sigma, S, P)$, where $\Sigma = \{a, b\}$ and P is

$$S \to abA \mid aB,\ A \to aaS \mid bA,\ B \to aA \mid b.$$

13. Given the following grammars with some left recursion rules, find out their equivalent grammars having *no* left recursive rules:

a. $S \to A \mid B$
   $A \to aaB \mid Aab \mid Aba$
   $B \to bB \mid Bb \mid aba.$
b. $S \to A \mid B$
   $A \to AAA \mid a \mid B$
   $B \to BBb \mid b.$

14. Given the production for a CFG as

    $S \to bbA$
    $A \to Bb$
    $B \to aAa \mid \varepsilon$
    Show that the word *bbaabaab* is not in the language generated by this grammar.

B. Analysis-based Problems

15. Are the following grammars ambiguous? If yes, suggest their equivalent unambiguous grammars.

    a. $E \to EE \mid (E) \mid \varepsilon.$
    b. $P = \{E \to F - E \mid E - F \mid F,\ F \to a \mid b\}.$

16. Explain why the grammar shown below, which generates strings with equal number of 0's and 1's, is ambiguous.

$$S \to 0A \mid 1B$$
$$A \to 0AA \mid 1S \mid 1$$
$$B \to 1BB \mid 0S \mid 0$$

17. * Give context-free grammar for each of the following languages:

a. $\{a^{3i}b^i \mid i \geq 1\}$.
b. $\{a^ib^j \mid i \geq j \geq 0\}$.
c. $\{w \mid w \in \{a, b\}^* \wedge \#a(w) = 2\#b(w)\}$.

18. Give the regular grammar for the language denoted by the regular expression $(aa + bb^*a + abb^*a)^*$.
19. "A CF Grammar having no rule like $A \to xBCy$ is *operator precedence*". How?
20. * Derive the arithmetic expression $a * (a + a)/a - a$ using CFG $G = (V, \Sigma, S, P)$, where

$V = \{E\}$, (E stands for expression)
$\Sigma = \{+, -, *, /, (,), a\}$
$S = E$, and
P is

a. $E \to E + E$.
b. $E \to E - E$.
c. $E \to E/E$.
d. $E \to E * E$.
e. $E \to (E)$.
f. $E \to a$.

21. Construct context-free grammars that accept the following languages over the alphabet $\{a, b\}$.

a. $\{w : w$ starts and ends with the same symbol$\}$.
b. $\{w : |w|$ is odd$\}$.
c. $\{w : |w|$ is odd and its middle symbol is $a\}$.
d. $\{0^n1^n : n > 0\} \cup \{0^n1^{2n} \mid n > 0\}$.

22. How will you check whether an arbitrary context-free grammar generates an empty set? Give logical steps.
23. A language L is called a *palindrome languages* if $L = L^R$. Give the algorithmic steps to determine whether a given language L is a palindrome language.

C. Proof-based Problems

24. If $G = (V, \Sigma, S, P)$ is a grammar with only productions as: $A \to xB$ and $A \to x$, where $A, B \in V$, and $x \in \Sigma\Sigma^*$. Show that $L(G)$ is a regular language. [Hint: Try to show that $L(G)$ can be generated by a regular grammar.]

25. Prove the following statements:

a. If a language is regular then it can be generated by a regular grammar.
b. If a language is generated by a regular grammar then it is regular language.

26. Given the productions for a CFG G as: $S \rightarrow aSb \mid ab \mid SS$, show that if $x \in L(G)$ and $x = uv$, then $u \neq abb$. [Hint: Use mathematical induction.]
27. Give a procedure about how to generate all the sentences for the grammar used in Example 6.7, Sect. 6.6.
28. Using the mathematical induction to prove that language strings corresponding to CFG given below have number of a's more than number of b's.

$$A \rightarrow a \mid Aa \mid bAA \mid Aab \mid AbA.$$

29. * Show that following CFGs are ambiguous:

a. $S \rightarrow abb \mid bb \mid aS \mid a.$
b. $S \rightarrow SaSaS \mid b.$

30. Show that following CFG generates palindrome language and it is unambiguous. $S \rightarrow aSa \mid bSb \mid a \mid b \mid \varepsilon.$
31. Show that the context-free languages are closed under Reversal, Homomorphism, and Inverse Homomorphism.
32. Show that it is not decidable whether a given CFG is ambiguous.
33. Show that the sentence, "The man worships the god with a flower", has two leftmost derivations for the CFG $G = (V, \Sigma, S, P)$, given the set P as

$$\begin{aligned}
&S \rightarrow NP\ \ VP,\\
&NP \rightarrow Cmp\text{-}N \mid Cmp\text{-}N\ \ Preph,\\
&VP \rightarrow Cmp\text{-}V \mid Cmp\text{-}V\ \ Preph,\\
&Preph \rightarrow Prep\ Cmp\text{-}N,\\
&Cmp\text{-}N \rightarrow Art\ \ N,\\
&Cmp\text{-}V \rightarrow V \mid V\ \ NP,\\
&Art \rightarrow a \mid the,\\
&N \rightarrow man \mid god \mid flower,\\
&V \rightarrow worships,\\
&Prep \rightarrow with.
\end{aligned}$$

34. Show that following grammar generates only the language $\{a^m b^n \mid m \neq n \text{ and } m, n \geq 0\}$.

$$\begin{aligned}
&S \rightarrow AE \mid EB\\
&E \rightarrow aEb \mid \varepsilon\\
&A \rightarrow aA \mid a\\
&B \rightarrow bB \mid b
\end{aligned}$$

35. * Given the regular languages A, B, a *Cartesian product language* is defined as: $A \times B = \{xy \mid x \in A \text{ and } y \in B, \text{ and } |x| = |y|\}$. Show $A \times B$ is context-free language.
36. * Show that the language $L = \{w \in \{a, b\}^* \mid \#a(w) = \#b(w)\}$ is an unambiguous context-free language. Here $\#a(w)$ stands for number of a's in w.
37. * If L_1 and L_2 are context-free languages, then show that $L_1 \cup L_2$, L_1L_2, and L_1^* are also context-free languages.
38. "L is CFL generated by an unambiguous grammar and R is regular set, then $L \cap R$ is a CFL generated by an unambiguous grammar". Prove this statement.
39. * Show that CFL are not closed on intersection.
40. * Consider following productions of a precedence grammar:

$$\begin{aligned} S &\rightarrow A \\ A &\rightarrow A + B \mid B \\ B &\rightarrow B * C \mid C \\ C &\rightarrow (A) \mid \varepsilon \end{aligned} \tag{6.22}$$

Find out the complete matrix of precedence relations for this grammar.

D. Multiple choice Questions

41. Consider the CFG $G = (V, \Sigma, S, P)$ where $V = \{S, A, B\}$, $\Sigma = \{a, b\}$, and set of productions as

$S \rightarrow aB \mid bA \mid bAA$
$A \rightarrow a \mid aS$
$B \rightarrow b \mid bS \mid aBB$

a. Which of the following strings are generated by this grammar?
(A) *aabbab*, (B) *aabbbb*, (C) *aaaabb*, (D) *abbbba*

b. For the correct strings in above grammar, how many derivation-trees can be there in each case?
(A) 1, (B) 2, (C) 3, (D) 4

42. * In the table given below, match the entries (a-d) to those on right side (1–4):

a. Number of formal parameters in a function declaration agrees with the actual parameters in its use	1. $L_1 = \{a^n b^m c^n d^m \mid n \geq 1, m \geq 1\}$
b. Arithmetic expressions with matched pairs of parentheses	2. $S \rightarrow bSb \mid cSc \mid \varepsilon$
c. Palindromes	3. $L_2 = \{wcw \mid w \in (a \mid b)^*\}$
d. Identifiers are declared before their use	4. $X \rightarrow XbX \mid XcX \mid dXf \mid g$

(A) $a : 3, b : 1, c : 4, d : 2$, (B) $a : 1, b : 3, c : 2, d : 4$,
(C) $a : 3, b : 1, c : 2, d : 4$, (D) $a : 1, b : 4, c : 2, d : 3$

43. Given productions of a grammar as: $S \rightarrow aSa \mid bSb \mid a \mid b$, the language generated by this grammar over the alphabet $\{a, b\}$ is the set of
    (A) Strings that begin and end with the same symbol.
    (B) All palindromes.
    (C) All odd length palindromes.
    (D) All even length palindromes.
44. * If P is language p^*q^* and $Q = \{p^n q^n \mid n \geq 0\}$, which of the following is always regular language? (A) $P - Q$, (B) $P \cap Q$, (C) $\Sigma^* - Q$, (D) $\Sigma^* - P$

E. Advanced Knowledge Assessment Problems

45. Create a context-free grammar that generates the language of all balanced parentheses expressions. For example, your grammar should generate strings like "()()", "((()))", but not "())(" or "(()".
46. Explore and explain how CFGs are used in programming languages. Provide examples of syntax rules in a programming language represented by a CFG and discuss how parsers use CFGs to validate and interpret source code.

References

1. Aho AV, Ullman JD (1975) Deterministic parsing of ambiguous grammars. Commun ACM 18(8):441–452
2. Aho AV, Ullman JD (1975) Translations on context-free grammars. Inf Control 19(5):439–475
3. Bar-Hillel Y et al (1961) On formal properties of simple phrase structure grammars. Zeitschrift für Phonetik, Sprachweissenshaft und Kommunika-tionsforschung 14:143–172
4. Cantor DG (1962) On the ambiguity problem of backus systems. J ACM 9(4):477–479. ISSN:0004-5411
5. Floyd RW (1962) On ambiguity in phrase structure languages. Commun ACM 5(10):526–534
6. Floyd RW (1963) Syntactic analysis and operator precedence. J ACM 316–333
7. Ginsburg S, Ullian J (1966) Ambiguity in context free languages. J ACM 13(1):62–89
8. Gruska J (1969) Some classifications of context-free languages. Inf Control 14(2):152–179
9. Chowdhary KR (2018) Lecture notes on context-free languages and grammars. http://www.krchowdhary.com/toc/8-cfg-cfl.pdf, seen on Aug. 02, 2022
10. Maurer HA (1967) A direct proof of the inherent ambiguity of a simple context-free language. J ACM 16(2):256–260
11. Révész GE (1991) Introduction to formal languages. Courier Corporation
12. Crespi Reghizzi S, Mandrioli D (2012) Operator precedence and the visibly pushdown property. J Comput Syst Sci 78(6):1837–1867

Chapter 7
Normal Forms of Context-Free Grammars

Abstract In context-free grammars, the left-hand part of every production is a nonterminal symbol, while the right-hand part comprises terminals as well as nonterminals, of any length and order. These variable length productions, when used in parsing, may produce ever-expanding parse trees, adding to excessive complexity in the parsing algorithms. However, these grammars can be transformed into standard forms: either to Chomsky Normal Form (CNF) or to Greibach Normal Formal (GNF), which have only linear time complexities, while their generating capability of language strings remains the same. A normalized form of grammar is useful in many proofs related to some interesting properties of context-free grammars. This chapter presents simplifications of context-free grammars, which are prerequisites for normalization, and the proofs that show that normal forms of the grammars generate the same language as the original one. The pumping lemma for context-free languages is presented along with worked-out problems. In addition, self-review questions along with the number of classified exercises at the chapter end, are aimed to make overall learning an interesting one.

Keywords Normal-forms · Chomsky normal form · Greibach normal form · Transformation of grammars · Null-productions · Unit-productions · Useless productions · Binary standard form · Invertible grammars · Decision problems · Leftmost derivation · Chain rule · Pumping lemma for CFLs

7.1 Introduction

The context-free grammars (CFGs) are a class of grammars whose production rules have a head as a single nonterminal and the body of the rules have no restriction, i.e., it can have any number of terminals and nonterminals in any order. The results of this type are of general interest because if we want to show that some set is context-free, it becomes easier to do so if we can employ full generality of context-free grammars. Further, this approach helps us to exploit all the rules of null productions ($A \rightarrow \varepsilon$), unit productions (chain rules, i.e., like, $A \rightarrow B$), left-recursions, etc. On the other hand, if one wishes to show that some property of grammar does not hold,

K. R. Chowdhary, *Theory of Computation*,
https://doi.org/10.1007/978-981-97-6234-7_7

it is convenient to restrict the type of grammar, so that the complexity of proof is reduced. Complexity here means in respect of time and space consumed by the algorithm. As an example, instead of a grammar being $A \rightarrow \alpha$,[1] if it is $A \rightarrow BC$, the parse-tree will be a binary tree, and there are efficient algorithms available for processing binary trees, also the binary trees can be more easily analyzed.

This chapter will show some normal formats of context-free grammars that are capable of generating all the context-free languages. Accordingly, we will be interested in transforming any grammar into these normal forms. In addition, we will impose certain restrictions on the production. However, in spite of restrictions due to normal forms, and certain other restrictions, the generative power of the grammars remains unchanged. If G is a CFG, its corresponding context-free language $L(G)$ can be generated with following restrictions on G:

1. Each variable and each terminal symbol of G appears in the derivation of some word of $L(G)$.
2. There are no productions of the form $A \rightarrow B$, called *unit production* or *chain rule*, where A and B are nonterminals.
3. If $\varepsilon \notin L(G)$, then there is no need of productions of the form $A \rightarrow \varepsilon$.

In addition, there are some *normal forms*, if applied to the grammars, they will still generate the same language as the original grammar [3].

Definition 7.1 (*Chomsky Normal Form*) A context-free grammar $G = (V, \Sigma, S, P)$ is in Chomsky normal form (CNF) if each production is one of these forms:

$$A \rightarrow BC \mid a, \tag{7.1}$$

where $A, B, C \in V$, and $a \in \Sigma$. □

Another normal form is called the Greibach Normal Form (GNF).

Definition 7.2 (*Greibach Normal Form*) For a CFG $G = (V, \Sigma, S, P)$ with $\varepsilon \notin L(G)$ is Greibach normal form (GNF) if all the production rules are of the form,

$$A \rightarrow a\alpha, \tag{7.2}$$

where $\alpha \in V^*$ and $a \in \Sigma$. □

If a CFG is in normal form then it cannot have infinite left-going structure. In addition, using the normal form we can give particularly elegant proofs of the connection between context-free languages and, pushdown-store machines.

---

[1] Let the grammar is $G = (V, \Sigma, S, P)$, where V is set of nonterminals, Σ is set of terminals, S is started symbol, and P is set of productions. A production rule $A \rightarrow \alpha$ is in CFG, where $\alpha \in (V \cup \Sigma)^*$.

Learning Outcomes of this Chapter:

1. Simplification of grammars. [Knowledge]
2. Transformation of grammars. [Synthesis]
3. Chomsky normal forms. [Analysis]
4. Greibach normal forms. [Analysis]
5. CNF vs. CFG. [Comprehension]
6. Removal of ε-productions, unit productions. [Apply]
7. Removal of useless symbols and productions. [Apply]
8. CFG to CNF. [Synthesis]
9. CFG to GNF. [Synthesis]
10. Pumping lemma for CFL. [Synthesis], [Analysis]
11. Decidable properties of CFLs. [Analysis]
12. Closure properties of CFLs. [Analysis]

7.2 Simplification of Grammars

We shall show that any language L that does not contain ε-string and it can be generated by CFG, can also be generated by a CFG in CNF format. We shall also show that every language L such that $\varepsilon \notin L$, and can be generated by CFG, can also be generated by CFG in Greibach Normal Form. We will first show that language L, not containing empty words and generated by CFG, can be generated using CNF of context-free grammar. We begin with two Lemmas, the first which demonstrates the flexibility of derivations in CF languages, and shows that if we have the derivation $\alpha\beta \Rightarrow^* \gamma$, where $\alpha, \beta, \gamma \in (V \cup \Sigma)^*$ and α, β may be treated separately, then we may derive $\gamma_1\gamma_2 \Rightarrow \gamma$.

Lemma 7.1 *Let $G = (V, \Sigma, S, P)$ be a grammar and $\alpha\beta \Rightarrow^* \gamma$ be derivable in G with n steps, where $\alpha, \beta, \gamma \in (V \cup \Sigma)^*$. Then γ can be expressed as $\gamma_1\gamma_2$, where $\alpha \Rightarrow^* \gamma_1$, and $\beta \Rightarrow^* \gamma_2$ are the derivations in G, both containing at most n steps.*

Proof We make use of *Induction* on the number of steps in the production. Assume that there is one step. Then any one nonterminal can be replaced using a production. Assume that it is $A \to uBv$. Either A is in the string α or it is in β. Without loss of generality, assume that it is in α, so,

$$\alpha = XAY$$

and

$$\alpha \Rightarrow XuBvY = \alpha'.$$

Further,

$$\alpha\beta \Rightarrow XuBvY\beta = \alpha'\beta.$$

So, let $\gamma_1 = \alpha'$ and $\gamma_2 = \beta$ we are done.

Assume that lemma is true for all derivations with less than k-steps. Assume $\alpha\beta \Rightarrow^* \gamma$ contains k-steps. As above, assume the first step is $\alpha\beta \Rightarrow \alpha'\beta$, where $\alpha \Rightarrow \alpha'$. Note that $\alpha'\beta \Rightarrow \gamma$ uses $k - 1$ steps. By induction there are derivations $\alpha' \Rightarrow^* \gamma_1, \beta \Rightarrow^* \gamma_2$ containing at most k steps. Therefore, $\alpha \Rightarrow \alpha', \alpha' \Rightarrow^* \gamma_1, \beta \Rightarrow^* \gamma_2$ are required derivations. □

One result of this lemma is that we can get from $\alpha\beta \Rightarrow^* \gamma$ by derivation,

$$\alpha\beta \Rightarrow^* \gamma_1\beta \Rightarrow^* \gamma_1\gamma_2,$$

where $\gamma = \gamma_1\gamma_2$ since if $X_1 \Rightarrow X_2$ is derivation, then so are $X_1\beta \Rightarrow X_2\beta$, and $\alpha X_1 \Rightarrow \alpha X_2$.

The next lemma shows that in applying productions, the order in which we apply the productions is not particularly important. In fact, we can derive any word w in the language generated by grammar G by replacing the leftmost nonterminal with the right part of a production at each step in the derivation. This is called as *leftmost derivation*.

Lemma 7.2 *Let $w \in L(G)$, the language generated by grammar $G = (V, \Sigma, S, P)$, then there exists a leftmost derivation of w.*

Proof For the proof, we make use of the induction of the number of steps n in the derivation. If $n = 1$, the derivation $S \Rightarrow w$ is obvious leftmost derivation. If $n = k - 1$, and $S \Rightarrow^* w$, let $S \Rightarrow \alpha\beta$ where $\alpha, \beta \in (V \cup \Sigma)^*$. By Lemma 7.1, there exists derivation $\alpha \Rightarrow^* w_1$ and $\beta \Rightarrow^* w_2$, where $w = w_1w_2$. Since, both of these derivations contains less than k-steps, there exist leftmost derivations containing less than k-steps, and there exists leftmost derivations $\alpha \Rightarrow^* w_1$ and $\beta \Rightarrow^* w_2$. Then, $S \Rightarrow \alpha\beta \Rightarrow^* w_1\beta \Rightarrow^* w_1w_2$ is leftmost derivation of w. □

In the following we will show that if a language L generated by context-free grammar G does not contain empty word ε, then L can be generated by a context-free grammar which does not contain any productions of the form $A \to \varepsilon$. The latter we call as *null productions*. Note that the only purpose of such production is to remove A from the sentential form. For example, if we have the productions $C \to abBaAa$ and $A \to \varepsilon$, we can derive $C \Rightarrow^* abBaa$ [1].

Suppose we have productions $A \to aB$, $B \to C$, $C \to aa$, and $C \to \varepsilon$. If we add a production $B \to \varepsilon$, we have created a new ε-production. If we remove just $C \to \varepsilon$, we are not in a position to derive a.

Definition 7.3 A nonterminal X is called *nilpotent* if $X \Rightarrow^* \varepsilon$. □

If there is no ε-string in the language, then we should remove all *nilpotents* and not just the ε-productions. Thus, in the sequence of productions, $A \rightarrow aB$, $B \rightarrow C$, $C \rightarrow aa$, and $C \rightarrow \varepsilon$, if $C \rightarrow \varepsilon$ is removed from these productions, we will have to remove $B \rightarrow C$, and also $A \rightarrow aB$, but $A \rightarrow a$ needs to be added.

The first requirement in the grammar can be to determine the nilpotents of the grammar. Let the set of all the nilpotents of the grammar G is θ. The following steps of an algorithm determine the nilpotents of a grammar by examining the productions.

1. If $A \rightarrow \varepsilon$ is a production, then add A into θ.
2. If $A \rightarrow A_1A_2...A_n$, where $A_1, A_2, ..., A_n \in \theta$ then add A to θ.
3. repeat step (2) until no new nilpotents are left to be added to θ.

The nonterminals in θ can be removed from the grammar. In the following, we consider all possible aspects.

7.2.1 Removing Null-Productions

If language $L(G)$ contains the ε-strings, certainly all the productions of the form $A \rightarrow \varepsilon$ cannot be eliminated from the CFG G. However, if there are no null-strings in $L(G)$, it is possible to eliminate all the ε-productions from the grammar. However, if $\varepsilon \in L(G)$, then we could eliminate all the null productions (null rules) and get a grammar for $L(G) - \varepsilon$, because the ε-strings have no use in any language.

The method for removing the null productions consists of finding a variables A for which $A \Rightarrow^* \varepsilon$ holds. In that case, the variable A is called *nullable* (also nilpotent). In such cases, each production of the form $B \rightarrow X_1X_2 \ldots X_n$ can be replaced by production formed by eliminating some X_i that are nullable. But, if there is a production like $B \rightarrow \varepsilon$, it is not considered nullable even if all X_i in $B \rightarrow X_1X_2 \ldots X_n$ are nullable.

The empty string plays a singular role in many theorems and proofs. Therefore, it is often necessary to give special attention to the null string. However, we prefer to remove it from a language without losing its generality.

Let L be a context-free language and $G = (V, \Sigma, S, P)$ be the corresponding context-free grammar with $\{\varepsilon\} \subseteq L(G)$. It is possible to obtain $G' = (V', \Sigma, S', P')$ using G, with no ε-productions such that G' will generate the same language L. Hence, $L(G') = L(G) - \{\varepsilon\}$. Instead, we may eliminate all null rules except $S \rightarrow \varepsilon$ and further restrict the new grammar so that S does not appear in any right-hand side of a production. For all practical purposes, there is no difference between context-free languages, which include ε-string, and those that do not.

Definition 7.4 Let $G = (V, \Sigma, S, P)$ be a context-free grammar, and let $A, B \in V$. Then B is said to be *reducible* from A if $A \Rightarrow^* B$ for $\alpha, \beta \in V^*$. □

We have the following idea of an algorithm to find the symbols that are nullable, i.e., derives to ε.

1. Initially, mark all variables C with production $C \rightarrow \varepsilon$.
2. If there is a production $A \rightarrow B_1 B_2 \dots B_m$, where all B_i's are nullable, then mark A as nullable. This can be done in linear time as follows:

   2.1 for each production of the form $A \rightarrow B_1 B_2 \dots B_m$, assign a counter denoting the number of nullable variables on the right-hand side, which is initially zero;

   2.2 for each variable A, store a list of pointers to all productions whose right-hand side contain A, and when A becomes nullable, update the corresponding counters.

Lemma 7.3 *Let G be a grammar such that $\varepsilon \notin L(G)$. Then a new grammar G' can be formed by:*

1. *removing all ε-productions (i.e., $A_i \rightarrow \varepsilon$),*
2. *for each production $A \rightarrow \alpha$ in G, where $\alpha = w_1 X_1 w_2 X_2 ... w_n X_n$, and nilpotents $X_1 ... X_n$ (which may all be not distinct), let P be a power set of $\{1, 2, ..., n\}$, and for $p \in P$, form productions $A \rightarrow \alpha_p$, where α_p is the string α in which $\{X_i \mid i \in p \text{ and } X_i \rightarrow \varepsilon\}$, are removed.*
   In this case, the language generated by G' is the same as that generated by G.

Proof Let us assume that L is the language generated by $G = (V, \Sigma, S, P)$, and L' be the language generated by $G' = (V, \Sigma, S, P')$. The language $L' \subseteq L$, since any production in G' that is not in G can be replaced with the original productions in G used to define it.

To show that $L \subseteq L'$, let $w \in L$. Using induction on the number of steps in derivation, we show that if $S \Rightarrow^* w$ using productions in P, then $S \Rightarrow^* w$ using productions in P'. If there is one step in derivation ($n = 1$), then $S \rightarrow w$ is obviously a production in P', since $w \neq \varepsilon$. Assuming $n = k$, the $S \Rightarrow^* w$ is a derivation in G containing k steps. Let $S \Rightarrow Y_1 Y_2 ... Y_m$ be the first derivation where $Y_i \in (V \cup \Sigma)$. Therefore,

$$S \Rightarrow Y_1 Y_2 ... Y_m \Rightarrow^* w$$

is the derivation $S \Rightarrow^* w$.

From Lemma 7.1 (Sect. 7.2), there exists a derivation $Y \Rightarrow^* w_i$ in G, for $1 \leq i \leq m$, where $w = w_1 w_2 ... w_m$ and each derivation has less than k steps. Using induction, if $w_i \neq \varepsilon$, there exists a derivation $Y_i \Rightarrow^* w_i$ in G' for $1 \leq i \leq m$. If Y_i is a terminal, then $Y_i = w_i$ and $Y_i \Rightarrow^* w_i$ has zero steps. Let $Y_i' = Y_i$ if $w_i \neq \varepsilon$ and $Y_i' = \varepsilon$ if $w_i = \varepsilon$. Then, $S \Rightarrow Y_1' Y_2' ... Y_m' \Rightarrow^* w_1 Y_2' ... Y_m' \Rightarrow^* w_1 w_2 Y_3' ... \Rightarrow^* w_1 w_2 ... w_m$ is derivation in grammar G'. □

For more clarifications, it is to be noted that if one follows the above proof carefully, we will see that if $L(G)$ comprised an empty word ε, the only difference between $L(G)$ and $L(G')$ is that, $L(G)$ has empty word while $L(G')$ does not. The nonterminal S is a nilpotent that does not get removed. However, if $S \to \varepsilon$ is a production, the production is removed.

The productions which are in *chain form*, called *trivial productions* or *unit productions*, and their removal are explained below.

Example 7.1 Eliminate the null productions in the following grammar:

$$
\begin{aligned}
S &\to AbB \mid C,\\
B &\to AA \mid AC,\\
C &\to b \mid c,\\
A &\to a \mid \varepsilon.
\end{aligned}
$$

We note that the nonterminal A and hence the nonterminal B is also nullable. We obtain the intermediate grammar as follows. Note that $\not{A}$, $\not{B}$ shows that these symbols are replaced by ε.

$$
\begin{aligned}
S &\to AbB \mid \not{A}bB \mid Ab\ \not{B} \mid \not{A}b\ \not{B} \mid C,\\
B &\to AA \mid \not{A}A \mid A\ \not{A} \mid \not{A}\ \not{A} \mid AC \mid \not{A}C,\\
C &\to b \mid c,\\
A &\to a.
\end{aligned}
$$

In the above, we have done the *inline expansion*, also called *inlining*[2] After dropping $\not{A}$, and $\not{B}$, we get:

$$
\begin{aligned}
S &\to AbB \mid bB \mid Ab \mid b \mid C,\\
B &\to AA \mid A \mid AC \mid C,\\
C &\to b \mid c,\\
A &\to a.
\end{aligned}
$$

In the new grammar, we have not retained the new rule $B \to \varepsilon$, which should be due to $B \to \not{A}\ \not{A}$, but $B \to \varepsilon$ has already been dropped, and it does not affect any other rule.

The new grammar has no ε-productions, and still, it produces the same language strings as the original grammar. It is left as an exercise for the student to generate all

[2] Inline expansion is similar to macro expansion, but occurs during compilation, without changing the source code. However, macro expansion occurs prior to compilation and produces a modified text, which is later processed by the compiler.

the strings in both the grammars and verify that these are the same. It is important to note that there is no recursion in the grammar (there is no same nonterminal in the left and right sides of any production). □

7.2.2 Removing Unit Productions

In simplification of context-free grammars, another important step is to make the given context-free grammar as *unit-rule* free. This is essential for the applications in compilers, as the compiler spends time on each rule used in parsing by generating semantic routines, having unnecessary unit rules will increase the compiler's time.

Lemma 7.4 *Let G be a CFG, then there exists a CFG G' without unit rules such that $L(G) = L(G')$.*

Proof Elimination of unit productions is somewhat similar to the elimination of ε-productions. When unit productions are eliminated we must be sure that the same strings can be generated by the grammar as earlier. Sometimes, there is a requirement to add a production when a unit production is removed. Consider the following productions.

$$A \rightarrow B$$
$$B \rightarrow bB \mid c$$

The unit production $A \rightarrow B$ can be deleted and we add production:

$$A \rightarrow bB \mid c$$

For this, we need a systematic view to find all the pairs of the variable (A, B) such that $A \Rightarrow^* B$. If there are no null productions in G, such pairs can be easily located by a sequence of unit productions, for all the variables pairs. But, if these are null productions, then finding unit productions is somewhat difficult, because $A \Rightarrow^* B$ may be derived through $A \Rightarrow BC \Rightarrow B$, where $C \rightarrow \varepsilon$. Therefore, before removing the unit productions, it is necessary that all the ε-productions be removed. Thus, first G' is obtained from G so that G' is free from ε-productions, and $L(G) = L(G')$.

Once G' is without ε-productions, we can find for each variable A, all variables B such that there is a derivation $A \Rightarrow^* B$. This can be achieved by drawing a dependency graph with edges (v_i, v_j) whenever the grammar has a unit production $v_i \rightarrow v_j$, where $v_i, v_j \in V$. Thus, $A \Rightarrow^* B$ holds whenever there is walk-through in the graph from A to B.

Let G has some unit productions, and the equivalent grammar obtained from G after having removed the unit productions is $G' = (V', \Sigma, S, P')$. The G' can be constructed as follows.

1. First add into P' all non-unit productions of P,
2. Next, for all A and B satisfying $A \Rightarrow^* B$, we add into P' the production $A \rightarrow \alpha_1 \mid \alpha_2 \mid \cdots \mid \alpha_n$,

where $B \rightarrow \alpha_1 \mid \alpha_2 \mid \cdots \mid \alpha_n$ is already in P'. Since this is already in P', none of the α_i are single variables because only the non-unit productions were added into P' in advance. Therefore, no unit productions are created in P'. The same process can be used for adding the remaining productions from P to P'. This completes the construction of G'. □

In the next lemma, we show that, the context-free languages $L(G)$ and $L(G')$ are equal.

Lemma 7.5 *If $G = (V, \Sigma, S, P)$, and language $L(G)$ generated by G does not contain an empty word, then there exists a grammar G' with no ε-productions, and no unit productions, such that $L(G) = L(G')$.*

Proof Let us assume that G has no ε-productions. We create G' by removing the unit productions whenever $A1 \rightarrow A_2 \rightarrow ... \rightarrow A_m \Rightarrow^* B$ occurs, where each $A_i \rightarrow A_{i+1}$ is a unit production, and there is $B \rightarrow w'$, then remove all the trivial (unit) productions, and include $A_1 \rightarrow B$; here $A_1, A_2, ..., A_m \in V$.

By construction, there is $L(G') \subseteq L(G)$.

Conversely, assume that $S \Rightarrow^* w$ occurs in G. We use induction on the number of trivial derivations, to show that there is a derivation $S \Rightarrow^* w$ in G'. Obviously if there is no unit production then derivation is in G'. Assume that there are k unit productions in the derivation, and let derivation is a leftmost derivation in w. Assume that $S \Rightarrow^* w$ has the form,

$$
\begin{aligned}
S &\Rightarrow^* X_1 A_1 X_2 \Rightarrow w_1 A_1 X_2 \Rightarrow w_1 A_2 X_2 \Rightarrow w_1 A_3 X_2 \\
&\Rightarrow^* \ldots \\
&\Rightarrow^* w_1 A_m X_2 \Rightarrow^* w_1 w' X_2 \Rightarrow^* w_1 w' w_2,
\end{aligned}
$$

where $A_1 \rightarrow A_2 \rightarrow ... \rightarrow A_m$ is the sequence of unit productions in the derivation, and $A_m \rightarrow w'$. Then there is a derivation,

$$X_1 \Rightarrow^* w_1,\ X_2 \Rightarrow^* w_2 \text{ in } G,$$

and

$$S \Rightarrow^* X_1 A_1 X_2 \Rightarrow^* w_1 A_1 X_2 \Rightarrow w_1 w X_2 \Rightarrow^* w_1 w w_2,$$

has no unit productions. Hence, using induction hypothesis there is a derivation $S \Rightarrow^* w$ in G'. □

7.2.3 Removing Useless Symbols and Productions

Certain symbols from the grammar can be eliminated without affecting the generating capability of the grammar. At the same time, it simplifies the grammar. Let $G = (V, \Sigma, S, P)$ be the CFG. A symbol $X \in V$ is called a *useful symbol* if there is a derivation like,

$$S \Rightarrow^* \alpha X \beta \Rightarrow^* w,$$

where $\alpha, \beta \in (V \cup \Sigma)^*$. The X is useful because it appears at least in one derivation from start symbol S to a word $w \in L(G)$. If this is not the case, then X is *useless symbol*. The justification for this is that a terminal string must be derivable through X.

Another condition for X to be useful is that it should derive a string $u \in \Sigma^*$, i.e., $X \Rightarrow^* u$. These two conditions are necessary, but they are not sufficient. However, the usefulness of a symbol has to be tested in the two steps above.

In the productions given below, variable B is not reachable through derivations from S, hence it is useless. The production $B \rightarrow bB$ is called *useless production* in the grammar:

$$S \rightarrow aSb \mid \varepsilon,$$
$$B \rightarrow bB.$$

When productions that do not take part in the derivation process are removed, it results in simplified grammar.

Consider another set of productions P for a grammar as given below.

$$S \rightarrow aSb \mid A \mid \varepsilon,$$
$$A \rightarrow aA.$$

Here, the production $S \rightarrow A$ has no role because if A appears in a sentential form, it cannot be eliminated while generating a terminal string. Hence, the productions $S \rightarrow A$ and $A \rightarrow aA$ both can be removed. The resulting grammar is simpler compared to earlier, and given by

$$S \rightarrow aSb \mid \varepsilon.$$

Theorem 7.1 *Let there be a context-free language $L = L(G)$ where $G = (V, \Sigma, S, P)$ such that $\varepsilon \notin L(G)$, then there exists a CFG G', such that (i) G' generates L, and (ii) G' does not have useless productions, (i.e., which are not substitutable in any derivation), (iii) G' does not have ε-productions and unit productions.*

Proof Using Lemma 7.3, ε-productions can be removed from G without losing its generating capability. Next, construct a new set of productions P' from P by first including only non-unit productions from P. Let $A \Rightarrow^*_G B$, for $A, B \in V$. Add to P' all the productions of the form $A\alpha$, where $B\alpha$ is a non-unit production, and $B\alpha$ is already in P'. Therefore, as per Lemma 7.3 we get a modified grammar $G' = (V', \Sigma, S, P')$. Next, eliminate unit productions symbols in V and get V', thus $G = (V', \Sigma, S, P')$.

Since all these three operations do not change the generating power of the grammar G' obtained from G, hence $L(G) = L(G')$. This proves the theorem. □

Example 7.2 Remove useless symbols and productions in the following grammar:

$$S \rightarrow A$$
$$A \rightarrow aA \mid \varepsilon$$
$$B \rightarrow bA.$$

We note that variable B cannot appear in any sentential form during the derivation of any string. Though a derivation from B leads to a primary string, this is of no use if B does not appear in any sentential form after starting from S. Therefore, variable B and production $B \rightarrow bA$ can be removed without affecting the generating power of grammar G. The resulting simplified grammar as per Lemma 7.4 is

$$S \rightarrow A$$
$$A \rightarrow aA \mid \varepsilon.$$

□

Theorem 7.2 *Let CFG* $G = (V, \Sigma, P, S)$ *contains productions of the form*

I. $A \rightarrow \alpha B\beta$
II. $B \rightarrow a \mid b \mid c,$

where $A, B \in V$.

Then, there exists an equivalent CFG $G' = (V', \Sigma, S, P')$ *where* P' *is obtained by deleting productions I and II from P and using only the production III.*

III. $A \rightarrow \alpha a\beta \mid \alpha b\beta \mid \alpha c\beta.$

In this case, the language strings generated by two grammars will be the same, i.e., $L(G) = L(G')$.

Proof Let $w \in L(G)$, such that $S \Rightarrow^*_G w$. If rules I and II are not used in this derivation, and instead, III is used, the rest of the grammars G and G' are the same. Hence, $S \Rightarrow^*_{G'} w$. A derivation in G is

$$S \Rightarrow^*_G uAv \Rightarrow_G u\alpha B\beta v \Rightarrow_G u\alpha b\beta v.$$

If the production $A \rightarrow \alpha B\beta$ is used in derivation $S \Rightarrow_G^* w$, then B so introduced in the sentential form is ultimately replaced. Nothing is lost if this is immediately removed. Since in grammar G', B is immediately replaced by b in a sentential form $\alpha B\beta$, the corresponding derivation is

$$S \Rightarrow_{G'}^* uAv \Rightarrow_{G'} u\alpha b\beta v.$$

Since, using either of the approaches we reach the same sentential form, hence the proof. □

Example 7.3 Simplify the grammar with productions,

$$A \rightarrow a \mid aaA \mid abBc,\ B \rightarrow abba \mid b.$$

The simplified grammar after applying Theorem 7.2 is

$$A \rightarrow a \mid aaA \mid ababbac \mid abbc.$$

□

Theorem 7.3 *Given a CFG $G = (V, \Sigma, S, P)$ with $L(G) \neq \phi$, there exists an equivalent CFG $G' = (V', \Sigma, S, P')$ such that for every variable $A \in V'$ there is derivation $S \Rightarrow^* \alpha A\beta \Rightarrow^* w$, for $w \in \Sigma^*$, where $\alpha, \beta \in (\Sigma \cup V')^*$. In other words, the equivalent CFG G' does not contain any useless symbols and productions.*

Proof A useless symbol does not appear in any derivation $S \Rightarrow^* w$, for $w \in L(G)$, hence, useless symbol is not reachable in a parse-tree.

We identify useless symbols as follows First initialize the sets $V' = \phi$, $P' = \phi$. Next, consider variables $A_i \in V$ such that $A_i \rightarrow u \in P$, and $u \in \Sigma^*$. Since $A_i \Rightarrow^* u$ holds, we move A_i to V' and $A_i \rightarrow u$ to P'. This is shown by level $k-1$ in the tree, in Fig. 7.1. Since only the dependent nodes are connected, this is *dependency graph*.[3]

Next, consider the productions $A_j \rightarrow X_1X_2 \ldots X_n \in P$, such that when X_i is nonterminal, it is necessary that X_i has been already added into V', else X_i need to be a terminal. In both cases, a terminal string can be generated with a derivation $A_j \Rightarrow X_1X_2 \ldots X_n \Rightarrow^* u$. The above situation is also illustrated in Fig. 7.1, and corresponds to levels $k-2$.

Explanation: To start with, we consider the level $k-1$ in this tree. Since $A_i \rightarrow ab$, therefore this production is moved into P' and variable A_i is moved into V'. A similar process is repeated for all the variables at $k-1$ level. Next, for level $k-2$, the symbols A_i are already in V'. We repeat the same process at $k-2$ to move the nonterminal symbols (A_j) into V' and productions $(A_j \rightarrow A_icd)$ into P'. Repeat this up to level 0 in the tree.

[3] A dependency graph is least likely to be a tree, because there will be productions like $A \rightarrow uAv$, which forms a loop at nonterminal A.

Fig. 7.1 Dependency graph

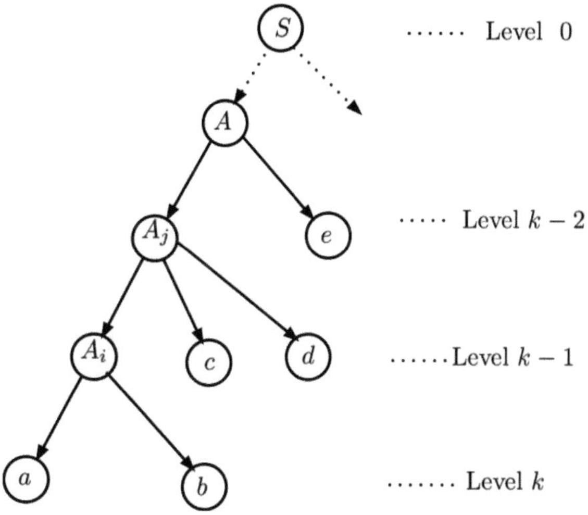

This results in the generation of CFG G'. Due to this, the variables and productions that are not part of this dependency graph, are automatically eliminated. Now, $V' \subseteq V$, $P' \subseteq P$ and $G' \subseteq G$. However, G' will generate the strings of the same language that were generated using G, because only the useless symbols and productions which were not contributing in the generation of strings earlier have been deleted. Therefore, $L(G') = L(G)$, and G' is simplified versions of G. □

Definition 7.5 (*Perfectly Reduced Grammar*) A Grammar G' obtained from Grammar G is said to be perfectly reduced if the following conditions of G' are satisfied [5]:

1. $L(G) = L(G')$'
2. G' is null free, i.e., it has no productions like $A \rightarrow \varepsilon$,
3. G' has no unit productions, like $A \rightarrow B$, where $A, B \in V$, and
4. G' is reduced and has no useless symbols and useless productions. □

7.3 Chomsky Normal Form

The CFGs have no restrictions on the right-hand side part of every production $A \rightarrow \alpha$, where $\alpha \in (V \cup \Sigma)^*$. The normal forms of these grammars state that all the context-free grammars are equivalent to grammars with some restrictions on the right side of each production. Many proofs can be simplified if the right-hand (α) are bounded to be of length two; then no grammar tree ever has more than binary branching.

Definition 7.6 A context-free grammar $G = (V, \Sigma, S, P)$ is in *Chomsky normal form* (CNF) if each production is one of these forms:

$$A \rightarrow BC \mid a, \tag{7.3}$$

where $A \in V$; $B, C \in V - \{S\}$, and $a \in \Sigma$. In addition, the start symbol S may appear only on the left-hand side of the rules. □

The CNF is also called *Binary standard form.*.

A grammar G in CNF has the property that any string w, with $|w| = n$, can be derived through $2n - 1$ number of derivation steps. This is because, its derivation steps strictly make use of binary productions like, $A \rightarrow BC$ and unary productions like $A \rightarrow a$. Figure 7.2 shows the derivation steps of a tree for string, $w = a_0a_1a_2...a_{n-1}$, where $|w| = n = 2^m$ for integer m. We note that derivation in CNF is a binary tree.

Example 7.4 Generate the string *ababab*, for the following grammar, which is in CNF:

$$S \rightarrow AB \mid SS,$$
$$A \rightarrow a,$$
$$B \rightarrow b.$$

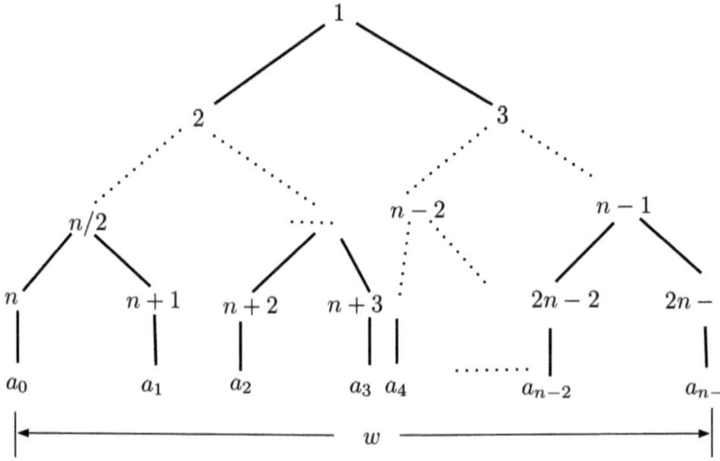

Fig. 7.2 Derivation steps for a parse-tree using CNF grammar

The derivation is

$$\begin{aligned} S \Rightarrow & SS \Rightarrow SSS \Rightarrow ABSS \Rightarrow aBSS \Rightarrow abSS \\ \Rightarrow & abABS \Rightarrow abaBS \Rightarrow ababS \Rightarrow ababAB \\ \Rightarrow & ababaB \Rightarrow ababab. \end{aligned}$$

Here, $|w| = 6$, hence, number of steps should be $2n - 1 = 12 - 1 = 11$. Note that, the actual steps carried out in generating the string are also 11. □

Theorem 7.4 *For each context-free grammar $G = (V, \Sigma, S, P)$ without null productions, unit productions, and useless productions, there is a grammar $G' = (V', \Sigma, S, P')$ such that $L(G) = L(G')$, where G' is in Chomsky Normal Form (CNF).*

Proof Let G be a CFG, which generates strings of context-free language L, and $\varepsilon \notin L$. Also, we assume that G does not have unit productions and useless productions. In case this does not hold, one can always convert a grammar with ε-productions, useless productions, and unit productions, into an equivalent grammar that does not have these. For proofs, see Theorem 7.1.

Now consider the productions P. If a production has a single symbol on the right-hand side, this will be a terminal symbol because unit productions do not exist in G. Hence this production is already in CNF. Next, consider a production in P of the form $A \rightarrow X_1X_2 \ldots X_n$, where $n \geq 2$ and $X_i \in (V \cup \Sigma)$. If X_i is a terminal symbol, say a, then substitute X_i by C_i and introduce a new production $C_i \rightarrow a$, where C_i is a newly defined nonterminal. After making these changes for all the productions, let the new set of variables be V' and the new set of productions be P'. Let us call this CFG as $G' = (V', \Sigma, S, P')$. However, G' is still not CNF as it has production of the form:

$$\begin{aligned} & A \rightarrow a \\ & A \rightarrow C_1C_2 \ldots C_i \ldots C_n, \end{aligned}$$

where $A, C_i \in V', a \in \Sigma$ and n is some integer greater or equal to $|V|$. However, we have $L(G) = L(G')$, as due to the above changes the generating power of remains same as that of G.

In second step, additional variables are introduced, and productions of the form $A \rightarrow C_1C_2 \ldots C_n$ are reduced to $A \rightarrow BC$, as explained in the following.

The productions of the form $A \rightarrow C_1C_2$ (already a CNF) are retained unmodified in G' along with their variables. Next, for the productions of the form $A \rightarrow C_1C_2 \ldots C_n$, for $n > 2$, new variables are introduced and productions are modified in G' as follows.

$$
\begin{aligned}
A &\rightarrow C_1 D_1 \\
D_1 &\rightarrow C_2 D_2 \\
&\dots \\
D_{n-3} &\rightarrow C_{n-2} D_{n-2} \\
D_{n-2} &\rightarrow C_{n-1} C_n
\end{aligned}
$$

The above productions are as per the CNF, hence they are added to P', and all corresponding variables are added to V'.

If the above process is repeated for all the productions in P', these productions get transformed into CNF in G'. This proves that $L(G') = L(G)$, and that G' is in CNF. □

We have discussed above that, before we proceed to the conversion of a CFG to CNF, some transformations in the grammar are necessary; these are: removal of ε-rules, unit rules, and removal of useless symbols and productions. In addition, for parsing to be started always from the start symbol, the symbol S should not be there in the right hand of any rule. The latter we call as *start* rule.

7.3.1 Application Order of Transformation

We will see that it is necessary to follow some order to apply these transformations, because some transformations may destroy the result achieved by other ones. For example, introducing the *start* rule will re-introduce a unit rule if it is applied after removing the unit productions. Consider that productions are

$$\{Exp \rightarrow Exp + Exp, Exp \rightarrow Exp * Exp, Exp \rightarrow a\},$$

where no unit rule exists. If we consider Exp as the start symbol, it exists on the right side of the productions. Hence, we apply *start* rule, by adding a new production $S \rightarrow Exp$. But, this adds a unit of production!

To follow a certain order of application of rules, let us first name the transformations as follows:

- *start*: Start rule, i.e., introducing $S \rightarrow var_1$, where var_1 is some nonterminal.
- ε : Eliminate ε-rule.
- *Unit*: Eliminate unit rule.

We construct a table where rows represent rules X and corresponding columns represent rule Y. If at a position (X, Y), the transformation X preserves the transformation Y, then the position is marked as $\surd$, else marked as $\times$. For example, the "start-rule" does not preserve the transformation of ε-rule, and the "unit-rule", but ε-rule preserves the transformation of "start-rule" and not the "unit-rule", and so on. The mark $(\surd)^*$ indicates that unit-rule preserves the results of ε-rule, i.e., elimination of unit productions can be done after the elimination of null productions if start-rule has been called before.

There are two more transformations, but we have taken them as necessary (steps) part of the CNF transformations. These are:

- *Term*: Elimination of terminal symbols except in right-hand sides of size 1;
- *Bin*: Reduction to rules that have right-hand side sizes ≤ 2.

The following example demonstrates the conversion of given grammar into CNF format and also considers the transformation rules while doing so.

Example 7.5 Obtain the CNF of the following Grammar:

$$\begin{aligned} E &\rightarrow T \mid E + T \\ T &\rightarrow F \mid T * F \\ F &\rightarrow a \mid (E), \end{aligned}$$

where nonterminals E, T, F stand for *expression*, *term*, and *factor*, respectively. The symbols a, $+$, $*$, (,) are terminals.

Since there is no null production in the grammar, the null rule is not applicable.

First of all, we carry out *Start* step of transformation by adding $S \rightarrow E$ in the grammar. Next, we carry out the transformation using *Term*.

$$\begin{aligned} S &\rightarrow E \\ E &\rightarrow T \mid \ E \ \ Add \ \ T \\ T &\rightarrow F \mid \ T \ \ Mult \ \ F \\ F &\rightarrow a \mid \ Open \ E \ Close \\ Add &\rightarrow + \\ Mult &\rightarrow * \\ Open &\rightarrow (\\ Close &\rightarrow) \end{aligned}$$

Next, we apply the *unit-rule* (Rule no. 1, 2 Sect. 7.2.2), which gives the following transformations:

$$
\begin{aligned}
S &\to E \\
E &\to E \ \ Add \ \ T \\
T &\to T \ \ Mult \ \ F \\
F &\to Open \ E \ Close \\
E &\to T \ \ Mult \ \ F \\
T &\to Open \ E \ Close \\
E &\to a \\
T &\to a \\
F &\to a \\
Add &\to + \\
Mult &\to * \\
Open &\to (\\
Close &\to)
\end{aligned}
$$

In the next step, we apply the *Bin*-rule, so that right-hand side of every production is ≤ 2.

$$
\begin{aligned}
S &\to E \\
E &\to E \ \ AddT \\
AddT &\to Add \ \ T \\
T &\to T \ \ MultF \\
MultF &\to Mult \ \ F \\
F &\to Open \ EClose \\
EClose &\to E \ \ Close \\
E &\to T \ \ MultF \\
T &\to Open \ EClose \\
EClose &\to E \ \ Close \\
E &\to a \\
T &\to a \\
F &\to a \\
Add &\to + \\
Mult &\to * \\
Open &\to (\\
Close &\to)
\end{aligned}
$$

The above grammar is in CNF, with the exception of $S \to E$ rule, which we introduced to add unique start symbol S.

The following derivation shows that, the string $(a + a) * a$, which we were able to generate in original grammar, can also be generated using this CNF grammar.

$$\begin{aligned} S \Rightarrow & E \Rightarrow T\ MultF \Rightarrow Open\ EClose\ MultF \Rightarrow (EClose\ MultF \\ \Rightarrow & (E\ \ Close\ MultF \Rightarrow (E\ \ AddT\ \ Close\ MultF \Rightarrow (a\ \ AddT\ \ Close\ MultF \\ \Rightarrow & (a\ \ Add\ \ T\ \ Close\ MultF \Rightarrow (a + T\ \ Close\ MultF \Rightarrow (a + a\ \ Close\ MultF \\ \Rightarrow & (a + a)\ MultF \Rightarrow (a + a)\ Mult\ \ F \Rightarrow (a + a) * F \Rightarrow (a + a) * a \end{aligned}$$

□

7.3.2 Complexity Analysis of CNF Grammar

Complexity of a Grammar G is defined by the size of that grammar. The size $|G|$ of a context-free grammar is defined as follows.

Definition 7.7 The size $|G|$ of context-free grammar G is

$$|G| = \sum_{A \to \alpha \in P} \lg(A\alpha), \tag{7.4}$$

where $lg(A\alpha)$ is length of the string $A\alpha$. □

It is important to note that the complexity of transformation to CNF depends on the size of the grammar as well as on the order in which these steps of normalization are carried out. For the sake of simplicity, we shall concentrate only on the three rules given in Table 7.1.

1. The blow-up in grammar size depends on the order between the elimination of ε-rules and application of *Bin*. It may be exponential when ε-rules elimination is done first but is linear otherwise.
2. Unit rule can incur a quadratic blow-up in the size of the grammar.

Hence, except for *Term*-rule, which gives a linear increase in grammar size, the order in which the single transformation steps are to be carried out should be: *Bin* $\to \varepsilon \to$ *Unit*. This will yield a grammar of size $O(|G|^2)$, where $|G|$ is size of the grammar, i.e., number of rules. However, the order $\varepsilon \to$ Unit $\to$ Bin, yields a grammar of *time complexity* $O(2^{2|G|})$ [3, 8].

Table 7.1 Allowed Transformations' orders

$X \downarrow \mid Y \rightarrow$	Start-rule	ε-rule	Unit-rule
Start-rule	–	×	×
ε-rule	√	–	×
Unit-rule	√	(√)*	–

7.4 Greibach Normal Form

Several algorithms have been proposed that utilize some forms of pushdown store machines for syntactic analysis of natural or artificial languages. These algorithms have a common feature—they place some restriction on context-free grammars. In order to work efficiently and in some cases to work at all, these algorithms forbid infinite left-going structures resulting from generations like $A \Rightarrow^* A\varepsilon$. It has been hypothesized that natural languages do not permit infinite loops of this kind. One can avoid such structures in designing the syntax of programming languages. It has been proved that every context-free grammar is strongly equivalent to one that does not contain structures of left recursions. Also, the Greibach Normal Form (GNF) shows that every context-free grammar is strongly equivalent to one that does not contain such structures [4].

In the multiple-path predictive analysis of the English language, a special kind of nondeterministic Pushdown-store automaton (PDA) is used. In an analysis of a given input string, the machine scans the input strictly from left to right of a given sentence. At each transition in PDA, it performs the operations shown below:

1. scans a new input symbol,
2. scans and erases the top symbol on the pushdown store,
3. adds a (possibly null) string of symbols to the pushdown store,
4. prints an output.

A context-free grammar can be rewritten so that the head (first symbol) of the replacement string of each production in the rewritten grammar, is a terminal symbol, i.e., of the form $A \rightarrow aB^*$, where a is terminal, and B is nonterminal. This results in the Greibach Normal Form. Greibach's procedure requires the obtaining of regular expression from a flow graph. However, using some matrix equations same normal form can be obtained in a systematic manner where the entire grammar is rewritten at one time and no regular expression needs to be evaluated [9].

Note that, in the general model of Pushdown-store automata, the machine is allowed to perform an infinite series of actions without advancing the input tape.

Let CFG be (V, Σ, S, P), where V is set of nonterminals, Σ is set of terminal symbols, S is started symbol, P is set of productions: $A \rightarrow X_1X_2...X_n$, $X_i \in (V \cup \Sigma)$. All generation: $S \Rightarrow \alpha_0 \Rightarrow \alpha_1 \Rightarrow ... \Rightarrow \alpha_n = w$, proceed from left to right, expanding the leftmost member of V first.

Definition 7.8 (*Standard form of CFG*) A CFG (V, Σ, S, P) is in standard form iff all the rules of P are of the form:

$$A \rightarrow a$$
$$A \rightarrow aB_1...B_n, \quad n \geq 1, a \in \Sigma, B_i \in V.$$

□

If a CFG is in standard form then there exists no infinite left-going structures. Using standard from, we can give particularly elegant proofs of the connection between CFLs, PDAs, and deterministic LBAs.

If $G = (V, \Sigma, S, P)$ is CFG, then its language can be expressed as

$$L(G) = \{w \mid S \Rightarrow^* w \text{ and } w \text{ is string in } \Sigma^*\}.$$

Using this we define *admissible* CFG as as given below.

Definition 7.9 (*Admissible CFG*) A CFG (V, Σ, S, P) is admissible if and only if either it is null $(P = \phi)$ or else following conditions are satisfied:

1. each $a \in \Sigma$ appears in some terminal string,
2. each $A \in V$ is used in generation of some terminal string,
3. each rule is used in the generation of some terminal string, and
4. any string in $V \cup \Sigma$ gets generated by the rules of P can be completed, i.e., can be expanded by rules of P to a terminal string. □

No generality is lost by restricting the Admissible CFG to generate strictly from left to right.

7.4.1 Removing Left-Recursion

A context-free phrase-structure generator is in *standard form* if and only if all of its rules are of the form $Z \rightarrow aY_1Y_2 \ldots Y_m$, where $Z, Y_i \in V$ and $a \in \Sigma$. This format will help in processing one input symbol at each step. A standard form is always convenient for computer manipulation of context-free languages. This standard form is called *Greibach normal form*. The proof of this theorem (refer [4]) states that every context-free phrase-structure generator is strongly equivalent to one in GNF.

Theorem 7.5 *For each context-free grammar* $G = (V, \Sigma, S, P)$ *with production* P *defined as*

$$A \rightarrow A\alpha_1 \mid A\alpha_2 \mid \cdots \mid A\alpha_n,$$

where $\alpha_i \neq \varepsilon$ *for all* i, $1 \leq i \leq n$, *be all the rules with variables A on the left such that the leftmost symbol of the right-hand side of the rule is A every where. The remaining rule is*

$$A \to \beta_1 \mid \beta_2 \mid \cdots \mid \beta_n,$$

then there exists a CFG $G' = (V, \Sigma, S, P')$ *such that* $L(G) = L(G')$, *where*

$$V' = V \cup \{B\}$$

and, P' *is given as*

$$\begin{aligned} A &\to \beta_1 B \mid \beta_2 B \mid \cdots \mid B_n B \mid \beta_1 \mid \beta_2 \cdots \mid \beta_n \\ B &\to \alpha_1 B \mid \alpha_2 B \mid \cdots \mid \alpha_n B \mid \alpha_1 \mid \alpha_2 \mid \cdots \mid \alpha_n. \end{aligned}$$

In other words, for each grammar with left recursions in the productions, there exists an equivalent grammar without left recursions.

Proof The effect of this construction is to eliminate the left recursion in the variable A. In each place, we have a new right-recursive variable B. We note that none of the new A-rules in P' are directly left-recursive because none of the β_i begin with A. In addition, with $\beta_i \neq \varepsilon$, one cannot get the left-recursion on A by going through B. Also, we note that B is not the left-recursive variable because $\alpha_i \neq \varepsilon$ for all i and because none of the α_i begin with B.

Let us consider a derivation using G:

$$\begin{aligned} A &\Rightarrow A\alpha_{i_1} \Rightarrow A\alpha_{i_2}\alpha_{i_1} \\ &\Rightarrow \cdots \Rightarrow A\alpha_{i_p}\alpha_{i_{p-1}} \ldots \alpha_{i_1} \\ &\Rightarrow \beta_j\alpha_{i_p}\alpha_{i_{p-1}} \ldots \alpha_{i_1} \end{aligned}$$

The above derivation in G can be obtained using G' as

$$\begin{aligned} A &\Rightarrow \beta_j B \Rightarrow \beta_j\alpha_{i_p} B \Rightarrow \beta_j\alpha_{i_p}\alpha_{i_{p-1}} B \\ &\Rightarrow \cdots \Rightarrow \beta_j\alpha_{i_p}\alpha_{i_{p-1}} \ldots \alpha_{i_2} B \\ &\Rightarrow \beta_j\alpha_{i_p}\alpha_{i_{p-1}} \ldots \alpha_{i_1}. \end{aligned}$$

This proves the theorem. □

In *recursive descent* parsers, the presence of left-recursion causes the device to go into an infinite loop. Thus elimination of left-recursion is of practical importance in such parsers.

7.4.2 Parsing Using GNF Grammar

A CFG $G = (V, \Sigma, S, P)$ is in Greibach normal form if and only if all of the rules of P are of the forms:

$$A \rightarrow a$$
$$A \rightarrow aB_1B_2 \dots B_n, \text{ for } n \geq 1, a \in \Sigma, \text{ and } B_i \in V.$$

Example 7.6 Simple example of converting CFG into GNF.

$$S \rightarrow BC,$$
$$B \rightarrow bB \mid aC \mid a,$$
$$C \rightarrow a.$$

The above CFG is not GNF, but applying Theorem 7.5, these productions can be transformed into an equivalence grammar, which is GNF.

$$S \rightarrow bBC \mid aCC \mid aC$$
$$B \rightarrow bB \mid aC \mid a$$
$$C \rightarrow a$$

which is GNF. □

It is easy to generate a language string using the above grammar, just like any CFG or CNF grammar. For example, we can generate $w = bbaaa$, as

$$S \Rightarrow bBC \Rightarrow bbBC \Rightarrow bbaCC \Rightarrow bbacC \Rightarrow bbaaa,$$

through application of rules $S \rightarrow bBC, B \rightarrow bB, B \rightarrow aC, C \rightarrow a, C \rightarrow a$, respectively. However, for this, the rule application sequence is to be correctly selected, else it requires a backtrack, but ultimately the string w will get generated. In the following example, we see how a pushdown automata (PDA) is more helpful for this derivation.[4]

[4] For the idea of how a PDA works, it is advised to refer to the next chapter.

Example 7.7 Recognize the string $w = bbaaa$, using the grammar given below and a PDA, where the grammar is a lookup table, with rules as follows:

1. $S \to bBC$
2. $S \to aCC$
3. $S \to aC$
4. $B \to bB$
5. $B \to aC$
6. $B \to a$
7. $C \to a$

Steps for recognizing the string $w = bbaaa$:

1. push S on top of stack (tos), and PDA head points to 1st b in the input string,
2. Since input b does not match with tos, so pop tos (i.e., S), push bBC (rule 1), so stack is bBC, where b is at top,
3. Current input symbol and tos matches, as both are b. **print** b, pop tos (b), advance PDA head. Now input = $baaa$, stack = BC,
4. Current input symbol is b; tos is BC; so no match. Pop B from tos, push bB (rule 4), so stack is bBC,
5. Input symbol b matches with tos b; advance input head; pop tos (b), **print** b. Now input = aaa, stack = BC,
6. Input symbol a does not match with tos B; pop B; push aC (rule 5). So stack is aCC,
7. Input symbol a matches with tos a; advance input head; pop tos; **print** a; now input left is aa; stack = CC,
8. Input symbol does not match with tos, so pop C push a (rule 7). Now stack = aC,
9. Input symbol matches with tos (a), advance input; pop stack; **print** a, so input = a, stack = C,
10. Input and tos do not match, so pop stack (C), push a (rule 7),
11. Input is a; tos = a; both match; advance input; pop tos; **print** a,
12. Input is fully scanned, stack is empty, and print queue is = $bbaaa$,
13. This completes the recognition.

We may note some important points. Every time we select the rule, it is chosen such that the head symbol of the production is the same as the current input symbol so that they will match in the next step. This makes the recognition, a *deterministic* process. Since the process has correctly selected a rule, it is also called *predictive parser*. However, sometimes it requires backtracking, e.g., in rules 2 and 3 head symbol of both the productions is a. □

7.5 Converting CNF to GNF Grammar

One approach to convert from CFG to Greibach Normal Forms is the matrix equations-based algorithm [9]. For this conversion, the CFG should not have null productions, unit productions, useless productions, and rules.

A simpler algorithm for the construction of Greibach normal form is as follows: For the input, we have grammar $G = (V, \Sigma, S, P)$ in CNF, with no null productions, unit productions, and useless productions and symbols. Also, the grammar G has no left-recursion, if it were, it was removed using the method discussed earlier as Theorem 7.5 (see Sect. 7.4.1). As another precondition, that G is in CNF, if it is not, we can easily convert it to CNF, using the method (Theorem 7.4).

Theorem 7.6 (Greibach Normal Form) *Every context-free language L can be generated by a grammar for which every production is of the form $A \to a\alpha$, where A is variable, a is terminal, and $\alpha \in V^*$.*

Proof Let $G = (V, \Sigma, S, P)$ be a grammar in CNF. Let $V = \{V_1, V_2, ..., V_m\}$. The first step in the construction is to modify the productions so that if $A_i \to A_j\gamma$ is a production, then $j > i$. This will be done as follows, starting with A_1 and proceeding to A_m. Assume that the productions have been modified so that, for $1 \le i \le k$, $A_i \to A_j\gamma$ is a production only if $j > i$. That means productions up to $A_k \to A_j\gamma$ have been modified. So, now we modify the A_{k+1} productions [6].

If $A_{k+1} \to A_j\gamma$ is a production, with $j < k + 1$, we generate a new set of productions by substituting for A_j the RHS of each A_j-production. By repeating the process $k - 1$ times at most, we shall obtain productions of the form $A_{k+1} \to A_l\gamma, l \ge k + 1$. The productions with $l = k + 1$ are left-recursive, hence replaced accordingly, i.e., converted into right-recursive.

By repeating the above process for each variable in V, we will have productions of the forms:

1. $A_k \to A_l\gamma$, and $l > k$
2. $A_k \to a\gamma$, and $a \in \Sigma$
3. $B_k \to \gamma$, and $\gamma \in (V \cup \{B_1, B_2, ..., B_n\})^*$.

For a production to be in GNF, the leftmost symbol on the RHS of any production for A_m must be terminal. Then, a leftmost symbol on the RHS of any production for A_{m-1} must be either A_m or a terminal. If it is A_m, then we can substitute the RHS of a production of A_m, as that has a terminal at the first position of its RHS. All the productions must have the first symbol of RHS as terminal, for it to be GNF. This we get when we proceed to the productions for $A_{m-2}, ..., A_2, A_1$.

In the last step, we examine the productions for the newly created variables $B_1, B_2, ..., B_n$. These productions start with either a terminal or a variable in V. We perform the substitutions in the productions $B_n, ..., B_1$ in a similar way, by ensuring that they are in GNF. □

Theorem 7.6 can be used to construct an algorithm to obtain a GNF from a given CNF. Let us consider that $V = \{V_1, V_2, ..., V_m\}$ is set of nonterminals, and $V_1, ..., V_m$ is their order.

The steps for conversion to GNF are as given as Algorithm 7.1.

Algorithm 7.1 CNF-to-GNF

1: Modify the production rules in P so that, if $V_i \to V_j\gamma \in P$ then $j > i$
2: Starting with V_1 and proceeding to V_m is done as follows:
3: **while** there exists $p \in P$ and p is not in GNF or there is left-recursion in p **do**
4: Assume that productions have been modified so that for $1 \le i \le k$, $V_i \to V_j\gamma \in P$ only if $j > i$.
5: If $V_k \to V_j\gamma$ is a production with $j < k$, generate a new set of productions, substituting for the V_j by the RHS of each V_j production
6: Repeating step 5 above at most $k - 1$ times we obtain rules of the form $V_k \to V_p\gamma$, $p \ge k$
7: **end while**
8: Replace rules $V_k \to V_k\gamma$ by removing left-recursive rules.
9: Perform the substitutions so that every rule is like, $A \to a\alpha$, where $a \in \Sigma$ and $\alpha \in V^*$

Example 7.8 Consider the following example, with Grammar,

$$S \to AA|a$$
$$A \to SS|b.$$

We shall follow the Algorithm 7.1 to convert the given CNF to GNF, hence to start with, first rename the variables as

$$A_1 \to A_2A_2|a$$
$$A_2 \to A_1A_1|b. \tag{7.5}$$

Three of these productions are in the required format of step 4 of the Algorithm 7.1, while $A_2 \to A_1A_1$ corresponds to the rule (5) of this algorithm, accordingly we change it through substitution as

$$A_2 \to A_2A_2A_1|aA_1|b,$$

where original A_1 (in Eq. 7.5) has been replaced using the production $A_1 \to A_2A_2|a$. But now, it has created a left-recursion, so we use Theorem 7.5 to rewrite A_2 as

$$A_2 \to aA_1B|aA_1|bB|b$$
$$B \to A_2A_1B|A_2A_1,$$

where aA_1B and bB are result of substitutions for removing left-recursion. So now the complete grammar looks like:

$$\begin{aligned}A_1 &\rightarrow A_2A_2|a,\\ A_2 &\rightarrow aA_1B|aA_1|bB|b,\\ B &\rightarrow A_2A_1B|A_2A_1.\end{aligned}$$

Now we must fix A_1, so that it starts with terminals:

$$A_1 \rightarrow aA_1BA_2|aA_1A_2|bBA_2|bA_2|a$$

Since A_2 rule is already in GNF, we must modify rule B in a similar fashion (replacing initial occurrences of A_2):

$$B \rightarrow aA_1BA_1B|aA_1A_1B|bBA_1B|bA_1B|aA_1BA_1|aA_1A_1|bBA_1|bA_1$$

and now we have the following grammar:

$$\begin{aligned}A_1 &\rightarrow aA_1BA_2|aA_1A_2|bBA_2|bA_2|a\\ A_2 &\rightarrow aA_1B|aA_1|bB|b,\\ B &\rightarrow aA_1BA_1B|aA_1A_1B|bBA_1B|bA_1B|aA_1BA_1|aA_1A_1|bBA_1|bA_1,\end{aligned}$$

which is in GNF. □

For the above example, we derive *aaaa* using new grammar as

$$A_1 \Rightarrow aA_1A_2 \Rightarrow aaA_2 \Rightarrow aaaA_1 \Rightarrow aaaa.$$

Also, with original grammar we have

$$S \Rightarrow AA \Rightarrow SSA \Rightarrow AAAA \Rightarrow^* aaaa.$$

Similarly, for many other strings, if a string w can be generated by original grammar, then it can also be generated by the new grammar.

7.6 Complexity Analysis of GNF Grammar

Rewriting of a context-free grammar to an equivalent grammar in required form/normal form will most likely cause a change in parameters of the grammar, such as number of rules, number of nonterminals, length of the productions, etc. For instance, the ε-rule removal substantially increases the number of rules of context-free grammars, while the total length of the grammar may increase as much as ten-times [3].

It has been found that number of nonterminals needed to describe a language by a grammar in GNF does not exceed twice the number of nonterminals needed to describe it by ε-free, unit-rule free, reduced grammar.[5] However, for language description by position-restricted grammars,[6] the increase in the number of nonterminals, the number of rules, the number of *grammatical levels* cannot be bounded by any function [7].

Increasing of productions and total length of grammars in GNF is at most cubic in the number of productions or in the total length of grammars in total length of ε-free unit rule-free reduced grammars.

Since a Context-free Grammar $G = (V, \Sigma, S, P)$ has many roles in the corresponding language $L(G)$, for example, for syntax analysis, parsing, semantic analysis, and language translation, it is obvious that if the grammar G is complex (difficult—computation intensive), the other operations will be inefficient.

In the grammar, the productions P are of the form $A \to \alpha$, where $A \in V$ and $\alpha \in (V \cup \Sigma)^*$. The size $|G|$ of the context-free grammar G is defined by

$$|G| = \sum_{A \to \alpha \in P} \lg(A\alpha),$$

where $\lg(A\alpha)$ is the length of the string $A\alpha$.

In addition, there are other parameters to specify the size of CFG:

$$Var(G) = |V|, \text{ (the number of nonterminals)}$$
$$Prod(G) = |P|, \text{ (the number of productions)}$$

For most purposes, it is sufficient to consider only ε-free languages. Following is the ε-free definition of a normal form grammars.

Definition 7.10 A grammar $G = (N, \Sigma, S, P)$ is *weak Greibach normal form* if all its productions are of type $A \to a\alpha$ for $A \in V, a \in \Sigma$ and $\alpha \in (V \cup \Sigma)^*$. □

---

[5] A reduced grammar is one without useless productions and symbols.

[6] The GNF is position-restricted grammar, as the position of terminals and nonterminals in the right-hand side of every rule is fixed.

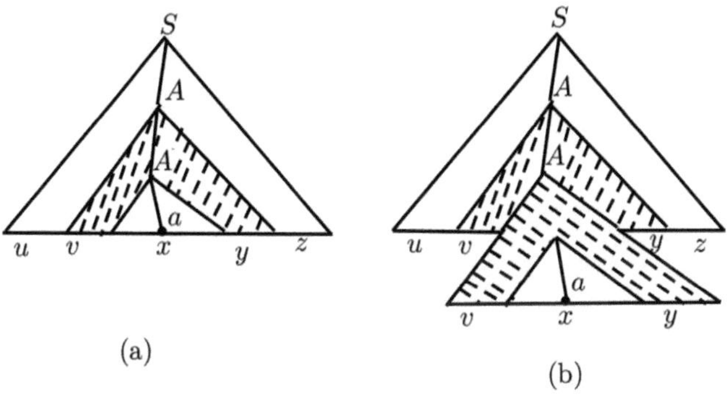

Fig. 7.3 Parse tree for: **a** $w = uvxyz$, **b** $w = uv^2xy^2z$

7.7 Pumping Lemma for Context-Free Languages

The pumping lemma for context-free languages is used to show that, for example, the language $\{a^n b^n c^n \mid n \geq 0\}$ cannot be generated by context-free grammars. Roughly speaking, the pumping lemma for CFLs claims that if we represent some part of the string in context-free language, then the resulting string also should remain in the language [2].

Figure 7.3 shows how this happens since a string w has a long path, from the root with start symbol S, to a leaf node with a terminal, say a. Assume that the grammar corresponding to this figure is

$$S \rightarrow uAz$$
$$A \rightarrow vAy$$
$$A \rightarrow a.$$

Let us consider that substrings are: $u = b$, $v = c$, $x = a$, $y = c$, and $z = e$. However, in our discussion, we will assume only the value of x, and the values of terminal substrings u, v, y, z as undeclared, to give emphasis on the structure of the string $w = uvxyz$, as a general structure.

In the parse-tree, there exists a nonterminal, say A, that appears at least twice on the path (Fig. 7.3a). This divides the string w into five parts, u, v, x, y, z, so that the string obtained by repeating 2nd and 4th part still remains in the language, as shown in Fig. 7.3a, while in Fig. 7.3b these parts appear twice. Due to the nature of productions that cause *recursions*, even if the parts v and y are repeated an arbitrary number of times, the string w should still belong to the language. This derivation is expressed by

$$S \Rightarrow^* uv^i xy^i z \Rightarrow^* w, \text{ for any } i \geq 0.$$

Lemma 7.6 *Pumping Lemma for CFLs. For every context-free language L there is an integer m such that for every string $w \in L$, and $|w| \geq m$,*

1. *there exists u, v, x, y, z such that $w = uvxyz$,*
2. *$vy \neq \varepsilon$,*
3. *$|vxy| \leq m$, and*
4. *for all i, $uv^i xy^i z \in L$.*

□

Theorem 7.7 *Proof of Pumping Lemma for CFLs.*

Proof Assume that the grammar $G = (V, \Sigma, S, P)$ is a Chomsky Normal Form (CNF). In case, the grammar is not in CNF, it can always be transformed into CNF format.[7]

Let us examine the relationship between the height of a parse tree and the length of the string generated by that tree. For this, we try to analyze the parse-trees of heights[8] 1 through 3, for productions:

$$P = \{A \rightarrow BC \mid a, B \rightarrow BB \mid b, C \rightarrow CC \mid c\}. \tag{7.6}$$

Parse-tree of height 1: $A \Rightarrow a$. (for this, $|w| = 1$) (Fig. 7.4a).

Parse-tree of height 2: $A \Rightarrow BC \Rightarrow^* bc$. ($|w| = 2$) (Fig. 7.4b)

Parse-tree of height 3: $A \Rightarrow BC \Rightarrow^* bbcc$. ($|w| = 4$) (Fig. 7.4c)

In CNF, the length of a string w generated by a parse-tree of height h is at most 2^{h-1}. In other words, we claim that generating a string $|w| = 2^{h-1}$ requires a parse-tree of height at least h.

Considering that $|V|$ is the number of variables in the CNF grammar. Thus, the maximum height of the parse-tree can be $h = |V| + 1$, which happens when only one variable is expanded in the path from the root node to the terminal node. Let this latter condition exist, and the height be $h = |V| + 1$. This parse-tree generates a string w of at least $2^{h-1} = 2^{|V|+1-1} = 2^{|V|}$. Hence, length of string w is $|w| = m = 2^{|V|}$, where m is some integer. Then, we can conclude that any parse-tree that generates a string w of length at least m, has a path from the root to a terminal, of length at least $|V| + 1$. Note that such a path consists of one node as a terminal, and at most $|V|$ nonterminal nodes. Since the grammar G has only $|V|$ nonterminals, there can be at the most $|V|$ number of productions. Hence, one nonterminal, say, A (see Fig. 7.3a and b) appears at least twice on this path. For condition $|vxy| \leq m$ (i.e., *condition 3*), in the theorem to hold, let A is chosen from lower $|V| + 1$ nonterminals in the path.

[7] Chomsky normal form is $A \rightarrow BC \mid a$, where $A, B, C \in V$, and $a \in \Sigma$. Every grammar with no null production has an equivalent CNF grammar, that generates the same language as the original.

[8] Height of a parse-tree is the largest number of edges from the root to the most distant leaf node. It is also equal to the length of the longest path from the root. A similar concept is the depth of the tree.

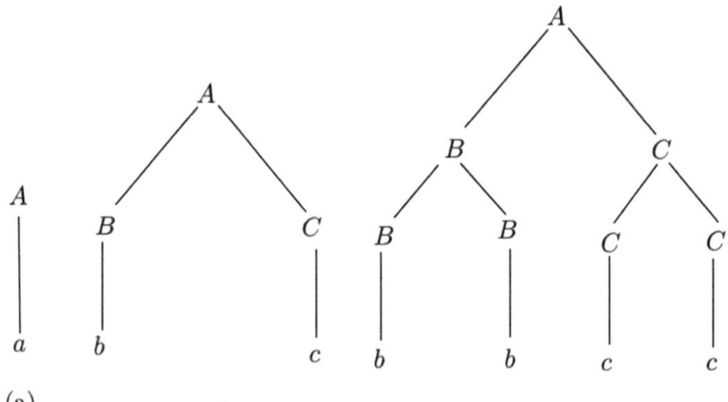

(a) (b) (c)

Fig. 7.4 Parse trees constructed using production given in (7.6)

As per Fig. 7.3a we have

$$\begin{aligned} A &\Rightarrow^* \alpha A \beta \\ &\Rightarrow uvAyz \Rightarrow^* uvxyz, \end{aligned}$$

where $\alpha \Rightarrow^* u$, $\beta \Rightarrow^* z$, $A \Rightarrow^* uAy$, and $A \rightarrow x$.

But, using these derivations, one can construct the derivation (see Fig. 7.3b) as

$$S \Rightarrow uvxyz \Rightarrow^* uvvAyyz \Rightarrow^* uv^i xy^i z$$

for any positive integer i.

Now we take the individual conditions of the pumping Lemma 7.6:

Condition 1: The height of upper A in Fig. 7.3a is at most $|V| + 1$, hence length of vxy that A generates is at most $2^{|V|+1-1} = 2^{|V|} = m$. This proves the condition 1 of the theorem.

Condition 2: $|vy| \neq \varepsilon$, i.e., $|vy| \geq 1$. The only possible ε-rule is $S \rightarrow \varepsilon$, and S does not appear in any right-hand side of a production rule. Hence, S does not appear in the tree except at the root.[9]

Let $A \rightarrow BC$ be the rule that is applied to the upper A in the left side of the tree (see Fig. 7.3a). Then at least one of the v and y contain substring s such that $X \Rightarrow^* s$ for $X \in \{B, C\}$, $s \in \Sigma^*$ such that $|s| \geq 1$. This completes the proof for condition (2), i.e., $|vy| \geq 1$.

[9] In arriving to CNF $A \rightarrow BC \mid a$, the ε-productions are removed, and when $w \neq \varepsilon$, $S \rightarrow \varepsilon$ is also removed.

Condition 4: For $i \geq 0$, $w = uv^i xy^i z \in L$. For any arbitrary number i, we can construct a parse-tree that generates $uv^i xy^i z$ by patching the region corresponding to v and y, i times. For $i = 0$, we have to eliminate the entire hashed region in Fig. 7.3a and b.

This proves the theorem. □

Theorem 7.8 *The set of strings of the form* $0^n 1^n 0^n$ *is not context-free.*

Proof We shall use the similar argument we used to show that $a^n b^n$ is not regular in Chap. 5 (Sect. 5.7). Let us assume that strings of the form $0^n 1^n 0^n$ are in context-free language. Next, we apply the pumping lemma for CFL and try to show that there is some integer m such that for any string of the length at least m, and of the form $0^n 1^n 0^n$ satisfies the conditions of the pumping lemma. We will see that it arrives at a contradiction. Let this string be $0^m 1^m 0^m$. We know that pumping lemma assumes that:

(a) $\exists u, v, x, y, z$ such that $w = uvxyz = 0^m 1^m 0^m$,
(b) $vy \neq \varepsilon$, and
(c) $\forall i, uv^i xy^i z$ is of the form $0^n 1^n 0^n$.

We now observe that either v and y each contain only one kind of symbol (0 or 1), or at least one of them contains some 0s and some 1s. In either case the string $uv^2 xy^2 z$ cannot be of the form $0^n 1^n 0^n$ (See footnote[10]). This is because, either the runs of 0s and 1s will not be of the same length, or there will be more than three sequences. This contradicts the assumption $\forall i, uv^i xy^i z \in 0^n 1^n 0^n$. Hence the proof of the theorem. □

Theorem 7.9 *The family of context-free languages is not closed under the operation of intersection.*

Proof Let there be two context-free grammars:

G_1	G_2
$S \to AB \mid A$	$S \to BA \mid A$
$A \to 0A1 \mid 01 \mid 0B$	$A \to 1A0 \mid 10$
$B \to 0$	$B \to 0B \mid 0$

It is evident that the languages generated by these grammars are the sets of strings of the form $0^n 1^n 0^m$ and $0^m 1^n 0^n$ for $m, n \geq 1$. The intersection of these languages is $0^n 1^n 0^n$, which is not context-free, as we have already proved in Theorem 7.8. □

[10] For example, if $w = 0^3 1^3 0^3$, let us pump $v = 00$, and $y = 00$, both to be pumped twice. Then, $w = 0^5 1^3 0^5 \notin L$.

Example 7.9 The languages of primes $L = \{a^n \mid n \geq 1,\ \text{and}\ n\ \text{is prime}\}$ is not a context-free language.

We know that a prime number is divided by 1 and by itself, and by no any other number.

Assume for the contradiction that L is a context-free language. We apply the pumping lemma for context-free language. Let m be the parameter of the pumping lemma. Let p be a prime such that $p \geq m$. We choose to pump the string $a^p \in L$. Since $a^p = uvxyz$, we have $v = a^k$ and $y = a^l$, with $k + l \geq 1$ (as $|xy| \geq 1$). From the pumping lemma we have $uv^{1+p}xy^{1+p}z \in L$, and therefore, $a^{p+kp+lp} \in L$. Subsequently, $a^{1+k+l} \in L$, which is impossible since $p(1 + k + l)$ is not a prime. Thus, we have a contradiction, and the language L is not context-free. □

7.8 Decidable Properties of Context-Free Languages

There are some properties of CFLs that are decidable, i.e., there exist algorithms to answer yes/no about those properties and give a corresponding context-free grammar. Following are some properties, for which we describe algorithms.

Membership Problem is Decidable

For a CFG G, find out if $w \in L(G)$ is called membership problem. The membership algorithm can be specified as: Let the given string be $|w| = n$. Convert the grammar G into CNF, and generate all the possible derivations of height (of parse-tree), i.e., $\log n$. Note that, there will be only a finite number of derivations of parse-tree whose height is $\log n$. After trying all these exhaustively, if we are successful in generating w, then $w \in L(G)$, else not. Hence, the membership problem is decidable.

Empty Language Problem Decidable

Empty Language Problem Decidable
This decision problem is to decide if $L(G) = \phi$? If the corresponding CFL is empty, then no string can be derived when started from symbol S. This means, there is some variable that is the root of a sub-tree, but all of its children do not lead to terminals. This can be verified using the dependency graph (Sect. 7.2.3). Thus, the empty language problem is decidable.

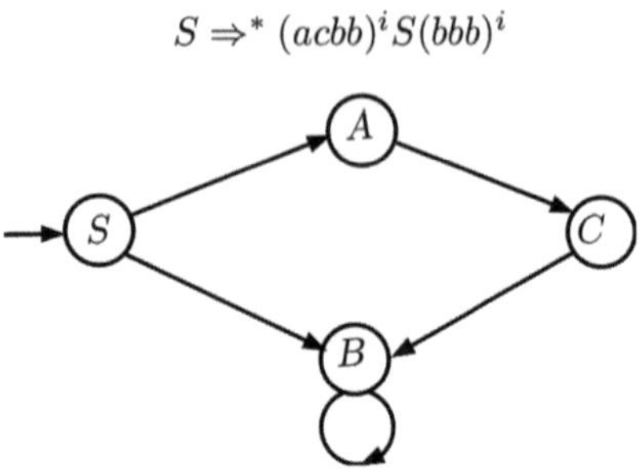

Fig. 7.5 Infinite language dependency graph

Infinite Language Problem is Decidable

Infinite Language Problem is Decidable
For a context-free grammar G, find out if $L(G)$ is infinite. The algorithm is as follows:

1. Remove useless symbols and productions,
2. Remove and unit productions,
3. Create dependency graph for variables,
4. If there is a loop in the dependency graph, then the language is infinite.

Another approach can be as follows: Let G is CNF, and V is a set of nonterminals. Without repeating any variable, longest word can be 2^{V-1}. Try the words of length between $2^{|V|}$ and $2^{|V|+1}$. If any of them is in $L(G)$, then the language $L(G)$ is infinite, else it is finite.

Example 7.10 Show that the language corresponding to the grammar $\{S \rightarrow AB, A \rightarrow aCb \mid a, C \rightarrow cBS, B \rightarrow bB \mid bb\}$ is infinite.

The graph shown in Fig. 7.5 indicates that there is an infinite loop in the dependency graph. Thus, the language corresponding to the above grammar is infinite.

This can also be found out by generating an arbitrary length string, e.g.,

$$S \Rightarrow^* (acbb)^i S(bbb)^i.$$

□

The following properties of CFLs are undecidable:

- Given a CFG, it is not decidable whether its language is Σ^*.
- The equivalence of two CFGs is not decidable.
- It is not decidable whether a given CFG is ambiguous.
- It is not decidable whether a given CFG generates a Regular Language.

7.9 Summary

The definition of context-free grammar is very general—every production has the left part as nonterminal and the right part has any number of terminals and nonterminals. Thus, it is not specific—being specific has simplicity in processing. An example of specific can be a fixed length right part, and further specialization can be a fixed type of symbols in the right part of the production. This approach has the benefit that analysis of strings produced as well as the complexity of derivations using these grammars is simple.

The normal forms of CFGs are CNF (Chomsky normal form), where the right-hand part of every production is either a terminal or two nonterminals, and GNF (Greibach normal forms) where the right-hand part of every production is a terminal optionally followed by a string of nonterminals.

This chapter has presented proofs as well as methods to transform any given context-free grammar into CNF or GNF, and it has been shown that after transformation, the new grammar, called a normal form of earlier, maintains the same language-generating capability as the original grammar.

Before a grammar is transformed into its normal form, it is necessary that null productions (e.g., $A \rightarrow \varepsilon$) be eliminated, including their dependencies, from the grammar.

In addition, the unit productions, of the form $A \rightarrow B$ be removed since they produce the chain rules, and unnecessarily consume the processing time in parsing.

The third thing that needs to be eliminated in the set of productions in the process of simplifications (normalization) is useless symbols and their productions, i.e., those nonterminals whose expansion does not lead to terminals.

Once the above three steps are completed, the normalization is applied either through CNF or GNF.

Like regular grammars, context-free grammars have also a pumping lemma, which states that, for every context-free language, L and $w \in L$, for $|w| \geq m$, for some integer m, there exist strings u, v, x, y, z such that $w = uvxyz$, $vy \neq \varepsilon$, $|vxy| \leq m$, then for all integers i, there is $uv^ixy^iz \in L$.

The above pumping lemma for CFLs states that for infinite size context-free languages, the substrings v and y or one of that can be repeated in concatenated form an arbitrary number of times to generate longer and longer strings in the given CFL. This generating of strings can be proved considering the CNF form of the grammar.

Given any grammar, if it cannot be represented in the form uv^ixy^iz, for $i \geq 0$, then this is a proof that the grammar and corresponding language are not context-free.

The family of context-free grammars is not closed under the operation of *intersection* and *complementation*.

The *membership problem* of CFL, i.e., given a string w, and CFG G, whether $w \in L(G)$ is decidable.

The *empty language problem* for CFL, i.e., if $L(G) = \phi$ is decidable, for context-free grammar.

The *infinite language problem* for a context-free grammar G is decidable, i.e., whether the language $L(G)$ has infinite number of strings.

Self Review Questions

1. Why ε-productions must be removed before the unit productions and not after?
2. What is the meaning of "useless symbols" in a CFG?
3. Why unit productions are not good in a CFG?
4. What is *dependency graph*?
5. In a grammar which has no useless productions, can there exist a useless symbol?
6. Give any two advantages of CNF grammar?
7. Give any two advantages of GNF grammar?
8. What is Invertible Grammar?
9. Given that grammar is in CNF, what is the maximum length of generated string $|w|$, in each of the following cases?

   a. Parse-tree height 1.
   b. Parse-tree height 3.
   c. parse-tree height h.

10. Which of the following productions are not allowed in: 1) CNF, in 2) GNF?

    a. $A \rightarrow aA$
    b. $A \rightarrow Aa$
    c. $A \rightarrow AB$
    d. $A \rightarrow aa$
    e. $A \rightarrow aBCD$

11. Give a logical explanation as to how a grammar with unit productions is equivalent to a grammar without unit productions.
12. What is the application of Pumping Lemma for CFLs?
13. Since Regular languages are a subset of the CFLs class, can you test if a language is regular using the Pumping Lemma for CFLs?

Exercises

A. Concepts based Problems

Note: The $*$ marked exercises are provided with solutions at the end of this book.

1. $*$ Remove the useless symbols and productions from the following grammar:

$$S \rightarrow aS \mid A \mid B,$$
$$A \rightarrow a, \quad C \rightarrow bb, \quad B \rightarrow aBa.$$

2. $*$ Convert the CFG $G = (V, \Sigma, S, P)$, with productions given below, into Chomsky normal form.

$$S \rightarrow aA \mid bB$$
$$A \rightarrow aaA \mid b$$
$$B \rightarrow bbB \mid a$$
$$\Sigma = \{a, b\}$$
$$V = \{S, A, B\}$$
S is start symbol.

3. For a CFG given below, find an equivalent CFG with no useless symbols and productions.

$$S \rightarrow BA \mid CB$$
$$A \rightarrow AC \mid BA$$
$$B \rightarrow a$$
$$C \rightarrow aA \mid b$$

4. Eliminate all the ε-productions from the following grammars.

a. $S \rightarrow AaB \mid aB$
$A \rightarrow \varepsilon$
$B \rightarrow bA \mid \varepsilon$

b. $S_0 \rightarrow S$
$S \rightarrow ASA \mid aB \mid a$
$A \rightarrow B \mid S \mid \varepsilon$
$B \rightarrow b \mid \varepsilon$

5. For each of the following grammars, find the equivalence grammars with no ε-productions and no unit productions.

a. $S \rightarrow ABA$
$A \rightarrow aA \mid \varepsilon$
$B \rightarrow bB \mid \varepsilon$

b. $S \rightarrow A \mid aba \mid bbb$
$A \rightarrow aBb \mid bBa$
$B \rightarrow aB \mid bB \mid \varepsilon$

6. $*$ Given the CFG $G = (V, \Sigma, S, P)$, where $V = \{A_1, A_2, A_3\}$, $\Sigma = \{a, b\}$, $S = A_1$, and P is:

$$A_1 \rightarrow A_2A_3$$
$$A_2 \rightarrow A_3A_1|b$$
$$A_3 \rightarrow A_1A_2|a.$$

Convert this CFG into Greibach Normal form.

7. Find equivalent CNF grammars for the following CFGs.

   a. $S \rightarrow bSb \mid SSb \mid b$
   b. $S \rightarrow aXX$
   $X \rightarrow aS \mid bS \mid b$

8. Construct a CNF equivalent to the following grammars:

   a. $S \rightarrow aBa$
   $B \rightarrow Sb \mid bcc \mid DaB$
   $C \rightarrow abb \mid DD$
   $E \rightarrow aC$
   $D \rightarrow aDB$

   b. $S \rightarrow aAC$
   $A \rightarrow aB \mid bAB$
   $B \rightarrow b$
   $C \rightarrow c$

9. Find GNF grammar, which is equivalent to the following grammar:

   $S \rightarrow aSbS$
   $A \rightarrow bBSa \mid bBaB$
   $B \rightarrow AbaA \mid C$
   $C \rightarrow ABS \mid ab$

10. Convert the following CNF grammars into GNF grammars:

    a. $S \rightarrow AB \mid BC$
    $A \rightarrow AB \mid a$
    $B \rightarrow AA \mid CB \mid b$
    $C \rightarrow a \mid b$

    b. $S \rightarrow AB$
    $A \rightarrow BB \mid CC$
    $B \rightarrow AD \mid CA$
    $C \rightarrow a$
    $D \rightarrow b$

B. Analysis-based Problems

11. Given any arbitrary Context-free grammar, how will you reduce it? Suggest steps or write down an algorithm in your own language.
12. Write descriptive steps for the following:

    a. to list all useless symbols in a grammar,
    b. to list all useless productions in a grammar.

13. Give algorithms or descriptive logical steps for the following:

    a. to remove ε-productions,
    b. to remove unit productions,
    c. to remove useless-symbols,
    d. to remove useless-productions.

14. For the following grammars, find the equivalence grammars that generate non-null strings, however, there can be a null production as part of the grammar.

    a. $S \rightarrow AB \mid \varepsilon$
       $A \rightarrow aAsB \mid a$
       $B \rightarrow bS$
    b. $S \rightarrow aA \mid \varepsilon$
       $A \rightarrow bA \mid \varepsilon$

15. Suggest an algorithm/logic to decide whether a given CFG generates null string.
16. Explain the validity of the statement, "It has been proved that, every context-free grammar is strongly equivalent to one that does not contain infinite loop statements".
17. What is the worst-case complexity of conversion from CFG to CNF? Consider that original grammar which is Non-CNF, has n number of productions of varying lengths.
18. Which of the following grammars is infinite? [Hint: Make use of graph-based technique, Fig. 7.5.]

    a. $A \rightarrow AB$
       $B \rightarrow BC$
       $C \rightarrow c$
    b. $A \rightarrow BC$
       $B \rightarrow aC$
       $C \rightarrow a$

19. We have discussed three decidable properties of CFLs in this chapter, namely, membership, empty language, and infinite language, can you try some intuitive steps to check the following undecidable properties of CFLs?

    a. Whether the language is Σ^*?
    b. Equivalence of two CFGs.
    c. Whether a given CFG generates a regular language?

20. Construct a reduced grammar equal to the following productions:

    $S \rightarrow aSbS$
    $A \rightarrow bBSa \mid bBaB$
    $B \rightarrow ABaA \mid C$
    $C \rightarrow ABS \mid ab$

21. $*$ Write an algorithm for construction of dependency graph shown in Fig. 7.1 (Sect. 7.2.3).
22. $*$ Give a linear-time algorithm for CFG to find out all symbols that would appear in some sentential form.
23. Write descriptive steps of an algorithm for conversion of a GNF grammar to CNF grammar.
24. $*$ Give an algorithm to decide the following: "Is $L(G)$ finite, for a given CFG G?

C. Proof-based Problems

25. Show that, for every context-free grammar G with left-recursion, there exists an equivalent context-free grammar G' with right-recursion.
26. Prove that every context-free language L is generated by a CFG G such that $L = L(G)$.
27. Let $G = (V, \Sigma, S, P)$ be a context-free grammar in Greibach Normal form (GNF). If $v, w \in \Sigma^*$, $\alpha \in V^*$ and $S \Rightarrow^+ w$, then show that every derivation of $S \Rightarrow^+ v\alpha$ has exactly $max\{1, \log(v)\}$ steps. Here V is set of nonterminals, excluding S.
28. Show that the complexity of generating CNF grammar is exponential in the worst case and it is linear in special cases [Hint. refer to Sect. 7.3.2].
29. Which of the following languages are context-free languages? For those that are not context-free, prove it using the Pumping lemma for CFLs.

    a. Set of all strings of balanced parenthesis, i.e., each left parenthesis has a corresponding balanced right parenthesis.
    b. $\{a^n b^m \mid n \neq m, \text{ and } m, n \geq 0\}$
    c. $\{a^n b^m \mid n \geq m\}$
    d. $\{w \in \{a, b\}^* \mid w = w^R\}$
    e. $\{w \in \{a, b\}^* \mid w$ has number of a's twice the number of b's$\}$
    f. $\{a^l b^m c^n \mid \text{ for } l, m, n \geq 1\}$
    g. $\{\{a\}^* \{b\}^*\}$

30. Let $L = \{xy \mid x, y \in \{0, 1\}^* \text{ and } |x| = |y|\}$. Show that L is context-free language.
31. Using pumping Lemma for CFLs shows that the language $L = \{a^n b^n c^n \mid n \geq 0\}$ is not context-free.
32. Use pumping Lemma for CFLs show that the following languages are not context-free:

    a. $\{0^n 1^n 0^n 1^n \mid n \geq 0\}$
    b. $\{0^n \# 0^{2n} \# 0^{3n} \mid n \geq 0\}$

33. If $G = (V, \Sigma, S, P)$ is a CNF grammar, $w \in L(G)$, and a derivation $S \Rightarrow^p w$, that takes p steps. What can be the maximum and minimum length of w?
34. Show that grammar $G = (V, \Sigma, S, P)$ whose productions P are

$$A \rightarrow a \mid aB \mid aBC,$$

generates every context-free language. Here $A, B \in V$ and $\Sigma = \{a\}$. [Hint: It can be seen that the grammar is in CNF.]

D. Multiple choice Questions

35. Given the statements about some grammars' properties,

    I. Every left-recursive grammar can be converted to a right-recursive and vice-versa.
    II. All ε-productions can be removed from any context-free grammar by suitable transformations.
    III. The CNF of CFG always generates binary trees.
    IV. The language generated by a context-free grammar is always regular, if all the productions are of the form: $A \rightarrow w$ or $A \rightarrow wB$. Here, w is a string of terminal, B is a nonterminal, and A is start symbol.
    Which combinations of these statements are true?

    (A) I, III and IV only (B) I, II and IV only
    (C) I, II, III and IV (D) II, III and IV only

    $[Hint : Answer : A]$.

E. Advanced Knowledge Assessment Problems

36. Compare the complexities of transforming a CFG into a CNF versus transforming it into a GNF. Analyze the number of steps required and the potential challenges in each transformation.
37. Identify challenging CFGs that resist straightforward conversion into normal forms. Discuss the obstacles and limitations in achieving normal forms for these grammars.
38. Given a context-free grammar in CNF, develop an algorithm to identify and eliminate any recursive productions (direct or indirect). Provide the resulting CNF grammar after the removal of recursion.

References

1. Anderson JA (2006) Automata theory with modern applications. Cambridge University Press
2. Bar-Hillel Y, Prles M, Shamir E (1965) On formal properties of simple phrase structure grammars. Z. Phonetik, Sprachwissen. Komm. 15:143–172 (1961). Bar-Hillel Y, Language and information. Addison-Wesley, Reading, Mass, pp 116–150
3. Gray JN, Harrison MA (1972) On the covering and reduction problems for context-free grammars. J ACM 19(4):675–698
4. Greibach Sheila A (1965) A new normal-form theorem for context-free phrase structure grammars. J ACM (JACM) 12(1):42–52
5. Gruska J (1969) Some classifications of context-free languages. Inf Control 14(2):152–179
6. Hopcroft JE, Ullman JD (1969) Formal languages and their relation to automata. Addison-Wesley Longman Publishing Co., Inc
7. Kelemenová A (1983) Complexity of normal form grammars. Theoret Comput Sci 28(3):299–314
8. Lange M, Leiß H (2009) To CNF or not to CNF? An efficient yet presentable version of the CYK algorithm. Informatica Didactica 8(2009):1–21
9. Rosen krantz DJ (1967) Matrix equations and normal forms for context-free grammars. J ACM (JACM) 14(3):501–507

Chapter 8
Pushdown Automata and Parsers

Abstract The pushdown automata (PDA) has the largest number of applications in recognition of computer languages, called context-free languages. Since context-sensitive languages are not well understood yet, the PDA is used for the recognition of these languages also. Regular languages can be recognized by PDA, but without making use of the pushdown stack. Unlike finite automata, a PDA is by default a nondeterministic machine. This chapter presents models of PDA, its simulation program, deterministic and nondeterministic PDAs, and language acceptability by PDA. It is shown that context-free grammars and PDA are equivalent—the principle has been used to show that context-free grammars can be directly converted to PDA. Important properties of PDA and context-free languages have been proved. Parsers, also called translators, make use of stack automata and contribute to language processing in computer languages and human languages, particularly they dig up the syntax in the language sentence and to some extent, the semantics, have been presented in detail. Since the process of parsing consumes a relatively large share of time among all the steps in compilation, its complexity/run time is important. The chapter also introduces basic concepts of parsing— bottom-up and top-down parsing and derives the complexity results of brute-force parsing. This is followed with more efficient k-symbols look-ahead grammars, i.e., LL(k) and LR(k) grammars, which eliminate the time-consuming backtracking in the application of rules. The chapter ends with self-assessment preview questions, followed by a list of classified exercises.

Keywords Pushdown automata · Context-free grammar · Context-free language · Deterministic PDA · Nondeterministic PDA · Acceptance by PDA · PDA = CFG · CFG-to-PDA · Parsing · Top-down parsing · Bottom-up parsing · Shift-reduce parser · Parallel-parsing · Unrestricted grammar

8.1 Introduction

We have discussed in previous chapters that finite automaton machines accept languages generated by regular expressions. These regular expressions specify the regular languages that are subsets of context-free languages (CFLs). Similarly, the Regular grammars are a proper subset of context-free grammars.

K. R. Chowdhary, *Theory of Computation*,
https://doi.org/10.1007/978-981-97-6234-7_8

Like a Finite Automata, a Pushdown Automata (PDA) can also be deterministic or nondeterministic. The context-free language $\{a^n b^n \mid n \geq 0\}$ can recognized by a Deterministic PDA (DPDA), as it can decide when the characters read from the input string switches from a to b. The corresponding grammar is $S \rightarrow aSb \mid \varepsilon$. The DPDA and nondeterministic PDA (NPDA) are not equivalent in power. The NPDA is strictly more powerful than a DPDA.

Let us consider a CFL $L = \{u = ww^R \mid w \in (a, b)^*\}$. This language is nondeterministic Context-Free Language (NDCFL), because in a PDA that recognizes this language, nondeterminism is necessary to guess the center point in ww^R. This language can be generated by CFG $G = (V, \Sigma, S, P)$, where P is given as

$$S \rightarrow aSa \mid bSb \mid \varepsilon. \tag{8.1}$$

We note that CFL $L = L(G)$ in above is a palindrome language, because in each string $u \in L(G)$, there is a mirror image of the string from the center of u on each side with length $|w|/2$. Therefore, any device that can recognize the string u, must read it from left to right, and store the first half of it in some form, then compare the second half of the input when read, with the previously stored half input in reverse order, i.e., the last symbol stored is compared first. If there is a perfect match, then $u \in L(G)$, else $u \notin L(G)$. Note that, for this purpose, the recognizing device needs to store one-half of the input string, which may be of arbitrary length. However, finite automata cannot recognize L, as the latter does not have memory. This is one proof that the strings generated by grammar (8.1) are not in regular language.

A PDA has a Last-In-First-Out (LIFO) memory, called *stack*, as will be shown later. The purpose of the stack is to allow the PDA to remove the letters in the word that it has read so that it can duplicate them with the other letters/symbols.

A machine that is a modified and upgraded version of a finite automata, and capable of accumulating the input symbols as they are read by appending them one at a time to a stored string, can recognize the palindrome language. In a string of language of grammar (8.1), it somehow (non-deterministically) finds that the center of the input string has reached. Thereafter, as it reads the remaining part of the string and every time a symbol is read, another symbol is taken off from the already stored string, in LIFO order, and compared with the current symbol read from input. In this way, the rest half of the input symbols are compared with the symbols already read and stored. The string is considered acceptable by this new version of finite automata called Pushdown Automata, if there is a match in all the second half of the symbols with the first half, in reverse order.

The Pushdown automata have several applications in computer science. Here are some of these applications:

- The PDAs are primarily used to recognize and parse context-free languages. Context-free grammars are widely used in programming languages, compilers, and natural language processing. The PDAs provide theoretical a theoretical framework for parsing and analyzing the structure of context-free languages.

- Specifically, the PDAs are used in the design and implementation of parsers for parsing languages. The PDAs are used in conjunction with context-free grammars.
- The PDAs can be used for syntax checking and validation in various applications. For example, they are used in web development to parse HTML (HyperText Markup Language) or XML (Extensible Markup Language) documents against their respective grammars. The PDAs can help in identifying syntax errors and can ensure that input sentences conform to the grammar of that language.
- The PDAs have applications in NLP (Natural Language Processing), like in parsing and understanding natural language sentences. Like in computer languages, the PDA can recognize and analyze the syntactic structure of NLP sentences.
- PDAs can be used to process and evaluate the arithmetic expressions.

The above are just few examples of the applications of PDA. Majority of these topics we shall be discussing in this chapter.

Learning outcomes of this chapter.

1. Pushdown automata. [Knowledge], [Application]
2. PDA model. [Knowledge]
3. Acceptance by PDA. [Evaluation]
4. Nondeterministic PDA. [Comprehension]
5. PDA Simulation. [Analysis]
6. PDA types. [Analysis]
7. PDA = CFG. [Proof], [Synthesis]
8. CFG to PDA. [Analysis]
9. Language Parsing. [Comprehension]
10. Top-down and Bottom-up parsing. [Knowledge]
11. LL(k) Parser. [Synthesis], [Apply]
12. LR(k) Parser. [Synthesis], [Apply]
13. Parallel parsing. [Knowledge]
14. Parallel lexical analysis. [Knowledge]

8.2 The Idea of Parsing

Consider a CFG (Context-free Grammar) G with productions $S \rightarrow SS \mid (S) \mid \varepsilon$, which generates strings of balanced parentheses, is a non-regular language. To recognize the language strings of this grammar, a PDA can be used, which inserts (pushes) every left parenthesis read from the input string into the stack and retrieves a pushed symbol from the top of the stack when a right parenthesis is read from the input. When the stack is empty and at the same time the end is reached of the input sequence of symbols in the tape, which shows that the input string has balanced parentheses, and hence the string is accepted. Otherwise, the string is rejected, indicating that it is not a balanced parenthesis sequence. A typical derivation sequence of string for this grammar can be:

$$S \Rightarrow SS \Rightarrow (S)S \Rightarrow (S)(S) \Rightarrow (SS)(S)$$
$$\Rightarrow ((S)S)(S) \Rightarrow ((S)(S))(S) \Rightarrow^* (()())()$$

which is a balanced parentheses string. If we have input string as $w = (()())()$, and try to recognize this using the approach discussed above—push when '(' is seen in the input and pop (retrieve the top symbol) when ')' is seen in the input, we will find that w is accepted ultimately.

We note that unless we count the number of parentheses, we cannot determine the center of this string. However, there is no provision for counting in PDA, but still, it can recognize such strings.

Parsing algorithms are used in all sorts of applications; web browsing, text processing, compilation, and language processing are some of the most common domains. Parsing is an essential step in all the languages' processing. The programming languages are continuously increasing in their capacity and complexity, which underlines the need for more efficient language processing tools, like *lexical analyzers* and *parsers*. However, the parsers with the brute-force approach have exponential time complexity, which means no general compiler can be realized using the brute-force method, hence the need for more efficient algorithms for parsers, with the capability of *parallel processing*.

The year 2007 was the 50th anniversary of IBM's release of the first optimizing compiler [7]. Its focus was limited to the translation of high-level language programs and to the optimization of space and time requirements of programs. Since then, a vast body of knowledge has been created about program analysis and transformations, automatic code generation, and runtime services. Compiler algorithms and techniques are now commonly used to facilitate software and hardware development, improve application performance, and detect and prevent software defects and malware. The compiler field is increasingly intertwined with other disciplines, including computer architecture, programming languages, formal methods, software engineering, and computer security.

Compiler algorithms for parsing, type checking and inference, data-flow analysis, loop transformations based on data-dependence analysis, register allocation based on *graph coloring* [4], and software pipelining, are among the more elegant creations.

For natural language parsing, probabilistic parsing is common now, mainly due to the wide-spread availability of corpora (or treebanks), which have served as benchmarks for empirical works, however, the probabilistic parsing is still less understood fields [3].

The simplest parser is called *brute-force parser*. Type of parsers works not only for the restricted grammars (context-free grammars, and context-sensitive grammar) but also for unrestricted grammars. A simple unrestricted grammar is

$$\begin{aligned} S &\rightarrow aaS \\ S &\rightarrow \varepsilon \\ aa &\rightarrow b \end{aligned} \tag{8.2}$$

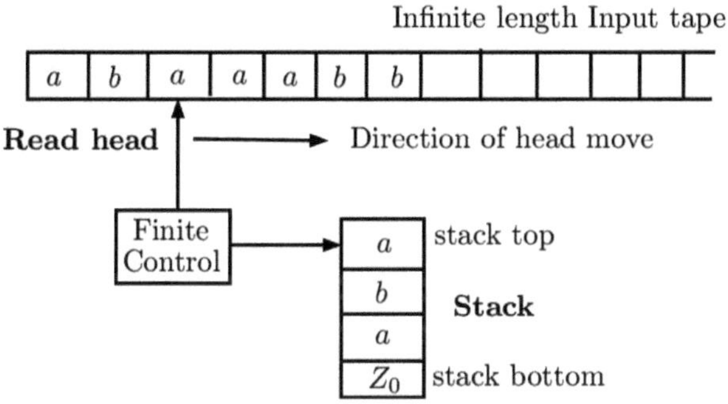

Fig. 8.1 Model of pushdown automata

It parses by first accepting parse, if not successful then it backtracks from the first disagreement with respect to the input string, and tries all alternatives of substitutions in the order the rules are listed. Thus, this method of parsing takes a very long time since it explores every possibility of substitution of variables. In case of unrestricted grammar, since this language is equivalent to *Turing recognizable languages*,[1] there is no guarantee that the brute-force parser will ever stop. For example, the grammar in (8.23), if used to parse the string $w = ab$, it will never terminate.

8.3 Pushdown Automata Model

The diagram of the pushdown automata reading the input string "*abaaabb*" is shown in Fig. 8.1. The storage device used in the pushdown automata is called *stack* or *pushdown store*, which inserts (stores) the symbols at the top as they are read from input.[2] When it reads these back from the store, they are retrieved from the top in LIFO order only.

A pushdown automaton consists of three parts: a read-only input tape, finite-state control, and a read-write pushdown store, called a stack. Depending on the state this automaton is in, the input symbol it is reading, and the symbol at the top of the stack, the PDA may make a transition to any one of the finite set of states, and write a finite number of symbols on the stack. Writing a null symbol corresponds to erasing the top-most symbol.

In addition, the automata may make transitions and write symbols on the stack without reading symbols from the input. Such transitions are called ε-moves. Thus, a PDA can manipulate the stack without reading any input. In fact, it can be proved that

---

[1] Turing recognizable language: If a string belongs to the language, then the machine accepts and halts, if not, the machine may keep on searching, without halting ever.

[2] A PDA may also write a different alphabet from what has been read from the input (Σ). The stack alphabet is represented by Γ.

for a PDA with ε-moves there exists an equivalence PDA without ε-moves, which accepts the same language. It is assumed that the Pushdown automata has potentially unbounded tape memory, and unbounded stack, it is the only fact that its access to stack memory is highly restricted, i.e., LIFO (Last in First Out) manner. Due to this reason, the PDA is not equivalent to a Turning machine, as discussed in the next chapters.

A Pushdown automata is a 7-tuple [12],

$$M = (Q, \Sigma, \Gamma, \delta, q_0, Z_0, F), \tag{8.3}$$

where

Q is a finite non-empty set of states,
Σ is a finite non-empty set of input symbols,
Γ is finite non-empty set of stack symbols, and $\varepsilon \in \Gamma$,
$q_0 \in Q$ is initial state,
$Z_0 \in \Gamma$ is initial symbol on the pushdown stack,
$F \subseteq Q$ is set of final states,

and δ is transition function, defined as

$$\delta : Q \times (\Sigma \cup \{\varepsilon\}) \times \Gamma \rightarrow \text{ finite subsets of } Q \times \Gamma^*. \tag{8.4}$$

The transition function δ shows that a PDA, while in state $q_i \in Q$ and reading an input symbol or null (nothing has been read) and with some symbol on top of stack, will cause a transition to new state $q_j \in Q$. Like this, there may be one or more transitions to the next state. And, while going in transitions through these states will write a finite number of symbols (or null, i.e., no symbol) on the stack. This is the meaning of $Q \times \Gamma^*$.

The right-hand side of the function δ, also means $2^{Q\times\Gamma^*}$, which indicates that PDA can non-deterministically assume one of the many subsets of $Q \times \Gamma^*$, i.e., "state $\times$ string" pair.[3] In each move, a PDA may or may not read an input symbol, but must read the top of the stack in every move, as there is no ε associated with Γ like its is with Σ.

However, there are variations where PDAs read ε from top of stack, and in such case the δ is as given below [13, 14].

$$\delta : Q \times (\Sigma \times \{\varepsilon\}) \times (\Gamma \times \{\varepsilon\}) \rightarrow 2^{Q\times\Gamma^*} \tag{8.5}$$

However, such variations do not change the power of PDA. In the standard PDA, we pop the stack any number of times, because it yields an intuitively clear algorithm for converting PDA to CFGs. There are basically two approaches for accepting in

---

[3] Recall that in NFA, 2^Q for $Q = \{q_0, q_1\}$, is the set $\{\phi, \{q_0\}, \{q_1\}, \{q_0, q_1\}\}$. Actually, $2^{Q\times\Gamma}$ for $\Sigma = \{a, b\}$ becomes, (q_0, ab), or (q_1, abb), or (q_1, ε), etc.

PDA, (1) when the entire input is read, and (2) when the entire input has been read and stack emptied.

Example 8.1 Consider a grammar with productions $S \rightarrow (S) \mid \varepsilon$. Some strings that can be generated using this grammar are,

$$S \Rightarrow (S) \Rightarrow ((S)) \Rightarrow (())$$
$$S \Rightarrow (S) \Rightarrow ((S)) \Rightarrow (((S)))) \Rightarrow ((()))$$

Since all the left parentheses get exhausted before the start of the first closing parenthesis, the center of the string can be determined with certainty. Therefore a PDA that can recognize these strings is deterministic. □

In the following, we will discuss about essential terminologies and foundational concepts of Pushdown automata, that are essential for understanding the remaining material of this chapter.

8.4 Formalism of PDA

An Instantaneous Description (ID) of PDA is an element of $Q \times \Sigma^* \times \Gamma^*$. An initial ID is a member of $\{q_0\} \times \Sigma^* \times \{Z_0\}$. Therefore, $(q, ax, Z\alpha)$ is an ID of PDA in state $q \in Q$, currently reading input $a \in \Sigma$, string $x \in \Sigma^*$ is yet to be read, symbol $Z \in \Gamma$ on the stack, and $\alpha \in \Gamma^*$ is symbols sequence in the stack below the symbol Z. In a special case a may be ε, in that case, the PDA will make a ε-move, that is, the input (read head) is not advanced, but may write on stack, and make a transition to next state [12].

8.4.1 Transition Function

The transition function δ for PDA is defined as a mapping $\delta : Q \times (\Sigma \cup \{\varepsilon\}) \times \Gamma$ to finite subset of $Q \times \Gamma^*$, which can be expressed as

$$\delta(q, a, Z) = \text{ Subset of } \{(p_1, \beta_1), (p_2, \beta_2), ..., (p_m, \beta_m)\}. \tag{8.6}$$

Hence $(p_1, \beta_1) \in \delta(q, a, Z)$, or in general $(p_i, \beta_i) \in \delta(q, a, Z)$. Here q, $p_i \in Q$, $a \in \Sigma$, $Z \in \Gamma$, $\beta_i \in \Gamma^*$ for $0 \leq i \leq m$. The above transition indicates that a PDA, which is in state q with input symbol a, the Z as the top symbols on stack can for any i enters state p_i and replaces the symbol on top of stack by a string β_i and advances the read head by one step. In particular, if $m = 0$, the right-hand side of the above equation is the empty set, which means that no next move is defined. It is convention that the left symbol in the sequence β_i is on the top of the stack, and its remaining part is in the stack below the top symbol. For an input x, the read head points to the leftmost symbol in x in the start.

Furthermore, in Eq. (8.6),

- if $a = \varepsilon$, the input head does not move,
- if $Z = \varepsilon$, the symbol at top of stack is empty,
- if $\beta_i = \varepsilon$, nothing is written (pushed) to stack.

Since, by default a PDA is nondeterministic, therefore it can manipulate the symbols on the stack without any input. This is expressed by state transition,

$$\delta(q, \varepsilon, Z) = \{(p_1, \beta_1), (p_2, \beta_2), ..., (p_m, \beta_m)\}, \tag{8.7}$$

where current input symbol read is ε (i.e., no input has been read, and therefore the read head of PDA does not advance), q is current state, and Z is a symbol on top of the stack. With this input, the PDA moves to state p_i and the symbol Z on the top of the stack is replaced by sequence β_i, where $1 \le i \le m$.

In general, if state q with input a, a symbol on top of stack as Z, causes the PDA to move to state p and symbol on top of the stack is written as β, then we express it as $(p, \beta) \in (q, a, Z)$.

Figure 8.2a, b, c shows some of the transitions in a PDA. The symbols "a, Z/β" in a transition in Fig. 8.2c shows that the PDA currently in state q reads symbol a on tape, with symbol Z on top of the stack, will write β on top of the stack, and will move to state p. The pair Z/β indicates that Z is replaced by β. Only way to insert new values at top of the stack is to replace top symbol ε by β. For example, in Fig. 8.2a, A/ε in the transition edge indicates that A is replaced by ε, which means A is erased. Similarly, in (b) it says that ε is replaced by A, i.e., A is pushed onto the stack.

8.4.2 *Moves of PDA*

Let $M = (Q, \Sigma, \Gamma, \delta, q_0, Z_0, F)$ be a PDA. We define a relation, called "move relation" by

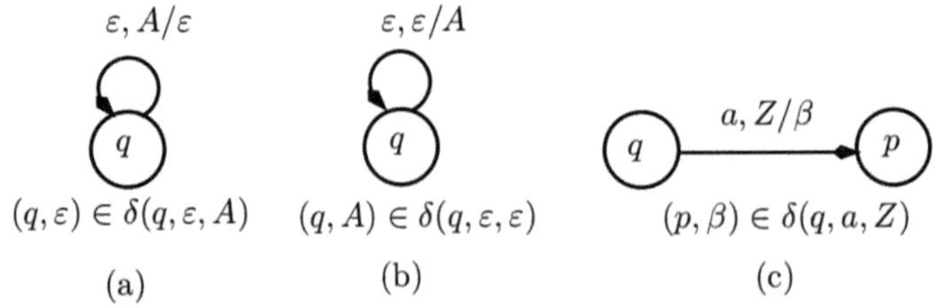

Fig. 8.2 Some transitions in PDA

$$(q, ax, Z\alpha) \vdash_M (q', x, \beta\alpha) \tag{8.8}$$

if $(q', \beta) \in \delta(q, a, Z)$ for any $q, q' \in Q$, any $a \in \Sigma \cup \{\varepsilon\}$, any $x \in \Sigma^*$, and $\alpha, \beta \in \Gamma^*$ and $Z \in \Gamma$.

Example 8.2 Construct a PDA that recognizes the language $L = \{a^n b^n \mid n \geq 0\}$.

Assume that the PDA recognizing this language is $M = (Q, \Sigma, \delta, s, F, \Gamma, Z_0)$. Here $\Sigma = \{a, b\}$, $s = q_0$, and Z_0 is top most character on stack at start. The other parameters are yet to be determined.

The language L states that there are a certain number of a's in the input string, and it is followed by exactly the same number of b's. This can be recognized by, first reading all a's, and for each a read, a fixed symbol (say $A \in \Gamma$) is written into the stack. When the second part of the input string (containing characters b) is read, the already stored symbol A is retrieved back from the stack for each b read from input. If the end of the input string and emptying out stack (retains original Z_0) coincides, we say the input is accepted. Accordingly, Q, δ, F, are defined as follows:

$Q = \{q_0, q_1, q_2, q_3\}$, $F = \{q_0, q_3\}$, $\Gamma = \{\varepsilon, A, Z_0\}$,
$\delta(q_0, \varepsilon, \varepsilon) = (q_1, Z_0)$
$\delta(q_1, a, \varepsilon) = (q_1, A)$
$\delta(q_1, b, A) = (q_2, \varepsilon)$,
$\delta(q_2, b, A) = (q_2, \varepsilon)$,
$\delta(q_2, \varepsilon, Z_0) = (q_3, \varepsilon)$.

These transitions are shown in Fig. 8.3.

Since $L = \{a^n b^n \mid n \geq 0\}$, the final state may occur at q_0 for $n = 0$, and at q_3 for $n > 0$. An input string $aabb \in L$ is thus accepted as follows.

$$\begin{aligned}(q_0, aabb, \varepsilon) &\vdash_M (q_1, aabb, Z_0)\\ &\vdash_M (q_1, abb, AZ_0)\\ &\vdash_M (q_1, bb, AAZ_0)\\ &\vdash_M (q_2, b, AZ_0)\\ &\vdash_M (q_2, \varepsilon, Z_0)\\ &\vdash_M (q_3, \varepsilon, \varepsilon), \text{ (The PDA accepts).}\end{aligned}$$

This shows that for the input $aabb$, when the tape string has been fully read, the pushdown stack contents also become null (Z_0 is not counted, being the end character of the stack). This satisfies the condition of acceptability, hence $aabb \in L$. □

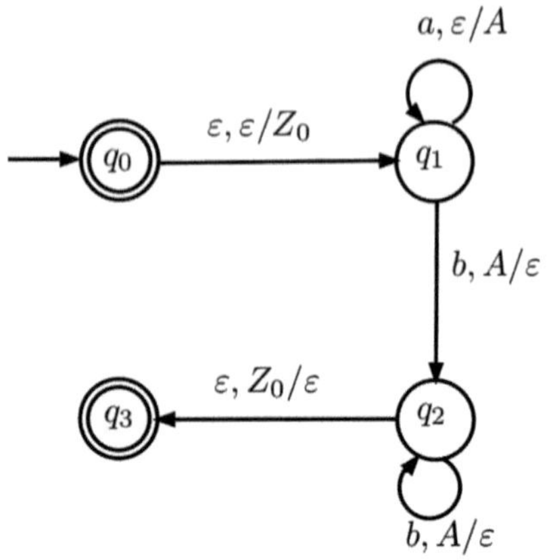

Fig. 8.3 PDA recognizing language $\{a^n b^n \mid n \geq 0\}$

8.4.3 Reflexive-Transitive Closure

The symbol sequence $\vdash_M^*$ is called *reflexive-transitive* closure of M. This is because, $I \vdash_M I$ for each ID I, $I \vdash_M J$ and $J \vdash_M K$ imply $I \vdash_M^* K$. We write a sequence of moves as $I \vdash^i K$ if ID I reduces to K after exactly i number of moves.

Note that, in

$$(q, ax, Z\alpha) \vdash_M (q', x, \beta\alpha), \tag{8.9}$$

there is $|Z\alpha| \geq 1$. This corresponds to the assumption that automata cannot make a move when the stack is empty. Also, $\beta = \varepsilon$ indicates that the top-most symbol Z of the stack has been erased.

As per the reflexive-transitive closure of the move relation, if,

$$(q, x, \alpha) \vdash^* (q', \varepsilon, \beta), \tag{8.10}$$

then, for any $y \in \Sigma^*$,

$$(q, xy, \alpha) \vdash^* (q', y, \beta). \tag{8.11}$$

Thus,

$$(q, x, \alpha) \vdash^* (q', \varepsilon, \beta) \Rightarrow (q, xy, \alpha) \vdash^* (q', y, \beta).$$

The converse is also true for the above, i.e., if Eq. (8.11) holds then (8.10) also holds. That is,

$$(q, xy, \alpha) \vdash^* (q', y, \beta) \Rightarrow (q, x, \alpha) \vdash^* (q', \varepsilon, \beta).$$

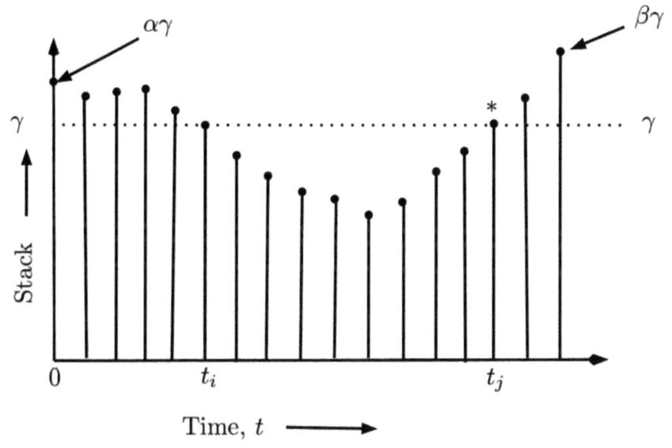

Fig. 8.4 Build-up of stack in pushdown automata

We may think of a similar relation for the stack. For example, for $\beta, \gamma \in \Gamma^*$, and $x, y \in \Sigma^*$, other symbols have the same meaning as earlier, if we have

$$(q, xy, \alpha) \vdash^* (q', y, \beta), \tag{8.12}$$

which means, during the time input x is processed, the stack contents α gets replaced by β, then we can say that,

$$(q, xy, \alpha\gamma) \vdash^* (q', y, \beta\gamma). \tag{8.13}$$

The latter means, when α gets replaced by β on the stack, the information γ below the α remains undisturbed.

However, the converse of the above is not necessarily true. That is, if Eq. (8.13) holds then it does not necessarily imply equation (8.12). Equation (8.13) may also mean that during the moves of the automata, possibly some part of the stack, i.e., γ was partly destroyed and then rewritten, such that final value of γ is same as it was earlier. In this process, if some computation step is reached without complete γ on the stack, the computation would block at the point marked as "*" in Fig. 8.4.

8.5 Pushdown Automata Simulation

Like we simulated deterministic finite automata, in Chap. 2, we will try to simulate a PDA also through a program. This program will simulate a PDA that recognizes the language $\{a^n b^n \mid n \geq 0\}$. The simulation first creates two data structures, $w[1000]$, and $stk[1000]$ for input tape and stack, respectively, of finite sizes. The tape is first initialized with all blank characters, i.e., 'B's. Let the states through which the

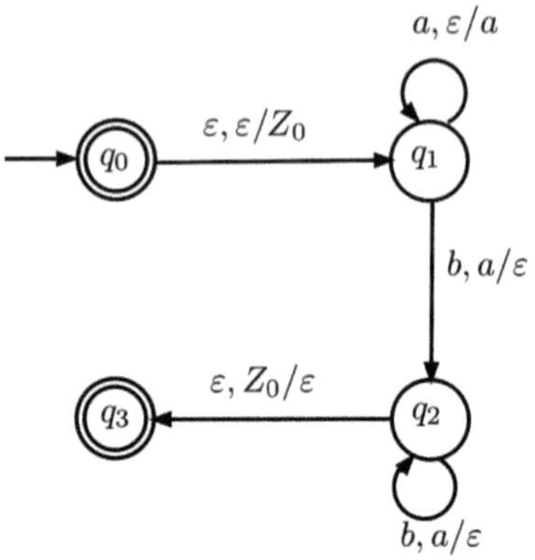

Fig. 8.5 PDA recognizing language $\{a^n b^n \mid n \geq 0\}$

machine goes through are q_0, q_1, q_2, q_3. For convenience, we have redrawn Fig. 8.3 as Fig. 8.5, of the corresponding PDA, the only difference is that here we have written the same input symbol(s) a onto the stack.

In the following, we have the listing of the PDA simulation program, *anbn.c* written in ANSI C. The PDA states and the program line numbers have been mapped as follows:

i. State q_0 (initializing): lines 8–11 correspond to initialization of tape pointer (i.e., head), writes the entire tape with B's, then writes input string $w = a^n b^n$ on to tape, for given value of n.
ii. Transition $q_0 \rightarrow q_1$: line 12, Initializes bottom of the stack
iii. Transition $q_1 \rightarrow q_1$ (loop): lines 15–18, read each input a from tape, and push it onto stack, advance the tape head and stack pointer, carry on for all a's are read from input tape.
iv. At q_0: Lines 21-23, if input is of zero length, Print "Yes", and exit.
v. Transition $q_1 \rightarrow q_2$: program lines 25–31, read 1st b character from tape and compare with stack.
vi. Transition $q_2 \rightarrow q_2$ (loop): program line 32–34, compare all the remaining characters "b" from tape with "a" on the stack, and advance tape head and stack pointer every time.
vii. Transition $q_2 \rightarrow q_3$: program lines 36–37, check stack bottom, and print "yes" if correct, otherwise print "No".

The program lines which are not part of the above discussion are for housekeeping. We can note the abstracted PDA in Fig. 8.5, which is far simplified compared to its implementation in this program. However, the abstract model serves its purpose for all the discussions and analyses.

```
/* anbn.c */
1. #include <stdio.h>
2. #include <stdlib.h>
```

```
int main(){
 int const MAX = 1000; //tape length of pda
 char w[MAX]; // tape of pda
 char stk[MAX]; // stack of pda
 char ch;
 int i=0, j;
 while(i < MAX) w[i++]= 'B'; //write all blanks on tape
 i = 0;
 while((ch=getchar())!='\n') w[i++] = ch; //initialize
                                               tape with w
 stk[0] = 'z'; //initialize bottom of stack
 i=0; //tape head points to first char
 j=1; //stack points to first location
 while(w[i] == 'a'){  //push a's on stack
   stk[j]=w[i];
   i++;
   j++;
 }
 j--; //stk points to top filled position
 // when input is null
  if (w[i]=='B'){
    printf("Yes\n");
    exit(0);
  }
 if (w[i]=='b' && stk[j]=='a'){  // compare 1st i/p 'b' char
                                                     with stack
   i++; j--;
   }
   else{
      printf("No\n");
      return 0;
 }
 while(w[i]=='b' && stk[j]=='a'){ //compare stk & II half
                                                      of w
   i++;
   j--;
 }
 if(stk[j]=='z' && w[i]=='B') // Is stk empty & tape end?
    printf("Yes\n");     // if yes, then input valid
 else
    printf("No\n");      //otherwise, input is not accepted
 return 0;
 }
```

The above program anbn.c is compiled and run to simulate a deterministic PDA, as follows.

```
$ gcc  anbn.c
$
$ ./a.out
 aaabbb
 Yes
$ ./a.out
 aabbb
 No
$
```

For null input, i.e., $|w| = 0$ ($n = 0$):

```
$ ./a.out
<press enter>
Yes
$
```

8.6 Types of PDAs

The PDA's accept input based on reaching to final state, or on the criteria of exhausting input w, or both of these. Further, PDAs can be deterministic, or nondeterministic types.

8.6.1 Deterministic PDA

We define Deterministic pushdown automata (DPDA) by fulfilling two conditions: (1) restrict the choice of next state after transition to single state only, and (2) take into account the ε-moves. In order to permit the automata to perform operations on its pushdown store without reading inputs, instead of simply disallowing ε-moves, a null move is permitted from a given state if and only if there does not exist a *non-null* move. The above conditions can be defined for a DPDA,

$$M = (Q, \Sigma, \Gamma, \delta, q_0, F, Z_0), \tag{8.14}$$

where $(q, a, Z) \in Q \times (\Sigma \cup \{\varepsilon\}) \times \Gamma$, as

1. $|\delta(q, a, Z)| \leq 1$; i.e., the choice of next state is one state only, where $a \in \Sigma$, or $a = \varepsilon$, and $Z \in \Gamma$.

2. For all $a \in \Sigma$, if $\delta(q, a, Z)$ does not produce non-null move then $\delta(q, \varepsilon, Z) = \phi$. That is, there are moves for all $a \in \Sigma$, then ε-move does not exist. The latter is called $\delta(q, \varepsilon, Z) = \phi$.

In the above, condition 1 restricts a choice of transition for any (q, a, Z) or (q, ε, Z) to single state only. We note that unlike the FA unless it is specified, a PDA is *nondeterministic*. Condition 2 prevents the possibility of a choice between a move independent of the input symbol (ε- move) and a move involving an input symbol.

If one can obtain a DPDA for a language, then that language is not inherently ambiguous (IA). This is because, for an IA language, there are two or more parse-trees, which means that there cannot be a deterministic PDA for that language.

Definition 8.1 A language L is called deterministic CFL (DCFL) if there is some DPDA M such $L = L_F(M)$. Two DPDAs M and M' are said to be equal to each other if $L_F(M) = L_F(M')$. □

There are CFLs that are not DCFLs. For example, $S \rightarrow aSb \mid bSa \mid \varepsilon$, is grammar for CFG but not DCFG, because we cannot find the center point of a string of these languages, i.e., ww^R unless we guess it. Hence, an NPDA is required to recognize this language. Further, this language (ww^R) is not ambiguous, as there can be only one parse-tree to parse the string of this language.

Example 8.3 Let us consider the grammar G as

$$S \rightarrow aSa \mid bSb \mid c.$$

Find out the language accepted by this PDA.

The above grammar generates a CFL, which is deterministic, as will be shown shortly. And, therefore, the corresponding Automata is DPDA.

The language generated by this grammar is a palindrome language with the character c as the center marker in each string of this language. Such language is a set made of strings,

$$L = L(G) = \{wcw^R \mid w \in \{a, b\}^*\}.$$

Let the corresponding DPDA be M. Intuitively, the automaton M will copy each symbol onto its pushdown stack as it reads and will remain in the same state. When it encounters input c, it will change to a new state q_1 without copying c onto the stack. Now onwards, every time the next symbol is read from the input, it is compared with the symbol at the top of the stack. If both are equal, the automaton will continue else it halts. If the PDA in this way reaches to the configuration $(q_1, \varepsilon, \varepsilon)$, i.e., there is no input symbol left and the stack is empty, then the input was certainly of the form wcw^R, and this causes the transition to final state q_2, and PDA accepts, as shown in Fig. 8.6. On the other hand, if the PDA encounters a mismatch between input and stack, or the input gets exhausted before the stack is emptied, then the input is rejected.

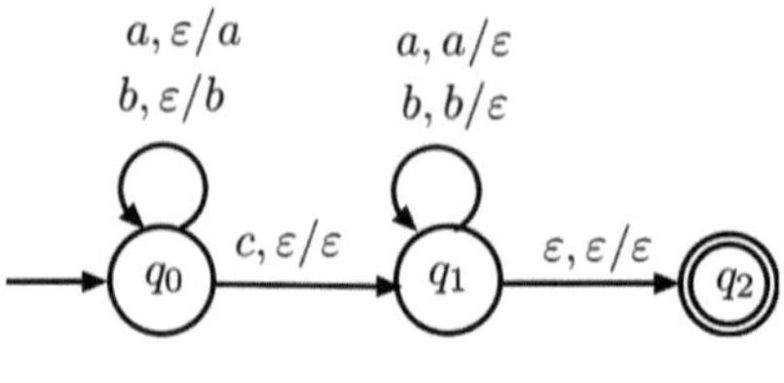

Fig. 8.6 PDA recognizing palindrome language

If the string is a palindrome, there will be the match, and the machine goes into the final state. This automaton M can be expressed as,[4]

$$M = (Q, \Sigma, \Gamma, \delta, q_0, F),$$

where

$$\begin{aligned}
Q &= \{q_0, q_1, q_2\}\\
\Sigma &= \{a, b, c\}\\
\Gamma &= \{a, b\}\\
F &= \{q_2\}.
\end{aligned}$$

Note that symbol c is only the center marker and it is not pushed onto the stack.

Let us designate different transitions (δ) by some unique identification number 1-6:

1. $\delta(q_0, a, \varepsilon) = (q_0, a)$; push input character a onto stack,
2. $\delta(q_0, b, \varepsilon) = (q_0, b)$; push input character b onto stack
3. $\delta(q_0, c, \varepsilon) = (q_1, \varepsilon)$; center character c is detected in the input,
4. $\delta(q_1, a, a) = (q_1, \varepsilon)$; compare and erase (tape and stack symbols are both a),
5. $\delta(q_1, b, b) = (q_1, \varepsilon)$; compare and erase (tape and stack symbols are both b),
6. $\delta(q_1, \varepsilon, \varepsilon) = (q_2, \varepsilon)$; Accept the input.

To show how this pushdown automaton recognizes, consider an input string $w = aabcbaa$. The corresponding moves of this automaton are shown below as well as in Table 8.1.

$$\begin{aligned}
(q_0, aabcbaa, \varepsilon) &\vdash (q_0, abcbaa, a)\\
&\vdash (q_0, bcbaa, aa)\\
&\vdash (q_0, cbaa, baa)\\
&\vdash (q_1, baa, baa)\\
&\vdash (q_1, aa, aa)\\
&\vdash (q_1, a, a)\\
&\vdash (q_1, \varepsilon, \varepsilon)\\
&\vdash (q_2, \varepsilon, \varepsilon)
\end{aligned}$$

[4] For the sake of simplicity, we have not used the symbol Z_0 that represents the bottom of the stack.

Table 8.1 Sequence of moves in PDA

Current state	Unread input	Stack (left is TOS)[a]	Transition no.
q_0	$aabcbaa$	ε	Initial state
q_0	$abcbaa$	a	1
q_0	$bcbaa$	aa	2
q_0	$cbaa$	baa	3
q_1	baa	baa	4
q_1	aa	aa	5
q_1	a	a	6
q_1	ε	ε	7 (next state is q_2)

[a]TOS: top of stack is always leftmost character

At this point the automaton halts at $q_2 \in F$, and therefore,

$$(q_0, aabcbaa, \varepsilon) \vdash^* (q_2, \varepsilon, \varepsilon).$$

In the above sequence of moves for the input string w, every move is deterministic, hence $L = L(G)$, M is a deterministic PDA, and G is context-free grammar that generates L. □

Example 8.4 Construct a PDA to recognize the language $\{a^i b^j c^k \mid i, j, k \geq 0$ and if $i = 1$ then $j = k\}$.

Solution Hint: Check that the first symbol on input tape is a, then push all b's and when input switches to c, start popping b's from stack. If exhausting of input (b's) coincides with that on the stack (c's), the language is accepted, else not. □

8.6.2 *Nondeterministic PDA*

A transition in a nondeterministic PDA is represented by

$$\delta(q, a, Z) = \text{ Subset of } \{(p_1, \beta_1), (p_2, \beta_2), ..., (p_m, \beta_m)\}, \tag{8.15}$$

which shows that any number of transitions may occur due single read from the input, where the input may be null also, and the stack may be written any number of times.

Example 8.5 Find out the language, and construct a PDA for the grammar G whose productions are

$$S \rightarrow aSa \mid bSb \mid \varepsilon.$$

The language generated by the grammar G is given as

$$L = L(G) = \{ww^R \mid w \in \{a, b\}^*\},$$

which is a CFL with every string a palindrome. The language L in this example differs from the Example 8.3 (Sect. 8.6.1) only in the sense that this has no center marker symbol. Therefore, if the PDA crosses over the center to find the center position of the input string, it may not be detected and may proceed just like the previous reads. With a little intuition, a reader will be convinced that since the input is one way with its length unbounded, a DPDA cannot find the center of the input. Therefore, it will "guess" for the center and if the guess works, then PDA will also work correctly. It should be ensured that if the PDA makes a wrong guess it should not accept the input string. There can be the following two extreme cases for the guess:

CASE I: If the Automaton guesses too frequently, it will pop the stack erasing the topmost character every time. This way it will empty the stack, while the input is not exhausted. Hence, the input string will not be accepted.

CASE II: If the Automaton guesses too late, the input may be exhausted while the stack is not empty and therefore the input string will still not be accepted.

Let the PDA be

$$M = (Q, \Sigma, \Gamma, \delta, q_0, Z_0, F),$$

where

$Q = \{q_0, q_1\}$
$\Sigma = \{a, b\}$
$\Gamma = \{a, b, Z_0\}$, $F = \phi$,

and δ is given by following for $d \in \{a, b\}$, and $\alpha \in \Gamma^*$.

$\delta(q_0, d, Z_0) = \{(q_0, dZ_0)\}$, push the first alphabet into the stack.
$\delta(q_0, d, \alpha) = \{(q_0, d\alpha)\}$, continue pushing the input
$\delta(q_0, \varepsilon, Z_0) = \{(q_1, Z_0)\}$, accept ε input string
$\delta(q_0, d, d) = \{(q_1, \varepsilon), (q_0, dd)\}$, guess what to do !!
$\delta(q_1, d, d) = \{(q_1, \varepsilon)\}$, compare and drop
$\delta(q_1, \varepsilon, Z_0) = \{(q_1, \varepsilon)\}$, accept.

To see the working of this PDA consider the input string $ww^R = baab$. The possible sequence of moves for the PDA is given below.
CASE I.

$$\begin{aligned}(q_0, baab, Z_0) &\vdash (q_0, aab, bZ_0)\\ &\vdash (q_0, ab, abZ_0)\\ &\vdash (q_0, b, aabZ_0)\\ &\vdash (q_0, \varepsilon, baabZ_0); \text{(Guesses too late)}\end{aligned}$$

CASE II.

$$\begin{aligned}(q_0, baab, Z_0) &\vdash (q_0, aab, bZ_0)\\ &\vdash (q_0, ab, abZ_0)\\ &\vdash (q_1, b, bZ_0)\\ &\vdash (q_1, \varepsilon, Z_0)\end{aligned}$$

The set of move sequences of PDA in CASE II exhausts the input string and empties the stack. Therefore the input string *baab* is accepted. It may be noted that M accepts input by *empty stack*, and the machine is nondeterministic. The machine has no final states, hence $F = \phi$. □

Example 8.6 Construct PDA to recognize the language $\{ww \mid w \in \{0, 1\}^*\}$.

To recognize this language it is necessary to recognize the center point or the first symbol of 2nd w in the ww string, which in the presence of many 0's and 1's in any order and frequency of occurrence in each w, is not possible by a deterministic PDA. Therefore, a nondeterministic PDA is needed to recognize this language. The remaining solution is similar to the Example 8.5. □

8.7 Language Acceptability by PDA

One of the criteria for acceptance by the PDA is: that there are some input strings for which some sequence of moves causes the PDA to empty the stack. This language is referred to be a language accepted by *empty stack*.

Another way to define the criteria for acceptance of a language is similar to that of FA (finite automata). As per this, for a set of inputs, some choice of the moves causes the PDA to enter the *final state*. It can be proved that, in fact, the above two criteria of acceptance of a language are equal. Because, if a language is accepted by the empty stack of one PDA then it is also accepted by another PDA by moving into the final state, and vice-versa. This fact we will prove shortly.

8.7.1 Acceptance by Final State

Let there be a PDA $M = (Q, \Sigma, \Gamma, \delta, q_0, Z_0, F)$. This M may be considered accepting input string w if upon reading it completely, the PDA moves to the final state. The contents of the stack are irrelevant. We denote $L_F(M)$ be the language accepted by final state by M. Thus,

$$L_F(M) = \{w \in \Sigma^* \mid (q_0, w, Z_0) \vdash^* (q_f, \varepsilon, \alpha)\} \tag{8.16}$$

for some $q_f \in F$, $\alpha \in \Gamma^*$. Here q_f is final state. This is the default criteria for acceptance and has been used in Example 8.2.

For $w = xx^R$, where $x \in \{0, 1\}^*$, the accepting computations of M on the criteria of final state is as given below.

$$(q_0, xx^R, Z_0) \vdash^* (q_0, x^R, x^R Z_0) \vdash (q_1, x^R, x^R Z_0) \vdash^* (q_f, \varepsilon, Z_0) \quad (8.17)$$

Note that when x is read and pushed onto stack, it appears back in reverse order. Next, with null (ε) input M goes to state q_1, and matches x^R input with same string (x^R) on its stack. Finally, on finding null input at q_1, it goes to accepting state q_f.

8.7.2 Acceptance by Empty Stack

A PDA $M = (Q, \Sigma, \Gamma, \delta, q_0, Z_0)$ accepts a language $L_E(M)$ on the criteria of empty stack if for a string w there exists some finite sequence of moves that exhaust w, and at the same time empties the stack. In this case, the automata will halt since it cannot make any move when its store (stack) is empty. The language $L_E(M)$ is defined as

$$L_E(M) = \{w \in \Sigma^* \mid (q_0, w, Z_0) \vdash^* (q, \varepsilon, Z_0)\} \quad (8.18)$$

for some $q \in Q$, i.e., any state. For $w = xx^R$, where $x \in \{0, 1\}^*$, the accepting computations of M on the criteria of final state is

$$(q_0, xx^R, Z_0) \vdash^* (q_0, x^R, x^R Z_0) \vdash (q_1, x^R, x^R Z_0) \vdash^* (q_1, \varepsilon, Z_0) \vdash (q_2, \varepsilon, Z_0) \quad (8.19)$$

At state q_0 the PDA reads input x and stores it on the stack in reverse order. Next, with null (ε) input, M goes to state q_1, and matches x^R input with same string (x^R) on its stack. Finally, on finding null input at q_1, it empties the stack, remain in state q_1, and accepts $w = xx^R$, by moving to state q_2.

8.7.3 Acceptance by Final State and Empty Stack

A PDA $M = (Q, \Sigma, \Gamma, \delta, q_0, Z_0, F)$ accepts a language $L_{EF}(M)$ by the criteria of both final state and empty stack together if on exhausting the input string w it reaches to the final state and also empties the stack.

$$L_{EF}(M) = \{w \in \Sigma^* \mid (q_0, w, Z_0) \vdash^* (q_f, \varepsilon, Z_0\} \quad (8.20)$$

for some $q_f \in F$. For $w = xx^R$, where $x \in \{0, 1\}^*$, the accepting computations of M on the criteria of final state is

$$(q_0, xx^R, Z_0) \vdash^* (q_0, x^R, x^R Z_0) \vdash (q_1, x^R, x^R Z_0) \vdash^* (q_1, \varepsilon, Z_0) \vdash (q_f, \varepsilon, Z_0) \tag{8.21}$$

At state q_0 the PDA reads input x and stores it on the stack in reverse order. Next, with null (ε) input M goes to state q_1, and matches x^R input with same string (x^R) on its stack. Finally, on finding null input at q_1, it empties the stack, goes to state q_f, and accepts w.

Theorem 8.1 *For every PDA accepted by an empty stack, there exists an equivalent PDA that accepts on final state.*

Proof Let there be a deterministic PDA $M = (Q, \Sigma, \Gamma, \delta, q_0, Z_0, \phi)$ which accepts on an empty stack. We want to show that there exists an equivalent deterministic PDA $M' = (Q, \Sigma, \Gamma', \delta', q_0, Y_0, \{q_f\})$ that accepts on final state. Let $L_E(M)$ be a language accepted by M and $L_F(M')$ be the language accepted by M'.

Let there is a string $x \in L_E(M)$. Our claim is, if $x \in L_E(M)$, then $(q_0', x, Y_0) \vdash^*_{M'} (q_f, \varepsilon, \varepsilon)$.

We define M' in terms of the states of M as

$$M' = (Q \cup \{q_0, q_f\}, \Sigma, \Gamma \cup \{Y_0\}, \delta', q_0', Y_0, \{q_f\}),$$

where $q_0' \in Q$, $Y_0 \notin \Gamma$, and δ' is given by

1. $\delta'(q_0', \varepsilon, Y_0) = \{(q_0, Y_0 Z_0)\}$, add new bottom symbol Z_0 in stack of M'.
2. For all $(q, a, Z) \in Q \times (\Sigma \cup \{\varepsilon\}) \times \Gamma$, there is $\delta'(q, a, Z) = \delta(q, a, Z)$, i.e., simulate M in M'.
3. $\delta'(q, \varepsilon, Y_0) = \{(q_f, \varepsilon)\}$ for all $q \in Q$, erase Y_0 and accept.

Certainly M', whose language is $L_F(M)$, accepts the language $L_E(M)$ of M. This is because M' first enters from its initial configuration to the initial configuration of M (step 1 above) without consuming any input symbol. Then it carries out the simulation of M in M', as shown by step 2 above. Finally, when M empties its stack, M' enters into its final state, as shown by step 3 above.

Claim: If $x \in L_E(M)$, then $(q_0', x, Y_0) \vdash^*_{M'} (q_f, \varepsilon, \varepsilon)$.

If $x \in L_E(M)$, then

$$(q_0, x, Z_0) \vdash^*_{M'} (q, \varepsilon, \varepsilon) \text{ for some } q \in Q.$$

But, since $\delta_M \subseteq \delta_{M'}$, we have

$$(q_0, x, Z_0) \vdash^*_{M'} (q, \varepsilon, \varepsilon).$$

In the above move(s) the pushdown stack is possible to be emptied on in the last move, accordingly, we can write all the moves as

$$(q_0', x, Y_0) \vdash_{M'} (q_0, x, Y_0Z_0) \vdash_{M'}^* (q, \varepsilon, Y_0) \vdash_{M'} (f, \varepsilon, \varepsilon)$$

Accordingly, for $x \in L_E(M)$, there exists $(q_0', x, Y_0) \vdash_{M'}^* (qf, \varepsilon, \varepsilon)$. This proves the claim. □

Theorem 8.2 *For every PDA accepted by the final state, there exists an equivalent PDA that accepts on an empty stack.*

Proof Let there be a deterministic PDA $M' = (Q', \Sigma, \Gamma', \delta', q_0', Y_0, \{q_f\})$ that accepts on final state. We want to show that there exists an equivalent deterministic PDA $M = (Q, \Sigma, \Gamma, \delta, q_0, Z_0, \phi)$ which accepts on empty stack. Let us assume that languages accepted by M' and M are $L_F(M')$ and $L_E(M)$, respectively.

Claim. If $(q_0, x, Y_0) \vdash_{M'}^* (q_f, \varepsilon, \varepsilon)$, then $x \in L_E(M)$.

If $(q_0', x, Y_0) \vdash_{M'}^* (q_f, \varepsilon, \varepsilon)$, then from the construction of M', the construction must be of the form,

$$(q_0, x, Y_0) \vdash_{M'} (q_0, x, Y_0Z_0) \vdash_{M'}^* (q, \varepsilon, Y_0) \vdash_{M'} (f, \varepsilon, \varepsilon) \tag{8.22}$$

for some $x \in Q$. Since, it is not possible to rewrite Y_0 in the computation (q_0, x, Y_0Z_0) $\vdash_{M'}^* (q, \varepsilon, Y_0)$, we must have $(q_0, x, Z_0) \vdash_{M'}^* (q, \varepsilon, \varepsilon)$, or $x \in L_E(M)$. Therefore, we can say that,

$(q_0', x, Y_0) \vdash_{M'}^* (f, \varepsilon, \varepsilon)$ implies that $x \in L_E(M)$.

This concludes that $L_F(M) \subseteq L_E(M)$. □

Theorem 8.3 *A PDA will accept on the final state if and only if there exists an equivalent PDA accepting on an empty stack.*

Proof We have verified in Theorem 8.1 that for a PDA accepting on the empty stack, there exists a PDA, which accepts the same language on final state. That is, $L_E(M) \subseteq L_F(M')$, where $L_E(M)$ is language accepted by PDA with empty stack, and $L_F(M')$ is language accepted by PDA on final state.

We have verified the converse in Theorem 8.2 that $L_F(M') \subseteq L_E(M)$.

Using the above two verifications we conclude that $LF(M') = L_E(M)$. Also, if the languages accepted by two PDAs are equivalent then the two PDAs are also equivalent. □

Theorem 8.4 *For each CFL L, there exists a PDA M such that* $L = L_E(M)$.

Proof Let $L = L(G)$ for some CFG $G = (V, \Sigma, S, P)$. Now construct a PDA M such that,

$$M = (\{q\}, \Sigma, V, q, S, \phi),$$

where δ is given by

1. $\delta(q, \varepsilon, Z) = \{(q, \alpha^R) \mid Z \to \alpha \in P\}$,
2. For each $a \in \Sigma$, $\delta(q, a, a) = \{(q, \varepsilon)\}$.

It is clear that M performs a standard top-down parse. There is no left recursion problem because M is nondeterministic. □

8.8 Equivalence of PDA and Context-Free Grammar

A pushdown automaton (PDA) and Context-free Grammar (CFG) look completely different from computational models. However, since a PDA recognizes CFL and that CFL can be generated by a CFG, there should be possible equivalence between PDA and CFG. It can be shown that these two models are in fact equivalent in power in specifying languages. Once equivalence is proved then a context-free language can be defined to be generated by a CFG or to be a language accepted by PDA. Hence, when we need to prove that the language is context-free, we can either prove that the language is generated by CFG or it is accepted by PDA. We prefer that both options are open to us, as certain CF languages may be more easily described using CFG, while there are CF languages that can be more easily accepted by a PDA [11].

We shall prove the equivalence of PDA and CFG in the following discussions, and show that given either the CFG or PDA, we can construct the other in the substantially same way, as the given one, that way we can conclude that the two satisfy the same language.

Theorem 8.5 *A language is generated by a CFG if and only if the language is accepted by PDA.*

Proof In this proof, we shall simulate a CFG by a PDA, by constructing a PDA M that is equivalent to a given CFG G. Let the string to be recognized by PDA is $w = a_0a_1...a_{n-1}$, hence it should be made available on its tape at the start. For the given CFG, we consider a typical parse-tree that should generate the same string $w = a_0a_1...a_{n-1}$ (Fig. 8.7). Let $G = (V, \Sigma, S, P)$, $V = \{S, A_1, ..., A_{13}\}$, $\Sigma = \{a_0, a_1, ..., a_{n-1}\}$, and productions are $A \to A_1A_2$, $A_1 \to A_3A_4$, ..., $A_7 \to a_0a_1$, ..., as shown in Fig. 8.7. Note that all the productions are in Chomsky Normal Form (CNF).[5]

[5] See Chap. 7 for CNF. As per this, any CFG can be converted into CNF grammar, i.e., the form with production rules like, $A \to BC|a$, while generating power of CNF based grammar remains the same as that of original.

In the following, we shall show that PDA M simulates derivation based on the grammar G. The transition in PDA is divided into two parts, (a) and (b). We call these two states, the PDA may occupy.

(a) Transitions of, first popping a nonterminal from the top of the stack, which is the head of production in the CFG, and then pushing the corresponding body of the production onto the stack. For example, if top of stack is A and rule is $A \rightarrow X_1X_2$, then X_1, X_2 are pushed with X_1 at top of stack.
(b) Transitions of popping of a terminal symbol from the top of the stack when this symbol is equal to (terminal symbol at the) current tape head position. This roughly corresponds to moving from left to right of the parse-tree (see the area covered in a loop of dashed line ('-') in Fig. 8.7.)

Now we show, how the operations in PDA match with the operations in the parse-tree. The *state* (a)[6] of PDA has the following operations, which correspond to derivations in the parse-tree:

- pop the start symbol S, and push A_1A_2 with A_1 at top. The Z_0 symbol is initially inserted in the stack to indicate the bottom of the stack.
- pop A_1 and push A_3A_4, with A_3 at top,
- pop A_3 and push A_7A_8, with A_7 at top,
- pop A_7 and push a_0a_1, with a_0 at top.

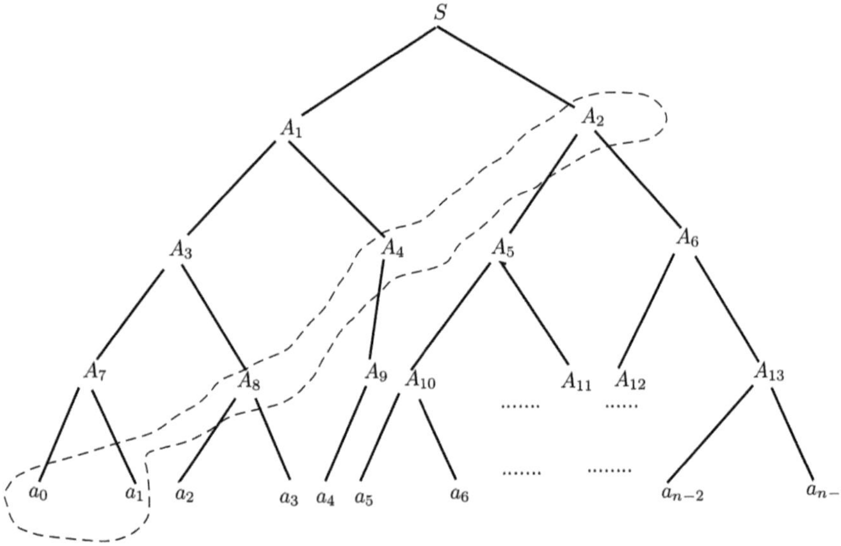

Fig. 8.7 Parse-tree to show the equivalence of PDA and CFG

[6] Truly speaking, it is not equal to a transition state, but bigger with many operations.

In this instance, two symbols of input match with the top two symbols on the stack, and the two symbols are popped off the stack. This latter part is performed in two transitions in state (b). now, A_8 is at the top of stack, and the PDA is ready to pop A_8 and push a_2a_3 onto stack with a_2 at top of the stack. This simulates the production rule $A_8 \rightarrow a_2a_3$.

Here is the detailed working of PDA M. To begin with, M pushes SZ_0 onto empty stack with S at top,

$$\delta(q_0, \varepsilon, \varepsilon) = (q_1, SZ_0),$$

the Z_0 will indicate that bottom of the stack is reached. The q_0 is start state of PDA and q_1 is state that simulates the derivation in G. The Table 8.2 shows the transition function (δ) of the PDA.

In general, a transition of the first stage is specified as

$$\delta(q_1, \varepsilon, A) = (q_1, \alpha),$$

for each rule $A \rightarrow \alpha$ of G, which means to apply the rule without input. Here $\alpha \in (V \cup \Sigma)^+$.

To perform a transition of state (a), the top of the stack comprises a nonterminal that is required to be replaced. However, if there is a terminal on top of the stack, this is compared with input, and removed when both are equal. In general, a transition of state (b) is

$$\delta(q_1, a, a) = (q, \varepsilon).$$

Thus, we note that PDA M performs the transitions that are chosen from state (a) and (b), depending on whether the symbol on top of the stack is a nonterminal or terminal, respectively. Figure 8.8 shows the transitions of the PDA. If the string to be generated by parse-tree is on the tape of M, then after this input has been processed, M is left with end character Z_0 on the stack.

If a transition function performs the operation,

$$\delta(q_1, \varepsilon, Z_0) = (q_2, \varepsilon),$$

then, PDA M moves to state q_2, with empty stack, and q_2 is accepting state of M. It should be noted that the PDA is not provided with the parse-tree, hence it should

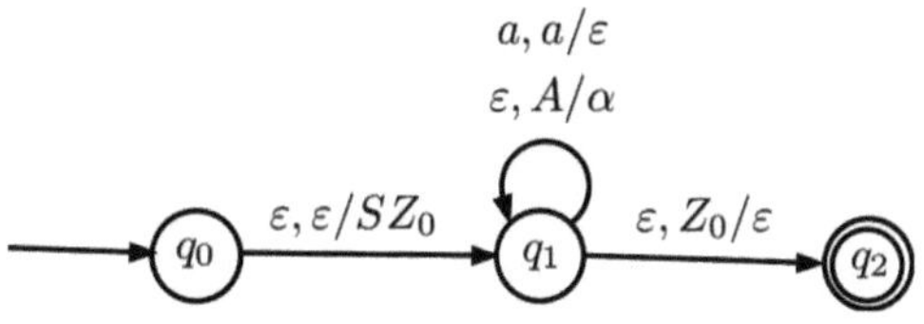

Fig. 8.8 Stages in state q_1 of a PDA corresponding to Parse-tree shown in Fig. 8.7

Table 8.2 The PDA simulates the CFG in CNF

Progressive contents of stack	Corresponding rule applied to derive parse-tree
$S \Rightarrow A_1 A_2$	$(\delta(q_1, \varepsilon, S) = (q_1, A_1 A_2))$
$\Rightarrow A_3 A_4 A_2$	$(\delta(q_1, \varepsilon, A_1) = (q_1, A_3 A_4))$
$\Rightarrow A_7 A_8 A_4 A_2$	$(\delta(q_1, \varepsilon, A_3) = (q_1, A_7 A_8))$
$\Rightarrow a_0 a_1 A_8 A_4 A_2$	$(\delta(q_1, \varepsilon, A_7) = (q_1, a_0 a_1))$

correctly guess the parse-tree and simulate the derivation by choosing the transitions properly.

In the above discussions, given the CFG G, we first constructed PDA M that simulates G.[7] Then we assumed that CFG G generates the string $a_0 a_1 ... a_{n-1}$, according to parse-tree shown in Fig. 8.7, and we derived PDA M that accepts that string.

In another way, we can assume that PDA M accepts $a_0 a_1 ... a_{n-1}$ then it is clear that there exists parse-tree based on the transitions of M like shown in Fig. 8.7, that generates the string. This is possible because, to make the stack empty at the end of the computation, the transitions of the first state somehow simulate derivations of a certain parse-tree, and input string to M coincides with the string that parse-tree generates, so as to pop off all the contents on the stack. □

Note that the parsing we have constructed in Fig. 8.7 corresponds to *top-down parsing* because we have started from the top (root node) and derive to sub-trees and ultimately match the bottom level terminals with the input, i.e., tape of the PDA. Truly, though it appears a parse-tree-like approach, actually we have used a PDA to recognize the input sentence.

In the next chapter, we will see a reverse approach, where we will make use of a PDA to recognize the given language sentence and travel from the bottom to the top of such a tree. Here, we will assemble the substrings, e.g., $a_0 a_1$ to A_7, $A_7 a_8$ to A_3, and so on. We will call this approach bottom-up parsing.

8.8.1 Direct Conversion of CFG to PDA

Given the option of choosing PDA vs CFG for recognition of CFL, what we should choose? Based on what we have studied so far, we will prefer to choose the CFG-based approach because the CFG-based approach appears easy. However, there exists a direct conversion algorithm to convert the CFG into PDA. This algorithm is in fact, a nondeterministic parsing algorithm. The opposite conversion (i.e., CFG to PDA), however, is more involved, and shall not be considered here. The below given theorem states that if a language is generated by a CFG then there exists a PDA that accepts the language.

[7] Reader may do so by constructing a PDA given the grammar $S \rightarrow aSb \mid \varepsilon$, and given any string in this grammar.

Theorem 8.6 *If a language is generated by a context-free grammar then there exists a pushdown automaton that accepts the language.*

Proof Let $G = (V, \Sigma, S, P)$ be a CFG that generates the language L. Based on G a PDA $M = (Q, \Sigma, \Gamma, \delta, q_0, Z_0, F)$ that accepts CF language L can be defined as follows. Consider states,

$$Q = \{q_0, q_1, q_2\}, F = \{q_2\},$$

and

$$\Gamma = \Sigma \cup V \cup \{Z_0\}.$$

Let the transition function δ be as shown in Fig. 8.8. The corresponding to transitions from q_1 to q_1 for every rule $A \to \alpha$ can be specified as

$$q_1 \xrightarrow{\varepsilon, A/\alpha} q_1$$

and for every $a \in \Sigma$, it can be given as follows:

$$q_1 \xrightarrow{a, a/\varepsilon} q_1$$

Then clearly, $L(M) = L(G)$. This completes the proof of the theorem. □

Finding a CFG to PDA conversion, there is an exponential time algorithm for any CFG $G = (V, \Sigma, S, P)$. The conversion is achieved through backtracking searches whenever the PDA comes across a nondeterministic choice. Here, a piece of code is rearranged that recursively searches for one of the paths that accepts. In fact, the computer works as a DTM (Deterministic Turing Machine) that simulates an NPDA [15].

8.8.2 CFG to PDA Conversion Algorithm

In the CFG to PDA conversion algorithm, the nonterminals (V) and terminals (Σ) of the grammar G are together taken as stack alphabet of the PDA.

Steps for conversion from CFG to PDA work as given in the Algorithm 8.1.

Since a language generated by context-free grammar is a context-free language, and every deterministic PDA is a subset of nondeterministic PDA, Theorems 8.5 and 8.6 can also be stated as below.

Theorem 8.7 *A set of strings is a context-free language if and only if it is accepted by a nondeterministic pushdown storage automaton [16].*

Proof The proof hint for this theorem is Theorem 8.6. □

Algorithm 8.1 CFG-to-PDA Conversion

1: Start with start state q_0 of PDA with Z_0 on the top of the stack.
2: From q_0, jump to state q' (some non-start state), with start symbol S of CFG on top of the stack and Z_0 below it.
3: **while** in state q' **do**
4: if top of stack is Z_0, jump to $q_f \in F$, the only accepting state,
5: if top of stack is terminal symbol $a \in \Sigma$, jump back to state q', without restoring the a on top of stack. By this, parsing goal of a is fulfilled.
6: if top of stack is non-terminal $X \in V$, and there is a rule, $X \rightarrow \alpha$, where $\alpha \in (V \cup \Sigma)^+$, then jump to q' state by popping X and pushing α on top of stack. By this, essentially, we have converted the parsing goal of X into zero or more sub-goals.
7: **end while**
8: End

8.8.3 Some Closure Properties of Formal Languages

Theorem 8.8 *Intersection of CFLs and Regular Languages is CFLs.*

Proof Let M_1 be a NPDA that accepts L_1 by final state, and let M_2 be the DFA that accepts the regular language L_2. Another NPDA M recognizing $L_1 \cap L_2$ can simulates M_1 and M_2 in parallel, and accepts, if both M_1 and M_2 accept the input. Figure 8.9a shows the finite transitions of M_1, M_2, and M. Like in a "cross-product" construction of DFA, states of the new machine M have pairs of states, where one element of pair corresponds to the state of M_1 and other corresponds to the state of M_2.

Figure 8.9b shows the ε-transition. Whenever, an input symbol is read, both M_1 and M_2 are simulated; if M_1 needs to make a ε-move, the M_2 remains stationary, and M makes a ε move.

Figure 8.9c shows start of state M_1, M_2, M and Fig. 8.9d shows the final states in three machines.

Since all the states in M, which is intersection of an NPDA M_1 accepting on final state and the DFA M_2, have been determined, this proves the theorem. □

8.9 Parsers

Today's parsing techniques are based on formal languages and automata theory, enabling the systematic development of compiler front ends. Likewise, early work on restructuring compilers used ad-hoc techniques for dependency analysis and loop transformation. Today, this aspect of compilers has been revolutionized by powerful algorithms based on integer linear programming.

Against the common belief of the context-sensitiveness of natural languages, natural languages are not necessarily not context-free. Considering that natural languages are non context-free, a fairly comprehensive grammar for a subset of natural

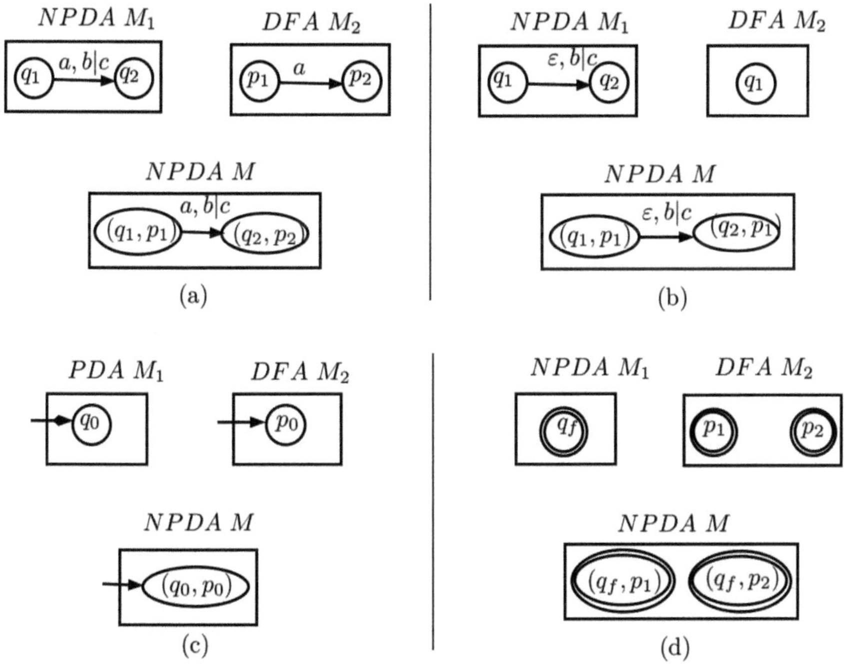

Fig. 8.9 **a** Finite transitions in M_1, M_2, and M, **b** ε-transition in M_1, **c** Single-state M_1, M_2, M, **d** Final-state in M_1, M_2, M

languages is sufficient for practical systems and can be written in context-free phrase structure.

The incremental generators of parsers,[8] based on LR techniques, for arbitrary context-free grammars, are based on a pseudo-parallel LR parsing algorithms. The yacc (yet another compiler compiler) generates faster parsers than IPG (incremental parser generator), but IPG takes less time for parser generation. It is found that IPG is more appropriate in the context of interactive language definition systems.

Definition 8.2 *Parser.* A parser is a recognizer, which also outputs the set of all legal derivation-trees of a sentence string. □

Against the common belief of context-sensitiveness of natural languages, natural languages are not necessarily context-free. Considering that natural languages are non-context-free, a fairly comprehensive grammar for a subset of natural languages is sufficient for practical systems and can be written in context-free phrase structure.

Definition 8.3 *LL Parser.* An LL parser is a top-down parser for a subset of context-free languages. It parses the input sentence from left to right and performs the leftmost

[8] There are tools, e.g., yacc (yet another compiler compiler), that can generate a parser, relieving from the need of writing code for writing a parser.

derivation of the sentence. An LL parser is called LL(k) parser if it uses k tokens of look-ahead when parsing a sentence. □

Definition 8.4 *LR Parser.* An LR parser is a type of bottom-up parser, that scans the input sentence left-to-right and constructs the rightmost derivation in reverse. The LR parser is called LR(k) parser if it uses k tokens of look-ahead when parsing a sentence. □

Definition 8.5 *Shift-reduce parser.* Table driven, bottom-up parsing methods used for parsing programming and natural languages, and use LR parsing and its variants, are shift-reduce parsers. □

The simplest parser is called *brute-force parser*. Type of parsers works not only for the restricted grammars (context-free grammars, and context-sensitive grammar) but also for unrestricted grammars. A simple unrestricted grammar is

$$
\begin{aligned}
S &\rightarrow aaS \\
S &\rightarrow \varepsilon \\
aa &\rightarrow b
\end{aligned}
\tag{8.23}
$$

It parses by first accepting parse, if not successful then it backtracks from the first disagreement with respect to the input string, and tries all alternatives of substitutions in the order the rules are listed. Thus, this method of parsing takes a very long time since it explores every possibility of substitution of variables. In case of unrestricted grammar, since this language is equivalent to *Turing recognizable languages*,[9] there is no guarantee that the brute-force parser will ever stop. For example, the grammar in (8.23), if used to parse the string $w = ab$, it will never terminate.

Parsers are basically two types, top-down parsers and bottom-up parsers. The top-down parser builds a parse-tree top-down, i.e., starts from the root of the tree and expands each node either in DFS (depth-first search) mode or BFS (breadth first search) mode by applications of production rules. Since each production rule in a context-free grammar (CFG) is of the form $A \rightarrow \alpha$, where A is nonterminal and α is string in $(V \cup \Sigma)^*$, it constructs sub-tree with children nodes as α under the parent node A. Consider the grammar $G = (V, \Sigma, S, P)$, where V is set of nonterminals, Σ is set of terminals, i.e., language symbols, S is started symbol, and P is set of production rules. If there is more than one rule like, $A \rightarrow \alpha$, with the same head symbol A, for top-down parsing, it will lead to backtracking if the correct rule is not selected. Apart from backtracking, which takes an exponential amount of time, the top-down parsing suffers from left recursion (left factoring) and stops when it finds a single derivation. Further, there is no semantic knowledge employed in the top-down parsing.

[9] Turing recognizable language: If a string belongs to the language, then the machine accepts and halts, if not, the machine may keep on searching, without halting ever.

A bottom-up parser builds a parse-tree reverse, i.e., starts from the bottom (children) of the tree and builds upward, and the final step is installing the root node. Thus, every time it assembles a subsequence β_k in the current sentential α_j such that $A \rightarrow \beta_k$, then β_k in sentential α_j is substituted with A to get new sentential α_i, and the process goes on until α_i becomes $\alpha_0 = S$. Hence, bottom-up parsing is a derivation from *right to left* in the derivation (8.24):

$$S = \alpha_o \Rightarrow \alpha_1 \Rightarrow ... \Rightarrow \alpha_i \Rightarrow \alpha_j \Rightarrow ... \Rightarrow \alpha_n = w \tag{8.24}$$

Opposite to bottom-up parsing is top-down parsing, where derivation is carried out from left to right in Eq. (8.24).

8.9.1 Top-Down Parsing

Following is an informal description of the algorithm as a *recognizer*. It scans an input string comprising X_1, X_2, ..., X_n from left to right looking ahead some fixed number k ($k \geq 0$) of symbols in the input.[10] As each symbol X_i is scanned, a set of states S_i is constructed, which represents the condition of the recognition process at that point in the scan. Each state in this set represents:

- a production, showing that we are currently scanning a portion of the input string, which is derived from the production's right (i.e., aBc of $A \rightarrow aBc$),
- a point in that production, which shows how much of the production's right side we have recognized so far,
- a pointer back to the position in the input string at which we begin to look for that instance of the production, and
- a k-symbol string, which is a syntactically allowed successor to that instance of the productions.

A *derivation-tree* represents a clear view of the parsing process. In addition, it shows the structure of the strings generated in the form of various substring components. The tree also represents the association among the various components of the language [5].

Starting node of a parse-tree represents the symbol S in the CFG, internal nodes represent the *Nonterminal symbols* or *variables* in V, and terminal nodes represent the alphabet of CFG or just the null string symbol ε. A node labeled by ε is the only child of its parent. If an interior node A is root of a parse-tree and $A \rightarrow X_1X_2...X_n$ is a production in CFG then X_1, X_2, ..., X_n will be child nodes of A, shown in Fig. 8.10.

[10] For example, it is difficult to decide, as which one to choose out of the productions, $A \rightarrow a$ and $A \rightarrow bA$, for a substitution in the current sentential form $S \Rightarrow^* abaA$, for top-down parsing, given that final string is $w = ababba$. It is clear that if we look ahead next symbol b in the sentential form, it would be helpful in deciding the production rule to be applied here. Hence, we choose $A \rightarrow bA$ two times, followed with $A \rightarrow a$. If this order of substitution is not followed, and we selected $A \rightarrow a$ instead, it would require backtracking.

8.9.2 *Bottom-Up Parsing*

The bottom-up parsing methods are locally described as algorithms that scan an input stream while computing with a pushdown store and a bounded amount of additional memory. At each stage, the algorithm performs one of the following actions [6]:

1. reads an input symbol onto the stack; this continues until a complete phrase resides in the stack; or
2. replace the phrase in the stack with a nonterminal which generated it. For example, if production is $A \to aBc$, and the phrase on the stack is aBc, then aBc is replaced by A.

In the above, the first action is called *phrase detection* while the second operation is called *phrase reduction*. The entire algorithm can be represented by a flow-chart shown in Fig. 8.11.

However, this simple procedure is not powerful enough to parse all the context-free languages. The bottom-up parsing techniques are discussed toward the end of this chapter.

8.10 LL(k) and LR(k) Grammars

The Context-free languages have aroused the widest interest as they serve approximate models for Natural Languages and computer Programming Languages, among others. There is a subset of CFLs which are called *translatable from left to right*, i.e., we read the characters of a string from left to right, and look for a given finite number of characters ahead, we are able to parse the given string without ever backing up to consider a previous decision.[11]

For a given word w and a non-negative integer k, we define w/k to be w if length of w is less than or equal to k, and we define w/k to be the string consisting of first k symbols of w if w has more than k symbols. If A is nonterminal, $w \in (V \cup \Sigma)^*$, and

Fig. 8.10 A derivation-tree

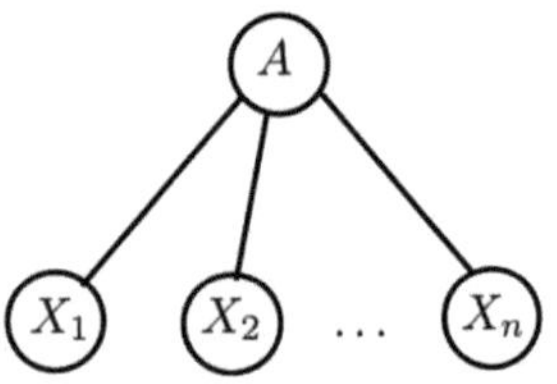

[11] For example, if the productions are $A \to aB$, $A \to bB$, $B \to c$, and we have to substitute A in the current sentential form $\alpha = abaABA$, with given $w = ababcac$. If we use a production rule arbitrarily, say the first production $A \to aB$, we will be wrong and will require backtracking later. However, if we look ahead, and try to match "b" of $A \to bB$ at **b** in $aba\mathbf{b}cac$, we will have correctly chosen the substitution rule.

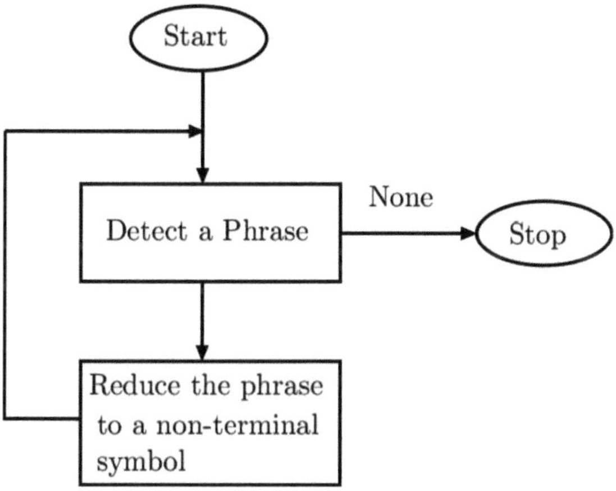

Fig. 8.11 Bottom-up parsing flow-chart

p is name of production in G, we write $A \Rightarrow w(p)$ if and only if w can be derived from A after applying production p. The alternate definitions of LL(k) and LR(k) grammars are given below.

Definition 8.6 A grammar is called $LL(k)$ if, for all $w_1, w_2, w_2', w_3, w_3' \in \Sigma^*$, $A \in V$, and $p, p' \in G$, $S \Rightarrow w_1Aw_3$, $S \Rightarrow w_1Aw_3'$, $A = w_2(p)$, $A = w_2'(p')$, and $(w_2w_3)/k = (w_2'w_3')/k$ imply that $p = p'$. □

An $LL(k)$ grammar is similar except that a production and its leftmost descendant can be identified from the symbols to the left of this leftmost descendant and the k symbols which follow (counting the leftmost descendant terminal as the first symbol).

An LL Parser (left-to-right, leftmost derivation) is a top-down parser for a subset of context-free languages.

Definition 8.7 An LL parser is called $LL(k)$ *parser* if it looks ahead k number of strings in the current sentential, beyond the current position of nonterminal symbol. □

An LR(k) (left-to-right, rightmost derivation in reverse, k-symbols look ahead) are the largest class of grammars for which left-to-right and bottom-up deterministic parsing is possible.

Definition 8.8 *LR(k) Grammar.* The LR(k) is a grammar for which parser scans the input sentence w from left to right and generates the reverse rightmost derivation, and it takes a decision about reduction by looking k symbols only, in w. □

Such languages are particularly important in the case of computer programming since this condition means a parsing algorithm can be mechanically constructed which requires an execution time at worst proportional to the length of the string being parsed [8].

The most common parsing algorithms fall into two categories: *top-down* and *bottom-up*, which means the way a derivation-tree is constructed for a given input sentence. This sentence is always read from left to right. Hence, the step-by-step development of derivation-tree represents the leftmost derivations in the case of the top-down construction of parse-tree, whereas it produces the rightmost derivation in a reverse sense when bottom-up parsing is used. In a bottom-up construction, we carry the lists of items (in fact, developing a forest) that are candidates at that point for being applied later when more of the input is seen. The power of this approach is precisely due to this parallel (forest) handling of those alternatives which are still open at any given point. This approach we can compare with top-down, where we may use trial-and-error methods for the selection of production rules to be applied in which backtracking will be necessary after each unsuccessful trial.

An optimal solution requires finding the correct production rule when more than one alternative production rule is available (e.g., $E \rightarrow E + T$ v/s $E \rightarrow T$) in every step of the parsing process so that the parsing can be carried out in deterministic and sequential manner without backtracking. But, choosing the correct production rule is difficult when we have not seen the rest of the input word. However, we can find the important subclass of grammars where a limited look-ahead is enough to make the correct decision at any given point in the parsing process.

8.10.1 LL(k) Grammar

A CFG is called LL(k), for left-to-right scan, if it produces leftmost derivation with k symbols look-ahead and we can always make a correct decision by examining at most the first k symbols in the right-hand side of the current production rule that is going to be used in the sentence w being derived [9].

For example, grammar is LL(1) if whenever $A \rightarrow \alpha$ and $A \rightarrow \beta$ are distinct productions, the following two conditions hold: (1) There is no terminal a such that both α and β derive strings beginning a. (2) At most one of α or β derives ε, the empty string.

The LL(1) grammar has been used very often for the construction of compilers. An $LL(1)$ grammar can be easily converted into a deterministic Pushdown Automata that accepts the corresponding language. For this, we choose the arrangement shown in Fig. 8.12.

Consider the grammar $G = (V, \Sigma, S, P)$, whose tuples have standard meanings. Additionally, $A \in V, \alpha, \beta \in (V \cup \Sigma)^*$. Initially, the start symbol S is stored on the stack. Each time we find a nonterminal $A \in V$ on top of the stack, we replace it with α, so that from the top of stack what we see is α, and β is stored below it. If the top of the stack is a terminal symbol, we compare it with the next input symbol on the tape, that is, the first letter of substring v, and if they match then the top of the stack (terminal) symbol is popped (removed), and while that time the tape head is shifted to the right to read the next input symbol.

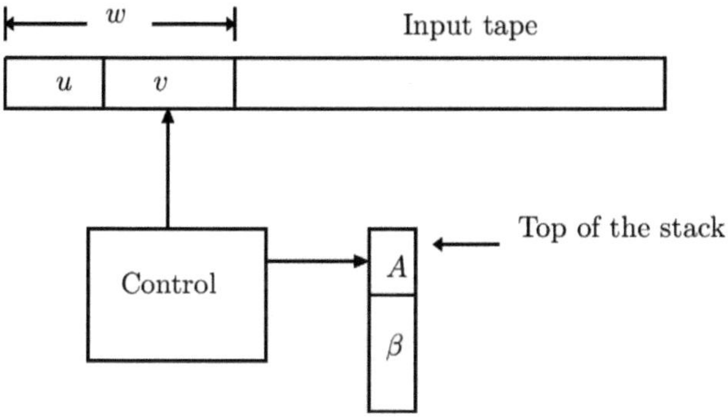

Fig. 8.12 PDA as LL(1) language recognizer

It is interesting to note that, the Greibach Normal Form (GNF).[12] appears to provide solution to the LL(1) parsing, i.e., for first letter of α (in $A \rightarrow \alpha$) must be a terminal symbol. Thus, the LL(1) condition is obviously satisfied if for each variable A the corresponding set of rules are like this,

$$A \rightarrow \alpha_1 \mid \dots \mid \alpha_m. \tag{8.25}$$

The above rule has the property that the first letter of α_i is different from that of α_j whenever $i \neq j$. It is important to note that if this condition fails, we may not be able to make the correct decision as to which rule to apply, even by using more information on β and v.

A formal definition of LL(k) grammar makes use of the notation $w : k$, which means k letter long initial segment of input w. Hence $aaaabbb : k = aaa$, for $k = 3$. Thus,

$$w : k = \begin{cases} u, & \text{if } w = uv, \text{ for } u, v \in \Sigma^*, \text{ with } |u| = k, \\ w, & \text{if } |w| \leq k. \end{cases} \tag{8.26}$$

Definition 8.9 *LL(k) Grammar.* A CFG is LL(k) if and only if, every pair of leftmost derivations is of the form,

$$S \Rightarrow^* uA\alpha \Rightarrow u\beta\alpha \Rightarrow^* uv, \tag{8.27}$$

where $u, v \in \Sigma^*$; $A \in V$; $\alpha, \beta \in (V \cup \Sigma)^*$, $A \rightarrow \beta$ and

$$S \Rightarrow^* uA\alpha \Rightarrow u\gamma\alpha \Rightarrow^* ux, \tag{8.28}$$

for $A \rightarrow \gamma$ and $x \in \Sigma^*$.

---

[12] See Definition 7.2, Sect. 7.1 for GNF.

The equality $v : k = x : k$ implies $\beta = \gamma$. A Context-free Grammar is LL(k) if it is generated by LL(k) grammar. □

For LL(k) grammar, if there are two productions $A \to \beta$ and $A \to \gamma$, then first k symbols of β and γ do not match. However, if they match, then the remaining parts should also match, i.e., $\beta = \gamma$.

The LL(k) grammars form the subsets of deterministic context-free grammars (DCFGs), and there are corresponding deterministic context-free languages (DCFLs).

The C language grammar is not LL(1). Consider the following code in the box:

$int\ v;\ main()\{$
$= 0; \}$
$\{v$
$:\ return\ 0; \}$

A compiler considers the code line as input string $w =$ "$intv;\ main()$". The bottom part of this code shows that parser has digested these tokens:

$$int\ v;\quad main()\{$$

and, it is about choosing a rule to derive the nonterminal statement. Looking only at the *first look-ahead* token "v", it cannot decide which of the two alternatives for the statement to choose, because there are two input continuations possible. They can be discriminated peeking at the *second look-ahead token*, which is either "=" or ":".

The LL parsers are table-based parsers, similar to LR parsers. The LL grammars can alternatively be characterized as precisely those that can be easily written by hand.

Theorem 8.9 *Every LL(k) grammar is unambiguous.*

Proof The theorem immediately follows from the Definition 8.9, because an ambiguous grammar has more than one leftmost derivation for some sentence w. But, LL(k) condition is obviously violation for two derivations of the same sentence w.

The exercise 23 (solution provided) shows that the following grammar is not LL(k).

$$\begin{aligned}
&S \to A \mid B\\
&A \to aAb \mid ab\\
&B \to aBc \mid ac
\end{aligned}$$

Hence, the proof.

□

8.10.2 LR(k) Grammar

To understand the process of left-to-right translation of languages, we consider intermediate symbols as V and terminals as Σ; the uppercase letters $A, B, C, \ldots$ are for intermediate symbols or nonterminals and lowercase letter $a, b, c, \ldots$ are for terminals. The letters X, Y, Z denote the either intermediates or terminals, S denotes the principle intermediate character. The string characters are denoted by letters $u, v, w, \ldots$, and empty string by ε. The Greek letters $\alpha, \beta, \gamma, \ldots$ represent strings on $V \cup \Sigma$. Let a language defined over context-free grammar G be,

$$L = \{w \mid S \Rightarrow^* w, \text{ and } w \text{ is string over } \Sigma\}.$$

We have the following definition for $LR(k)$ Grammar. We may note that in the abbreviation LR, the letter L stands for *left-to-right*, and R stands for *rightmost derivation in reverse*. Here is a formal definition of $LR(k)$ grammar.

Definition 8.10 A grammar is called $LR(k)$ if it is unambiguous and for all $w_1, w_2, w_3, w_3' \in \Sigma^*$, there is $A \in V$, $S \Rightarrow w_1 A w_3$, $A \Rightarrow w_2$, $S \Rightarrow w_1 w_2 w_3'$ and $w_3 : k = w_3' : k$ then it imply that $S \Rightarrow w_1 A w_3'$. □

In the above, $w_3 : k = w_3' : k$ means w_3 and w_3' are identical for upto first k number of characters.

When stated in terms of parsing, $LR(k)$ grammar is context-free grammar such that for any word in the language each production in its derivation can be identified, and its descendants determined with certainty by inspecting the word from its beginning (left) to the kth symbol beyond the rightmost derivation.

We take the following example to parse a sentence using LR(1) grammar.

Example 8.7 The productions,

$$S \rightarrow AE,\ A \rightarrow aC,\ B \rightarrow bce,\ C \rightarrow BF,\ E \rightarrow g,\ F \rightarrow f, \tag{8.29}$$

define a language consisting of a single string "abcefg", and there is only one parse-tree for this grammar.

A grammar is said to be *unambiguous* if every sentential form has a unique derivation tree. Two possible derivation sequences of grammar in (8.29) are

$$S \Rightarrow AE \Rightarrow aCE \Rightarrow aBFE \Rightarrow abceFE \Rightarrow abcefE \Rightarrow abcefg \tag{8.30}$$

and

$$S \Rightarrow AE \Rightarrow Ag \Rightarrow aCg \Rightarrow aBFg \Rightarrow aBfg \Rightarrow abcefg \tag{8.31}$$

However, if we look at the corresponding parse-tree in Fig. 8.13, we get only one parse-tree. □

In order to avoid the unimportant difference between sequences of derivations corresponding to the same tree, we can stipulate a particular order, such as insisting that we always substitute for the leftmost nonterminal as done in Eq. (8.30) or the rightmost one, as in Eq. (8.31).

For LR(k) parsing, we must start with the terminal string $abcefg$ and try to reconstruct the derivation leading back to S. For this derivation, an important concept of *handle* is used.

Definition 8.11 *Handle* of a tree to be the leftmost set of adjacent leaves forming a complete branch in a sentential. □

For example, in the tree in Fig. 8.13, the handle is bce. In other words, if X_1, X_2, ..., X_k, are the leaves of the tree (where each X_i is nonterminal symbol), we look for the smallest k such that the tree has the form as shown in Fig. 8.14, for some i and Y.

If we consider going from terminals $abcdefg$ backward to reach S, we can imagine starting with a tree in Fig. 8.13, and "pruning off" its handle "bce" then next prune off the handle "f" of the resulting tree, then "BF", and so on until only the root S remains. This process of pruning the handle at each step corresponds exactly to the derivation shown in derivation (8.31) in reverse. It can be easily verified that the process of "handle pruning" always produces, in reverse, the derivation obtained by replacing the *rightmost* nonterminal symbol at each step, and this may be regarded as an alternative way to define the concept of handle. Note that, if we begin with all the leaves as terminals, all the symbols to the right of the handle are terminals. For example, to parse the string "$w = abcefg$" following are the sententials:

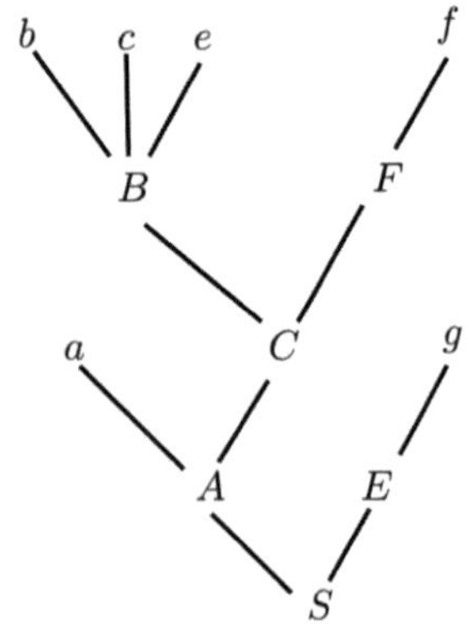

Fig. 8.13 A derivation tree in reverse

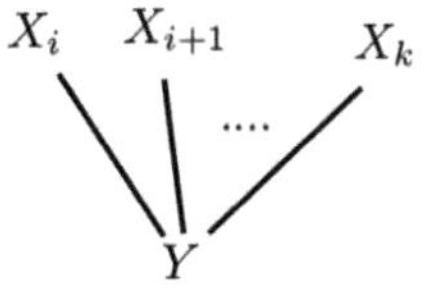

Fig. 8.14 A handle

$$\begin{aligned} &abcefg; \text{ hangle is ``bce''} \\ &\Leftarrow aBfg; \text{ handle is ``}f\text{''} \\ &\Leftarrow aBFg; \text{ hangle is ``}BF\text{''} \\ &\Leftarrow aCg; \text{ handle is ``}aC\text{''} \\ &\Leftarrow Ag; \text{ handle is ``}g\text{''} \\ S &\Leftarrow AE; \text{ handle is ``}AE\text{''} \end{aligned} \tag{8.32}$$

We are interested in algorithms for parsing, and thus we want to be able to recognize the handle when only the leaves of the tree are given. Suppose, productions are numbered as $1, 2, ..., s$, in some arbitrary manner and let $\alpha = X_1...X_n...X_t$ be the present sentential form. Further, let there is a derivation tree in which the handle is $X_{r+1}...X_n$, obtained by application of the pth production, for $0 \leq r \leq n \leq t$ and $1 \leq p \leq s$. We will say (n, p) is *handle* of α. A formal definition of LR(k) is given below.

Definition 8.12 *LR(k) Grammar.* A grammar is said to be *translatable from left to right with bound k* (called as "LR(k) grammar") under the following conditions:

1. There is $k \geq 0$, and "$\dashv$" is a symbol not in $\Sigma \cup V$,
2. The current sentential form is k sentential form (i.e., a sentential form followed by k "$\dashv$" symbols),
3. $\alpha = X_1X_2...X_nX_{n+1}...X_{n+k}Y_1...Y_u$ and $\beta = X_1X_2...X_nX_{n+1}...X_{n+k}\ Z_1...Z_v$ be k sentential forms, where $u \geq 0$, $v \geq 0$, and none of $X_{n+1}, ..., X_{n+k}, Y_1, ..., Y_u, Z_1, ..., Z_v$ is a nonterminal symbol. Since the handle is $X_{r+1}...X_n$, the sequence $X_{n+1}...X_{n+k}$ are k the number of look-ahead symbols in the input w, which match with the k number of right-hand side of production being substituted.
4. If (n, p) is handle in α and (m, q) is handle in β, then we require that $m = n$ and $p = q$. □

In step 3, once the handle is pruned, the k number of symbols after and before pruning remains the same, i.e., $X_{n+1}...X_{n+k}$ and $Y_{n+1}...Y_{n+k}$. The symbols $Y_1...Y_n$, and $Z_1...Z_k$ are obviously the terminal symbols as they fall at the rightmost part of the sentential form, and handle is to be searched.

In other words, the grammar is LR(k) if and only if, any handle in a sentential form is always uniquely determined by the string to its left and the k terminal characters.[13] to its right. Note that the position of the handle is marked by its rightmost symbol in the sential and not the leftmost symbol.

[13] These are the terminals in the construction process and not the final parse-tree.

The above definition of the handle is clear if we take a particular value of k, say, $k = 1$. Suppose we are constructing a derivation sequence such as in derivation (8.31) in reverse, and the current string (followed by the delimiter "$\dashv$" for convenience) has the form $X_1 ... X_n X_{n+1} \alpha \dashv$, where the tail end "$X_{n+1}\alpha \dashv$" represents parts of the string we have not yet examined; but all possible reductions have been made at the left of the string before X_{n+1}, so that the right boundary of the handle must be at position X_r for $r \geq n$.

8.10.3 LR(k) Versus LL(k) Grammars

Briefly, LL(k) and LR(k) grammars are those that can be realized top-down and bottom-up, respectively, by deterministic pushdown automata, scanning from left to right [10].

More precisely, for LR(k) grammars [8], the following hold.

1. Any context-free language that has an LR(k) grammar can be recognized (bottom-up) by a (deterministic) pushdown automata. The machine uses grammar in the recognition process and can be said to recognize each production, and
2. Conversely, given any pushdown automata, there is an effective procedure for finding an LR(1) grammar for the language recognized by the machine.

For LL(k) grammars, any context-free language that has an LL(k) grammar can be recognized (top-down) by a (deterministic) pushdown automata. The machine uses a prediction recognition scheme and, in a manner that can be precisely defined, "uses" the grammar in the recognition process, and can be said to recognize each production.

The LL(1) and LALR(1) (Look-ahead LR) grammar classes are pre-eminent among the sub-context-free classes for practicability and usefulness of their parsing algorithms. There is always one production for any element of the canonical collections of LR(0) items for a null free LL(1) grammar.

Size of a grammar G, whose productions are $A \rightarrow \alpha$ ($A \in V$, and $\alpha \in (V \cup \Sigma)^*$) is defined as

$$\sum_{A \rightarrow \alpha \in P} \log(A\alpha) \tag{8.33}$$

8.11 LL Parser

The languages the LL grammars accept are a proper subset of LR languages. There is at least one dangling-*else*, which is not representable by LL grammar. The LL(1) grammar is parsed by the device, shown in Fig. 8.15, called *predictive parser*. The predictive parser is actually one state pushdown automaton that may scan an input symbol without consuming it.

A simple deterministic automaton, shown in Fig. 8.15, called a predictive parser, can find the leftmost (left parse) of any string in the language. There is an input tape which holds the string to be parsed, with end marker \$. The input pointer indicates the current input symbol. The parser also has predictive *parsing table* (See Table 8.3), and a stack. The rows of the parsing table are nonterminals of the rules, and columns are the first symbol of the right-hand side of productions, and position *row* × *column* is the production rule applicable. For example, if a rule is $A \rightarrow aB$, then the row will be A, the column will be a. The stack initially contains only the start symbol \$, with the top of the stack at the left. Thus, in the stack shown Fig. 8.15, the symbol A is at the top of the stack.

At every instant of time, if input (xay in Fig. 8.15) is in the language, then portion of the input over which the input pointer has moved (i.e., x) followed by $A\alpha$ (stack contents) will be called as the *left sentential* form represented by the parser [1].

Consider that the grammar is $G = (V, \Sigma, S, P)$, the $A \in V$, and $\alpha, \beta \in (V \cup \Sigma)^+$, and $x, y \in \Sigma^+$. The moves of the parser are of three types.

1. If the current input symbol matches the top stack symbol then pop the stack and advance the input pointer to the next symbol on the right. This move is made only with a terminal symbol on top of the stack. This move does not change the left sentential represented by the parser.
2. If there is a nonterminal, say A, on top of the stack, and a is the current input symbol, consult a parsing table to determine a particular production $A \rightarrow \beta$ associated with A and a. Replace the top of the stack with string β. The input pointer

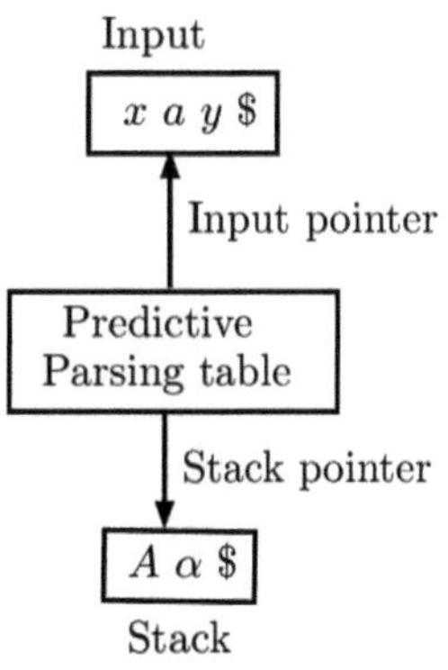

Fig. 8.15 Predictive parser

Table 8.3 A $LL(1)$ predictive parser table

	a	b	$
S	$S \rightarrow aA$	$B \rightarrow bB$	–
A	$A \rightarrow a$	–	–
B	–	$B \rightarrow b$	–

Table 8.4 Moves in a LL(1) parser

Input	Stack	Left sentential form
$aa\$$	$S\$$	S
$aa\$$	$aA\$$	aA
$a\$$	$A\$$	aA
$a\$$	$a\$$	aa

is not advanced in this case. This move causes the parser to represent the next sentential form.

3. If the current input symbol is $ and stack contains only $, then parser halts and accept the original input $w = xay$.

The following example demonstrates the working of LL(1) parser.

Example 8.8 Given the grammar productions $\{S \rightarrow aA|bB,\ A \rightarrow a,\ B \rightarrow b\}$, with S as start symbol, we construct the parsing Table 8.3 for $LL(1)$ parser.

Let the input be $w = aa$, there will be moves as shown in Table 8.4 of the parser:

If the input scanned so far after any move is x and the content of stack is β, then the left sentential form is equal to $x\beta$. This also holds true in the above. The generation of w can also be verified as

$$S \Rightarrow aA \Rightarrow aA \Rightarrow aa.$$

□

8.12 LR Parser

We shall discuss LR(1) parser as it is one of the most widely used deterministic parsers. Figure 8.16 presents a general LR parser. Input to an LR parser consists of the string to be parsed, terminated by an end marker $, where $\$ \notin \Sigma$. The input pointer indicates the current input symbol, shown as a, the sequence x has been processed, while ay is yet to be processed. The LR parser makes use of a *parsing*

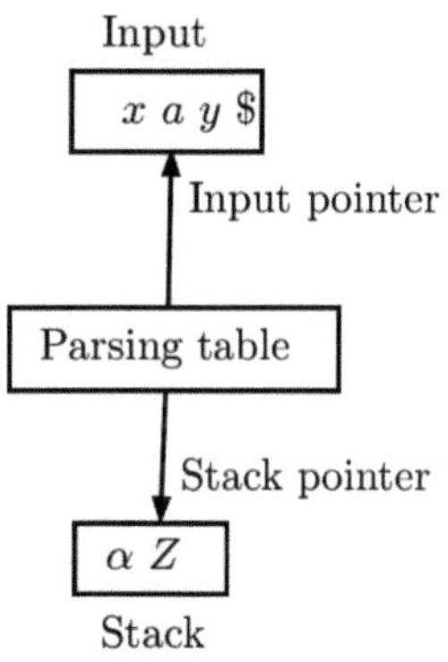

Fig. 8.16 An LR parser

table and a *stack*. We assume that the top of the stack is the rightmost symbol (shown as Z here) in the box shown as a stack.

Moreover, at every point in time if input is in the language, then αZ (grammar symbols on the stack) followed by ay (portion of the input not yet read) will be called the *right sentential form*.[14] In the Fig. 8.16, αZay is the right sentential form. Note that derivation of αZ is x and if ay is appended to αZ, it becomes αZay, that derives the sentence xay.

However, in addition to putting grammar symbols on the stack, an LR parser places special symbols, called *states* on the stack. In fact, at all times, the contents of the stack is a sequence of the form $s_0 X_1 s_1 X_2 s_2 ... X_m s_m$, where each s_i is a state and each X_i is a grammar symbol. The next move of the parser is dictated by s_m (the state on top of the stack) and a, the current input symbol. This move, for (a, s_m) is found in the parsing table, latter consists of two parts, an *action table* and a *goto table*. The type of move is determined by the entry for s_m and a in the action table. The move can be one of the four types:

1. *Shift* s. The current input symbol a is shifted onto the stack and the state numbered s is then placed on top of the stack. This move has the effect of advancing the input pointer one symbol to the right.
2. *Reduce by production* $A \rightarrow \alpha$. Suppose the right side β is of length $r \geq 0$. Then $2r$ symbols are popped off the stack (r symbols and r states). Thus, the sequence $X_{m-r+1} s_{m-r+1} ... X_m s_m$ is removed from the stack, leaving $s_0 X_1 s_1 ... X_{m-r} s_{m-r}$. The nonterminal A is placed on top of the stack. The goto table for s_{m-r} is then consulted and the state in the entry for s_{m-r} and A is placed on top of the stack. In a properly constructed LR parser, when a reduction by the production $A \rightarrow \beta$ is called for, $X_{m-r+1} ... X_m$, the string of grammar symbols removed from the stack, will match β, the right side of the production.
3. *Accepts*. The parser halts and announces the successful completion of parsing.

[14] If a derivation is like, $S \Rightarrow \alpha_1 ... \alpha_n$, starting from S, the sentential forms α_i are called *left sentential* form. However, if a derivation is from α_n to S, i.e., bottom up, the sentential forms are called *right sentential forms*.

4. *Error.* The input string is not in the language being parsed; the parser transfers control to an error recovery routine.

In a shift move the right sentential form, represented by the parser, does not change, but changes in the "reduce" move. Let,

$$S \Rightarrow^*_{rm} \alpha Aay \Rightarrow_{rm} \alpha\beta ay \Rightarrow^*_{rm} xay \tag{8.34}$$

is a rightmost derivation in the grammar. An LR parser would represent the right sentential form $\alpha\beta ay$ with $\alpha\beta$ on the stack and ay as the unexpended input. After a reduction by the production $A \rightarrow \beta$, the parser would represent the right sentential form αAay with αA on the stack.

Initially, an LR parser has an input string to be parsed, on the input tape, and the input pointer to the leftmost symbol in this string. The stack contains only the initial state s_0. The parser then makes a sequence of moves until either an accept action or an error action is called for. The sequence of reductions made by the parser up to an accepted action is the parse produced by the parser for the input string [1].

The following example explains the shift-reduce (LR(1)) parsing.

Example 8.9 Parsing using Shift-reduce parser, i.e., LR(1) parser.

Consider the following grammar, with production rules numbered from (1) to (6):

(1) $E \rightarrow E + T$

(2) $E \rightarrow T$

(3) $T \rightarrow T * F$

(4) $T \rightarrow F$

(5) $F \rightarrow (E)$

(6) $F \rightarrow a$

The *Parsing action* table and *goto* tables are shown jointly as Table 8.5 (separated by vertical line "|"). In the parsing action table, the symbol \$ represents the right end marker. The symbol "-" stands for "error," "sh i" stand for "shift i," and "red i stand for "reduce using production rule number (i)". In the goto table (the last three columns of the above table), the blank entries are never referenced.

An LR parser using these actions and goto table would parse the string $a + a * a$ in the way it is shown in Table 8.6, for which the explanation is as follows: In the beginning the input pointer points to a and state 0 is initially at top of stack. For $(a, 0)$, the action table shows entry *sh 5*, which means shift $a5$ to stack. This makes stack content as $0a5$, with state 5 at stack top. With, the input left is $+a * a\$$.

With next input symbol as $+$ and state on stack as 5, the $(+, 5)$ entry in action table corresponds to action *red 6*, i.e., reduce using the rule number 6. This reduces input to $F + a * a$, shown in Table 8.6, and the input string to be processed remains unchanged. Note that in the reduce operation, $2r$ symbols are popped from the stack in this operation, r symbols and r states. Since the right side of the production $F \rightarrow a$

Table 8.5 An LR Parser table to parse the expression $a + a * a$ using grammar rules (1)–(6)

(a) Action table							(b) Goto table		
State	+	$*$	(	)	*a*	$	*E*	*T*	*F*
0	–	–	*sh* 4	–	*sh* 5	–	1	2	3
1	*sh* 6	–	–	–	–	*accept*			
2	*red* 2	*sh* 7	–	*red* 2	–	*red* 2			
3	*red* 4	*red* 4	–	*red* 4	–	*red* 4			
4	–	–	*sh* 4	–	*sh* 5	–	8	2	3
5	*red* 6	*red* 6	–	*red* 6	–	*red* 6			
6	–	–	*sh* 4	–	*sh* 5	–		9	3
7	–	–	*sh* 4	–	*sh* 5	–			10
8	*sh* 6	–	–	*sh* 11	–	–			
9	*red* 1	*sh* 7	–	*red* 1	–	*red* 1			
10	*red* 3	*red* 3	–	*red* 3	–	*red* 3			
11	*red* 5	*red* 5	–	*red* 5	–	*red* 5			

is 1, only two symbols, i.e., $a5$ are removed from the stack. And, the nonterminal F is placed on top of the stack, the goto table is consulted, and the state 3 is pushed onto the stack. This makes the stack content as $0F3$.

Next, action table is checked for (3, +), which shows the action as *red 4*, i.e., reduce using the rule 4 (i.e., $T \rightarrow F$). So, again there is a reduced operation, which can be explained just as above. The complete process of LR(1) parsing process, for all the steps, is shown in Table 8.6.

Note that the parse produced by this parser for the input string $a + a * a$ is the reverse of the sequence of productions used in a rightmost derivation of $a + a * a$:

$$\begin{aligned} E &\Rightarrow_{rm} E + T \Rightarrow_{rm} E + T * F \Rightarrow_{rm} E + T * a \\ &\Rightarrow_{rm} E + F * a \Rightarrow_{rm} E + a * a \Rightarrow_{rm} T + a * a \\ &\Rightarrow_{rm} F + a * a \Rightarrow_{rm} a + a * a \end{aligned}$$

This concludes the shift-reduce parsing, also called LR parsing (here it is LR(1)). □

8.13 Parallelization

The literature on parallel parsing and lexical analyzers is vast and extends over half a century [1]. With the advent of parallel machines (such as multi-cores), it may be possible to view the relation between syntax and semantics in natural language parsing in a wholly new way. The processes which control the syntactic aspect can be separated

Table 8.6 LR(1) parsing steps for $a + a * a$

Stack (Top is RHS)	Unexpended input	Right sentential form represented by the parser
0	$a + a * a\$$	$a + a * a$
$0a5$	$+a * a\$$	$a + a * a$
$0F3$	$+a * a\$$	$F + a * a$
$0T2$	$+a * a\$$	$T + a * a$
$0E1$	$+a * a\$$	$E + a * a$
$0E1 + 6$	$a * a\$$	$E + a * a$
$0E1 + 6a5$	$*a\$$	$E + a * a$
$0E1 + 6F3$	$*a\$$	$E + F * a$
$0E1 + 6T9$	$*a\$$	$E + T * a$
$0E1 + 6T9 * 7$	$a\$$	$E + T * a$
$0E1 + 6T9 * 7a5$	$\$$	$E + T * a$
$0E1 + 6T9 * 7F10$	$\$$	$E + T * F$
$0E1 + 6T9$	$\$$	$E + T$
$0E1$	$\$$	E

from those that control the semantic aspect, such that the syntactic processes contain no semantic information in themselves, but receive it by communication with the semantic processes, and vice-versa. The advantage of this approach is that transparent algorithms can be written that are dedicated to only one aspect of parsing, while the desirable effects of integrating syntax and semantics can be achieved through the communication of processes. Using this approach, semantic constraints can be enforced on syntactic processors in order to avoid the combinatorial explosion of producing all legal possibilities.

The communication between the above two components can be the focus of designing a parallel parser. The communication between syntax and semantics can take place at three levels: word level, phrase level, and sentence level.

8.13.1 Parallel Parsing

In addition to being ubiquitous, there are also significant exceptions to the syntax and semantic-based trends, toward the exploitation of parallel architectures. The most likely reason for the lack of practical parallel parsers is the intrinsically sequential nature of the classical deterministic LL and LR algorithms. For example, consider a language $L = L_1^*$ and $L_1 = \{0a^n b^n \mid n \geq 1\} \cup \{1a^{2n} b^n \mid n \geq 1\}$ to be parsed using a deterministic *shift-reduce* parallel algorithm. For this need, a pre-scanner will decide whether the string belongs to the first set or the second, by checking the first character as "0" or "1". After this, there is a second stage to find out if the global sentence belongs to L or not. However, since the substrings belonging to L can be arbitrarily long, any random or fixed policy to split the input into substrings is likely to be far from optimal; it may even be impossible to determine whether ab or aab groups are to be reduced in case a substring contains no 0's or 1's. To cope with these issues, two straightforward approaches can be pursued: nondeterministic computations or pre-scanning.

The former approach non-deterministically performs the parsing computations for all the possible cases: for example, it may carry two parsing processes depending on whether the current substring is of type $0a^n b^n$ or $1a^{2n} b^n$, and discards the result of incorrect computation as soon as possible. However, this method is not efficient. The latter approach involves a first lightweight scanning of the input to determine the viable splitting points: for example, it would look for the occurrence of 0 and 1 and split the input right before them. But, this approach introduces an overhead for the preliminary scanning which could require pre-scanning over the whole input string. To sum up, the first approach may require a computational overhead to cope with the nondeterminism which is potentially more significant than the benefits provided by the parallelism, while the latter implies an $O(n)$ worst-case preprocessing which, in case of simple languages, may take as a sequential parsing process.

To overcome the impasse we can use operator-precedence grammar which is the foundation for deterministic bottom-up parser. The most notable example is the GNU Compiler Collection *gcc*, which actually employs an Operator Precedence parser to handle expression parsing in C [2].

In the present time, there is much demand for real-time speech processing and real-time natural language processing. Both of these demand parallel processing, i.e., parallel finite automata for speech processing and parallel parsing for natural language processing, taking maximum advantage of available hardware resources to speed up the processing.

8.13.2 Parallel Lexical Analysis

The lexical analysis (scanning) takes place before parsing and translation. We studied the lexical analysis (recognition of tokens) in Chap. 2), the complexity of lexical analysis is $O(n)$, where n is length of input. The gain in performing parallel parsing alone would be small without coupling it with parallel lexical analysis and preprocessing. Further, apart from a few idiosyncrasies of some languages—which tend to go unused by programmers—lexical analysis is even better suited for parallel execution. However, to achieve this goal a few non-trivial technical difficulties must be tackled.

A distinguishing feature of the parallel lexical analyzer is that it produces a stream of tokens, which, rather than being compatible with the original BNF (Backus-Naur Form) of the source language, is ready to be parsed according to the operator-precedence (OP) version of the grammar [2]. This results in an advantage from both the performance point of view and an adaptation to the operator-precedence parsing point of view. Typically such a preprocessing allows for disambiguating some terminals that are overloaded in the language and would induce conflicting relations in the operator-precedence matrix: depending on the context in which they occur, the lexical analyzer can associate them to distinct token classes, so that the resulting string of tokens can be parsed according to the OP version of the syntactic grammar. Note that such disambiguation is complementary to the usual operations performed in the lexical-analysis phase to cope with the presence of ambiguities in the lexical grammar (e.g., in the presence of reserved words and identifiers corresponding to the same lexical pattern). However, this is hidden from the user who does not have to worry about the internal format.

8.14 Summary

A Pushdown Automata (PDA) consists of an infinite tape to hold the input string, a control with a set of states, a read head, and a pushdown read-write stack. While reading the input, the pushdown stack can be written or read any number of times for each input symbol read.

While recognizing any string, a PDA moves through configurations, where a configuration comprises the state it is in, input yet to be read, and contents of stack recognized when the input is completely read and together it is in the final state or stack is empty with input completely read, or both of these conditions are true together. At this point, the input is accepted by the PDA.

Regular Languages are a proper subset of context-free languages. Since a PDA recognizes context-free languages, hence it can be shown that it also recognizes regular languages—the stack of the PDA will be ignored for this recognition. A PDA recognizes parenthesized languages, which is a property of all the high-level programming languages.

A PDA can be a deterministic or nondeterministic machine. However, by default, it is considered nondeterministic, unlike the finite automata, which is by default a deterministic machine.

A PDA can be simulated through a program, by defining certain data structures of: tape and stack with head and stack values.

A deterministic PDA has only one next state for a given tuple, i.e., (state, input symbol, stack symbol), while a nondeterministic PDA has more than one equally likely next state for this tuple, and PDA chooses any one of them non-deterministically after a transition is performed. But there can be only a finite number of such next states. A nondeterministic PDA needs to guess the next state.

A PDA can accept a language by being at the final state, with an empty stack, or by satisfying both these conditions together. However, these two conditions are equal, and a PDA accepting the final state can always be converted into one accepting an empty state, and vice-versa.

For each context-free language, there exists a PDA that accepts it on an empty stack.

A Pushdown Automata and context-free grammar are equivalent in specifying languages. A context-free language can be defined to be generated by a CFG or to be a language accepted by PDA.

A language is generated by a CFG if and only if the language is accepted by a PDA. This approach can be used to directly convert a CFG into a PDA.

The intersection of a CFL and Regular languages is a CFL.

Parsing algorithms are everywhere, in compilation, human and machine language processing, web browsing, text processing, etc. Ordinary (brute force) parsers consume exponential time, hence, their efficiency is important. The new parsing techniques use formal languages and automata theory. There is a common belief that natural languages are not context-free, but a comprehensive grammar—a subset of natural languages is sufficient for practical systems and can be written in context-free phrase structure grammar.

The incremental generators of parsers based on LR techniques, for arbitrary context-free grammars are based on pseudo-parallel LR parsing algorithms. The Incremental Parser Generator (IPG) takes less time for parser generation.

Basically, there are two approaches to parsing: i) top-down parser builds a parse-tree top-to-bottom starting from the root node. But, if there is more than one rule with the same left-hand variable in a rule, it will lead to backtracking when the correct rule is not selected. ii) The Bottom-up method builds a parse-tree starting from the bottom of the tree and building upward, and the final step is the installation root node. The bottom-up parsing is a derivation from right to left in a sentential.

There is a subset of CFLs, called translatable from left to right that looks for a given finite number of characters ahead, making it possible to parse without ever backtracking. All LL(k) (left-to-right leftmost derivation) parsers are in this class that look for k number of characters ahead.

Every LL(k) grammar is an unambiguous grammar.

The LR(k) (left-to-right, rightmost derivation in reverse) with k symbols look ahead are the largest class of grammars, for which left-to-right and bottom-up deterministic parsing is possible. Such parsers can be mechanically constructed.

The LR(k) grammar is also unambiguous. In order to avoid the unimportant difference between sequences of derivations corresponding to the same tree, we can stipulate a particular order of substitution. For substitutions, we make use of a concept of *handle*. If sentential form is $abCdeF$ and production is $A \rightarrow bCd$, then bCd is handle, to be substituted in the sentential form, to get $aAeF$.

The LR(1) is one of the most widely used deterministic parsers. It uses a parsing table, a stack pointer, and the input sentence to be parsed and makes four types of moves: shift, reduce, accept, and error in the algorithm. The stack holds the states in it, instead of input symbols.

With the advent of parallel machines (such as multi-cores), it may be possible to view the relation between syntax and semantics in natural languages in totally a new way—the process that control the syntactic aspects can be separated from those that control the semantic aspect. The advantage of this is that transport algorithms can be written that are dedicated to only the two aspects of the above. Communication between the above two components can focus on the design of a parallel parser.

Self Review Questions

1. Why an NPDA is considered more powerful than a PDA?
2. From Eq. 8.6 (Sect. 8.4.1), if $\delta(q, a, z) \in (p_i, \beta_i)$, what are the values of state, input symbol, and top of the stack, before the transition, and these values after the transition?
3. Can there be a two-stack PDA?
4. Is the PDA corresponding to grammar "$S \rightarrow aSb \mid bSa \mid a$", a DPDA?
5. What is *reflexive-transitive closure* in PDA? Explain.
6. List five strings, in lexicographic order, for the CFL language whose grammar is $S \rightarrow aSb \mid bSa \mid \varepsilon$.
7. Is the CFG, $S \rightarrow aSb \mid bSa \mid a$, an ambiguous grammar?
8. Is the PDA that recognizes the language ww^R, $w \in \{a, b\}^*$, a nondeterministic PDA?
9. What is the property of the language that is accepted by an empty stack?
10. There are more than one language acceptability criteria for PDA (see section 8.7). Which criteria are considered as the default criteria?
11. If a language is accepted by a DPDA then its complement is also accepted by a DPDA (True/False).
12. If a language is accepted by NPDA then its complement is also accepted by NPDA (True/False).
13. Why a nondeterministic Pushdown automata is more powerful than a deterministic pushdown automata?
14. What is a special property of DPDA in reference to the parsing of languages?
15. What are the *phrase-detection* and *phrase-reduction* processes?
16. What is meaning of LL in LL parser?
17. What is difference between $LL(0)$ and $LL(1)$ parser?
18. Is the pair productions $A \rightarrow aB$, $A \rightarrow aC$ allowed in the $LL(1)$ predictive parser?
19. What is LR(0) parsing? How it differ from $LR(1)$ parser?
20. Which is most widely used parser, LL(1) or LR(1)?
21. What is a handle?
22. What is handle pruning?
23. What is the condition for a grammar to be LR(k)?
24. What is the condition for a grammar to be LL(k)?
25. What constructs of C language cannot be checked through parsing? How such constructs are handled by a Compiler?

Exercises

A. Concepts based Problems

Note: The $*$ marked exercises are provided with solutions at the end of this book.

1. Construct a pushdown automata that recognizes the language generated by the following grammars:

   a. $S \to aAA,\ A \to aS \mid bS \mid b.$
   b. $S \to aA,\ A \to aAB,\ A \to a,\ B \to b,\ B \to \varepsilon.$

2. * How the stack store is helpful in recognizing CFLs? Give a general explanation.
3. Initially the tape contents of a PDA is w. Can we use the part of the tape beyond this contents as a stack? If yes, what changes are needed in the working of the tape and the head?
4. * What are the conditions for a PDA to be deterministic?
5. Given the grammar: $E \to E + T \mid T; T \to T * F \mid F; F \to (E) \mid id$, derive the expression $(id * id) + (id * id)$, using,

   a. LR(1) parsing,
   b. LL(1) parsing.

6. Which algorithm uses a combination of top-down together with bottom-up methods of parsing?
7. Construct a PDA that accepts string w with number of a's equal to number of b's.
8. Designate the following grammars as $LL(1)$ or $LL(2)$:

   a. $S \to aA \mid bB,\ A \to aB \mid cB,\ B \to bC \mid aC,\ C \to bD,\ D \to d$
   b. $S \to abB \mid aaA,\ B \to d,\ A \to c \mid d.$

B. Analysis-based Problems

9. How the CFL and PDA are equivalent?
10. Give an algorithm for the conversion of CFG to PDA.
11. Give an algorithm for the conversion of PDA to CFG.
12. Given any arbitrary context-free grammar, how will you reduce it?
13. a. What is the meaning of the following expression in a PDA?
    $(q, x, \alpha) \vdash^* (q, \varepsilon, \beta)$
    b. Are the following implications true for a PDA?
    (i) $(q, x, \alpha) \vdash^* (q', \varepsilon, \beta) \Rightarrow (q, xy, \alpha) \vdash^* (q', y, \beta)$
    (ii) $(q, xy, \alpha) \vdash^* (q', y, \beta) \Rightarrow (q, x, \alpha) \vdash^* (q', \varepsilon, \beta)$

14. * Explain the significance of stack operations shown in Fig. 8.4 (Sect. 8.4.3).

15. Construct PDAs in each of the following cases, which recognize the languages generated by the grammars: $G = (V, \Sigma, S, P)$, $V = \{S, A, B\}$, $\Sigma = \{a, b, c\}$, and productions P are:

    a. $S \to AB,\ A \to acA \mid aAa \mid \varepsilon,\ B \to bcB \mid bB \mid \varepsilon$
    b. $S \to AB,\ A \to aAc \mid AaA \mid \varepsilon,\ B \to bBc \mid bB \mid \varepsilon$

16. Construct a pushdown automata that accepts the language:

$$\{a^i b^j \mid i, j \geq 0 \text{ and } i \neq j\}.$$

17. * Construct a Pushdown automata that accepts the language:

$$\{a^i b^j c^k \mid i, j, k \geq 0 \text{ and } i = j, \text{ or } j = k\}.$$

18. Given the productions: $E \to E + E \mid E - E \mid E * E \mid E/E \mid (E) \mid id$, find out whether the grammar of these productions is LL(0) or LL(1) or LL(2).
19. Is the following grammar LL(1)?

$$E \to T + E \mid T - E \mid T$$
$$T \to F * T \mid F/T \mid F$$
$$F \to num$$

20. * The following grammars generate the same language, however, they have many different characteristics. What are these characteristics?

$$S \to aAc,\ A \to bAb,\ A \to b.$$
$$S \to aAc,\ A \to Abb,\ A \to b.$$

C. Proof-based Problems

21. Prove that every regular set accepted by a finite automation of n states may also be accepted by the following PDAs:

    a. a PDA with n states and one pushdown symbol.
    b. a PDA with 1 state and n pushdown symbols.

22. Show that the following grammar is not LL(1).

$$E \to E + E \mid T$$
$$T \to T * T \mid num$$

23. * Show that the following grammar is not LL(k).

$$S \to A \mid B$$
$$A \to aAb \mid ab$$
$$B \to aBc \mid ac$$

24. Show that $S \to (S)S \mid \varepsilon$ is LL(1) grammar.

D. Multiple choice Questions

25. * Let $G = (V, \Sigma, S, P)$ is a context-free grammar, where $V = \{S\}$, $\Sigma = \{a, b\}$, and P is $S \rightarrow aSb \mid SS \mid \varepsilon$.

    Which of the following statements is true for the above grammar:?

    (A) There exist $u, v \in L(G)$ such that $uv \notin L(G)$
    (B) There exists a DPDA that accepts $L(G)$
    (C) There does not exist a DPDA that accepts $L(G)$
    (D) G is not an ambiguous grammar

26. Which of the following statements is True?

    (A) There is a unique minimal DFA for every regular language
    (B) Complement of every context-free language is a CFL.
    (C) Every NPDA can be converted to an equivalent DPDA.
    (D) Every NFA can be converted to an equivalent PDA.

    [Hint: A is true from the knowledge of Chap. 4, B is false (see Sect. 6.5), C is false because DPDA $\neq$ NPDA, and D is true.]

27. Given the productions of a context-free grammar G as $P : S \rightarrow SS \mid ab \mid ba \mid \varepsilon$, consider the following statements about it:

    I. G is unambiguous
    II. G can be accepted by an NPDA
    III. All the strings produced by G have equal number of a's and b's

    Which combination of the following are the true statements about G?

    (A) I and III only
    (B) I, II and III
    (C) II and III only
    (D) I and II only

    [Hint: Answer is C]

28. Let $S \rightarrow aSa \mid bSb \mid a \mid b$. The language generated by this grammar over $\Sigma = \{a, b\}$ is the set of one or more of the following:

    (A) All even length palindromes over a, b
    (B) All odd length palindromes over a, b
    (C) $w \in \Sigma^*$ and every w begin and end with the same symbol
    (D) None of the above

    [Hint: Answers are B and C]

29. Given the grammar productions $\{S \rightarrow AA, A \rightarrow aA \mid b\}$, the corresponding grammar is,
(A) SLR(1) but not LL(1) (B) LL(1)
(C) LR(l) but not LALR(1) (D) LALR(1) but not SLR(1)
[Hint: Answer is B]

E. Advanced Knowledge Assessment Problems

30. Can a two-stack PDA recognize the language $\{a^n b^n c^n \mid n \geq 0\}$? If yes, explain the logic.
31. Can a two-stack PDA recognize the language $\{a^n b^n c^n \mid n \geq 0\}$? If yes, explain the logic.
32. If M_1 and M_2 are PDAs accepting the languages L_1 and L_2, respectively, by final state, describe the procedures to construct PDAs in each of the following cases, to accept these languages on final state.
    a. $L_1 \cup L_2$
    b. $L_1 L_2$
33. Match all items in Group A with the correct options from those given in Group B.

Group A	Group B
Dataflow analysis	Code generation
Pushdown automata	Lexical analysis
Register allocation	Syntax analysis
Regular expression	Code optimization

References

1. Alblas (1994) A bibliography on parallel parsing. SIGPLAN Not, Jan 1994, pp 54–65
2. Barenghi et al (2015) Parallel parsing made practical. Sci Comput Program 112:195–226
3. Charniak et al (1996) Artificial intelligence, vol 85, pp 45–57. Elsevier
4. Chowdhary KR (2020) Constraint satisfaction problems. In: Fundamentals of artificial intelligence. Springer, New Delhi. https://doi.org/10.1007/978-81-322-3972-7_10
5. Feldman J, Gries D (1968) Translator writing system. Commun ACM 11(2):77–113
6. Gray JN, Harrison MA (1972) On the covering and reduction problems for context-free grammars. J ACM 19(4):675–698
7. Hall M, Padua D, Pingali K (2009) Compiler research: the next 50 years. Commun ACM 52(2):60–67
8. Knuth Donald E (1965) On the translation of languages from left to right. Inf Control 8:607–639
9. Beatty JC (1979) On the relationship between the LL(1) and LR(1) grammars, CS-79-76 October 1979
10. Lewis PM II, Stearns RE (1968) Syntax-directed translation. J ACM 15(3):465–488
11. Maruoka A (2011) Concise guide to computation theory. Springer Science & Business Media
12. Ginsburg S, Greibach SA, Harrison MA (1967) Stack automata and compiling. J ACM 14(1):172–201

13. Michael S (2012) Introduction to the theory of computation, 2012. Cengage learning
14. JFLAP (2020) http://jflap.org/ Seen on May 09, 2020
15. Gopalakrishnan G (2006) Computation engineering: applied automata theory and logic. Springer Science & Business Media
16. Schützenberger MP (1963) On context-free languages and push-down automata. Inf Control 6(3):246–264

Part IV
Turing Computations and Chomsky Hierarchy

In one sense, the theory of computation starts with Turing machine (TM) because the languages accepted by finite automata and those accepted by pushdown automata are a subset of those accepted by TM. As per the Church-Turing thesis, TM is the ultimate model of computation—no other model has invalidated this over the last 87 years, since the publication about TM model in 1936.

The first chapter in this part explains the concept of time and space complexity, and based on the concept of human computation builds the concept of TM computation, that can do computations as well can recognize languages, called type-0 or unrestricted languages. The corresponding grammars are unrestricted grammars. This approach of no restriction promises to incorporate all possible languages, even those of future about which we do not know anything yet.

The Turing machine has been shown to be capable of doing computations as well as recognizing languages. It has been shown how TM can be constructed to carry out all computations, using the TM models of basic computations. The Post machine—a variant of TM, has also been introduced by mathematician Emil Post.

The next chapter presents variants of TM models, like multitape TM, and other models. It has been shown that no such model adds any special computing capability to the TM, they only help in better modeling of problem solutions.

Interestingly, like a program can be loaded in the memory of a modern computer, a TMM can be loaded with the encoding of another TM, say M', and M will simulate M'. Such a TM (M) is called Universal TM.

A TM with bounded memory is called LBA (linear bounded automata), this machine is more closer to modern (practical) computer than the standard TM model. The LBA recognizes context-sensitive languages. This last chapter of this part also gives a detailed treatment to Chomsky-hierarchy grammars and languages, and many other grammars that fall between context-free and context-sensitive. These have been introduced here looking at the intensive research in NLP, language models, particularly the LLM (large language models), that are used in NLP and machine learning. Such grammars are, Indexed grammars, regulated rewriting grammars, and conjunctive grammars.

The nature of exercises, their categories, and solutions are in the same pattern as in previous chapters.

Chapter 9
Turing Machine and Computability

Abstract The Turing Machine (TM), introduced by Alan M. Turing through his landmark paper: "On Computable Numbers with an Application to the Entscheidungsproblem", is the foundation of the Theory of computation. This chapter introduces the TM Model, explains its working principle, its configurations, computations, and language acceptability, and shows that TM also accepts the languages accepted by finite automata and by Pushdown automata. Solutions to the number of standard problems of formal languages and computations have been illustrated through simple examples. The complexity of language recognition as well as of simple arithmetic has been illustrated. The Turing Machine is an algorithm, hence its analogy with modern computers has been convincingly justified. Finally, the Church-Turing thesis and its role in computability conclude that the Turing Machine is the ultimate computing machine. The Post machine, which performs the same functions as a TM, except that its instructions are quadruples against TMs quintuple format, has been briefly introduced. The chapter ends with a discussion on computation beyond the Turing limit, followed by a number of self-review questions, and exercises of varying difficulty levels.

Keywords Turing machine · TM configurations · Acceptability by TM · Computability · Computational complexity · Formal languages · Church-turing thesis · Post machine · TM simulator

9.1 Introduction

The study of Turing machines is crucial in computer science as it forms the foundation of theoretical computer science and helps in understanding the limits and capabilities of computation. The concept of a Turing machine was introduced by Alan Turing in 1936 and is considered one of the fundamental models of computation. Following are some reasons why the study of Turing machines is important in computer science:

- *Computational Complexity*: Turing machines provide a theoretical framework for analyzing the complexity of algorithms and problems. By studying Turing

K. R. Chowdhary, *Theory of Computation*,
https://doi.org/10.1007/978-981-97-6234-7_9

machines, we can classify problems as computationally solvable (decidable), unsolvable, or requiring exponential time to solve.

- *Computability Theory*: Turing machines are central to computability theory, which deals with what can and cannot be computed. Through Turing machines, we can explore the notion of undecidable problems, including the famous *halting problem*, which states that there is no general algorithm to determine if an arbitrary program will ever halt or not.
- *Algorithm Design and Analysis*: Turing machines provide insights into algorithm design and analysis. They help in understanding the concept of computable functions and the efficiency of algorithms in terms of time and space complexity.
- *Formal Language Theory*: Turing machines are closely connected to formal languages and automata theory. They help in defining and analyzing various language classes, such as regular languages, context-free languages, recursive and recursively enumerable languages.
- *Artificial Intelligence*: Turing machines have influenced the new fields, like, artificial intelligence. They form the basis for designing intelligent systems, machine learning algorithms, and computational models for understanding cognition and intelligence.

In this chapter, we will explore the power and limits of computation without regard to resource usage. That is, we seek to study which problems the computers can solve. To be more precise, the goal is to provide a model of computation powerful enough to be representative of an algorithm. The primitive automata we discussed in the previous chapters motivate this problem. The finite automata compute memory-less algorithms. While the regular languages are quite interesting and useful, the finite automata fail to decide context-free languages, like, $L_1 = \{a^n b^n \mid n \in \mathbb{N}\}$. Hence, when the infinite stack is added to the finite automaton we get *pushdown automaton*, which accepts precisely the context-free languages, including the language L_1 above. We again find the languages beyond the capability of the pushdown automata, e.g., $L_2 = \{a^n b^n c^n \mid n \in \mathbb{N}\}$, which cannot be recognized by a pushdown automata, also this language does not satisfy the *Pumping Lemma* for Context-Free languages.

It is quite simple to design an algorithm to verify if an input string is of the form specified by language L_1 or L_2, as this program is of very elementary nature. Thus, both the FA and PDA are not suitable for representing the algorithm in the most general form. To convince ourselves, why it is so, consider computing $x = a + b$; $y = x + c$; which requires replacing the value in memory x by the sum of values at a and b. Then, take the value from memory location x by revisiting it, and take value c, sum them, and place this result at the location y. We should be convinced that no such specific locations can be handled by the algorithms of FA and PDA because we cannot revisit those locations on the tape! To this end, we introduce the Turing Machine—the model of computation that serves to extend the limits of FA as well as PDA, as it allows to modify the locations by visiting those again and again, i.e., the head is read/write instead of read-only, and it can move left as well as right on the tape.

There are in fact, numerous models of computation, which are vastly different from the Turing Machine, but none of them have been found to be more powerful than the Turing Machine. The latter corresponds to the Church-Turing thesis, which conjectures that no model of computation is more powerful than the Turing Machine. However, the exception is *hyper-computation model*, but this model is yet not properly understood and not physically realizable, which further strengthens the idea of Church-Turing thesis.

In this chapter, we will study the machines, which can recognize the languages we have studied in the previous chapters and even more complex languages. These machines are called Turning Machines (TMs) after their inventor (Alan M. Turing). In 1936 Alan M. Turing defined a class of logical machines that he used as an aid in proving certain results in mathematical logic, and which should prove of interest in connection with the theory of control and switching system [1]. He had shown that given any logical arithmetic computation for which complete instructions for carrying out these computations are supplied, it is possible to design a TM, which can perform all this computation. Turing suggested that such a machine is an abstract mathematical model of a human being that is assumed to perform a computation with the *states* of mind of the human, and the *symbols* on tape corresponding to the numerical answers and to the intermediate results on the scratch paper.

These machines are similar to the machines we discussed earlier but are more general than those. A TM consists of finite control like FA (Finite Automata) and PDA (Pushdown Automata), a tape for reading and writing on it, and a head that can read from this tape and write on it, while doing this the head can move right and left on the tape.[1]

These machines are very simple in structure. In spite of this, they need not to be augmented for doing complex tasks. The access in the Turing Machine is always sequential. Still, machines, that appear more attractive, like those with random access capability, in fact, do not increase the computing power. These, visibly more powerful machines can be simulated by the Turing Machine, and have no extra computation power than standard TM. Other alternative and powerful TMs seem to form a stable and maximal class of computing devices in terms of the computations they perform. It may be noted that computing power here means not the speed of computation, but the capability of problem solvability through the machine, given the sufficient time to solve it.

[1] In many texts, and particularly the older texts, the tape is considered moving left or right and head remains stationary at the same position. This, in principle, is not different from moving the head, because moving the head right is nothing but moving the tape left, and vice-versa. In fact, keeping the head stationary and moving tape under has an analogy with most punch tape systems and magnetic tape systems like in audio recording-playing. However, in our discussions, which are followed in most current texts, we will consider that the head is moving, and tape is fixed, and the head moves one square left or right or remains stationary, in every transition of the machine.

Learning Outcomes of this Chapter:

1. TM (Turing Machine) Model. [Knowledge]
2. TM as an Algorithm. [Analysis]
3. Standard TM. [Knowledge]
4. Language recognition by TM. [Evaluation]
5. Computability. [Synthesis]
6. Arithmetic using TM. [Synthesis]
7. Church-Turing thesis. [Comprehension]
8. Turing Machine as an ultimate computing machine. [Analysis]
9. Post Machine. [Knowledge]
10. Computer simulation by TM. [Synthesis]
11. Computation beyond Turing limit. [Knowledge]

9.2 Algorithmic Complexity

We typically measure the computational efficiency algorithm as a number of basic operations it performs, as a function of its input length. That is, the efficiency of an algorithm can be captured by a function t from the set of natural numbers $\mathbb{N}$ to itself such that $t(n)$ is equal to the maximum number of basic operations that the algorithm performs on inputs of length n. For example, a linear search in an array of size n will require n steps to find an element in it, in the worst case. If one is lucky, the required element may be the first element of the array. Similarly, a bubble sort requires $n(n-1)/2$ steps in the worst case, and for quick-sort it is $n \log n$ steps in the worst. These are called *worst-case* complexities or *upper bound* of complexities.

However, the function $t(n)$ sometimes becomes overly dependent on the low-level details of the definition of a basic operation. For example, the addition algorithm will take about three times more operations if it uses the addition of single-digit binary (i.e., base 2) numbers as a basic operation, as opposed to decimal (i.e., base 10) numbers. To help us ignore these low-level details and focus on the big picture, the following well-known notations are useful.

In the following definitions, we assume that input is of size n, and the f and g are functions from $\mathbb{N}$ to $\mathbb{N}$, where $\mathbb{N} = \{1, 2, ..., i, ...\}$. The $\mathbb{N}_0 = \mathbb{N} \cup \{0\}$. However, we shall often mean $\mathbb{N}$ to stand for $\mathbb{N}_0$.

Definition 9.1 (*BIG-OH-notation*) $f(n) = O(g(n))$ if there exists a constant c such that $f(n) \leq c.g(n)$ for every sufficiently large n. □

The "Big Oh" is an asymptotic upper bound notation for an algorithm, for the input of size n.

Example 9.1 Following are examples of big-Oh notation:

1. If $f(n) = 100n \log n$ and $g(n) = n^2$ then we have the relations $f(n) = O(g(n))$.
2. If $f(n) = 100n^2 + 16n + 2 \log n$ and $g(n) = n^2$ then $f(n) = O(g(n))$, which we often write as $f(n) = O(n^2)$. We also have the relation $g(n) = O(f(n))$. □

Definition 9.2 (*Ω-notation*) $f(n) = \Omega(g(n))$ if $g(n) = O(f(n))$. □

Example 9.2 If $f(n) = 100n \log n$ and $g(n) = n^2$ then $f(n) = O(g(n))$. We also have the relation $g(n) = \Omega(f(n))$. □

Definition 9.3 (*θ-notation*) $f(n) = \theta(g(n))$ if $f(n) = O(g(n))$ and $g(n) = O(f(n))$. □

Example 9.3 If $f(n) = 100n^2 + 16n + 2 \log n$ and $g(n) = n^2$ then $f(n) = O(g(n))$. We will often write this relation as $f(n) = O(n^2)$. We also have the relation $g(n) = O(f(n))$ and hence $f(n) = \theta(g(n))$ and $g(n) = \theta(f(n))$. □

Definition 9.4 (*SMALL-OH-notation*) $f(n) = o(g(n))$ if for every $\epsilon > 0$, $f(n) \leq \epsilon.g(n)$ for every sufficiently large n. □

Example 9.4 If $f(n) = 2^n$ then for every number $c \in \mathbb{N}$, if $g(n) = n^c$ then $g(n) = o(f(n))$. Similarly, we also write $h(n) = n^{O(1)}$ to denote the fact that h is bounded from above by some polynomial. That is, there exist a number $c > 0$ such that for sufficiently large n, $h(n) \leq nc$. □

Definition 9.5 (*ω-notation*) $f(n) = \omega(g(n))$ if $g(n) = o(f(n))$. □

9.3 Analysis of Human Computation

Turing, in his seminal 1936 paper [1], analyzed human computation "from the bottom up", which builds complex procedures from the most primitive of operations on single symbols. As per that, computation proceeds by sequential symbol manipulation, and argued that any such computation can be mimicked by a symbolic computation with the following properties:

- *Deterministic behavior*: The behavior of the computer at any instance is determined by the symbol(s) which he (human) is observing and the state of his mind at that time.
- *Finitely many internal states*: If we admitted an infinite number of states of mind, some of them will be *arbitrarily close* to each other and will be confusing. (This restriction is not one which seriously affects computation, since the use of more complicated states of mind can be avoided by writing more symbols on the tape).
- *A finite symbol space*: If we were to allow an infinite number of symbols, then there would be symbols differing to an arbitrarily small extent. The effect of this restriction on the number of symbols is not very serious, as it is always possible to use sequences of symbols in place of single symbols.

- *Finite observability and local action*: Let us imagine the operations performed by the computer to be split up into simpler operations, which are so elementary that it is not easy to imagine them further divided; we may suppose that there is a bound to the number of symbols or squares which the computer can observe at one moment. If he (human) wishes to observe more, he must use successive observations.
- *Linear external memory*: The two-dimensional nature of paper (which we use for computation) is not essential for computation. We assume that the computation is carried out on one-dimensional paper.

9.4 Turing Machine Model

A Turing Machine satisfies the following three general criteria:

- It is an automata, i.e., its function and construction are in similar lines to the automata discussed earlier,
- It should be as simple as possible, to define formally, describe, and reason about them, and
- It should be as general as possible so that any computation can be represented using it.

A Turing Machine is usually regarded as a small computer with a finite number of states and a (potentially) infinite tape marked off into discrete squares. Upon each square of the tape is written one symbol selected from a finite alphabet; all but a finite number of the squares contain symbol B (blank). The operation of the Turing Machine is as follows: at a given time, the machine would be in some state and would be scanning a square on the tape. For each state-symbol pair, there would be either a well-defined operation or a command to halt. A non-halting operation (step) would consist of three suboperations:

- A new symbol (possibly the same as the previous one) would be written on the square being scanned.
- The scanning head of the machine would move to the left or to the right one square on the tape. However, we can also allow the machine to stay on the same square.
- The machine would enter a new state (possibly the same as the previous one).

The machine would then be scanning a new symbol, and to the new state-symbol pair there would correspond another operation, etc.

A slightly more formal approach to the above version of a Turing Machine is to define a machine as a set of quintuples $\langle q_i, a_j, a_k, D, q_t \rangle$ with the five components of the quintuple representing present state, present symbol being scanned, new symbol written, direction moved on tape, and next state, respectively. By convention, the machine halts if it reaches a state-symbol convention configuration for which there is no quintuple. In order for the machine to be well defined, q_i and q_t must be selected from a finite set of states $\{q_1, q_2, ..., q_n\}$, and a_j, a_k must be selected from a finite set of symbols $\{a_o(= B), a_1, a_2, ..., a_{m-1}\}$, and D must be either L, R or N (left, right, or no head motion. Furthermore, no two distinct quintuples of the machine may have as their leftmost two components the same state-symbol pair. Often the possibility, $D = N$ is excluded from the characterization of Turing Machines. It is well known that this entails no loss of generality[2] [5].

Definition 9.6 A Turing Machine has a *blocking loop* (or simply a *loop*) if for some k there exists integers $i_1, i_2, ..., i_k$ and $j_1, j_2, ..., j_k$ such that machine includes the k tuples:

$$\langle q_{i_1}, a_{j_1}, a_{j_2}, N, q_{i_2}\rangle, \langle q_{i_2}, a_{j_2}, a_{j_3}, N, q_{i_3}\rangle, ..., \langle q_{i_k}, a_{j_k}, a_{j_1}, N, q_{i_1}\rangle.$$

□

The above configuration sequence leads to a loop because the first state and last states are both q_{i_1}.

Clearly, one can tell effectively whether or not a Turing Machine has a blocking loop, although one cannot in general tell whether or not the loop will ever be entered. A machine in a blocking loop is not halted, but except for the square being scanned at that time, the tape will undergo no further changes. Therefore, one can dispense with the ability of a machine to enter a blocking loop without weakening its computing ability.

The developments since the time of Turing's paper [1], have been in the direction of digital computers which show a much more direct resemblance to Turing Machines than to human beings. In fact, several earlier computers comprised magnetic tape or perforated paper tapes as auxiliary memories. The one-tape machines are called Turing Machines.

By analogy of TMs with modern computers is as follows: the tape of the TM is equal to the memory of computers, and the read-write head is equal to the CPU (Central Processing Unit).

9.4.1 *Standard Turing Machine*

The standard Turing Machine has many similarities with the finite-state automaton. Just like the finite automaton, the Turing Machine solves decision problems—it decides whether a string belongs to the given language. Both the finite automaton and Turing Machine have a finite number of states, a tape of infinite length, and one head. But, unlike the finite automaton, the TM head is read/write, it can move left as well as right on the tape or may remain stationary. In addition, the TM has unlimited read/write memory, which can be written as well as can be read an arbitrary number

---

[2] A N-move of the head can be modeled as "L, R" move sequence or "R, L" move sequence.

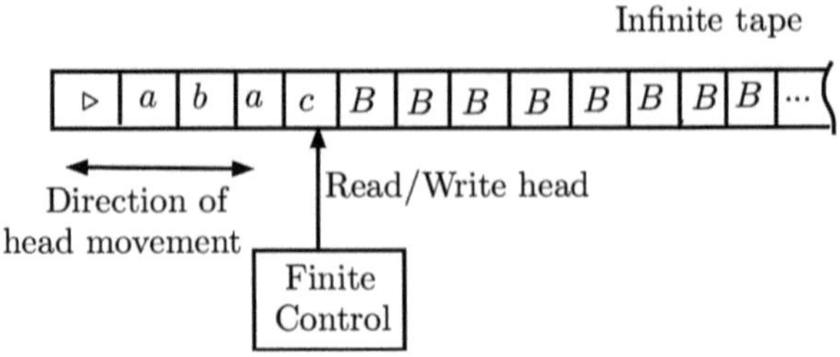

Fig. 9.1 Turing machine model

of times. This allows one to parse characters multiple times and develops a notion of iteration in computations being carried out. It has explicit accept and reject states which take effect immediately upon reached.

A Turing machine computing model (Fig. 9.1) consists of a finite-state control, a tape, and a read-write head. The read-write (RW) head reads the input symbols from the tape, as well as writes or modifies the symbols on the tape.

The finite control operates in discrete steps, where, in each step, it performs the following operations that are decided by the current state of the finite control and the tape symbol currently read by the read/write head:

1. Write a symbol on a square on the tape the position from which it has just read a symbol, thus replacing the previous symbol,
2. Change of state of the control to a new state, and
3. Move the RW head to the left or write. The direction of the move will be decided by the current state and the symbol the RW head has just read.

The tape of the TM ends at its left but extends to the right without any limit. Thus, to prevent the read-write head from moving beyond this left end, an end-marker symbol ($\triangleright$) indicates the left end of the tape. The end marker is not counted as a symbol in the alphabets of input. We will use R (right) and L (left) characters as short forms to indicate the direction of the head movement. Input to the TM is supplied by writing the string on the tape in advance, starting immediately after the symbol $\triangleright$ and extending toward right up to any length. Note that, at many places in our text, we will be using B (for blank) symbol in place of $\triangleright$.

The rest of the tape squares, after the string end are blank, indicated by B symbols. The TM is free to alter its input string in any way it sees fit and can write symbols beyond it. Since the machine's head makes only one square move after reading each square, therefore, for any finite computation only a finite number of squares will be scanned on the tape.

Mathematical Model of a Turing Machine is a 6-tuple defined as

$$M = (Q, \Sigma, \Gamma, \delta, s, H) \tag{9.1}$$

where

Q is finite set of states
Σ is set of input symbols
Γ is set of tape symbols, and $\Gamma = \Sigma \cup \{B, \triangleright\}$, here B is for blank space, and $\triangleright$ is left-end marker symbol on tape. Since B can also be written and read, hence the tape symbols are $\Gamma = \Sigma \cup \{B\}$
$s \in Q$ is start state
$H \in Q$ is a set of halting states,[3] and,
δ is transition function, which is a mapping,

$$\delta : (Q - H) \times \Gamma \rightarrow Q \times \Gamma \times D, \tag{9.2}$$

where $D = \{L, R\}$ indicates that head takes left or right move. Thus, a transition in TM can be represented by

$$\delta(p, a) = (q, b, d), \tag{9.3}$$

where $p \in Q - H$, $q \in Q$, terminals $a, b \in \Gamma$,[4] and the displacement $d \in \{L, R\}$. A transition indicates that a TM in the state p (not a halting state), and symbol on the tape square being read is a then TM replaces a by b on that square, changes the state to q, and moves the head one square to left or to right depending on the value of d. If $q \in H$ then the TM has halted. Once the TM is halted then it does not cause further transitions anymore, hence is not defined for $\delta(p, a)$, where $p \in H$, and a is any symbol in Γ.

If the head moves to the extreme left end of the tape then δ is defined as

$$\delta(p, \triangleright) = (q, \triangleright, R) \tag{9.4}$$

This shows that the leftmost symbol $\triangleright$ on the tape is never erased. Also, the machine does not write $\triangleright$ on the tape except at the extreme left end of the tape. Unlike in pushdown automaton, transition function $\delta(q, a)$ for a TM is always a single value (not a set). Therefore, a TM is by default a deterministic machine, and $\delta(q, a)$ is not defined for halting state (H). However, nondeterministic TMs are possible as variations of basic TMs, but these are in no way more powerful than the standard Turing Machines.

---

[3] A halting state is not necessarily an accepting state, as TM may halt in accepting state or rejecting state, in case of language acceptance. For a computation, as TM has to halt. However, depending on the nature of the problem, a TM may continue indefinitely without halting.

[4] Though the input alphabet are Σ, the head can read and write all the characters in Γ.

9.4.2 Configurations and Moves of TM

A *Configuration* of a TM is denoted by $\alpha_1 q \alpha_2$, where $\alpha_1 \in \Sigma^*$ is a string which extends from head position to left, up to end marker, and $\alpha_2 \in \Sigma^*$ is a string which extends from RW head up to rightmost non-blank symbol. It is assumed that the head is pointing to the leftmost symbol of α_2. If $\alpha_2 = \varepsilon$ then the head is pointing to blank (B). The tape symbols include Σ along with blank character B and left-end marker symbol $\rhd$, i.e., $\Gamma = \Sigma \cup \{\rhd, B\}$. Let $X_1, X_2, ..., X_i, ...$ stand for symbols on tape, where X_i is at ith position from left.

A *move* of a TM M is

$$X_1 X_2 \dots X_{i-1} q X_i X_{i+1} \dots X_n \vdash_M X_1 X_2 \dots X_{i-2} p X_{i-1} Y X_{i+1} \dots X_n, \qquad (9.5)$$

where TM moves ($\vdash_M$ is a symbol for move) from one configuration to another configuration. A configuration is $\alpha_1 q \alpha_2$, as mentioned above. The detail of a configuration is also called ID (Instantaneous Description) of the Turing Machine—a combination of symbols before the head, the symbol head is pointing, the symbols after the head, and what is the current state of the machine. We can equally well say that TM is in so and so configuration or say that the ID of the TM is so and so. Let us assume that

$$X_1 X_2 \dots X_{i-1} q X_i X_{i+1} \dots X_n$$

be an instantaneous description of a TM shown in Fig. 9.2, where head points to symbol X_i. Consider that there is a transition

$$\delta(q, X_i) = (p, Y, d).$$

It shows that when a TM is at state q and head is pointing to symbol X_i, TM writes symbol Y in place of X_i, changes its state to p and the R/W head takes a displacement d (i.e., left or right). If $i - 1 = n$ then $X_i = B$. If $i = 0$ then $X_i = \rhd$ and the head will move to right, else it will fall off the tape or we say it crashes. If $i > 1$ and $i = n$ then for $d = L$, the move is as follows.

$$X_1 X_2 \dots X_{i-1} q X_i X_{i+1} \dots X_n \vdash_M X_1 X_2 \dots X_{i-2} p X_{i-1} Y X_{i+1} \dots X_n$$

Alternatively, for $i > 1$ and $d = R$, the move is written as

$$X_1 X_2 \dots X_{i-1} q X_i X_{i+1} \dots X_n \vdash_M X_1 X_2 \dots X_{i-1} Y p X_{i+1} \dots X_n.$$

For $i - 1 = n$, the entire string exists to the left of q, and $X_i ... X_n$ part is empty comprising all B symbols. If two IDs are related by the move operation $\vdash_M$, then we say that the second ID results from the first by a single move. If two IDs are

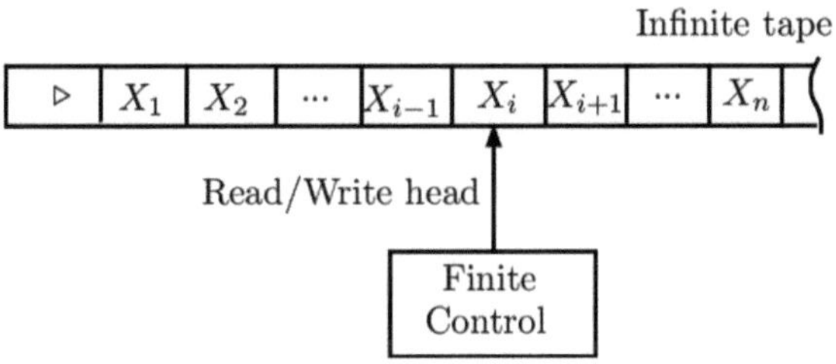

Fig. 9.2 TM with $ID = X_1X_2 \dots X_{i-1}qX_iX_{i+1} \dots X_n$

related by $\vdash_M^*$ then we say that the second ID results from the first ID by zero or more number of moves, but certainly by the finite number of moves.

Consider that language $L = L(M)$ accepted by the TM M is such that at start, head points to the leftmost square of the tape (i.e., just after $\triangleright$), the start state is q_0, and ultimately the M enters into the final state. Thus, language L is formally represented as

$$L = \{w \mid w \in \Gamma^*,\ q_0w \vdash_M^* \alpha p\beta \text{ for some } p \in H \text{ and } \alpha, \beta \in \Gamma^*\}. \tag{9.6}$$

Naturally, a TM has to pass through a sequence of configurations to accept any input string such that finally it is in an accepting configuration, i.e., the machine has halted and the state is the final (accepting) state. These configurations must be finite, and no configuration must repeat else the machine will loop forever. Note that, in a run, a state may repeat but not the configuration.

The following is the formal definition of acceptance by a Turing Machine.

Definition 9.7 (*Acceptance by Turing Machine*) A TM M accepts a string w if there exists a sequence of configurations $C_0, C_1, C_2, \dots, C_n$ such that,

1. C_0 is starting configuration of M on input w, expressed as $C_0 = q_0w$,
2. C_n is accepting configuration, expressed as uq_hv, and $u, v \in \Gamma^*$, q_h is halting or accepting state,[5] and
3. for each $0 \leq i \leq n$, C_i yields C_{i+1}, then

$L(M)$, the language of M is set of all strings recognized by M. □

A *configuration* of a Turing Machine M specifies the state, contents of all the tapes, and positions of all the access heads. The sequence of configurations $C_0, C_1, \dots, C_i, \dots, C_n$ is called *computation path*. If M has no infinite computation paths, then M *always halts*, and may halt in either accepting state or rejecting state.

[5] In TM, when we say it halts on input w, it means machine has halted and accepted the input w. This is opposite to the case where a TM runs forever for certain inputs and does not halt. However, there are languages for which TM always halts – if a string w is in the language L, the TM accepts and halts, and when $w \notin L$, TM halts in a rejecting state. Such Languages are called *Recursive* or *Decidable* Languages.

M accepts an input word if there exists an accepting computation path that starts from the initial configuration C_0 in which w is on the input tape. M rejects w if the only halting computation paths are rejecting.

In addition to deciding languages, shown by Eq. 9.6 above, deterministic TMs can compute functions. For this, we consider two tapes, tape-1 holds the input x and tape-2 is the output tape. If M halts on input word x, then word on tape-2 is output of M. If the function to be computed is f, then this output is $f(x)$. The multi-tape TMs and the other variants of TMs are discussed in Chap. 10.

Definition 9.8 A function f is *total recursive* if there exists a deterministic Turing Machine M that always halts such that for each input word x, the output of M is the value of $f(x)$. □

Example 9.5 Turing Machine as an algorithm to erase the memory content.

Consider a TM, $M = (Q, \Sigma, \Gamma, \delta, s, H)$, where $Q = \{q_0, q_1\}$, $\Sigma = \{a\}$, $\Gamma = \{a, B, \triangleright\}$, $s = q_0$, $H = \{q_1\}$ and transition function δ is given as

$$\delta(q_0, a) = (q_0, B, R)$$
$$\delta(q_0, B) = (q_1, B, L).$$

For an input string $w = aaaa$, the corresponding IDs and moves are as follows:

$$\begin{aligned} q_0aaaaB &\vdash Bq_0aaaB \\ &\vdash BBq_0aaB \\ &\vdash BBBq_0aB \\ &\vdash BBBBq_0B \\ &\vdash BBBq_1BB \end{aligned}$$

Therefore, the above TM simply erases all the characters of the input string and then halts. Figure 9.3 shows the transition diagram of this Turing Machine. □

Conceptually, a TM can be used as a language recognizer, as a computing machine to compute something, or in general as a functioning computer.

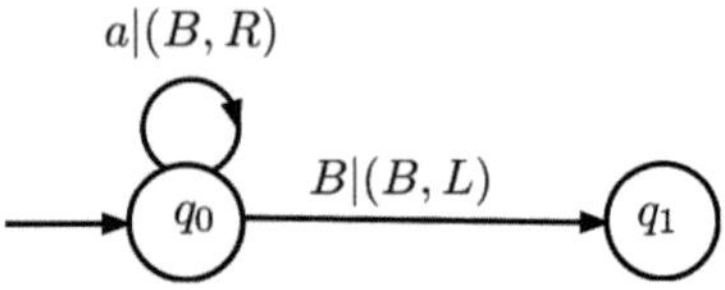

Fig. 9.3 TM erasing its tape contents

9.5 Language Recognition by Turing Machine

We introduce the following notions of language acceptance.

Definition 9.9 (*Language Acceptance*) A Turing Machine M *accepts* the language $L = L(M)$ if it halts on every string w, irrespective of whether w is or not in $L(M)$. □

Definition 9.10 (*Language Recognition*) A Turing Machine M *recognizes* a language $L = L(M)$ if it halts on every string $w \in L$ and accepts, but for $w \notin L$ it may continue indefinitely. □

The above definitions sharply distinguish the properties of language acceptance and language recognition. The languages in the first category (acceptance) are called Recursive (R) languages, while those recognizable are called Recursively Enumerable (RE) languages. Naturally, the R languages are decidable, while the RE languages are semi-decidable, and they are related by the relation $R \subseteq RE$.

Definition 9.11 (*Recursively Enumerable Language*) A language L is said to be *recursively enumerable* (RE) if there exists a deterministic Turing Machine M, and $L = L(M)$, such that if $w \in L$, then M halts in accepting mode on w as input. However, for $w \notin L$, the M need not to halt. □

Definition 9.12 (*Recursive Language*) A language $L = L(M)$ is recursive iff the TM M accepts and halts if there is $w \in L(M)$ and M rejects and halts if $w \notin L(M)$. □

Definition 9.13 (*Decidable Language*) A language L is said to be *decidable* if there exists some Turing Machine M such that for $L = L(M)$ the TM M halts on all inputs $w \in L$, as well for $w \notin L$. For such a language we say *M decides L*. □

The *Recursive languages* are decidable, and *Recursively Enumerable* languages are recognized by Turing Machines. Further, we note that every decidable language is recursively enumerable, however, the converse is not true.

In the following, we will discuss a number of examples of languages as sets, and corresponding Turing Machine in each case that recognizes the given set.

Example 9.6 Construct a TM that accepts the language $L = \{a^n b^n \mid n \geq 0\}$.

Let $M = (Q, \Sigma, \Gamma, \delta, s, H)$ be a Turing Machine, which accepts the language L. Let us assume that the string $w = a^n b^n$ exists on the tape for some integer n, followed by an infinite number of blank characters B. The working of M to recognize w is explained in following steps:

1. M replace leftmost a by X, and then head moves to right until it encounters leftmost b.

Table 9.1 Transition Table for $L = \{a^n b^n \mid n \geq 0\}$

state	a	b	X	Y	B
q_0	(q_1, X, R)			(q_3, Y, R)	(q_4, B, L)
q_1	(q_1, a, R)	(q_2, Y, L)		(q_1, Y, R)	
q_2	(q_2, a, L)		(q_0, X, R)	(q_2, Y, L)	
q_3				(q_3, Y, R)	(q_4, B, L)

2. Replaces this b by Y, and then moves left to find the rightmost X. Then moves one step right to leftmost a.
3. Repeat Step 1 and 2 in order, i.e., 1, 2, 1, 2, ...
4. When searching for b, if M finds a blank character B (i.e., $|a^n| = |b^n|$) then M halts without accepting.
5. If a is not found but it finds b ($a^n \neq b^n$), then M halts without accepting.
6. After changing b to Y, if M finds no more a then it checks that no more b remains. If this is true then $a^n b^n$ is accepted by M (i.e., $|a^n| = |b^n|$).

Based on the above procedure, Turing Machine M can be specified as follows:

$$
\begin{aligned}
Q &= \{q_0, q_1, q_2, q_3, q_4\} \\
\Sigma &= \{a, b\} \\
\Gamma &= \{\triangleright, a, b, X, Y, B\} \\
s &= q_0 \\
H &= \{q_4\}
\end{aligned}
$$

The transition table for this machine is given as Table 9.1.

Figure 9.4 shows a transition diagram for this TM accepting language $L = \{a^n b^n \mid n \geq 0\}$.

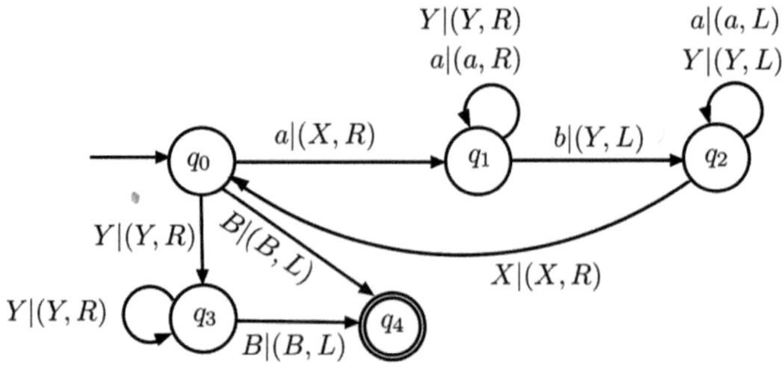

Fig. 9.4 TM accepting the Language $L = \{a^n b^n \mid n \geq 0\}$

Let $w = aabb$. The following are a sequence of moves, which leads to the acceptance of w. A character B after $aabb$ indicates the end of the input string.

$$\begin{aligned} q_0aabbB &\vdash Xq_1abbB \vdash Xaq_1bbB \vdash Xq_2aYbB \\ &\vdash q_2XaYbB \vdash Xq_0aYbB \vdash XXq_1YbB \vdash XXYq_1bB \\ &\vdash XXq_2YYB \vdash Xq_2XYYB \vdash XXq_0YYB \vdash XXYq_3YB \\ &\vdash XXYYq_3B \vdash XXYq_4YB \end{aligned}$$

The reader may verify that strings aab, $abab$, abb etc., are not accepted. □

9.5.1 *Complexity of Language Recognition*

The time complexity of a Turing Machine is how much time it takes to arrive at a solution in the worst case. Therefore, this time complexity is called worst-case time complexity, i.e., the maximum number of steps (transitions) the Turing Machine takes for that problem. Since a Turing Machine is an algorithm, and it is problem-specific, so time complexity of an algorithm or the time complexity of a given problem is one and the same. The time complexity is calculated as a function of the size of the input. Thus, if input w is of length $|w| = n$, then worst-case time complexity $O(n)$ is *linear time complexity*, while $O(n^2)$ is *quadratic*, and $O(2^n)$, $O(3^n)$ are *exponential* time complexities.

If a Turing Machine having input w takes the worst-case tape space equal to size of w ($|w| = n$), then worst-case space complexity for that problem is $O(n)$.

In the following example, we calculate the worst-case time complexity of a problem. Note that, since there can be more than one algorithm for solving any given problem, hence the corresponding Turing Machines also, will have different time complexities.

In the following example, we find out the time complexity of a given problem, based on how many transitions the corresponding Turing Machines take.

Example 9.7 Complexity of TM for $L = \{a^n b^n \mid n \geq 0\}$.

The time (number of transitions) taken by a 1-tape Turing Machine for this language can be calculated as follows [7]:

1. Assume that R/W head is initially pointing to input symbol a of a^n. In the first run, the machine performs total $n - 1$ transitions while scanning a's and 1 transition in b (total n transitions), while moving in forward direction, and equal numbers while moving in reverse direction; total $2n$ transitions (see Fig. 9.5).
2. This scan is repeated n-times, making total of $2n * n = 2n^2$ transitions.
3. When entire input string is crossed (a's by X's and b's by Y's), there are n-transitions more—from q_0 to q_3 including loop at q_3, and one transition from q_3 to q_4 (see Fig. 9.4).

After forward scan	B	a	a	a	a	a	b	b	b	b	b	B	B	B	B	B
1	B	X	a	a	a	a	Y	b	b	b	b	B	B	B	B	B
2	B	X	X	a	a	a	Y	Y	b	b	b	B	B	B	B	B
3	B	X	X	X	a	a	Y	Y	Y	b	b	B	B	B	B	B
4	B	X	X	X	X	a	Y	Y	Y	Y	b	B	B	B	B	B
5	B	X	X	X	X	X	Y	Y	Y	Y	Y	B	B	B	B	B

Fig. 9.5 Scans of TM Head to recognize $w = a^5b^5$

4. Thus, total transitions are $2n^2 + n + 1$ to recognize the string $a^n b^n$. For an input $|w| = n$, this value is $n^2 + n/2 + 1$. This gives a time complexity of $O(n^2)$. □

Example 9.8 Show that $L = \{a^n b^n \mid n \geq 0\} \in TIME(n \log n)$.

We cross off every other a and every other b. If the number of as and bs left on the tape is odd, we reject the input, else if none is left, we accept.

This shows that a one-tape TM cannot decide L in less time than $O(n \log n)$. Note that we have not indicated states here, which are obvious from the previous examples. □

If $f(n) = o(n \log n)$, then $Time(f(n))$ contains only regular languages. Here o is the lower bound of the time, against the O as worst-case time-bound.

Example 9.9 Show that the language $L = \{a^n b^n c^n \mid n \geq 0\}$ is accepted by a TM.

We have just seen that language $a^n b^n$ can be accepted by a TM. In that process $a^n b^n$ gets converted to $X^n Y^n$ before the TM halts.

To design a TM to accept $a^n b^n c^n$, we use almost the previous technique and perform the following conversions:

1. $aa...abb...bcc...c$ is converted to $Xa...aYb...bZc...c$,
2. ...
3. In the scan last but one, the tape contents are $XX..aYY...bZZ...c$,
4. Finally, the tape contents are $XX...XYY...YZZ...Z$.

The above can be carried out by adding one more state after q_2, say q_5. Hence, this proves that language $a^n b^n c^n$ is accepted by a TM shown in Fig. 9.6. □

Note that time complexity of this Turing Machine is again quadratic, i.e., $O(n^2)$.

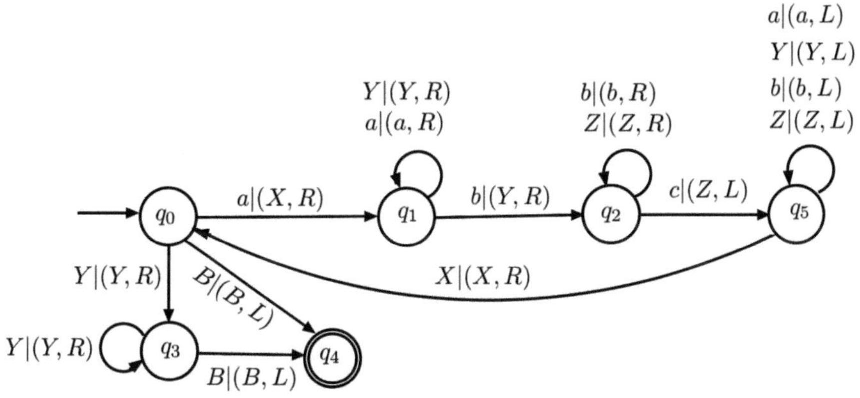

Fig. 9.6 TM accepting the Language $L = \{a^n b^n c^n \mid n \geq 0\}$

9.5.2 *Palindrome Languages*

All the strings w in a palindrome language L have the property that $w = w^R$, that is, every string $w \in L$, where L is palindrome language, is identical when read forward as well as backward (reverse).

See "Proof Based Problems" (Exercise no. 24b) for constriction of standard Turing Machines that accept even and odd styles of palindrome languages.

In the Examples 9.6, 9.7, 9.9 we solved above, we assumed formal definition of some language $L \in \Sigma^*$, and demonstrated that there exists some Turing Machine M such that for any string $w \in \Sigma^*$ if $w \in L$ then $M(w)$ = "yes" and for $w \notin L$, $M(w)$ = "No". If above holds, we say that M *decides* L. If L is decided by some Turing Machine M then L is called a *Recursive Language* (see Definition 9.12).

A language is called *Recursively Enumerable* (RE) , if for $w \in \Sigma^*$ and also $w \in L$ then $M(w)$ = "Yes"; however, for $w \notin L$, $M(w)$ is either "No" or it undecidable.

Theorem 9.1 *Prove that the language L made of all strings of well-matched parenthesis is recursive.*

Proof We try to give a recursive definition for the language L containing all strings of well-matched parenthesis.

- *Basis step:* $w = () \in L$.
- *Induction step:* If $w \in L$ then $w()$, $()w$, (w) are all in L.

Let f is defined as $f : \Sigma^* \rightarrow \Gamma^*$, and let M be a Turing Machine with alphabet Σ. We say that M computes f if for any $w \in \Sigma^*$, there exists $M(w) = f(w)$. If such M exists, then f is *recursive function*. □

9.5.3 Copy a String

String copy is one of the most widely operations in the recognition of languages, often, to reuse the original string we need to copy it somewhere. For example, how to copy the input string $w \in \{a, b\}^*$ to a location immediately after its current position, but separated by a hyphen symbol "-"? For this we would like to construct a TM as follows: As each symbol position is copied to a new location and its original position, say, a is replaced by X, and b by Y. The new symbol X and Y marks the positions that these have been copied. Finally, these modified symbols are replaced by the original symbols a and b. The final tape contents will be w-w.

Example 9.10 Figure 9.7 shows a TM that produces the output w-w for an input w, at the end the Read/Write head remains pointing to the first character of original w. Note that the machine remains in the state q_8 while the head moves on to left as long as it sees X or Y on the tape; on seeing B, head remains stationary (indicated by S), with q_9 as accepting state.

It can be verified that this copy operation works for ε input also, in that case noting is copied. □

The Turing Machines are equivalent in computation power to arbitrarily general (recursive) computer programs. Turing Machines can be thought of as algorithms for solving string-related problems. But, calculations are expressed as, e.g., "1110 + 111".

To solve the problems with Turing Machines, whose instances are mathematical objects, like, graphs, networks, numbers, etc, the first requirement is to represent an

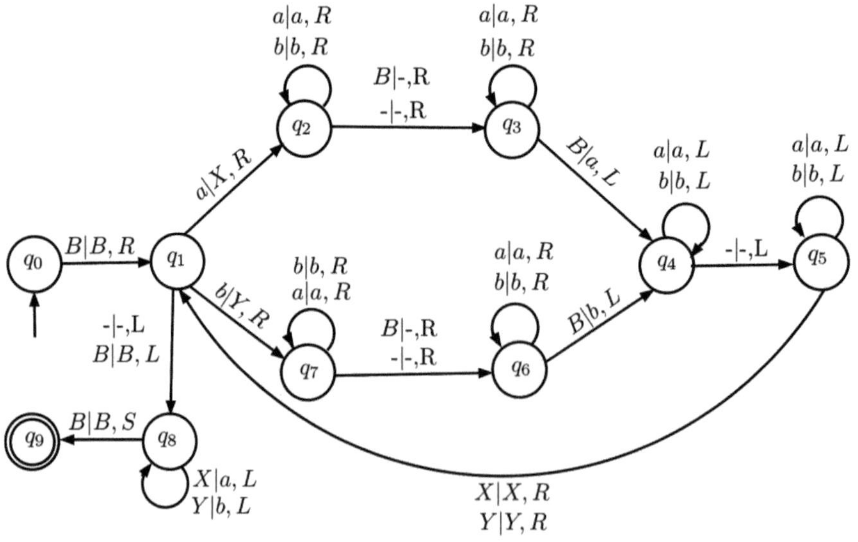

Fig. 9.7 TM to Copy a string w to make w-w

instance of the problem with a string. Then, the algorithm for a decision problem is a Turing Machine that decides the corresponding language made of these strings.

9.6 Turing Machines and Formal Languages

We shall first try to pay our attention to the Turing machine as a language accepter. We have already defined two classes of languages, i.e., Recursive Languages (R) and Recursively Enumerable languages (RE), depending on whether string membership in the respective languages can be *decided* or merely *accepted.*

One approach to categorizing the languages is using the (phrase structured) grammars. But, how do these language classes compare in relation to those defined by types of Turing Machines? We have seen how to characterize these languages using machines. For instance, *regular languages* are recognized by finite-state automata. We have also discussed that the inverse of a regular language can be recognized by exchanging the final and non-final states of the corresponding finite automaton. In the following, we shall show the relation between Turing machine and regular languages, and that way between Turing machines and Finite automata.

Turing machines are important because (it is generally believed that) anything that can be done by any mechanical procedure or algorithm can in principle be done by a Turing machine (as per the Church-Turing thesis). For example,

- Any language $L \subseteq \Sigma^*$ that can be "recognized" by some mechanical procedure can be recognized by a TM.
- Any mathematical function $f : \mathbb{N} \to \mathbb{N}$ that can be computed by a mechanical procedure can be computed by a TM (for example, representing integers in binary, and requiring the TM to write the result onto the tape.)

9.6.1 TMs and Regular Languages

We can simulate the FA (finite automata) using a Turing machine, such that simulating a Turing machine will only read the string w and the tape head will move only in the right-hand direction on tape. Such a Turing machine, after reaching to last symbol of input, will accept the input if the corresponding FA accepts this string, else rejects it. This shows that regular languages are accepted by TM. However, we have not been able to say anything about halting TM when it rejects the input w.

Consider the following approach. We construct Turing machine M that accepts the regular language $L = L(M)$, and for $w \in L$ it accepts and halts. Similarly, since there exists a FA that accepts language $\overline{L}$, the $\overline{L}$ is regular. We construct Turing machine $\overline{M}$ that accepts regular language $\overline{L} = L(\overline{M})$ and halts. As next step, we construct a Turing machine M' which combines Turing machines M and $\overline{M}$, such that $L' = L \cup \overline{L}$, and $L' = L(M')$. Because of construction of the Turing machine M', if M accepts input w and halts then M' accepts and halts, also if $\overline{M}$ accepts and halts then also M' accepts and halts. Thus, for both the situations, $w \in M$ and $w \notin M$ ($w \in \overline{M}$), the TM M' halts. This leads us to conclude that regular languages are in the class of *Recursive languages*, because they always make the Turing machine to halt. This observation is complete by noting that a Turing machine can easily act as finite-state automata, where all the transitions need to be of the form,

$$\delta(q_i, a) = (q_j, R),$$

where we only read from the tape and transition internally from one state to the other, never writing on the tape or moving in any other directions. This brief and informal analysis allows us to affirm our intuition that regular languages (L_{Reg}) are included in Recursive languages (L_{Rec}), i.e., $L_{Reg} \subseteq L_{Rec}$.

We have discussed that palindrome languages are *Decidable languages*, and by above-discussed fact, we conclude that they are included in the Recursive languages. We also know that they cannot be recognized by FA, and need more powerful machines, called Pushdown automata. This further allows us to establish strictly that, $L_{Reg} \subset L_{Rec}$.

9.6.2 TMs and Context-Free Languages

The context-free languages are those that are generated by the context-free grammars, i.e., the grammars whose production rules are of the form $A \rightarrow (V \cup \Sigma)^*$, where A is variable (nonterminal) symbol, V is set of variables, and Σ is set of terminal symbols. These languages are recognized by the machines, called Pushdown automata. Most of the machines we considered in Chap. 8 are actually nondeterministic PDAs. We will make use of this information to show how the Turing machines can recognize CFLs.

The relation we would like to show is as follows: there is a strict inclusion of CFL in recursive language. To show this, we would have to demonstrate that:

1. There are recursive languages that are not context-free, and
2. Every CFL can be decided by some TM.

To show that the first point above is valid, we have to only show one incident in favor of this point. The CFG can be converted to Chomsky Normal Form (CNF) where derivations of string w are bounded by $2|w| - 1$ steps. This is the case of $L_{\text{CFG}} \subseteq L_{\text{Rec}}$. Another fact is, that $\{a^n b^n c^n \mid n \geq 0\}$ is in L_{Rec} but, is not in L_{CFG}. This is the case of context-free languages are a subset of recursive languages, i.e., $L_{\text{CFG}} \subseteq L_{\text{Rec}}$. This shows that the set of recursive languages is strictly larger than that of context-free languages. The language $\{a^n b^n c^n \mid n \geq 0\}$ satisfies our need of one case in favor. Note that we have shown that the above language cannot be generated by any CFG, however, we have shown that this language can be decided by a Turing machine (Example 9.9, Sect. 9.5.1), which means it is Recursive language.

This leaves us with the last task to show that CFL is decidable by a Turing machine. For this we try to prove a weaker result, namely, that every CFL is included in the set of Recursively Enumerable Languages. We have the following Lemma to prove it.

Lemma 9.1 *Every CFL can be recognized by some Turing Machine.*

Proof We know that CFLs are recognized by Pushdown Automata. So we shall show that any PDA can be simulated by a Turing machine. We use the 2-tape Turing machine, which works as follows:

- The first tape of the Turing machine simulates the tape of Pushdown automata, such that for the 1st tape of this Turing machine, the head moves only to the right, without writing anything,
- As the head moves on 1st tape, the head of 2nd tape may push a symbol on 2nd tape or it may pop it, based on the state the TM is in, together with the symbol it has read from the first tape. □

We have the following detailed explanation of the Lemma above.

If a language is Context-free, then there exists an NPDA that can recognize it. Unfortunately, the nondeterminism in NPDAs does not permit us to say much about the termination of every run of such a machine. What all NPDA recognition gives us is that there exists some sequence of transitions that accepts the strings in the recognized CFL. That is, we only have a termination guarantee for strings in the language and the nondeterminism of the machine prohibits us from stating anything about decidability.

But, there is no problem, as we can use the 2-tape Turing machine to easily simulate an NPDA, where the 1st tape is used as the input tape to hold the input string undisturbed, and the head always moves to the right in that. The 2nd tape of this Turing machine is used to simulate the NPDA stack, such that the symbols are added and removed from the rightmost position of the string on this 2nd tape. To keep the simulation simple, we can use a nondeterministic Turing machine. Such a simulation guarantees that there exists some deterministic Turing machine that can simulate the NPDA. Such a simulation guarantees that there exists some deterministic TM that can simulate the NPDA and therefore recognize the context-free language.

9.7 Computability

We have represented a deterministic Turing Machine as $M = (Q, \Sigma, \Gamma, \delta, q_0, H)$ and input as $w \in \Gamma^*$. This input results in finite computation (configurations) sequence $C_0, C_1, C_2, \ldots, C_m$, where each C_i is a configuration of M and C_0 is initial configuration. If this Turing Machine M succeeds to configuration C_m and halts, then the computation is successful with computation length m. We say, M has computed the result for the given input w, and this result is $f_M(w)$. Since M is deterministic, for inputs $w = x$, $f_M(w) = f_M(x)$.

Definition 9.14 (*Partial function*) If, for some $w \in \Sigma^*$, $f_M(w)$ is not defined because M halts and fails or does not halt, then f_M is a *partial function* from Σ^* to Γ^* and f_M is a function computed by M. □

Definition 9.15 (*Turing Computable function*) A function $f : \Sigma^* \rightarrow \Gamma^*$ is *Turing Computable*, if and only if there is a Turing Machine M, such that $f = f_M$. □

Definition 9.16 A set A is *computable* if there exists a TM M that behaves as follows:

$$M(x) = \begin{cases} 1, & \text{if } x \in A, \\ 0, & \text{if } x \notin A. \end{cases} \tag{9.7}$$

The computable sets are also called decidable or solvable. The TM like M is said to decide A.

Some examples of computable sets are:

1. The primes.
2. Fibonacci numbers (i.e., 1, 1, 2, 3, 5, 8, ...).
3. (x, y, n) such that TM $M_x(y)$ halts with n stops.
4. In fact, most of the sets we think are computable.

Are there any noncomputable sets? In fact, the number of SETS is uncountable, but the number of Computable SETS is countable. Thus, there must be some sets that are not computable! In fact, they are uncountable! We will discuss these in Chap. 12.

In general, a TM may be viewed as a computer of functions from integers to integers, that is

$$f : \mathbb{N}_0 \rightarrow \mathbb{N}_0. \tag{9.8}$$

The approach uses a representation of integers in unary format for $i \geq 0$, where integer i is represented by a string 1^{i+1}. If a function has k arguments $i_1, i_2, \ldots, i_k$, these arguments are initially placed on the tape separated by 0's, in the form:

$$1^{i_1}01^{i_2}0\ldots01^{i_{k-1}}01^{i_k}. \tag{9.9}$$

Given this initial tape contents, and the initial state of the machine as q_0, if the TM halts in state q' with ID (Instantaneous description) $q'1^{m+1}$, then it shows that the value m has been computed by the function f:

$$f(i_1, i_2, ..., i_k) = m. \tag{9.10}$$

Example 9.11 Turing Machine computes functions.

The function $\mathbb{N}_0 \times \mathbb{N}_0 \rightarrow \mathbb{N}_0$ defined by $f(x, y) = x + y$ is Turing computable. Also, a Turing Machine can be constructed to compute the function $f : \mathbb{N}_0 \times \mathbb{N}_0 \rightarrow \mathbb{N}_0$ defined by $f(x, y) = x * y$.

In the same line, any polynomial function $f : \mathbb{N}_0 \rightarrow \mathbb{N}_0$ defined by $f(x) = a_0 + a_1x + a_2x^2 + \cdots + a_nx^n$ can be computed by a Turing Machine, hence the function is Turing computable. □

It may be noted that TM can compute a function of one argument or a different function of two or more arguments. For a function of k arguments, all the k-tuples need not have values. A function with all the arguments present, is called *total recursive function*, whereas a function with some of the tuples having values, is called *partial recursive function*. All the arithmetic functions, like $[\log n]$, n^2, 2^n etc., are total recursive functions.

The total recursive functions correspond to Recursive Language, which causes the TM to halt always, whereas the partial recursive functions are like Recursively Enumerable languages and correspond to TMs that may not halt on every input.

9.7.1 TM as Adder

Example 9.12 Given two positive integers x and y, construct a Turning Machine to computes the sum $x + y$.

We first choose a convenient way to represent x and y on the tape. We use a unary notation so that *weight* of each number is represented by a sequence of 1's, i.e., $\{1\}^+$. Therefore, $w(x), w(y) \in \{1\}^+$, $|w(x)| = x$, and $|w(y)| = y$.

It is assumed that $w(x)$ and $w(y)$ are placed on the tape in sequence with a "0" separating them. Initially, the TM is in state q_0, and the read-write head is positioned to the first character of $w(x)$. When computation is over, the result $w(x + y)$ is placed on the tape with the read-write head positioned to the first character of the result $w(x + y)$ and a blank (B) is placed after result. Therefore,

$$q_0w(x)0w(y) \vdash^* q'w(x + y)B, \tag{9.11}$$

where q' is a accepting state at which TM halts. We note that the addition operation is simple. What is required is to move the separator 0 to the end, and replace it with B,

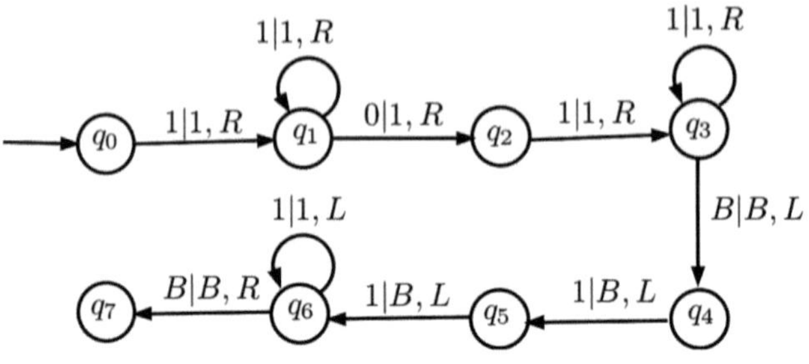

Fig. 9.8 TM to add two integers in unary format

so that $w(x)$ and $w(y)$ are concatenated. This results in $w(x + y)$. It is important to note that in the process of concatenation, one extra "1" gets appended, which needs to be removed, so that:

$$1^{m+1}.1^{n+1} \text{ results to } 1^{m+n+1} \text{ and not } 1^{m+n+2}.$$

Let the TM be,

$$M = (Q, \Sigma, \Gamma, \delta, q_0, H),$$

where

$Q = \{q_0, q_1, q_2, q_3, q_4, q_5, q_6, q_7\}$, $H = \{q_7\}$,
$\Sigma = \{0, 1\}$ and
$\Gamma = \{0, 1, B\}$.

The corresponding TM is shown in Fig. 9.8 and the transition function δ is given in Table 9.2.

In the process of moving 0 from middle of $w(x)$ and $w(y)$ to right, 1 gets added extra, this is deleted later.

Table 9.2 Transition table for unary addition

State	0	1	B
q_0	–	$(q_1, 1, R)$	–
q_1	$(q_2, 1, R)$	$(q_1, 1, R)$	–
q_2	–	$(q_3, 1, R)$	–
q_3	–	$(q_3, 1, R)$	(q_4, B, L)
q_4	–	$(q_5, 1, L)$	–
q_5	–	(q_6, B, L)	–
q_6	–	$(q_6, 1, L)$	(q_7, B, R)
q_7	–	–	–

Let us consider $x = 2$ and $y = 3$, hence $w(2) = 111$, and $w(3) = 1111$. All the moves, in sequence, of the TM are given as follows:

$$\begin{aligned} Bq_0 11101111 &\vdash B1q_1 1101111B \vdash B11q_1 101111B \vdash B111q_1 01111B \\ &\vdash B1111q_2 1111B \vdash B11111q_3 111B \vdash B111111q_3 11B \\ &\vdash B1111111q_3 1B \vdash B11111111q_3 B \vdash B1111111q_4 1B \\ &\vdash B111111q_5 1BB \vdash B11111q_6 1BBB \vdash B1111q_6 11BBB \\ &\vdash B111q_6 111BBB \vdash B11q_6 1111BBB \vdash B1q_6 11111BBB \\ &\vdash Bq_6 111111BBB \vdash q_6 B111111BBB \vdash Bq_7 111111BBB \end{aligned} \tag{9.12}$$

This shows that, the sum of the numbers 2 and 3 is computed as 5 ($wt(5) = 11111 = 1^6$). □

Note that, we have considered x and y as finite numbers (greater than zero). When zero is one of the arguments, the representation is unary 1. For $|x| + |y|$ the final result is 1^{x+y+1}.

Further, the number of the configurations through which the TM goes are 19 (see Eq. 9.12), and number of transitions or moves are 18. However, the unique transitions are 10, thus, total 10 *elementary instructions* have been executed to compute the function $f(x, y) = f(2, 3)$. Note that, as the size of numbers x and y increases, the looping along the states q_1, q_3 and q_6 will increase linearly. However, the total number of unique transitions (number of unique instructions) will remain unchanged, i.e., the size of the program remains unchanged. Also, the Turing Machine to add two integers will remain unaltered irrespective of the size of the numbers being added.

Example 9.13 Find an expression for the number of steps (i.e., elementary instructions) carried out by the Turing Machine to sum two positive integers m and n.

For this we refer to Fig. 9.8. The counts of steps (moves) with respect to different states, including loops, as follows:

q_0 to q_1: 1
q_1 to q_1: m
q_1 to q_2: 1
q_2 to q_3: 1
q_3 to q_3: n
q_3 to q_4: 1
q_4 to q_5: 1
q_5 to q_6: 1
q_6 to q_6: $m + n + 1$
q_6 to q_7: 1

The sum total of the above steps is $2(m+n)+8$, where $m+n+2$ is total length of the input arguments, is same as the length of the input w. This gives complexity[6] of $O(n)$, for input $|w|=n$. □

9.7.2 TM as Subtracter

Example 9.14 Show that function $f : \mathbb{N}_0 \times \mathbb{N}_0 \rightarrow \mathbb{N}_0$ defined by $f(x, y) = x - y$ is Turing Computable.

The subtraction of $f(x, y) = x - y$ is performed as follows: if $x > y$, $f(x, y) = x - y$, else it is zero.

To demonstrate that the above subtraction function is Turing computable, we construct a Turing Machine that computes $f(x, y)$. We represent the integers x and y as unary numbers. The approach shall be: search the beginning of y and for each 1 in y go back to the start of x and delete a symbol 1. For subtraction to be possible, x should be always greater than y.[7] □

9.7.3 TM as Incrementer

Example 9.15 Construct a TM that increments a given binary number by unity.

Let the TM be $M = (Q, \Sigma, \Gamma, \delta, s, H)$, where $Q = \{q_0, q_1, q_2, q_3\}$, $s = q_0$, and $q_3 \in H$. We store the binary number to be incremented, in reverse order on the tape, i.e., its LSB (least significant bit) at the start of the tape. So, if number to be increased is 13 (i.e., 1101), it is stored on tape as 1011, with initial configuration as $Bq_0 1011B$. The possible transitions of this machine are given below.

1. While the RW head is moved to right, every 1 is replaced by 0, and when 0 is encountered, it is replaced by 1 and head moves back to begin without changing any bit value on tape.
2. If all bits are 1 then they are replaced by 0, and at end B is replaced by 1, and head scans back to begin of the string.
3. If there is only one B on tape, it is replaced by 1, and tape head returns back to first bit.

Figure 9.9 shows the transition diagram, and Table 9.3 is the transition table for this Turing Machine.

Note that, if $w = 101110$, it becomes 101111, and for $w = 110111$ the result is 111000, and for $w = 111111$, result is 1000000. □

---

[6] The term complexity will mean worst-case time complexity unless until it is specifically mentioned.

[7] For a negative result, the approach is same except that the negation sign has to be stored somewhere.

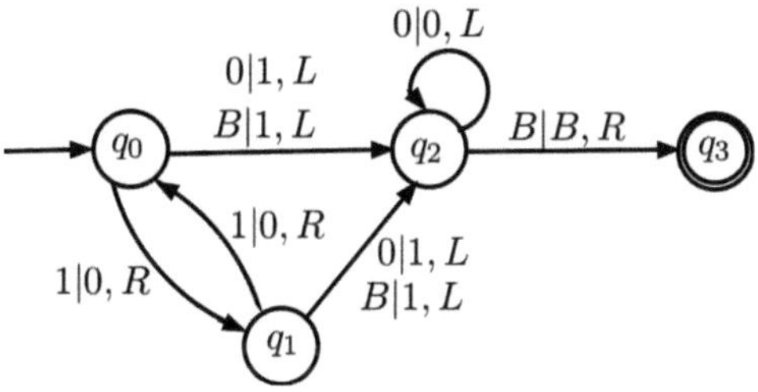

Fig. 9.9 TM to increment a binary number

Table 9.3 Transition table for Fig. 9.9

State	0	1	B
q_0	$(q_2, 1, L)$	$(q_1, 0, R)$	$(q_2, 1, L)$
q_1	$(q_2, 1, L)$	$(q_0, 0, R)$	$(q_2, 1, L)$
q_2	$(q_2, 0, L)$	–	(q_3, B, R)
q_3	–	–	–

9.7.4 TM as Concatenater

Example 9.16 Turing Machine to compute the concatenation function.

We compute the binary function of the concatenation of strings $u, v \in \{a, b\}^*$. The initial configuration is $q_0 BuBvB$. One or both or none of u and v may be null. The final configuration is $q_f BuvB$. The TM to concatenate two strings is shown in Fig. 9.10. □

9.8 Church-Turing Thesis

The intuitive notion of an algorithm is that it is an unambiguous mechanical procedure, with simple instructions for carrying out a computational task. This intuitive notion is adequate when we are required to design an algorithm to compute a problem. And, with this, we are always sure about whether a procedure is an algorithm or not. However, when we say that there exists no algorithm to compute a certain problem, the intuitive notion of an algorithm is not sufficient. Here, we require a precise definition of the algorithm. This is because when we say that no algorithm exists to solve it, we must be sure of all algorithms. That is impossible to answer unless, we have a precise definition of algorithm [2, 3].

The precise definition of an algorithm is given based on the Church-Turing thesis, which gives a connection between the informal nature of the algorithm and its formal (mathematical) counterpart, the computation. The Church-Turing thesis claims that what an algorithm computes is exactly, what TM computes, i.e.,

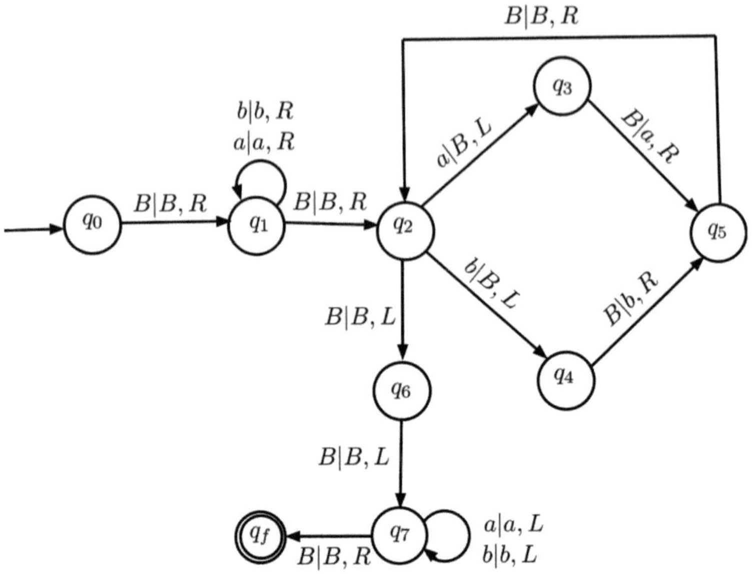

Fig. 9.10 TM to concatenate two strings

"Being computed by an algorithm ⇔ Being computed by TM".

As a definition, this can be specified as follows.

Definition 9.17 (*Church-Turing Thesis*) A function can be computed by an algorithm *iff* it can be computed by a Turing Machine. □

This above statement has two parts: "algorithm ⇒ TM", and " algorithm ⇐ TM". We can intuitively accept "⇐" of the Church-Turing thesis, because no matter what Turing machine is given, we can compute mechanically using it, to obtain the output.

The direction "⇒" means, whatever algorithm is given, we can describe a TM to infer this. However it is impossible to prove this direction because we do not have a precise definition of the algorithm. In other words, we cannot give counterexamples, i.e., there exist procedures as algorithms but cannot be described as Turing machines.

The Church-Turing Thesis takes the direction "⇒" as granted on the assumption that if it can be computed by an effective algorithm, then the Turing machine can compute it. Thus, the Church-Turing thesis is not what we can prove, but what we can admit.

However, there is evidence for this admitting:

1. no algorithm exists, which cannot be described by TM,
2. any algorithm can be described by TM,

3. several models have been defined independently, to define algorithms, which have been proved equivalent in power to TM (like RAM (Random Access Machine) model, RASP (Random Access Stored Program) machine), and,
4. all the independent models reveal that these models are natural, and robust, in the sense that their power is invariant.

9.8.1 Defining Church-Turing Thesis

The Church-Turing thesis has been defined in three different platforms:

(a) *Church-Turing thesis for Decision problem:* There is an effective procedure to solve a decision problem if and only if, for this, the TM halts for all input strings. The language accepted by this TM is Recursive (R).

A variant of this definition is: TM may halt for all instances of the decision problem for which the solution is Yes, and when No, it may halt or continue forever. Thus, it is a partial solution. Such a procedure is effective but not *complete*. In such case, the solution is formulated as membership to *recursively enumerable* (RE) language.
(b) *Church-Turing Thesis for Recognition problems:* A decision problem is partially solvable if and only if there exists a TM that accepts all instances of the problem whose answer is Yes.
(c) *Church-Turing thesis for Computable functions:* A function is effectively computable (Turing computable) if and only if there is a TM available that computes it.

As discussed above, the Church-Turing thesis is not a mathematical theorem, hence it cannot be proved. This would require a formal definition of the intuitive notion of effective procedure: a procedure which is *mechanistic, complete*, and *deterministic*.

The claim could however be disproved. This could be done by finding an effective procedure that cannot be computed by TM. However, due to the following reasons, such a procedure cannot be found:

1. The equivalence of TM to other algorithmic systems,
2. Robustness of TM architecture, and
3. the lack of any counter-example.

A proof (solution) by Church-Turing thesis is often a shortcut, in evidence of decision algorithm. Rather than constructing a TM solution to a decision problem, we describe an intuitively effective procedure that solves the problem. For complicated machines, we simply give a description of the actions of a computation of a machine, and we assume that a complete machine could be explicitly constructed.

9.8.2 *The Ultimate Computing Machine*

The Church-Turing thesis—a prevailing paradigm in computation theory, states that no realizable computing device can be "globally" more powerful, that is, aside from relative speed-ups than a Universal Turing Machine.[8] It is a thesis, and not a theorem, as it relates an informal notion—a realizable computing device, which is a mathematical notion. Rephrasing, the Church-Turing Thesis states that the Universal Turing Machine is an adequate model for discrete computation. Here are some reasons why the Church-Turing Thesis is universally accepted, and the TM is the ultimate computing machine:

- *Philosophical argument:* Due to Turing's analysis it seems very difficult to imagine some other method that falls outside the scope of this description.
- *Mathematical evidence:* Every mathematical notion of computability, which has been proposed was proven equivalent to Turing computability.
- *Sociological evidence:* No example of a computing device that cannot be simulated by Turing Machine has been given by anyone, i.e., the thesis has not been disproved or contradicted despite having been proposed over 70 years ago.

The Church-Turing Thesis includes a syntactic as well as physical claim. In particular, it specifies which types of computations are physically realizable.

9.9 Post Machine

A popular variant of Turing's formalism is due to mathematician Emil Post. In this formalism a machine is represented by a set of quadruples of the form $\langle q_i, S_j, X, q_t \rangle$, where q_i, S_j and q_t have the same meaning as in the quintuple model (i.e., the Turing Machine), i.e., q_i is current state, S_j is symbol under head position, and q_t is next state after transition has taken place. The X is either L, R or some symbol S_k. Other criteria for "well-definedness" are as before. If X is L or R the machine leaves the symbol under scan alone and moves left or right on the tape. If X is a symbol S_k then S_k is written on the square being scanned, i.e., S_j, but the machine does not move. Thus, in a single operation, a Post machine can only perform two of the three possible suboperations of a Turing Machine and it can never perform both suboperations (1) (i.e., a new symbol is written) and (2) (the scanning head moves to left or right), in the same transition.

Since many of the operations in a "typical" Turing Machine program tend to be searches along the tape for a specific symbol or combination of symbols, one seldom takes advantage of the quintuple machine's ability to write and to move on the same step. Thus, the number of quadruples in a Post machine would often be of the same order of magnitude as the number of quintuples in an equivalent Turing Machine, and

[8] The Universal Turing Machine is discussed in the next chapter in detail.

the description of the Post machine would take fewer characters than the description of the Turing Machine. For this reason, the Post formulation has been used relatively more often in the literature of computability theory [5].

Let us now seek some more precise statements about the relationship between Turing Machines and Post machines. The theorem is elementary.

Theorem 9.2 *For every m-symbol n-state Turing Machine there exists a Post machine with m symbols and at most* 3*n states which simulates the Turing Machine.*

Proof Let $S_0, S_1, ..., S_{m-1}$ be the symbols of the Turing Machine and $q_1, ..., q_n$ be its states. Then, the Post machine will have the same symbols as the Turing Machine and will have as states $q_1, ..., q_n$; $q_{1,L}, q_{2,L}, ..., q_{n,L}$; $q_{1,R}, ..., q_{n,R}$. For each quintuple $\langle q_i, S_j, S_k, D, q_t \rangle$ in the Turing Machine, the Post machine will have a quadruple $\langle q_i, S_j, S_k, q_{t,D} \rangle$. In addition, the Post machine will have mn quadruples of the form $\langle q_{l,L}, S_k, L, q_t \rangle$ and mn quadruples of the form $\langle q_{l,R}, S_k, R, q_t \rangle$ $(l = 1, 2, ..., n; k = 0, 1, ..., m - 1)$. The verification that the Post machine is well defined and exhibits the correct computational behavior (when given the same initial instantaneous description as the Turing Machine) is trivial. □

Although one can map Turing Machines into equivalent Post machines without increasing the number of symbols, it is not possible in general to find equivalent Post machines for Turing Machines without increasing the number of states.

In fact, there are other equivalences of the Turing Machines, e.g., the *D-Machines*, *S-Machines*, *U-Machines*, Universal Post Machine, and Universal Turing Machine [5], but they are not being covered here, the interested reader may consult the given reference. The Universal Turing Machine is covered in the next chapter.

9.10 Turing Machine Simulation

The Turing Machines can be simulated by programs written for a computer. The instruction set from which these programs are constructed consists of operations of two types: first type are *operations on the tape*, and the second are *program control* operations. There are no instructions that allow for program modifications during execution time.

In writing complicated programs for any computer it is desirable and often necessary to have an actual computer to check (debug) them on. This is true for programmed Turing Machines. As originally conceived by Turing, this abstract computer is equipped with a potentially one-way infinite tape that is divided up into squares. It performs its calculations on this tape by writing characters in the squares, and being able at any time to make decisions based on the finite number of characters (tape content) already written on the tape. The read-write head scans one character at a time.

Translating this general idea of a computer into a specific form we now specify: (1) the set of characters which may be written on the tape, (2) the programming language that it can interpret, and (3) conventions for using the tape.

1. *The Character Set*: The character set chosen was determined by programming and hardware considerations of the specific computer which is used in the simulation.

2. *The Programming Language:* This language consists of a certain basic set of instructions that are written down in the specified format. A Program is a basic sequence of these basic instructions. The basic instructions that were chosen were:

- Shift the head right or left for a specified number of positions,
- Write a character at the current position,
- Conditional transfer (i.e., if current symbol is so and then transfer control to specific instruction's address),
- Unconditional transfer to a specific address.

In writing the program for the Turing Machine, the instructions are listed in sequence and executed in sequential order except as changed by the transfer instructions. The symbolic address is written to the left of the instruction designated. The END signifies the program-end and causes the tape contents to be printed on the type-writer of the computer or teletype [6].

3. *Tape Conventions:* In the simulator, the Turing Machine tape consists of a finite string of digits in the RAM memory of the specific modern computer, two digits per tape square. The simulator initializes the tape by marking B's (blanks) in each square. Then the programmer's initial tape contents (i.e., data from the program) are read starting at the left end of the tape. When control is passed over to the machine program, the leftmost square is scanned first. Thus, the simulator provides a tape extending to the right. However, the programmer may use multiple tapes or a two-way open tape by marking off the tape in sections and programming accordingly. Note that B's are read in as part of the data.

The simulator program also handles the subroutines with variable arguments. More details can be seen in the reference [6], which describes a Turing Machine simulator, programmed on the IBM 1620 machine, but can be realized on any modern computer.

9.11 Computing Beyond the Turing Limit

The Church-Turing thesis, the prevailing paradigm in computer science, states that no realizable computing device can be more powerful than the Turing Machine. This excludes the relative polynomial speed-ups that are the result of richer instruction sets or parallel computation.

Extensive efforts have been made to prove that the Church-Turing thesis, which suggests that all realizable physical and dynamical systems cannot be more powerful than the classical models of computation. It is said that a highly chaotic dynamical system called *analog shift map*, has the computational power beyond the Turing limit. This machine computes exactly like neural networks and analog machines. The proposed model builds on a particular chaotic dynamical system, by applying the system to computer science, a "super-Turing" model can be developed. This model has practical and theoretical implications. Theoretically, it could open the doors for theories of computation that go beyond the Turing model. On the practical level, computers designed and built on the basis of super-Turing theories should be capable of modeling phenomena that existing computers are not powerful enough to model well.

The nonuniform Turing Machines exemplify such models: The machines receive on their tape, in addition to the input, another sequence w_n to assist in the computation. For all possible inputs of the same length n, the machine receives the same advice sequence w_n, but different advice is provided for input sequences of different lengths. The focus here is on nonuniform machines that compute in polynomial time, and use a polynomial long device, denoted by P/ply. For example, a super-Turing function that appears in P/poly is the "unary halting" function. Given a unary encoding of a computer program f and a sequence $x \in \{1\}^*$, the function determines whether the program terminates when acting on the sequence x. If both advice and time are exponentially long, i.e., 2^n, the advice can be used to indicate the desired response for each of the 2^n possible input strings of length n, and thus to compute all functions $f : \{0, 1\}^* \rightarrow \{0, 1\}$, including noncomputable ones [4].

9.12 Summary

The Turing Machine (TM) is an abstract mathematical model of the human brain; symbols on its tape correspond to numerical answers and to the intermediate results on the scratch paper used by humans to carry out such computations.

A TM consists of a read/write head that can move left and right, an infinite tape, and a control with a finite number of states. At any instance, a TM's head is pointing to a tape symbol, and the machine is in one of these states. The transition to the next state is decided by the current state and current symbol pointed to by the read-write head; on the transition to a new state, the head may modify the current symbol or may not. Since the head may move to left or right, it is not necessary for the read-write head to reach to end of the input string—the acceptance of input or "computation over" is indicated by a special state, called *halting state*.

The Turing Machine is a model of computation that serves to extend the limits of FA (Finite Automata) and Pushdown Automata, as it allows us to modify the tape locations by visiting them again and again, as we do in conventional programming languages. This is due to the read-write feature of the head.

The Church-Turing thesis says that in spite of having so many models of computation, no model is more powerful than the Turing Machine, thus the TM is the ultimate computing model.

A configuration in a TM is represented by quintuple $\langle q_i, a_j, a_k, D, q_t \rangle$, with q_i as current state and a_j as current symbol on tape, the head will write the symbol a_k

at the current position, and the machine will transit to next state q_t, and head will move to a position represented by symbol D, which may be equal to, head moves to right or left or remain stationary (no move). While processing the input, a Turing Machines moves from one configuration to another configuration. A configuration is $\alpha_1 q \alpha_2$, where strings α_1, α_2 are in tape alphabet, q is the current state of the machine, and head of the TM points to first symbol in α_2.

The tape of the Turing Machine has a left-end marker, however, to the right it may extend to infinity. Thus, it can hold arbitrarily large size input strings. The tape positions beyond the input are filled with blank characters, usually represented by "B".

The TM accepts the input if that input is given on the tape, the head is pointing to the first symbol, and with this, the machine goes through a sequence of configurations, and the last configuration is the halting configuration.

Similarly, a TM completes a computation, given the input on tape, if a sequence of configurations leads to the halting configuration. The tape contents at the end will be the result of computation.

A TM M accepts the language $L = L(M)$ if it halts on all the input w irrespective of whether w is or not in L, however it halts in an accepting configuration if $w \in L$. In the latter, it is said that TM *decides* L.

A language is called Recursively Enumerable (RE) if the corresponding TM halts on all the strings in that language, and for strings outside the language, it may loop indefinitely.

A decidable language is also called a Recursive (R) language.

A Turing Machine can compute a function, if it goes from its initial configuration to the final configuration through a sequence of steps, and the final configuration is accepting configuration.

The Church-Turing thesis emphasizes the above point further—a function can be computed by an algorithm iff it can be computed by a Turing Machine. In other words,

"Being compute by an algorithm $\Leftrightarrow$ Being computed by TM".

For any computation or language recognition carried out using TM, the total number of transitions/steps (elementary instructions) can be easily worked out in terms of the size of the input. A general expression for this is called the difficulty level of computation, or the *time complexity* of the computation.

The *Post machine* is a popular variant of Turing Machine, where a configuration, unlike the Turing Machine, is quadruple $\langle q_i, S_j, X, q_t \rangle$, where q_i, S_j, and q_t have same meaning as in the TM, and stand for previous state, symbol on tape, and new state, respectively. The X is either L or R or some symbol S_k, which shall be written at the correct head position.

Since the Post machine requires separate transitions for moving (left/right) and writing a symbol on the tape, compared to TM which performs write operations as well as left/right head moves in the same transition, the number of transitions or the elementary instructions executed in the Post machine for a given algorithm shall be more than the TM. So, the length of the program shall also be longer in the

Post machine. But, in the Post machine, each instruction is compact (4-tuple), which makes the description of the Post machine more compact than the TM.

A TM can be simulated on a modern computer; for this, the character set used in TM can be represented in encoded form, a program can interpret the TM instructions, and tape (one or more) can be represented as character array(s) in the computer's memory.

It has been undisputedly established that no realizable device can be more powerful than the Turing Machine. However, it may exclude one—it is said that a highly chaotic dynamical system called *analog shift map*, has computational power beyond the Turing Machine.

Self Review Questions

1. The tape of a TM is analogous to what component of modern computers?
2. Explain the following terms: Recursive Languages, Recursively Enumerable languages.
3. What is meaning of term "head crash", in a TM?
4. What is difference between *language acceptance* and *language recognition.*
5. Can some configuration of a Turing Machine repeat when it goes through a sequence of configurations? If yes, what are its consequences?
6. Can a general-purpose computer be simulated by a Turing machine?
7. What is upper bound of complexity $100n \log n$?
8. Can a Turing Machine ever write the blank symbol (B) on its tape?
9. Is it possible that for a TM that its tape alphabet $\Gamma = \Sigma$ (the input alphabet)?
10. Can the head of a Turing Machine ever stay on the same cell for two consecutive steps of a computation?
11. For the transition diagram given in Fig. 9.10:
    a. What is the number of configurations through which this TM goes?
    b. What is program size in terms of low-level instructions (transitions)?
12. Can a TM ever have only one state?
13. Can palindrome be recognized in linear time?
14. Can a TM recognize Palindromes in real time?[9]
15. Can a TM perform string matching in real time?
16. Give three examples in each:
    a. Total recursive functions.
    b. Partial recursive functions.
17. Is the *language acceptability*, a property of a TM or of the language?
18. What is the difference between the Post machine and the Turing Machine?
19. What is the idea of super-TM?

[9] A real-time Turing Machine is called *online* machine, and in addition, it makes only a constant number of steps between two readings.

Exercises

A. Concepts based Problems

Note: The $*$ marked exercises are provided with solutions at the end of this book.

1. What is difference between the complexity notations: Big-O, Ω, θ, small o, and ω? Give one example for each.
2. What are the characteristics of an effective procedure?
3. Construct a Turing Machine to invert the input, e.g., given any input string "10110" change it to "01001".
4. Show that the function $f : \mathbb{N}_0 \times \mathbb{N}_0 \rightarrow \mathbb{N}_0$ defined by $f(x, y) = x - y$ is Turing computable.
5. Give the transition table and draw the transition graph for the Turing Machine, for each of the following, for input alphabets $\Sigma = \{a, b\}$.

   a. Concatenate two input strings which are already there on the tape separated by a single blank symbol.
   b. Double the string $w \in \{a\}^*$ available on the tape (i.e., to transform into ww).
   c. Locate the first occurrence of consecutive characters aa in the input string, halt in accepting state on locating. If not found, halt in a non-accepting state.
   d. Recognize all strings consisting of even number of a's.
   e. Replace all the even position occurrences of as by bs.
   f. Insert a in the begin of string.
   g. Find out whether a given string is a palindrome.
   h. Accept all odd palindromes.

6. Let M be a Turing Machine defined by transition Table 9.4, with Read/Write head pointing to symbol B initially, and q_2 is the halting state.

   a. Give the state diagram for M.
   b. Trace the computations for inputs: $aabb$, $abab$, $bbaa$.
   c. Describe the language recognized by M.

7. Let $\Sigma = \{a, b\}$, and $u \in \{a, b\}^*$. Construct Turing Machines that compute each of the following functions:

   a. $f(u) = aaaa$
   b. $f(u) = u^R$.

8. Modify the TM in the Example 9.6 (Sect. 9.5), to recognize the following languages:

   a. $L = \{a^m b^n \mid m > n\}$.
   b. $L = \{a^m b^n \mid m < n\}$.

Table 9.4 Transition table for a TM

δ	B	a	b
q_0	q_1, B, R		
q_1		q_1, b, R	q_2, a, R
q_2			q_2, a, R

9. Modify the string copy operations shown in Fig. 9.7 (Sect. 9.5.3) to obtain *ww*, given that tape originally comprises string *w*.
10. Why the Church-Turing Thesis is universally accepted?

B. Analysis-based Problems

11. How the TM is considered as ultimate computing machine?
12. Explain the concept of the Church-Turing thesis. Why this is called a thesis and not a theorem?
13. For any given problem, will the Turing Machine have more instructions or the Post Machine?
14. What is the meaning of the following terms in the definition of *effective procedure*?

    a. mechanistic,
    b. complete, and
    c. deterministic.

15. In TM vs. Post Machine, which program will be longer for a given problem?
16. How will you convince that the following program segment cannot be implemented using pushdown automata but can be implemented using Turing Machine?

    - $x = 5;$
    - $y = x + 10;$
    - $x = x + 1;$
    - $y = y - 1;$

17. Are there computers or models more powerful than the Turing Machine? If yes, explain it.
18. For a given algorithm, which machine TM or Post machine, will have more number of:

    a. Configurations?
    b. Transitions?
    c. Unique transitions?

Table 9.5 Transition Table for some TM M

	a	b	B
q_0	q_1, b, R	q_1, b, R	Halt
q_1	q_1, b, R	q_0, b, L	q_0, B, L

19. Construct a TM to subtract unary number 1^{i+1} from 1^{j+1}. Both the numbers are available on the tape as $1^{i+1}\#1^{j+1}$, separated by symbol "#". Store the result at the end of the original input while separating the original input and result by symbol \$. The result is 1^{j-1+1} if $j \geq i$, else 1 (zero).

C. Proof-based Problems

20. Show that TMs that cannot write on the portion of the tape containing the input string, recognize only regular languages.
21. How a Turing Machine can be used as both a language recognizer and a function computer?
22. What is the difference between the Turing Machine and Post Machine? How they are equal to each other?
23. * Show that the function $inv(w)$ (string inversion), where $w \in \{a, b\}^*$, is Turing computable.
24. * Construct TMs for followings:

    a. * Recognizes a binary strings having equal number of 0's and 1's.
    b. * Recognize the language $\{ww^R \mid w \in \{0, 1\}^*\}$.
    c. * Recognize the language $\{w\#w \mid w \in \{0, 1\}^*\}$.
    d. * Multiplies two positive integers that are given in unary notation.

25. Which of the following languages is RE and the other is not? Give a logical explanation.

    a. $L_1 = \{M \mid L(M)$ contains at least 100 elements$\}$
    b. $L_1 = \{M \mid L(M)$ contains at most 100 elements$\}$

26. Show that the language $L = \{M \mid M$ halts on all inputs of length less than $100\}$ is RE.

D. Multiple choice Questions

27. A Turing Machine M has two states q_0 and q_1, of which q_0 is the starting state. The tape alphabet $\Gamma = \{a, b, B\}$ and its input alphabet is $\Sigma = \{a, b\}$. Table 9.5 is the transition table.

Which of the following statements is true about M?
(A) M halts on all strings ending with a
(B) M does not halt on any string in $(aa + b)^*$
(C) M halts on all strings ending with b
(D) M does not halt on any string in $(a + b)^+$

28. Which of the following statements is true for the language $L = \{a^p \mid p \text{ is a prime}\}$?
(A) L is not context-free, but a TM will accept it
(B) L is not accepted by any Turing Machine
(C) L is context-free but not regular
(D) L is regular but not context-free

E. Advanced Knowledge Assessment Problems

29. Give a design approach as to how you will construct a Turing Machine simulator on a modern computer.
30. Why the following problems are undecidable?
    a. Whether any given two algorithms compute the same function?
    b. Whether a given algorithm will ever get into an infinite loop on a given input x?
31. If a Turing Machine has n number of states, then an equivalent Post machine will have more or less a number of transitions. Derive an expression that shows this relation.

References

1. Turing AM (1936) On Computable numbers, with an application to the Entscheidunds problem. Proc Lond Math Soc Ser 2(24):230–265
2. Cooper BS (2012) Turing's titanic machine? Commun ACM 55(3):74–83
3. Dershowitz N, Gurevich Y (2010) A natural language approximation of computability and proof of Church's thesis. Bull Symb Logic 14(3):299–349
4. Siegelman HT (1995) Computation beyond the turing limit. Science 268:545–548
5. Fischer Patrick C (1965) On formalism for turing machines. J ACM 12(4):570–580
6. Curtis MW (1965) A turing machine simulator. J ACM 12(1):1–13
7. Hartmanis J (1968) Computational complexity of one-tape turing machine computations. J ACM 15(2):325–339

Chapter 10
Extensions of Basic Turing Machine

Abstract There exists many extensions/variants of standard Turing machine Model. These are 2-tape, 3-tape, and k-tape TMs; two-dimensional and multidimensional TMs; multi-track and two-way infinite tape TMs; nondeterministic TM and Universal TM. It is shown that these extension machines have the same problem-solving capability as the standard TM, in other words, they are in no way more powerful than the standard TM. These machines, however, require fewer number of steps (transitions) in comparison to standard TM, hence the complexity/difficulty of problem-solving through these machines may be lesser. This is due to the reason that most of these machines have capability to read/write on many tapes together, and make head movements together; in effect, do the parallel processing, like most modern computers do. The chapter also presents Universal TM, where the tape can hold encoding of some other TM; thus, a TM can be designed to simulate any other TM, in effect, it is like a subroutine/function call in conventional computer programs. The halting problem of TM proves that it is undecidable whether a TM will halt for some or all the inputs. The explanation of extended TMs are supported with worked out problems to strengthen their concepts. Also, there are number of exercises at the end of the chapter for practice, and review questions for self-assessment.

Keywords Multi-tape turing machine · Nondeterministic TM · Universal TM · Variants of turing machines · k-tape turing machine · Multi-track turing machine · Post-machine · Church–turing thesis · Turing machine encoding · Multidimensional turing machine · Turing machine simulation · Halting problem · Complexity of turing machine variants

K. R. Chowdhary, *Theory of Computation*,
https://doi.org/10.1007/978-981-97-6234-7_10

10.1 Introduction

Variations of Turing machine have been proposed to enhance the power of the Turing machine. It has been proved that the problems solved by these new models can also be solved by standard TM.[1] The solution processes used by these variants are mechanical procedures, and any mechanical procedure can be simulated on a basic Turing machine. This gives further strength to the basic TM that it is the ultimate TM [1]. Hence, TMs with multiple tapes, or multiple dimensions, or random access memory have problem-solving capability no better than the basic TM. In fact, a TM with nondeterminism is in no way better than the basic TM, though it guesses and therefore does not work purely on mechanical procedure. This fact was not verified even by Alan Turing himself.

One problem, which was not immediately solved by Turing's thesis was—different problem solvability by TM at different times. This corresponds to *rewritability* of programs in modern computers and the corresponding machine is called Universal Turing Machine.

Many variations have been proposed for TM extensions, over the standard Turing machine. The major extensions are as follows [6]:

1. *Post-Davis.* The machine cannot do both the works together, i.e., cannot change the symbol under scan and move along the tape on the same step. This is also called Post-Machine.
2. *Multiple-tape Turing Machine.* In this variant more than one tape is permitted, each tape having its own read–write head. Action of the machine depends on the internal state and the symbol scanned by each of the read–write head. The tape heads' motion directions are independent—in a step one tape head may move left, other right, while some other may remain stationary.
3. *Multiple-track Turing Machine.* There are multiple tracks, but there is only one read–write head which can move right–left on a track, and can move up–down to access different tracks.
4. *Multidimensional Turing Machine.* The tapes are multidimensional structures. In two-dimensional case, the place is marked off into squares and the permissible head motions are in four directions: $x, -x, y, -y$. For higher dimensions, higher coordinate system is used.
5. *Two-way infinite tape.* The tape is allowed two-way infinite (x and $-x$), with single read-write head.
6. *Nondeterminic Turing Machine.* The transitions are nondeterministic in nature.
7. *Universal Turing Machine.* When a Turing machine M can imitate the behavior of any other Turing machine M', then M is called Universal Turing Machine.

The fact that operations of a TM allow that all the above extensions can be simulated by a standard TM, suggests that the extensions do not give more power than a

[1] We will be using the terms "basic Turing machine" and "Standard Turing machine" both, as they are commonly used for the same purpose.

TM. The statement—"The extensions do not give us machines more powerful than the standard TM" is a theorem in the theory of computation. In the course of time, as we progress, we will be supported by evidences that this theorem is holds true. At some point of time, we will prove this theorem. The "powerful" here means problem-solving capability, and not the relative speed at which the TM computes. However, the extensions are helpful in designing machines to solve some particular problems.

Learning Outcomes of this Chapter:

1. Variants of TM. [Knowledge]
2. Two-tape TM. [Application], [Synthesis]
3. Multi-tape TM. [Application], [Knowledge]
4. Simulation of 3-tape TM by standard TM. [Application]
5. Nondeterministic TM. [Evaluation]
6. Universal TM and its simulation. [Analysis], [Evaluation]
7. Simulation of computer on TM. [Evaluation], [Analysis]
8. Halting problem. [Analysis]
9. Linear speedup. [Analysis]

10.2 Multi-tape Turing Machine

A Multi-tape Turing machine is an extension of the basic TM, it consists of more than one tapes and number of read-write heads equal to number of tapes, and each tape extending in infinite in one direction. Each tape is similar to the tape in a standard Turing machine, with cells that can hold symbols, and a read/write head that can move left or right. However, in a multi-tape TM, there are multiple independent tapes that can be read from or written to separately. On a single move, depending on the state of the finite control and symbol read from each tape, the machine performs following operations:

1. change the state to a new state,
2. write a symbol at the current head position on each tape, and,
3. each head either moves to right or left or remain stationary on the corresponding tape.

However, many a time one tape is considered for the original input string, and only read operation takes place on that, while manipulation of symbols takes place on other tapes through read-and-write operations. In each step (transition), the TM reads symbols scanned by two heads depending on the head positions, subsequently each head writes and moves R (right) or L (left), or remains stationary and the control-unit enters into a new state. Actions of R–W heads are independent of each other [5].

Table 10.1 Transition table of a 2-tape TM

δ	$[a, a]$	$[B, a]$	$[a, B]$	$[B, B]$
q_0	$(q_1, [a, b], [L, R])$	$(q_2, [b, B], [L, L])$	$(q_0, [b, B], [L, R])$	...

There are some key aspects and uses of multi-tape TM:

- They provide enhanced computational power—with multiple tapes, the machine can perform parallel operations and manipulate different pieces of information simultaneously. This can lead to more efficient algorithms and solutions for certain types of problems.
- Multi-tape Turing machines are particularly useful for language recognition tasks, such as parsing and analyzing programming languages and natural languages. E.g., each tape can represent a different aspect of the input or hold different types of information, allowing for more efficient and structured processing of the language.
- The multi-tape TMs are useful in study of computational complexity theory—they can define complexity classes and analyze the computational difficulty of problems that benefit from multi-tapes.
- The multi-tape TMs can simulate the parallel systems or processes. This is helpful for study and analysis of complex systems and their behaviors.

Let the head positions in a 2-tape TM are $[a, b]$, and the transition function δ is given by:

$$\delta(q_i, [a, b]) = (q_j, [a', b'], [d, d]),$$

where $d \in \{L, R\}$. Various moves of this 2-tape Turing machines can be typically given as shown in Table 10.1.

The multi-tape TMs are better suited for specific applications, e.g., copying string from one tape to another tape. However, their time-complexity remains P (Polynomial) only.

Figure 10.1 shows a k-tapes Turing machine , presently in state q_i, and k different heads points to k tapes.

A transition in a k-tape Turing machine, for number of tapes $k \geq 2$ is:

$$\delta : (Q - H) \times \Gamma^k \rightarrow Q \times \Gamma^{k-1} \times \{L, R\}^k. \tag{10.1}$$

There are k-tapes in the machine, and by convention the first one is *read-only*. It is the input tape containing the input to the machine. In the start configuration, it is assumed that all the reaming $k - 1$ tapes are empty. For function computation, the value of the computed function will be available on the kth tape at he end of the computation.

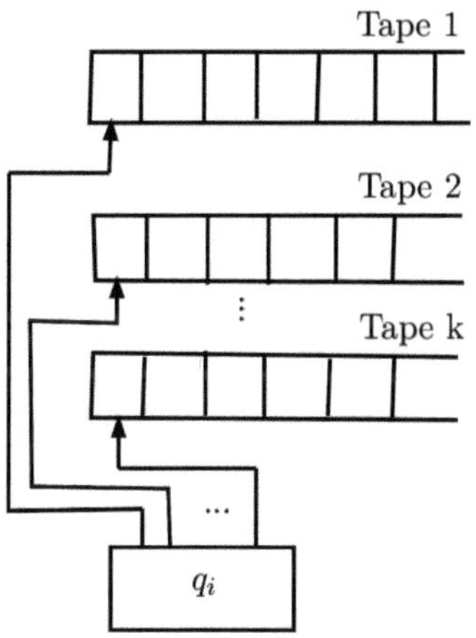

Fig. 10.1 k-tape turing machine

A specific transition is given by

$$\delta(q_i, a_1, \ldots, a_k) = (q_j, (a_1, b_2, \ldots, b_k), (d_1, \ldots, d_k)), \tag{10.2}$$

where $a_1, \ldots, a_k$ are original symbols on tapes $T_1, \ldots, T_k$, and $b_2, \ldots, b_k$ are new symbols written on these tapes T_2 to T_k, where as symbol a_1 remains unchanged on tape T_1. The heads of all tapes takes movements (displacements) d_1, ..., d_k, respectively, where $d_i \in \{L, R\}$.

Our first goal is to show that the standard deterministic Turing machine is as powerful as k-tape Turing machine, for any $k \in \mathbb{N}$, where $\mathbb{N}$ is natural number greater or equal to 1. We need to show that the languages accepted (decided) by the deterministic Turing machines are exactly those languages, which are accepted (decided) by the multi-tape TM. Formally, we show that for any multi-tape TM there exists a deterministic TM, and for any deterministic TM there exists a multi-tape TM. In other words, we show that one model simulates the other and vice versa, and that means the language accepted (decided) by one model is precisely the same as that of other model.

A computation is a sequence of configurations consisting of state, head position, and contents of tapes. The machine does not move after entering a *halt* state. A configuration with halt state is called *halting configuration*. A machine may never enter a halt state and run forever. Often our machines are deciders (compute total functions). Such machines halts on every input.

The machine accepts an input $w \in \Sigma^*$ if it starts from a start configuration and reaches an accept–halt configuration in finite number of steps given by

$$(q_0, w, u_{0_1}, \ldots, z_{0_{k-1}}) \vdash^* \ldots (q_h, (w, u_{n_{k-1}}, \ldots., z_{n_{k-1}}), (d, d, \ldots, d)), \tag{10.3}$$

where $d \in \{L, R\}$, $\vdash$ (called move) may be viewed as one-step computation, and $\vdash^*$ is reflexive–transitive closure of $\vdash$. We assume that tape-1 is read-only tape and there are total k tapes, which hold initially the contents w, u_{0_1}, ..., $z_{0_{k-1}}$, which in n transitions becomes w, $u_{n_{k-1}}$, ..., $z_{n_{k-1}}$.

Theorem 10.1 *A language is recursively enumerable if and only if some multi-tape Turing machine accepts it.*

Proof We know that language accepted by standard TM is RE (Recursively Enumerable). We begin by showing that the multi-tape Turing machine model is as powerful as the standard Turing machine. Clearly, a standard Turing machine is a 1-tape Turing machine. So every language accepted by a standard deterministic Turing machine is also accepted by some multi-tape Turing machine. For this, we simply ignore all the tapes in multi-tape TM except the first.

To prove the converse, i.e., for every multi-tape Turing machine $M = (Q, \Sigma, s, \delta, \Gamma, H)$, there exists an equivalent standard Turing machine M', we need to show that M'accepts the same language as that is accepted by M. As M has k-tapes, it is necessary to represent the strings on each of the k-tapes on to a single tape. It is also necessary to represent the placement of each of the k-tape heads of M on single tape of M'. This is done by using a special marker to mark the position of virtual heads in M' to represent the k-heads' positions of k-tapes. For each symbol $\gamma \in \Gamma$, we include two symbols γ and γ' in Γ', where γ' indicates the tape head position in M that is pointing to the character γ. We then have a special delimiter symbol # in M', that separates the strings of each of the k-tapes on single tape of M'. Considering that Γ' as tape alphabet of M', there is $|\Gamma| = 2|\Gamma| + 1$. The standard Turing machine M' simulates the k-tape TM M in the following manner:

- M' scans the tape from first delimiter to the last delimiter to determine which symbols are marked as under the tape heads on M,
- M' then evaluates the transition function of M, then makes a second pass along the tape to update the symbols on the tape,
- If at any point, the tape head of M' falls on a delimiter #, M would have reached the end of that specific tape. So M' shifts the string, cell by cell, starting at the current delimiter inclusive. A blank symbol is then overwritten on the delimiter.

Thus, M' simulates M. Hence any language accepted by a multi-tape Turing machine is accepted by a standard Turing machine. This proves the theorem. □

10.2.1 Two-tape Turing Machine

A 2-tape Turing machine has two read/write tapes, and corresponding two read/write heads and control, that occupies one of the states at a time. After each transition, the read/write heads will write a symbol in their current positions, then moves to right both or left both, or one left and other right, and the machine changes state from q_i to q_j [4].

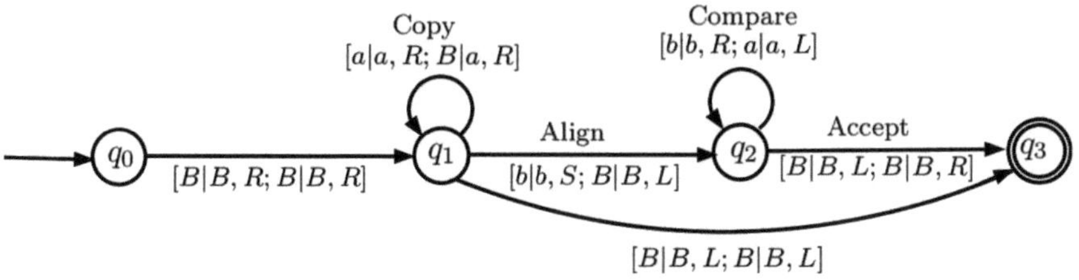

Fig. 10.2 Two-tape TM to recognize language $L = \{a^n b^n \mid n \geq 0\}$

$$\delta(q_i, [a, b]) = (q_j, [a', b'], [d, d]),$$

and $d \in \{L, R\}$.

Example 10.1 Construct a 2-tape TM to recognize the Language $L = \{a^n b^n \mid n \geq 0\}$.

The approach which we will use is as follows: We copy all the a's from input tape to tape 2. By this the read/write heads on both the tapes are at the middle. Next, we align the first head to 1st b and 2nd head to last a on their tapes, and move these in opposite directions. If both the heads reach to symbol B together, then number of a's and B's are equal, and all b's follow to a's. So, input must be accepted.

With the original string w on tape 1, the transitions (instructions) performed by the TM are shown in Fig. 10.2, and major steps are as follows:

1. *Copy:* Copies the string of all a's on tape-1 to tape-2.
2. *Align:* Moves head 1 to begin of b's on tape-1, and head-2 on last a on tape-2.
3. *Compare:* Compares number of b's tape-1 (while moving the head to R direction) with number of a's on tape-2 by moving this head in L direction.

The *time complexity* of this TM is computed as follows: There are total $1 + (n) + 1 + (n) + 1 = 2n + 3$ transitions for an input string $|w| = 2n$. Thus, for $|w| = n$, number of transitions are $n + 3$, as the constant factor 3 remains unchanged. So, the time-complexity is $O(n + 3) = O(n)$, which is *Polynomial* in time, i.e., P. Therefore, $\{a^n b^n \mid n \geq 0\}$ can be decided in time $O(n)$ with a 2-tape TM. Note that for $n = 0$ the TM reaches to halting state in two transitions. □

Compare the above computed complexity with that of example (Sect. 9.5.1), of $O(n^2)$ for standard TM for the same problem. We note that in 2-tape TM it is linear, i.e., its complexity increases proportional to size of input, while in standard TM it increases quadratically with the size of the input, however in both the cases it is in P.

10.2.2 Simulation of 3-Tape TM using a Standard TM

Example 10.2 Simulation of a 3-tape Turing machine M by standard deterministic Turing machine M'.

Let the contents of a 3-tape TM M be as follows:

1. Tape 1 holds: $\mathbf{0}1010B$
2. Tape 2 holds: $aa\mathbf{a}B$.
3. Tape 3 holds: $\mathbf{b}aB$.

The bold symbols in all the above three tapes indicate the position of R/W head.

Let a standard Turing machine M' simulates the 3-tape Turing machine M. The contents of standard Turing machine, having single tape shall be as follows:

$$\mathbf{0}1010\#aa\mathbf{a}\#\mathbf{b}aB.$$

Here, # is separator for contents of three tapes when kept on single tape. In practice, the tape of Standard TM M' leaves an extra blank before each symbol in strings (01010, aaa, ba) to record the position of virtual read-write heads corresponding to original Tapes 1, 2, 3. The R/W head of M' reads the symbols under the three virtual heads left to right. Next, the head on M' makes a second pass to update the tapes according to the way the transition function of M dictates [5].

If, at any point of time, Turing machine M' moves any of the virtual heads to the right of symbol #, it implies that head has moved to unread blank portion of that tape. So, M' writes a blank symbol in the right most of that tape, then continues to simulate. Using this approach, we simulate the 3-tape Turing machine M on standard Turing machine M'. However, it is clear that control will require a lot more states in standard TM when it simulates a 3-tape TM.

It is left as an exercise as what will be the complexity of M' when 3-tape TM M is simulated on M'. □

In 3-tape TM, tape-1 holds the input, the 2nd is used as working tape (scratch pad), and the 3rd is for simulations. In the next example, we make use of 3-tape TM to recognize the input w whether it belong to the language of perfect squares $\{a^1, a^4, a^9, a^{16}, \ldots\}$.

Example 10.3 Construct a 3-tape TM to recognize the set $\{a^n \mid n \text{ is a perfect square}\}$.

Tape T_1 holds the input, tape T_2 holds progressive a^{k^2} (for $k = 1, 2, 3...$) and tape T_3 the progressive a^k, for $k = 1, 2, 3, ...$ (see Fig. 10.3).

1. Initialize tapes $T_2 = T_3 = a$. (i.e., $k = 1$)
2. Input tape T_1 (i.e., $|T_1|$) is compared with that of T_2, by scanning both tapes. If $|T_2| = |T_1|$, accept and terminate, else if $|T_2| > |T_1|$, reject input and terminate (else it is, $|T_2| < |T_1|$, so go to next step).

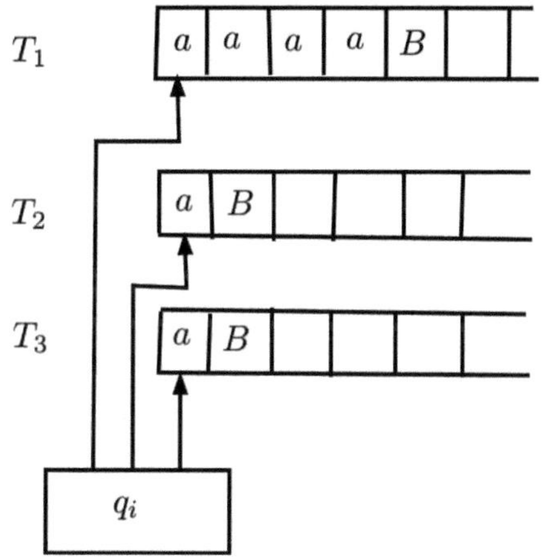

Fig. 10.3 Three-tape TM to recognize the language a^{k^2}

3. Append tape T_2 with $2 \times T_3$. This changes tape T_2 contents from current value a^{k^2} to a^{k^2+2k}.
4. Append the symbol a to tape T_2 as well to T_3. This changes contents of T_2 to $a^{k^2+2k+1} = a^{(k+1)^2}$, and tape T_3 to $k + 1$.
5. Go back to Step-2
6. End.

We have shown that the tape T_3 increments its contents to next integer $k + 1$ every time, and tape T_2 builds the its square $(k + 1)^2$. At any moment, if $T_2 = T_1$ then T_1 is holding a square number, else if $T_2 > T_1$, then we have exceeded the input size, hence the process should be terminated with rejection of input. □

The students are advised to take $w = a^4$, $w = a^{16}$ and $w = a^{10}$, and manually run the steps of above algorithm to see that its works correctly.

10.2.3 k-Tape Turing Machine

If the k-tape Turing machine takes n-steps for solving a problem (for input $|w| = n$), then each tape uses at most $n + 1$ steps. So, the equivalent standard Turing machine constructed in the proof of Theorem 10.2 takes total

$$n.(n + 1)^2 = O(n^2)$$

steps, i.e., time $DTIME(n^2)$. This is time-complexity of standard TM, i.e., for the deterministic Turing machine.

Theorem 10.2 *Let L be decided by k-tape Turing machine M in time $t(n)$. Then L can be decided by a single-tape Turing machine M' in time $ck(t(n)^2)$, where c is some constant.*

Proof Let us take $k = 3$. The 3-tape Turing machine M has the following initial configuration on input $x = a_1a_2...a_n$.

$$(q_{0M}, (\#x, B), (\#, B), (\#, B)). \tag{10.4}$$

Let the tape alphabet of M be $\Gamma = \{\#, B\} \cup \Sigma$, where Σ is input alphabet, B is blank, and # is left-end marker on tape. We take $\Gamma \cup \overline{\Gamma}$ as the tape alphabet of the single-tape Turing machine M', where $\overline{\Gamma} = \{\overline{\gamma} : \gamma \in \Gamma\}$. These new symbols represent virtual heads' positions of k-tapes of M on M'. The encoding of the initial configuration of single-tape machine M' is $(q_{0M'}, (\#x, B))$ as usual. But M' converts it to encode the initial configuration of M as

$$(p_{0M}, (\#\#\ x\ \#\ \#), B), \tag{10.5}$$

where three #s indicate three virtual heads' positions of M in M', and the leftmost # is for the left-end marker on tape.

Let the following be a general configuration of M:

$$(q, (\#\gamma_{11}...\gamma_{1i_1}..., i_1), (\#\gamma_{21}...\gamma_{2i_2}..., i_2), (\#\gamma_{31}...\gamma_{3i_3}..., i_3)). \tag{10.6}$$

This is encoded in M' as

$$(p, (\#\#\gamma_{11}...\overline{\gamma}_{1i_1}...\#\gamma_{21}...\overline{\gamma}_{2i_2}....\#\gamma_{31}...\overline{\gamma}_{3i_3}..., B)), \tag{10.7}$$

where three heads' positions are captured by $\overline{\gamma}_{1i_1}, \overline{\gamma}_{2i_2}, \overline{\gamma}_{3i_3}$, respectively. The beginning of virtual tapes $k = 1, 2, 3$ are marked by "#", and the left-end marker of tape of M' is shown by leftmost #.

To simulate a move of M, the machine M' scans the input and identifies the symbols corresponding to three heads of M, and go to a corresponding state. Note that if Γ has m symbols, then Γ' has $(2m).k$ symbols. In the second pass it makes three updates by shifting head positions of M and modifying the symbols under the head and comes back to the leftmost cell [7].

If M at some point writes in the first blank cell at the end of the ith tape, then in M' the contents of $(i + 1)th$ tape onwards are to be shifted by one cell.

Since the maximal number of cells in use is the running time of M, i.e., $t(n)$, M' will spend maximum time $2t(n)$ for a single operation of M. Since there are k-tapes, this time shall be $k.2t(n)$. Considering some house keeping operation corresponding to each move of M, maximum time for M' is $c2kt(n)$, for $c > 1$.

Yet other simple, direct inference is: each move of M is simulated in $t(n)$ time on M', thus to simulate $t(n)$ moves of M, the M' requires $t(n)^2$ time. □

10.3 Linear Speedup

The linear speedup theorem, also known as the *time-hierarchy* theorem, is a result in the theory of computation that states that for certain types of computational problems, there exist algorithms that can solve them faster with more resources. More specifically, the theorem states that, given a problem that can be solved by a Turing machine within a certain time bound, there exists a Turing machine that can solve the same problem within a shorter time bound, specifically in a linear speedup. The time complexity of the problem is reduced by a constant factor, resulting in a faster algorithm.

The linear speedup theorem is significant in the theory of computation as it shows that for certain problems, there is room for improvement in terms of time complexity. It suggests that by utilizing additional computational resources or employing more sophisticated algorithms, it is possible to achieve faster solutions. This result helps establish the theoretical possibilities of optimizing algorithms and provides insights into the relationship between time complexity and computational resources.

The linear speedup theorem says that, for any constant c, you can decide the language c times faster. It does not say that you can make it faster by some non-constant function. The speedup theorem works for a TM M, by defining a new Turing machine N, that writes c characters of the old Turing machine in a single-tape cell, and then adjusting the transition function so that it simulates in a single step everything that the original machine did between entering and leaving each c-character block. If c is a constant, it does not depend on the input, so you just compute the new machine once and use it on whatever input you want.

Definition 10.1 The *linear speedup theorem* for Turing machines states that given any real number $c > 0$ and any k-tape Turing machine solving a problem in time $t(n)$ (t is a time function of n), there is another k-tape machine that solves the same problem in time at most $t(n)/c + 2n + 3$, where $k > 1$. □

If the original machine is nondeterministic, then the new machine is also nondeterministic. The concrete constants 2 and 3 in $2n + 3$ can be lowered, for example, to $n + 2$.

The construction of new Turing machine N is based on packing several tape symbols of the original machine M into one tape symbol of the new machine.[2] It has a similar effect as reading and processing longer instructions in parallel processing machines, thus, it speeds up the computations but increases the machine size. How many symbols of machine M are packed to construct a new symbol of N depends on the desired speedup.

Theorem 10.3 *Let M be a k-tape Turing machine, $k > 1$, that accepts language L with time $t_M(n) = t(n)$, for input of size n. For any constant $c > 0$, there is another k-tape Turing machine N that accepts L with time $t_N(n) = \lceil ct(n) \rceil + 2n + 3$.*

---

[2] This is similar to shifting from 16-bit machine to 32-bit or 64-bit in modern computers, such that instead of reading/writing 16-bits, the machine reads/writes 32-bits or 64-bits together.

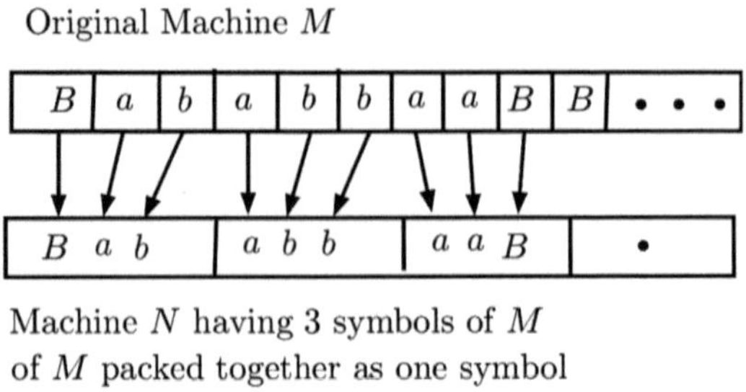

Fig. 10.4 Linear speedup

Proof If alphabet of old machine M with k-tape ($k > 1$) is Σ and new machine N with k-tape packs three old symbols ($m = 3$) as one symbol then alphabet of the new machine is $\Sigma \cup \Sigma^3$. A state of N consists of the following components:

- the state of M;
- for each of the k tapes, m-packed symbols corresponding to the symbols on original tape at head position, and m-tuple to left and m-tuple to right of head (Fig. 10.4 shows this for $k = 2$), and
- in each of the $i = 1, ..., k$ tapes, a position i_j in the m-tuple currently scanned by M that corresponds to currently scanned m-tuple in N.

The new machine N starts with encoding the original input into a new alphabet, due to which its alphabet must include Σ.

The steps of operation of new machine N are as follows:

1. The machine N packs a tuple of three old symbols (e.g., B, a, b into a new symbol (B, a, b)) and copies it to the second tape, while erasing the first tape. This leaves the original tape blank (see Table 10.2). This takes $n + 1$ steps, where input $|w| = n$. The symbol following the w is B, and # is left-end marker of tape). Thus, effectively this compresses the input w to the size of n/m.
   Table 10.2 shows the tape configuration of 2-tape machine M and corresponding input configuration of 2-tape machine N:
2. At the end of the initialization, the *new machine* directs its head to the beginning. This takes $1 + n/m$ steps.

Table 10.2 Linear speedup: symbols mapping from machine M to N

	Machine M	Machine N
Tape-1	[$\#BababbaaB$...]	[$\#(B, B, B)\ (B, B, B)\ (B, B, B)$...]
Tape-2	[$\#BBBBBBBBB$...]	[$\#(B, a, b)\ (a, b, b)\ (a, a, B)$...]

Overall, this takes $n + 1 + 1 + n/m = n + 2 + n/m$ steps.
Now the machine N simulates the machine M.

i. There are 4-steps: (L, R, R, L) to read relevant symbols of left and right, "remember" in state,
ii. 2-steps (L, R or R, L) to make N's changes.

Together, these makes 6-steps.
The accounting of time is as follows:

- copying along with packing: $n + 2$ steps,
- returning back to original place: n steps,
- simulation: $6(f(n)/m)$ steps,
- Set $m = 6/c$, thus, total = $cf(n) + 2n + 2$ steps. □

As in the case of k-tape to 1-tape reduction, encode k-tuple of symbols of M as single symbols of M' (effectively increasing the size of alphabet). First, rewrite the input in this form (this takes $n + n/k + 2$ steps). Now, to simulate k-steps of the old machine, notice that k-steps of the old machine effect only three cells of the new machine. It takes 6-steps of the machine to read and overwrite these cells with new information, as for three symbols, there are three virtual heads, making it six. Now, set $k = 6/c$. Then the total time of M' on input of size n is at most $cT_M(n) + n + 2$. This proves the theorem.

We have noted that in solving the problem using standard TM (i.e., one tape) it took $DTIME(n^2)$ time, while using two tapes it is $DTIME(n^1)$. Both the terms are in polynomial form. All the polynomial forms are from set $\{n^k \mid k \in \mathbb{N}\}$. This is called a polynomial class of problems, i.e., a class consisting of those problems that are solvable in polynomial time, and expressed as

$$\mathsf{P} = \bigcup_{k\in\mathbb{N}} DTIME(n^k). \tag{10.8}$$

The time to recognize the language $\{a^k b^k \mid k \geq 0\}$ using standard Turing machine is $O(n^2)$, i.e., $DTIME(n^2)$, while for the language $\{a^k \mid k \mod 5 = 0\}$ it is $O(n)$ or $DTIME(n)$. Using linear speedup theorem we know that for k-tape Turing machine ($k \geq 2$), by varying the tape count there is only linear speedup, hence its worst-case computation time remains polynomial in time.

We have following lemma from above theorem.

Lemma 10.1 *A k-tape TM provides a linear speedup for any problem that is solved on single-tape deterministic Turing machine.*

Proof *Proof idea.* One step of new k-tape Turing machine is linear in running time of the standard TM, i.e., $t(n)$. Hence the total time in standard TM for n-steps in k-tape machine will be, $t(n).t(n) = O((t(n))^2$. □

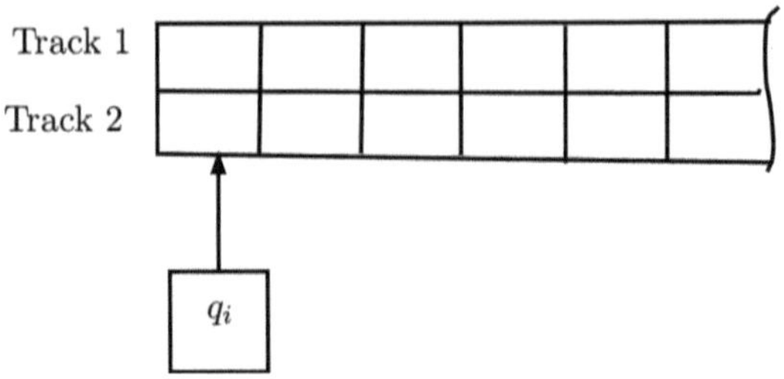

Fig. 10.5 Two-track turing machine

10.4 Multiple-track Turing Machine

Figure 10.5 show a two-track TM, where a tape is divided into two tracks. In general a tape position in n-track tape contains n symbols from tape alphabets at the head position. A head position in two-track is represented by $[a, b]$, where a is symbol in track-1 and b is in tack-2. The tuple Q, Σ, Γ, q_0, F of a two-track machine is same as for standard machine. A transition in a two-track machine reads and writes the entire position on both the tracks.

The transition function δ is defined as: $\delta(q_i, [a, b]) = [q_j, [a', b'], d]$, where $d \in \{L, R\}$. The input for two-track is put at track-1, and all positions on track-2 are initially blank. The acceptance in multi-track is by final state.

The languages accepted by two-track machines are *Recursively Enumerable* languages.

Theorem 10.4 *A language is accepted by a two-track TM M' if and only if it is accepted by a standard TM M.*

Proof *Part 1* : If L is accepted by standard TM M then it is accepted by two-track TM M' also.

For this, simply ignore 2nd track. Hence, track content is tuple $[a, B]$.

Part 2: If a language L is accepted by 2-tape TM M', then it is also accepted by a standard TM M.

Let $M' = (Q, \Sigma, \Gamma, \delta', q_0, H)$ be two-track machine, we want to find one equivalent standard TM M. For this, create ordered pair $[a, b]$ on single-tape machine M, where

$$M = (Q, \Sigma \times \{B\}, \Gamma \times \Gamma, \delta, q_0, F)$$

with δ as

$$\delta(q_i, [a, b]) = \delta'(q_i, [a', b']).$$

This proves the theorem. □

10.5 Nondeterministic Turing Machine

A nondeterministic Turing machine (NTM) is a theoretical construct in computation. While a deterministic Turing machine follows a single path of execution for a given input, a NTM can have multiple possible paths of execution for the same input. In other words, NTM can explore multiple possible paths of execution for the same input, simultaneously. The primary use of NTM is in complexity theory, specially in classification of computational problems based on their difficulty level. The non-determinism allows for exploration of different paths and provides potentially more efficient algorithms for solving certain problems.

Some of the common applications of NTM are as follows:

- NTMs help define the complexity classes, such as P and NP, which play crucial role in understanding the tractability of computational problems and existence of such efficient algorithms. The nondeterminism can be a useful concept for designing algorithms and problem-solving strategies,
- it allows for exploring multiple potential solutions in parallel, which can lead to more efficient algorithms in certain cases,
- NTMs can be used to verify correctness of algorithms, because they can explore all possible execution paths simultaneously and can determine if a given solution exists for a particular problem, and
- NTMs can be used to study the properties and limitations of computation as they provide a powerful tool for understanding the boundaries of what can and cannot be computed efficiently.

In practice, deterministic algorithms are typically used for solving real-world problems, but NTMs help in understanding of computational complexity and the theoretical possibilities of efficient computation.

Prototypical examples of difficult problems are those belonging to the class that can be solved in polynomial (P) time if a hypothetical Turing machine—named nondeterministic Turing machine (NTM)—could be built. They are classified as nondeterministic polynomial time (NP) problems, and the machine is hypothetical because, unlike a deterministic Turing machine, it requires a fictitious "oracle" that chooses which path the machine needs to follow to get to an appropriate state. In Fig. 10.7b there are many alternate likely paths for NTM, but it some how through oracle, chooses the correct path and accepts the input, when input is in the language of the machine. However, in DTM (Fig. 10.7a) there is only one path for a given input.

To date, it is not known whether NP problems can be solved in polynomial time by a deterministic Turing machine. If that were the case, we could finally provide an answer to the most outstanding question in computer science, namely, whether $\mathsf{NP} = \mathsf{P}$.

A nondeterministic TM (NTM) M has the same structure as that of a basic Turing machine with finite control, read-write head, and one-way infinite tape (see Fig. 10.6). The only difference is that, for a given present state and input symbol pointed by

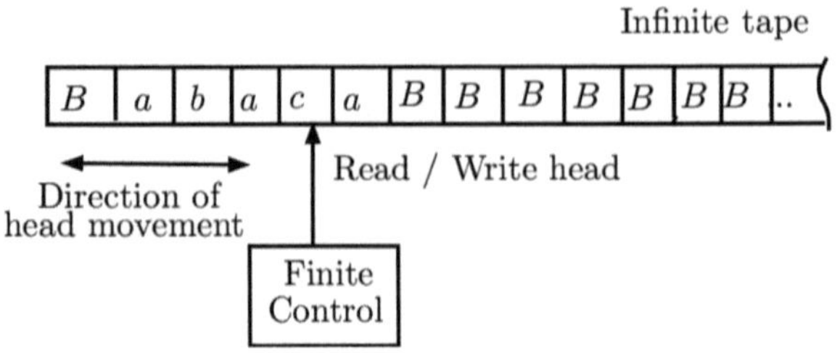

Fig. 10.6 Nondeterministic turing machine model

read/write head, instead of a single next state there is a set of next states, a set of symbols written, and set of left–right head movements, represented by the following transition:

$$\delta(q, a) = \text{ subset of } \{(q_1, a_1, d_1), (q_2, a_2, d_2), \ldots, (q_n, a_n, d_n)\}, \tag{10.9}$$

where $q_i (i = 1, n)$ is a next state, a_i is a symbol written in place of a, and $d_i \in \{L, R, S\}$, is displacement for $1 \leq i \leq n$.

Alternatively, it is also represented by

$$\delta : (Q - H) \times \Gamma = 2^{Q \times \Gamma \times \{L, R, S\}}. \tag{10.10}$$

Similar to DFA, addition of nondeterminism to Turing machine does not make it able to recognize new languages, nor does it give it capability to perform any new computations. Neither, adding new features like multiple tapes and heads, two-way infinite tape, etc., give any additional power to a Turing machine. The power here means the problem-solving capability, and not the number of computing steps or the speed of computation.

We will show that the deterministic and nondeterministic variants of the Turing machine are equally powerful. The proof of this is by simulation. Before we go for the proof, let us conceptualize this fact. In the 1st chapter we introduced graph theory, and in the Chap. 2 we arrived at the intuition for understanding of what is meant by a string to be accepted by a machine. We also discussed about what we mean by acceptance of string by a nondeterministic automaton. The definition of string acceptance by a nondeterministic Turing machine says about existence of a choice string such that the nondeterministic Turing machine would reach to accepting state q_f from the starting state q_0. The graph theory analog for this is existence of a path for the input string from q_0 to q_f.

The way a deterministic Turing machines can simulate a nondeterministic Turing machine is through, essentially a BFS (breadth first search). A multi-tape deterministic Turing machine is used to simulate a nondeterministic Turing machine.

An NTM M has finite number of choices of moves from any given configuration, but it has same parts as the standard TM, and may have more than one moves for any "input, state pair" ($Q \times \Gamma$). To be precise, a nondeterministic Turing machine may proceed according to several possibilities, and the machine accepts a string if there exists a path from start configuration to an accepting configuration.

Nondeterminism in NTM is like it is in FA and PDA. A NTM machine accepts by halting if there is at least one computation sequence that halts normally when run with input w.

10.5.1 Computation Paths

Figure 10.7a shows the transitions of computations in a deterministic Turing machine M', where there is only one path, based on input and that decides the problem. For example, to find out if a given integer is in the set of primes. The answer is "Yes" or "No" depending on the integer being prime or not; if "Yes", the machine halts in accepting configurations, else it halts in rejecting configuration.

If above problem is solved using NTM M, there may be more than one paths of sequence of transitions for a given input, which may terminate in rejecting configuration. But, if there is at least one path that leads to accepting configuration, then the input is accepted (see Fig. 10.7b). However, if no sequence of transitions lead to an accepting configuration, the given input is rejected. Obviously, to solve any problem in a deterministic way, that is solvable on NTM, one needs to generate all possible sequences for a given input sentence to find out if at least one of them is an accepting configuration.

Fig. 10.7 Computation steps of: **a** DTM M', **b** NTM M

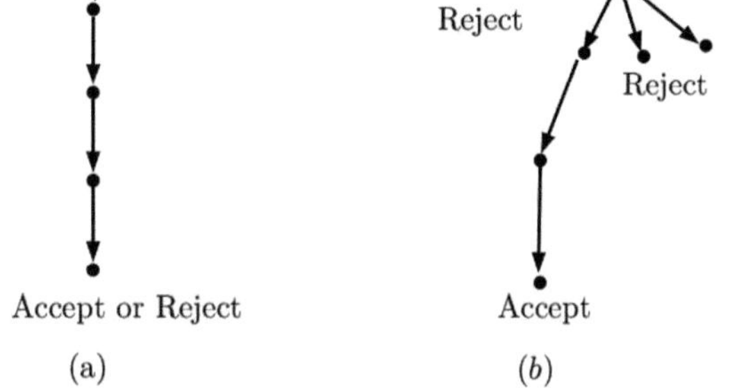

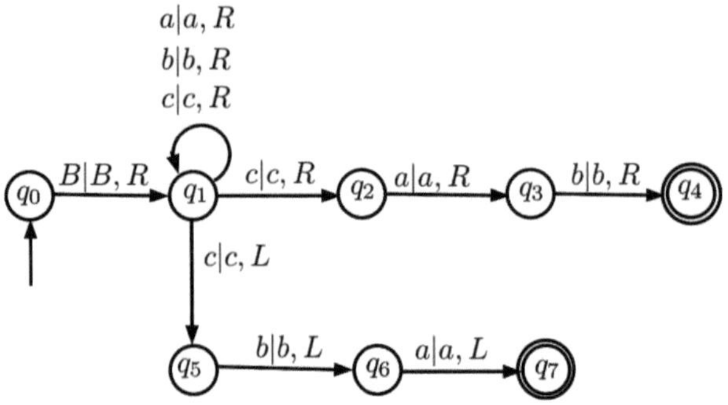

Fig. 10.8 NTM to accept strings $w = ucv$, where $u|v = ab$

As an example, to find if a graph of n nodes has a connected subgraph of k nodes, there is no efficient algorithm for this problem, and only an exhaustive check method works. However, a non-exhaustive-based solution of *Guess and check* is possible using NTM. The approach for this can be as follows:

1. Arbitrarily choose a move when more than one possible moves exists for the transition $\delta(q_i, a)$ in the graph.
2. Accept the input if there is at least one computation sequence that leads to accepting state.

In our next example, we construct a NTM that recognizes all the inputs where we need to *guess* about the input.

Example 10.4 Construct a NTM that accepts a substring ab preceded or followed with c, i.e., in the input $w = ucv$, the symbol c is preceded by or followed by ab, and $u, v \in \{a, b, c\}^*$.

The approach used shall be as follows: Read input a, b, c and write a, b, c respectively, and move to Right (R) in each step. Then, with input c non-deterministically decide c, a, b by moving Right in three states transitions or decide c, b, a by moving Left (L) in three other states transitions (see Fig. 10.8). □

10.5.2 Complexity of Nondeterministic TM

Consider that a NTM M shown in Fig. 10.7b is a decider machine, that is, its all branches when started from root, halt on all the inputs. Given this, we can define the running time of such Turing machine as follows:

Definition 10.2 The running time or *time-complexity* of NTM M is the function $f : \mathbb{N} \rightarrow \mathbb{N}$, where $f(n)$ is the maximum number of steps that M uses on any branch of its computation for any input of length n. □

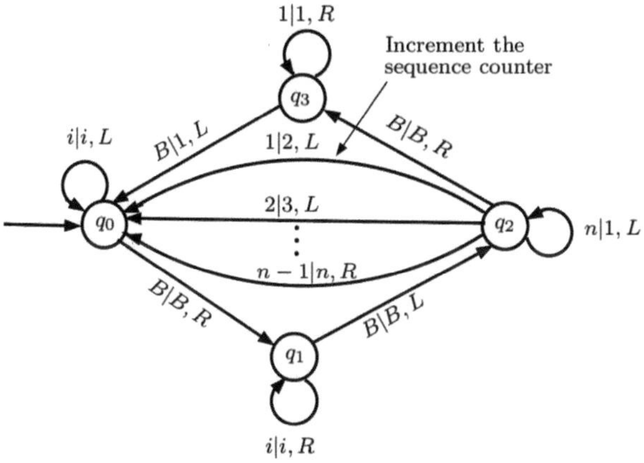

Fig. 10.9 Generating lexicographic sequences $(1, 2, ..., n)^+$ by TM

Theorem 10.5 *Let $t(n)$ be a function, and $t(n) \geq n$. Then, every $t(n)$-time nondeterministic single-tape TM has an equivalent $2^{O(t(n))}$ deterministic single-tape TM.* □

We will discuss the proof of this theorem shortly, in our discussions that follows.

We can define the class of problems solvable on nondeterministic Turing machines in time $t(n)$ as follows:

Definition 10.3 If $t(n)$ is time taken by a nondeterministic Turing machine M to decide a language L, then the time complexity for the Nondeterministic TM is,

$$NTIME(t(n)) = \{L \mid L \text{ is decided by a } O(t(n))\text{-time NTM.}\} \quad (10.11)$$

The $NTIME$ is related with the $DTIME$ by

$$DTIME(t(n)) \subseteq NTIME(t(n)). \quad \square \quad (10.12)$$

The intuition for the above definition is that deterministic TM computation time $DTIME(t(n))$ is contained in the time of nondeterministic TM's time to carry out that computation. This becomes clear from Fig. 10.7a and b.

Example 10.5 Generating Lexicographic Sequences.

Sequence generator is a TM, with no input, but output is set of sequences:

$BBBBBBBB...$
$1BBBBBBB...$
...

$nBBBBBBB...$
$nB1BBBBB...$
.....
$nBnBBBB...$
$nBnB1BB...$
....
$nBnBnBB...$
...

Figure 10.9 shows the sequences generation of finite length integers from 1 to n, at each position, then 1 to n in next position of the tape, and so on. The transitions $1|2, L$,..., indicates incrementing the count at the same position, while $n-1|n, R$ indicates incrementing a position to final value, and head moves to next right position. We assume that each position can hold an integer of arbitrary size, up to n. The alphabet can be unary, so that 1, 2, ..., n are 1^2, 1^3, ..., 1^{n+1}. The notation i/i in this figure stands for $1/1$, ..., n/n. Note that the machine will keeps on generating the sequences indefinitely. □

10.5.3 Simulation of Nondeterministic Turing Machine

Theorem 10.6 *For each nondeterministic Turing machine there exists a standard TM (deterministic Turing machine) that accepts same language as the original machine.*

Proof To accomplish the transformation of a NTM into a deterministic TM, we show that multiple computations of a single input string can be sequentially generated and examined.

A NTM produces multiple computations for a single string w. We show that multiple computations $m_1, \ldots, m_i, \ldots, m_k$ for input string w can be sequentially generated and applied (see Fig. 10.10). (A computation m_i is $\delta(q_i, a) = [q_j, b, d]$, where $d \in \{L, R, S\}$. To make it more clear, say a transition in NTM is, $\delta(q', a) = \{(q_i, b, L), (q_j, c, R), (q_k, d, L)\}$. Now, what is needed is to apply each of these three configurations, corresponding to states q_i, q_j, and q_k. There in, for q_i there will be sequence of configurations, when all exhausted, then q_j is applied, and similarly, q_k. Since in each case, the configurations are finite, the total computation will be finite.

These computations can be systematically produced by adding alternative transitions for each $Q \times \Gamma$ pair. Each m_i may produce a subset of configurations out of $|Q| \times |\Gamma| \times |d| = n$ (e.g., c_1, ..., c_n). If the machine reaches to any configuration which is halting in accepting mode, the machine accept. If machine halts in rejecting state or for any $a \in \Gamma$ there is $\delta(q_i, a) = \phi$, the TM rejects the input. □

Using the ability to sequentially produce the computations, a *NTM M* can be simulated by a *3-tape* deterministic TM M'.

An idea of simulation of NTM M using a 3-tape DTM M':

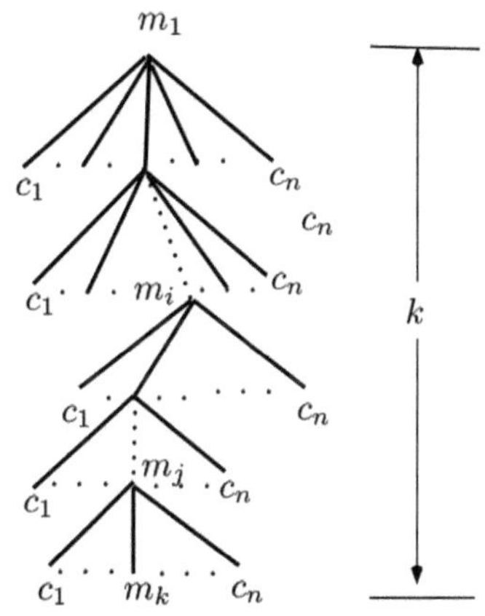

Fig. 10.10 Simulation of a NTM on standard TM

1. The input string w is put on tape-1,
2. Copy w from tape-1 to tape-2,
3. Based on the current head position on tape-2 and the machine's state, sequence $(m_1, ..., m_k)$ is generated on tape 3,
4. Tape-2 is simulated for the moves (sequence) available on tape 3.
5. If any move leads to a halting state, the machine is halted and w is accepted, else goto next step,
6. Advance the head on tape 2 (L, R, S) and repeat the process from step 3.

Note that sequence generation is nonterminating, like we have shown in the Example 10.5 above. Hence, if $w \notin L$, the process will continue indefinitely. This conclusion we are using in the next theorem to show that languages accepted by NTM are Recursively Enumerable (RE).

Theorem 10.7 *A language is recursively enumerable if and only if it is accepted by some nondeterministic Turing machine.*

Proof A deterministic Turing machine is clearly nondeterministic with only one path, for each string in the language, in its transition graph. So it suffices to show that every nondeterministic Turing machine has an equivalent deterministic Turing machine. To prove the converse, we use Theorem 10.1 that states that a multi-tape Turing machine can be used to construct an equivalent TM for every nondeterministic Turing machine.

Let M be a nondeterministic Turing machine (NTM) such that for each pair of a state and input there are only finite number of possible transitions. Let these transitions be ordered and they are represented as $1, 2, \ldots, n$. Not all these sequences are possible because generally only a subset of these is possible.

Let the deterministic TM M' has 3-tapes, where tape-1 holds the input w, tape-3 generates the possible sequences $1, 2, \ldots, n$. For each sequence generated on tape-3, the TM M' copies the input onto tape-2, then it simulates the NTM M on tape-2 using the sequences on tape-3 to dictate the moves of M. For example, if M enters in the accepting state, M' will also enter.

Hence, if there are sequences of choices, which lead to acceptance in M, it will ultimately be generated on tape-3, and M' will accept when it simulates M. If no sequence of choices of M leads to acceptance, then M' will reject the input. This proves the theorem. □

10.6 Turing Machine and Type-0 Grammars

Definition 10.4 (*Unrestricted Grammar*) A grammar $G = (V, \Sigma, S, P)$ is unrestricted grammar, provided that tuples of G have standard meaning, and $P \subseteq (\Sigma \cup V)^* \times (\Sigma \cup V)^*$ is finite set of production rules. Given this, we say, $\gamma_1\alpha\gamma_2 \Rightarrow_G \gamma_1\beta\gamma_2$ iff $(\alpha \rightarrow \beta) \in P$. And, $L(G) = \{w \in \Sigma^* \mid S \Rightarrow_G^* w\}$. □

Note that there is no restriction of $|\alpha| \leq |\beta|$, which exists in context-sensitive grammar, with at least one variable symbol in α.

In the following, we shall show that a language is recognized by Turing machine if and only if it is generated by a type-0 grammar. To prove the "if" part, we construct a nondeterministic Turing machine that will non-deterministically choose a derivation in the grammar, and see whether or not the result of that derivation is the input string to the TM. If yes, the Turing machine accepts input. To show that the "only if" part, we construct a grammar which will non-deterministically generate the representation of a terminal string, and then simulate the TM on that string. If the string is accepted by the TM, the string is converted to the terminal symbols it represents.

We would like to show that a language is accepted by a TM iff it is generated by a type-0 grammar. The two parts are proved through two theorems, as follows.

Theorem 10.8 *Part I: If a language L is generated by a type-0 grammar, then L is recognized by a Turing machine.*

Proof Let $G = (V, \Sigma, S, P)$ be a type-0 grammar, and $L = L(G)$. We informally describe a Turing machine M accepting L, as follows. Let M be nondeterministic TM,

$$M = (Q, \Sigma, \Gamma, \delta, q_0, F), \tag{10.13}$$

where $\Gamma = V \cup \Sigma \cup \{B, \#\}$.

The symbols B, #, S are not in $V \cup \Sigma$. We shall not enumerate all the states in Q, but designate some of them when it is necessary.

To begin, M has input $w \in \Sigma^*$ on its tape. The M inserts # before w and shifts the entire w to right one cell. Then appends w with #S#, so that the tape contents becomes #w#S#.

As next step, M will non-deterministically simulate a derivation in G starting with start symbol S. Each sentential form in the derivation will appear in turn between two "#" symbols, these symbols initially enclose S, and the new sentential produced replaces the S. If some choice of moves leads to a string of terminals there, that string is compared with w. If they match, M accepts w.

Formally, let M has $\#w\#A_1A_2...A_k\#$ on its tape, M moves its head through $A_1A_2...A_k$, non-deterministically choosing a position i and a constant r between 1 and the maximum length of the left side of any production in P. Then M examines the substring $A_iA_{i+1}...A_{i+r-1}$. If $A_iA_{i+1}...A_{i+r-1}$ is the left-hand side of some production in P, it may be replaced by the right-hand side of that production. The TM M may have to shift $A_{i+r}A_{i+r+1}...A_k\#$ either to left or right to make room to fill up space, should the right side of the production used have a length other than r.

From this simple simulation of derivation in G, it should be noted that M will print on its tape a string of the form $\#w\#\alpha\#$, and $\alpha \in (\Sigma \cup V)^*$ when $S \Rightarrow^* \alpha$. Also, if $\alpha = w$, then M accepts. □

Theorem 10.9 *If L is recognized by a Turing machine, then L is generated by a type-0 grammar.*

Proof Part II: We present the approach for formal proof, without going into the detailed proof. Let L be accepted by a Turing machine $M = (Q, \Sigma, \Gamma, \delta, q_0, H)$. We construct a grammar G, which non-deterministically generates two copies of a representation of some word in Σ^* and then simulate the action of M on one copy. If M accepts the word, then G converts the second copy to a terminal string. If M does not accept, the derivation never results in a terminal string. □

10.7 Universal Turing Machine

A Universal Turing Machine (UTM) is designed to read the description of any other Turing machine, called the input program, and simulate its execution. It can interpret and execute the instructions of the input program on its own tape, effectively emulating the behavior of the simulated machine. This property makes the universal Turing machine capable of performing any computation that can be described by a Turing machine, regardless of the specific details of the simulated machine.

The concept of a UTM is significant in the field of computer science and the theory of computation because it demonstrates the idea that a single machine can simulate the behavior of any other machine. This forms the foundation of the Church–Turing thesis, which suggests that any computation that can be algorithmically performed can also be carried out by a Turing machine or an equivalent computational model.

Alan M. Turing described a UTM, as a single ordinary Turing machine that could perform all operations performed by an ordinary Turing machine, even in case the ordinary machine was more complicated than this Universal machine. In other words, the UTM imitates the operations of an ordinary TM. This ability to make a relatively

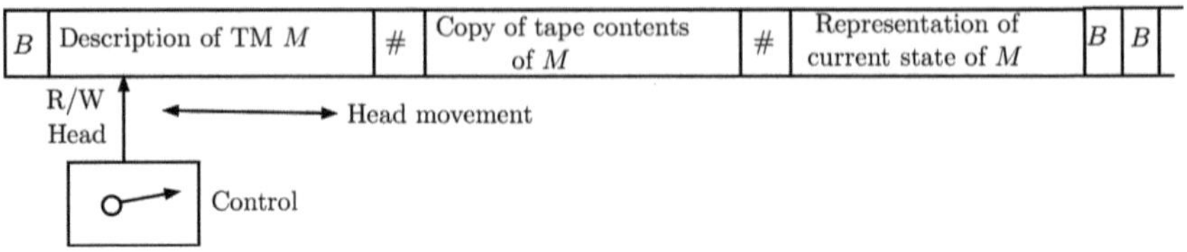

Fig. 10.11 Universal turing machine imitating other TM

simple machine to act like a more complicated machine, is achieved by giving the complicated instructions to the simple machine. In particular, a UTM is provided on one part of its tape a complete symbolic description of the machine it is expected to imitate. The UTM stores on another part of its tape (for instance on alternate squares) a copy of the tape that would be on the imitated machine, and makes the changes on this part of the tape whenever the imitated machine would make. The remaining part of the tape must be used for intermediate *scratch work*, for instance, to record what state the imitated machine is in, what are the intermediate results, etc. The internal structure of the UTM has to include instructions to use the various kinds of data, and to move back and forth between the different parts of its tape. Figure 10.11 shows that UTM M' imitates another TM M [2, 5].

Since the method of storing all this information on one tape is rather complicated, the internal structure of the UTM is also rather complicated, requiring a large number of states. Therefore, a simplification could be to use all this information on multi-tapes, which requires lesser complicated instructions, but this alternative machine has no any capability of higher computing power than what can be computed on a TM.

Let the ordinary Turing machine be defined as 6-tuple, $M = (Q, \Sigma, \Gamma, \delta, s, H)$, which is a special purpose computer, designed to solve a particular problem. It is possible to design a reprogramable Turing machine called Universal Turing Machine M'. Given an input description of any ordinary Turing machine M and a string w, the UTM M' can simulate the computation of M. To construct such a UTM, we first choose a standard way of describing a Turing machine M without any loss of generality. We assume that,

$$Q = \{q_1, q_2, ..., q_n\} \text{ and}$$
$$\Gamma = \{a_1, a_2, ..., a_m\},$$

where q_1 is start state, q_n is single accepting state, and a_1 is blank character. Now, select an encoding of states and symbols such that q_1 is 1, q_2 is 11 etc, and $a_1 = 1$, $a_2 = 11$ and so on. For right (R) and left (L) move, the symbols 1 and 11, respectively, are used.

The Universal Turing machine M' stores five tuples $\delta(q_i, a) = (q_k, b, d)$ of each transition function of Turing machine M, on its tape in encoded format, where d is displacement, which is either L, R or S. The symbol 0 is used as field separator of the tuples on the tape of UTM. Since, start state, final states, and other states are specified, Turing machine M can be described completely by the details of its transition function δ. The transition function δ can also be encoded according to this scheme with arguments and the result in some prescribed sequence. For example, a transition $\delta(q_1, a_3) = (q_4, a_2, R)$ may appear as follows:

$$...1011101111011010...,$$

where 1 is for q_1, 111 is for a_3, 1111 is for q_4, 11 is for a_2, and 1 is for R. All these fields are separated by 0's. Having this, any Turing machine (i.e., its δ function) can be encoded using finite encoding on $\{0, 1\}^+$. In addition, given a finite encoding of Turing machine, it can be decoded also.

Apart from this description of M, a UTM has an input alphabet sequence string also in $\{0, 1\}^+$.

10.7.1 Encoding of a TM

The description is encoding of a Turing machine, it refers to the representation of a Turing machine as a string or a sequence of symbols. It is a way of encoding the structure, states, transitions, and behavior of a Turing machine in a format that can be stored, manipulated, or transmitted. There are different encoding schemes that can be used to represent a Turing machine. One common approach is to use a formal notation such as the Turing machine description in the form of a transition table or a set of production rules. This notation specifies the states, symbols, and transitions of the Turing machine.

Another encoding method represents a Turing machine as a binary string or a sequence of symbols from a specific alphabet. In this approach, each component of the Turing machine, such as states, symbols, and transitions, is assigned a unique binary code or symbol sequence. By concatenating these codes or symbol sequences together, the complete encoding of the Turing machine is formed.

The encoding of a Turing machine is important in various contexts, such as theoretical analysis, algorithmic complexity, and computer simulations. It allows the representation of Turing machines in a standardized format that can be processed by other computational tools or algorithms. Additionally, encoding enables the study of properties and behaviors of Turing machines, as well as the development of algorithms that manipulate or simulate Turing machines.

Because of the ability to encode arbitrary symbols as strings over $\{0, 1\}$, we consider Turing machine with inputs $\Sigma = \{0, 1\}$ and tape symbols $\Gamma = \{0, 1, B\}$. The states of M are assumed to be $\{q_1, \ldots, q_n\}$.

Table 10.3 Encoding TM symbols

Symbol	Encoding
0	1
1	11
B	111
q_0	1
q_1	11
...	...
q_n	1^{n+1}
L	1
R	11

Table 10.4 Encoding of TM transitions

Transition	Encoding
$\delta(q_0, B) = (q_1, B, R)$	101110110111011
$\delta(q_1, 0) = (q_0, 0, L)$	1101010101
$\delta(q_1, 1) = (q_2, 1, R)$	110110111011011
$\delta(q_2, 1) = (q_0, 1, L)$	1110110101101

In general, a TM is defined by its transition function: $\delta(q_i, a) = (q_j, b, d); q_i, q_j \in Q; a, b \in \Gamma$; and $d \in \{L, R\}$. For the TM M we can have encoding for alphabets Σ, states Q, transition function δ, as given in Table 10.3.

Let $en(z)$ denote the encoding of z. Hence, Transition $\delta(q_i, a) = (q_j, b, d)$ is encoded by string:

$$en(q_i)0en(a)0en(q_j)0en(b)0en(d).$$

The symbol "0" separates the five components of δ.

A representation of machine M is constructed from encoded transitions. Two consecutive 0's separate one transition from other, e.g., two different transitions can be, $\delta(q, a) = (q', b, R)$ and $\delta(q', a) = (q'', b, L)$. Beginning and end of complete representation are defined by three 0's. Consider the transitions for the Turing machine M as given in table 10.4

As per the encoding, we consider, the machine M can be represented by encoded string as follows:

000101110110111011 00110101010100 11011011101101100
1110110101101000.

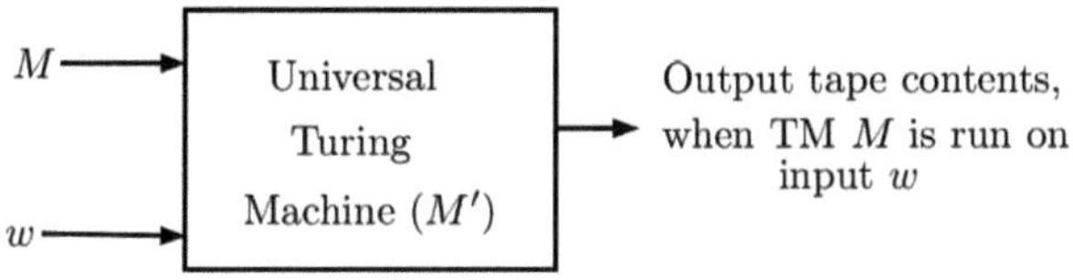

Fig. 10.12 Universal turing machine simulates other TM M

Note that this string is nothing but the transition table above for states q_0-q_2. Thus we conclude that encoding of a TM is a long binary string, which satisfies a certain norms, e.g., 0 as separator of tuples of a transition, and 00 as separator for all given transitions. A three zeros pair delimits this big integer representing the entire transition table. Since, a large integer number is representation of TM, every TM is nothing but a large integer number [4].

10.7.2 Conceptual Representation of Universal Turing Machine

Figure 10.12 shows the concept of Universal Turing machine. Let there is ordinary TM M that accepts by halting. Then, UTM M', that simulates M has input string $R(M)w$, where $R(M)$ is representation of M and w is input to M.

Without loss of generality, we represent the UTM in Fig. 10.12 with two outputs, as shown in Fig. 10.13.

1. Output-1: *Accept* (indicates that M halts with input w),
2. Output-2: *loops*, i.e., M does not halt with input w, i.e., computation of M' does not terminate.

This way, the machine M' is Universal TM, as computation of any Turing machine M can be simulated by M' (See Fig. 10.13).

Fig. 10.13 Recognition of string $R(M)w$ by universal turing machine

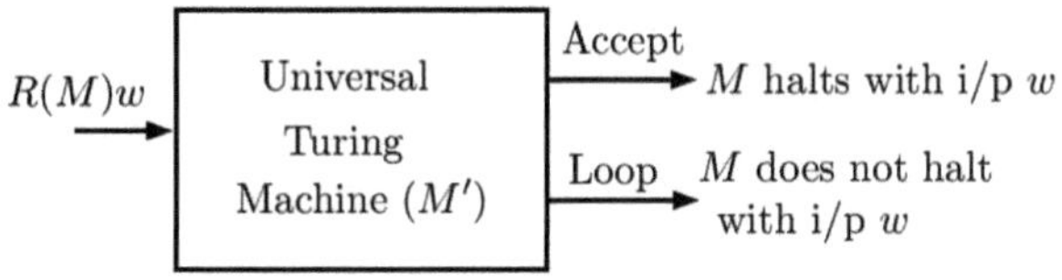

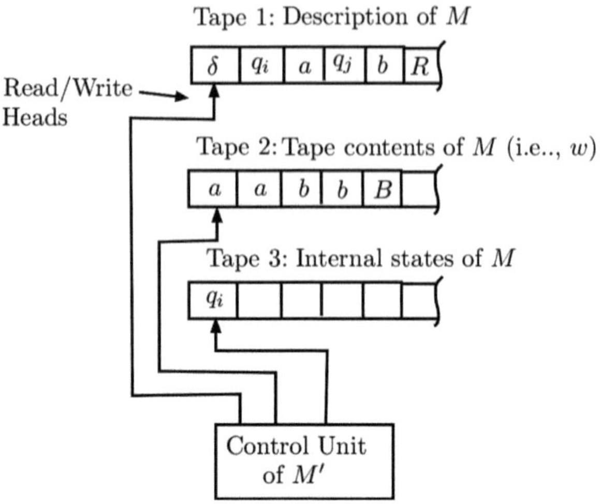

Fig. 10.14 Universal turing machine simulates other TM

10.7.3 Simulation of Universal TM on 3-Tape TM

To simplify the structure of information on the tape of a UTM, we use a 3-tape TM to simulate the UTM (Fig. 10.14).

To simulate an ordinary TM M using a UTM M', we need representation of all transitions of M; let this be $R(M)$, called encoding/representation) of M. The tape-1 of UTM holds $R(M)w$, tape-2 simulates computations of M for input w, and tape-3 is used as working tape, which holds the current state of M when w is processed on tape-2. If input on tape-1 is not of the form $R(M)w$ (for deterministic TM M and string w), the M' moves to right forever, i.e., loops.

The working of this 3-tape UTM is as follows: first, w from input $R(M)w$ on tape-1 is copied onto tape-2, with tape head of tape-2 held at first character of w. The tape-3 stores the initial state of M and later the current state. Encoding of q_1, i.e., 1 is written to tape-3, to indicate that machine M is in state q_1.

The steps to be followed for each transition are as follows:

The UTM M' looks at current state q on tape-3 and current symbol $a \in \Sigma$ tape-2 to determine the next state of M. Then, looks for corresponding $\delta(q, a)$ on tape-1 to determine the result (q', b, L) or (q', b, R). Based on this result, the current symbol on tape-2 is modified to b, tape-2 makes a move to R or L, and the state of M is modified simultaneously on tape-3 to q'. This process is repeated until there is halting state of M on tape-3.

Further to note that a 3-tape TM can always be simulated using single-tape TM, where different areas are selected on the tape to represent the contents of tape-1, tape-2 and tape-3, but finite control will cause the transitions based on current symbol at virtual head position on tape-2 and the current state on tape-3. In fact, there will be need of virtual head positions in these three areas on single tape. Note that virtual heads of three tapes are recorded on the single tape of standard TM when 3-tape TM is simulated on standard TM (see Sect. 10.2.2).

In the above discussions, we have seen that the Universal TM can do complicated logical operations using fairly small number of components. However, this requires a far larger amount of memory (tape)[3] than the original machine being simulated [5].

10.8 The Halting Problem of TM

The "Halting Problem" is a fundamental problem in the field of computer science and the theory of computation. It was first formulated by Alan Turing in 1936 and proved to be undecidable, meaning that there is no general algorithm that can solve it for all possible cases. The halting problem is concerned with determining whether, given a particular program and input, the program will eventually halt (terminate) or will run indefinitely (loop forever).

The halting problem is a very strong, provably correct, statement that no one will ever be able to write a computer program or design a Turing machine that can determine if a arbitrary program will halt (stop, exit) for a given input.

This is NOT saying that some programs or some Turing machines cannot be analyzed to determine that they, for example, always halt. The halting problem says that no computer program or Turing machine can determine if ALL computer programs or Turing machines will halt or not halt on ALL inputs. To prove that halting problem is unsolvable, we will construct one program and one input for which there is no Turing machine.

We make use of some powerful mathematical concepts and do the proofs for both a computer program and a Turing machine. The mathematical concepts we need are:

- *Proof by contradiction*: Assume a statement is true, show that the assumption leads to a contradiction. Thus, the statement is proven false.
- *Self-referral.* Have a computer program or a Turing machine operate on itself, well, a copy of itself, as input data. Specifically we shall use is diagonalization, taking the enumeration of Turing machines and using M as input to M, and
- *Logical negation.* Take a black box that accepts input and outputs true or false, put that black box in a bigger black box that switches the output so it is false or true respectively.

Alan Turing's proof of the undecidability of the halting problem was based on a clever *diagonalization* argument. He demonstrated that if there were a universal algorithm that could solve the halting problem for all programs, then it would be possible to construct a paradoxical program that would lead to a contradiction. This

---

[3] In conventional computers there is hierarchy of memories: registers, cache, primary, secondary, etc. However, in the TM model of computation, there is a simplistic representation of all memory types by one memory, i.e., tape memory.

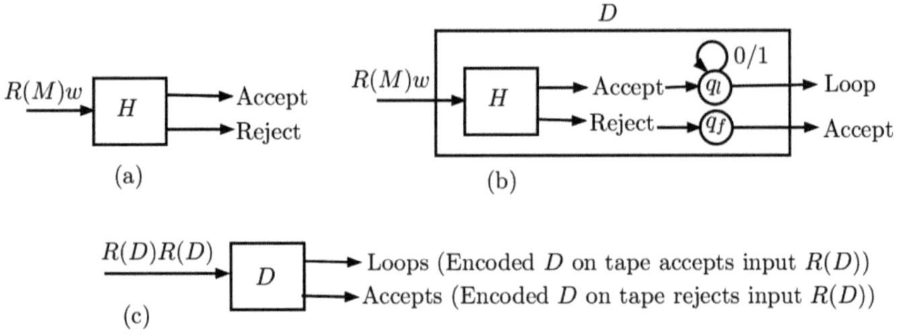

Fig. 10.15 Halting problem

contradiction arises when considering the behavior of the paradoxical program when fed with its own description as input.

If there exists *no* Turing machine that eventually halts for all instances of the problem and decides Yes/No, for all instances of a given problem, then the problem is called as *undecidable*. The problem is called *halting problem*, that seeks the answer to the question, whether any Turing machine will eventually halt or run forever. We will show in the remaining discussion in this section that halting problem is undecidable.

Theorem 10.10 *Show that halting problem is undecidable.*

Proof Assumption: There exists a Turing machine, H, such that, when the input tape contains the encoding of a TM, M, followed with string $w \in L(M)$, the TM H accepts if TM M accepts with input w and H rejects if M is not a Turing machine or M rejects with input w.

We assume that Turing machine H always halts and either accepts or rejects.

For modeling the halting problem, let the tape of H consists $R(M)Bw$, where $R(M)$ is representation of M in encoded form, followed with space ("B") and input string w. When H is run with this tape input, it prints "accept" if M accepts w, and prints "Reject" if M rejects w. This is shown in Fig. 10.15a.

Next, we do minor modification in H as follows: The Accept state of H is fed into a new state q_l, and for each tape symbol (0 or 1), the transition from q_l loops back to q_l. We call this state as "loop" state, i.e., the machine loops if it had gone to Accept state. Additionally, the output of Reject state is fed to a new state q_f, which is new Accept state. After modification, we call the new machine as D. It is shown in Fig. 10.15b.

As next modification, we replace the tape contents of D by $R(D)BR(D)$, i.e., string w is replaced by encoded representation of D, i.e., $R(D)$. This is shown by Fig. 10.15c. Now we have Turing machine D that operate on tape, that has $R(D)$ as the input machine and $R(M)$ as input data.

Consider two mutually exclusive cases of D:

Case 1: The encoded Turing machine D accepts ($w = R(D)$), thus D (Fig. 10.15b) enters the state q_l. This means, by the definition, the D halts with input D. But, we are running D on input "D with input D". So, we see that TM acceptance causes TM D to loop forever, thus not halting. This is contradiction, because this case says that TM D does not halt when given input "$R(D)$ with input $R(D)$. So, let us try other case.
Case 2: The encoded TM D rejects ($w = R(D)$), thus TM D enters in state q_f (Fig. 10.15b). Since, we are running D on input "$R(D)$ with input $R(D)$" and so we see that the TM H's rejecting cause $R(D)$[4] to reject. Hence, the machine D accepts and halts (Fig. 10.15c). Since $R(D)BR(D)$ is tape content of D, the D accepts and halts. This is a contradiction to our original statement which said that D does not halt when given input "$R(D)$ with input $R(D)$".

There are no other cases, as a TM either accepts or rejects. Thus, what must be wrong is our assumption "there exists a TM H such that it decides that a TM M accepts input w. □

The halting problem is important in theory of computation for several reasons:

- *Undecidability*: The halting problem was the first problem to be proven undecidable, meaning that there is no general algorithm that can solve it for all possible cases. This result demonstrated the limits of what can be computed algorithmically. It highlighted the existence of problems that cannot be solved by any algorithm, regardless of the computational resources available.
- *Program analysis and verification*: The halting problem has direct implications for program analysis and verification. It shows that there is no general algorithm that can determine, in all cases, whether a program will halt or run indefinitely. This poses a challenge when it comes to reasoning about program behavior, identifying potential infinite loops, or proving the termination of programs. It also highlights the inherent complexity of program analysis and the difficulty of ensuring correct and reliable software.
- *Limits of formal systems*: The undecidability of the halting problem also has implications for formal systems and logic. It demonstrates that there are statements or propositions within a system that cannot be proved or disproved within the system itself. This insight connects to Gödel's incompleteness theorems, which showed the inherent limitations of formal axiomatic systems to fully capture the truths of arithmetic or more complex domains.
- *Turing completeness*: The halting problem is closely related to the concept of Turing completeness, which characterizes the computational power of a system. If we can solve the halting problem for a given computational model, it implies that we can determine whether any program written in that model will halt or not.

[4] That is, the encoded $R(D)$ on tape rejects input $w = R(D)$.

Conversely, if the halting problem is undecidable for a computational model, it means that the model is Turing complete, capable of performing any computation that can be algorithmically described.

In conclusion, the halting problem proves that there is no *general* algorithm that can determine the halting behavior of all programs. This result has important consequences in fields such as program analysis, compiler design, and software verification, as it highlights the inherent difficulty in reasoning about the behavior and correctness of programs.

10.9 Modern Computer Simulation on Turing Machine

Let us compare the Turing machine and the common computer that we use daily. Since the notion of "a common computer" is not well defined mathematically, the arguments in this section shall be informal. A Turing machine can simulate a computer, and can do that in an amount of time, that is, at most some polynomial in the number of steps taken by the computer.

We have some assumptions on how a typical computer operates. First, we shall suppose that the storage of a computer consists of an indefinitely long sequence of words, each with an address. We shall not put a limit on the length of a word. Addresses will be assumed to be integers 0, 1, 2, and so on. Although, in a real computer there is a limit on the number of words it can hold in its "memory", but we shall assume there is no limit to the number of words. We assume that the program of the computer is stored in some of the words of the memory. Each of these words represent a simple instruction, as in case of machine or assembly language of a typical computer.

We assume that each instruction involves a limited (finite) number of words, and that each instruction changes the value of at most one word. A typical computer has registers, which are memory words with especially fast access. Often, operations such as addition are restricted to occur only in registers. We shall not make any such restrictions, but will allow any operation to be performed on any word in its memory.

In TM, we consider that first tape represents the entire memory of the computer. Addresses of memory words are in numerical order, *alternate* with the contents of those memory words. Both addresses and contents are *written* in binary forms. In addition, the marker symbols * and # are used to make it easy to find the ends of addresses and contents (i.e., words). Another marker, $, indicates the beginning of the sequence of addresses and contents.

The second tape is used as "instruction counter", and holds one integer number in binary form, that represents one of the memory locations on tape-1. The value stored in this location is the next computer instruction to be executed.

The third tape holds a "memory address" or the contents of that address after the address[5] has been located on tape-1. To execute an instruction, the TM must find the contents of one or more memory addresses (operands) that hold data. First, the desired address is copied onto tape-3 and compared with the addresses on tape-1, until a match is found. The contents of this address is copied onto the third tape and moved to wherever it is needed.

An Instruction to be executed is searched on tape-1 as follows:

1. search tape-1 for an address that matches the instruction number on tape-2,
2. for this, start at the $ sign on the tape-1 and move right, comparing[6] each address with the contents of tape-2. The address must be found.

When the Instruction's address is found, examine its value. Let us assume that when a word is an instruction, its first few bits represent the action to be taken (e.g., *copy, add, branch*). The remaining bits code an address or addresses that are involved in the action (e.g., in the Instruction *ADD adr1, adr2*).

If the instruction requires the value of some address (Indirect Addressing) then that address will be part of the instruction. Copy that address onto the tape-3, and mark the position of the Instruction using a second track of the first tape.[7] Now, search for the memory address on tape-1 and copy its value onto tape-3.

The next step is to execute the Instruction or the part of the instruction involving this value. After performing the Instruction, and determining that the instruction is not a *jump*, add 1 to the Instruction counter on tape-2 and begin the instruction cycle again. The latter is like action of Program Counter (PC) in ordinary computers.

10.9.1 Sample Instruction Execution

The followings are some of the most common Instructions in any CPU, and many other instructions can be derived from these Instructions.

Copy Instruction. We get the second address from the Instruction as where we need to copy. This address is found by putting it on tape-3 and searching for this address on tape-1. When we find the match, we copy the value into the space reserved for the value of that address. If more space is needed for the new value, or the new value uses less space than the old value, change the available space by shifting over. As a special case, the address may not yet appear on the first tape. In this case, we find the place and store both the address and the new value there.

---

[5] This address is operand of the Instruction found on tape-1.

[6] The comparison of addresses on the two tapes is easy, as we have already discussed in the 2-tape machine.

[7] We consider here two tracks in a tape to store more than one value at a head position. Alternatively, consecutive values can be stored on the same tape. However, the first one is easy to visualize.

Add Instruction. An add Instruction has two operands, which may be a values or locations. Following are the steps to simulate in a 3-tape machine.

1. go back to the Instruction to locate the other address,
2. find this address on tape-1,
3. perform a binary addition of the value of that address and the value stored on tape-3.

By scanning the two values from their right ends, a TM can perform a ripple-carry addition. Should more space be needed for the result, use the shifting over technique. *Jump Instruction.* Simply copy tape-3 to Tape-2 and begin the Instruction cycle again.

10.9.2 Comparison of Running Times

We shall use the TM not only to examine what can be computed at all, but what can be computed with enough efficiency to be used in practice. The dividing line between the *tractable* from the *intractable* is generally held to be between what can be computed in polynomial time and what requires more than any polynomial running time. Thus, we need to assure ourselves that if a problem can be solved in polynomial time on a typical computer, then it can be solved in polynomial time by a Turing machine, and conversely

10.10 Computing Frameworks

We may call it types of computations or even computing frameworks. Investigation into properties of computability has resulted into number of approaches for solving any given problem:

String transformations. The string transformation-based computing exists in Markov chains, unrestricted grammars, and Post-machines.

Evaluation of functions. The examples of computations that are based on evaluation of functions are: Recursive functions, Recursive enumerable functions, and Lambda calculus.

Abstract computing machines. The computing performed through an abstract machine may use these machines: TM, Register Machine, and Stack Machine.

Programming Languages. The programming languages are example of high levels of computations, that are close to humans thinking to perform computations. The programming languages make use of various constructs, like, *if... then...else*, *while...do*, *repeat...until*, *switch...case*, etc.

All the above methods have not resulted in any different problem-solving capability, the reason being that the problem solution part is inherent feature of every problem itself and not of some algorithmic system. Church–Turing thesis validates this intuition.

The only difference between the above four types of computations is that they perform different types of operations on different types of data, but there are equivalences in operations and data both, in one system of computation to other system. Like unary vs decimal, and addition vs concatenation of unary stings, etc.

In fact there is no single definition of algorithm and no single system for performing effective computation. However, there are well defined bounds that can be bounds on what can be accomplished in each system. The Church–Turing thesis formalizes this fact in a general statement about the capabilities and limitations of algorithmic computations.

10.11 Summary

At different times, number of variants of standard Turing machine have been proposed claiming to enhance the power of standard (1-tape, 1-head) Turing machine. These machines are: multi-tape Turing machine, multi-track Turing machine, nondeterministic Turing machine, two-way Turing machine, and Universal Turing Machine.

All these machines also use mechanical procedures, like the Turing machine, hence they all can be simulated by standard Turing machine. Thus, they cannot do any thing more than the standard Turing machine. This emphasizes that the standard Turing machine (or just the Turing machine) is the ultimate computing machine. The exception is nondeterministic Turing machine, because it does not work purely using mechanical procedure.

A nondeterministic Turing machine guesses the next state correctly. Thus, instead of searching a solution, like searching a tree, a nondeterministic TM correctly guesses the solution, and will be able to solve a problem with tape input $|w| = n$, in n steps. However, a nondeterministic TM can always be simulated by a standard TM. This will do the job in finite and exponential time in the worst case.

A multi-tape Turing machine may be a 2-tape, 3-tape or in general k-tape Turing machine. Since it can read and/or write many tapes simultaneously, it has time complexity of $O(kn)$ where the standard Turing machine has this complexity $O(n^2)$.

A language is recursively enumerable if and only if some multi-tape Turing machine accepts it.

For a 3-tape Turing machine, there exists an equivalent standard Turing. This can be demonstrated by simulating a 3-tape Turing machine by a standard Turing machine.

A multi-track Turing machine, e.g., a n-track Turing machine can read/write n-symbol at the current head position.

A Universal Turing Machine can simulate any other Turing machine. This is done by storing entire encoding of transition table of that Turing machine onto the tape of the Universal Turing Machine along with the input w.

A Universal Turing Machine of 3-tape can simulate any standard Turing machine by storing the encoding of standard Turing machine on one tape, storing input w on other tape, and one tape is used as a scratch tape.

The "Halting Problem" is a fundamental problem in the field of computer science and the theory of computation. It is concerned with determining whether, given a particular program and input, the program will eventually halt (terminate) or will run indefinitely (loop forever). The halting problem says that no computer program or Turing machine can determine if ALL computer programs or Turing machines will halt or not halt on ALL inputs. Thus, the halting problem is unsolvable. This result has important consequences in fields such as program analysis, compiler design, and software verification, as it highlights the inherent difficulty in reasoning about the behavior and correctness of programs.

A 3-tape TM can simulate a modern computer, and can do so in an amount of time that is at most polynomial in number of steps taken by the computer. For this, the tape-1 of the TM represents the entire memory of the computer, the addresses of memory words are in numerical order, and alternate with the contents of these memory words. The tape-2 is used as Instruction Counter (also called Program Counter), and holds the address of next instruction to be executed, on tape-1. The tape-3 holds the data location of tape-1, once it is located.

Thus, a TM can simulate execution of one address or two address instructions, like, ADD adr1 or ADD adr1, adr2.

Various computing frameworks are:

(i) *String transformations*, based on Markov chains, unrestricted grammars, and Post-Machine.

(ii) *Evaluation of functions*, like, in Recursive Functions, Lambda Calculus, Recursively Enumerable Function,

(iii) *Abstract computing machine*, like, TM, Register Machine, Stack Machine, and

(iv) *Programming Languages*, which are the highest level of computations, and are close to humans' thinking about performing computations. The Programming Languages make use of various constructs, like, if ... then ... else, while do, repeat ... until, switch ... case.

All the above methods have not resulted in any different problem-solving capability, and they can be simulated by standard Turing machine. The Church–Turing thesis validates this Intuition.

Self Review Questions

1. When extensions of TM give no powerful machine than the standard TM, how these extensions are useful?
2. Can a TM T store its own description on itself, as well as input w and its states, and imitate its own behavior?
3. Can a Universal TM really exists?
4. What is Post-Davis Machine?
5. A Total Recursive function corresponds to Recursively Enumerable languages. (True/False)
6. While simulating a modern computer on 3-tape TM,
   a. What the tape-2 holds?
   b. What the tape-3 holds?
   c. What the tape-1 holds?
7. Can a k-tape ($k > 1$) perform computation faster than a single-tape TM?
8. Why only a 3-tape Turing machine is more convenient to simulate any other TM, rather than a 4 or 5 tape machine?
9. If a 2-tape TM is considered convenient to recognize the language $\{a^n b^n \mid n \geq 0\}$, is it true that a 3-tape TM will be more convenient to recognize the language $\{a^n b^n c^n \mid n \geq 0\}$?
10. State the linear speedup in single sentence.

Exercises

A. Concepts based Problems

Note: The $*$ marked exercises are provided with solutions at the end of this book.

1. Construct a 2-tape TM to replace all b's by c's on the input tape, for alphabets $\Sigma = \{a, b, c\}$.
2. Construct 2-tape TMs that enumerate the following languages:
   a. $\{a, aa, aaa, ..., a^i, ...\}$
   b. ab^*
   c. $\{w \mid a^{i^2} \text{ for } i \geq 0\}$
   d. $\{wcw^R \mid w \in \{a, b\}^*\}$
3. Construct a 2-tape TM that enumerates the language $\{1, 3, 5, ...\}$ written in unary number format.
4. Write the steps of a Turing machine that enumerates all the primes in unary.
5. * Construct a 2-tape TM to recognize language $L = \{ww^R \mid w \in \{a, b\}^*\}$.
6. Describe a 2-tape TM that generates the binary strings in lexicographic order, with the sequence in the beginning as $\{0, 1, 00, 01, 10, 11, 000, 001, ...\}$.

7. * Construct a 2-tape TM to recognize the language $L = \{ww \mid w \in \{a, b\}^*\}$.
8. Describe a multi-tape TM that recognizes the language $\{x^i y^j z^k \mid i, j, k \geq 1 \text{ and } k = i.j\}$.
9. Answer the following, considering that a real-life computer is simulated on TM:

   a. How the addresses are stored in TM?
   b. Considering that an ordinary computer is programmed in Assembly language, how the Instructions and their Addresses are stored on tape?
   c. How the data of real computer are stored in TM?
   d. How the CPU registers are realized in the TM?
   e. How the end, and the beginning of data and program are recognized in TM?

10. What are the important applications of nondeterministic Turing machine?

B. Analysis-based Problems

11. Describe a 2-tape TM that accepts the strings set (u, v), where u is a substring of v.
12. The Example 10.3 (Sect. 10.2.2) shows a solution using 3-tape TM to recognize the language $\{1, 4, 9, 16, ...\}$. Is this a Recursive or Recursively Enumerable language?
13. If there are $|Q| = n$ number of states in a NTM M, and it solves a problem in m steps,

   a. What can be the number of steps when NTM M is simulated on a standard TM?
   b. What is the length of input w?
   c. What is possible largest number of configurations in standard TM when NTM is simulated by standard TM?

14. How you justify that when an ordinary computer is simulated on TM, the time taken for solving any problem is only polynomial of what it takes on the real computer.
15. What are the consequences of linear speedup?
16. It is said that halting problem has important applications in program testing, program verification, and compiler writing. Explain, how these applications may be related to halting problem?

C. Proof-based Problems

17. Show that, if a k-tape Turing machine ($k > 1$) has time complexity of $O(n)$ for solving some problem, then the equivalent standard deterministic Turing machine will have time complexity of $O(n^2)$ for that problem.
18. Show that 2-tape Turing machine can be simulated by the standard TM.
19. Given a TM with a double-ended tape, show that it can be simulated by single-ended tape.

D. Multiple choice Questions

20. Which of the following statements are true?
    (A) Every NTM has an equivalent DTM
    (B) Every NFA has an equivalent DFA
    (C) Every regular language is in the set of context-free languages
    (D) Every subset of a recursively enumerable set is a recursive set

21. Which of the following pairs of machines have same computing power?
    (A) Deterministic FAs and nondeterministic FAs
    (B) Single-tape TMs and multi-tape TMs.
    (C) Deterministic TMs and Nondeterministic single-tape TMs
    (D) Deterministic PDAs and nondeterministic PDAs

22. Which of the following definitions about NTM are correct?

    (A) A NTM M accepts input w if no computation of M on w halts in the state q_{reject}.
    (B) A NTM M accepts input w if for every computation of M on w is such that M halts in state q_{accept}.
    (C) A NTM M accepts input w if there exists more than one computation of M on w such that M halts in the state q_{accept}.
    (D) A NTM M accepts input w if there exists a computation of M on w such that M halts in the state q_{accept}.
    (E) A NTM M accepts input w if there is exactly one accepting computation of M on w.

E. Advanced Knowledge Assessment Problems

23. The real computer consists words (data) and addresses. How these words and addresses are stored in TM when we simulate ordinary computer on TM?
24. Considering the simulation in Sect. 10.9, explain how you will simulate following 8085 Microprocessor's assembly language instructions [3], on 3-tape TM:

    a. *ORA* r (logically OR accumulator with register r, the result remains in accumulator)
    b. *MOV r1, r2* (move the contents of register $r2$ to $r1$)
    c. *ADD* r (add register r into accumulator)
    d. *INR* r (increment register r)

25. Give skeleton of a C program that can simulate a halting machine.

References

1. Turing AM (1936) On computable numbers, with an application to the Entscheidunds problem. Proc Lond Math Soc Ser 2(24):230–265
2. Davis M (1958) Computability and unsolvability. McGraw-Hill
3. Kaushik DK., (2010). An introduction to microprocessor 8085. New Delhi.: Dhan-pat Rai Publishing Company. 2010;536
4. Sudkamp TA (2005) Languages and machines: an introduction to the theory of computer science, 3rd edn. Addison-Wesley Longman Publishing Co., Inc. ISBN: 0321322215
5. Moore EF (1952) A simplified universal turing machine. In: Proceedings of the 1952 ACM national meeting (Toronto), pp 50–54. https://doi.org/10.1145/800259.808993
6. Fischer PC (2003) Turing machine. In: Encyclopedia of computer science. Wiley Ltd, p 1799. ISBN: 0470864125
7. Biswas G (2015) Lecture notes - basic complexity classes. https://cse.iitkgp.ac.in/~goutam/toc/lect/basicCompClass.pdf, Autumn Sem 2014-15, IIT Kanpur

Chapter 11
Linear-Bounded Automata and Context-Sensitive Languages

Abstract The Linear-Bounded Automata (LBA) was developed as models for actual computers rather than for the analysis of computational processes. An LBA is a space-bounded Turing machine, where for its computation it cannot consume space more than the size of original input. An LBA decides the language strings for *accept/reject* unlike the Turing machine which *recognizes* the language strings. The LBA decides regular languages, context-free languages, and context-sensitive languages. When compared with other two machines, i.e., Finite Automata and Pushdown Automata, the LBA accepts all recursive languages (decidable languages). In addition to LBA, this chapter presents the analysis of some decidable languages having theoretical significance: the language of all regular expressions, empty language, language of DFA pairs, and the language of grammar-and-strings pairs. The chapter also covers topics like, some non-closure properties of context-free languages, context-sensitive languages and grammars, standard and extended Chomsky-hierarchy, decidable and closure properties of context-sensitive languages. In addition, the topics that are not so common but provides a foundation for advanced studies, have been also covered, like, indexed grammars, regulated rewriting grammars, programmed grammars, matrix grammars, conjunctive grammars, and at the end, an analysis has been given about universal versus Chomskian grammars, followed with self review questions and exercises.

Keywords Linear-bounded automata · Space-bounded machine · Decidable languages · Recognizable languages · Context-sensitive languages · Context-sensitive grammars · Chomsky-hierarchy · Indexed grammars · Regulated rewriting grammars · Programmed grammars · Matrix grammars · Universal grammars · Chomskian grammars · Conjunctive grammars

11.1 Introduction

One of the main problems in the design of computer algorithms and in their implementation is that of producing efficient programs, under the restrictions given by the available resources. In the beginning years of computing, the memories of the

K. R. Chowdhary, *Theory of Computation*,
https://doi.org/10.1007/978-981-97-6234-7_11

computers were limited and there were no provision of virtual memories; one of the standard approach in the implementation of applications was of choosing data structures that required only a small amount of extra memory, over and above the memory needed by the actual data. To cope with a restricted memory space we were forced to choose data structures that were not efficient from the point of view of the time used by the algorithms manipulating them.

In the last two decades, due to abundance of memory available, now one can write very large programs, and can use sophisticated algorithms and advanced data structures, and programs can use memory hierarchy to manipulate huge amount of data. However, still in many situations, the space is critical resource, for example memories in embedded systems, like, mobile devices. Thus, the investigation of computing with restricted resources is always an interesting and important topic. From a theoretical point of view, this area has been explored by studying and comparing the power of machine models using certain amounts of resources [1].

A restricted computational model is 1-tape *offline* Turing machine. This machine has just one semi-infinite tape (there is left end marker, but to the right it is infinite length) which at the beginning of the computation contains the input string. Due to the fact that entire input is provided before the computation begins, and not as needed, the machine is called *offline* TM. The content of the tape can be modified during the computation. Hennie [2] proved that if a machine of this kind works in *linear time* then the accepted language is regular. Hence, the capability of storing data on the tape is useless under this time restriction. A *stronger bound* on the time is that, in order to recognize nonregular languages the time must grow at least as $n \log n$.[1]

In an *online* computation, input data are supplied to the machine, one symbol at a time, at a special input terminal. Corresponding to each input symbol, the machine produces, at a special output terminal, an output symbol. In general the machine does not do it immediately, but must spend a number of time units to compute the required output symbol. However, the next new symbol is supplied at the input terminal until the machine has produced the output symbol corresponding to the previous input symbol. Thus, each output symbol is a function solely of the preceding input symbols. However, in an offline computation, all of the input symbols are written on one of the machine's tapes prior to the start of the computation. The results of the computation are obtained only when and if the machine halts, and may be taken to be either a *pattern* of symbols appearing on one of the tapes or else the *internal state* of the machine at the end of the computation. In the latter, there are two possible outcomes, represented by the symbols 0 and 1, which may also be thought of as being associated with the non-accepting and accepting states of the machine.

The Linear-Bounded Automata (LBA) are restricted space machines, they were originally developed as models for actual computers rather than models for the computational process. They have become important in the theory of computation even though they have not emerged in applications to the extent, which pushdown automata enjoy.

[1] Note that $O(n \log n) \in O(n^2)$.

In 1960, Myhill introduced an automation model today known as deterministic linear-bounded automaton [3]. Shortly thereafter, Landweber proved that the languages accepted by a deterministic LBA are always context-sensitive. In 1964, Kuroda introduced the more general model of (nondeterministic) linear-bounded automata, and showed that the languages accepted by them are precisely the context-sensitive languages [4].

As usual, we denote by Σ^* the set of all strings over a finite alphabet Σ, and by $|w|$ the length of a string $w \in \Sigma^*$. A language L is a subset of Σ^*. The L is said to be a *unary* or *tally language* if Σ contains only one element. In this case we stipulate $\Sigma = \{a\}$. Given a language L and an integer n, we denote by $L^{\leq n}$ the set of strings of length at most n belonging to L.

We will consider 1-tape offline Turing machines. At the beginning of the computation, the input string is written on the tape starting from the leftmost tape square, while the remaining squares contain the blank symbol. At each step of the computation, the machine writes a symbol on the currently scanned square of the tape (possibly changing its content), and moves its head to the left, to the right, or keeps it stationary, according to the transition function. The machine never writes the blank symbol.[2] Hence, it is able to modify the part of the tape that, at the beginning, was containing the input string. Special states are designed as accepting and rejecting states. We assume that in these states the computation stops.

Learning Outcomes of this Chapter:

1. Turing machine and grammars. [Knowledge]
2. Linear-bounded automata. [Synthesis]
3. Language acceptability by LBA. [Comprehension]
4. Halting problem for LBA. [Analysis]
5. Space bounds of LBA. [Analysis]
6. Chomsky-hierarchy of grammars. [Knowledge], [Comprehension]
7. Decidable problems. [Evaluation]
8. Classifying CFLs. [Analysis]
9. Context-sensitive grammars and languages. [Analysis], [Evaluation]
10. Indexed grammar. [Synthesis]
11. Regulated rewriting grammars. [Knowledge]
12. Conjunctive grammars. [Analysis]
13. Universal versus Chomskian grammars. [Analysis]

[2] The TM computes and in the process modifies the original contents in 1-tape machine, so that at the end of computation only the result remains on the tape. No blank symbol is over-written on a symbol in Σ, simply because a blank has no meaning in the output.

11.2 Linear-Bounded Automata Model

A linear-bounded automaton (LBA) is a computational model that operates similarly to a Turing machine but with a finite memory. Thus, LBAs are the machines to study computational power of machines with finite amount of memory. The key characteristic of an LBA is that the amount of tape it can use is limited by a linear function of the input size. This limitation distinguishes LBAs from Turing machines, which have an unlimited amount of tape. The linear restriction reflects practical scenarios where memory is limited, such as in real-world computers.

A linear-bounded automaton is a multi-track Turing machine which has only one tape, and this tape is exactly the same length as the input. That seems quite reasonable. We allow the computing device to use just the storage it was given at the beginning of its computation.[3] As a safety feature, we shall employ end-markers ("<" on the left and ">" on the right) on LBA tapes and never allow the machine to go past them. This will ensure that the storage bounds are maintained and help keep our machines from leaving their tapes.

Definition 11.1 (*Linear-bounded Automata*) A Turing machine that uses only the tape space occupied by the input is called a linear-bounded automaton (LBA). □

At this point, the question of accepting sets arises. Let's have linear-bounded automata accept just like Turing machines. For an LBA halting means accepting or rejecting. Unlike the Turing Machine, the LBA always halts.

For these new machines, computation is restricted to an area bounded by a constant (the number of tracks) times the length of the input (k_n, for $|w| = n$ and k tracks). This is very much like a programming environment where the sizes of values for variables is bounded.

A linear-bounded automaton (LBA) is a nondeterministic Turing machine $M = (Q, \Sigma, \Gamma, \delta, s, H)$ (see Fig. 11.1) such that:

- There are two special tape symbols '<'and '>'(the left end marker and, right end marker).
- Σ is input alphabet, Γ is tape alphabet, $\Gamma = \Sigma \cup \{<, >\}$.
- The TM begins in the configuration $(s, < x >, 0)$, where s is start state, the R/W head points to 1st symbol of input $x = a_1 a_2 ... a_n$, and there is "0" or "B" after ">" end marker symbol.
- The TM cannot replace "<" or ">" with any other symbol, nor move the tape head left of "<" or right of ">".
- $H = \{t, r\}$ is set of halting states, t is accept, and r is reject state.
- $\delta : (Q - \{t, r\}) \times \Gamma \rightarrow Q \times \Gamma \times \{L, R\}$.

The productions of CSG (context-sensitive grammar) are: $\alpha \rightarrow \beta$, where $\alpha \in (V \cup \Sigma)^* V (V \cup \Sigma)^*$, $|\alpha| \leq |\beta|$, and $\beta \in (V \cup \Sigma)^*$.

[3] For example, space consumed by a C program is equal to size of program code in machine language, plus the sum of size of all the data defined, provided that program does not create dynamic storage.

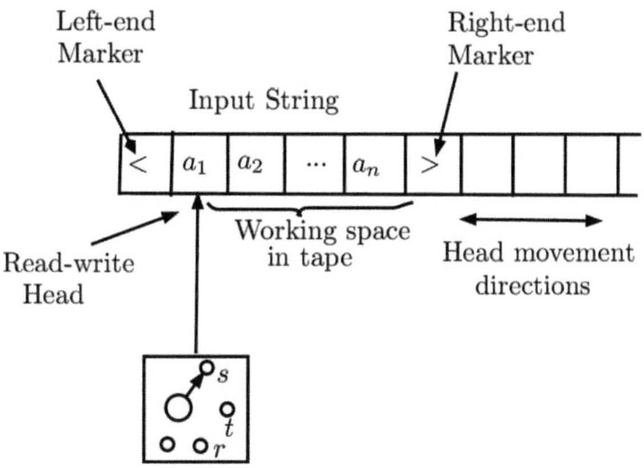

Fig. 11.1 Model of linear-bounded automata

A linear-bounded automaton, as defined by Myhill [3] and, following him, by Landweber [5], is a deterministic automaton specified by a tuple $(Q, \Sigma, \Gamma q_0, \delta, H)$, where the set Q of states, tape symbols Γ and input alphabet Σ are finite sets, the initial state q_0 is an element of Q, the set H of final states is a subset of Q and, finally, the behavior function δ is a function from $(Q - H) \times \Gamma \rightarrow Q \times \Gamma \times \{L, S, R\}$ where $\Gamma = \Sigma \cup \{B, <, >\}$, satisfying the condition: $\delta(<, s) = (<, s', k)$, where $k = R$. Here "<" is a symbol outside Γ and called the boundary symbol.[4] Similar is the case with right boundary symbol ">".

The automaton works as follows: It has input, a tape blocked into squares containing a string $< x >$, where x is a string in Σ and "<", ">" are the boundary symbols. Before operating on the input, the LBA is set in the initial state q_0. While in the initial stage, it reads left boundary in the state q_0. In general, if it is reading a symbol a in a state q and if $\delta(q, a) = (a', q', k)$, it prints a' in the scanned square, and makes a k move, i.e., one square to the right, one square to the left, or no move at all. Accordingly, the k is 1, -1 or 0, respectively, and enters in the state q'. Continuing the computation in this way, if it runs off the right end of the given tape and at this time it finds itself in one of the final states of H, then by definition the string x is *accepted*, or otherwise, *rejected*. The set of all strings accepted by the automaton is *language accepted* by the automaton.

Now, if we allow the behavior function to be multivalued, we have a nondeterministic automaton. We understand, henceforth, by *linear-bounded automaton* a possibly nondeterministic automaton thus obtained. Only when there is possibility of confusion, we use the phrase "nondeterministic linear-bounded automaton" as a synonym of "linear-bounded automaton" . A linear-bounded automaton in Myhill's sense is referred to as a deterministic linear-bounded automaton. We then mean by a string accepted by a nondeterministic automaton M, a string for which there is a computation of M which, given the string as input, ends up off the right end of the tape in a final state. On the other hand, a string is said to be rejected by M if there is a

[4] This condition means that the symbol "<" is not effected during the computation.

computation of M which, given the string as input, never ends, or ends up off the left end of the tape, or, finally, ends up off the right end of the tape in a non-final state. Because of the nondeterminacy of M, a string can in general be both accepted and rejected by M . The set of all strings accepted by M is called the *languages accepted* by M. The set of all strings rejected by M is called the *language rejected* by M.

11.3 Language Acceptability by LBA

In the following we will go through some important proofs about LBA. Because of finite number of blocks on tape or restricted length tape, the total configurations under which an LBA can go are finite, hence the language accepted by LBA is decidable. On the same grounds it can be shown that the *Halting Problem* is decidable for an LBA. Every LBA accepts context-sensitive language (CSL) and for every CSL there exists an LBA that accepts it, i.e., a language is accepted by LBA if and only if it is CSL.

Definition 11.2 (*Context-sensitive Grammar and Language*) If a grammar G has rules of the form $\varphi \rightarrow \psi$, where length of ψ is not smaller than that of φ, then the grammar G is *context-sensitive grammar*, and it generates the context-sensitive language $L(G)$. □

Theorem 11.1 *A language is accepted by an LBA iff it is context-sensitive.*

Proof **Part 1**. If L is a CSL, then L is accepted by some LBA:

1. Let $G = (V, \Sigma, S, P)$ be the given grammar such that $L(G) = L$, which is CSL and we need to show that there is an LBA that accepts L.
2. Construct LBA M with tape alphabet as pairs: $\Sigma \times \{V \cup \Sigma\}$ (for 2- track machine), such that first track holds input string w, and second track holds a sentential form α, $S \Rightarrow^* \alpha$.
3. if $w = \varepsilon$, M halts without accepting.
4. Repeat:

   a. Non-deterministically select a position i in α.
   b. Non-deterministically select a production $\beta \rightarrow \gamma$ of G.
   c. If β appears beginning in position i of α, replace β by γ there.
      If the sentential form is longer than w, LBA halts without accepting.
   d. Compare the resulting sentential form on track 2 with w on track 1. If they match, accept. If not go to step 4a.

Part 2. If there is a linear-bounded automaton M accepting the language L, then there is a context-sensitive grammar generating $L - \{\varepsilon\}$.

Following is the approach to proof. Let the grammar of the following language simulates the moves on LBA.

1. Derivation simulates moves of LBA
2. Three can be three types of productions in this grammar:
   a. Productions that can generate two copies of a string in Σ^*, along with some symbols that act as markers to keep the two copies separate.
   b. Productions that can simulate a sequence of moves of M. During this portion of a derivation, one of the two copies of the original string is left unchanged; the other, representing the input tape to M, is modified accordingly.
   c. Productions that can erase everything but the unmodified copy of the string, provided that the simulated moves of M applied to the other copy cause M to accept. □

On the other hand, a language rejected by a linear-bounded automaton will also be shown to be context-sensitive language. Indeed we can construct another linear-bounded automaton which accepts this language. When, in particular, it is rejected by a deterministic automaton, a linear-bounded automaton which accepts it can also be deterministic, and since it is nothing but the complement of the language accepted by the automaton, it follows that the class of languages accepted by deterministic linear-bounded automata forms a Boolean algebra.

Example 11.1 Show that the language $L = \{a^n b^n c^n \mid n \geq 0\}$ is context-sensitive.

The production rules, we will be making in use are listed without any specific order as

1. $S \to abc \mid aAbc$
2. $Ab \to bA$
3. $Ac \to Bbcc$
4. $bB \to Bb$
5. $aB \to aa \mid aaA$

As per the Definition 11.2, these production rules are of a context-sensitive grammar.

For $w = aabbcc$, derivation can be obtained as follows:

$$S \Rightarrow aAbc \Rightarrow abAc \Rightarrow abBbcc$$
$$\Rightarrow aBbbcc \Rightarrow aabbcc.$$

Note that above strings also be generated using the set of productions: $\{S \rightarrow SBc \mid abc, cB \rightarrow Bc, bB \rightarrow bb\}$. The reason for this being—we can always transform one grammar into other through simplification, normal forms, and reductions. We note that both of these grammars are context-sensitive grammars. □

The limitation (of size of storage) of LBA makes the LBA a more accurate model of computers that actually exists, than a Turing machine whose definition assumes unlimited tape.

Example 11.2 Determine the upper limit of number of configurations of an LBA.

Let an LBA M has $|Q|$ number of states, m number of symbols in the tape alphabets, and input $|w| = n$. Then, LBA can have at most $\alpha(n)$ configurations:

$$\alpha(n) = m^n * n * |Q|, \tag{11.1}$$

where m^n is maximum possible number of tape contents, n is maximum possible number of head positions for the input of length n, and $|Q|$ is number of states. □

From the above example and the proof in exercise 15 (in Exercises), we get two following corollaries.

Corollary 11.1 *The membership problems for sets accepted by linear-bounded automata are decidable.*

Proof This problem can be expressed as

$$A_{LBA} = \{\langle M, w\rangle \mid M \text{ is an LBA that accepts } w\},$$

and M is deterministic machine.

Consider that set of deterministic machines is $\{\langle M_1, w_1\rangle, \langle M_2, w_2\rangle, ..., \langle M_i, w_i\rangle, ...\}$. A new 3-tape LBA M can simulate each of pairs $\langle M_i, w_i\rangle$, where tape-1 holds the description of M_i, tape-2 holds w_i, and tape-3 holds current state. Since every LBA and input pair $\langle M_i, w_i\rangle$ can have only finite number of configurations, hence the 3-tape machine that simulates M_i will also have finite number of configurations, and it can decide and say "Yes" or "No", depending on whether w_i is accepts M_i or not. Hence, the membership problem for LBA is decidable. □

Corollary 11.2 *The sets accepted by linear-bounded automata are all recursive.*

Theorem 11.2 *Every Context-Sensitive Language is Recursive.*

Proof Construct a 3-tape deterministic TM M to simulate the derivation using context-sensitive grammar G:

1. Let the tape-1 is read only, and it holds input string w and the grammar G.
2. Generate all possible derivations on tape-3 for w using grammar G.
3. Tape-2 holds sentential form generated by each simulated derivation.

Finally, if $w \in L(G)$, we will reach to the accepting configuration, else not. Since, we will be in a position to decide, the language is recursive. □

11.3.1 Space Bounds of LBA

The length restriction in CSGs has some intuition: what is the motivation for the restriction $|\alpha| \le |\beta|$ in context-sensitive rules $\alpha \to \beta$? The Idea is that, in a context-sensitive derivation $S \Rightarrow ... \Rightarrow \alpha_i ... \Rightarrow w$, all the sentential forms α_i are of length at most $|w|$. This means that if L is context-sensitive, and we are trying to decide whether $w \in L$, we only need to consider possible sentential forms of length $\le |w|$. So intuitively, we have the problem under control, at least in principle.

Note that, in the sentential form,

$$S = \alpha_a \Rightarrow \alpha_1 \Rightarrow ... \Rightarrow \alpha_i ... \Rightarrow \alpha_n = w,$$

there can be at the most only $(|\Gamma| + |V|)^{|w|}$ number of derivations, which is a finite number.

By contrast, without the length restriction, there is no upper limit on the length of intermediate forms that might appear in a derivation of w. So if we are searching for a derivation for w, how do we know when to stop looking? Intuitively, the problem here is wild and out of control. We will see this intuition made more precisely as we proceed.

The machine therefore has just a finite amount of memory, determined by the length of the input string. We call this a linear-bounded automaton. An equivalent definition of an LBA is that it uses only k times the amount of space occupied by the input string, where k is a constant fixed for the particular machine. However, it is possible to simulate k tape cells with a single tape cell, by increasing the size of the tape alphabet.

At the bottom level of the Chomsky-hierarchy, it makes no difference: every NFA can be simulated by a DFA. At the top level, the same happens. We have defined a "deterministic" version of Turing machines—but any "nondeterministic Turing machine" can be simulated by a deterministic one.

At the context-free level, there is a difference—we need NPDA (Nondeterministic Pushdown Automata) to account for all context-free languages. For example, $\Sigma^* - \{ww \mid w \in \Sigma^*\}$ is a context-free language whose complement is not context-free. However, if L is accepted by a DPDA (Deterministic Pushdown Automata) then so is its complement—can just swap the accepting and non-accepting states.

What about the context-sensitive level? Are NLBAs (nondeterministic LBAs) strictly more powerful than DLBAs? This is still an *open problem!* (Cannot use the same argument because it turns out that CSLs are closed under complementation—it was only shown in 1988).

11.3.2 Detecting Non-acceptance in LBA

Suppose the machibe M is an LBA. How might we detect that w is not in $L(M)$? Clearly, if there is an accepting computation for w, there is one that does not pass through exactly the same machine configuration twice, if it did, we could shorten it.

Since the tape is finite, the total number of machine configurations is finite (though may be large). So in theory, if M runs for long enough without reaching the final state, it will enter the same configuration twice, and we may as well abort it. Note that on this view, repeated configurations would be spotted "not by M itself", but by "us watching", or perhaps by some super-machine spying on M.

For Turing machines with unlimited tape space, this reasoning does not work. There are no general ways of spotting that a computation in a TM is not going to terminate.

11.4 Context-Sensitive Grammars and Languages

We have discussed other types of languages besides those in the "classical" Chomsky-hierarchy. For example, we noted that nondeterministic pushdown automata (NPDA) were more powerful than deterministic Pushdown Automata (DPDA). Table 11.1 shows some of the language classes that fit readily into this hierarchy.

Not all languages' classes fit neatly into a hierarchy. For example, the *linear languages*, which (like deterministic context-free languages) fit neatly between the regular languages and the context-free languages. However, there are languages that are linear but not deterministic context-free, and there are languages that are deterministic context-free but not linear.

Table 11.1 Extended Chomsky-hierarchy

S. no.	Language	Machine
1.	Regular language	Deterministic or nondeterministic finite-state automata
2.	Deterministic context-free language	Deterministic pushdown automaton
3.	Context-free language	Nondeterministic pushdown automaton
4.	Context-sensitive language	Linear-bounded automaton
5.	Recursive language	Turing machine that halts
6.	Recursively enumerable language	Turing machine

In fact, mathematicians have defined dozens, maybe hundreds, of different classes of languages, and how these relate to one another. We should know at least the four "classic" categories that are taught in almost every textbook on the subject.

Definition 11.3 A *family of grammars* $G = (\Sigma, V, S, P)$ is defined by restrictions placed on the form of production rules. We have studied that a regular grammar is defined as consisting only productions of the form,

$$A \to aB \mid a \mid \varepsilon, \tag{11.2}$$

where $A, B \in V$ and $a \in \Sigma$.

A CFG is defined as

$$A \to \beta, \tag{11.3}$$

and in context-sensitive grammars, the productions are,

$$\alpha \to \beta, \tag{11.4}$$

where $A \in V$, $\beta \in (V \cup \Sigma)^*$ and $\alpha \in (V \cup \Sigma)^*$ with atleast one non-terminal symbol.

Note that condition of context-sensitiveness is fulfilled due to terminals and non-terminal both in the left-hand side of a productions. For example, in $A \to \alpha$ there is no context, while in the rule $Cb \to bC$, the b is context for C in Cb. In addition, in CSG there is $|\alpha| \le |\beta|$. □

Definition 11.4 A context-sensitive grammar is of *order-n* if there appears no string of length greater than n in any rule of the grammar. □

For example, if $\alpha \to \beta$ be a rule in context-sensitive grammar, then this grammar is of order-n if longest length of any β is n. Any two grammars G and G' are equivalent if they generate the same languages, i.e., $L(G) = L(G')$.

Lemma 11.1 *For any order-n context-sensitive grammar G* ($n \ge 3$) *there exists an order* $n - 1$ *context-sensitive grammar* G' *equivalent to* G.

Proof We can assume that no rule of G has a terminal symbol unless it is of the form $A \to a$. Let $\varphi \to \psi$ is a rule in G. If $|\psi| < 3$ then it is in G', else, we can write $\varphi = A\varphi'$ and $\psi = BCD\psi'$, where A, B, C, D are nonterminals. If $\varphi = I$, introduce two new symbols and rules, as follows:

$$\begin{aligned} A &\to A_1 A_2 \\ A_1 &\to BC \\ A_2 &\to D\psi'. \end{aligned} \tag{11.5}$$

and add them in G'. If $\varphi' \ne I$, write $\varphi' = E\varphi''$ (E is nonterminal), which makes $\varphi = A\varphi' = AE\varphi''$. Now introduce two new symbols A', E', and add following rules in G' (see rule set 11.5):

$$\begin{aligned} AE &\rightarrow A'E' \\ A' &\rightarrow B \\ E'\varphi'' &\rightarrow CD\psi'. \end{aligned} \tag{11.6}$$

This G' obtained is of order $n - 1$ and equivalent to G. □

By repeated use of Lemma 11.1 we shall get a CSG of order-2. Following is lemma for order-2 CSG.

Lemma 11.2 *A context-sensitive grammar is equivalent to an order-2 grammar.*

Proof Note that if, for each rule $AB \rightarrow CD$ of an order-2 context-sensitive grammar, we introduce a new symbol A' and replace the rule by three rules: $AB \rightarrow A'B$, $A'B \rightarrow A'D$ and $A'D \rightarrow CD$, we get a new grammar which is equivalent to the old one and context-sensitive. □

The rules of order-2 length preserving grammar are one of the following types:

$$\begin{aligned} A &\rightarrow C \\ AB &\rightarrow CD \\ S &\rightarrow EF, \end{aligned}$$

where C, D are not the initial symbol.

Example 11.3 The language $\{a^n b^n c^n \mid n \geq 0\}$, which we know that it cannot be derived using context-free grammar, can be generated by following context-sensitive grammar.

$$\begin{aligned} &V = \{S, A, C\}, \Sigma = \{a, b, c\}, S \rightarrow aAbc \mid \varepsilon \\ &A \rightarrow aAbC \mid \varepsilon, Cb \rightarrow bC, Cc \rightarrow cc. \end{aligned}$$

Applying the above rules, we get

$$\begin{aligned} S &\Rightarrow aAbc \\ &\Rightarrow aaAbCbc \text{ (using } A \rightarrow aAbC) \\ &\Rightarrow aabCbc \text{ (using } A \rightarrow \varepsilon) \\ &\Rightarrow aabbCc \text{ (using } Cb \rightarrow bC) \\ &\Rightarrow aabbcc \text{ (using } Cc \rightarrow cc) \end{aligned}$$

□

Based on the derivations above of context-sensitive grammar, we can give one more definition of context-sensitive grammar.

Definition 11.5 A *context-sensitive* (CS) grammar $G = (\Sigma, V, S, P)$ has productions of the form $u \rightarrow v$, where $u, v \in (V \cup \Sigma)^*$, $|u| \leq |v|$, and u consists at least one nonterminal symbol in it. □

Theorem 11.3 *Every context-free language is context-sensitive.*

Proof The productions of a context-free grammar have the format $A \rightarrow v$, where $v \in (\Sigma \cup V)^*$. The productions of a context-sensitive grammar have the form $xAy \rightarrow xvy$. Thus, in $A \rightarrow v$, with x, y as ε, it is context-sensitive grammar. □

Every context-free grammar is also context-sensitive but not the reverse.

Theorem 11.4 *There exists a context-sensitive language that is not context-free.*

Proof The language $\{a^n b^n c^n \mid n \geq 0\}$ is not context-free. We used pumping lemma to show this (see Sect. 7.7). We can show that this language is context-sensitive, by providing an appropriate context-sensitive grammar for this. Following are the productions for one such grammar. Note that it is different set from Example 11.3, and ε-production has been removed.

$$
\begin{aligned}
&S \rightarrow aXBC \mid aBC \\
&X \rightarrow aXBC \mid aBC \\
&CB \rightarrow BC, \;\; aB \rightarrow ab \\
&bB \rightarrow bb, \;\; bC \rightarrow bc, \;\; cC \rightarrow cc.
\end{aligned}
$$

Using these rules we can generate the string $aabbcc$.

$$
\begin{aligned}
S &\Rightarrow aXBC \Rightarrow aaBCBC \Rightarrow aabCBC \\
&\Rightarrow aabBCC \Rightarrow aabbCC \Rightarrow aabbcC \Rightarrow aabbcc
\end{aligned}
$$
□

Are there different grammars for the same language $a^n b^n c^n$, as demonstrated in Example 11.3, and Theorem 11.4? Truly not. In such situations, where the language is same, a grammar can be transformed into another grammar, or both can be transformed into some standard format such that they are identical.

11.5 Non-context-free Properties of Programming Languages

We have so far considered the programming languages as context-free types. Truly speaking, the general case is contrary to this assumption. For example, in C language we can declare a *function prototype* with arbitrary number of arguments.[5] In the

---

[5] An argument of a function is pointer to strings, like, **argv[]*.

definition of this function prototype these arguments must appear in the same order and type. These two parts of a function we may call as "define/use" structure. This can be captured in the definition, e.g.,

$$L = \{ww \mid w \in \{0, 1\}^*. \tag{11.7}$$

This language is not CFL, but context-sensitive, which can be accepted by the Linear-Bounded Automata (LBA). To recognize *ww* strings, the LBA can have marking bits on its tape, which it can mark while moving the head forward and backward. This approach can easily recognize the boundary of two *w*'s on the tape.

The symbol table in a compiler follows similar process where pointers move forward and backward to identify the tokens in the input. This structure of symbol table associated with the search process, give the compilers the power of LBA. The approach also helps the compilers to handle the C prototypes definitions [6].

Based on the method, how the strings *ww* are recognized by compilers in HLLs (high level languages), it is clear that strings 11.7 are not in CFLs, but in fact in the context-sensitive languages. Let us try to find out the complement of this language in the following example.

Example 11.4 If $L = \{ww \mid w \in \{0, 1\}^*\}$, then $\overline{L}$ is CFL.

We are given the language L which has even length strings *ww*, of 0's and 1's. The complement $\overline{L}$ is therefore those strings of 0's and 1's that are not in *ww*. These strings of $\overline{L}$ are made of 0's and 1's, which are of odd length, in addition $\overline{L}$ also comprises even length string that do not repeat from center, i.e., that are of even length but not like *ww*. The following grammar can be verified to be generating such strings (not in $\overline{L}$).

$$\begin{aligned} S &\to AB \mid BA \mid A \mid B \\ A &\to CAC \mid 0 \\ B &\to CBC \mid 1 \\ C &\to 0 \mid 1 \end{aligned}$$

The first production in the above states that, either the strings are odd (due to $S \to A \mid B$), hence not in *ww*, or they are even (due to $S \to AB \mid BA$). When it is $S \to AB$, it is even, but not in *ww*, and same is case with $S \to BA$. This shows that language for this grammar does not generate strings in *ww*. Also, from the structure of this grammar, where LHS is non-terminal and RHS is in $(V \cup \Sigma)^+$, where V is non-terminal symbols and Σ is terminal symbols, it is clear that this grammar is CFG (as per the definition of CFG), and the corresponding language as CFL. □

11.6 Chomsky-Hierarchy Grammars and Languages

The Chomsky-hierarchy is a classification system of formal grammars and languages, named after the linguist Noam Chomsky, comprises four types of languages and their associated grammars and machines, as shown in Fig. 11.2. The context-sensitive languages are also called decidable languages.

These languages form a strict hierarchy, that is,

$$\begin{aligned}\text{Regular languages} &\subset \text{Context-free languages}\\ &\subset \text{Context-sensitive languages}\\ &\subset \text{Recursively enumerable languages.}\end{aligned}$$

The Chomsky-hierarchy provides a framework for understanding the relationships and limitations between different types of formal grammars and the languages they generate. It illustrates the trade-offs between generative power and complexity, with each level of the hierarchy encompassing the languages generated by the levels below it while adding more expressive capabilities.

The Table 11.2 characterize Chomsky-hierarchy of languages and grammars, and describes the nature of language and grammar for each machine. We note that just by varying the production rules, we can obtain all types of grammars and languages of Chomsky-hierarchy. The following definition covers all four types of languages and grammars.

Definition 11.6 (*Grammars*) Type 0, 1, 2, 3.

For $i = 0, 1, 2, 3$, a grammar $G = (V, \Sigma, S, P)$ is of type i iff the restrictions (i) on productions as given below are satisfied:

For $i = 0, 1, 2, 3$, a language is of type i iff it is generated by a grammar of type i. The family of languages of type i is identified $\mathscr{L}_i$ [7]. □

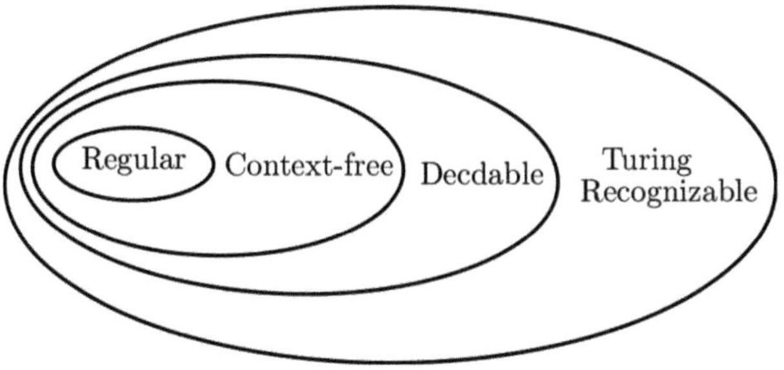

Fig. 11.2 Chomsky-hierarchy of languages

Table 11.2 Chomsky-hierarchy of grammars

S. no.	Language	Grammar	Machine	Language example
1.	Regular language (type-3 language)	Regular grammar: Right-linear grammar/Left-linear grammar	Deterministic or nondeterministic finite-state automata	a^*
2.	Deterministic context-free language (type-2 language)	Context-free grammar (There is no null symbol in productions, i.e., all productions are deterministic)	Deterministic Pushdown Automata	$\{a^n b^n \mid n \geq 1\}$
3.	Context-free language (type-2 language)	CFG (Each left-hand side has only one non-terminal)	Nondeterministic PDA	$\{ww \mid w \in \{a, b\}^*\}$
4.	Context-sensitive (type-1 language)	Context-Sensitive Grammar. For a production, $\|LHS\| \geq 1$, and $\|LHS\| \leq \|RHS\|$	Linear-bounded Automata	$\{a^n b^n c^n \mid n \geq 0\}$
5.	Recursively enumerable (type-0) language	Recursivley Enumerable Grammar. All the above grammars are allowed, and there can be $\|LHS\| \geq \|RHS\|$	Turing machine	Any computable function

In the followings, we describe each of these grammars and languages.

Type-3. These are called *Regular languages*. These are having grammars with production, where productions have following properties,

- there is one non-terminal in the LHS of each production,
- there is only one terminal in the right hand side,
- the RHS is having on-terminal and a terminal (left-linear) or terminal and a non-terminal (right-linear),
- the non-terminals are the states of a NFA that realizes the given regular languages.

These productions are expressed as

$$X \rightarrow a, \text{ or}$$
$$X \rightarrow aY,$$

where $a \in \Sigma$, and $X, Y \in V$.

Type-2: Deterministic CFL. The corresponding DPDA and DCFGs parse the sentences without backtracking, i.e., deterministically. For example, in $\{a^n b^n \mid n \geq 0\}$, the language is deterministic, since we can deterministically switch to comparing b's. Each production in P is of the form,

$$X \rightarrow \alpha$$

where $X \rightarrow V$, and α is word over $V \cup \Sigma$.

Type-2: Context-Free Languages. These languages are more general than deterministic CFLs, since the restriction of determinism is removed in the corresponding machines and grammars. The language $L(G)$ for the grammar G: $S \rightarrow aSa \mid bSb \mid \varepsilon$, is nondeterministic CFL, because nondeterminism is required in order to guess the midpoint for the corresponding language strings $L = \{ww^R \mid w \in \{a, b\}^*\}$. Also, the language $\{a^n b^m c^n d^m \mid n, m \geq 0\}$ is a CFL (i.e., nondeterministic).

Type-1: Context-Sensitive Languages. These are the languages which are recognized by linear-bounded automata. The LBAs are restricted TMS, which can write only in the space equal to the length of input string w. In addition, the LBA can always decide whether the string w is accepted or not. However, the latter is not guaranteed for TM.

The context-sensitive grammar (CSG) have productions with left-hand side with one or more non-terminals along with zero or more terminal symbols, but the length of the LHS of every production rule for that grammar is less or equal to the right hand side of that production. Such CSG specifies a pattern on the LHS and sentential form on the RHS. For example, we have rules in CSG like, $aBc \rightarrow abcd$ or $bBc \rightarrow Def$, which means in the first case when context is a, c the sentential form is $abcd$, in second case, when the context is b, c, the sentential is Def. These are the two different expansions of B, one when it is surrounded by a, c, and other when it is surrounded by b, c. Hence, the there is context sensitivity of the interpretation of B. The length of space used is restricted to $|w|$ to ensure the decidability of input sentence w.

Each production in P is of the form,

$$\alpha X \beta \rightarrow \alpha \gamma \beta,$$

where α, β are words over the alphabet $(V \cup \Sigma)$, $X \in V$, and γ is non-empty word over $(V \cup \Sigma)$. There is possible exception of production $X_0 \rightarrow \varepsilon$, whose occurrence in P implies, however, that X_0 does not occur on right side of any production in P.

Type-0: Recursive Enumerable (RE) languages. These languages are also called *Turing recognition* languages, and form the most general class of Chomsky-hierarchy. The TMs recognize these languages, and the corresponding grammar have unrestricted form of productions. That is, they are like the productions in Context-Sensitive grammars, but there is no restriction like $|LHS| \leq |RHS|$ in the productions [6].

The CFGs and CFLs are fundamentals to computer science because they describe the nested structure of all programming languages. The basic characteristic of CFLs is "nested structures", e.g., the nesting occurs in expressions (if...then...else) and in many other statically scoped structures in the computer programs.

We must distinguish the *iteration* from *nesting*. The basic characteristic of regular languages is "iteration" (i.e., looping). The C language program structure is an example of nesting.

$$\text{Lang} - C \rightarrow \text{main } () \; \{\text{braces}\}$$
$$\text{braces} \rightarrow \{\text{braces}\} \mid \varepsilon$$

11.7 Closure Properties of Context-Sensitive Languages

It is well-known that the class of regular languages are closed under complementation but that neither the class of *recursively enumerable* sets nor the class of *context-free* languages are closed under complementation. It is, however, not known whether the class of context-sensitive languages is closed under complementation!

Furthermore, it is known that nondeterministic finite automata and nondeterministic Turing machines are not essentially more powerful than (deterministic) finite automata and Turing machines, respectively, although nondeterministic pushdown storage automata are essentially more powerful than deterministic pushdown storage automata. However, we do not know if nondeterministic linear-bounded automata are essentially more powerful than deterministic linear-bounded automata. If nondeterministic linear-bounded automata are not essentially more powerful than deterministic linear-bounded automata, the class of context-sensitive languages is closed under complementation, and hence is a Boolean algebra.

In contrast to the unrestricted grammar and languages, the context-sensitive languages are decidable. That is, given any string w and any context-sensitive grammar G, we are in a position to decide whether or not the given grammar G generates w.

Theorem 11.5 *There is an algorithm for deciding whether or not a string $w \in L(G)$, is generated by type-1 grammar $G = (V, \Sigma, S, P)$.*

Proof By definition of type-1 grammars, it is obvious that $\varepsilon \in L(G)$ iff the production $S \rightarrow \varepsilon \in P$. Thus, we may assume that $w \neq \varepsilon$ and $w \in \Sigma^*$. We consider the sequence of the form,

$$S = \alpha_0, \alpha_1, ..., \alpha_{n-1}, \alpha_n = w, \tag{11.8}$$

where $n \geq 1$, are pairwise distinct words over $(V \cup \Sigma)$, and for $0 \leq i \leq n-1$, $|\alpha_i| \leq |\alpha_{i+1}|$. Clearly, the number of subsequences is finite. It is also obvious that $w \in L(G)$ iff for some sequence (11.8),

$$S = \alpha_0 \Rightarrow \alpha_1 \Rightarrow \ldots \Rightarrow \alpha_n = w. \tag{11.9}$$

Thus, it suffices to check, for each of the finitely many sequences (11.8), whether or not the subsequence (11.9) is satisfied. This can be accomplished because for any two words α_i, α_j and a grammar G, we can decide by checking through the productions in G whether or not $w_i \Rightarrow_G w_j$ holds [7]. □

The context-sensitive languages are closed under the following operations:

- Union
- Concatenation
- Reversal
- Kleene star
- Intersection.

Theorem 11.6 *If L_1 and L_2 are two context-sensitive languages, then their union $L = L_1 \cup L_2$ is also a context-sensitive.*

Proof Let the LBAs M_1, M_2 accepts the languages L_1, L_2, respectively. We construct an LBA M that works as follows: Given an input w, M stores w, say, on the lower half of its tape and computes on the upper half, by simulating M_1. If M_1 accepts w then M accepts. Else, if M_1 does not accept, M goes back to the left end and starts computation on the lower half, simulating this time M_2. If M_2 accepts w then M accepts. If none of M_1 or M_2 accept, M rejects. Hence, the language M accepts is the union of L_1 and L_2. □

Theorem 11.7 *If L_1 and L_2 are two context-sensitive languages, then their intersection $L = L_1 \cap L_2$ is also a context-sensitive.*

Proof Let the linear-bounded automata M_1 and M_2 respectively, accept the languages L_1 and L_2. We can construct an LBA M that works as follows: Given an input w, M stores w, say, on the lower half of its tape and computes on the upper half, by simulating M_1. If M_1 accepts w then M goes back to the left end and starts computation on the lower half, simulating this time M_2. If M_2 also accepts w then M is made to accept w. In other cases M is not made to finish calculation successfully. Hence, the language M accepts is the intersection of L_1 and L_2. We should note that space occupied by w will not overflow its size. □

The ideas used to show that context-sensitive languages (CSLs) are closed on union and intersection, can be extended to prove that CSLs are also closed on reversal, concatenation, and Kleene star operations.

11.8 Indexed Grammars

Indexed grammar, also known as an Attribute Grammar, defines and analyze context-free grammars with associated attributes or semantic information. Unlike traditional context-free grammars, which only specify the syntax of a language, indexed grammars associate additional information (attributes) with each grammar symbol. These attributes can be used to represent the semantics of the language being described. In an indexed grammar, production rules are augmented with semantic rules that specify how attributes are computed and propagated throughout the parse-tree during the parsing process. Each attribute may depend on the attributes of other symbols involved in the production rule. This dependency relationship forms a directed acyclic graph known as the *attribute dependency graph*.

Some applications of indexed grammars are as follows:

- *Compiler Design*: Indexed grammars are commonly used in compiler construction. They allow the definition of syntax and semantics in a unified manner, which is essential for constructing a compiler that not only checks for syntactic correctness but also performs semantic analysis and generates intermediate code.
- *Type checking*: Indexed grammars useful in type checking during the compilation of programs. The attributes associated with the grammar symbols can represent the types of expressions and variables, facilitating type checking and error detection.
- *Code Optimization*: Indexed grammars are helpful in various code optimization, such as constant folding, common subexpression elimination, and dead code elimination. The attributes can carry information about the values and dependencies of expressions, aiding in identifying opportunities for optimization.
- *Program Analysis*: Indexed grammars are employed in program analysis tasks, such as data-flow analysis, control-flow analysis, and dependency analysis. The attributes can store information about program properties, which helps in understanding program behavior and finding bugs or inefficiencies.

Overall, the indexed grammars provide a formal and powerful framework for combining syntax and semantics in language definition and processing. They are widely used in the design and implementation of compilers, interpreters, and other language processing tools to facilitate code analysis, optimization, and transformation.

The languages generated by indexed grammars are called *indexed languages*. An indexed grammar is an extension of context-free grammar. The indexed languages include properly all the CFLs and yet is a properer subset of context-sensitive languages (see Fig. 11.3). The indexed languages resemble the CFLs in the sense that many of the closure properties and decidable results of both class of languages are the same.

Partly the interest in larger classes of languages is due to the inadequacy of context-free grammars in specifying all the syntactic structures found in many algorithmic programming languages. For automatic compiler writing systems to be practical reality there should be a reasonable scheme of representing the complete syntactic structure of a language. The indexed languages includes all the CFLs and some

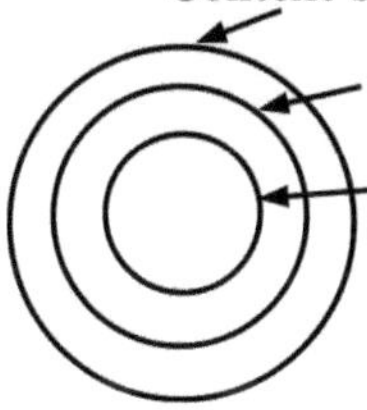

Fig. 11.3 Indexed grammar versus CFG and CSG

context-sensitive languages, yet it is a proper subset of the class of context-sensitive languages.

All four grammars in Chomsky-hierarchy grammars, i.e., type-0, 1, 2, and 3, generate the family of languages, which correspond to the family of sets recognized by the particular automata, i.e., TM, LBA, PDA, and FA, respectively. The indexed languages also enjoy this dual representation. An automata model, called *nested stack automaton*, provides additional characterization. Such automata is one-way nondeterministic nested stack automata, and it recognizes indexed language. This automata and indexed language have one-to-one correspondence.

Definition 11.7 (*Index Grammar*) An indexed Grammar is, $G = (V, \Sigma, S, P, F)$, where

V is finite non-empty set of non-terminals,
Σ is finite set of terminals,
S is start symbol, $S \in V$,
F is finite set of flags, each element of which is a finite set of ordered pairs of the form (A, χ), where $A \in V$ and χ is in $(V \cup \Sigma)^*$. An element $f \in F$ is called *index* or *flag*. An ordered pair (A, χ) in f is written as $A \rightarrow \chi$ and called as *index production* contained in f.
P is finite ordered pairs of the form $(A \rightarrow \alpha)$, it is called Production, where $\alpha \in (VF^* \cup \Sigma)^*$. □

Let $G = (V, \Sigma, S, P, F)$ be the indexed grammar. A derivation in G is a sequence of derivation strings, $\alpha_1, \alpha_2, ..., \alpha_n$, with each $\alpha_i \in (VF^* \cup \Sigma)^*$, where α_{i+1} is derived from α_i by the application of either one production or one index production. Except the manner in which indices and strings of indices are manipulated, a derivation in G proceeds in exactly same manner as in context-free grammar. The difference is that, for a derivation in an indexed grammar each non-terminal in V can be immediately followed by a string of indices in F^*. A string of symbols of the form $A\xi$, where $A \in V$ and $\xi \in F^*$, is called as an *indexed non-terminal*. A string α in $(VF^* \cup \Sigma)^*$ is called as sentential form, and labeled as α. Note that, in a sentential form there is one or more flags (also called *index*), of the kind $A \rightarrow \chi$, after each variable (i.e., in V) but there is no such flag after the terminals symbols (i.e., in Σ).

For the indexed Grammar $G = (V, \Sigma, S, P, F)$, we make use of following notation of symbols:

$$A, B, C, D \in V,$$
$$a, b \in \Sigma \cup \{\varepsilon\},$$
$$X \in (V \cup \Sigma),$$
$$w, x \in \Sigma^*,$$
$$f, g, h \in F,$$

$$\chi \in (V \cup \Sigma)^*,$$
$$\xi, \eta, \theta \in F^*,$$
$$\alpha, \beta, \gamma, \delta \in (VF^* \cup \Sigma)^*.$$

A sentential form α is said to be directly generating (i.e., deriving) a sentential form β, i.e., $\alpha \rightarrow_G \beta$, if one of the following two is satisfied.

1. $\alpha = \gamma A \xi \delta$, where

$$A \rightarrow X_1\eta_1 X_2\eta_2 \ldots X_k\eta_k$$

is a *production* in P, then β due to $\alpha_a \rightarrow \beta$ is,

$$\beta = \gamma X_1\theta_1 X_2\theta_2 \ldots X_k\theta_k\delta,$$

where, for $1 \leq i \leq k$, $\theta_i = \eta_i\xi$ if $X_i \in V$, or $\theta_i = \varepsilon$ if $X_i \in \Sigma$.

Here, η_i is flag of X_i, and ξ is string of flags following it. Since, for non-terminals there is no flags, hence if $X_i \in \Sigma$, the flags string is ε.

2. $\alpha = \gamma A f \xi \delta$, where

$$A \rightarrow X_1 X_2 \ldots X_k$$

is an *index production* in the index f, and β in $\alpha \rightarrow_a \beta$ is,

$$\beta = \gamma X_1\theta_1 X_2\theta_2 \ldots X_k\theta_k\delta,$$

for $1 \leq i \leq k$, $\theta_i = \xi$ if $X_i \in V$, or $\theta_i = \varepsilon$ if $X_i \in \Sigma$.

In both the above cases 1 and 2, the non-terminal A is said to be expanded. In case 2, the index f is said to be consumed by non-terminal A. Note that the terminal symbol can never have a string of indices immediately following to it in any line of the derivation.

If $A\xi$ is an indexed non-terminal and $A \rightarrow aB\eta C\theta b$ be a production in P, then $A\xi$ can directly derive the sentential form $aB\eta\xi C\theta\xi b$ in G. Here, the index string ξ distributes over the indexed non-terminals $B\eta$ and $C\theta$, but none over the terminal symbols a and b in the production.

If $Af\xi$ is an indexed non-terminal and index f contains the index production $A \rightarrow aBC$, then $Af\xi$ can directly derive the sentential form $aB\xi C\xi$ in G. Note that in such a step, the index f is removed from the next line of the derivation, and the index string ξ distributes over the non-terminals B and C, but not over the terminal a.

The operation $\alpha \rightarrow \beta$ given above is a transitive relation. A sequence of derivation,

$$S = \alpha_0 \Rightarrow \alpha_1 ... \alpha_n = w, \text{ for } w \in L(G), \tag{11.10}$$

is called derivation of length n.

We illustrate a derivation using the Indexed grammar, in the following.

Example 11.5 Find out the indexed grammar for derivation of all the strings in the language $\{a^n b^n c^n \mid n \geq 1\}$.

Let $G = (V, \Sigma, S, P, F\}$ be the grammar, where

$$\begin{aligned} V &= \{S, A, B\} \\ \Sigma &= \{a, b, c\} \\ F &= \{f, g\} \end{aligned}$$

and P is: $S \rightarrow aAfc, A \rightarrow aAgc, A \rightarrow B$ and F is: $f = [B \rightarrow b], g = [B \rightarrow bB]$. The first production is supposed to be applied once only.

$$S \Rightarrow aAfc$$

Now we apply the second production on the sentential form number of times:

$$\begin{aligned} aAfc \Rightarrow & aaAgfcc \\ \Rightarrow & ... \\ \Rightarrow & a^n Ag^{n-1} fc^n \\ \Rightarrow & a^n Bg^{n-1} fc^n. \end{aligned}$$

Note that we have applied the second production $n - 1$ times. Next, we apply the third production once.

$$a^n Ag^{n-1} fc^n \Rightarrow a^n Bg^{n-1} fc^n. \tag{11.11}$$

Next, we expand B by consuming the indices.

$$Bg^{n-1} f \Rightarrow bBg^{n-2} f \Rightarrow ...b^{n-1} Bf \Rightarrow b^n.$$

Substituting the above result in (11.11), we get $S \Rightarrow^* \{a^n b^n c^n \mid n \geq 1\}$ in $2n + 1$ steps. Note that this indexed grammar is deterministic. □

11.9 Regulated Rewriting Grammars

The family of four grammars—type 3, 2, 1, 0—was obtained by imposing restrictions on the format of productions. A natural generalization is to restrict also the manner in which grammar is allowed to generate the sentences, that is, to impose restrictions also on how the productions should be used. Hence, every derivation of terminal word starting from start symbol should not be acceptable. There can be *control device* which lets through accepted derivations only. In the following we shall study such control devices. For example,

- An application of a production may determine which productions are applicable at the next step. This is called *Programmed grammar*.
- Only certain previously specified production strings are allowed to be applied. This is called *Matrix Grammar*—a grammar with control languages.
- Some productions cannot be applied if some others are applicable. This is called *ordered grammar*.
- At the ith step of derivation, only a subset of whole set of productions P can be applied. This is called *time varying grammar*.

These are the formal grammars that extend the concept of context-free grammars (CFGs) by incorporating additional rules that regulate the application of production rules during the derivation process. A regulated rewriting grammar consists of all four tuples of context-free grammars, and in addition they contain *Regulation rules*. These rules impose additional constraints on the application of production rules. Regulation rules control how many times a particular production rule can be used, the order in which rules can be applied, and other conditions governing the derivation process. Presence of these regulation rules introduce an extra layer of control and coordination during the derivation process.

The languages generated by regulated rewriting grammars are known as *regulated languages*. These languages are a proper superset of context-free languages and can describe certain phenomena that context-free grammars cannot capture efficiently.

The study of regulated rewriting grammars and regulated languages contributes to the broader field of formal language theory and helps in understanding the computational power and limitations of different types of grammars.

These grammars are useful in many rewriting systems, e.g., in heuristic/intelligent compilers, leading to regulated rewriting. Rather than these grammars working independently, they can be supplemented to CFG in the form of additional control device. This control device remarkably increases the generating capability of the grammar. In the following, we discuss each one of them ranging from brief introduction to more elaborate discussions [8].

11.9.1 Programmed Grammars

The *Programmed grammars* are used in defining *recursive languages* larger than the class of context-free languages, while device oriented definitions of such a class are provided by various kinds of stack automata [9].

The programmed grammars are a generalization of phrase structure grammars where each production has a label, a core consisting of an ordinary phrase structure production, and two associated sets of production labels. These grammars lie between context-free and context-sensitive grammars in their generative power. The cores of this grammar has single symbol on the left-hand side and a non-null string on the right.

In a programmed grammar, the derivation process is guided by a program or control mechanism that determines which production rules are applied at each step, based on the current state of the derivation and the symbols encountered so far. This control mechanism provides additional flexibility and allows for more sophisticated language generation compared to regular context-free grammars.

The programmed grammars have the property that after applying a production of a programmed grammar to sentential form in a derivation, one is restricted as to which production rule may be applied next. Each production rule has a label, a core consisting of a regular phrase structure production, and two associated "go-to" fields of two subsets $\sigma(f)$ and $\phi(f)$ of the entire production sets F of G referred to as the success and failure fields of f, respectively. If possible, the production is applied (as far to the left as possible) to the sentential form in a derivation. The next production to be used is selected from the first go-to field, which is called the *success field*. If the production cannot be applied to the string, the next production is selected from the other go-to field.

The programmed grammar model is useful as it permits the specifications within the grammar as to the order in which productions can be used in generating a sentence. A major advantage of using programmed grammars is that grammars can often generate the sentences of a language in a manner which corresponds to the way in which humans would envision the generation. This is particularly true for context-sensitive languages where a phrase structure grammar might have to trace out the detailed maneuvers of a linear-bounded automata. In writing and using the phrase structure for a particular language, all the productions must be constantly checked to see if they are applicable at a given point. Writing a programmed grammar for a given language is similar to writing a program for the generation of its sentences [10].

In the first class of programmed grammar the cores have single symbol on the left-hand side and non-null string on the right, i.e., $A \to \beta$, and it can handle many context-sensitive features of a programming language, and acts in more natural manner than the phrase structure grammar. The other class have identical success and *failure fields*. A more general programmed rule is $\alpha \to \beta$, where $\alpha, \beta \in (V \cup \Sigma)^+$, with α has at least one symbol from V.

A Programmed grammar is $G = (V, \Sigma, S, P, J)$, where the new symbol J is set of production labels. With each r in J there is associated a unique production (r, α, β, M, N), where M, N are in J. A production is written in the following format:

$$(r) \quad \alpha \rightarrow \beta \quad S(M)F(N). \tag{11.12}$$

Note that production format is some what similar to the format of FORTRAN language, where beginning columns 1–7 are label of the sentence, and the last field, 73–80 columns are for comments, which may be sentence serial number, next sentence number, etc.

In applying the production to a sentential form, say θ, the θ is first scanned to see if it contains α as a substring. If so, the leftmost occurrence of α in θ is replaced by β, and the next production is to be applied to the resulting string is selected from M. If θ does not contain α, then no change is made and the next production is selected from N. Since the next production is selected from N if the scan is successful, M is called *success field*, and N is called *failure field*. If M or N is absent from the explicit statement of a rule, the corresponding set of labels is the empty set. If at any point in a derivation, the next production label must be selected from the empty set, the derivation comes to a halt.

Since the success and failure fields can contain several production labels, and different choices from a field can lead to different sentences, a grammar is capable of generating an infinite number of sentences.

Some additional notations will now be introduced. If θ and ω are strings over $V \cup \Sigma$, r and p are the rule labels, and a rule r is,

$(r) \quad \alpha \rightarrow \beta \qquad S(M)F(N)$,

we shall write $(\theta, r) \rightarrow (\omega, p)$ if either of the following two conditions is satisfied:

1. rule r succeeds on θ, producing ω, and $p \in M$; or
2. rule r fails on θ, $\omega = \theta$; and $p \in N$.

If ω consists entirely of terminal symbols, we can also write $(\theta, r) \Rightarrow \omega$. In addition, if production r applied to θ produces the string ω, but the set of labels from which the next production is to be selected is empty, we write $(\theta, r) \Rightarrow \omega$.

Now $(\theta, r) \Rightarrow (\omega, p)$ if there is a chain such that,

$$(\theta, r) = (\theta_1, r_1) \Rightarrow (\theta_2, r_2) \Rightarrow ... \Rightarrow (\theta_n, r_n) = (\omega, p). \tag{11.13}$$

The language generated by the grammar is the set of terminal strings w such that $(S, r) \Rightarrow^* w$, where r is a rule which has on S on the left-hand side of its core. In the case of productions with cores which are not context-free, the # can be used endmarker, and $L(G)$ is the set of terminal strings w not containing # such that $(\#S\#, r) \Rightarrow \#w\#$ for an r which is applicable to $\#S\#$.

Example 11.6 The following is an example of programmed grammar where $\Sigma = \{a, b, c\}, V = \{S, A, B, C\}$. The language generated is the set of sequence of the form $a^n b^n c^n$ with $n \geq 1$. This is context-sensitive language which cannot be generated by any context-free phrase-structure grammar.

Following are the production rules in the format of Eq. 11.12:

(1) $S \rightarrow ABC$	S(2, 5)
(2) $A \rightarrow aA$	S(3)
(3) $B \rightarrow bB$	S(4)
(4) $C \rightarrow cC$	S(2, 5)
(5) $A \rightarrow a$	S(6)
(6) $B \rightarrow b$	S(7)
(7) $C \rightarrow c$	

In the right hand side of the production rules, there are restrictions defined, as how the rules are to be applied. At the end of first rule, $S(2, 5)$ indicates that the rules 2, or 5 is to be applied. If we apply rule 5, we will generate *abc* (as we jump to rule 5 then subsequently to rule 6 and 7). However, if we apply rule 2, which causes iterations, then after rules 2, $S(3)$ indicates that next rule 3 is to be applied, and so on.

Consider generating the sentence $a^2b^2c^2$. The steps are as follows:

Derivation sequence	Rule used
$A \Rightarrow ABC$	1
$\Rightarrow aABC$	2
$\Rightarrow aAbBC$	3
$\Rightarrow aAbBcC$	4
$\Rightarrow aabBcC$	5
$\Rightarrow aabbcC$	6
$\Rightarrow aabbcc$	7

Hence, $S \Rightarrow^* aabbcc$. □

From the given rules above, it is straight forward to see that we can generate strings $a^n b^n c^n$.

11.9.2 Matrix Grammars

Matrix grammars are a type of formal grammar that extends the concept of context-free grammars (CFGs) by using matrices to specify production rules. Each entry in the matrix can be either a terminal symbol or a nonterminal symbol. The Matrix grammars are more expressive than context-free grammars, as they can describe certain languages that cannot be generated by context-free grammars alone. They are particularly useful in the study of formal language hierarchy and the relationship between different classes of formal languages. However, it is worth noting that matrix grammars are not as commonly used as context-free grammars in practical applications due to their complexity and less intuitive nature. The matrix grammars are primarily of theoretical interest in the field of formal language theory.

In *matrix grammars*, instead of isolated and independent productions, there exists a finite set of finite sequences of productions, where instead of separately applying the productions, a whole sequence of productions is applied. To apply such sequence, one first rewrites according to first productions, then according to second productions, and on, until one has written according to the last production. These sequences are referred to as *matrices* [7].

The language generated by a matrix grammar is the set of strings that can be obtained by starting with the start symbol S and applying the production matrices repeatedly until no nonterminal symbols remain. The derivation process in matrix grammars involves matrix multiplication, where the current string is represented as a row vector (or column vector) of nonterminal symbols. To apply a production matrix to the current string, the matrix is multiplied with the string vector, resulting in a new string vector. This process continues until the string vector contains only terminal symbols.

Definition 11.8 A matrix grammar is ordered quadruple $G = (V, \Sigma, S, M)$, where V, Σ, S have the same meaning as in generative grammars, and M is finite set of finite length non-empty sequences whose elements are pairs,

$$(P, Q) = P \in (X^*AX^*), \text{ and } Q \in (V \cup \Sigma), \tag{11.14}$$

where $X \in (V \cup \Sigma)$, $A \in V$, and the pairs (P, Q) are referred to as productions, and written as $P \to Q$. The sequences are referred to as matrices and written as

$$m = [P_1 \to Q_1, ..., P_n \to Q_n],\ n \geq 1. \tag{11.15}$$

The language generated by the matrix grammar G is defined as

$$L(G) = \{w \mid S \Rightarrow^* w \text{ and}, w \in \Sigma^*\}. \tag{11.16}$$

We are mostly concerned with grammars of type-2, as the generative capability of matrix grammars is remarkably larger than that of context-free grammars. We will represent the family of context-free ε-free matrix grammars by $\mathscr{M}$. We consider the following example to illustrate this cabability.

Example 11.7 Matrix grammar for the language $L = \{ww \mid w \in \{a, b\}^*\}$.

Let $G = (V, \Sigma, S, M)$ be the matrix grammar, with $V = \{S_0, S_1\}$, $S = S_0$, $\Sigma = \{a, b\}$, and M is,

$$\{[S_0 \rightarrow S_0S_1],$$
$$[S_0 \rightarrow aS_0,\ S_1 \rightarrow aS_1],$$
$$[S_0 \rightarrow bS_0,\ S_1 \rightarrow bS_1],$$
$$[S_0 \rightarrow a,\ S_1 \rightarrow a], [S_0 \rightarrow b,\ S_1 \rightarrow b]\}.$$

This grammar generates the language $L = \{ww \mid w \in \{a, b\}^*\}$, and $w \neq \varepsilon$. Note that the language is not context-free. Using this grammar we can generate the words in L, as illustrated below.

$$\begin{aligned} S_0 &\Rightarrow S_0S_1 \\ &\Rightarrow aS_0aS_1 \\ &\Rightarrow abS_0abS_1 \\ &\Rightarrow abaaba \in L. \end{aligned}$$

□

It is important to note that we have used the productions in sequence which are specified in matrices, i.e., in "[" and "]" parentheses symbols. Verify that we are able to generate the language L in the above example as $\{aa, bb, abab, abaaba, ...\}$. Further, note that the top level production $S_0 \rightarrow S_0S_1$ is to be used only once.

On the other hand every grammar can be regarded as a matrix grammar whose matrices consist of single productions. Further, it has been proved that each matrix grammar can be generated by a parallel communicating system. The matrix grammars have applications in *Register Machines* and vector addition systems. In fact, the Register machines and matrix grammars have been proved equivalent [11].

11.10 Conjunctive Grammars

The generative power of context-free grammars is generally considered to be insufficient for denoting many languages that arise in practice; most natural languages contain non-context-free constructs, while there is many times a non-context-freeness found in programming languages also. The context-sensitive and indexed grammars are also the potential solutions for these scenarios.

The conjunctive-grammars use a more general and uniform approach of allowing the explicit use of *intersection* operation in the body of any rule of the grammar. This increases the generative power even beyond the finite intersections of context-free languages, and at the same time allows the model to remain no less convenient for practical use than ordinary CFLs. The semantics of conjunctive grammar is characterized by system of languages equations with unrestricted concatenation, union, and intersection. The conjunctive languages are known to be closed under union, intersection, concatenation, and *inverse-homomorphism* [12].

A subclass of conjunctive grammars, called *linear conjunctive grammars*, is known to be computationally equivalent to automata, such grammar exist for language $\{a^n b^n c^n \mid n \geq 0\}$, $\{wcw \mid w \in \{a, b\}^*\}$, and language of all accepting computation of a given Turing machine.

A conjunctive grammar is defined as $G = (V, \Sigma, S, P)$, where V, Σ, S have same meaning as in CFG, while the production rules P, is an *ordered pair* $(A, \{\alpha_1, ..., \alpha_n\})$ of non-terminal and a finite non-empty subset of $(\Sigma \cup V)^+$, and written as

$$A \rightarrow \alpha_1 \& ... \& \alpha_n. \tag{11.17}$$

For every rule $A \rightarrow \alpha_1 \& ... \& \alpha_n \in P$, for every i $(1 \leq i \leq n)$, a pair of the form (A, α) is called *conjunct*, and denoted as $A \rightarrow \alpha_i$.

A collection of rules for a single non-terminal is specified using the notation,

$$A \rightarrow \alpha_{11} \& ... \& \alpha_{1n} \mid ... \mid \alpha_{m1} \& ... \& \alpha_{mn}.$$

Similar to the context-free case, a conjunctive grammar is called *linear conjunctive* if every rule it contains is either of the form,

$$A \rightarrow u_1 B v_1 \& .... \& u_n B v_n, \tag{11.18}$$

where $n \geq 1$, $u_i, v_i \in \Sigma^*$, $B_i \in V$; or of the form,

$$A \rightarrow w, \tag{11.19}$$

where $w \in \Sigma^*$.

The semantics of conjunctive grammar is defined using derivations, generally in the same way as in the context-free grammar case. The only difference is in the nature of the objects being transformed; while context-free derivations operate with strings over $\Sigma \cup V$ in the form of concatenations, the conjunctive grammar uses formats over *concatenation* and *conjunction*.

For a conjunctive grammar $G = (V, \Sigma, S, P)$, the following holds:

- ε is conjunctive formula,
- every symbol from $V \cup \Sigma$ is a formula,
- if A and B are formulas, then AB is a formula.
- If $\mathsf{A}_1 ..., \mathsf{A}_n$ $(n \geq 1)$ are formulas, then $\mathsf{A}_1 \& ... \& \mathsf{A}_n$ is a formula.

Conjunctive formulas are defined by script capital letters from the beginning of the alphabets: A, B, C. The derivability is as follows:

$$s_1 \mathsf{A} s_2 \Rightarrow_G s_1 (\alpha_1 \& ... \& \alpha_n) s_2,$$

where $s_1, s_2 \in (\Sigma \cup V \cup \{``(", ``\&", ``)"\})^*$. For $\mathsf{A} \in V$, if $s_1 \mathsf{A} s_2$ is formula then for all $\mathsf{A} \rightarrow \alpha_1 \& ... \& \alpha_n \in P$,

$$s_1 \mathsf{A} s_2 \Rightarrow_G s_1 (\alpha_1 \& ... \& \alpha_n) s_2.$$

Also, conjunction of several identical terminal strings enclosed in parentheses can be replaced by one such string.

A language ($L_G(\mathsf{A})$) generated by a grammar G is set of all strings over Σ derivable from A in zero or more steps.

$$L_G(\mathsf{A}) = \{w \mid w \in \Sigma^*, \text{ and } \mathsf{A} \Rightarrow_G^* w\}. \tag{11.20}$$

A language generated by the grammar G is set of all strings over Σ derivable from its start symbol. Hence, $L(G) = L_G(\mathsf{A})$.

We take two simple examples to demonstrate the theory of conjunctive grammar. These examples are from non-context-free grammars: (1) $\{a^n b^n c^n \mid n \geq 0\}$, which represents multiple agreements, and (2) $\{a^m b^n c^m d^n \mid m, n \geq 0\}$ (cross agreement). Both languages are intersections of two context-free languages, and therefore, a conjunctive grammar for each of them can be contsructed by using a simple conjunction on top level.

Example 11.8 Consider the language: $\{a^n b^n c^n \mid n \geq 0\}$. The productions for conjunctive grammar for this language are given below:

$$\begin{aligned} &S \rightarrow AB \,\&\, DC,\ A \rightarrow aA \mid \varepsilon,\ B \rightarrow bBc \mid \varepsilon \\ &C \rightarrow cC \mid \varepsilon,\ D \rightarrow aDb \mid \varepsilon. \end{aligned}$$

In the above production rules, AB and DC generate $\{a^i b^j c^k \mid j = k\}$ and $\{a^i b^j c^k \mid i = j\}$, respectively. And, therefore, S generates $\{a^n b^n c^n \mid n \geq 0\}$.

$$\begin{aligned} &AB \Rightarrow aAB \Rightarrow abBc \Rightarrow abbBcc \Rightarrow abbcc, \text{ and} \\ &DC \Rightarrow aDbc \Rightarrow aaDbbc \Rightarrow aabbc. \end{aligned}$$

Combining the above two,

$$\begin{aligned} S &\Rightarrow AB \,\&\, DC \Rightarrow abbcc\&DC \\ &\Rightarrow abbc\&aabbc \Rightarrow aabbcc. \end{aligned}$$

□

Consider another language: $\{a^m b^n c^m d^n \mid m, n \geq 0\}$, with cross agreement. The productions for conjunctive grammar for this language are:

$$\begin{aligned} &S \rightarrow XD \,\&\, AY, X \rightarrow aXc \mid B, Y \rightarrow bYd \mid C \\ &A \rightarrow aA \mid \varepsilon, B \rightarrow bB \mid \varepsilon \\ &C \rightarrow cC \mid \varepsilon, D \rightarrow dD \mid \varepsilon \end{aligned}$$

The derivation of this second language is left as an exercise.

11.11 Universal Versus Chomskian Grammars

Chomskyan linguistics, beginning with his Syntactic Structures—a distillation of his Logical Structure of Linguistic Theory, challenges the structural linguistics and introduce *transformational grammar*. This theory takes utterances (sequences of words) to have a syntax which can be characterized by a formal grammar; in particular, a context-free grammar extended with transformational rules.

Children are hypothesized to have an innate knowledge of the basic grammatical structure common to all human languages. Under this hypothesis it is assumed that any language which the children encounter is of a certain restricted kind. This innate knowledge is often referred to as *universal grammar*. It is argued that modeling knowledge of language using a formal grammar accounts for the "productivity" of language. With a limited set of grammar rules and a finite set of terms, humans are able to produce an infinite number of sentences, including sentences no one has previously said. Chomsky has always acknowledged his debt to *Panini* for his modern notion of an explicit generative grammar.

The Principles and Parameters approach (P & P)—make strong claims regarding universal grammar. As per these, the grammatical principles underlying languages are innate and fixed. The differences among the world's languages can be characterized in terms of parameter settings in the brain (such as the pro-drop parameter, which indicates whether an explicit subject is always required, as in English language, or can be optionally dropped, as in Spanish language), which are often linked to switches. In this view, when a child learns a language, he needs only acquire the necessary lexical items (words, grammatical morphemes, and idioms), and determine the appropriate parameter settings, which can be done based on a few key examples.

The advocaters of this view argue that the pace at which children learn languages is inexplicably rapid, which is not possible unless children have an innate ability to learn languages. The similar steps are followed by children all across the world when learning languages. The fact that children make certain characteristic errors as they learn their first language, whereas other seemingly logical kinds of errors never occur.

Chomsky also theorizes that unlimited extension of a language such as English is possible only by the recursive device of embedding sentences in sentences.

Generative Grammar—the Chomskian approach toward syntax, often termed generative grammar, studies grammar as a body of knowledge possessed by language users. Since the 1960s, Chomsky has maintained that much of this knowledge is innate, implying that children need only learn certain parochial features of their native languages. The innate body of linguistic knowledge is often termed Universal Grammar. From Chomsky's perspective, the strongest evidence for the existence of Universal Grammar is simply the fact that children successfully acquire their native languages in so little time. He argues that the linguistic data to which children have access radically underdetermine the rich linguistic knowledge which they attain by adulthood.

Today there exists many different branches of generative grammar; one can view grammatical frameworks such as head-driven phrase structure grammar, lexical functional grammar and combinatory categorical grammar as broadly Chomskian and generative in orientation, but with significant differences in execution.

11.12 Summary

This chapter is devoted to expansive coverage of formal grammars and their properties, in addition to the linear-bounded automata machines.

The Linear-Bounded Automata (LBA) were originally developed as models for actual computers rather than models for the computational process; even though they have become important in the theory of computation, but have not emerged to the extent the pushdown automata have.

An LBA is nothing but TM with bounded memory, i.e., the space used will never be more than the original input string w. That makes an LBA more realistic than the TM having infinite memory. However, that allows the TM to use an arbitrary amount of memory to compute without any memory bounds.

When we compare LBA with finite automata, they will look same if we restrict LBA further, to allow it to move head to right only on the tape, and allow to only read the tape contents. Hence, the LBA with these restrictions can simulate a finite automata, and will accept only regular language.

The LBA always halts for any given input string; if it accepts it, it halts and accept, and if it rejects it, then it halts and rejects. Thus, an LBA decides a language, and not merely recognize, like TM, which may continue indefinitely in some cases when input is not accepted.

The LBA accepts recursive languages.

The recursive languages are strictly larger set than that of context-free languages.

An LBA accepts context-sensitive languages like $\{a^n b^n c^n \mid n \geq 0\}$.

Every context-free language can be accepted by an LBA; this can be done with two tapes of LBA—the first holds original string w as read only, and second simulates the pushdown stack, which is read–write tape, but from one end of tape only.

To make the LBA tape-bounded, there are two end markers for input w, making it $< w >$, or $< a_1, a_2, ..., a_n >$, where $<, >$ are left and right end markers on the tape, and disallows the read/write head to go beyond these markers.

For its space-bounded feature, $\alpha \rightarrow \beta$ as production, there is restriction of $|\alpha| \leq |\beta|$.

A language is accepted by LBA if and only if it is context-sensitive.

Due to tape-bounded and decidable (recursive) features of LBA, the halting problem is solvable for linear-bounded automata.

The consequent of Chomsky-hierarchy of grammars is a relation of proper subset between languages, as follows:

$$\text{Reg. lang} \subset \text{context-free lang.} \subset \text{context-sensitive lang} \subset \text{recursively rnumerable lang.}$$

The following languages are decidable:

- The language of regular expressions;
- An empty language;
- The language for which every element is a pair of: DFA and string accepted by it;
- The language where every element is pair of strings—first element is description of a grammar G, and second is string w generated by G; and
- A context-free languages, i.e., A_{CFG}.

The CFLs can be classified in one way, according to minimal number of variables (non-terminals) in the grammar of that language, and other on number of production rules in the grammar, number of grammatical levels, and maximal depth of grammatical levels.

The context-sensitive languages are closed under union, concatenation, reversal, Kleene star, and intersection operations.

Following are other grammars, having practical significance, but these do not exactly fit in the Chomsky-hierarchy grammars:

The indexed grammars specify a device or algorithm for recognizing well-formed sentences instead of generating a parse-tree. Alternatively, set of properties can be specified, and the language obey these properties. The indexed grammar lie between CF grammars and context-sensitive grammars.

The grammars of types, 3, 2, 1, 0 are obtained by imposing some restrictions on the production rules. An idea is to have a control device that lets through accepted derivations only.

If application of productions may determine which productions are applicable at next step, then this is called *programmed-grammar*.

When only certain previously specified production strings are allowed to be applied, then this grammar is called *matrix grammar*.

When some productions cannot be applied, when others are applied, then the grammar is called *ordered grammar*.

At the ith step of derivation, when only a subset of the whole set of productions are applied, then the grammar is called *time varying grammar*.

The generative power of context-free grammars is generally considered insufficient for denoting many languages that arise in practice; the natural languages contain non-context-free constructs, while there are many programming languages also, having non-context-free constructs. The context-sensitive and indexed grammars are potential solutions for this.

The *conjunctive grammar* allows the operation of set intersection in the body of any rule of the grammar. This increases its generative power even beyond the finite intersection of context-free languages.

The Chomskian linguistics, beginning with syntactic structures, challenges the structural linguistics and introduce the transformational grammar. This theory gives syntax to utterances, i.e., sequence of words that are characterized by formal grammar. This is extension of context-free grammar with transformational rules.

It is hypothesized that the children have innate knowledge of basic grammatical structure common to all human languages. This innate knowledge is referred to as *universal grammar*. When equipped with this, having limited set of grammatical rules humans are able to produce an infinite set of sentences, even those which no one has previously said.

Self Review Questions

1. List the differences between LBA and Turing machine.
2. What is Tally language?
3. Why the computation in LBA is called tape bounded?
4. How the tape-bounded property of LBA justifies it to recognize the context-sensitive language?
5. How the regular languages are proper subset of recursive languages?
6. What is an *offline* computation?
7. What is an *online* computation?
8. What is *indexed non-terminal*?
9. How a derivation in an indexed grammar is different from that in the context-free grammar?
10. How a non-terminal in an indexed grammar is different from that in the context-free grammar?
11. How a sentential in indexed grammar is different from that in the context-free grammar?
12. Which automata recognizes the indexed languages? [Ans. Nested stack automata]
13. In what way the matrix grammar is different from standard generative grammar?
14. What is universal grammar? Why it is called universal?
15. Conjunctive grammars are closed on what set operations?

Exercises

A. Concepts based Problems

Note: The $*$ marked exercises are provided with solutions at the end of this book.

1. What are the analogous of Online and Offline computations of TM, in the modern computation?
2. Construct a linear-bounded automaton that accepts the language $\{a^m b^n a^m b^n \mid m, n \in \mathbb{N}\}$.
3. Construct a linear-bounded automaton that accepts the language $\{a^{2^n} \mid n \in \mathbb{N}\}$, i.e., the language of powers of two, in unary coding.

4. Construct a linear-bounded automaton that accepts the set of primitive words over the alphabet $\{a, b\}$. (Note: A word w is primitive if it is not of the form u^n for any word $u \neq w$, where u is a word, and n is an integer).
5. In what way a Pushdown automata can be viewed as an LBA?
6. * Generate the language for the following matrix grammar: Let, $G = (V, \Sigma, S, M)$, where $S = S_0$, $\Sigma = \{a, b, c\}$, and $M = \{[S_0 \rightarrow S_0 S_1], [S_0 \rightarrow aS_0b, S_1 \rightarrow cS_1], [S_0 \rightarrow ab, S_1 \rightarrow c]\}$.
7. Give one special characteristic for each of the following grammars:

    a. Programmed grammar
    b. Matrix Grammar
    c. Ordered grammar
    d. Time varying grammar.

8. How you will simulate a Pushdown Automata using an LBA?

B. Analysis-based Problems

9. Describe the LBA that accepts the language $L = \{a^i \mid i \text{ is not prime}\}$.
10. How you will show that language 11.7 (Sect. 11.5) is not a context-free language?
11. Consider the grammar $G = (V, \Sigma, S, P)$, with Unary language (also called Tally language), $\Sigma = \{a\}$ and productions are as follows:

$$\begin{aligned} &S \rightarrow ACa\# \mid a \mid \varepsilon,\ Ca \rightarrow aaC,\ AD \rightarrow AC \\ &C\# \rightarrow D\# \mid E,\ aD \rightarrow Da,\ aE \rightarrow Ea \\ &AE \rightarrow \varepsilon. \end{aligned}$$

    Find out the few derivations due to G and determine the language $L(G)$.
12. Give a context-sensitive grammar that generates the strings in language $\{ww \mid w \in \{0, 1\}^*\}$.
13. Given the grammar G below, can you prove that language $L(G)$ is empty?

$$\begin{aligned} S &\rightarrow aAB,\ B \rightarrow ab \\ Aa &\rightarrow SaB,\ B \rightarrow SA \\ bB &\rightarrow a,\ Ab \rightarrow SBb. \end{aligned}$$

C. Proof-based Problems

14. Show that LBA can decide the membership of the language $\{a^n b^n c^n \mid n \geq 0\}$. Also justify that this languages is space bounded. [Hint: The solution to space boundedness can be proved by nature of productions used, i.e., in productions $\alpha \rightarrow \beta$, there is $|\alpha| \leq |\beta|$, where $\alpha, \beta \in (V \cup \Sigma)^+$.]
15. * Prove that *Halting Problem* is solvable for Linear-Bounded Automata.
16. Show that an LBA can decide of the language $\{a^n b^{n^2} \mid n \geq 0\}$.
17. Prove that every context-free language is recognized by a deterministic LBA.

18. Show that regular languages are Recursive Languages. [Hint: See the logical approach, on Sect. 9.6.1]
19. Prove that every context-free language is accepted by deterministic LBA.
20. * What is grammar for the language $\{a^p \mid p \text{ is prime}\}$?
21. Show that every context-free language can be recognized by a 2-tape LBA machine.
22. Let M be an LBA. Show that there exists an LBA M_1, that accepts the same language as M, always halts, irrespective of whether its input is accepted or not.
23. Let C be a class of devices of some type, and there is an enumeration, $M_1, M_2, \ldots$ of all the devices in C. Show that there can be an algorithm that, given a device $M \in C$ and an input x, can determine if M accepts x.

D. Multiple choice Questions

24. * Intersection of two context-sensitive languages is:
    (A) Context-sensitive (B) Unrestricted
    (C) Regular (D) Context-free

25. * Which automata and Indexed languages have one-to-one correspondence?
    (A) Nondeterministic PDA (B) One-way NPDA with nested-stack
    (C) One-way nested-stack PDA (D) Deterministic PDA

26. * Which of the following are True, given that: G_{CF} is CFG, L_{CF} is set of context-free languages, I_G is indexed grammar, I_L is set of indexed languages, L_{CS} is set of context-sensitive languages,
    (A) $L_{CF} \subset I_L$ (B) $I_L \subset L_{CS}$
    (C) $G_{CF} \subset I_G$ (D) All above

27. * Let L_1 and L_2 be languages defined as follows: $L_1 = \{a^i b^j c^k \mid i, j, k \geq 0\}$, $L_2 = \{a^m b^m c a^n b^n \mid m, n \geq 0\}$. Then, $L = L_1 \cap L_2$ is:
    (A) Recursively enumerable but not context-free
    (B) Recursive but not context-free
    (C) Context-free and Regular
    (D) Context-free but not regular

E. Advanced Knowledge Assessment Problems

28. Explain the concept of nested one-way nondeterministic stack automata.
29. "The matrix grammar has applications in *register machines* and in *vector addition* system." Explain the application. (Hint: See Ref. [11].)
30. Show that register machines and matrix grammar are equivalent. (Hint: See Ref. [11].)

References

1. Pighizzini G (2015) Guest column: one-tape Turing machine variants and language recognition. ACM SIGACT News 46(3):37–55 Sep 1
2. Hennie FC (1965) One-tape, offline Turing machine computations. Inf Control 8(6):553–78
3. Myhill J (1960) Linear bounded automata (WADD Technical Note). Wright Patterson AFB, Wright Air Development Division, Ohio
4. Kuroda Sige-Yuki (1964) Classes of languages and linear-bounded automata. Inf Control 7(2):207–223. https://doi.org/10.1016/s0019-9958(64)90120-2
5. Landweber PS (1968) Three theorems on phrase structure grammars of type 1. Inf Control 6(2):131–136. https://doi.org/10.1016/s0019-9958(63)90169-4
6. Gopalakrishnan G (2006) Computation engineering: applied automata theory and logic. Springer Science & Business Media
7. Salomaa A (1977) Formal languages. ACM monograph series. Academic Press, New York, San Francisco, and London, 1973
8. Greibach S (1969) An infinite hierarchy of context-free languages. J Assoc Comp Mach, 91–106
9. Aho AV (1968) Indexed grammars—an extension of context-free grammars. J ACM 1968:647–671
10. Daniel JR (1969) Programmed grammars and classes of formal languages. J ACM 16(1):107–131
11. Freund R et al (2005) Matrix languages, register machines, vector addition systems, Fénix Editora
12. Okhotin A (2004) An overview of conjunctive grammars. In Current trends in theoretical computer science: the challenge of the new century vol 1: algorithms and complexity vol 2: formal models and semantics. World Scientific, pp 545–566

Part V
Decidability and Undecidability

This part is for the topics that are philosophical in nature and are at the same time having the practical importance. There is only one chapter in this part—It talks about what can and what cannot be computed; in some problems, even it cannot be decided whether computation will ever lead to the solution, whatever may be the power of computing machine is dedicated for such problem—with abundant memory and time resources.

In general, the problems are classified as decidable, semi-decidable, and undecidable. The first, called decision problems, always halt the machine with solution, or provide Yes/No answer when it is case of membership problem, e.g., whether a given number is a prime number. The semi-decidable problems halt the machine when solution is found and may continue the machine forever if solution is not found or does not exist—this is no different from infinite loop.

The Gödel numbering provides encoding of TMs, using which a TM can be encoded and decoded back to TM, thus Turing machine can be said to be a large integer number in $\mathbb{N}$.

Many interesting problems have been presented that make us realize that there are no solutions possible for many problems, i.e., they are undecidable and unsolvable.

Chapter 12
Decidability, Undecidability, and Unsolvability

Abstract An important question in algorithmic solution is whether a given problem's solvability is *decidable* or *not*. The problems of decidable type have answer in the form of Yes/No, while for the undecidable type, no algorithm can exist for their solution. This chapter takes us from foundational concepts to theories about this question, and introduces with what problems are solvable (decidable)/semi-decidable/undecidable, how to formulate them, and presents the characteristics of an effective procedure. In addition, we shall arrive to relation between decision problems vs. recursive languages, what are the decidable and closure properties of formal languages. We will see how the recursive languages differ from recursively enumerable, what are the properties of computable, non-computable, countable, and uncountable sets. The undecidability theory starts with Hilbert—one of his problems seeks to answer about an arbitrary diophantine equation with rational integral coefficients, whether it has a solution in rational integrals. As per Gödel, the symbolic logic problems can be transformed into positive integers in recursive set. Therefore, whether a problem is solvable or not, amounts to say whether the problem of positive integers is solvable or not in the set of integers. The chapter presents how to represent a formula into a number, Gödel's Incomplete theorem, and the unsolvability has been illustrated through examples, particularly through diagonal language, Barber's paradox, and through undecidability of halting problem. Many undecidability results have been proved through Rice's theorem. The chapter concludes with its summary, self review questions and exercises.

Keywords Decision problems · Recursive languages · Recursively enumerable languages · Computable sets · Decidable problems · Semi-decidable problems · Undecidable problems · Non-computable sets · Diophantine equation · Completeness · Unsolvability · Diagonal language · Barber's paradox · Rice's theorem

K. R. Chowdhary, *Theory of Computation*,
https://doi.org/10.1007/978-981-97-6234-7_12

12.1 Introduction

In this chapter,[1] we will examine the limits of computation as a means to solve the problems. This consideration is important due to many reasons: (i) the problems which cannot be solved need to be simplified to a formulation such that computation can be applied, (ii) the techniques used in proving the languages to be undecidable, like, reductions and diagonalizations appear very often in the complexity theory, and (iii) the undecidability is an interesting topic in the computation theory.

The canonical results in the computability theory is "undecidability of the halting problem." It has been proved intuitively that no algorithm can exist to decide if a Turing machine halts on an arbitrary string. This result however seems unimportant and abstract, but it has far reaching effects.

The software designers seek better ways to determine the correctness of their programs. The undecidability of the halting problem provides the impossibility of certain results for software developers. There does not exist such technique as halting problem to validate any arbitrary program.

Computability theory also helps in establishing the existence of undecidable problems that cannot be solved in principle, regardless of the amount of time invested. In contrast, complexity theory establishes the existence of decidable problems that, although solvable in principle, cannot be solved in practice, because the time and space required would be larger than the age and size of the known universe.

Let us go to basics. But, to catch the much needed concept we may occasionally jump between different topics. We know that integers are enumerated on the basis of their *base*, which in decimal system is 10, octal it is 8, and so on, there can be arbitrary and infinitely large number of bases. The set of these bases, say O, is therefore enumerably infinite, and can be indeed effectively generated in sequence of distinct elements,

$$O : B_1, B_2, B_3, \ldots$$

Since each base B_i defines a unique *recursively enumerable* set of positive integers and each such set is defined by at least one B_i, O is also an ordering of all recursively enumerable sets of positive integers, though each set will indeed recur an infinite number of times in O above. We may then say, in classical terms, that, whereas there are $2^{\aleph_0}$ arbitrary sets of positive integers (i.e., all the subsets of $\aleph_0$), there are but $\aleph_0$ recursively enumerable sets, i.e., $B_1, B_2, \ldots$.

By the *decision problem* of a given set of positive integers we mean the problem of effectively determining for an arbitrarily given positive integer whether it is, or is not, in the set. While, in a certain sense, the theory of recursively enumerable sets of positive integers is potentially as wide as the theory of general recursive functions,[2] the decision problems for such sets constitute a very special class of decision problems.

[1] A Diophantine equation is an equation in which only integer solutions are allowed.

[2] A function that can be computed by a computer program whose loops are all "for" loops.

One of the problems posed by German mathematician David Hilbert in his Paris address of 1900 [problem 10] is the problem of determining for an arbitrary *diophantine*[3] whether the equation has a solution with all unknowns taking integer values. For example, the Diophantine equation $3x^2 - 2xy - y^2z - 7 = 0$ has an integer solution: $x = 1, y = 2, z = -2$. But, the Diophantine equation $x^2 + y^2 + 1 = 0$ has no integer solution.

If the variables in a diophantine equation be chosen from a given enumerably infinite set of variables, it is clear that the set of diophantine equations are enumerably infinite. Indeed these equations can be effectively put into one-one correspondence with the set of positive integers. Since, for any one diophantine equation, and assignment of integral values to its variables, it can be effectively determined whether or not the equation is satisfied by those values. Based on this, a set of diophantine equations having rational integral solutions can be generated. The corresponding integers under the above one-one correspondence can then also be generated, and, indeed, constitute a recursively enumerable (RE) set of positive integers. And, under that correspondence, Hilbert's problem is transformed into the decision problem of that recursively enumerable set [6].

More generally, a wide variety of decision and other problems are transformed into problems about positive integers. And, whether those problems are, or are not solvable in the intuitive sense is equivalent to whether they are or are not recursively solvable.

Gödel's classic theorem on the *incompleteness* and extendibility of symbolic logic led to the *recursive unsolvability* of a generalization of the above problem of Hilbert. Alonzo Church explicitly formulated the concept of recursive unsolvability, and arrived at the unsolvability of a number of problems; certainly, he proved them recursively unsolvable [1, 2].

Learning Outcomes of this Chapter:

1. Recursive and recursively enumerable languages. [Analysis]
2. Decidable languages. [Proof]
3. Decidability. [Proof]
4. Computable Sets. [Knowledge]
5. Effective procedure. [Comprehension]
6. Formulating decision problems. [Comprehension]
7. Language Enumeration. [Application]
8. Undecidability. [Evaluation], [Proof]
9. Gödel's Incomplete theorem. [Knowledge], [Analysis]
10. Diagonal language. [Evaluation]
11. Unsolvability. [Proof]
12. Halting problem. [Proof]
13. Barber's paradox. [Analysis]
14. Rice's theorem. [Analysis], [Proof]

---

[3] *Diophantine equation*: A polynomial equation with rational integral coefficients, whose variables are permitted only to assume integer variables.

12.2 Recursive and Recursive Enumerable Sets

The *decision problem in logic*, more precisely its *deducibility problem*, is a problem of determining of an arbitrary member x of E whether it is, or is not, deducible from a set of logic formulas A. Granting that every generated set is effectively enumerable, the members of E can be effectively set in one-to-one correspondence with the set of positive integers. The positive integers corresponding to the members of A, then, constitute a generated, and hence, under our generalization, a recursively enumerable set of positive integers. And, under that correspondence, the decision problem of the symbolic logic is transformed into the decision problem of this recursively enumerable set of positive integers.

Closely related to the technical concept, *recursively enumerable* set of positive integers is that of a *recursive* set of positive integers. This is a set for which there is a recursive function $f(x)$ such that $f(x)$ is say 1 when x is a positive integer in the set, 0 when x is a positive integer not in the set. We may also make this the definition of the decision problem of the set being *recursively solvable*. For 1 and 0 may be regarded as the two possible truth-values, true, false, of the proposition: "positive integer x is in the set," and the definition of recursive set is equivalent to this truth-value being recursively calculable for all positive integers x.

Definition 12.1 (*Recursive Set*) A set is recursive if it possesses a recursive characteristic function. That is to say, set A is recursive if and only if there exists a recursive function f such that for all x, it holds that $x \in A \Rightarrow f(x) = 1$, and $x \notin A \Rightarrow f(x) = 0$. □

Intuitively, A is recursive if there exists an effective procedure for deciding, given any x, whether or not $x \in A$.

Following are the recursive sets:

i. The set $\{0, 2, 4, ...\}$ of even numbers;
ii. $\mathbb{N}$ and ϕ;
iii. Any finite set;
iv. Any set with finite complement.

The sets (i), and (ii) are straight forward, as the elements and their order are explicit, hence required element can be found out using a characteristic function, e.g., the characteristic function can recursively generate consecutive numbers, and when a higher number is generated without generating the given number, it can be concluded that given number is not in the set (i). The sets in (ii) are also explicit. The sets (iii) and (iv) are recursive, since explicit listing of the appropriate finite set can be used to give instructions for the characteristic function.

There are $\mathbb{N}$ recursive sets, as all these will have finite number of elements. By cardinality, nonrecursive sets must exist (since there are $2^{\mathbb{N}}$ subsets of $\mathbb{N}$ in all).

Definition 12.2 (*Recursively enumerable Set*) A set A is recursively enumerable if it constitutes the range of recursive function, i.e., if there exists a recursive function f that can eventually generate any element in A. Any recursive set is also recursively enumerable. □

Alternatively, a recursively enumerable set is a set where you can write a program that will output each element in the set. It is okay if this program never stops.

We usually talk about this in the context of languages. Thus, recursively enumerable language is a language where you could write a program that writes out every valid string in that language.

Imagine, however, that we do not want to generate all the strings in a language or all the elements in a set, but, we just want to check and see if a given string is in the language, say L. The problem is that we would never know for sure that the string is not in the language L. If it was required to write a compiler for this language L, the compiler would work just fine on valid inputs, but invalid inputs may make this compiler hang forever as it searches through an infinite list for something that is not there.

The set of *recursive languages* or *recursive sets* are sets where you can write a program that tells you whether the given input is in the set or not. All recursive languages are also recursively enumerable because you can just enumerate every string, and then output it if it is in your set. Recursive languages are also called decidable because you can decide for sure if an element is in it or not. This is not the case with the more general recursively enumerable sets.

In general, it is easier to prove that a set or language is recursively enumerable or is recursive, but harder to prove that it is not recursive but recursively enumerable.

The relationship between these two concepts is revealed by the following theorem.

Theorem 12.1 *A set of positive integers is* recursive *if and only if, both it and its complement with respect to the set of all positive integers are* recursively enumerable.

Proof For the sake of simplicity, we assume that both the set S and its complement $\overline{S}$ to be infinite. If S is *recursive*, there is an effective procedure of telling about any positive integer x whether it is, or not in S. The procedure is as follows: generate the positive integers $1, 2, 3, \ldots$ in their natural order, and, as soon as a positive integer is generated, test its being or not in S. Each time a positive integer is thus found to be in S, write down it as belonging to S. Thus, an effective process is set up for effectively enumerating the elements of S. Hence, S is recursively enumerable. Likewise $\overline{S}$ can be shown to be *recursively enumerable.*

Conversely, let both S and $\overline{S}$ be *recursively enumerable*, and let $n_1, n_2, n_3, \ldots$ be a recursive enumeration of S; and $m_1, m_2, m_3, \ldots,$ of $\overline{S}$. Given a positive integer x, generate in order $n_1, m_1, n_2, m_2, n_3, m_3, \ldots$. Since x must be either in S or in $\overline{S}$, in a finite number of steps we shall thus come across an n_i or m_j identical with x, and accordingly discover x to be in S, or $\overline{S}$. An effective method is thus set up for determining of any positive integer x whether it is, or is not, in S. Hence, S is *recursive*. □

12.3 Computable Sets

There are two ways to look at the Sets: (i) From *Computability* point of view, and (ii) From *Compressibility* point of view. The *tractability* is a notion which describes that a set is "nearly computable". Given any function f, assume that we can compute it, i.e., there is an algorithm, but only with some external information that we need from a set A, expressed as $f \leq_T A$ (f is reducible to A). Assume that, in addition, A is computable, i.e., there is an algorithm to compute A. We can build together both programs into one program that directly computes f. In other words: if A is computable then all f that are computable in A are computable, too.

In computability theory, a set of natural numbers is called *recursive/computable/decidable* if there is an algorithm which terminates after a finite amount of time and correctly decides whether a given natural number belongs to the set.

A more general class of sets is called *recursively enumerable sets*, also called *semi-decidable sets*. For these sets, it is only required that there is an algorithm that correctly decides when a number is in the set; the algorithm may give no answer (but not the wrong answer) for numbers not in the set. A set which is not computable is called *noncomputable* or *undecidable*.

Definition 12.3 (*Computable set*) A subset S of the natural numbers $\mathbb{N}$ is called recursive if there exists a *total computable* function f such that $f(x) = 1$ if $x \in S$ and $f(x) = 0$ if $x \notin S$. In other words, the set S is recursive if and only if the *indicator function*[4] 1_S is computable. □

The following sets are computable:

a. Every finite or co-finite subset of the natural numbers is computable;
b. The above can be modified to include these special cases:
    i. The empty set is computable,
    ii. The entire set of natural numbers is computable,
    iii. Each natural number (as defined in standard set theory) is computable, that is, the set of natural numbers less than a given natural number is computable;
c. The set of prime numbers is computable;
d. A recursive language that is recursive subset of a formal language, is computable;
e. The set of stings that correspond to well-formed programs is computable.

Note that any finite object can be encoded as a natural number (e.g., an algorithm, a program, a large prime number, a large composite number, code of a Turing Machine, etc.). Hence, as per the definition of computable set, all these objects are computable.

Given sets $A, B \subseteq \mathbb{N}$, we say that "$A$ is computable in B", which we write as $A \leq_T B$, if there is a computable procedure that can tell whether an element is in A

[4] An indicator function or a characteristic function is defined on a set X that indicates membership of an element in a subset A of X. It has value 1 for all elements of A and the value 0 for all elements of X not in A. That is, $1_A(x) = 1$, if $x \in A$, else 0 for $x \notin A$.

or not, using B as an *oracle*. We call this also as "A is Turing reducible to B". That is, problem A is polynomial time reducible to problem B. We say that A is Turing equivalent to B, and we write $A \equiv_T B$ if $A \leq_T B$ and $B \leq_T A$.

The following three sets are Turing equivalent.

a. The set of pairs (set-of-generators, relations), of non-trivial groups;
b. The set of finite triangulations of simply connected manifolds;
c. The set of programs that halt.

What is a computable set? We fix some model of computation (typically Turing machines), and also fix a set $A \subseteq \mathbb{N}$, and the TM can answer Yes if a given integer $x \in A$, else the answer is No.

Theorem 12.2 *Show that infinite set T_∞ of all Turing machines is computable.*

Proof Turing machines have definite representation (see Universal TMs, in Chap. 10). For any x, if $x \in T_\infty$, we first choose format of x, if it is not as per the representation of TM, we reject it. Otherwise, we check for membership of x step by step in T_∞. Let the set T_∞ is arranged lexicographically. In the search process of x, if $|x| > |T_i|$, where $T_i \in T_\infty$, then reject x, else keep on searching it in T_∞. When found, accept x. □

There also exists *non-computable* sets. Following are some examples of non-computable sets:

- *The word problem:* Consider the *groups* (group theory) that can be constructed with a finite set of generators ($\mathcal{G}$) and a finite set of relations between the generators ($\mathcal{R}$). The set of pairs $\langle \mathcal{G}, \mathcal{R} \rangle$, of *non-trivial* groups is not computable. For example, the generators can be grammars' set, and relations can be acceptability/rejection relation between grammar and strings.
- *Simply connected manifolds:* The set of finite triangulations of *simply connected* manifolds is not computable.
- *The Halting problem:* The set of programs that halt, and do not run for ever, is not computable.

Countable and Uncountable Sets

Let a set of strings $S = \{s_1, s_2, \ldots, \}$ is countable. The s_i are generated through enumerating procedure. We can show that the power set for S is 2^S, is not countable. Let some subsets of power set be: $\{s_1\}$, $\{s_1, s_3, s_4\}$, $\{s_2, s_3\}$, etc. We can encode the elements of power set as binary strings of 1s and 0s. Let $t_1 = \{s_1\}$, $t_2 = \{s_1, s_3, s_4\}$, and so on, in lexicographic order (see Table 12.1). Thus power set is $\{t_1, t_2, ..., t_i, ...\}$. In he following we show the proof that power set is not countable.

Table 12.1 Enumerating the power set elements

Power set elements' names	Power Set elements	Encoding				
		s_1	s_2	s_3	s_4	...
t_1	$\{s_1\}$	1	0	0	0	...
t_2	$\{s_1, s_3, s_4\}$	1	0	1	1	...
t_3	$\{s_2, s_3\}$	0	1	1	0	...
...	...		...		...	

Theorem 12.3 *Power set is not countable.*

Proof We would prove it by contradiction. Let us assume that power set is *countable*.[5] Thus, we can enumerate its elements, as shown in Table 12.1, such that all the subsets of S are considered.

For our proof we shall consider only the last column in this table, comprising the encoding of every element of the power set. Let us consider the diagonal elements' string of 1s and 0s of this power set, let it be x. Now, consider $\overline{x}$, it is complement of the power set diagonal elements (bits). This $\overline{x}$ is not t_1 because its first bit differs with first bit of t_1, it is also not t_2 because its second bit differs from 2nd bit of t_2, and in general, it is not t_i because its ith element differs from ith bit of t_i.

Hence, this new element must be some element t_j of power set (since we assume that $P(S)$ is enumerated). However, that is impossible, because all the elements of power set have been considered—a contradiction to our assumption. Hence, we conclude that power set is *uncountable*. □

12.4 Recursive and Recursively Enumerable Languages

A language L is *Recursively Enumerable* (RE) if there is an *effective procedure* that lists only the words in L with or without repetitions. By effective procedure we mean a finite set of instructions which describe in an unambiguous and detailed way how the task is performed. There are no restrictions on space or time needs to carry out the procedure, although the amount of information available at each step of the procedure is finite.

We wish to study recursively invariant properties of sets of integers, in particular those properties which have to do with solvability and unsolvability. Most basic is the property of possessing a recursive function [15]. Consider an enumerable finite language L, whose sentences[6] can be listed in the order of their mapping with some

[5] A countable set is one whose elements can be enumerated with one-to-one mapping to the elements of set of natural number $\mathbb{N}$.

[6] However, for the sake of simplicity we say strings or words.

set S, such that $|S| = n$, and $n \in \mathbb{N}$. To find out whether, for some string $x \in S$, we can think of an algorithm, which can list all the elements of S, and, at the end, the algorithm halts. If, in this process the string x is produced, we conclude that $x \in S$, else $x \notin S$. Since, S is finite, the time to answer, "Is $x \in S$?", will also be finite.

12.4.1 Recursive Languages

Definition 12.4 (*Recursive Language*) A language is recursive if there exists an algorithm, that when given an input word x, will determine in a finite amount of time whether $x \in L$ or not. □

Naturally, Recursive (R) languages are *decidable languages*, as one can decide (in finite time) whether a string is in the language or not.

Consider an infinite language L, whose elements have *bijection* with the set $\mathbb{N}$. Since L has bijection with $\mathbb{N}$, the language L is enumerable, and its elements can be exhaustively listed. However, being infinite it may not terminate. To find out, whether some string x is in L, we may think of an algorithm which will produce a list of members of L in order of their mapping with set $\mathbb{N}$, and in the process if x is produced, the algorithm halts, and we are in a position to conclude that $x \in L$. And if x is not produced (the algorithm will not halt) we may have to wait for an indefinite amount of time to see if ever the string x gets listed. Thus, this kind of recognition is *semi-decidable*. Here, the word *halting of an algorithm* is *synonymous* to halting of a machine running the algorithm.

The Table 12.2 shows the listing of some Recursive Languages

It is obvious that these are not a mathematical definition of Recursive languages. For an adequate definition, the intuitive notion of an effective procedure be replaced by a formalized notion, such as Turing machine. On the other hand, the above intuitive definition is adequate for the purpose where only it is required to show the existence of an effective procedure.

To illustrate an effective procedure, we take the following example.

Example 12.1 Procedure to enumerate the elements x, y, z, n that satisfy the equation $x^n + y^n = z^n$ for $n \geq 3$.

We consider ordered quadruples (x, y, z, n) of natural numbers in $\mathbb{N}$ satisfy the conditions,

Table 12.2 Recursive languages

S. no.	Recursive languages
1.	Any finite language
2.	Set of Prime numbers
3.	Set of programs that terminate on any input

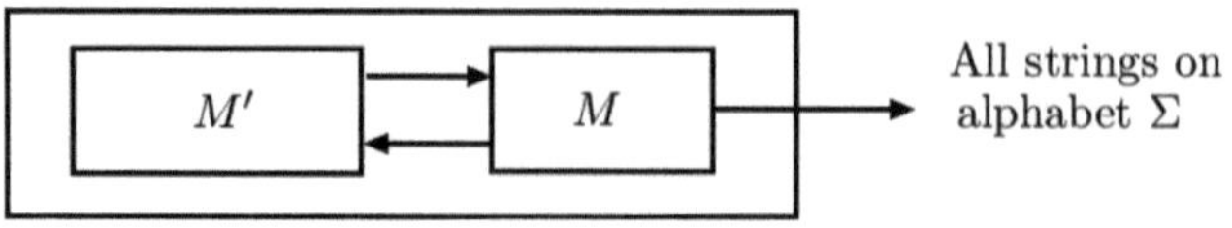

Fig. 12.1 Enumerating a recursive language

$$x^n + y^n = z^n, \quad n \geq 3. \tag{12.1}$$

We associate with each such quadruple the word $w = x\#y\#z\#n$, where x, y, z and n are in binary form. Let L be the language over the alphabet $\{0, 1, \#\}$ consisting of all such words w. Then L is recursive because given any word w, we can determine whether or not w is of the form $x\#y\#z\#n$, where x, y, z and n are non-empty words over the alphabet $\{0, 1\}$, and if it is of this form, determine whether or not the integers represented by x, y, z and n satisfy the relation (12.1).

The language L above is also *recursively enumerable*, as explained in the following: To list the words in L, we consider all words over $\{0, 1, \#\}$ in some specified order. For instance, we may order them according to their length, and the words of same length in lexicographic order. For each word, we apply the algorithm described above for deciding whether or not the word is in L. The word is added to the list if it is not in L, after which next word is considered. Clearly, this procedure does not terminate. □

Because of its decidable property, every recursive language can be enumerated. The following theorem shows this.

Theorem 12.4 *If a language L is recursive then there exists an enumeration procedure for it.*

Proof Let TM M recognizes language L, hence $L = L(M)$. If $\Sigma = \{a, b\}$, then a TM M' can enumerate strings: $a, b, aa, ab, ba, bb, aaa, \ldots$, in lexicographic order (see Fig. 12.1).

The enumeration procedure is as follows. The machine M' generates string $w \in \Sigma^*$. Next, the TM M checks "if $w \in L$?" is yes, then it outputs w else ignore it. Let $L = \{ab, aabb, bb, aaabbb, \ldots\}$ be the language of TM M. Let the M' outputs in lexicographic order as $\{a, b, aa, ab, ba, bb, aaa, ...\}$. Every word w, generated by M' is input to M; if M accepts it then M outputs it, else not. Naturally, the word sequence output of M is in lexicographic order, and it is the language of M, and it is enumerated . □

Example 12.2 Enumerate all the strings of language $L = \{a^n b^n c^n \mid n \geq 0\}$.

We consider a 2-tape Turing machine T, with both tapes empty initially, i.e., all the cells have B written. The language L can be generated on tape 1, following these steps:

1. Write ## on tape 1 to indicate that there is null string between two # signs, for $n = 0$, while tape 2 is empty.
2. append a on tape-2 after its content.
3. Write following on tape-1: as equal to string length on tape 2, then by same length bs, then by same length cs, then # is written.
4. goto step 2.

We find that tape 1 contents grow as $\#abc\#aabbcc\#aaabbbccc\#$.... and the tape 2 contents grow as $Baaa$...., and this process goes on indefinitely, because $n \geq 0$.

The language $L = \{a^n b^n c^n \mid n \geq 0\}$ is, say, recognized by a TM M (see Example 9.9). An enumerator T generates all the strings of L, shown in Fig. 12.2. □

The recursive languages are closed under set operations of union, concatenation, intersection, Kleene star, complement, and set difference.

Theorem 12.5 *If a language L is recursive then its complement $\overline{L}$ is also recursive.*

Proof Let the language L is decided by the Turing machine $M = (Q, \Sigma, \Gamma, \delta, s, \{y, n\})$. Let M' be another Turing machine, such that,

$$M' = (Q, \Sigma, \Gamma, \delta', s, \{n, y\}).$$

If L is recursive, then $L = L(M)$ for some TM M that always halts. We transform M into M' so that M' accepts when M does not and vice versa. Therefore, M' always halts and accepts $\overline{L}$. Thus, $\overline{L}$ is recursive.

Construction of M' (Fig. 12.3) is as follows: The accepting states in M are made non-accepting states in M' with no transitions, i.e., here M' will halt without accepting also. Thus, if q' is new accepting state in M', then there is no transition from this state.

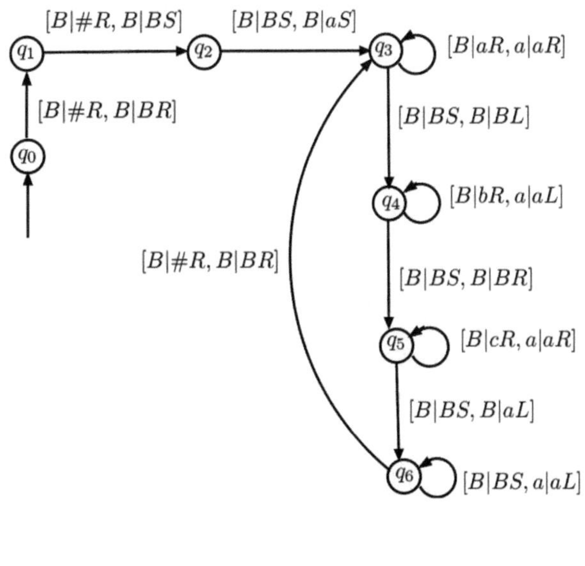

Fig. 12.2 TM T as enumerator for the language $L = \{a^n b^n c^n \mid n \geq 0\}$

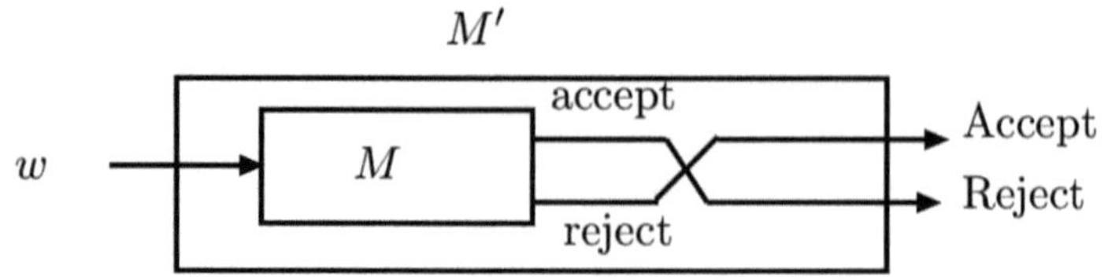

Fig. 12.3 Co-recursive is recursive

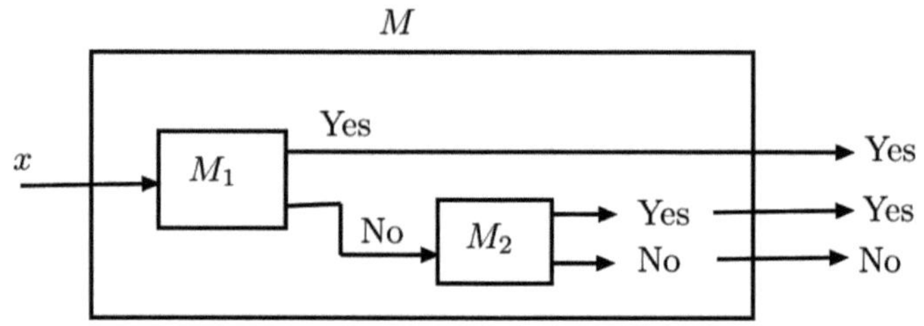

Fig. 12.4 Union operation of recursive languages

The transition function δ' is expressed as

$$\delta'(q,a) = \begin{cases} n, & \text{if } \delta(q,a) = y, \\ y, & \text{if } \delta(q,a) = n, \\ \delta(q,a), & \text{otherwise} . \end{cases} \tag{12.2}$$

It is clear that $M(w)$ yields y iff $M'(w)$ yields n. Thus, M decides the language $\overline{L}$. This proves the theorem. □

Theorem 12.6 *Every context-sensitive Language is Recursive.*[7]

Proof This follows from Theorem 11.5 (Sect. 11.7). A context-sensitive grammar is noncontracting; moreover, for any integer n there are only a finite number of sentential forms of length n. Therefore, for any string w we can set a bound on the number of derivation steps required to generate w, hence a bound on the number of possible derivations. Thus any string w is in the language if and only if one of these derivations produces w. Since we always get the answer whether w is in the language or not, the context-sensitive language is recursive. □

Theorem 12.7 *Union of two Recursive languages is recursive.*

Proof The TM corresponding to this must halt always. Let L_1 and L_2 be sets accepted by M_1 and M_2, respectively. Then $L_1 \cup L_2$ is accepted by TM M, where $x = w_1 \cup w_2$, for $w_1 \in L_1$ and $w_2 \in L_2$ (see Fig. 12.4). □

[7] A different proof of this was presented in Theorem 11.2, Sect. 11.3.

12.4.2 Recursively Enumerable Languages

Based on the above conclusions, now we construct the following definition for Turing Recognizable and decidable languages.

Definition 12.5 (*Turing recognizable*) A language L is Turing recognizable (also called, Recursively Enumerable (RE)) if there exists a TM M which halts if and only if its input $w \in L(M)$. It is possible for this TM to never reach a halting configuration on some input $w \notin L(M)$, and it might instead loop for ever. □

Figure 12.5a shows *Post machine*[8] with tape contents as 1111000011..., with read-/write head pointing to 1st zero symbol in the current configuration. The transition diagram in Fig. 12.5b shows that it terminates its execution in state q_2, but in (c) it loops forever and switches between states q_0 and q_1. Note that, unlike the TM, the Post machine's R/W head either moves left/right with no change of tape symbol, and when symbol changes on the tape, the head stays, i.e., it does not move. The symbol m in the transition diagram stands for head move, while c stands for change of tape symbol. For example, 0, mR indicates that on 0 on the tape, the head moves to Right, and 1, $c0$ indicates that when 1 is found, it is changed to 0.

As we have seen above, in case of a language as Turing recognizable, there are three possible outcomes for any given input: 1. TM *accepts*, 2. TM *rejects*, or 3. TM *loops*.

Since the properties of recursive languages also exists in recursively enumerable languages, and the recursively enumerable languages have additional property of running the TM indefinitely, the recursive languages are subset of recursively enumerable languages. Fig. 12.6 shows the relation between recursive, recursively enumerable, non-RE and diagonal languages. The Non-RE and diagonal languages are discussed toward the end of this chapter. It is important to note that the non-RE and diagonal languages cannot be recognized by TM, they are undecidable languages.

If M is a Turing Machine that recognizes recursive language L, then M can be easily modified to recognize recursively language, just by changing output to loop when it is not accepting the input.

The terms Turing recognizable and recursively enumerable, are used interchangingly, as they mean the same. A language L is Turing recognizable if it is the language of some TM M (i.e., $L = L(M)$). A language is recursively enumerable if there exists a TM M that can enumerate string in L, on its tape or say on output tape, such that $x \in L$ is generated to appear in a finite amount of time.

Example 12.3 Show that the problem of not equality of CFGs is Turing recognizable.

[8] For details about Post Machines, refer Chap. 9, Sect. 9.9.

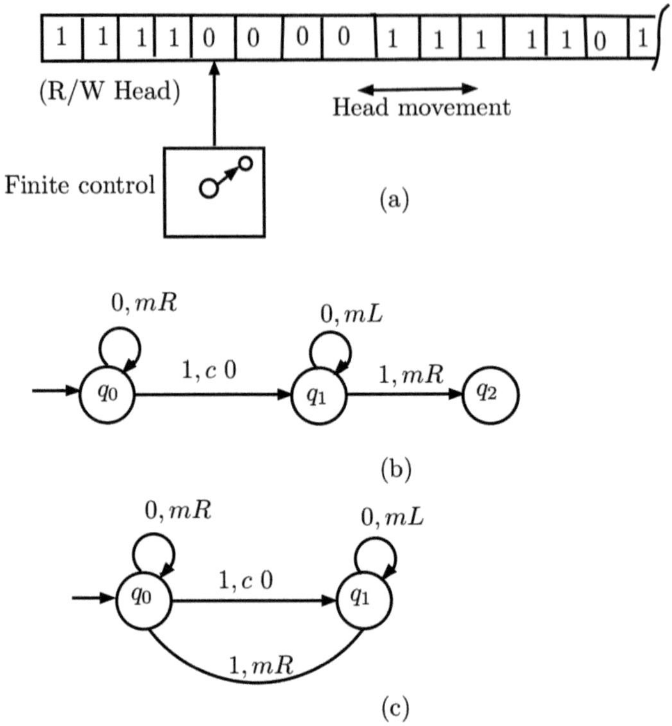

Fig. 12.5 **a** Post machine's initial input, **b** Post machine terminates execution, **c** Post machine loops forever

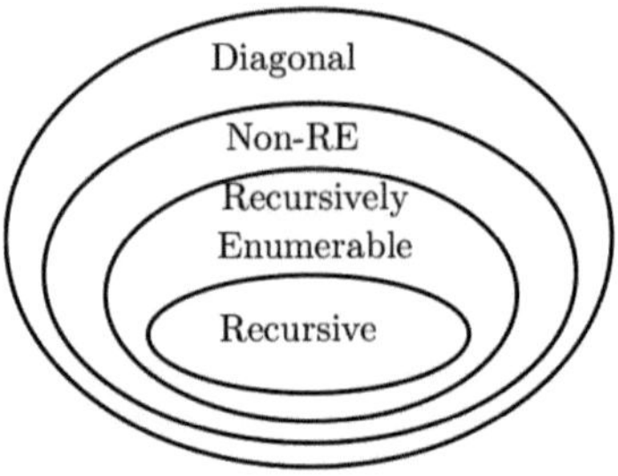

Fig. 12.6 Relation between classes of languages

For any two context-free grammars G_1, G_2 it is required to show that,

$$NEQ_{CFG} = \{\langle G_1, G_2 \rangle \mid G_1, G_2 \text{ are } CFGs \text{ and } L(G_1) \neq L(G_2)\}$$

is Turing recognizable.

A TM for this language is defined as follows:

1. Input: $\langle G_1, G_2 \rangle$
2. Output: If $\langle G_1, G_2 \rangle \in NEQ_{CFG}$, then *accept* else *loop*

The method is as follows:

1. Generate language strings $x \in \Sigma^*$ in lexicographic order, feeding x to a Parser (PDA) for G_1 and another for G_2.
2. For each such x, if x can be parsed by G_1 and not by G_2 (or vice versa), *accept* else loop.

Hence, this a case of recursively enumerable. □
Note that parser grammar is CFG.

Theorem 12.8 *Every type-0 language is Recursively Enumerable.*

Proof Let us assume that G is a type-0 grammar. For each k, there is only a finite number of derivations according to $G = (V, \Sigma, S, P)$ that are beginning from the start symbol S and having length k. Hence, we may check through all derivations of length k for $k = 1, 2, \ldots$. Whenever the last word in a derivation is over in the terminal alphabet, it is added into $L(G)$. Thus, this list of $L(G)$ constitute an effective listing procedure (note that repetitions may occur). This proves that type-0 language is recursively enumerable. □

However, we must understand the important difference between the two. The language of type-0 grammar $G = (V, \Sigma, S, P)$, is generated by using unrestricted production rules $\alpha \rightarrow \beta$, where $\alpha, \beta \in (V \cup \Sigma)^*$ with atleast one variable necessarily present in α. But, the recursively enumerable language is defined using TM that may not halt on non-member input strings.

Theorem 12.9 *The union of two recursively enumerable languages (RE) is recursively enumerable language.*

Proof Let L_1 and L_2 be sets accepted by Turing machines M_1 and M_2, respectively. Then $L_1 \cup L_2$ is accepted by TM M, where $x = w_1 \cup w_2$, for $w_1 \in L_1$ and $w_2 \in L_2$.

To determine if M_1 or M_2 accepts x, we run both M_1 and M_2 simultaneously using a 2-tape TM M. The M simulates M_1 on the first tape and M_2 on the second tape. If either one enters the accepting state, the input is accepted (see Fig. 12.7). □

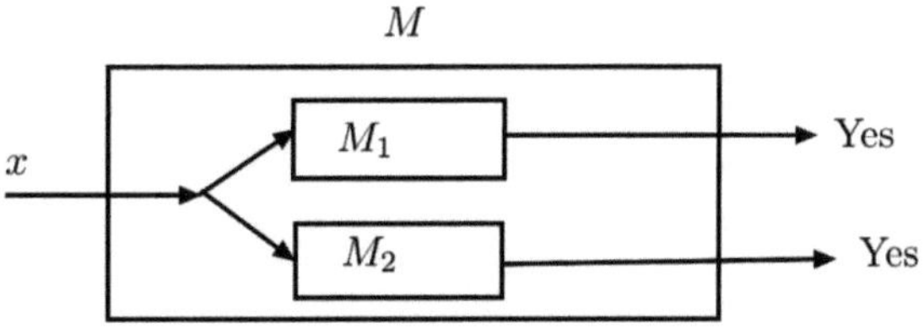

Fig. 12.7 Union of two *RE* languages

12.5 Decision Problems

A decision problem a is membership problem, like, “Is $w \in L$?”, whose answer is Yes/no. Since, *completeness* (see Sect. 12.5.2) requires that the corresponding TM should terminate on every input string, hence, the language recognized by this is *Recursive* (R). In other words, every TM solution to a decision problem defines a recursive language. The duality between solvable decision problems and recursive languages can be exploited to broaden the techniques available for establishing the decidability of a decision problem. For example, the decision problem of determining whether any given number is perfect square, is *decidable*.

Definition 12.6 (*Decision Problem*) By the decision problem of a given set of positive integers, we mean the problem of *effectively* determining for an arbitrary positive integer whether it is, or is not, in the set. □

Definition 12.7 (*Turing Decidable*) A language L is Turing-decidable or simply *decidable*, if there is a Turing machine M that decides L. Such TMs halts on every input $w \in \Sigma^*$. □

About the answer of “What problems are solvable”, we will proceed in a systematic manner. However, we take a sudden jump, and consider the problem(s) of this form: Given a function,

$$f : \mathbb{N}^k \to \mathbb{N}, \tag{12.3}$$

compute $f(x)$ for the input argument x. The reason for straight way choosing this problem are many: the functions on natural numbers or equivalently, on real numbers, are well-defined, and are the natural objects of study of mathematics. Once we have understood the functions on natural numbers to be computable, we can use this understanding to address other problems that are not based on recursion theory. Other approach, which is more important: many problems can often be encoded into natural numbers in such a way that we can use our knowledge of latter to reason about the new problems.

Theorem 12.10 *A language L is decidable if and only if L and $\overline{L}$ are both recursively enumerable.*

Proof Let us consider that L is decidable, and let M be the Turing machine that decides L. Since M decides L, M also accepts L. Thus, L is recursively enumerable.

As next step, we define a Turing machine M' such that on input w, the M' simulates M. The simulation is constructed as follows: M' accepts w iff the Turing machine M rejects w, and M' rejects w iff M accepts w. We note that as M is decider for L, and the M' is also a decider for $\overline{L}$. Hence, $\overline{L}$ is also recursively enumerable.

Conversely, let L and $\overline{L}$ be recursively enumerable. Let us assume that T and T' be the Turing machines that accepts L and $\overline{L}$, respectively. Now construct a Turing machine T_2 to decide L, whose working is as follows: on input w, the TM T_2 simulates

T and T' in parallel on input w. Since, L and $\overline{L}$ are recursively enumerable, at least one Turing machines T or T' will halt and accept the input w. Thus, if T accepts w, then so does the Turing machine T_2. Otherwise T' will accepts w and T_2 rejects. Hence, T_2 decides the language L. This proves the theorem. □

12.5.1 Effective Procedure

We have chosen to study the functions over natural numbers is due to their level of difficulty, i.e., simplicity. But, we still need to define what we mean by "solution"? In fact, what we are after is some *effective procedure*, which takes as input possible instances of the problem, and produces the correct answer. This procedure should be *complete*, *deterministic*, and should consist of simple steps, which can be done by hand.

Definition 12.8 (*Effective Procedure*) An effective procedure is one, which is *mechanical, deterministic, and complete.* □

The kind of simple steps may be, e.g., adding 1 to a given number, given two numbers discard the first and select the second, testing whether a given number is zero, etc. In other words, we are looking for the explanation of effective procedure in terms of elementary mechanical computation steps, each of that involves the manipulation of finite amount of data.

Deterministic means each step should have at most one unambiguous outcome, and *complete* means, it should work for the entire domain of input and not selective part of that.

A function that can be computed using such a procedure is called *effectively computable* function.

There are two approaches to handle this effective procedure. First approach is mathematical in nature, and starts with few simple and well-understood objects. These objects are some very simple functions which are *intuitively computable*, called primitive recursive functions (PRF).[9] Using these functions as basic building blocks, we gradually build more complicated objects, the process is called *recursion*. Thus, the answer to the questions: "Which functions are effectively computable", is recursive functions, which is general case of PRFs.

A simple example of decision function is an arbitrary polynomial $P(x_1, x_2, \ldots, x_n)$, with non-negative integral coefficients, which are not identically zero. If the x's are assigned arbitrary positive integral values, for example, in the Arabic notation, the algorithms comprising of addition and multiplication in that notation enable us to calculate the corresponding positive integral value of the polynomials. That is, $P(x_1, x_2, \ldots, x_n)$ is an *effectively calculable* function of positive integers. The importance of the technical concept—*recursive function* derives from the

[9] Basic primitive functions are: zero, increment and projection. When these functions are operated on by composition operation, the resultant value is also a primitive recursive functions.

overwhelming evidence that it is coextensive with the intuitive concept effectively calculable function.

The second approach to handle the effective procedure is practical, and may be regarded as belonging to the field of computer science. This approach is concerned with theoretical framework for computation, and study of what can be computed in the framework, and models the actions of an idealized human computing agent, so that we can systematically analyze the possibilities and limitations of the same. Among such several frameworks, the Turing machine is the best-known framework. The purpose of this framework is to study computations in an idealized setting, i.e., there is no limitation of time and memory size, which is sufficiently general but technically simple, so that the study is not overly complicated.

12.5.2 Formulating Decision Problems

In the previous chapters, we designed machines to detect patterns in strings, (for example palindromes, $a^n b^n c^n$, etc.) and recognized the languages based on these patterns. Many higher level problems can be posed based on these pattern recognition of strings and string manipulations. For example, we may be interested in the answers of following questions:

"Is a given natural number perfect square?"
"Is a given natural number prime?"
"Does a given graph has cycle?"
"Does the computation of a given TM halt before 25th transition?"

Each of these general questions describes a *decision problem*. Formally, a decision problem P is a set of *related questions* p_i, each of which has Yes/No answer. For example, to determine if a natural number x is a perfect square, requires answering following questions, and we carry on the process until we reach to that natural number[10] i, such that $i^2 = x$.

p_1: Is $1^2 = x$?
p_2: Is $2^2 = x$?
p_3: Is $3^2 = x$?
...
p_i: Is $i^2 = x$?
...

[10] For example, to answer if 20 is perfect square, we generate the sequence of 1, 2, 3, ..., and compare each number's square with 20, and carry on as long as the squared number is less than 20. After getting square of 4, when next square is 25, we note that it is greater than 20, hence we terminate the process and declare 20 as not a perfect square. However, if any generated square matched with the given number, we would say it is success.

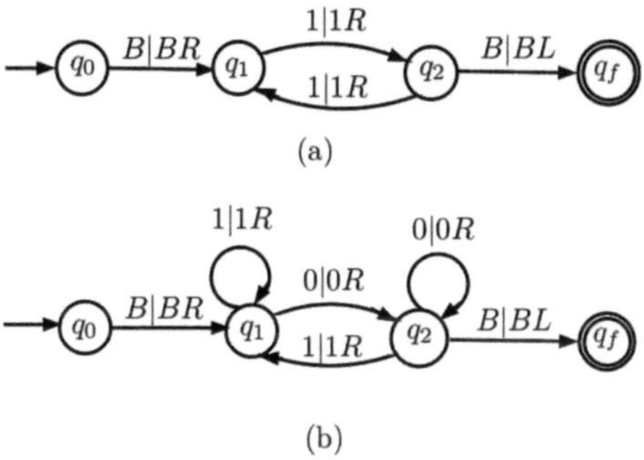

Fig. 12.8 TM recognizing: **a** even unary numbers, **b** even binary numbers

Each of the p_i is an *instance* of the problem P. The solution of a decision problem P is an algorithm that determines the answer of every question "Is $p_i \in P$"? (a membership problem). A *decision problem* is *decidable*, if it has a solution.

While, in a certain sense, the theory of recursively enumerable sets of positive integers is potentially as wide as the theory of *general recursive functions*. Since decision problem's solution requires an algorithm, an intuitive notion of algorithm is essential. Following are the properties of such algorithms.

- *Complete*: Correct answer is computable for every problem instance,
- *Mechanistic*: Consists of finite sequence of instructions, each can be carried out without requirement of insight, ingenuity, or guesswork, and
- *Deterministic*: With identical input, the identical computation is carried out.

A standard TM is an effective algorithm if it is mechanistic, deterministic, and complete. However, it is complete only if, it halts on every input. Thus, TM can be used to solve decision problems. To solve a problem using TM, we need to translate the problem instances into strings, called, representation of the decision problem. A problem instance is answered by a TM, if TM accepts and halts, or rejects and halts.

The *Church–Turing* thesis for decision problem states that TM can be designed to solve a decision problem if it is solvable by an *effective procedure*.

The Table 12.3 shows the general representation of problem P, in the form of its instances $p_1, ..., p_i$, with inputs to TM as $w_1, ..., w_i$, and for each instance the TM gives output Yes/No, when it completes the processing.

The Table 12.4 shows the representation of a problem: "acceptance of unary numbers strings", that represent even numbers.

In general, 1^i, such that i is odd, is an even number in unary format. The TMs for acceptance of even numbers can be constructed for unary and binary numbers, as shown in Fig. 12.8a and b. In case of input as a unary number, when TM reaches to blank symbol at the end of input, it will halt at state q_f if the number is even. In case of binary number as input, which should be terminated by 0 for input to be an even number, it halts in q_f on finding B at the end of input (see Fig. 12.8b). Note that B is tape symbol, and not the part of input string.

Table 12.3 General format for problem instances

Problem instance	TM input	Answer of Turing machine once computation is done
p_1	w_1	Yes/No
p_2	w_2	Yes/No
...	...	...
p_i	w_i	Yes/No

Table 12.4 Problem instances with solutions

Decimal input	Equivalent unary	Is number even?
0	1	Yes
1	11	No
2	111	Yes
3	1111	No
...	...	...

12.6 Some Standard Problems and Their Intuitive Algorithms

We start by asking a grand question: "What problems are solvable?" However, we find it a very general and vague question, it is required to be more precise. To be precise, we give certain examples of problems.

1. Given any natural number $n \in \mathbb{N}$, determine if n is prime.
2. Given a formula θ in the language of *propositional logic*, find out whether θ is satisfiable?
3. Given a formula θ in the language of *propositional logic*, find out whether θ is tautology.
4. Given a formula ψ in *predicate logic*, find out whether ψ is provable using the natural deduction. To be precise, given the collection of predicate formulas Θ, can we deduce $\Theta \vdash \psi$?
5. Given a polynomial $P(x_1, ..., x_n)$ of n variables with integer coefficients, determine whether $P(x_1, ..., x_n) = 0$ has *integer solutions*, i.e., are there $x_1, ..., x_n$ as integers that satisfy the equation?
6. Given a C program P, determine whether this program will ultimately halt when some definite input is given, or it will loop forever?
7. Given a C program Q, determine whether Q will ultimately halt on every input?
8. Given a natural number $n > 0$ and $n \in \mathbb{N}$, determine whether there exists n consecutive 3's in the decimal expansion of π?

All these questions further raise interesting questions, which we will clarify in our future discussions. However, one thing is clear that they are all *decision-based* problems, which requires some decision is to be made in the form of Yes/No.

For each of the above problems, there are instances that we can solve easily. For the problem 5 it is easy to find the roots. For the predicate logic-based problem 4 we can use deduction to find out the solution. For the problem 8, we can generate the decimal value of π, and when n consecutive 3's come, the process can be terminated. All these are the given instances of the problems, which can be easily solved. However, we are interested for a general solution to these problems so that it works for all the instances of the problem.

In the problem 1, a program can receive an input, and a fixed algorithm can check if it is prime, then prints Yes or No depending on the result of that program. This is a completely mechanical procedure. In the problem 2, one can construct truth-table, and if there is True in any row of the expression θ, it is satisfied else not. Similar is the case in the problem 3, where all the values in the column of θ must be True, for θ to be tautology. Hence, both these problems are decidable, as we can write a general programs to solve these problems, which can work for all the instances of the problems.

As we proceed through, we will discuss about the solution approaches for these problems, since each of them requires a different approach.

We can say that a problem is *decidable* or *solvable*, if there exists an effective procedure which gives the correct outcome for each of the possible instances of the problem.

12.6.1 Undecidable Problems

In contrast to problems, 1, 2 and 3, no recipes are available for problem 4. We can try for a natural deduction proof for the formula ψ, but after trying a lot if we do not succeed, we are not sure whether the lack of success is because ψ is not provable or because natural deduction just is not the strong point. Note that it may not be the case that we do not have good algorithm in hand, but there may not exist any algorithm at all!! In that case the problem's solution is undecidable.

Definition 12.9 (*Undecidable Problems*) A formally stated problem is *undecidable* if no total recursive function and thus, no Turing machine that always halts, can be constructed to decide the problem. □

Consider again the decimal expansion of π (problem 8). The best way we can do it is, to run the algorithm that computes π, till we get n number of 3's, for a given value of n (i.e., not for a general case). Thus, it is not sure whether the algorithms of problems 4 and 8 will ever terminate for the general case. Hence, these problems are called *undecidable problems*.

12.6.2 Semi-Decidable Problems

Definition 12.10 (*Semi-decidable*) Let $M = (Q, \Sigma, \Gamma, \delta, s, H)$ be a Turing machine and let $L \subseteq \Sigma^*$ be a language. In this case, M *semi-decides* L if for any string $w \in \Sigma^*$ the following holds: $w \in L$ if and only if M halts on input w. In addition, the L is recursively enumerable, i.e., for $w \notin L$, the TM M may loop indefinitely. □

If M is supplied with input $w \in L$, then M is required to halt eventually. However, it is not important as what halting configuration it reaches, it is all right as long as it reaches to some halting configuration. However, if $w \in \Sigma^* - L$, then M will never enter a halting state. This is because, if any configuration that is not halting, it yields some other configuration, and the machine will continue to run indefinitely.

Even though some of the problems may be difficult to solve, it may still be easy to decide whether a given answer of a problem is correct or not. For example, finding factors of a polynomial problem may be difficult, but checking whether the given sequence $n_1, ..., n_k$ is a solution, is straight forward. We may simply multiply the given factors, if we get original expression, the factors is the solution. As other problem, we might not be able to come up with a natural deductive proof for a given formula ψ, but if we are given the solution, then it is not hard to verify whether the solution is indeed correct, as $\Theta \rightarrow \psi$ implication will be *valid* if ψ is deducible from Θ.[11]

This suggests following strategy for the problem 4: start generating proofs in a systematic way, and make sure that we generate all the proofs eventually, and for each we check that it is a valid proof for the formula ψ. Clearly, if a proof exists for ψ, we will be able to generate the ψ. But, if really there does not exist a proof, we will be trying to generate more and more proofs, and we would never know if at all there is a proof ahead. Such problems are sometimes called *semi-decidable* problems. An example for semi-decidable problem is [7],

$$z^n = x^n + y^n, \tag{12.4}$$

where x, y, z, n are all integers. It is well known that for $n = 2$ there are many solutions, but, it is not known whether there exists any x, y, z for which this equation holds true for $n \geq 3$. The Eq. 12.4 is called *Fermat's last theorem*. The theorem states that exponential diophantine equation $x^n + y^n = z^n$ has no non-trivial solution for $n \geq 3$, has been an open question for many centuries, and has attracted a lot of attention. However, one of the most amazing results in number theory is the Andrew Wiles' proof [18] of this Fermat's last theorem.

[11] Given the proposition A, and given that $A \rightarrow B$ holds, they will deduce B, then $A \wedge (A \rightarrow B) \Rightarrow B$ is valid.

A C language program P, given an input (Problem 6), whether ultimately halts or not is semi-decidable: one can simply run the program P and wait for its response. If it halts, then we have found the solution, but if it does not halt, we cannot say, whether it is going to halt ultimately or may run forever!

The Problem 7 is not for one input, but for infinitely many inputs, for which we do not have time to test. May be it is not halted for one billion different inputs, we are not sure for the next input. Alternatively, the program may not require any input, in that case, say, the program has run continuously for one hundred year and not halted, who knows it may halt in the 22nd century if continuously run!

Hence, the Problems 6 and 7 are unsolvable[12] problems. However, for the Problem 8 it is yet unknown as to which class it belongs [16].

12.6.3 Modeling Decision Problems

Apart from the Turing machine, there is another machine—the *register machine* [14] that can model the computations using natural numbers. The *recursive functions* are exactly those which are computable by a register machine.[13] The same computation can be defined using Lambda-calculus. The theory of recursive functions derives its significance from the fact that recursive functions can be *effectively enumerated.* One can encode each of them as a natural number such that the code can effectively retrieve the function. This means, in *recursive functions theory*, the natural numbers appears in two guises: once as *code* of recursive functions, and other as *arguments* for these functions.

There are however, functions and sets that are not recursive. The sets whose membership can be effectively decided, are the *recursively enumerable* (RE) sets. A set is RE if there is an effective procedure for generating (enumerating) its elements, like in the Problems 4, 5, 6 listed on Sect. 12.6. Thus, if a given element belongs to an RE set, we can run this procedure and it will eventually confirm that the element is in the set. But if the element is not in the set, the procedure may search forever and we may never know that the element is not in the set. For this reason, the RE sets are sometimes called *semi-decidable*, or *semi-recursive* sets.

A set of positive integers is said to be RE if there is a recursive function $f(x)$ of one positive integral variable whose values, for positive integral values of x, constitute the given set of positive integers. The sequence $f(1), f(2), f(3), \ldots$ is then said to be a *recursive enumeration* of the set. The corresponding intuitive concept is that of an effectively enumerable set of positive integers. To prepare us in part for our

[12] It is not that these problems have no algorithms, but one cannot say by the nature of problem and input, as how long the C program will run. Therefore, the problem is unsolvable, and not undecidable.

[13] The concept comes from CPU registers, which hold the variables of loop counters and other memory variables.

intuitive approach, consider the following three examples of *recursively enumerable* sets of positive integers.

1. $1^2, 2^2, 3^2, \ldots,$
2. $1, 2, 2^{1+2}, 2^{1+2+2^{1+2}}, \ldots$
3. a. $1^2, 2^2, 3^2, \ldots$
   b. $1^3, 2^3, 3^3, \ldots$
   c. $1^4, 2^4, 3^4, \ldots$

In the first example, the set is produced by a recursive enumeration using the recursive function $f(x) = x^2$. In the second example, the set is generated in a linear sequence, each new element being effectively obtained from the elements previously generated, in this case by raising 2 to the power the sum of the preceding elements, e.g., in the third element, 2^{1+2} is obtained by raising the sum of previous elements $1 + 2$ over 2. This set is effectively enumerable, since given n, the nth element of the sequence can be found by regenerating the sequence through its first n elements.

In the third example with three series, we rather imagine the positive integers 1, 2, 3, ...generated in their natural order, and, as each positive integer n is generated, a corresponding process is set up which generates $n^2, n^3, n^4, \ldots$, all these to be in the set. Actually, the standard method for proving that an enumerable set of enumerable sets is enumerable yields an effective enumeration of the set. The series a, b, c in above are enumeration sets, and their union is also enumerated set [6].

12.7 Decidable Properties of Grammars and Languages

In this section we give some examples of languages that are decidable through algorithms. We will focus on languages concerning automata and grammars. For example, we can present an algorithm that tests whether a string is a member of a context-free language (CFL) or not. This is nothing but a parsing algorithm. These languages are important for several reasons: for example, the problem of testing whether a CFG generates a string, is related to the problem of recognizing and compiling programs. Certain other problems concerning automata and grammars are not decidable through algorithms. We will start with examples in which decidability is possible, it will helps us to understand the existence of undecidable problems.

12.7.1 Decidability of Grammar Problems

The close relationship between programming language syntax, context-free grammars and languages, parsing and compiling, is well known. It is interesting to note that many of the problems concerning to programming languages, parsing or compiling, that we may wish to solve are equivalent to *undecidable* or *computationally intractable* context-free grammar or language problems. Some of such problems are:

1. *Emptiness-of-intersection problem.* It is a problem of determining whether the intersection of languages generated by two grammars is empty.
2. *Grammar-class-membership problems.* That is, problems of determining, for a grammar G and grammar class C, whether G is an element of C.
3. *Language-class-membership problems.* That is, problems of determining, for a grammar G and class of languages $\mathcal{L}$, whether the language generated by G is an element of $\mathcal{L}$.
4. *Grammatical-similarity-relation problems.* That is, problems of determining for a grammar G, the binary relation rel ($=, \subseteq, \subset, \in$), and grammar class C, whether there exists a grammar $G' \in C$ such that "$G\ rel\ G'$" holds true.

12.7.2 Decidable Properties of Regular Languages

We begin with certain computational problems concerning finite automata and, suggest algorithms them. For example,

i. Whether a finite automaton B accepts a string w?
ii. Whether the language of a finite automaton A is empty?
iii. Whether two finite automata A and B are equivalent, i.e., accept the same language?

Note that we had chosen to represent various computational problems through languages. Doing so is convenient because we have already set up terminology for dealing with languages. For example, the acceptance problem for DFAs is of testing whether a particular deterministic finite automaton B accepts a given string w. It can be expressed as a language A_{DFA}, which contains the encoding of all DFAs together with strings that the DFAs accept [10].

Consider the language,

$$A_{DFA} = \{\langle B, w\rangle \mid B \text{ is a DFA that accepts input string } w\}. \tag{12.5}$$

The problem of testing whether a DFA B accepts an input w is the same as the problem of testing whether $\langle B, w\rangle$ is a member of the language A_{DFA}. Similarly, we can formulate other computational problems in terms of testing membership in a language. Hence, showing that the language is decidable is the same as showing that the computational problem is decidable.

In the following theorem we show that A_{DFA} is in fact decidable. Hence this theorem shows that the problem of testing whether a given finite automaton accepts a given string is decidable.

Theorem 12.11 *A_{DFA} is decidable.*

Proof We simply need to present a TM M that decides A_{DFA}, where M is described as follows:

The TM M receives input $\langle B, w\rangle$, where B is description/representation of a DFA in encoded form, and w is a string. Then TM M simulate DFA B with w as input to B. If in this simulation B accepts w then M accepts $\langle B, w\rangle$, else M rejects. Note that, A_{DFA} (acceptability by DFA) is a language whose elements are all such pairs $\langle B, w\rangle$. □

In the similar line, it can be easily shown that A_{NFA} is decidable language. For this, first it is necessary to convert NFA into DFA, then run the above algorithm, such that if decidability of $\langle N, w\rangle$ is to be decided, where N is an NFA, and whether w is acceptable by N or not. For this, a Turing machine T_1 first translates the NFA N into an equivalent DFA D, and then a Turing machine T_2 decides membership of $\langle D, w\rangle$ by simulating DFA D on T_2. If DFA D accepts w then T_2 accepts w, and NFA accepts. Otherwise, if DFA D simulated on T_2 does not accept w, then T_2 does not accept, which implies that NFA does not accept w. □

Similarly, we can determine whether a regular expression R generates a given string w. Accordingly, we may define a language $\langle R, w\rangle$ such that R is a regular expression, and it generates string w, as

$$A_{REX} = \{\langle R, w\rangle \mid R \text{ is a regular expression that generates string } w\}. \tag{12.6}$$

Following theorem proves that A_{REX} is decidable language.

Theorem 12.12 *A_{REX} is a decidable language.*

Proof Let T_1 be a TM that decides A_{REX}. Let $\langle R, w\rangle$ is input to T_1, where R is regular expression, and w is some string. Follow these steps to decide about A_{REX}.

1. Run T_1 to convert R into equivalent NFA A,
2. Input $\langle A, w\rangle$ to a TM T_2,
3. Run TM T_2 on input $\langle A, w\rangle$,
4. If T_2 accepts, then T_1 *accepts*, else *rejects*.

This proves the theorem. □

One decision problem about finite automata is about its acceptance of empty language, i.e., to determine whether a finite automaton accepts no strings, not even empty strings. We define the language E_{DFA} as follows:

$$E_{DFA} = \{\langle A\rangle \mid A \text{ is DFA and } L(A) = \phi\}. \tag{12.7}$$

Theorem 12.13 *E_{DFA} is decidable language.*

Proof A DFA accepts some string $w \in \Sigma^*$, iff when stared in its start state, and the transitions of w lead it ultimately to the accepting state. To test this condition, we can design a TM T that uses a marking algorithm.

Let T has input $\langle A \rangle$, and A is description of DFA A in encoded form. The steps are:

1. Mark the start state of A.
2. Mark every state that has a transition coming into it from any state that is already marked.
3. If no state other than start state is marked then *accept*; otherwise, *reject*. □

The next theorem states to determine "whether two DFAs recognize the same language, is decidable". The language of all pairs $\langle A, B \rangle$, where A and B are representation of two DFAs, which recognize the identical language, is expressed as

$$EQ_{DFA} = \{\langle A, B \rangle \mid A \text{ and } B \text{ are } DFAs \text{ and } L(A) = L(B)\}. \tag{12.8}$$

Theorem 12.14 *EQ_{DFA} is decidable language.*

Proof To prove this, we construct a DFA D from DFAs A and B, where D accepts only those strings that are accepted either by A or B, but not by both. Thus, if A and B accept the same language, D will accept nothing.[14] The language D can be expressed using languages A and B as

$$L(D) = (L(A) \cap \overline{L(B)}) \cup (L(B) \cap \overline{L(A)}). \tag{12.9}$$

Once we have constructed DFA D, we can use Theorem 12.13 to test whether $L(D)$ is empty. If empty, then $L(A)$ and $L(B)$ are equal. Let there is a TM T as defined below:

1. Input $\langle A, B \rangle$ to T,
2. Construct DFA D from these two DFAs A, B as per Eq. (12.9),
3. Run TM T (as defined in Theorem 12.13) on input D,
4. If T accepts, then *accept*, else *reject*. □

12.7.3 Decidable Properties of Context-Free Languages

Similar to the regular languages and finite automata, there exist properties of context-free languages and pushdown automata, and these can be algorithmically determined. For example, to determine whether a context-free grammar G generates a string w,

[14] If two sets are P and Q, then $P \oplus Q = (\overline{P} \cap Q) \cup (P \cap \overline{Q})$. If P and Q are equal, then as per this formula, $P \oplus Q = \phi$. The $\oplus$ is exclusive-OR operation on sets.

or to find out whether the language of a given CFG G is empty [9], are decidable problems. We can represent a language A_{CFG} consisting of tuples $\langle G, w\rangle$ as elements, as

$$A_{CFG} = \{\langle G, w\rangle \mid G \text{ is a CFG that generates } w\}. \tag{12.10}$$

The following theorem proves this.

Theorem 12.15 *A_{CFG} is decidable language.*

Proof Using an approach where CFG G will generate all its possible strings, and then it remains to find out if w is generated, is not an efficient solution because the computation may run indefinitely. Because, if G actually does not generate w, this algorithm would never halt due to the reason that it will keep on trying for infinitely long time. This idea for TM is as *recognizer* but not as *decider* of A_{CFG}.

To work as decider, the algorithm should try only a finite number of derivations. For this we make use of the knowledge of CNF (Chomsky Normal Form), which says that a string of length $|w| = n$ can be generated in maximum $2n - 1$ steps. Thus, only $2n - 1$ steps would be sufficient to see if w is in the given language. We have following steps to decide A_{CFG} using a TM T:

1. Input to TM T is $\langle G, w\rangle$, where G is grammar and w is string,
2. Convert G into equivalent CNF,
3. For string $|w| = n$, try its derivation; a derivation will not take more than $2n - 1$ steps. For $n = 0$, there is single step derivation,
4. If a derivation generate w, *accept* it, else *reject* it. □

In the following, we show that E_{CFG} (empty CF language) is decidable, i.e., a set whose members make CFGs, such that these CFGs generate no strings.

Theorem 12.16 *E_{CFG} is decidable language.*

Proof We understand that E_{CFG} being empty language means $E_{CFG} = \{\langle G\rangle \mid L(G) = \phi\}$. Consider that productions of G are $A \rightarrow \alpha$, where α is substring of terminals and non-terminals.

There are two conditions of a CFG grammar G, either of that should be satisfied for it to generate empty language:

- None of terminals in α have a path to start symbol: In that case no string shall be generated ultimately, as can be seen in Fig. 12.9a. To confirm this, connections from non-terminals to root node can be traced in the production rules, if no connection is found, the condition is satisfied.
- No non-terminal symbol should expand to a string of terminals: This is shown in Fig. 12.9b, and can be checked by forward searching in the grammars rules, but avoiding the substitutions that create loops. The dotted lines indicates paths. □

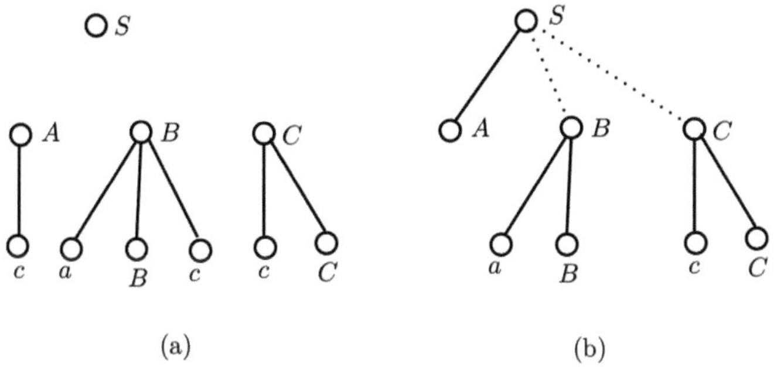

Fig. 12.9 Testing membership in E_{CFG}: **a** no terminal connects to start symbol, **b** no non-terminal expands to a terminal string

12.8 Enumeration of Languages and Turing Machines

We can enumerate Turing machines, by encoding each one of them as a big integer in binary form (refer to Chap. 10, Sect. 10.7.1). Assume that these big binary numbers, each representing a Turing machine, are converted into decimal numbers, and may, say, look like this:

- 50128478921234563456 is TM for the problem of balancing of parenthesis,
- 50256728933456723453 is TM for recognition of even number of 1's,
- 52563429393456734569 is TM that acts as Universal TM,
- 56239892129823489734 is TM which is equal to Windows XP,

  ...

  and so on.

In the above example we have just taken some hypothetical integers numbers as encoding of TMs, but actual integer numbers for these may be still larger. Similar examples in binary form, when five tuples of each transition $\delta(q, a) = (q', b, d)$ are encoded, and separated by 00 (shown as bold faced), and transition tables of all TMs are separated by commas, then it forms a language, like,

$$\begin{aligned}L = \{&0001010101101\mathbf{00}10110101011\mathbf{00}11010101101000,\\ &00010101101011\mathbf{00}1101011101101000,\\ &0001011011010 1\mathbf{00}10101101011\mathbf{00}10110110101000,\\ &\ldots\}.\end{aligned}$$

Note that first TM has transition table of size three, second of two and in third TM there are three transitions.

This language L of encoded TMs is *countable set* of infinite number of strings, because, we have enumerated all those binary strings whose format is matching with the encoding of TM functions. Thus, there is one-to-one correspondence between elements of the set of TMs and the corresponding natural numbers ($\mathbb{N}$).

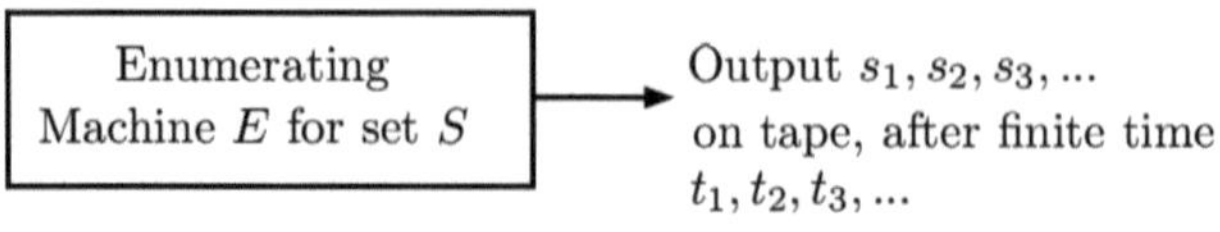

Fig. 12.10 An enumerator E for integer numbers as encoding of TMs

Let S be a set of strings in decimal format. An enumeration procedure for S may be a TM E that generates all strings of S one-by-one in lexicographic order, each within finite time. Let $S = \{s_1, s_2, \dots s_i, \dots\}$. Figure 12.10 shows an enumeration machine, and we can have an algorithm that obtains the next number in S that.

We can generate the encoding of all the Turing machines, i.e., language L, in lexicographic order for $\Sigma = \{0, 1\}$ by repeating the following steps indefinitely.

i. Generate next binary string of 1s and 0s in order,
ii. After every string is generated, check if the string describes a Turing machine (an encoding of some TM),
iii. if yes, print the string on output tape, else ignore it.

Theorem 12.17 *Set of All the Turing machines is countable.*

The proof of this theorem is enumeration procedure discussed above.

We have already discussed that Turing machine can be used as language generator and as language enumerator.

Theorem 12.18 *If a language L is enumerated by a TM E, then L is recursively enumerable.*

Proof Let L be generated by a k tape TM E, which also enumerates strings $w_i \in L$. As they are enumerated, they are written on tape-1 as: $\#w_1\#w_2\#...w_i\#....$ We add a new $(k+1)$th tape to this machine, and call this modified machine as M. Consider a string $x \in L$, which we write on $(k+1)$th tape. Every time the symbol # is written on tape-1 by machine E, and it starts generating next string w_i, simultaneously w_i is compared with x on tape $k+1$; if found equal, M halts otherwise the process of generating next $w_i \in L$ and comparing with x is repeated. Since, the machine M halts for $x \in L$ and otherwise it continues indefinitely, the language L is recursively enumerable.

For enumeration it is necessary that lexicographic order (lo) of strings is generated. We can generate all the strings on alphabet $\Sigma = \{a_1, \dots, a_n\}$ in lexicographic order using recursion:

$$lo(\varepsilon) = 0, lo(a_i) = i, \text{ for } i = 1:n$$
$$lo(a_i u) = i.n^{lenth(u)} + lo(u)$$ □

In the following we intuitively and procedurally demonstrate the enumeration process of string in Σ^*, in lexicographic order. However, we note that this is also the proof of theorem: "If a language is enumerated by TM then it is RE."

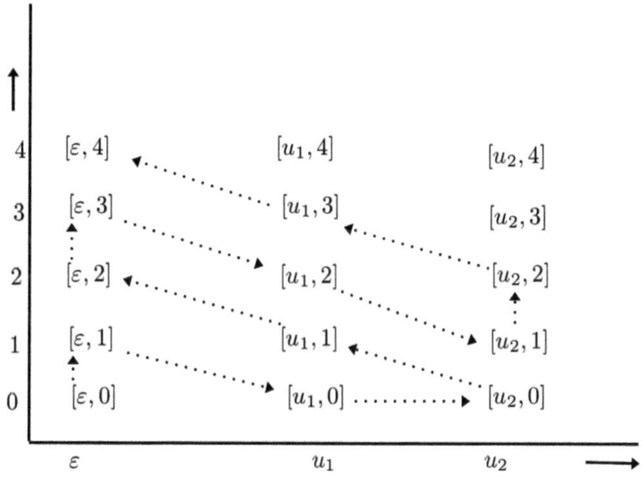

Fig. 12.11 Enumeration in lexicographic order

Theorem 12.19 *For any alphabet Σ, there exists a TM T_{Σ^*} that enumerates Σ^* in lexicographic order.*

Proof Let M be the TM that accepts L. The lexicographic ordering produces listing: ε, u_1, u_2, ..., $\in \Sigma^*$. We construct a table with columns as strings ε, u_1, u_2, ... and rows as natural numbers ($\mathbb{N}$), and the entries in this table are pairs $[a, b]$, where $a \in \Sigma^*$ and $b \in \mathbb{N}$, in the order, as shown in Fig. 12.11. The entries in the table are enumerated as indicated by connected dotted arrow lines as $[\varepsilon, 0]$, $[\varepsilon, 1]$, $[u_1, 0]$, $[u_2, 0]$, $[u_1, 1]$, $[\varepsilon, 2]$, ... Consider that we proceed in similar fashion when there are more number or infinitely large number of row and columns.

The $[a, b]$ entry in this table means "run the TM M for input u_a for b steps". The machine E is built to enumerate the language L such that enumeration of the ordered pairs are interleaved with the computation of M. The computation of E is a loop as follows:

i. generate an ordered pair $[a, b]$,
ii. run a simulation of M with input u_a for b transitions or until the simulation halts,
iii. If M accepts, write u_a on the output tape,
iv. continue with step *i*.

If $u_a \in L$, the computation of M with input u_a halts and accepts after $b = k$ transitions, for some number k. Thus, u_a will be written on output tape of E when ordered pair $[a, b]$ is processed. The 2nd element (b) ensures that simulation is terminated after b steps. Consequently, no non-nonterminating computation are allowed, and each string of Σ^* is examined. □

12.9 Gödel Numbering

It is possible to list all the sets of instructions by a procedure, comprising the instructions as quadruples (see Post machines, Chap. 9, Sect. 9.9) or quintuple (Turing machine) for listing all primitive recursive derivations. This procedure is itself algorithmic, and can be viewed as a procedure which associate with each integer x, the set of instructions falling at the $(x + 1)^{st}$ place in the list of all sets of instructions.[15] We assume that we have selected one such listing procedure [15].

Definition 12.11 (*Gödel numbers*) If P_x is the set of instructions associated with the integer x in a fixed listing of all sets of instructions, then x is called the *index* or Gödel number of P_x. □

12.9.1 Gödel Representation of a Formula

Adapting to the formal notation just described—a device which is due to Gödel, we associate with every formula a positive integer to represent it, as follows. Let us assume that we have, number 1 and the prime numbers corresponding to certain symbols:

1. to the symbol ε the number 1,
2. to each of the symbols {, (, [, we let correspond the number 11,
3. to each of the symbols },),], the number 13, and
4. to the variables $a, b, c, ...$ the prime numbers 17, 19, 23, ..., respectively.

In addition, a formula, which is composed of the n symbols $\tau_1, \tau_2, ..., \tau_n$, in order, we associate the number $2^{t_1}3^{t_2}5^{t_2}...p_n^{t_n}$, where t_i is the number corresponding to the symbol τ_i, and where p_n, stands for the n-th prime number.

This number $2^{t_1}3^{t_2}...p_n^{t_n}$ will be called the *Gödel representation* of the formula comprising the symbols $\tau_1, \tau_2, ..., \tau_n$ [1].

Example 12.4 Gödel number of a formula.

Let us consider to find the Gödel number for the formula "0 = 0". Let Gödel number for symbol 0 is 6 and for "=" it is 5. Then Gödel number for the formula "0 = 0" is $2^6 \times 3^5 \times 5^6 = 243, 000, 000$. □

The mapping works because no two formulas will ever end up with the same Gödel number. The Gödel numbers are integers, and integers only factor into primes in a single way. So the only factorization of $2^6 \times 3^5 \times 5^6$ is $243, 000, 000$. This means that there is only one possible way to decode the Gödel number.

It is readily proved that *no two distinct well-formed formulas can have the same Gödel representation*. It is clear, moreover, that there is an effective method by which,

---

[15] Each TM is a large binary integer or equivalent decimal integer, representing the encoding of some TM, i.e., some algorithm.

given any formula, its Gödel representation can be calculated; and likewise that there is an effective method by which, given any positive integer, it is possible to determine whether it is the valid Gödel representation of three well-formed formula and, if it is, how to obtain that formula.

In this connection the Gödel representation plays a role similar to that of the matrix of incidence in combinatorial topology. For there is, in the theory of well-formed formulas, an important class of problems, each of which is equivalent to a problem of elementary number theory obtainable by means of the Gödel representation.

12.9.2 Gödel's Incompleteness Theorem

Gödel's incompleteness theorems are two theorems of mathematical logic that demonstrate the inherent limitations of every formal axiomatic system containing basic arithmetic. These results, published by Kurt Gödel in 1931, are important both in mathematical logic and in the philosophy of mathematics. The theorems are widely, but not universally, interpreted as showing that Hilbert's program to find a complete and consistent set of axioms for all mathematics is impossible [5, 17].

The *first incompleteness theorem* states that, "no consistent system of axioms whose theorems can be listed by an effective procedure (i.e., an algorithm) is capable of proving all truths about the arithmetic of the natural numbers." For any such formal system, there will always be statements about the natural numbers that are true, but that are unprovable within the system. In other words, any *consistent formal system* F within which a certain amount of elementary arithmetic can be carried out is incomplete; i.e., there are statements of the language of F which can neither be proved nor disproved in F.

Employing a diagonal argument, Gödel's incompleteness theorems were the first of several closely related theorems on the limitations of formal systems. They were followed Church's proof that Hilbert's Entscheidungsproblem (The Decision problem) is unsolvable, and Turing's theorem that there is no algorithm to solve the halting problem.

The *second incompleteness theorem*, an extension of the first, shows that the system cannot demonstrate its own consistency.

12.9.3 Syntactic Form of the Gödel Sentence

The unprovable statement GF[16] referred to by the theorem is often referred to as "the Gödel's sentence" for the system F. The proof constructs a particular Gödel sentence for the system F, but there are infinitely many statements in the language

[16] G stands for Gödel's sentence or Gödel's number.

of the system that share the same properties, such as the conjunction of the Gödel sentence and any logically valid sentence.

The Gödel sentence is designed to refer, indirectly, to itself. The sentence states that, when a particular sequence of steps is used to construct another sentence, that constructed sentence will not be provable in F. However, the sequence of steps is such that the constructed sentence turns out to be GF itself. In this way, the Gödel sentence GF indirectly states its own unprovability within F.

To prove the first incompleteness theorem, Gödel demonstrated that the notion of provability within a system could be expressed purely in terms of arithmetical functions that operate on Gödel numbers of sentences of the system. Therefore, the system, which can prove certain facts about numbers, can also indirectly prove facts about its own statements, provided that it is effectively generated. Questions about the provability of statements within the system are represented as questions about the arithmetical properties of numbers themselves, which would be decidable by the system if it were complete.

Thus, although the Gödel sentence refers indirectly to sentences of the system F, when read as an arithmetical statement the Gödel sentence directly refers only to natural numbers. It asserts that no natural number has a particular property, where that property is given by a primitive recursive relation. As such, the Gödel sentence can be written in the language of arithmetic with a simple syntactic form. In particular, it can be expressed as a formula in the language of arithmetic consisting of a number of leading universal quantifiers followed by a quantifier-free body.

12.9.4 Formal System and Completeness

The incompleteness theorems apply to formal systems that are of sufficient complexity, to express the basic arithmetic of the natural numbers and, which are complete, consistent, and effectively axiomatized. In general, a formal system is a deductive apparatus that consists of a particular set of axioms along with rules of symbolic manipulation (or rules of inference) that allow for the derivation of new theorems from the axioms. One example of such a system is *first-order Peano arithmetic*—a system in which all variables are intended to denote natural numbers. In other systems, such as *set theory*, only some sentences of the formal system express statements about the natural numbers. The incompleteness theorems are about formal provability within these systems, rather than about "provability" in general.

The incompleteness theorems show that systems which contain a sufficient amount of arithmetic cannot possess all three of these properties, i.e., *completeness*, *consistency*, and *effective axiomatization*.

Definition 12.12 (*Complete*) A set of axioms is complete if, for any statement in the axioms' language, that statement or its negation is provable from the axioms. □

This is the notion relevant for Gödel's first Incompleteness theorem. It is not to be confused with semantic completeness, which means that the set of axiom proves all the semantic tautologies of the given language. In his completeness theorem, Gödel proved that first-order logic is *semantically complete*. But it is not *syntactically complete*, since there are sentences expressible in the language of first-order logic that can be neither proved nor disproved from the axioms of logic alone: for example, "the flower is pretty" (*pretty(flower)*), can neither be proved nor unproved.

In a mere system of logic it would be absurd to expect syntactic completeness. But in a system of mathematics, thinkers such as Hilbert had believed that it is just a matter of time to find such an axiomatization that would allow to either prove or disprove (by proving its negation) each and every mathematical formula.

12.10 Unsolvability

What makes some formal languages Undecidable? Why certain properties in language theory are undecidable? What are the specific peculiarities of the different families of languages? The answer is, many properties of languages are undecidable because the "ability to count" or "compare" in them is absent. Intuitively, if a family of languages contains the set $\{a^n b^n \mid n \geq 1\}$ and is closed under some simple closure properties, then it has the ability to count.[17] For example, the language generated by $\{a^n b^n \mid n \geq 1\}$ is such a family of languages. To capture this intuitive concept of counting, we define a counter machine and then relate the valid computations of a counter machine to Turing machine computations and families of languages containing the set $\{a^n b^n \mid n \geq 1\}$. Intuitively, a counter machine is a one register machine, where the register is capable of holding an arbitrary size integer, which can multiply the content of its register by one of the finite number of multiplicands, and causes branch if product is not integer.

Having given this counting property, it can be shown that every *recursively enumerable* language is a *homomorphic* image of the set of valid computations of some counter machine. In addition, if a family of languages $\mathcal{L}$ (with some closure properties) contains the set $\{a^n b^n \mid n \geq 1\}$ then the valid computations of any counter machine can be represented as an intersection of two languages in $\mathcal{L}$. These results can then used to derive several undecidability results of families of languages containing the set $\{a^n b^n \mid n \geq 1\}$. For example, for any recursive AFL (abstract family of languages)[18] containing $\{a^n b^n \mid n \geq 1\}$ the problem of containment, equivalence and equivalence to Σ^* are undecidable and of Turing degree 1 [8].

Definition 12.13 (*Unsolvability*) Unsolvability refers to the property of a specific problem for which no algorithm exists that can solve it within certain constraints or under certain conditions. □

---

[17] Given the start element ab, we can prepend and append the every successive element by a and b, respectively, to generate ab, a^2b^2, ..., a^ib^i, ...

[18] AFL is closed under $\cup$, ., $+$, ε-free, inverse homomorphism, and have intersection with regular sets.

An unsolvable problem is one that does not have a solution or an algorithm that can find a solution for all possible instances of the problem. The unsolvability may be due to various factors, such as its inherent complexity, restrictions on resources, or limitations of the computational model being used. Some problems may be solvable in certain cases but become unsolvable or computationally infeasible for larger instances or specific constraints. For example, exhaustive solution of a traveling salesman's problem (TSP) for 100 cities, which will have almost 100! routs in the worst case, is an unsolvable problem.

Definition 12.14 (*Provably Unsolvable*) A formally stated problem is provably unsolvable if it can be proved that no Turing machine exists to compute the solution. □

Other argument in support of existence of unsolvabilty is that, there are infinitely more number of problems than algorithms, and there are in fact infinitely many more problems than machines. So building a machine that is more powerful computer, would not help a bit. There would still be an infinite number of problems it would not be able to solve.

In the next, we list the steps to define some problems [11].

Defining Problem-I

We start by defining a Problem: A problem is described by its *inputs* and *outputs*. The *primality* testing problem, for example, is defined as:

Inputs: A natural number x.
Output: True, if x is prime, *False* otherwise.

Following are steps to define it:

1. We can define a problem as a function from its inputs to output, $y = f(x)$, where x is input, y is output, and f is function (an algorithm). To make matters more simple, we limit ourselves to an input that is a natural number and an output that is a digit (0, ..., 9).
2. The next step is defining, what is an algorithm? We define the algorithm as a text of finite length. It is clear that all algorithms are texts but there are many texts that are not algorithms.
3. The next step is to show one-to-one function from the algorithms onto the natural numbers ($\mathbb{N}$). In simple words, we show how to transform every algorithm into a natural number and vice versa. The transformation is simple: for example, assume that our alphabet has 1000 symbols that are encoded by the numbers 000 to 999. By concatenating the code of all the symbols in our text, we get an integer. For example: Our text is: "pizza", and the codes for p, i, z, a are: 632, 625, 642, 617, respectively. consequently, the text "pizza" can be encoded into the an integer: 632625642642617.
4. We may decode an integer to a text as follows: divide the digits in the integer into triplets and write a letter that each triplet represents. To avoid the problem of

leading zeros (the number 000123 is equal to 123) we take the *space* character to be coded as 000, and ban texts that begin with a string of spaces.
Therefore, one algorithm can be mapped to one and only one integer. In case it is found that two algorithms map to a single integer number $n \in \mathbb{N}$, then these algorithms are same. By above explanation it is clear that two different integers cannot map to a single algorithm.

Defining the problem II
The next problem is: try to show a one-to-one function from the set of problems on to the set of real numbers [0, 1]. We do this by concatenating the output digits of all possible inputs (one to infinity) of the problem of primality test mentioned above. The problem can be stated as

Input: Natural Number
Output: 1 if input is prime and 0 otherwise. Note that each output 0 or 1 is an instance of solution of a problem of primality test.

For input 1, output is 0, for input 2 the output is 1, for input 3 (prime), output is 1, and so on. The real number that corresponds to this problem is 0.0110101000101..., which is infinite in length. We have given it only for the first 13 integers. We may consider that for infinitely large number of problems, every problem will have some kind of representation, like this, which is a unique representation. □

The next step is to show how we compare cardinality of infinite sets. Obviously, the problem represented by a sequence like this of real numbers are *uncountably infinite*, whereas the number of algorithms are *countably infinite*. Using *Cantor's diagonalization* theorem (Chap. 1, Theorem 1.4), we conclude that there are more real numbers between 0 and 1, than (the number of algorithms).

Having described the steps and the logic above, we can easily conclude that there are infinite numbers of problems that cannot be solved (even by a most powerful computer), merely because there cannot exist algorithms for them!

12.11 Undecidability

Definition 12.15 (*Undecidability*) Undecidability refers to the property of a problem that cannot be solved by any algorithm, regardless of the amount of computational resources available. □

An undecidable problem is one for which there is no general algorithm that can determine the correct answer for all possible instances of the problem. This means that there is no algorithm that can always halt and output the correct answer (either "yes" or "no") for every input of the problem. The halting problem is a classic example of an undecidable problem.

When we compare the solvable vs. undecidable problems, the undecidability is a broader concept that refers to the property of a problem being unsolvable by any algorithm, while unsolvability specifically describes the lack of an algorithm to solve a particular problem. Undecidability is a more fundamental and general concept, while unsolvability refers to specific instances or problems that lack a solution within certain conditions or constraints.

In the following discussions, our objective will be those problems which cannot be solved by computer. In other words, we will be able to show that no Turing Machine exists to solve such problems.

12.11.1 Russell's Paradox

The Russell's paradox consider that there is a village and among other villagers there is a barber. The barber is also a villager, and has a special status as barber. After going through the problem, the statement of the problem leads to self contradiction. That means statement of the problem is false, i.e., there cannot be any village and a barber. *Statement of the problem.* A barber in a small town declares that he shaves every one in this town who does not shave himself, and that he does not shave any one who shaves himself.

We will see that barber's declaration leads to contradiction. This contradiction is heart of the argument to prove that the halting problem is undecidable [4].

Proof attempt. Let X denote how the barber behaves:

$X = 1$ means "to shave a villager", and
$X = 0$ means "not to shave a villager".

Similarly, Y denotes how the villager behaves:

$Y = 0$ means"not to shave himself", and
$Y = 1$ means "to shave himself.

Clearly, what barber declared is for any villager, including himself, so (X, Y) must be:

$(1, 0)$: Barber (X) shaves villager Y and villager Y does not shave himself, or
$(0, 1)$: Barber (X) does not shaves the villager and the villager Y shaves himself.

On the other hand, the barber shaves himself not only as barber, but also as "one of the villager". Therefore, if barber shaves himself, (X, Y) becomes $(1, 1)$. And, when barber does not shave himself, (X, Y) becomes $(0, 0)$. In either cases, this contradicts what barber has declared.

If the barber is not treated as villager, the contradiction would not occur. The contradiction in above results to *self reference* in the declaration [3].

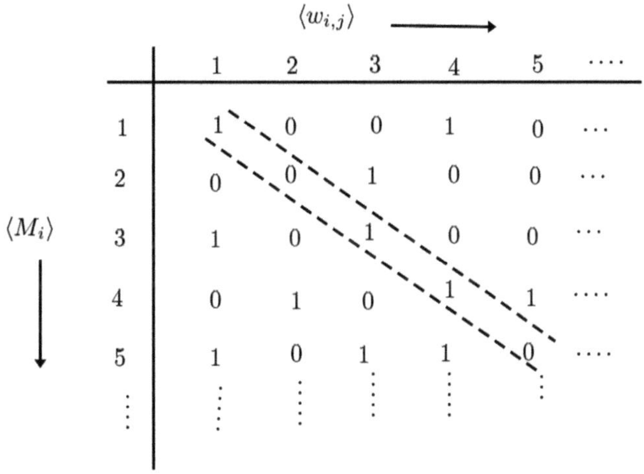

	1	2	3	4	5	....
1	1	0	0	1	0	...
2	0	0	1	0	0	...
3	1	0	1	0	0	...
4	0	1	0	1	1	....
5	1	0	1	1	0	....
⋮	⋮	⋮	⋮	⋮	⋮	

Fig. 12.12 Binary diagonal vector is diagonal language L_d

12.11.2 Diagonal Language

Consider that M is a TM with alphabet $\Sigma = \{a, b\}$, $w \in \Sigma^*$ and M accepts w. We had discussed that a TM M can be encoded as $en(M)$, and its input w as $en(w)$, accordingly, for the transition function δ, the encoding is:

$$\begin{aligned} &\delta(q_i, a) = (q_j, b, L) \\ &= 001^{i+1}01^201^{j+1}01^301^200. \end{aligned} \tag{12.11}$$

Similarly, all the transitions can be encoded. Hence $\langle M \rangle$ is encoded as $00m_i 00m_j00\dots00$, where m_i, m_j are a transitions, like shown in Eq. 12.11. We note that all the transitions of a TM, separated by 00 is a big integer number. If this process is followed, we can encode all the possible TMs. If a string is not a well-formed representation of any TM, we take this as encoding of a TM with null moves, hence every binary string, whether long or short, can be taken as representation of some TM. Therefore, all Turing machines can be represented by integers $\{1, 2, 3, \dots, i, \dots\}$, which is enumeration of Turing machines M_i, and are the countably infinite numbers.

Consider that language of a TM M_i is $L(M_i)$. For example, in a typical case $L(M_i) = \{1, 11, 100, 101, 110, 1001\dots,\}$. This is subset of lexicographic order binary set: $S = \{0, 1, 00, 01, 10, 11, 100, 101, 110, 111, 1000, \dots\} = \mathbb{N}$. Let us consider an encoded representation of $L(M_i)$ using set S as follows: If a word $w \in S$, is present in set $L(M_i)$, we indicate this by 1 in encoded representation in the position as per set S. If it is absent, then we show it by 0 in encoded form at that position. Thus, the encoded representation of, say, $L(M_4)$ (Fig. 12.12) is: $\{0, 1, 0, 1, 1, \dots\}$, where 0 in the begin indicates that "0" $\notin L(M_i)$, next 1 means "1" $\in L(M_4)$, next 0 means "00" $\notin L(M_4)$, and so on. Thus, strings of language $L(M_4)$, at columns

$j = 2, 4, 5, \ldots$, are $1, 01, 10, \ldots$. Note that, string corresponding to position of the column j where there is 0, are absent in the language $L(M_4)$.

In fact, the ith row is *characteristic vector* of language $L(M_i)$. When an integer along the axis $\langle M_i \rangle$ is not a valid encoding of TM, corresponding TM is taken as with single state machine having no final state, which does not accept any string.

Next, we consider the diagonal vector of matrix shown in Fig. 12.12, i.e., the sequence $[1, 0, 1, 1, 0, \ldots]$. This is a characteristic vector of some language $L_d = \{0, 00, 01, \ldots\}$, which is obvious by the definition of characteristic vector. As next step, take the *complement* of this diagonal vector, which is $\{0, 1, 0, 0, 1, \ldots\}$, and its corresponding language is $\overline{L_d} = \{1, 10, \ldots\}$, called *diagonal language*. Note that we can equally well write the $\overline{L_d}$ as a characteristic vector of some language $\overline{L_d} = \{0, 1, 0, 0, 1, \ldots\}$.

In the following we show that the diagonal language (in fact, the language which is complement of diagonal language) cannot be recognized by any Turing machine, in other words, there cannot exist any algorithm that recognizes the language $\overline{L_d}$, as, it is an undecidable language.

Theorem 12.20 *$\overline{L_d}$ is not recursively enumerable.*

Proof Let us assume that contrary is true, that is, $\overline{L_d}$ is recursively enumerable. Let $k \in \mathbb{N}$, such that some Turing machine M_k accepts the language $\overline{L_d}$. Let some string $w_{k,j} \in \overline{L_d}$. Then M_k accepts $w_{k,j}$, because $L(M_k) = \overline{L_d}$. However, $w_{k,j} \in \overline{L_d}$ implies that M_k does not accept $w_{k,j}$, a contradiction. This is due to Fig. 12.12, where Turing machines (in rows) are enumerated, and $\overline{L_d}$ disagrees with all machines.

Let us assume the reverse, $w_{k,j} \notin \overline{L_d}$. Then $w_{k,j} \notin L(M_k)$. Since M_k does not accept $w_{k,j}$, it follows by definition of $\overline{L_d}$ that $w_{k,j} \in \overline{L_d}$, which is again a contradiction. Thus, $w_{k,j} \in \overline{L_d}$ if and only if $w_{k,j} \notin \overline{L_d}$. This shows that no such Turing machine M_k can exist. Since M_k is general, therefore no Turing machine can exist that accepts the complement diagonal language $\overline{L_d}$. This shows that $\overline{L_d}$ is not recursively enumerable. □

Since, there does not exist any TM which recognizes $\overline{L_d}$, and therefore the diagonal language $\overline{L_d}$ is undecidable.

The definition of $\overline{L_d}$ is motivated by *Russell's paradox*, where in the definition of some specific set: $S = \{X \mid X \notin X\}$. Where as in Russell's paradox we had to conclude that there is no set as, here we conclude that $\overline{L_d}$ is not a Turing-acceptable set.

The Church–Turing Thesis (CTT) also has consequence for undecidability. If a problem cannot be solved by any TM, then it cannot be solved by any algorithm. A decision language having no algorithmic solution, is called *undecidable*.

There are countable TMs (i.e., Algorithms), but the number of problems are uncountable. It follows that there are languages whose membership are undecidable.

12.12 Undecidability of Halting Problem

First we recall a basic result from *computability theory* that there are undecidable languages. This can be argued as follows. There is a 1-1 correspondence between algorithms (TMs) and natural numbers. There is a 1-1 correspondence between languages (over the binary alphabet)[19] and real numbers in the interval [0, 1]. Since the set of reals ($\mathbb{R}$) is bigger than the set of natural numbers ($\mathbb{N}$) (as per Cantor's theorem, Sect. 1.4), there exists some undecidable languages. The problem with this argument is its non-constructiveness. We have exhibited such an undecidable language in Theorem 12.20. However, the most famous example of undecidability is in the form of *halting problem.*

The halting problem is stated as

$$Halt = \{\langle M, x\rangle \mid \text{Turing Machine } M \text{ accepts } x\}. \tag{12.12}$$

Thus, $Halt$ is set of $\langle M, x\rangle$ such that M halts on input x.

The contradiction in the proof of halting problem uses self reference and diagonalization. To obtain the standard relation table for a diagonalization argument, we consider every string $v \in \{0, 1\}^*$ to represent TM. If v does not have the form $R(M)$, the one state TM with no transition is assigned to it. Thus, Turing machines can be listed as M_0, M_1, ..., corresponding to strings ε, 0, 1, 00, 01, 10, ..., as vertical leftmost column as in Fig. 12.13, and their representation as $\langle M_0\rangle$, $\langle M_1\rangle$, ..., $\langle D\rangle$... as horizontal top row in this table. This means, if the string $\langle M_j\rangle$ is accepted by TM M_i then corresponding value in the matrix (i, j), where i is row count and j is column count, is 1 else 0. Then, we construct a diagonal vector of this matrix, shown between two dashed line.

Considering the machine M_i, infinitely large number of strings $\langle M_0\rangle$, $\langle M_1\rangle$, $\langle M_2\rangle$, ... $\langle M_j\rangle$, ..., which form the language strings of machine M_i, will have 1 in the row of TM M_i in the columns j.

Thus, entry in the cells of ith rows and jth column intersection is 1 if a TM M_i accepts its representation $\langle M_j\rangle$, else 0. Thus, (i, i)th entry in Fig. 12.13 is:

$$\begin{cases} 1, & \text{if } M_i \text{ halts when run with input, i.e., } \langle M_i\rangle \\ 0, & \text{if } M_i \text{ does not halt when run with i.e., } \langle M_i\rangle \end{cases}. \tag{12.13}$$

The Diagonal of the table in Fig. 12.13 represents the answers to the self reference question: "Does M_i halt when run on itself?" The machine D was constructed to produce contradiction in response to this question.

In the following theorem we show that *Halt* is undecidable.

Theorem 12.21 *Halt is undecidable.*

[19] See Fig. 12.12, each language's characteristic vector, e.g., $L(M_1)$ can be taken as 0.10010.... Such characteristic vectors of all the languages are unique in each language, and they fall in the interval [0, 1].

	$\langle M_0\rangle$	$\langle M_1\rangle$	$\langle M_2\rangle$	...	$\langle M_j\rangle$	...	$\langle D\rangle$	...
M_0	1	0	0	...	1	...	0	...
M_1	0	1	1	...	0	...	0	...
M_2	1	0	1		0	...	1	...
$\vdots$	$\vdots$	$\vdots$	$\vdots$		$\vdots$		$\vdots$	
M_i	1	0	1	...	0	...	0	...
$\vdots$	$\vdots$	$\vdots$	$\vdots$		$\vdots$		$\vdots$	
D	0	1	0	...	1	...	?	...
$\vdots$	$\vdots$	$\vdots$	$\vdots$		$\vdots$		$\vdots$	

Fig. 12.13 Does M_i halt when run on itself?

Proof We will prove the theorem in two stages:

1. First, we define a certain language $Diag$ and show that $Diag$ is undecidable,
2. Then we will show that $Diag$ is reducible to $Halt$,
   Conclusion: Hence, $Halt$ is also undecidable.

Stage 1: To define $Diag$, we consider an enumeration $x_1, x_2, x_3, ...$ of all binary strings. Let $M_1, M_2, M_3, ...$ be an enumeration of all Turing machines whose description are $x_1, x_2, x_3, ...$ Note that some binary strings corresponds to "broken" TMs. We will assume that a broken TM does not accept any string.

We define $Diag$ as follows:

$$Diag = \{M \mid M \text{ does not accept input } M\}. \tag{12.14}$$

Note that $Diag$ is same as $\overline{L_d}$ (Fig. 12.12), because we have already considered $\overline{L_d}$ by saying "M does not accept M". To show that $Diag$ is undecidable, our proof is by contradiction. Suppose some TM D decides $Diag$. Then we have one of two cases:

1. D accepts D, or
2. D does not accept D.

In the first case, $D \notin Diag$ (by definition of $Diag$). Since D decides $Diag$ (by our assumption), D does not accept D, a contradiction.

In the second case, we get $D \in Diag$ (by definition of $Diag$). Since D decides $Diag$ (by our assumption), D accepts D. Again a contradiction.

Thus, our assumption that $diag$ is decidable must be wrong.

Stage 2: Now we reduce $Diag$ to $Halt$. If $Halt$ were decidable by some TM H, then we could decide $Diag$ as follows:

"On input M, run the TM H on $\langle M, M\rangle$, and negate the output (i.e., Accept if H rejects, and Reject if H accepts)." It is clear that output of H is also undecidable when it has $\langle M, M\rangle$ input, where 1st M is machine which has M (description of M) as input, because $\langle M, M\rangle$ is undecidable.

Stage 1 of the proof deduces through contradiction that $diag$ is undecidable. In stage 2, we reduce $Diag$ to $Halt$, thus $Halt$ is also undecidable. This proves that, $Halt$ is undecidable. □

12.13 Rice's Theorem

Rice's theorem shows that a very large family of problems are all undecidable. The theorem is after Henry Rice, who proved these results [13]. The statement of the theorem is as follows.

Theorem 12.22 *If* S *is a non-trivial*[20] *property of Turing-recognizable languages, then the problem,*

"Given a TM M, does $L(M)$ have property S*?"*

is undecidable. □

An example of a property of Turing-recognizable languages could be, say, being a *regular language*. If we have an algorithm for determining, given a TM M, if $L(M)$ was regular language then we would have a tool that we could use to determine whether we could replace M by an equivalent finite automation machine. In fact, the problem is undecidable [12].

As other example, consider a language whose strings contained some specific sequence of characters. If we can determine if a TM M accepted all strings of this language, then we have a tool that has determined that all the data which we assumed to be correct, were correct. Unfortunately, this is also not possible, as algorithms that check certain properties of languages cannot exist!

To start with, we give a mathematical definition of the notion of property. In our setting, a property is simply a class of Turing-recognizable languages.

Definition 12.16 A class of languages S is called a property of Turing-recognizable languages if the members of S are Turing-recognizable languages, i.e., for every language $L \in \mathsf{S}$ there exists a TM that recognizes L. □

Example 12.5 The class of languages,

$$\mathsf{S}_{\text{Regular}} = \{L \mid L \text{ is regular}\} \tag{12.15}$$

is a property of Turing-recognizable languages, since all its members (L) are Turing-recognizable languages. □

[20] Trivial: of little value or importance. Non-trivial: (in mathematics) Having some variables or terms that are not equal to zero or an identity.

Example 12.6 The class of languages, which is set of two sets,

$$\mathsf{S}_2 = \{EQ_{TM}, A_{TM}\} \tag{12.16}$$

is not a property of Turing-recognizable languages, since EQ_{TM}[21] is a language in S which is not Turing-recognizable. □

The property S of Turing-recognizable languages is non-trivial property if some of these languages have this property while others do not have.

Definition 12.17 The property S is said to be non-trivial if there exists Turing-recognizable languages L_1 and L_2 such that $L_1 \in \mathsf{S}$ but $L_2 \notin \mathsf{S}$. □

If a property of Turing-recognizable languages is *not* non-trivial, then it is trivial.

Example 12.7 Show that the class of languages,

$$\mathsf{S}_{\text{Regular}} = \{L \mid L \text{ is regular}\}, \tag{12.17}$$

is a non-trivial property of Turing-recognizable languages.

Since the language say L_1, where $L_1 = \{a^n \mid n \geq 0\}$ is a member of $\mathsf{S}_{\text{Regular}}$, and also Turing-recognizable. Let $L_2 = \{a^n b^n \mid n \geq 0\}$. We note that L_2, though Turing-recognizable, it is not regular language. Hence, set (12.17) is an example of non-trivial property of Turing-recognizable languages. □

There are only two ways of violation of conditions of being non-trivial. These properties are,
(i). $\mathsf{S}_{\text{all}} = \{L \mid L \text{ is Turing-recognizable}\}$, and,
(ii). $\mathsf{S}_{\text{none}} = \phi$,
which are both trivial, and they are the only such properties. S_{all} is trivial, since there does not exist a Turing-recognizable language L_2 such that $L_2 \notin \mathsf{S}_{\text{all}}$. The S_{none} is trivial, since there does not exists a Turing-recognizable language L_1 such that $L_1 \in \mathsf{S}_{\text{none}}$. □

Some examples of non-trivial properties of Turing-recognizable languages are given below:

- The class $\{\phi\}$ whose only member is empty language. It is not same as S_{none}.
- The class $\{\Sigma^*\}$. Its members are all strings over Σ^*.
- Class of languages A, where $\varepsilon \in A$.
- The class of context-free languages.
- The class of Turing-decidable languages.

[21] $\langle T_i, T_j \rangle \in EQ_{TM}$ if T_i and T_j are Turing machines, and $L(T_i) = L(T_j)$.

12.13.1 Proof of Rice Theorem

Consider that S be a property of a language, then the language S_{TM} is set of all the Turing machines' encoding,

$$\mathsf{S}_{TM} = \{\langle M\rangle \mid L(M) \in \mathsf{S}\}. \tag{12.18}$$

What we are going to prove in the following is that, S_{TM} is undecidable whenever the property S is non-trivial.

As an example,

$$\mathsf{S}_{TM} = \{\langle M\rangle \mid L(M) \text{ is regular language}\}.$$

The approach shall be as follows. We will show that if S is a non-trivial property of Turing-recognizable languages, then we can reduce A_{TM} to S_{TM}, i.e., given $\langle M, w\rangle$ we can construct the description of a machine $\langle M'\rangle$ such that M accepts w if and only if $L(M') \in \mathsf{S}$.

Theorem 12.23 *If* S *is a non-trivial property of Turing-recognizable languages, then* S_{TM} *is undecidable.*

Proof Let S be a non-trivial property of some language. We pickup some language $L_1 \in \mathsf{S}$ and assume that some $L_2 = \phi$, hence $L_2 \notin \mathsf{S}$.

As a next step, given $\langle M, w\rangle$, we construct a TM M' such that if M accepts w then $L(M') = L_1$ and if M does not accept w, then $L(M') = \phi$.

It will not be a loss of generality to assume that $\phi \notin \mathsf{S}$, because, if we wanted to show that S was undecidable and $\phi \in \mathsf{S}$, we could simply consider the complementary property $\overline{\mathsf{S}}$. Obviously, $\overline{\mathsf{S}}_{TM}$ is decidable if and only if S_{TM} is decidable.

Since S_{TM} is a non-trivial property of Turing-recognizable languages (as per Eq. 12.17), there must be some $L_1 \in \mathsf{S}$. Since L_1 is Turing-recognizable, there exists a Turing machine that recognizes L_1. Let the recognizer for L_1 be a machine M_{L_1}. Given this, we can have a reduction from A_{TM} to S_{TM} as follows. From $\langle M, w\rangle$ and using M_{L_1}, we construct the description of a new machine M':

M' = "On input x,

1. Simulate M on w,
2. If M accepts w, then simulate M_{L_1} on x,
3. If M_{L_1} accept x, then accept."

Now we show that this reduction is correct, i.e., $\langle M, w\rangle \in A_{TM}$ if and only if $\langle M'\rangle \in \mathsf{S}_{TM}$:

First, suppose that $\langle M, w\rangle \in A_{TM}$, i.e., M accepts w. Then M' will accept its input x exactly when M_{L_1} accepts x. So, here $L(M') = L_1$, and $L_1 \in \mathsf{S}$ by assumption.

Now suppose that $\langle M, w\rangle \notin A_{TM}$, i.e., M does not accept w. Then M' will never reach the simulation of M_{L_1}, and consequently M' accepts no string. Hence, $L(M') = \phi$ and $\phi \notin \mathsf{S}$ by assumption.

We can now conclude that S_{TM} cannot be decidable. For if S_{TM} were decidable, we would have decider for it, say R, but then we could also build the following decider for A_{TM}:

H = "On input $\langle M, w \rangle$

1. Construct $\langle M' \rangle$ from $\langle M, w \rangle$
2. Feed $\langle M' \rangle$ to R
3. If R *accepts*, then accept. If R rejects, then *Reject*."

This proves the theorem. □

12.13.2 Undecidability Results of Rice's Theorem

From the Rice theorem and discussion made above, we have following problems, all of which are undecidable:

- Does M accept all inputs?
- Does M accept no input at all?
- Does M accept empty string?
- Is $L(M)$ regular?
- Is $L(M)$ Context-free?
- Is $L(M)$ Turing-decidable?

Example 12.8 Consider the following problem:
Given TM M, does M accept all the strings that are palindromes?

To use Rice's theorem, we reformulate this problem such that it talks about the "class of languages."

$$PALINDROMES_{TM} = \{\langle M \rangle \mid L(M) \text{ contains all palindromes}\}$$

Next, we represent the property, we are actually looking for as

$$S_{\text{PALINDROMES}} = \{L \mid L \text{ is Turing-recognizable and contains all palindromes}\}.$$

This is a class of Turing-recognizable languages. Also, it is non-trivial, since Turing-recognizable language of all strings over Σ^* is a member of this class, whereas the empty language ϕ (which is recognizable) is not a member of this class.
Using Rice's theorem we conclude that PALINDROMES$_{TM}$ is undecidable. □

12.14 Summary

This chapter has focused on decidable or decision problems, i.e., the problems about whose solution is in the form of Yes/No. The problems that we can include in this class are, for example, "Is a given number prime?", "Will a given program compile correctly?", "Is a given number perfect square?", "Can a given Graph be traversed without repeating any node?","Can a given graph be traversed without repeating any edge?", "Can a given sentence w be parsed using the given grammar G?", and so on.

The problems for which the answer can be decided in the form of Yes/No, are called *Recursive* or *decidable* problems. They are also called members-of-recursive language, because the elements of such languages can be generated through recursive procedure, and the membership can be tested though a mechanical algorithm.

On the other hand the *Recursively Enumerable* (RE) languages are those whose membership can be also algorithmically tested, but when there is no solution, e.g., given Γ as formulas and θ as a formula, an algorithm that tries to answer, if $\Gamma \vdash \theta$ holds? But, if $\Gamma \nvdash \theta$, then the algorithm may continue indefinitely. Such languages are called *Turing recognizable.* A language for this can be $\{(\Gamma_1, \theta_1), (\Gamma_2, \theta_2), ...\}$. These language are also called *semi-decidable.* Other example can be, whether there exists any integer numbers x, y, z and $n \geq 3$ which satisfies the equation $z^n = x^n + y^n$.

For any computation to be carried out we require an *effective procedure*—one, that is, *mechanical, deterministic*, and *complete.* An effective procedure can be constructed using functions that are intuitively computable—called *recursive functions.*

Other method of building an effectively computable procedure uses human like computing agent, and for this the *Turing machine* is the best-known framework. This is a general as well as simple approach, and has no limits of time and space, where time is run-time of the algorithm runs, and space is that which holds input, intermediate computation results and the output.

A decision problem needs to be formulated before we write a procedure for its solution. Examples of some decision problems are: "Is the given natural number a perfect square?", "Does a given graph has a cycle?", etc. Each such problem has problem instances, e.g., "Is 1 perfect square?", "Is 2 perfect square?", and so on.

There is a duality between *decision problems* and *recursive languages*; every decision problem corresponds to an input $w \in L$, where w is an element of recursive language L.

Turing recognizable are those languages, such that for $w \in L$ (L is recursively enumerable), the Turing machine will always halt, but for $w \notin L$, the machine may continue indefinitely or loop forever.

If a language is recursive, then its complement is also recursive.

A language is decidable if and only if that language and its complement are both recursively enumerable.

Some of the decidable properties of Grammars and language are: emptiness-of-intersection problem, grammar-class-membership problem, and language-class-membership problem.

Considering the regular languages and finite automata, the following are *decidable*:

- a language having elements like, $\langle B, w\rangle$, such that B is DFA that accepts w;
- a language having elements $\langle R, w\rangle$, such that regular expression R generates string w;
- a language having elements DFA as A, and language of A is empty string;
- a language with elements $\langle A, B\rangle$, both DFAs, and they are equivalent.

The following context-free languages are *decidable*:

- $L = \{\langle G, w\rangle \mid G \text{ is a CFG that generates } w\}$,
- membership of E_{CFG} is also decidable, i.e., whether $\langle G\rangle \in E_{CFG}$, such that the language generated by G is empty.

Union of Recursive languages is recursive, and union of two RE languages is also RE. Intersection of R and RE languages is RE language.

Every context-sensitive language is Recursive.

If a language L is recursive then there exists an enumeration procedure for it.

Since languages are sets, it is possible to define computability on sets. There are two ways to look at the sets: *computable* and *compressible*. If a function f is computable then there exists an algorithm to compute it. However, for this there may also be a need of some external set A, and we say f is computable through A, written as $f \leq_T A$ (f is Turing reducible to A), and $\leq_T$ stands for "Turing reducible".

In computability theory, a set of natural numbers is also called recursive or computable, if there is an algorithm that terminates after finite amount of time, and correctly decides if a given natural number is in the set or not.

The infinite set T_∞, of all Turing machines, is computable.

A set A is recursively enumerable if either $A = \phi$ or there exists a recursive function f such that A is equal to range of f. Further, if set A is recursive, then $\overline{A}$ is also recursive.

A Turing machine can be used as an enumerator. The set of all the Turing machines is countable.

About "how many problems are undecidable?", Rice's theorem says that in fact there are very large number of problems that are undecidable. The theorem states that if S is a non-trivial property of Turing-recognizable languages, then the problem,

"Given a TM M, does M have property S?"

is undecidable. From this we can conclude that a large number of problems are undecidable. Even, the language "$\mathsf{S} = \{\langle L\rangle \mid L \text{ is regular}\}$", is undecidable, because "regularity" is a non-trivial property.

Self Review Questions

1. Is it always the case that if a language is decidable then it is also recognizable?
2. What is an effective procedure?
3. What is completeness property of an algorithm?
4. How a recognition problem is different from recursive problems?
5. What is the Church–Turing thesis?
6. What are the three variants of Church–Turing thesis?
7. What is difference between unsolvability and undecidabilit?
8. Is barber's problem undecidable or unsolvable?
9. List any five problems that are decidable.
10. As per Gödel, first-order logic is *semantically* complete. (True/False).
11. Give two examples in each of the following:

    a. Computable sets,
    b. Non-computable sets.

12. What are the properties of an ideal algorithm?
13. What is a *diophantine* equation?
14. What is diagonal language?
15. Why the diagonal language $\overline{L_d}$ is not in RE language?
16. How the number of problems are *uncountable* while TMs are *countable*, despite the fact that both are infinite?
17. What is characteristic-vector of a language?
18. If characteristic vector of some language is {0, 1, 1, 0, 1, 0, 1, 0, 0, 0, 1, ...}, what is corresponding language?
19. What is conclusion of following statement?
    "Two formulas which appears distinct but have same Gödel representation?"

Exercises

A. Concepts based Problems

Note: The $*$ marked exercises are provided with solutions at the end of this book.

1. Is the language
   "$\overline{HALT} = \{\langle M, x\rangle \mid M$ is Turing machine that *does not* halt on input $x\}$,"
   Turing recognizable?
2. Is the language
   "$HALT = \{\langle M, x\rangle \mid M$ is Turing machine that *halt* on input $x\}$"
   Turing recognizable?

3. Represent the following formulas in the form of Gödel numbers:

   a. $(a + b + c)^2$
   b. $z^2 = x^2 + y^2$
   c. $S = \Sigma_{i=1}^{n} a_i$
   d. $z^n = x^n + y^n$

4. Determine which of the following languages are *Recursive* only and, which of these are *Recursively Enumerable*?

   a. $\{1, 3, 5, 7, \ldots\}$.
   b. $\{x \mid x \text{ is prime}\}$.
   c. $\{x \mid x \text{ is citizen of planet earth}\}$.
   d. Language of all possible mathematical functions.
   e. Power set all the sentences in English language.
   f. Set of all algorithms.

5. Describe construction of a TM M, which decides if a given natural number m is larger than some other natural number n. "Decide" here means, given $\#1^m\#1^n$, M halts and returns "Yes" if $m > n$, and halts with output "No" if $m \leq n$.
6. Give logical justification of following:

   a. The first-order logic is *semantically complete*.
   b. The first-order logic not *syntactically complete*.

7. Why the *property* of "Turing-recognizable languages" is non-trivial property.

B. Analysis-based Problems

8. Why the following problems are undecidable?

   a. Does some TM M accept all inputs?
   b. Does some TM M accept no input at all?
   c. Does some TM M accept empty string?
   d. Is language $L(M)$ of some TM M, a regular language?
   e. Is language $L(M)$ of some TM M, a Context-free language?
   f. Is language $L(M)$ of some TM M, Turing-decidable?

9. Give a logical explanation that the Hilbert's problem can be transformed into the decision problem of recursively enumerable set.
10. "A language $L(G)$ contains at least 10 strings, for a given CFG G." Is this problem decidable?
11. * Show that Turing Machine can be used as language enumerator.
12. For any Turing machine M, determine if the given language $\{\langle M \rangle\}$ is decidable:

   a. $\{\langle M \rangle \mid L(M) \text{ has exactly } n \text{ elements}\}$.
   b. $\{\langle M \rangle \mid L(M) \text{ is not recognizable}\}$.
   c. $\{\langle M \rangle \mid M \text{ has an even number of states}\}$.
   d. $\{\langle M \rangle \mid \text{a string } w \text{ is accepted by } M \text{ in less than } |w| \text{ transitions}\}$.

13. What are the ways of violation of condition of being non-trivial?
14. What is $\mathsf{S}_{\text{all}} = \{L \mid L \text{ is Turing-recognizable}\}$? Is it a trivial or a non-trivial property?
15. Let L_1, L_2 are decidable as well recognizable languages. Are the languages $L_1 \cup L_2$, $L_1 \cap L_2$ necessarily decidable and recognizable?
16. Which of the following are the non-trivial properties of Turing recognizable languages?

    a. Class of regular languages
    b. Class of context-free languages
    c. Class of context-sensitive languages
    d. Unrestricted languages

C. Proof-based Problems

17. * Prove that intersection R and RE languages is RE.
18. Show that class of Turing-decidable languages are closed under:

    a. Set Union,
    b. Set Intersection, and
    c. Kleene star.

19. * Show that decidable languages are closed under the operations of *union* and *intersection*.
20. Show that following problems are *decidable*:

    a. A DFA A accepts the string w, where $A = (Q, \Sigma, \delta, s, F)$, and $w \in \Sigma^*$.
    b. A given expression generates a string w.
    c. A DFA A accepts the language $L = \{\}$.
    d. A CFG generates all string in 1^*.
    e. $L = \{\langle G \rangle \mid G \text{ is CFG}, \Sigma = \{0, 1\}, \text{ and } \{1^*\} \subseteq L(G)\}$.
    f. All the finite languages.
    g. Determining whether a given DFA accepts a palindrome string.
    h. $L = \{1^n \mid n \text{ is a prime}\}$.
    i. $L = \{\langle M \rangle \mid M \text{ is DFA that accepts } w \in \Sigma^* \text{ with more } 1s \text{ than } 0s\}$.

21. Use the concept of halting problem to show that the sentence "this sentence is not True" is contradictory.
22. Show that there is no algorithm that determines whether an arbitrary Tuning Machine halts when run with the input string 101.
23. Show that property of being context-free is a non-trivial property.
24. Show that the language $\{a^{2^n} \mid n \geq 0\}$ is recursive.
25. * Show that the diagonal language L_d is recursively enumerable.
26. * Show that *Universality* of a language of CFG is undecidable.[22]

---

[22] A language is universal if $L = \Sigma^*$.

D. Multiple choice Questions

27. * Which of the following statements are decidable?
I. A given grammar is CFG.
II. Intersection of two regular languages is infinite.
III. A given Context-free language is regular.
IV. Two given pushdown automata accept identical language.
(A) I, II (B) II, III (C) I, IV (D) II, IV

28. * Given some language L, the following statements are decidable?
I. If L is context-free then also the $\overline{L}$.
II. If L is recursive then also the $\overline{L}$.
III. If L is regular then also the $\overline{L}$.
IV. None of above.
(A) I, IV (B) II, III (C) I, III (D) III, IV

29. If the sentences $w \in L$ can be effectively enumerated in lexicographic order, then following property holds for L:
(A) regular but may not be finite
(B) may not be regular but context-free
(C) recursive but may not be context-free
(D) finite

30. If L and $\overline{L}$ are recursively enumerable then L is
(A) regular (B) context-free
(C) context-sensitive (D) recursive

E. Advanced Knowledge Assessment Problems

31. Show that following problems are *undecidable*:

   a. Given that infinite diagonal of $\langle M_i \rangle \times \langle w_{i,j} \rangle$ is set D, then there does not exists a Turing machine that accepts the language corresponding to the characteristic vector $\overline{D}$.
   b. Given two Turing machines M_1 and M_2, is $L(M_1) \subseteq L(M_2)$?
   c. Given two Turing machines M_1 and M_2, is $L(M_1) \cap L(M_2) = \phi$?
   d. Determining if the languages generated by two CFGs are same?
   e. If two Turing machines M_1 and M_2 accept the same language?
   f. Neither the language $L = \{M \mid M \text{ halts on all inputs}\}$ nor its complement is recursively enumerable.
   g. Intersection of two given context-free languages is a context-free language.
   h. A Turing machine M halts on some input string w.
   i. Given L_1 and L_2 as CFLs generated by CFG G_1, G_2, respectively, the language $L = \{\langle w_1, w_2 \rangle \mid w_1 \in L_1, w_2 \in L_2, \text{ and } w_1 = w_2\}$ is undecidable.

32. * There is a table comprising of all rows as the characteristic vectors $\langle w_{i,j} \rangle$, where $(i, 1), ..., (i, j), ...$ is characteristic vector of ith language. And, corresponding to all these rows there is one column representing the characteristic vector of all the Turing machines $\langle T_i \rangle$, then "a characteristic vector constructed by complementing the diagonal vector of $\langle w_{i,j} \rangle$ cannot be characteristic vector of any language." Prove this statement.

References

1. Church A (1936) An unsolvable problem of elementary number theory. Am J Math 58(2):345–363
2. Bernays P, Church A (1936) An unsolvable problem of elementary number theory. Am J Math 58:345–363. J Symb Log 1(2):73–74
3. Burks AW, Copi IM (1950) Lewis Carroll's Barber shop paradox. Mind 59(234):219–222
4. Carroll L, Washburn M (1894) A logical paradox. Mind 3(11):436–438
5. Chaitin GJ (1971) Computational complexity and Gödel's incompleteness theorem. ACM SIGACT News 9:11–12
6. Post EL (1944) Recursively enumerable sets of positive integers and their decision problems. Bull Am Math Soc 50(5):284–316
7. Grechuk B (Mar 2022) Open problems column edited by William Gasarch. ACM SIGACT News 53(1)
8. Hartmanis J, Hopcroft JE (1 Aug 1970) What makes some language theory problems undecidable. J Comput Syst Sci **4**(4):368–376
9. Hunt III HB (Apr 1982) On the decidability of grammar problems. J ACM 29(2):429–447
10. Hopcroft JE, Ullman JD (Apr 1968) Decidable and undecidable questions about automata. J ACM 15(2):317–324
11. Gal-Ezer J et al (28–30 Jun 2004) Introducing undecidability. In: TiSCSE '04, Leeds, United Kingdom, ACM 1-58113-836-9/04/0006, p 276
12. Huttel H (Oct 2001) On Rice's theorem. Aalborg University. A note
13. Péter R, Rice HG (1954) Classes of recursively enumerable sets and their decision problems. Trans AMS 74:358–366
14. Peter S (7 Apr 2010) Godel without (too many) tears—5: primitive recursive functions. University of Canterbury, Christchurch, NZ, pp 1–9
15. Jr Rogers H (1987) Theory of recursive functions and effective computability. McGraw-Hill Book Company, NY
16. Seymour G, Rose GF (1962) Some recursively unsolvable problems in ALGOL-like languages*. J Assoc Comput Mach 29(2):429–447
17. Feferman Solomon (17 Nov 2006) The nature and significance of Gödels incomplete theorems. Institute for Advanced study, Princeton, Gödel Centenary Program, pp 1–16
18. Wiles A (1 May 1995) Modular elliptic curves and Fermat's last theorem. Ann Math 141(3):443–551

Part VI
Comlexity of Computations

This part presents the complexity theory and NP-completeness, in two chapters. Complexity of a solution or algorithm says about how much resources are needed in terms of time and space, as a function of size of the input to solve that problem. For most problems, and in fact for all the solvable problems, the time needed is polynomial (P) function of the input size, for example, for bubble sort, the complexity (time) for input of size n is $O(n^2)$, for quick sort it is $O(n\log n)$, and for ordinary $n \times n$ matrix multiplication it is $O(n^3)$, which are all polynomial in n. The space needed is equal to the size of input, i.e., n. In general, the complexities are classified as linear, sublinear, and superlinear.

The complexity theory presents major time complexities classes, P, EXP, DTIME, NP-complete and NP-hard for deterministic TMs and NP, NTIME, and NEXP for nondeterministic TMs.

Similarly, there are space complexities classes: LOGSPACE, DSPACE, PSPACE, E, EXPSPACE for deterministic TM, and NSPACE, NE, NEXPSPACE for nondeterministic TM.

Various complexity classes form a hierarchy of complexity classes, which include all the classes, including circuit complexity—a class based on computation through Boolean logic circuits, rather than using Turing machine.

Among all the complexity classes, the special significance is carried by the class of NP-completeness problems, as there exists large number of problems of this class, and they have critical applications in practical fields, like software testing, power distribution grid, matching entities of two groups based on large number of attributes, and for example, register allocation while compiling codes, etc.

The NP-complete problems are hard problems and have yet no polynomial (efficient) algorithm for their general solutions. Interestingly, if solution is presented for any such problem, then it is easy (polynomial time complexity) to verify that it is correct or not. Further, if a polynomial time general solution is found for one such problem, then all the NP-complete will have a polynomial (P) time solution.

Many general NP-complete problems have been discussed, including the Boolean satisfiability (SAT) problem. At the end, a new complexity class has been presented, called #P, #SAT, #P-hard, etc., which is based on counting all the possible solutions, rather than just finding a solution of a given problem.

Overall, this last part raises many questions in the mind of a reader and makes one think beyond, this course of theory of computations, as well as it has been designed to provide a great motivation to the learner.

Chapter 13
Computational Complexity Theory

Abstract The computational complexity theory is concerned with computational resources needed for solving the problems on computers. These resources are in the form of time and space (memory), where time is number of elementary steps required in solving the problem, and space is storage consumed in units of words. The important difference between these two resources is that space is reusable in nature while time is not. Despite the fact that there are infinite variety of problems, there are only limited classes of time and space complexity, into which all the known problems can be fitted. In fact, there is canonical hierarchy of complexities, which covers all the classes. The basic classes for time are P, NP and EXP, and for space are L (for log), PSPACE, NSPACE, and EXPSPACE. The complexity classes are defined for deterministic and nondeterministic TMs. The general case of all the type P is solvable on realistic machines in realistic time, while it is other way for type NP. An interesting principle, called problem reduction, states that a problem can be reduced from a more complex form to a simpler form. Thus, if an NP class problem can be reduced into a class P through a transformation that takes time in P, the original problem can in fact be solved in time, in P. The chapter also presents some specific type of problem called PRIMES and COMPOSITS in the NP class, introduces the classes NP-complete and NP-hard, and provides the chapter summary followed with number of exercises for practice.

Keywords Time bound · Space bound · Complexity classes · Circuit complexity · P · NP · EXP · L · PSPACE · NSPACE · EXPSPACE · PRIMES · COMOSITS · NP-Complete · NP-Hard · Problem reduction · Reducibility · Oracle TM

13.1 Introduction

The computational complexity theory is aimed to study the computational resources, such as *time* and *space* (memory), required to solve computational problems, and to *classify* the problems according to their difficulty level. Often, there are many possible algorithms to solve any given problem, like, evaluation of an algebraic expression, indexing a data, or parsing a sentence. With each of these algorithms,

K. R. Chowdhary, *Theory of Computation*,
https://doi.org/10.1007/978-981-97-6234-7_13

there are associated certain cost functions, e.g., how many computational steps are requited to compute the function for a given size of the problem, and what are the memory space requirements for the computation that function. By quantifying these computational resources, the complexity theory has profoundly affected our thinking about computation. In contrast, the complexity theory also establishes the existence of decidable problems that although are solvable in principle, but cannot be solved in practice, because the time and space required to solve such problems would be larger than the age and size, respectively, of this universe.

Given a computational problem P, we may have following questions about this: What are good algorithms that can solve P? Can one find and prove some lower bound for one of the cost functions time and space, which are associated with this algorithm? Is the problem P *intractable*, in a sense, that no algorithm can solve it in a realistic time? These questions may be asked for the average-case behavior as well as for the worst-case behavior of the algorithms for P. Though the resources often discussed are space (i.e., memory) and time, however, the challenge of the theory is to prove *lower bounds*, i.e., the problem is solvable without spending large amount of resources. Although it is not difficult to prove that inherently difficult problems exist, but it is much more difficult to show that any interesting problem is hard to solve. There has been success in finding strong evidence of intractability based on widely held conjectures [9].

Most of the lower bounds in complexity theory are *asymptotic* in nature. For example, to solve a particular problem of rapidly growing function t, it takes $\Omega(t(n))$ time on a Turing machine, where input $|w| = n$. For any algorithm to be solved using the Turing machine model, no other lower bound can be possible because Turing machines have the *linear-speed-up* property—i.e., complexity is multiplied by a constant factor—in effect, the complexity class is not changed when some more complex Turing machine is used, e.g., many tape TM. But the problem has a by-product—for any input $|w| = n$ there is a Turing machine that handles input w in just n steps, and each step is to look-up for the answer in a big table!

The meaning of these asymptotic lower bounds mentioned above is that they can be essentially translated into concrete lower bounds on, say, the number of components of a particular computer's technology, or the number of clock cycles on a particular make of the machine, that are required to compute a given function of any given input size. These bounds can be translated only for few general complexity classes, but for the large majority of important problems, it is difficult as no nontrivial lower bound on complexity is known for those problems.

The complexity theory has contributed in two ways: (1) it has partitioned the computation into complexity classes, and (2) there is sufficient evidence that these complexity classes are distinct. If this evidence can be reduced to proofs, then there is abundance of scope of interesting lower bounds. Typically, a complexity class is defined by three things collectively: (1) a *model* of computation, (2) a *resource* (or collection of resources), and (3) a *function* known as the complexity bound for each resource. For example, for a problem P, whether P is equal to "palindrome problem", using the Turing machine model of computation, *resource* is time taken by TM, and the time function is $O(n^2)$, where $|w| = n$, is size of input w.

The models that define complexity classes are mainly two types: (1) *machine-based* models and (2) *circuit-based* models. The TMs and *Random-Access Machines* (RAMs) are the two principal families in the machine-based models [4]. When we are interested to model a realistic computation, the deterministic machines and circuit models are our first preferences. There are two reasons for why consider the other models. First reason is the computational problems whose complexity we are interested to understand. The examples that can be called as most notorious are the known hundreds of NP-complete problems. To a large extent what we understand about complexity of these problems is due to the nondeterministic model of Turing machine. Though the nondeterministic Turing Machines do not model physical computations, but they can model real computational problems.

The second reason also comes from the first only. Our interest to understand real computational problems has motivated us to understand a range of computational models and the resource bounds for the problems. In order to understand the relation between these models and bounds, we combine and mix them and attempt to discover their relative powers. In the process, we discovered some new models that are found to be useful to model efficient parallel computation.

To solve a problem, we should have an algorithm. The notion of algorithm excludes the TMs that do not halt on some inputs. Therefore, Turing machines that halt on all inputs, are adopted as a precise notion corresponding to the intuitive notion of an "algorithm". Nothing is considered an algorithm if it *cannot* be represented in the form of a Turing machine that is guaranteed to halt on all inputs. All those machines that halt on all input will be called algorithms. This is what we call a Church–Turing thesis. It is not a theorem because it is not a mathematical result. It simply says that a certain informal concept, i.e., algorithm, corresponds to a certain *mathematical object*, called Turing machine. Since it is not a mathematical statement, it cannot be proved.

It is possible (conditionally) that Church–Turing thesis could be disproved by someone in future, if one proposes an alternate model of computation which becomes publicly acceptable as a possible and reasonable model of computation and at the same time provably capable of carrying computations that cannot be carried out by the Turing machine. But this is not considered likely to happen.

Learning Outcomes of this Chapter:

1. Computational complexity. [Application]
2. Time complexity. [Knowledge], [Analysis]
3. Space complexity. [Knowledge], [Analysis]
4. Time and space bounds. [Knowledge]
5. Time-bounded complexity classes. [Analysis]
6. Standard model of computation. [Application]
7. P and NP classes. [Knowledge], [Evaluation]
8. NP-complete class. [Knowledge]

9. P-Space and EXP Classes. [Knowledge], [Analysis]
10. Reducibility. [Knowledge], [Comprehend]
11. Canonical complexity classes. [Knowledge]
12. Primality and compositeness. [Knowledge]

13.2 Determining Time Complexity

We measure the time complexity by counting the elementary steps required for a machine to halt. The running time of a Turing machine M that halts on all inputs can be defined as follows.

Definition 13.1 The running time or time complexity of M is the function $f : \mathbb{N} \rightarrow \mathbb{N}$, where $f(n)$ is the maximum number of steps that M uses on any input w of length n. □

Given the language $L = \{a^k b^k \mid k \geq 0\}$, with input w of length n, a Turing machine accepts it in time $O(n^2)$. To be precise, it accepts in time $n^2 + (n+1)/2$ (see Example 9.7). But, if we compute the asymptotic value of this, it is close to n^2. Thus, time complexity for this is $O(n^2)$. Similarly, the asymptotic value of $5n^3 + 3n^2 + 20n + 10$ is $O(n^3)$.

BIG-O

Let the f and g be two functions $f, g : \mathbb{N} \rightarrow \mathbb{R}^+$. We say that $f(n) = O(g(n))$ if there exist positive integers c and n_0 so that for every integer $n \geq n_0$,

$$f(n) \leq cg(n).$$

When $f(n) = O(g(n))$, we say that $g(n)$ is an asymptotic upper bound for $f(n)$, "f is asymptotically NO MORE THAN g", then,

$$5n^3 + 3n^2 + 20n + 10 = O(n^3).$$

The other examples of asymptotic computations are as follows.

$$5n^{4.2} + 230405n^4 + 23 = O(n^{4.2}).$$

$$6n \log_2 n + 6n \log_2 \log_2 n = O(n \log_2 n).$$

$$n \log_{10} n^{35} = O(n \log_{10} n).$$

$$O(n \log_{10} n) = O(n \log_2 n) = O(n \log n).$$

Definition 13.2 If $TIME(t(n)) = \{L \mid L$ is a language decided by a $O(t(n))$ time Turing Machine, then $L = \{a^k b^k \mid k \geq 0\} \in TIME(n^2)$. □

In conclusion, that, Big-Oh notation is necessary, given a model of computation. The relation $f(n) = O(g(n))$ holds if there exists a constant c such that $f(n) \leq cg(n)$ for sufficiently large values of n. The TM model does not make distinctions between two *time* usage that differs by a constant factor. Similar is the case in space complexity when *space* differs by a constant.

13.3 Time Complexity of Arithmetic Operations

First of all we try to analyze the most common computation problems, the addition and multiplication, which is an important question that has undergone thorough analysis. A simple argument about *fan-in* in the gate logic shows that if gates with r inputs are used, then a circuit for addition of two n-bit numbers will require the addition time of at least $\log_r n$ (transitions). This is a lower bound, which is achievable.

It is important to note with respect to the analogy between *parallel algorithms* and *hardware algorithms*, that, one of the best results on circuits for addition is one that uses Boolean identities that are immediately translatable into an efficient parallel evaluation algorithm for polynomials. These results pertain to the binary representation of the numbers being added. Could it be that under a suitably clever coding of the numbers $0 \leq a < 2^n$, addition *mod* 2^n can be performed in time less than $\log_r n$. It has been found that under very general assumptions on the coding, the lower bound remains $\log_r n$.

While doing the multi-precision arithmetic, the question arise in connection with multiplication is, how much total number of bit operations are required in carrying out the multiplication of two n-bit numbers? The standard method takes n^2 bit-operations. Earlier attempts of improvement over this method employed simple algebraic identities and resulted in complexity of $O(n^{1.58})$ operations [9].

Let us consider computations steps for some standard computations.

Adding two n-digit numbers: It takes usually $n + 1$ steps. But if we look at minor steps then $5n + 1$ steps (n additions of digits, n additions of carry, n comparisons if sum of two digits and carry is greater than or equal to 10, n steps to print lower digit, n steps to save carry). The last step is for carry save from last sum.

Even further smaller steps are taken, it comes out to be $an + b$, where a, b are constants, not dependent on n. Thus, time complexity of add is $O(n)$.

Multiplication: To multiply x and y, one approach is add x to 0, y times. If both numbers are n digit long, then complexity of computation is $O(n.10^n)$.

Other method is $O(n^2)$ complexity, as for adding single n-digit number it is $O(n)$, and doing this n times, is $O(n^2)$. The best-known algorithm for multiplication is $O(n^{1.1})$.

Factoring: Let us try to find out factoring of an n-digit number. Sometimes the factoring is not well defined, for example, $1001 = 77 \times 13$ or it is 91×11. In this,

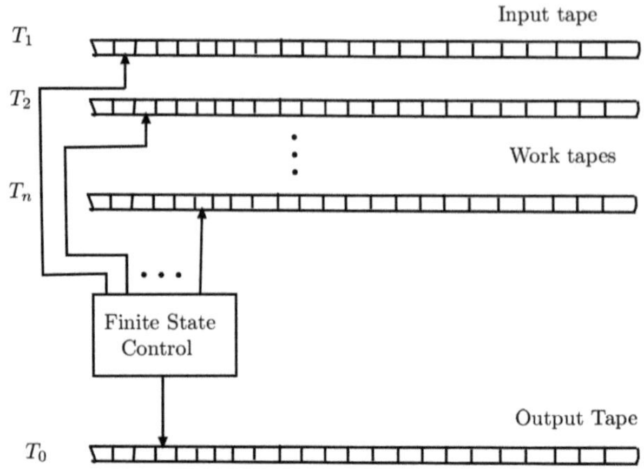

Fig. 13.1 An n-tape Turing machine

since factors are different, the complexity of each computation is different. To factor a decimal number Z we need to divide it by a range 2 to $Z - 1$. If $|Z| = n$, complexity is $O(10^n)$. However, there is no solution like, $O(n)$ or $O(n^c)$, where c is constant, is available for factoring.

13.4 Multi-tape Turing Machine Complexity

In the following, we shall define a multi-tape Turing machine, complexity classes with respect to this machine, and then work out for some basic properties of these complexity classes.

First, we give a description of our machine shown in Fig. 13.1. We consider a computing device that has the control unit as a finite automaton, attached to this control unit has fixed number of tapes that are linear, unbounded at both ends, with an infinite sequence of squares, each can hold one symbol. The control unit has one *read-write* head assigned to each of the $n - 1$ tapes, one *read* head assigned to the input tape (T_1), and each head rests on a single square of the assigned tape. There can be a finite number of distinct symbols that can appear on the tape squares. Each combination of symbols under all the read/write heads, together with the state of the control unit, determines a unique machine operation.

A machine operation consists of writing a symbol on each tape square under the current head positions,[1] shifting the heads independently either one square left, one square right, or no move, and then changing the state of the control unit. The machine is then ready to perform its next operation as determined by the tapes' symbols and

[1] The input tape T_1 is assumed to be read only tape so that its contents are not modified during the computation.

control state. One such operation constitutes basic unit of time spent by the machine for carrying out the computation. The output tape (T_0) is different, motion of head on this tape is restricted to one way only, it moves either one or no squares right. What is printed on the output tape and moved from under the head is therefore irrevocable and is isolated from further calculations.

The standard Turing machine has one tape, and if someone puts k successive 1's on the tape and started the machine, it would print some $f(k)$ 1's on the tape and stop. Here f is algorithm run by the machine.

A multi-tape machine is expected to print successively $f(1)$, $f(2)$, ... on its output tape, that means every time it prints something on the output tape, it computes some small function. Turing showed that such upgrades, like adding tapes or tape symbols do not increase the number of functions that can be computed by these machines. Since the techniques for establishing such equivalences are based on common knowledge, we take it as obvious that the functions computable by Turing's model are the same as those computable by other versions of a Turing machine. The reason that this model of n-tapes and one output tape, has been chosen is that it closely resembles the operation of present-day computers; and being interested in how fast a machine can compute, the extra tapes make a calculated difference.

To further clear up our doubts about this n-tape model, we give a formal definition.

Definition 13.3 (*n-tape Turing machine*) An n-tape Turing machine, M, is a set of $(3n + 4)$-tuples,

$$\{(q_i; a_{i_1}, a_{i_2}, ..., a_{i_n}; b_{j_0}, b_{j_1}, ..., b_{j_n}; m_0, m_1, ..., m_n; q_j)\} \tag{13.1}$$

which is a $(3n + 4)$-tuple expression, where each component can assume only a finite set of values, such that for every possible combination of the first $n + 1$ entries, i.e., current state and current values of input symbols, there exists a unique $(3n + 4)$-tuple in this set. The first entry, q_i presents the current state of machine; the next n entries, $a_{i_1}, ..., a_{i_n}$ represents symbols scanned on tapes $T_1, ..., T_n$, respectively; the next $n + 1$ are symbols $b_{j_0}, ..., b_{j_n}$, represents the new symbols to be written on tapes $T_0, ..., T_n$, respectively, by the corresponding heads; the next $n + 1$ entries represent the tape motions (left, right, stationary) of the $n + 1$ tapes with the restriction $m_0 \neq$ left; and the last entry is the next state of the machine. Tape T_0 is called the output tape. One tuple with a_{i_j} = 'B' (blank symbol), for $1 \leq j \leq n$ is designated as starting symbol [6]. □

Note that the output tape T_0 is not considered when we figure n. Thus, a zero-tape machine is a Turing machine whose outputs are written on the same tape that was holding the input. Without loss of generality, we assume that our machine starts with blank tapes ($T_2, ..., T_n$). For the sake of simplicity, we shall talk about binary sequences. We use the notation $\alpha = a_1 a_2....$ of symbols from input alphabet.

In the following definition, T-computable means time-computable, and $t(n)$ is a time function. For example, if n^2 is value of $t(n)$ for some input n, then n^2 is number of steps (time taken) to build n^2 give the input n.

Definition 13.4 (T-*Computable*) Let $t(n)$ be a computable function from integers into integers such that $t(n) \leq t(n+1)$ and, for some integer k, it holds that $t(n) \geq (n-k)$ for all n. Then, we say that a sequence $\alpha = a_1a_2a_3...$, is t-computable if and only if there exists a multi-tape Turing machine M that writes first n digits of the sequence α on its output tape in not more than $t(n)$ steps, $n = 1, 2, ...$, and allows for the possibility of printing a bounded number of digits on one square. We will denote the class of all t-computable binary sequences by S_T, and shall refer to $t(n)$ as a *time-function*, and S_T will be called a *complexity class*. □

It is important to note that when several symbols are printed on one square, we call them as components of that single symbol. Since these are bounded, the output symbols is a finite set. As long as the output comes out of the machine in a readily understood form, we do not regard it as unnatural that the output is not strictly binary.

The condition $t(n) \geq (n-k)$ is necessary because we do not wish to call the empty set as a complexity class. Because, the sequence $\alpha = a_1a_2...$ is in S_T and M is the Turing machine that prints it, there is bound k on number of digits per tape square on the output tape, and M can print at most kn_0 digits in n_0 steps. By assumption, $t(kn_0) \geq n_0$ or (substituting $n_0 = n - k$), $t(n) \geq (n-k)$. On the other hand, $t(n) \geq (n-k)$ implies that the sequence of all zeros is in S_T because we can print k zeros in each operation and thus S_T is not void.

13.5 Concepts of Time and Space Complexities

Dealing with the questions fundamental to complexity measures, *time* and *space*, were introduced. Both of them have been considered as functions of input. Informally, the *time complexity* of an algorithm working on an input is the number of "elementary" operations executed by the algorithm processing the given input. In other words, it is the amount of work done to arrive from input to the corresponding output. The *space complexity* of an algorithm is the number of "elementary" cells of the memory used in the computing process. Obviously, what does "elementary" means, depends on the formal model of algorithms one chooses (*machine models, axiomatic models, programming languages*, etc.). Since a *theory* always tries to establish results (*assertions*) that are independent of the formalism used and have general validity, this dependence on the measurement on the model does not seem welcome. Fortunately, the reasonable computing models used are equivalent, in the sense that the differences in the complexity measurement are negligible for the main concepts and statements of the complexity theory.

Here, we use Turing machine (TM) as the standard computing model to define the complexity measures. From the several versions of TM, we consider the off-line multi-tape Turing machine (MTM) consisting of one two-way read-only input tape, and finite number of working tapes each having its read-write head. A computing step of a MTM is considered to be an elementary operation of this model. In one step, a MTM M reads one symbol from each of these tapes and depending on them and current state of the M, M possibly changes its state, rewrites the symbols read from the working tapes and moves the heads at most one position to left or right.

A *configuration* is a set of global state of the machine, current contents of the tapes, and the position of heads on tapes. A *computation* of M is sequence of configurations $C_1, C_2, ..., C_m$ such that $C_i \rightarrow C_{i+1}$ (C_{i+1} is reached from C_i in one step).

The *language* of accepted by a Turing machine M is defined by:

$$L(M) = \{w \in \Sigma^* \mid M \text{ accepts } w\}. \tag{13.2}$$

Definition 13.5 A language $L \subseteq \Sigma^*$ is called *(Turing) recognizable* or *recursively enumerable*, if $L = L(M)$ for some Turing machine M. □

When Turing machine M is started with an initial input w on tape, there are three possible consequences: (i). M may accept w (i.e., reaches to its accepting configuration), (ii). M may reject w, hence it reaches the rejecting configuration, or (iii). M may *loop*, which means M does not halt. In both the second and third consequences, M may fail to accept either by rejecting or by looping. It is important to distinguish between taking long time to accept the input versus looping forever. However, in complexity theory, we are only interested in machines that halt on all the inputs, i.e., never loop. Such machines are called *deciders*.

Consider that M be a multi-tape Turing machine that recognizes the language $L(M)$ and let input string is $w \in \Sigma^*$, where Σ is the input alphabet of M. If $C = C_1, C_2, ..., C_k$ is finite sequence of configurations through which M goes, then the *time complexity* of the computation M (say t_M) on w is,

$$t_M(w) = k - 1.$$

If the computation of M on w is infinite, then

$$t_M(w) = \infty.$$

The *time complexity* of Turing machine M is a *partial function* from $\mathbb{N}$ to $\mathbb{N}$, defined as,

$$t_M(n) = \max\{t_M(w) \mid w \in \Sigma^n \cap L(M)\}, \tag{13.3}$$

where $\Sigma^n \cap L(M)$ means $|w| = n$ and $w \in L(M)$.

We assume that M reads all of its input strings, followed with the blank symbol ("B") after the right end of the input string, so $t_M(n) \geq n + 1$. In general, we shall refer it as $t(n)$, assuming that it is for Turing machine M.

The *space complexity* of one configuration C of TM M, $s_M(C)$, is the length of the longest word over the working alphabet stored on the working tapes in C. Thus, space complexity in a computation is largest space consumed during the computation.

Fig. 13.2 Linear, sublinear, and superlinear speeds

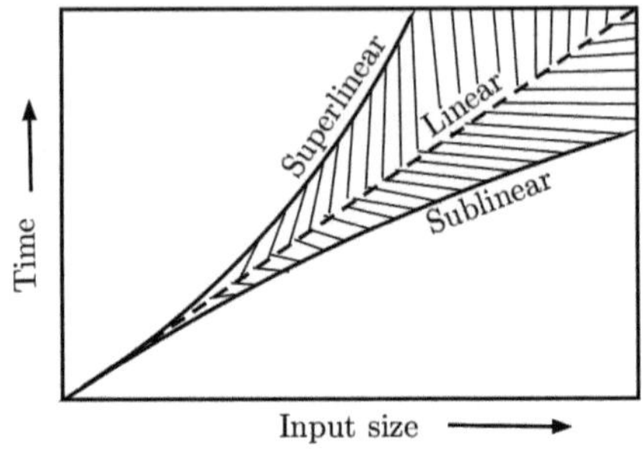

Hence, the space complexity of a computation $D = C_1, C_2, ..., C_m$ can be computed as,

$$s_M(D) = \max\{s_M(C_i) \mid i = 1, ..., m\}. \tag{13.4}$$

Definition 13.6 (*Worst case time complexity of M*) The worst case time complexity of M is the function $T_M : \mathbb{N} \rightarrow \mathbb{N} \cup \{\infty\}$ defined by

$$T_M(n) = \max\{t_M(x) \mid x \in \Sigma^*, |x| = m\}. \tag{13.5}$$

□

If the complexity expression T_M is polynomial in $|x|$, we say that Turing machine M runs in *polynomial time*. There are three possibilities in polynomial time: (i) if it is linear in $|x|$, then it is *linear time*. (ii) The *sublinear time* (see Fig. 13.2) is not meaningful for Turing machines that do not have random values to the input. The problem with random input is that, the machine cannot read the whole input on the tape: For M to be a deterministic Turing machine and for every input $|x| = n$, and $n \in \mathbb{N}$, the TM M reads at most $n - 1$ symbols of the input x. If there are words $w_1, w_2, ..., w_m$ with $|w_i| < n$ for $1 \leq i \leq m$, then the language of the Turing machine is expressed by,

$$L(M) = \bigcup_{i=1}^{m} w_i.\Sigma^*. \tag{13.6}$$

The space complexity of M on a word $w \in L(M)$ is $s_M(w) = s_M(D_w)$, where D_w is the computation of M on w.

The space complexity of M is the partial function from $\mathbb{N}$ to $\mathbb{N}$,

$$s_M(n) = \max\{s_M(w) \mid w \in \Sigma^n \cap L(M)\}. \tag{13.7}$$

Because few interesting languages can be decided by Turing machines of sublogarithmic space complexity, henceforth we will assume that $s(n) \geq \log n$.

The space complexity is defined in the same manner as time complexity (Eq. 13.5), but instead of the number of steps $t_M(x)$ we maximize the number of tape cells visited.

Considering a single value for complexity of any algorithm, one can suggest that the product function $t_M(w).s_M(w)$, as a function from $L(M)$ (i.e., input string) to $\mathbb{N}$ is a most precise and complete description of the complexity behavior of machine M. However, such a description is not useful for comparison of complexities of different algorithms, which is one of the essential requirements as how the algorithms fair in computations. Thus, we prefer to consider the complexity measures as functions of the input sizes rather than of specific inputs.

The time and space complexities are so called worst-case complexities because $t_M(n)s_M(n)$ is maximum of the complexities over all words of length n from $L(M)$ (i.e., M can recognize every input from $L(M) \cap \Sigma^n$ in time $t_M(n)$ and there exists $w \in L(M) \cap \Sigma^n$ such that $t_M(n) = t_M(w)$. In abstract complexity theory, we usually prefer this *worst-case* approach to define the complexity measures, but in the analysis of concrete algorithms, we are often interested to know the average behavior of the complexity on inputs of fixed length. In such case one has to make a probabilistic analysis of $t_M(w)$ and $s_M(w)$ according to probability distribution of inputs of a fixed length [2].

13.6 Computational Complexity

Due to use of computer in everyday life, the attention rose to the questions like—how to measure the effectiveness of computer programs (algorithms), how to compare the effectiveness of two algorithms, and how to measure the computational difficulty of computing problems. The theory of complexity is concerned with measuring the difficulty of computations. To do this, we must discuss what is meant by a complexity measure.

We are concerned with the computational complexity measures which are defined for all possible computations, i.e., for all *partial recursive functions* mapping the integers into the integers. Therefore, to define a complexity measure, we require an effective way of specifying all possible computations or algorithms (for the computation on of these functions). The complexity measure will then show how many "steps" it takes to evaluate any one of these algorithms on any specific argument. For example, our list of algorithms or computing devices could be a standard enumeration of all one-tape Turing machines (which we know are capable of computing all partial recursive functions), and the complexity measure of a given machine M_i (or algorithm) working on argument n could be the number of operations performed by M_i before halting on input n.

It should be noted that these complexity measures are associated with the algorithms and not directly with the functions they compute. The reason for this is that in computations we usually deal with algorithms that specify functions, and for each computable function there are infinitely many algorithms that compute it. Furthermore, there exists functions which have no "best" algorithm, and thus we cannot talk of complexity of function as that of its best algorithm [7].

The celebrated paper [10], by A. M. Turing showed the computability of sequences (functions) using mechanical procedures and further showed that the set of sequences can be partitioned into *computable* and *noncomputable* sequences. Some of these computable sequences are simple, use few steps and with bounded times, whereas other computable sequences seem to have an inherent difficulty level, such that the time and space needed to compute them are enormously high. In the following, we will discuss about classifying these sequences (or TMs) according to how hard they are to compute. This scheme can be generalized to classify numbers, functions, or recognition problems according to their computational complexity [6].

The *computational complexity* of a sequence is to be measured by how fast a multi-tape Turing machine can print the terms of the sequence on its output tape. This particular abstract model of a computing device, in the form of multi-tape Turing machine, is a modern digital computer. We can define the measure of printing speed of these terms in terms of a time function $t(n)$.

Definition 13.7 If $t(n)$ is a computable and monotonically increasing function of positive integers into positive integers and if α is a (binary) sequence, then we say that α is in complexity class S_T or that α is T-computable if and only if there is a multi-tape Turing machine M such that M computes the nth term of α within $t(n)$ operations. □

Each set S_T is *recursively enumerable* and so no class S_T contains all computable sequences. On the other hand, every computable α is contained in some complexity class S_T. This suggests that there exists a hierarchy of complexity classes. Furthermore, these classes are independent of *time-scale* or of the speed of the components from which the machines could be built. This is certain because the "speed-up" theorem states that $S_T = S_{kT}$ for positive numbers k, which means by adding more or faster resources, it is possible to speed-up a computation by a constant factor only, while the complexity classes are separated by a polynomial or exponential factor. Hence, the complexity class of a problem will not change due to linear speed-up.

There are many corollaries to the speed-up theorem, due to which there are several limiting conditions that establish containment between two complexity classes, i.e., nonzero intersection. One form of this result states that if (with miner restrictions), $T(n)$ and $U(n)$ are "nice" functions[2] and,

$$\lim_{n\to\infty} \frac{T^2(n)}{U(n)} = 0 \tag{13.8}$$

[2] A function is "nice" if it is a combination of polynomials times exponentials.

then set S_U is properly contains the set S_T [6, 8]. These results have shown that there are problems with very sharp, intrinsic computational complexity bounds. No matter what method and computational algorithm was used, the problem solution required, say n^2 operations for problem instance of size n. The intersection of two classes is again a class. The general containment problem, however, is *recursively unsolvable*. Many a times we are concerned about how a change in abstract machine model might effect the complexity classes. Some of these are related by a "square law", including the one-tape versus multitape relationship: that is if α is T-computable by a multitape Turing machine, then it is T^2-computable by a single tape Turing machine. It is interesting to note that some of the more obvious variations do not change the classes.

13.7 Time- and Space-Bounded Complexities

The decider machine has the property to halt on all inputs. We are particularly interested in decider machines that have computation resources (time and space) bounded by some function of the input size. In the following discussions, unless explicitly stated, by a TM we will mean a *multi-tape* TM. When we talk about the space used by a multi-tape TM, we only count the number of cells on the work-tape(s) that are touched by the TM head(s) during its computation. That is, we do not count the input tape or the output tape. We also assume that input tape is *read-only*, and the output tape is *write-only* (with one way access: after each write operation, the tape head moves one cell to the right, and can never move left). We shall denote the length of input as n.

13.7.1 Time-Bounded Complexity

There are Turing machines that compute function $F : \mathbb{N}_0 \rightarrow \mathbb{N}_0$, where $\mathbb{N}_0 = \{0, 1, 2, ...\}$. What is actually computed is the numerical of $F(n)$, from numerical of n as input. If we choose binary numerical, then we have the corresponding function $f : \{0, 1\}^* \rightarrow \{0, 1\}^*$, such that whenever x is a binary numerical of n, then $f(x)$ is the binary numerical of $F(n)$. The computation of F is equivalent to the computation of f.

Definition 13.8 Let M be a Turing machine that is deterministic and which may have several tapes. Let $x \in \Sigma^*$ be an input to M.

1. We define *computation* of M on x as follows:

   $Time_M(x) = \max\{$number of transitions on $p \mid p$ is a computation path of M on input $x\}$.

2. For $n \in \mathbb{N}$, we define *time complexity* of M as:

$$Time_M(n) = \max\{Time_M(x) : \ |x| = n\}.$$

□

Definition 13.9 (*$t(n)$-time bounded*) If a deterministic Turing machine M halts on every input $x \in \Sigma^*$, and takes at most $t(n)$ steps for all but finitely many inputs of length n, where function $t : \mathbb{N}_0 \to \mathbb{N}_0$, then the machine M is called *$t(n)$-time bounded*. □

Since for the TM M it takes at most $t(n)$ steps, naturally, $Time_M(n) \leq t(n)$.

A nondeterministic Turing machine is also time bounded in a similar way as deterministic TM, but in this, case computations on all its possible paths must be over within $t(n)$ steps.

If M is decider, then $L(M)$, the language of M, is decided in $t(|x|)$ time, where $x \in \Sigma^*$ is an input string. As a computer of functions, the M starts with x on the input tape, and when it halts, it has $f(x)$ on its output tape. We say that M computes $f : \{0, 1\}^* \to \{0, 1\}^*$.

A decision problem of a language $L \subseteq \Sigma^*$ may be viewed as a computation of some *characteristic function* $f_L : \{0, 1\}^* \to \{0, 1\}^*$, so that $f_L(x) = 1$ if and only if $x \in L$.

Definition 13.10 (*Time constructible*) A function $t : \mathbb{N}_0 \to \mathbb{N}_0$ is said to be *time constructible* if $t(n) \geq n$ and there exists a Turing machine that computes $x \mapsto t(|x|)$ in time $O(t(|x|))$, where $x \in \Sigma^*$ and $t(|x|)$ is in binary numeral. □

A time-constructible function t has the property that $t(n)$ can be constructed from n by a deterministic Turing machine in time $O(t(n))$, and the TM halts after that. The term "time-constructible" means, given n the Turing machine will construct (build) $t(n)$ in time $O(t(n))$.

Alternatively, a function t is called time-constructible if there exists a Turing machine M which, given a string 1^n, outputs the binary representation of $t(n)$ in $O(t(n))$ time.

Example 13.1 Let the tape of standard TM M has input string $x = 1^n$ (unary string), and we are interested to build the function $t(n) = n^2$. We can construct n^2 as follows:

1. write # after existing 1^n,
2. copy 1^n after #, let this be progressing string,
3. append 1^n to progressing string $n - 1$ times. This builds the progressing string to 1^{n^2}.

To copy the original string x for n times, we shall maintain a down counter 1111...n times ($=1^n$), such that every time, x is appended to progressing string, this counter is decremented by 1 by converting 1 to 0. It can be easily shown that total time to build 1^{n^2} from input 1^n is $O(n^2)$. □

This combined machine we call as M''.

Let $t(n)$ be a function that is time constructible by a deterministic Turing machine M. For every Turing machine M' that may have infinite computation paths, we can convert M' into M'' of time complexity $O(t(n))$, that always halts, as follows: for M', first make a copy of input word on a separate work tape; then concurrently run M' with M (combination is M''), and halt M' as soon as M halts. The total time taken for this run is $2n + O(t(n)) + O(1)$.[3] This time of M'' is $O(t(n))$ because $t(n) \geq 2n + 1$. In particular, for a deterministic (or nondeterministic) Turing machine M' that accepts each word in $L(M')$ in $t(n)$ time, but we may reject words by not halting. This construction produces deterministic (nondeterministic) Turing machine M'' of time complexity $O(t(n))$ that accepts the same language, i.e., $L(M'') = L(M')$, but M'' always halts.

Definition 13.11 DTIME$[t(n)]$ is the class of languages decided by deterministic Turing machines of time complexity $t(n)$. □

When we say $t(n)$ is time bounded TM M, that means TM takes at most $t(n)$ steps.

Definition 13.12 NTIME$[t(n)]$ is the class of languages decided by nondeterministic Turing machines of time complexity $t(n)$. □

We can abbreviate DTIME$[t(n)]$ as DTIME$[t]$ when t is taken to be a function, and no reference is made to the length of input, i.e., $|x| = n$.

13.7.2 Space-Bounded Complexity

Different from the time complexity, it is interesting to study the computation that run in *sublinear space*. For this, we will assume that a Turing machine has one extra input tape, which is *read only*[4] and not counted toward the consumption of space (see Fig. 13.3).

Definition 13.13 Let M be a deterministic Turing machine with additional input tape and several work tapes.

1. For $x \in \Sigma^*$ as an input to TM M and c as a configuration, the *space consumed* by the configuration c is defined as:

$$Space_M(c) = \max\{|w| : w \text{ is content of work tape during the configuration } c\}.$$

[3] The $2n$ steps are due to copy $|x| = n$ from M to M' and then coming back to begin on each machine, $O(t(n))$ is due to computation in M in parallel with M', and $O(1)$ is one step due to halt.

[4] A tape can be made as read only, if every time it writes the same symbol that it has read.

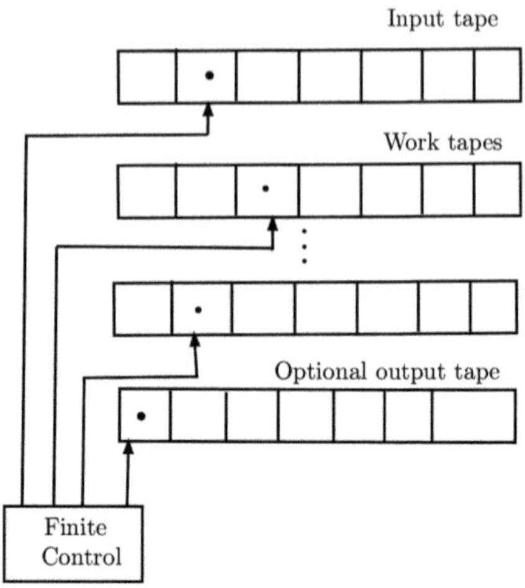

Fig. 13.3 Turing machine with additional read only input tape, many work-space tapes, and an optional output tape

2. The space consumption of x is defined by:

$$Space_M(x) = \max\{Space(c) : c \text{ is a configuration that occurs in a computation of } M \text{ on } x\}. \quad (13.9)$$

3. For $n \in \mathbb{N}$, we define *space complexity* of M as:

$$Space_M(x) = \max\{Space_M(x) : |x| = n\}. \quad (13.10)$$

In the above, if space grows without bounds, then $Space_M(x) = \infty$. □

Definition 13.14 (*$s(n)$-space bounded*) If a deterministic TM M halts on every input $x \in \Sigma^*$, and uses at most $s(n)$ cells on the $(k-1)$ work-tapes, for all but finitely many inputs of length $|x| = n$, then M is called *$s(n)$-space bounded*. The function s is $s : \mathbb{N}_0 \to \mathbb{N}_0$, and $Space_M(n) \le s(n)$ for all $n \in \mathbb{N}$. □

A nondeterministic TM is also space bounded in a similar way. But in this case, computations on each of its possible paths should not use more than $s(n)$ cells of work-tapes. If M is decider, then $L(M)$ is decided in $s(n)$ space.

Often it is necessary that these space and time binding functions should be *space constructible* and *time constructible*, respectively.

Definition 13.15 (*Space constructible*) A function $s : \mathbb{N}_0 \to \mathbb{N}_0$, where $s(n) \ge O(\log n)$, is called *space constructible*, if there exists a TM that takes 1^n as input and computes $s(n)$ using $O(s(n))$ work-tape cells. □

Note that the work-tape cells are maximum number of cells consumed at any stage in the process of constructing the function $s(n)$.

Functions such as $n, n \log n, n^k, 2^n$ are time or space constructible, as long as $t(n)$ or $s(n)$ is at least cn, for a constant $c > 0$.

Given that $s : \mathbb{N} \rightarrow \mathbb{N}$ be some space constructible function, we define the following.

Definition 13.16 $\mathsf{DSPACE}[s(n)]$ is class of languages decided by deterministic Turing machines (DTMs) of space complexity $s(n)$. Formally,

$$\mathsf{DSPACE}_k(s(n)) = \{L(M) \mid M \text{ is a } k\text{-tape DTM, with extra input tape, which is a decider and } s(n)\text{-space-bounded.}\} \quad (13.11)$$

□

Definition 13.17 $\mathsf{NSPACE}[s(n)]$ is class of languages decided by nondeterministic Turing machines (NTMs) of space complexity $s(n)$. Formally,

$$\mathsf{NSPACE}_k(s(n)) = \{L(M) \mid M \text{ is a } k\text{-tape NTM, with extra input tape, which is a decider and } s(n)\text{-space-bounded.}\} \quad (13.12)$$

□

Example 13.2 Consider that language $L = \{x \mid x \in \{a, b\}^*\}$, and number of a's in x is equal to number of b's in $x\}$. Then, L is in $\mathsf{DSPACE}(O(\log n))$.

Proof We give the construction of deterministic Turing machine that is $O(\log n)$-space-bounded and it decides the language L, as follows: We read the input from read-only tape from left to right, and we keep a binary counter on the working-tape. There are two events to operate this counter:

1. If a is read on the input tape, we increment the counter by 1,
2. If b has been read, we decrement this counter by 1.

We will accept the input if counter value is zero when input has been completely read. This clearly decides the language L.

The explanation for space consumption is as follows: Initially, we store binary zero on working tape, and in every step, we increment this if current input is a and decrement it if b. Thus, the space consumed by this counter is $\log |x|$ bits for input of length $|x|$. Note that incrementing and decrementing of counter do not cause space overhead. Thus, the Turing machine needs no more than $O(\log n)$ space. □

13.8 Time-Bounded Complexity Classes

Let M be a Turing machine that halts on all input $x \in \Sigma^*$. Let $t(n)$ (t is, $t : \mathbb{N}_0 \rightarrow \mathbb{N}_0$) be the *maximum* number of steps taken by M on different inputs of length n.

Definition 13.18 (*Time bounded*) The Turing machine M is said to be $t(n)$ time bounded. The running time of machine is $O(t(n))$. □

Definition 13.19 (*Time constructible*) A function $t : \mathbb{N}_0 \rightarrow \mathbb{N}_0$ is time constructible if $t(n) \geq n$ and there is a Turing machine M_t that computes the function $n \mapsto t(n)$ in time $t(n)$. □

In simple terms, a function $t(n)$ is time-constructible if there exists a deterministic Turing machine that halts after exactly $t(n)$ steps for every input of length n. In most texts, the functions $t(n) \geq n + 1$ are taken as time-constructible. Further, if $t_1(n)$ and $t_2(n)$ are time contructible, then so are $t_1 + t_2$, $t_1 t_2$, $t_1^{t_2}$, and c^{t_1} for every integer $c > 1$.

We shall only consider time-constructible functions as *time-bound*. Note that n, $\log n$, 2^n etc., are all *time-constructible*.

Example 13.3 Time-bound of Regular language.

Let L_1 be a regular language. The state transitions of a Turing machine mimics the state transitions of the corresponding DFA:

1. An input symbol is read.
2. The same symbol is written on the tape.
3. The state transition follows the transition of the DFA and the head moves toward right.
4. At the end of input, the state may be either *Accept* or *Reject* indicating acceptance or rejection of input.

It is clear that the running time of such a machine is bounded by $O(n)$, so the language L is also decided in time $O(n)$. □

13.8.1 Class P

We can also define DTIME for function computation in the following.

Definition 13.20 DTIME$[t(n)]$ is class of languages that have deterministic time complexity of $t(n)$. □

Let a language $L \subseteq \Sigma^*$, and L is *polynomial* if membership $w \in L$ can be determined in polynomial function of n, where $|w| = n$. A Polynomial time is defined in terms of number of transitions in TM M, where $L = L(M)$. The L is decidable in polynomial time if standard TM M can decide L in time $tc_M \in O(n^r)$, where r is natural number, not related to n. Then the family of L is called Class-P.

Definition 13.21 P : Class of membership problems for the languages in

$$\mathsf{P} = \bigcup_{k \geq 1} \mathsf{DTIME}(n^k). \tag{13.13}$$

□

Following are the examples of problems in class P:

1. *Acceptance of palindromes.* The output of this problem is Yes if $w \in \Sigma^*$ is a palindrome, else No. The Complexity class of this problem is P, as complexity is $O(n^2)$ for standard Turing machine.
2. *Path problem in directed graphs.* Input is $G = (V, E)$, and output is Yes if for $v_i, v_j \in V$, there is a path from v_i to v_j in the graph, else No. The complexity class is P, as time complexity of this problem is $O(n^2)$ due to Dijkstra's shortest path algorithm.
3. *Deriveability in CNF.* Input is Chomsky Normal Form grammar G and the sentence w, output Yes if $S \Rightarrow^* w$, else No. Complexity for this derivation is $O(n^3)$.

A language accepted by multi-tape TM in time $O(n^r)$ is accepted by standard TM in time complexity $O(n^{2r})$, which is also polynomial. This invariant property shows the robustness of TM.

The class P contains many familiar problems that can be efficiently solved, such as: sorting of numbers and strings, finding shortest path in a network, matrix multiplication, parsing context-free grammars, and the linear programming problems. As per its definition, the P contains all the problems that can be solved by deterministic Turing machine (equivalently, by deterministic programs) of reasonable worst-case time complexity.

The P also contains all problems that have worst case time complexity of as high as n^{1000}, for very large n but finite!! However, we know that such problems cannot be solved in realistic times. Following are the reasons due to which we include all the polynomial class problems in P:

- The main goal of proving that a problem is in P is to show the general notion that problem is in the class of feasible problems. However, if we have shown that a problem is not in P, then we must have shown in a very strong way that it is not solvable using deterministic methods.
- We know that if the functions f and g are to be computed in order, then the composite function is composition of these, and the resultant complexity is multiplication of the two. This can be applied in complexity-bound *reduction* (see Sect. 13.12.2).

For example, if complexity of any problem is $O(n^2)$, as most algorithms have, then all the problems having running times $n^4, n^6, n^8, \ldots$ are feasible, because reduction will take n^2 or if it is concatenation of some functions then it will take $n^4, n^6, \ldots$ time. Also, if the original problem of time n^2 calls as its instance another algorithm of time n^2, its time becomes n^4. Thus, we justify that if a problem of time n^2 is solvable (deterministically) then all n^k, for $k \in \mathbb{N}$, are solvable in deterministic times, hence a natural and generous notion of P.

- The polynomial time has served as the intellectual boundary between feasible and infeasible problems. The problems of time n^{1000} occur absolutely rare. However, the problems of time $O(n^4)$ or those of $\Omega(2^n)$,[5] occur often. Apart from this, once a polynomial-time algorithm for a problem is found, we have better prospectus to solve it—using some mathematical techniques there is scope to improve it—the linear programming is one of the best known technique. However, no known NP-complete problems, e.g., Hamiltonian path problem, have been found having complexity $O(n^{1000})$; in case that happens, there may need to redefine the whole complexity theory. However, for the time being, it seems unlikely.
- We know that our concept of complexity is based on the Turing machine as a standard model of computation and also that it was historically accidental to introduce the Turing machine as a model of computation. The class P has been defined on Turing machine. However, the natural notion of polynomial time for essentially all models of sequential computation yields the same class P. The *random access machine* and *register machine* can be simulated by a Turing machine in polynomial time, hence complexity of these machines remains ultimately polynomial. Thus, P gives a true notion of polynomial complexity. To be specific, a problem Π having time complexity polynomial when run on TM, take polynomial time when run on register machine, random access machine, and *pointer machine* model.
- Another reason that makes concept P as robust is that it is characterized by many concepts from logic and mathematics that do not mention about machine or time.

13.8.2 Class NP

Definition 13.22 NP. A language is in NP iff it is decided by some Nondeterministic Turing Machine (NTM) in Polynomial time. An NTM guesses the alternatives. Hence, NP is class of membership problems for languages in,

$$\mathsf{NP} = \bigcup_{P(n)} \mathsf{NTIME}(P(n)), \tag{13.14}$$

where $\mathsf{P}(n)$ stands for polynomial in n, e.g., $n, 5n^2, n^3 \in P(n)$. □

[5] The notation $\Omega(n)$ the lower bound of an algorithm's running time.

Polynomial solution for these problems is not known to exist. In an NDTM, the solution is selected non-deterministically rather than systematically examining all the possibilities. Therefore $\mathsf{P} \subseteq \mathsf{NP}$ because a P problem is also an NP (see Fig. 13.4).

Definition 13.23 (NP-*Complete*) A decision problem B is NP-complete if:

1. B is in NP, and
2. every problem A in NP is reducible[6] to B in polynomial time.

The problem B can be shown to be in NP by demonstrating that a candidate solution to B can be verified in polynomial time. □

Definition 13.24 A verification algorithm (or *verifier*) is a two argument algorithm V, where one argument is an ordinary input string x, and other argument is a binary string y called certificate. The algorithm V verifies x if there is a y such that $V(x, y) = 1$, else 0. □

The NP is the class of languages that have polynomial time verifiers.

Another way through which the class NP can be defined is through mathematics and not using a nondeterministic Turing machine—the NP is set of all the problems whose solutions can be *verified* quickly using deterministic Turing machine in polynomial time. In other words, NP is set of all those languages whose membership can be checked quickly. For example, it is difficult to find out the factors of a composite number, but if factors are given (or guessed by NTM) then one can quickly check their correctness by multiplying them, whether they correctly produce the given number. The difference between P and NP is, what is there between solving and checking, or between finding the proof of a mathematical theorem and testing whether a candidate proof is correct. In conclusion, NP represents a set of all the theorems whose proofs are short, i.e., polynomial length, while P represents all the theorems which can be proved or refuted quickly, from scratch.

Earlier, the problem of primality test was considered as NP, which is a hard class. However, the set of prime numbers is now known to be in P, owing to the efficient deterministic primality test due to [1].

Another important language in NP is set of all the *satisfiable* Boolean formulas, called Φ. This problem is called SAT. An example of a formula with three variables is: $\phi = x \wedge (y \vee \overline{z}) \wedge (\overline{x} \vee y \vee \overline{z}) \wedge (x \vee \overline{y} \vee z)$. This and any other such formula can be converted into its equivalent standard conjunctive normal forms (CNF), and with three variables they are called $3CNF$ or $3cnf$ [3].

Following are examples of NP problems:

1. *SATISFIABILITY Problem.* Input is Boolean expression u in CNF (Conjunctive Normal Form), and output is Yes, if there is an assignment that satisfies u else No. The Complexity in P for such a formula is unknown, while in NP is Yes. This problem is also called SAT problem. Thus,

$$SAT = \{\langle \phi \rangle \mid \phi \text{ is satisfiable Boolean formula}\}. \tag{13.15}$$

[6] The reduction is discussed later in this chapter.

2. *Hamiltonian Path Problem.* Input for this problem is a directed graph $G = (V, E)$, and output is Yes if there is a single cycle that visits all nodes of this graph, and No otherwise. It is unknown whether this problem belongs to the complexity class P, but for NP it is Yes. A Hamiltonian path problem is in NP, but its solution can be verified in polynomial (P) time.
3. *Subset-Sum Problem.* The input is set S, an integer number k, and output is Yes if there is a set $\mathsf{P} \subseteq S$ whose sum is k, else the output is No. Whether this problem belongs to Complexity class P, it is unknown, but about it being in NP, it is Yes.

13.8.3 Class EXPTIME

Definition 13.25 EXP or $\mathsf{EXPTIME}$ (deterministic exponential time) is class of membership problems which can be computed by deterministic TM in exponential time, expressed as,

$$\mathsf{EXP} = \bigcup_{P(n)} \mathsf{DTIME}[2^{P(n)}] \tag{13.16}$$

where $\mathsf{P}(n)$ stands for polynomial in n, e.g., $n^2, n^5, 6.5n \in P(n)$. □

The other exponential time is NEXP (nondeterministic exponential time), also called $\mathsf{NEXPTIME}$,

$$\mathsf{NEXP} = \bigcup_{P(n)} \mathsf{NTIME}[2^{P(n)}]. \tag{13.17}$$

Table 13.1 shows the various complexity classes for time.

Table 13.1 Complexity classes for time

Class	Machine	Time constraint
$\mathsf{DTIME}[t(n)]$	*DTM*	$t(n)$
P	*DTM*	$\mathsf{P}(n)$
$\mathsf{NTIME}[t(n)]$	*NDTM*	$t(n)$
NP	*NDTM*	$\mathsf{P}(n)$
$\mathsf{EXPTIME}$	*DTM*	$2^{P(n)}$
NEXP	*NDTM*	$2^{P(n)}$

13.8.4 Speedup Theorem

We have discussed about the linear speedup and the corresponding theorem (see Sect. 10.3, Chap. 10). It says that for any language L, it is possible to decide it c times faster compared to its recognition on a two-tape TM M, here c is any constant. The speedup theorem works for M, by defining a new Turing machine M' that writes c characters of the old Turing machine in a single tape cell, and then adjusting the transition function so that it simulates in a single step everything that the original machine did between entering and leaving each c-character block. Alternatively, we can have c-tapes in place of two tapes of Turing machine M, such that you can write c-characters at the same time.

The Speedup theorem is of general nature and provides a speedup of type other than linear.

Theorem 13.1 *There is a decidable language L such that for every machine M that decides L with running time $t_M(n)$, there is another machine M' that decides L much faster: its running time $t_{M'}(n)$ satisfies $2^{2^{t_{M'}(n)}} \leq t_M(n)$, for all but finitely many n.*

This statement, too, holds with any computable function $r(t)$ in place of 2^{2^t}. Put intuitively, the program M' running on an old IBM PC (personal computer) may turn out to be better than the program M running on the fastest hardware to date. Hence, the language L has no best algorithm, and no well-defined time-complexity function!!

The speedup phenomenon may hold for languages and time bounds of interest. For instance, a problem of time complexity bounded by $t(n) = n^{\log n}$, which is just above polynomial time (P), may have arbitrary polynomial speed-up—may have algorithms of time complexity $t_{M'}(n)^{1/k}$ for all $k > 0$.

One implication of the speedup theorem is that the complexities of some problems need to be sandwiched between upper and lower bounds. Actually, there is a sense in which every problem has a well-defined lower bound on time, that is decided by the nature of the problem itself. For every language L there is a computable function t_0 such that for every time-constructible function t, there is some machine that accepts L within time t if and only if $t = \Omega(t_0)$.[7] A catch, however, in that t_0 itself may not be time-constructible.

13.9 Space-Bounded Complexity Classes

A Turing machine solves a problem using $s(.)$ if, for every input x, the machine outputs the correct answer and uses only the first $s(|x|)$ cells of the tape. For a standard Turing machine (also called offline TM), we cannot do with better than linear space because the input x is already on the input tape. So we will consider a

[7] $\Omega(n)$ is lower bound of an algorithm's running time.

machine with multiple tapes, such that there is a read-only "input" tape, a "work" tape which is read-write, and a "output" tape, which is write only. Then we say that the machine uses space s if for input x, it uses only the first $s(|x|)$ cells of the input tape.

Definition 13.26 ($s(n)$) A function $s(n)$ is called *space constructible* if there exists an $s(n)$ space-bonded Deterministic Turing Machine that, for each input $|w| = n$ requires exactly $s(n)$ space. Therefore, $s(n)$ is space complexity of a deterministic Turing Machine. □

Simply said, a function $s(n)$ is space-constructible if there exists a deterministic Turing machine that uses exactly $s(n)$ work-tape cells for every input of length n. We denote by L the set of decision problems that are solvable in $O(\log n)$ space.[8] It is important to understand that for an input x of length n, the original space itself is of length n, then how it is possible to solve it in log-space? The answer is, due to representation. A unary representation for 7 is 1^8, but it can also be represented in 1000 in binary, which is $(\log_2 1000) = 3$. Thus, a unary number 1^n can be represented by $\lceil \log n \rceil$. Hence, in log-space, $s(n) = \log n$.

The NL is set of decision problems solvable by nondeterministic Turing machine using $O(\log n)$ space, while NPSPACE is set of decision problems solvable by a nondeterministic Turing machine in *polynomial space*.

In analogous way, we can say that NL are the problems whose solutions can be verified by the deterministic Turing machine with log-space, i.e., $O(\log n)$ for input of length n. But in that case NL would be equal to NP. This is because for NP (e.g., SAT) there is log-space algorithm that verifies the solution. But, NL cannot be equal to NP because the NL is contained in P.

An intuitive justification for above is as follows: A problem with log-space verifier cannot be simulated in NL because a NL machine does not have enough memory to keep track of all the non-deterministic choices made during the simulation process.

Definition 13.27 $\mathsf{DSPACE}(s(n)) = \{L \mid$ there is a $s(n)$ space bounded deterministic Turing machine M such that $L = L(M)\ \}$. □

Here, $s(n)$ space bounded means, L is decided by a TM that touches at most $s(n)$ cells of its workspace.

Definition 13.28 PSPACE. The class of membership problems for the languages decidable in polynomial space on deterministic Turing Machine are:

$$\mathsf{PSPACE} = \bigcup_{k \geq 1} \mathsf{DSPACE}(n^k) \tag{13.18}$$

□

[8] L is called *Log Space Class*.

Many texts limit attention to $s(n) \geq \log n$ for space bounds. There do exist sub-logarithmic space-constructible functions. Considering that, $s(n) = \log n$ is space-constructible, and if $s_1(n)$ and $s_2(n)$ are space-constructible, then so are the functions $s_1 + s_2$, $s_1 s_2$, $s_1^{s_2}$, and c^{s_1} for every integer $c > 1$, that are space-constructible. Many commonly used functions, like, $n \log n$, n^3, 2^n, $n!$ are also space-constructible.

The constructability helps to eliminate the use of an arbitrary choice in definition of basic time and space classes. For example, for general time functions t, the classes DTIME$[t]$ and NTIME$[t]$ may vary depending on whether the machines are required to halt within t steps on all computation paths or jut on those paths that accept. If the function t is time-constructible and the function s is space-constructible, then DTIME$[t]$, NTIME$[t]$, DSPACE$[s]$, and NSPACE$[s]$ can be defined without loss of generality, in terms of Turing machines that always halt.

As a general rule, any function $t(n) \geq n + 1$ and any function $s(n) \geq \log n$ that one is interested in as a time or space bound, is time- or space-constructible, respectively. It is important to note that, not much can be proved without restricting attention to constructible functions. This restriction still leaves a rich class of resource bounds.

Theorem 13.2 *If a machine always halts, and uses $s(.)$ space, with $s(n) \geq \log n$, then its runs in time $2^{O(s(n))}$.*

Proof For Turing machine M, let the input is x, and let the configurations sequences are $c_1, c_2, ..., c_t$, where c_i is configuration at time i, and t is running time. No c_i is equal to c_j, otherwise the machine will loop. The number of all the possible configurations are product of number of states $O(1)$ (the state count being a constant), number of tape-head positions (n), and the number of possible contents of the work tape, which is,

$$O(1).n.|\Sigma|^{s(n)} = 2^{O(s(n))+\log n} = 2^{O(s(n))}. \tag{13.19}$$

Note that the number of possible contents of the work tape also depends on number of allowable positions on input tape.

Since no configuration can be visited more than once during the computation, the computation will finish in $2^{s(n))}$ steps only. □

Definition 13.29 NSPACE$(s(n))$ = $\{L|$ there is a $s(n)$ space bounded nondeterministic Turing machine M so that $L = L(M)$ $\}$.

$$\text{NSPACE}(s(n)) = \{L \mid L \text{ is decidable by } O(s(n)) \text{ space on } NDTM\}.$$

□

Definition 13.30 EXPSPACE is the set of all decision problems solvable by a deterministic Turing machine in exponential space, i.e., in $O(2^{p(n)})$ space, where $p(n)$ is a polynomial function of n.

A decision problem B is EXPSPACE-complete if it is EXPSPACE and every problem in EXPSPACE has a polynomial-time reduction to B. □

Table 13.2 Space complexities

Class	Machine	Space constraint
L	DTM	$O(\log\ n)$
NL	$NDTM$	$\mathsf{P}(n)$
DSPACE$(s(n))$	DTM	$s(n)$
NSPACE$(s(n))$	$NDTM$	$s(n)$
PSPACE	DTM	$\mathsf{P}(n)$
EXPSPACE	DTM	$2^{P(n)}$
NEXPSPACE	$NDTM$	$2^{P(n)}$

The EXPSPACE-complete problems might be thought of as the hardest problems in EXPSPACE.

In terms of DSPACE and NSPACE, the EXPSPACE can be expressed as,

$$\mathsf{EXPSPACE} = \bigcup_{k \in \mathbb{N}} \mathsf{DSPACE}(2^{n^k}) = \bigcup_{k \in \mathbb{N}} \mathsf{NSPACE}(2^{n^k}). \tag{13.20}$$

Table 13.2 shows the details of various space complexities, where L stands for LOGSPACE and NL is same for nondeterministic Turing machine.

13.10 Canonical Complexity Classes

The following are the complexity classes in *canonical* order, with their formal definitions, and the relation between these classes is shown in Fig. 13.4.

Deterministic log space: $\mathsf{L} = \mathsf{DSPACE}[\log n]$.

Nondeterministic log space: $\mathsf{NL} = \mathsf{NSPACE}[\log n]$.

Polynomial time: $\mathsf{P} = \mathsf{DTIME}[n^{O(1)}] = \bigcup_{k \geq 1} \mathsf{DTIME}[n^k]$.

Nondeterministic polynomial time: $\mathsf{NP} = \mathsf{NTIME}[n^{O(1)}] = \bigcup_{k \geq 1} [n^k]$.

Polynomial space: $\mathsf{PSPACE} = \mathsf{DSPACE}[n^{O(1)}] = \bigcup_{k \geq 1} \mathsf{DSPACE}[n^k]$.

Deterministic Exponential space: $\mathsf{E} = \mathsf{DTIME}[2^{O(n)}] = \bigcup_{k \geq 1} \mathsf{DTIME}[k^n]$.

Nondeterministic Exponential space: $\mathsf{NE} = \mathsf{NTIME}[2^{O(n)}] = \bigcup_{k \geq 1} \mathsf{NTIME}[k^n]$.

Deterministic exponential time: $\mathsf{EXP} = \mathsf{DTIME}[2^{n^{O(1)}}] = \bigcup_{k \geq 1} \mathsf{DTIME}[2^{n^k}]$.

Fig. 13.4 Inclusion relationships among the canonical complexity classes

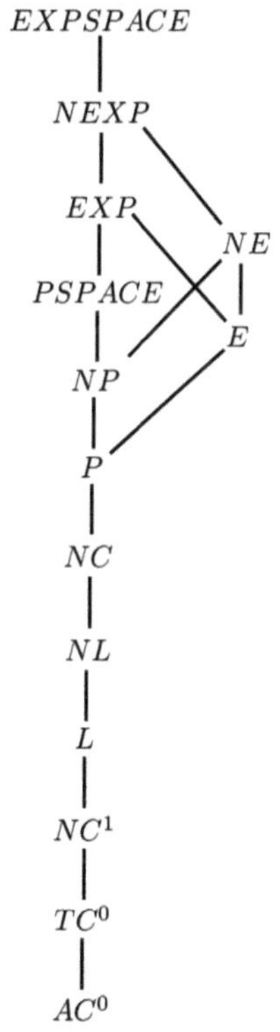

Nondeterministic exponential time: $\mathsf{NEXP} = \mathsf{NTIME}[2^{n^{O(1)}}] = \bigcup_{k\geq 1} \mathsf{DTIME}[2^{n^k}]$.

Exponential space: $\mathsf{EXPSPACE} = \mathsf{DSPACE}[2^{n^{O(1)}}] = \bigcup_{k\geq 1} \mathsf{DTIME}[2^{n^k}]$.

Nondeterministic exponential space: $\mathsf{NEXPSPACE} = \bigcup_{k\geq 1} \mathsf{NSPACE}(2^{n^k})$.

It is important to note that P is subclass of NP, and $\mathsf{P} \neq \mathsf{NP}$ is not known. The motivation for study of L, NL and PSPACE comes from their relations to P and NP. For example, L and NL are the largest space-bounded classes that are contained in P, and PSPACE is the smallest space-bounded class known to contain NP. Further, the EXP is of interest because it is the smallest deterministic-time class known to contain NP. However, the closely related class E is not known to contain NP. The complexity classes shown at the bottom in the Fig. 13.4 are explained in Sect. 13.11.

13.10.1 Relationships Between Complexity Classes

Considering all the time functions $t(n)$ and all the space functions $s(n)$, the following relations hold:

$$\mathsf{DTIME}[t(n)] \subseteq \mathsf{NTIME}[t(n)],$$
$$\mathsf{DSPACE}[s(n)] \subseteq \mathsf{NSPACE}[s(n)].$$

The above holds true because a deterministic machine is a special case of nondeterministic machine. In addition, the following relations also hold true:

$$\mathsf{DTIME}[t(n)] \subseteq \mathsf{DSPACE}[t(n)],$$
$$\mathsf{NTIME}[t(n)] \subseteq \mathsf{NSPACE}[t(n)].$$

This is because, at each step, a k-tape Turing machine can write on at most $k = O(1)$ previously unwritten cells. The following theorem presents additional important relationships between the complexity classes.

Theorem 13.3 *Let $t(n)$ be the time constructible function, and $s(n)$ be the space constructible function $s(n) \geq \log n$.*

$\mathsf{NTIME} \subseteq \mathsf{DTIME}(O(1)^t)$.
$\mathsf{NSPACE}(s) \subseteq \mathsf{DTIME}(n + O(1)^s)$.
$\mathsf{DTIME}(t) \subseteq \mathsf{DSPACE}(t/\log t)$.
$\mathsf{NTIME}(t) \subseteq \mathsf{DSPACE}(t)$.
$\mathsf{NSPACE}(s) \subseteq \mathsf{DSPAC}(s^2)$ *(This last is called Savitch's theorem, given in the following).*

13.10.2 Savitch's Theorem

It is not known whether introducing nondeterminism strictly increases the class of languages decidable in polynomial time, however, the Savitch's theorem says that for space classes, nondeterminism does not help by more than a polynomial time.

Theorem 13.4 (Savitch's Theorem) *If a Nondeterministic TM uses $f(n)$ space, it can be converted into a Deterministic TM that uses $f^2(n)$ space.*

As per Savitch's theorem: PSPACE = NSPACE, EXPSPACE = NEXPSPACE.

For nondeterinistic TM, if $f(n)$ is a maximum number of tape cells scanned in any branch of computation, then its complexity is $f(n)$.

The SAT problem, which is NP-$Complete$ in time, is linear in space, because the space is reusable.

$$\text{PSPACE} = \text{NSPACE},$$

$$\text{P} \subseteq \text{PSPACE},$$

$$\text{NP} \subseteq \text{NSPACE}.$$

Therefore, $\text{NP} \subseteq \text{PSPACE}$.

From above,

$$\text{P} \subseteq \text{NP} \subseteq \text{PSPACE} = \text{NSPACE} \subseteq \text{EXPTIME}.$$

□

Lemma 13.1 *Let $t, s : \mathbb{N} \to \mathbb{N}$ be two functions. Then following inclusions hold:*

$$\begin{aligned} \text{DTIME}(t(n)) &\subseteq \text{NTIME}(t(n)), \\ \text{DSPACE}(s(n)) &\subseteq \text{NSPACE}(s(n)), \\ \text{DTIME}(t(n)) &\subseteq \text{DSPACE}(t(n)), \\ \text{NTIME}(t(n)) &\subseteq \text{NSPACE}(t(n)). \end{aligned}$$

Proof Since any deterministic Turing machine is also a nondeterministic Turing one, the first two inclusions are obvious.

A Turing machine can only scan or write one cell (space) per step/transition (i.e. time). Hence, the tape usage is bounded by time also, which justifies the last two inclusions in the above. □

13.11 Circuit Complexity

So far we were concerned about the complexity classes that were defined in order to understand the sequential nature of computation. Apart from calling these machines of sequential computations, they may equally well be called "sequential algorithms", or the single processor machine-language programs. On the other side is hardware of electronic circuits, called sequential and combinational circuits built using the logic gates, can also be thought as computing machines. These circuits also capture the notion of non-branching straight-line computation.

The size of a Boolean circuit is also a measure of complexity of a function. It has been demonstrated that a close relation exists between circuit size and time taken on Turing machine to solve a problem. These circuits are appealing models of computation for proving lower bounds. Due to their relatively simple definition, circuit-based models are more amenable to combinatorial analysis and allow for natural variations and restrictions. Accordingly, the problems have been classified by the *size* and *depth* of Boolean circuits to solve them. This effort has developed into the field of *circuit complexity theory*, where classes of problems are defined in terms of constraints upon circuits solving them. This type of complexity measure has become important in recent times due to the connections between size and depth of Boolean circuits versus number of processors and running time on parallel computers.

In addition, the circuits also provide a good model of parallel computation—there are many models, complexity measures, and classes of parallel computations that have been devised based on these circuits.

A circuit (also called straight line program) that uses basic building blocks, like, AND, OR, and NOT, is a sequence of instructions, each producing a function by applying an operation from the basis to previously obtained functions. Initially, we start with functions naturally associated with each of the input variables. Each function is used at most once, and the circuit is called *formula*. Consequently, a problem in P will have a polynomial size family of circuits. To show that a problem is outside the class P, it would suffice to show that its circuit complexity is *superpolynomial*. A circuit of digital logic can be formalized as a directed acyclic graph with some number of sources (say, n), called *input nodes*, labeled as $x_1, x_2, ...x_n$, and one sink node, called *output node*. The output node value is Boolean function $f : \{0, 1\}^n \rightarrow \{0, 1\}^r$. The value of the output gate is $C(x)$. The circuit accepts x if $C(x) = 1$. All the computation in these circuits is the result of Boolean operators$\vee, \wedge, \neg$ on binary values.

The size of a circuit is equal to number of steps in a program. A more powerful view of logic gates is that they can act in parallel—every gate whose inputs come directly from the original input and compute the value, is called single step of computation. Such output joins together and becomes input to other gates and becomes the step 2, and so on. For example, for the expression $(x \vee \overline{y}) \wedge (\overline{x} \vee y) \wedge (x \vee y)$, the step-1 computes $(x \vee \overline{y})$, $(\overline{x} \vee y)$, and $(x \vee y)$, in parallel through three OR gates, and step-2 is AND operation whose three inputs are from outputs of three OR gates, and produces single output. This computation has circuit *depth* of two—at depth-1 it performs all three OR operations in parallel, and at depth-2 it performs the AND operation of three inputs. As it appears, the depth is a notion of *parallel time complexity*, because at every stage as we traverse the depth, the parallel computation is taking place. A circuit with small depth is a fast circuit.

13.11.1 Circuit Complexity Classes

The circuit complexity classes NC, TC, and AC refer to complexity classes in the context of parallel and distributed computing. A *circuit complexity family* C consists of a sequence of circuits $\{C_1, C_2, ...C_n\}$, where the circuit C_n has n input nodes. The language accepted by this family is,

$$L(\mathsf{C}) = \{x \mid \text{circuit } C_{|x|} \text{ has } |x| \text{ input nodes}\}. \tag{13.21}$$

The relations between various circuit classes are shown in Fig. 13.4 (Sect. 13.10.1). These complexity classes are defined in terms of Boolean circuits and include AC^0, AC, TC^0, NC^1, and NC. Input to a Boolean circuit is of *in-degree* 0 labeled by one of the n input bits, and an AND gate, OR gate or NOT gate. One of these gates is also an output gate. The Boolean circuits are called families, $C_1, C_2, ..., C_n$, where C_n accepts input of size n.

The AC^0 is the class of problems that have circuits of polynomial size and constant depth in a model with unbounded fan-in. It has been proved that exclusive OR function is not in AC^0, which separates it from NC^1.

Definition 13.31 AC^0 (Arithmetic Circuit Complexity) is the smallest complexity class in circuit complexity. It consists of all the circuits of depth $O(1)$, hence it is of polynomial size. □

Definition 13.32 NC stands for "Nick's Class (named after computer scientist Nick Pippenger), is a class of decision problems that can be efficiently solved in parallel on a parallel computer with a polynomial number of processors (i.e., in polylogarithmic time). □

The complexity class NC^1 consists of those Boolean functions from $\{0, 1\}^* \rightarrow \{0, 1\}$ which can be computed by circuits of fan-in two[9] and depth $O(\log n)$. Hence, a function f is in NC^1 if for each n there is a circuit C_n which computes f correctly on inputs of size n, and each C_n has a depth at most $c \log n$ for some constant c. The problems in NC^1 are usually considered easy to solve in parallel, and thus NC^1 is considered a small complexity class. There is a subclass of NC^1 for which separation results are known.

The TC_0 is the class of problems solvable by families of circuits of unbounded fan-in threshold gates, where circuit depth is bounded by a constant and circuit size by a polynomial in the input size [5].

The TC (Thue Complexity)[10] is a complexity class concerned with decision problems related to combinatorics on words, particularly dealing with infinite sequences of symbols. These problems can be decided by a deterministic Turing machine in logarithmic time.

Definition 13.33 TC is complexity class of decision problems that can be recognized by threshold circuits, which are Boolean circuits, with AND, OR, and majority gates.[11] For each fixed i, complexity class TC^i consists of all languages that can

[9] For example, if $n = 8$, with fan-in two, we can compute it in depth of $\log 8 = 3$, as follows: at stage-1, four AND/OR gates of fan-in 2, then two AND/OR gates of fan-in two, then one AND/OR gate of fan-in two. This makes depth 3.

[10] The class is named after Axel Thue—a Norwegian mathematician known for his work in combinatorics.

[11] The majority function is the Boolean function that evaluates to false when half or more arguments are false and true otherwise.

be recognized by a family of threshold circuits of depth $O(\log^i n)$,[12] a polynomial size, with no bounds on the *fan-in*. Hence, the class TC is,

$$\mathsf{TC} = \bigcup_{i \geq 0} \mathsf{TC}^i. \tag{13.22}$$

□

Thus, TC^0 complexity class is in circuit complexity, and first class in the hierarchy of TC classes.

The complexity classes TC, NC, and AC form a hierarchy of complexity classes. The relationship between the TC, NC, and the AC hierarchy can be summarized as follows:

$$\mathsf{NC}^i \subseteq \mathsf{AC}^i \subseteq \mathsf{TC}^i \subseteq \mathsf{NC}^{i+1}. \tag{13.23}$$

In the above, when $i = 0$, we have,

$$\mathsf{NC}^0 \subseteq \mathsf{AC}^0 \subseteq \mathsf{TC}^0 \subseteq \mathsf{NC}^1.$$

The first strict containment follows from the fact that NC^0 cannot compute any function that depends on all the input bits.

As an immediate consequence of these containments, we have NC = AC = TC.

13.11.2 Uniformity and Circuit Classes

A tricky aspect of the *circuit complexity* is that many functions that are not computable have a trivial circuit complexity. Consider that K is a non-computable set of numbers, such as the indices of *halting* Turing machines, and suppose language $A = \{x : |x| \in K\}$. For each n, if $n \in K$, we define C_n by attaching a NOT gate to input x_1 and and OR gate whose two wires come from the NOT gate and the x_1 itself. If $n \notin K$, then define C_n similarly, but with AND gate in place of OR gate. This circuit family $[C_n]$ accepts the language A and size and depth 2. The problem, however, is that there is no algorithm to tell which choice for C_n to define for each n. Indeed, every language is accepted by some circuit family $[C_n]$ with size complexity $2^{O(n)}$ and depth complexity 3. Thus, general circuit complexity is at most exponential, and depth complexity is at most linear.

---

[12] In most cases, logarithmic complexities are considered very efficient, and as i increases, the algorithm is likely to be even more efficient.

13.12 Reducibility

The goal of a reduction is to transform one problem A into another problem B. If we know the solution of problem B then this yields the solution for problem A. The reductions allow us to order the problems as how hard they are. However, if A is undecidable, the reduction will imply that B is also undecidable. Otherwise, a Turing machine could be used to decide B and that can be used to decide A. The reductions are also standard tool in complexity theory, where we can transform the problem of one bound on resources (complexity) into other bound. The bound may be on space or time. It is important to note that in computability theory, the bounds need to be computable.

We formalize the notion of reduction using the following two definitions.

Definition 13.34 (*Computable Function*) A function $f : \Sigma^* \to \Sigma^*$ is computable if there exists some Turing machine M, such that with input x, the M halts just when $f(x)$ is written on its tape. □

Definition 13.35 (*Reduction*) Given two languages A and B, a reduction from A to B is a computable function $f : \Sigma^* \to \Sigma^*$ such that $x \in A$ iff $f(x) \in B$. Then we say A is reducible to B, denoted by $A \leq B$, if there exists a reduction from language A (Set) to B. □

The steps for reduction are: First, original problem is represented using Turing machine, and then transform the original instances into those of target problem. In order to understand that the reductions are useful in computability theory, we need initially an *undecidable* problem. For example the *diagonalization theorem* (see Theorem 1.4). With the idea of reduction, we shall show that A_{TM} is undecidable. Note that A_{TM} is defined as,

$$A_{TM} = \{\langle M, w\rangle \mid w \in \Sigma^* \text{ is string and } M \text{ is Turing machine that accepts } w\}.$$

The following theorem shows that A_{TM} is undecidable.

Theorem 13.5 *A_{TM} is undecidable.*

Proof To prove this theorem it suffices to show that $L_d \leq A_{TM}$. □

Related to the question of *solvability* or *unsolvability* of problems is that of the reducibility or non-reducibility of one problem to another. Thus, if problem P_1 has been reduced to problem P_2, a solution of P_2 immediately yields a solution of P_1, while if P_1 is proved to be unsolvable, P_2 must also be unsolvable. For unsolvable problems, the concept of reducibility leads to the concept of *degree of unsolvability*. Two unsolvable problems being of the same degree of unsolvability if each one of them is reducible to other problems. And, one of them is of lower degree of unsolvability than another, if it is reducible to the other, but that, other is not reducible to it. They are of incomparable degrees of unsolvability if neither is reducible to the other.

A primary problem in the Recursively Enumerable (RE) sets is the problem of determining degrees of unsolvability of unsolvable decision problems. We introduce the concept of "recursive reducibility" of one problem to another. As per this, for any "recursively" defined unsolvable problem, there is another of higher degree of unsolvability. We have the following theorem.

13.12.1 *Oracle Turing Machines*

Some computational problems remain difficult even when solutions to the instances of a particular different decision problem are available free, and the latter is sub-problem of the original problem. When we study complexity of a problem whose sub-problem is about deciding the membership to a language L, we assume that answers about membership in L have been precomputed and stored in a (possibly infinite) table, such that there is no cost to obtain an answer to a membership query, e.g., "Is w in L"? In that case, the language L is called *Oracle*. Conceptually, an algorithm queries the Oracle whether a word w is in L, and it receives the correct answer.

An Oracle Turing machine M has a special oracle tape and special states QUERY, YES, and NO. The computation of the oracle TM M^L, with oracle language L, is same as that of an ordinary Turing machine, except that when M enters the QUERY state with a word w on the oracle tape, M enters either YES state if $w \in L$ or NO state if $w \notin L$, in one step. Further, during this step, the oracle tape is erased, so that the time for setting up each query is accounted separately.

13.12.2 *Problem Reduction*

A Turing reduction from problem A to problem B is a reduction that solves A, assuming the solution to B is already known. It can be understood as an algorithm that could be used to solve A if it had available to it a subroutine B. In other words, Turing reduction is a function computable by an *Oracle* machine for B. This reduction can be applied to *decision problems* as well to *function problems*.

Let there be problems A and B, with A not harder than B, is represented as $A \leq B$. Now, if A is *undecidable*, then B is also undecidable. Similarly, if B is decidable, then A is also decidable. Thus, given a hardness relation between two problems, and given one is hard or soft, we can conclude the hardness or softness of the other problem.

The relation $A \leq B$ means that problem A can be solved using the solution to B. To be precise, to get solution of A for the instance w, what we need to do is to modify w some how to obtain w' and then obtain solution to B for the instance w', so that the solution of B for w' turns out to be the solution of A for w also. In this case, "$A \leq B$" means that problem "A is reducible to problem B". Further, the correspondence between w and w' is a function f such that $w' = f(w)$.

Definition 13.36 Let A, B are both problems whose solutions are in the form of Yes/ No, and $A \leq B$ if there is a function $f : \Sigma^* \rightarrow \Sigma^*$, such that,

$$A(w) = Yes \Leftrightarrow B(f(w)) = Yes,$$

for all $w \in \Sigma^*$, then the function f is called *reduction* of A into B. □

Also, when A and B are membership problems of language, the language A is said to be reducible to language B, where languages are thought to be membership problems.

Whenever A and B are languages or problems, if reduction $A \leq B$ is computable by a TM, A is said to be mapping reducible to B, denoted by $A \leq_{mred} B$. Similarly, if the reduction is computable by a TM in polynomial time, we say $A \leq_P B$. Since, all the polynomial problems are computable, $A \leq_P B$ is simply written as $A \leq B$. In this reduction by TM using a reduction function $f : \Sigma^* \rightarrow \Sigma^*$, is polynomial if there exists integers k and m such that for $w \in \Sigma^*$, $f(w)$ is computed in $k|w|^m$ steps.

There is yet another concept of reducibility, called *Turing reducibility*. The Turing reducibility is defined in terms of an *Oracle*. An Oracle is a device that is equipped to a TM: when the TM asks the Oracle whether any string w is member of a certain language, say B, the oracle answers it Yes/No depending on whether $w \in B$ or $w \notin B$. Such a TM which has capability to query an oracle about membership, is called "Oracle TM", and denoted by M^B. To be specific, a Oracle TM queries an oracle by placing a string on a special oracle tape and then obtain Yes/No from Oracle in a single computation step.

A language A is Turing reducible to B if there exists an oracle TM with an oracle of B that decides A. This is denoted by $A \leq_{Turing} B$. This Turing reducibility can be thought of as a generalization of mapping reducibility. This is graphically explained in Fig. 13.5.

If $A \leq B$ holds for languages A and B, then,

$$w \in A \Leftrightarrow f(w) \in B,$$

where f is reduction.

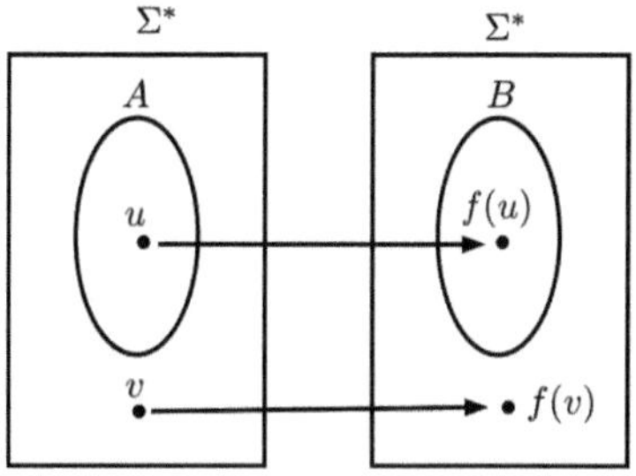

Fig. 13.5 Reduction concept explained using sets

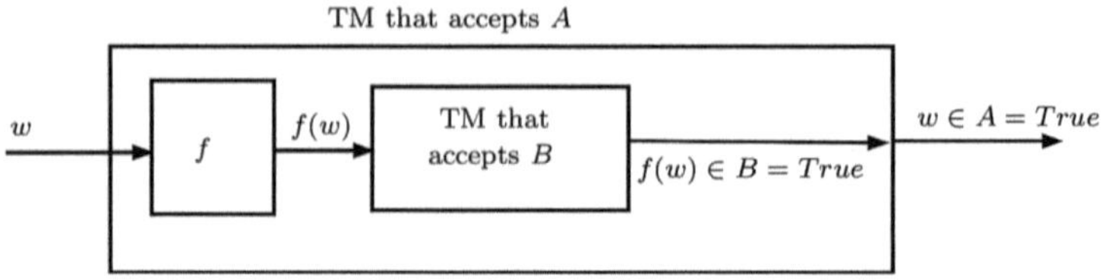

Fig. 13.6 Reduction concept explained using Turing machine

Fig. 13.6 illustrates how to construct a Turing machine that decides the membership problem for language A by using the Turing machine that decides the membership problem for language B. In other words, to test whether $w \in A$, we use the reduction f to map w to $f(w)$ and then test whether $f(w) \in B$.

Following are the properties of $\leq_{Turing}$ (or $\leq_T$) if $A \leq_T B$:

- If B is recursive then so is A.
- If B is recursively enumerable, then so is A.
- If A undecidable, then so is B.
- $A \leq_T A$ (reflexive property).
- If $A \leq_T B$ and $B \leq_T C$, then $A \leq C$ (Transitive property).

13.12.3 Polynomial-Time Reduction

Definition 13.37 Language A is *polynomial reducible* to language B, expressed as $A \leq_P B$, if there exists a polynomial function f such that $f : \Sigma^* \rightarrow \Sigma^*$ for every $w \in A \Leftrightarrow f(w) \in B$. □

Definition 13.38 (*Polynomial time solution*) If problem A reduces to problem B in polynomial time, and solution of B takes polynomial time, then solution of B be can be used to solve A in polynomial time. □

Definition 13.39 A function $f : \Sigma^* \rightarrow \Sigma^*$ is *polynomial time computable* if some polynomial time TM M, which when started with input $w \in \Sigma^*$, halts with $f(w)$ on tape. □

If one language is polynomial time reducible to a language already known to have polynomial time solution, we obtain a polynomial solution to original.

Theorem 13.6 *Given the languages A and B, if $A \leq_P B$ and $B \in P$, then $A \in P$.*

Proof Following are the steps for proof:

1. Let M be polynomial-time deterministic TM that decides B, and let f be a polynomial time reduction from A to B. We build a polynomial-time Turing machine M' that decides A as follows:
2. M' = with input w,

   a. compute $f(w)$ on TM R (reducer for function f),
   b. Run M on input $f(w)$.

Therefore, M' is polynomial because each of the above steps is polynomial (Note: Composition of two polynomial functions is polynomial). □

Theorem 13.7 *If $A \leq_T B$ and B is recursively enumerable, then A is also Recursively Enumerable.*

Proof Let f be a function from A to B and let M_B be a Turing machine recognizing B. Then, TM recognizing A can be constructed as:

On input w
  compute $f(w)$
  Run M_B on $f(w)$,
  Accept if M_B accepts, and reject if M_B rejects. □

Theorem 13.8 *(a) If $A \leq B$ and $B \leq C$ are mappings for problem A, B, C, then that $A \leq C$. (Note $A \leq B$ is called mapping reducibility). (b) Also, if $A \leq_P B$ and $B \leq_P C$, then $A \leq_P C$.*

Proof (a) Let $A \leq B$ and $B \leq C$ with reduction function f, g respectively. The $g(f(w))$ is reduction for $A \leq C$. This is possible as follows: For any input w to A,

$$\begin{aligned} A(w) = YES &\Leftrightarrow B(f(w)) = YES, \text{ for } A \leq B \\ &\Leftrightarrow C(g(f(w))) = YES, \text{ for } B \leq C \end{aligned}$$

Also, if f and g are computed by Turing machines M_f and M_g, respectively, then $g(f(w))$ can be computed by first converting input w to $f(w)$ by M_f then feeding $f(w)$ as input to M_g to obtain $g(f(w))$ as output. Let the TM M_{gf} computes this reduction of $A \leq C$.

(b) For polynomial time reducibility, suppose f and g are computed by TM M_f and M_g in time an^k and bn^l (both polynomial), respectively, where the input to A is $|w| = n$ and a, b, k, l are integer constants.

Then, since the length of an output is obviously upper bounded by the steps of M_f, we have $|f(w)| \leq an^k$. So the steps of M_g are upper bounded by $b|f(w)| \leq b(an^k)^l = ba^l n^{kl}$. Thus, M_{gf} computes the deduction $g(f(w))$ in at most $an^k + ba^l n^{kl}$ steps or time, which is in polynomial. This completes the proof. □

Theorem 13.9 *(a) If a language B is decidable and $A \leq B$ holds, then A is also decidable. (b) If B is computable in polynomial time, and $A \leq B$ holds, then A is computable in polynomial time.*

Proof (a) Let the reduction $A \leq B$ is done by function f and corresponding Turing machine is denoted by M_f. Let TM to compute B be denoted by M_B.

Having computed B, the A is computed for (a) and (b), by TM M_A as follows:

1. Input w,
2. run TM M_f on input w and yield $f(w)$ as output,
3. run TM M_B on input $f(w)$ and get its output as output of M_A.

As per the definition, TM M_A decides A.
(b) Now, if f and B are computable in polynomial time, then A is also computable in polynomial time.

This proves the theorem. □

13.13 Primality and Compositness

A prime number is one that can be divided by unity and itself only. A class of all the primes is called $\mathsf{P}RIMES$, and defined as,

$$PRIMES = \{x \mid x \text{ is a prime number}\}. \tag{13.24}$$

Similarly, a *composite* number is one that can be factored into integers, whose multiplication is that number. Obviously, the numbers in the factors are excluding that original number and unity. Thus, the set of all the composite number is,

$$COMPOSITS = \{y \mid y \text{ is a composite number}\}. \tag{13.25}$$

Therefore, $\mathsf{P}RIMES = \overline{COMPOSITS}$; also, if $COMPOSITS$ is NP then $\mathsf{P}RIMES$ is $Co\text{-}NP$ (i.e., complement of NP). The *compositness* can be determined by $NDTM$ by guessing it Nondterministically. Hence, compositeness is in NP but its solution can be verified in P time.

Theorem 13.10 *Fermat's Little theorem (for Primality Test): If p is prime and a is an integer, then: $a^p \equiv a(mod\ p)$, i.e., "$a^p - a$" is evenly divisible by p.*

The general case of this problem is NP because of exponential component a^p. As an example, we can check that $2^{11} - 2 = 2048 - 2 = 2046$ is divisible by 11. Sets of primes are in NP but not in *NP-complete*; similarly the $COMPOSITS$. The language of PRIMES is NP ∩ Co-NP, and hence of $COMPOSITS$ also belong to this class. Imagine, if that is not the case, there will be equivalence of NP = Co-NP.

Theorem 13.11 *COMPOSITS are* NP.

Proof 1. Let Input on nondeterministic Turing machine is p, $|p| = n$. *Guess* a factor f of at most n bits ($f \neq 1$, $f \neq p$). This part is non-deterministic, and the time taken by any sequence of choice is $O(n)$. (Note there are n ways of choosing an n-bit number non-deterministically).

2. Divide p by f, check if remainder is 0. Accept if so. This part step is deterministic with complexity $O(n^2)$ on a 2-tape TM.
Therefore the *COMPOSITS* are in NP. □

Theorem 13.12 *If there is a polynomial time algorithm for one* NP*-problem, then all* NP *problems are solvable in* P *time.*

Proof This is possible, because, if A is NP-complete, then all NP-problems are reducible to A. And, if $A \in P$, then all those NP are P. □

The above conclusion has advantage, as if one NP problem can be solved, then all rest are automatically solved; and for this one may choose only one of the most appropriate NP problem for solution.

13.14 Summary

Computational complexity theory is, (i) study of resources such as *time* and *space* (memory), required to solve computational problems and (ii) to classify the problems according to their difficulty level.

Given computational problem P, we may question about: What are good algorithms for solution of P? Can one establish and prove a lower bound for one of the cost functions associated with the algorithm? Is P perhaps intractable, in the sense, that no algorithm will solve it in practically feasible time?

The complexity theory has contributed in two ways: (i) it has partitioned the computation into complexity classes, and (ii) there is sufficient evidence that these complexity classes are distinct.

Typically, a complexity class is defined by three things collectively: (i) a model of computation, (ii) a resource (or collection of resources), and (iii) a function known as the complexity bound for each resource. The models fall into two categories: machine-based models (e.g., TM) and circuit-based models. This chapter has presented both, but more emphasis has been put on machine-based model—a multitape Turing machine.

The *time complexity* is measured by counting the elementary steps required for a machine to compute and halt. Various complexity classes are defined based on these criteria that give time spent by an algorithm as a function of size of the input, and this function is either asymptotic (sublinear), or linear, or exponential (superlinear) in time.

Based on the nature of problems, the TMs are space-bounded and time-bounded. A function t is time constructible, defined as $t : \mathbb{N}_0 \rightarrow \mathbb{N}_0$ if there exists a TM that computers $x \mapsto t(|x|)$ in time $O(t(|x|))$.

Based on the time complexity needed to recognize the languages on TM, classes of languages are defined. $\mathsf{DTIME}[t(n)]$ is the class of languages decided by deterministic TMs in time complexity $t(n)$. The class $\mathsf{NTIME}[t(n)]$ is defined in similar way for NDTMs.

Based on the space consumed for deciding the languages, these are called space constructible or space bounded, are their classes are $\mathsf{DSPACE}_k(s(n))$ and $\mathsf{NSPACE}_k(s(n))$, respectively for DTMs and NDTMs.

All the problems which can be solved in time $\mathsf{DTIME}[t(n))$ on DTM, where $t(n) = n^k$, make the class P, i.e.,

$$\mathsf{P} = \bigcup_{k \geq 1} \mathsf{DTIME}(n^k).$$

Similarly, all the problems which can be solved in time $\mathsf{NTIME}(P(n))$ on NDTM are in the class NP, and expressed as,

$$\mathsf{NP} = \bigcup_{\mathsf{P}(n)} \mathsf{NTIME}(\mathsf{P}(n)).$$

A problem is in NP-complete if it is in NP and every problem in NP can be reduced into this problem.

A Boolean expression u in CNF (Conjunctive Normal Form), and output is True, if there is an assignment that satisfies u, else it is False. This expression is called SAT problem. For this, the Complexity in P is unknown, while in NP is Yes. Thus,

$$SAT = \{< \phi >: \phi \text{ is satisfiable Boolean formula}\}.$$

The SAT is NP-complete problems (NPC). The Hamiltonian path problem, and subset sum problems are NPC.

The EXP or $\mathsf{EXPTIME}$ are class of problems which can be solved by deterministic Turing machine in exponential time, thus,

$$\mathsf{EXP} = \bigcup_{P(n)} \mathsf{DTIME}[2^{P(n)}].$$

Similarly, NEXP is defined for nondeterministic Turing machine, as,

$$\mathsf{NEXP} = \bigcup_{P(n)} \mathsf{NTIME}[2^{P(n)}].$$

Like, time bounds on the Turing machines, there are space bounds, and classes of space bounds. E.g., $\mathsf{DSPACE}(s(n))$ is a class of all languages which are decided by space-bounded deterministic TMs in space $s(n)$. The set of all such languages is called PSPACE,

$$\mathsf{PSPACE} = \bigcup_{k \geq 1} \mathsf{DSPACE}(n^k).$$

LOGSPACE is another complexity class, where the problem consumes $\log n$ space for input size $|w| = n$ for DTM and for NDTM the class is NL.

A hierarchy of complexity classes is called *Canonical* complexity classes. It also shows the relationship between various complexity classes as well as their order.

The size of a Boolean circuit is also a measure of complexity of a function. A close relation exists between circuit size and time taken on Turing machine to solve a problem.

A circuit (also called straight line program) uses basic building blocks, like, AND, OR, and NOT, is a sequence of instructions, each producing a function by applying an operation from the basis to previously obtained functions.

The circuit complexity classes NC, TC, and AC refer to complexity classes in the context of *parallel* and *distributed* computing.

Many times, a problem can be reduced to another form—a simpler form, and by solving the latter we can arrive at the solution of the original problem. A relation $A \leq B$ (A is reducible to B) means that problem A can be solved using the solution to B. However, if A is undecidable, then B is also undecidable.

If the solution of A and B is in the form of Yes/No, then $A \leq B$ if there is a function $f : \Sigma^* \rightarrow \Sigma^*$, such that,

$$A(w) = Yes \Leftrightarrow B(f(w)) = Yes.$$

If A can be reduced to problem B in polynomial time, then it is called polynomial reduction, represented by $A \leq_P B$. Also, we can say,

$$w \in A \Leftrightarrow f(w) \in B,$$

where f is reduction function.

The reduction is transitive, i.e., if $A \leq B$ and $B \leq C$, then $A \leq C$.

All the NPC (NP-Complete) problems carry lot of significance as they have number of important applications, hence there are abundant research efforts being made to find out efficient/near-polynomial solutions to these problems.

The NPC are a subset of NP-hard problems, the latter are the hardest known class of problems.

A prime number is one that can be divided by unity and itself only. A class of all the primes is called *PRIMES*. Similarly, a composite number is one that can be factored into integers, whose multiplication is that number. The set of all the composites is called *COMPOSITS*. They are related as follows:

$$PRIMES = \overline{COMPOSITES}.$$

Fermat's little theorem is used to test primality of any number, that is, whether it is prime or not.

Self Review Questions

1. If you add two n-digit numbers (decimal), what is the total number of basic operations performed?
2. Define the *time-constructible* function.
3. Define the *space-constructible* function.
4. Define the languages $\mathsf{DTIME}[t(n)]$ and $\mathsf{NTIME}[t(n)]$.
5. How $\mathsf{DTIME}[t(n)]$ and $\mathsf{NTIME}[t(n)]$ are different from classes of problems P and NP, respectively?
6. Give examples of two problems in each of the following: $t(n)$, DTIME, NTIME, P, NP.
7. Define verifier.
8. What is the difference between decidable and recognizable languages?
9. Is $\mathsf{P} \subseteq \mathsf{NP}$ or other way round?
10. Give an example of deterministic log space problem.
11. What is space complexity of storing a unary number whose decimal value is n?
12. What is space complexity of a binary number whose decimal value is n?
13. What is meaning of language $\Sigma^n \cap L(M)$?
14. What is an Oracle Turing Machine?

Exercises

A. Concepts based Problems

Note: The $*$ marked exercises are provided with solutions at the end of this book.

1. In what ways the complexity theory has contributed to the computer science?
2. The models that define complexity classes fall into what categories?
3. Show the relations between various complexity classes: P, NP, NP-complete, and NP-hard, making use of Venn Diagrams?
4. Show that for all recursive languages A, B, the relation $A \leq_T B$ holds (i.e., for all recursive languages A, B, there is $A \equiv_T B$).
5. Show that $\mathsf{NL} \neq \mathsf{NP}$.

6. Give examples of three problems having time complexity linear, sublinear, super linear, respectively, like, shown in Fig. 13.2.
7. What is meaning of $PRIMES = \overline{COMPOSITS}$?
8. What is difference between decidable language and recognizable language?

B. Analysis-based Problems

9. Explain the meaning of the function 13.8 given on Sect. 13.6.
10. Show that time complexity of addition of two n-digit numbers is $O(n)$.
11. * Find out the membership of a language that is decided in time $t(n) = 7.5n^2 + 100n \log n$.
12. The best-known algorithm for multiplication is $\theta(n^{1.1})$. Prove this.
13. For two n-digit decimal numbers, show that ordinarily the complexity of multiplication is $\theta(n.10^n)$.
14. Find out the complexity of n-bits addition of two n-bit binary numbers.
15. Find out the complexity of two n-bits multiplication of binary numbers.
16. What is circuit complexity of:

    a. Product of sum form (i.e., Conjunctive normal form, CNF)?
    b. Sum of product (i.e., Disjunctive normal form, DNF)?

17. If A and B are languages and such that $A \leq_T B$. Which of these are true?

    a. If B is recursive then so is A.
    b. If A is recursive then so is B.
    c. If B is recursively enumerable then so is A.
    d. If A is recursively enumerable then so is B.
    e. If A is undecidable then so is B.
    f. If B is undecidable then so is A.

C. Proof-based Problems

18. For a regular grammar G, show that $L(G) \in TIME(n)$.
19. For a context-free grammar G, show that $L(G) \in TIME(n^3)$.
20. Given the mathematical concept of TM, show that all the possible languages cannot be accepted by TMs, i.e., there are languages for which no Turing machines exist.
21. * If $A \leq_T B$ and B is a regular language, does that imply that A is a regular language?
22. * Show that $\mathsf{NL} \subseteq \mathsf{P}$.
23. Prove the followings:

    a. Show that n^2 and 2^n are time functions.
    b. Show that $(\log_2 n)^2$ is space function.

D. Multiple choice Questions

24. Nobody knows yet if $\mathsf{P} = \mathsf{NP}$. Consider the language L defined as follows.

$$L = \begin{cases} (0+1)^* & \text{if } \mathsf{P} = \mathsf{NP} \\ \phi & \text{otherwise} \end{cases}$$

Given this, which property holds true for L?

(A) It is not recursive, but recursively enumerable.
(B) It is not recursively enumerable.
(C) It is recursive.
(D) None of these hold true.

25. Let the languages L_1, L_2 be based on some alphabet Σ, and let $f : \Sigma^* \to \Sigma^*$ be a polynomial time computable bijection function such that $(\forall x)[x \in L_1$ iff $f(x) \in L_2]$. Given that f^{-1} is a polynomial time computable, which of the following statements are false?

(A) $L_1 \in \mathsf{NP}$ and $L_2 \in \mathsf{P}$.
(B) L_1 is recursively enumerable and L_2 is recursive.
(C) L_1 is undecidable and L_2 is decidable.
(D) $L_1 \in \mathsf{P}$ and L_2 is finite.

E. Advanced Knowledge Assessment Problems

26. Show that circuit complexity classes can model parallel computing.
27. Prove the hierarchy of circuit complexity classes shown in Eq. 13.23 (Sect. 13.11.1).

References

1. Agrawal M, Kayal N, Saxena N (1 Sep 2004) PRIMES is in P. Ann Math, 781–793
2. Aho AV, Hopcroft JE, Ullman JD (1975) The design and analysis of computer algorithms. Second printing
3. Chowdhary KR (2015) Fundamentals of discrete mathematical structures. PHI Learning Pvt. Ltd., Chapter 5, pp 84–106
4. Allender E, Loui MC, Regan KW (1999) Complexity classes: 27-1. Citeseer
5. Barrington DAM et al (1990) On uniformity within NC^1. J Comput Syst Sci 41(3):274–306. https://doi.org/10.1016/0022-0000(90)90022-D
6. Hartmanis J, Stearns RE (1965) On the computational complexity of algorithms. Trans Am Math Soc 117:285–306
7. Hartmanis J, Hopcroft JE (1971) An overview of the theory of computational complexity. J ACM 18(3):444–475
8. Hartmanis J (1995) On computational complexity and the nature of computer science. ACM Comput Surv (CSUR) 27(1):7–16
9. Rabin MO (1977) Complexity of computations. Comms ACM 20(9):625–633
10. Turing AM (1937) On computable numbers, with applications to the Entscheidungs problem. Proc Lond Math Soc 2(42):230–265

Chapter 14
NP-Completeness

Abstract The NP-complete problems are hardest problems in NP, so far no algorithm has been found for any of the NP-complete problems. But, due to their existence in many practical applications, their efficient solution carries a lot of significance. The interesting fact about all of them is that if any one of the NP-complete (NPC) problem is found to have a polynomial solution, all the NPC problems will have polynomial solution. One way to have an efficient solution to a problem is to reduce it into some simpler problem. The above are the topics of this chapter, in addition, it presents some of the standard NP problems to begin with, gives a more detailed deliberation about Satisfiability (SAT) problem, and shows that SAT is in NP. Next, the Cook–Levin theorem proves that SAT is in NP-complete, this is followed with various proofs about NP-complete, and introduction to number of NP-complete problems. Various approaches are presented about how to solve SAT problem. In the end, counting problems are introduced with their significance and their fields of applications, followed by self-review questions and exercises.

Keywords NP · NP-complete · SAT · $3SAT$ · Cook–Leven theorem · Problem reduction · Counting problem · Knapsack problem · Traveling Salesman problem · Hamiltonian Path problem · Subset-sum problem · Clique problem · Dominating Set problem · Vertex-cover problem · Independent-Set problem · Graph Coloring problem · Solving sat

14.1 Introduction

The class NP includes an enormous number pf practical problems that occur in business and industry [11]. A proof that an NP problem is NP-Complete (NPC) is a proof that the problem is not in P. Hundreds of fundamental problems, including many optimization problems of operations research, are NP-complete (NPC)—they are the hardest problems in NP. If there is a polynomial-time algorithm for any one NPC problem, then there would be polynomial-time algorithms for all the NPC problems. Despite the efforts made during the last many decades, no any polynomial-time algorithm has been found yet for any NPC problem. Although no one knows

K. R. Chowdhary, *Theory of Computation*,
https://doi.org/10.1007/978-981-97-6234-7_14

whether P is different from NP, showing that a problem is NPC, provides strong evidence that the problem is computationally infeasible and only the alternatives left for solving it are through heuristic and probabilistic approaches.

Membership of a language in NP can be determined in polynomial time on a nondeterministic TM, and the verification, i.e., the proof that the membership computed is correct, can be determined in polynomial time on deterministic TM. Consider a language of composite numbers written in binary format. A nondeterministic TM can solve this NP problem in polynomial time and its solution can be verified in polynomial time on deterministic TM. For example, on input z, a nondeterministic Turing machine for computing composite numbers can guess z_1 and z_2[1] and can also *deterministically* computes their product to check whether $z_1 z_2 = z$.

Another language in NP is the set of *Satisfiable Boolean* formulas, called SAT. A Boolean formula ϕ is satisfiable if there exists a truth assignment of True or False to each variable such that the resulting value of ϕ is True. For example, $x \wedge (\bar{x} \vee y)$ is satisfiable for $x = 1, y = 1$ but $x \wedge \bar{y} \wedge (\bar{x} \vee y)$ is not satisfiable any value of x, y pair, i.e., for $(x, y) = (0, 0); (0, 1); (1, 0)$ and $(1, 1)$. A nondeterministic Turing machine for SAT guesses a truth assignment and then deterministically evaluates ϕ for this truth assignment [15].

A commonly used approach to solve any new complex problem is to *reduce* it to a problem whose solution is known (see Sect. 13.12). Frequently, every instance of the new problem is formulated completely in terms of an instance of the problem whose solution is known. For instance, a language L' is NPC if $L' \in$ NP and every language L in NP can be reduced to L' in the following manner: for each L in NP, there exists a function f, which is computable in polynomial time such that for every word w, $w \in L$ if and only if $f(w) \in L'$. If there is a polynomial-time algorithm A' to decide membership in L', then there is a polynomial-time algorithm to decide membership in L as follows: for an input word w, first compute $f(w)$ and then run A' on $f(w)$. It is well known that SAT is NPC. Suppose, if deciding SAT becomes easy (i.e., it can be solved in polynomial time), then factoring integers also becomes easy—a surprising connection between two unrelated problems!

The NP-Completeness concept has become quite common throughout the literature of mathematics, numerous sciences, and engineering disciplines because many of their computational problems are NP-Complete.

Learning Outcomes of this Chapter:

1. NP-completeness. [Analysis], [Evaluation]
2. P and NP classes. [Knowledge], [Evaluation]
3. PSPACE and EXP classes. [Analysis]
4. NP-Complete problems. [Application]
5. Reduction. [Application]
6. Reducibility. [Proof]
7. Reducing a classic known NP-complete problem. [Application]

[1] The z_1 and z_2 are ≥ 2.

14.2 Class NP

Definition 14.1 (NP) A language is in NP iff it is decided by some Nondeterministic Turing Machine (NDTM) in polynomial time. An NDTM guesses the alternatives. Hence, NP is class of membership problems for languages in,

$$\mathsf{NP} = \bigcup_{P(n)} \mathsf{NTIME}(P(n)), \tag{14.1}$$

where P(n) stands for polynomial in n, e.g., $n, 5n^2, n^3 \in P(n)$. □

Polynomial solutions for these problems are not known to exist. In an NDTM, the solution is selected nondeterministically rather than systematically examining all the possibilities. Therefore P ⊆ NP, because a P problem is a special case NP (see Fig. 13.4, Sect. 13.10.1).

Definition 14.2 (NP-*Complete*) A decision problem B is NP-complete if:

1. B is in NP, and
2. Every problem A in NP is reducible[2] to B in polynomial time.

The problem B can be shown to be in NP by demonstrating that a candidate solution to B can be verified in polynomial time. □

Another way through which the class NP can be defined is through mathematics and not using a nondeterministic Turing machine—the NP is a set of all the problems whose solutions can be *verified* quickly using deterministic Turing machine in polynomial time. In other words, NP is set of all those languages whose membership can be checked quickly. For example, it is difficult to find out the factors of a composite number, but if factors are given (or guessed by NDTM) then one can quickly check by multiplying them whether they correctly produce the given number. The difference between P and NP is that between solving and checking, or between finding the proof of a mathematical theorem and testing whether a candidate proof is correct. In conclusion, NP represents the set of all the theorems whose proofs are short, i.e., polynomial length, while P represents all the theorems that can be proved or refuted quickly, from scratch.

Earlier, the problem of the primality test was considered as NP, which is a hard class. However, the set of prime numbers is now known to be in P, owing to the efficient deterministic primality test due to [1].

An important language in NP is a set of all the *satisfiable* Boolean formulas, called SAT. For example, the formulas with three variables, $\phi_1 = x \wedge (y \vee \overline{z})$ and $\phi_2 = (\overline{x} \vee y \vee \overline{z}) \wedge (x \vee \overline{y} \vee z)$ are in SAT. These can be converted into their equivalent conjunctive normal forms (CNF), and with three variables they are called $3CNF$ or $3cnf$ [5].

---

[2] The reduction is discussed later in this chapter.

Following are some examples of NP problems:

1. *SATISFIABILITY Problem.* Input is Boolean expression u in CNF and output is Yes, if there is an assignment that satisfies u, else No. The complexity in P is unknown for this problem, while in NP is Yes. This problem is also called SAT problem.

   A consequence of this definition is that if we had a polynomial time algorithm on a Universal TM, for problem B (see Definition 14.2 of NP-complete), we could solve all problems in NP in polynomial time.

   A Boolean expression $\phi = \{\bar{x} \vee y) \wedge (x \vee \bar{z})$ is satisfiable for $x = 0$, $y =$ don't care, $z = 1$, as it evaluates ϕ to True.

   SAT is languages of all satisfiable formulas,

$$SAT = \{\langle \phi \rangle \mid \phi \text{ is satisfiable Boolean formula}\}. \tag{14.2}$$

   The Cook–Levin theorem (see Theorem 14.2) links the complexity of SAT problem to complexities of all problems in NP. Using this, any NP problem can be converted into SAT in polynomial time.
2. *Hamiltonian Path Problem.* Input for this problem is a directed graph $G = (V, E)$, and output is "Yes" if there is a single cycle that visits all nodes of this graph, and "No" otherwise. It is unknown whether this problem belongs to the complexity class P, but for NP it is "Yes". A Hamiltonian path problem is in NP, but its solution can be verified in polynomial (P) time.
3. *Subset-sum Problem.* The input is set S, an integer number k, and output is "Yes" if there is a set $P \subseteq S$ whose sum is k, else the output is "No". Whether this problem belongs to Complexity class P, it is unknown, but about it being in NP, it is "Yes".

All these three problems are NP-Complete also.

The notion of NP-completeness applies to sets, and a proof that a set is NP-complete is usually interpreted as a proof that it is intractable. There are, however, a large number of apparently intractable functions for which no NP-completeness proof seems to be relevant. For these problems, a notion #P-completeness is defined. Proving that a function is #P-complete shows that it is apparently intractable to compute. This is similar to proving that a set is NP-complete shows that it is apparently intractable to recognize it. For instance, if #P-complete function is computable in polynomial time, then P = NP. One of the interesting example of #P-complete problem is permanent of an integer matrix.[3]

[3] It is like determinant and equal to the sum of products of sets of matrix entries that lie in distinct rows and columns.

14.3 Boolean Satisfiability

There are many real-life situations where one needs to satisfy many constraints, which are potentially conflicting. For example, determining a schedule for a series of games that satisfy the condition of availability of players and venues, or for example, finding a seating arrangement at a dinner that is consistent with various rules the host has imposed. Such examples are also found in computing applications, for example, ensuring that a hardware/software system functions correctly with its overall behavior constrained by the behavior of its components and their composition, or finding an optimum path plan for a robot's moves that is consistent with various restrictions laid down [8]. While these applications may seem varied, at the core they all often have a large number of variables whose values we need to determine (for example, the person sitting at a given seat at dinner) and constraints that these variables must satisfy (for example, the host's seating rules) [16].

The satisfiability (SAT) problem is concerned with truth values of propositional formulas in propositional logic. It was shown to be the first decision problem that is NP-complete. The objective of satisfiability problem is to determine whether there is an assignment of truth values to propositions that make a CNF (conjunctive normal form) formula as True. A CNF formula is $u_1 \wedge u_2 \wedge \cdots \wedge u_n$, where u_i is a clause (i.e., consisting of disjunction of variables, say, $u_i = V_{i_1} \vee V_{i_2} \vee \cdots \vee V_{i_k}$, where V_{i_j} is an atom) [5].

Many constraint satisfaction problems, which have variables of non-Boolean nature, can be relatively easily translated into *SAT* problems. For example, consider the classic *graph coloring* problem where an n-vertex graph needs to be checked for 4-colorability, that is, determining whether each vertex can be colored using one of four possible colors such that no two adjacent vertices have the same color. Let us consider that variables in this problem are colors $\{c_0, c_1, c_2, ..., c_{n-1}\}$ for the n vertices, and the constraints are that adjacent vertices must not have same colors. It is clear that variables for this problem are not of Boolean nature, and the constraints are also not directly expressible with the operators $\{\wedge, \vee, \neg\}$. The variables and constraints in this problem can be encoded into a propositional formula as follows: Two Boolean variables, c_{i0}, c_{i1}, can be used in a two-bit encoding (00, 01, 10 and 11) to encode four possible values of the colors for vertex i. Let i and j be adjacent vertices. The constraint $c_i \neq c_j$ can be expressed as,

$$\neg((c_{i0} == c_{j0}) \wedge (c_{i1} == c_{j1})), \tag{14.3}$$

where "==" represents equality and thus this condition checks that both bits in the encoding do not have the same value for i and j. Further, $(c_{i0} == c_{j0})$ can be expressed as $(c_{i0} \wedge c_{j0}) \vee (\neg c_{i0} \wedge \neg c_{j0})$, that is, both variables are 1 or 0. Similarly for $(c_{i1} == c_{j1})$. If we take the conjunction of the constraints on each edge, then the resulting formula is satisfiable if and only if the original graph coloring problem has a solution.

Like in the above example, encoding is necessary for translating problems from wide range of domains to SAT, for example, scheduling a basketball match, planning in artificial intelligence, validating a software model, routing in field programmable gate arrays, and synthesizing consistent network configurations.

A deterministic solution to a satisfiability problem can be obtained by checking every truth assignment. For n number of Boolean variables, the number of truth assignments is 2^n, which results to exhaustive search, and the complexity is exponential.

Example 14.1 A satisfying assignment is a setting of the variables that makes the formula true, e.g.,

$$\phi = (\neg x \wedge y) \vee z.$$

The assignment $x = 1, y = 1, z = 1$ is a satisfying assignment for ϕ, because $(\neg 1 \wedge 1) \vee 1 = 0 \vee 1 = 1$. □

A Boolean formula is satisfiable if there exists a satisfying assignment for it.

$$SAT = \{\phi \mid \phi \text{ is a satisfiable Boolean formula}\}. \tag{14.4}$$

A 3cnf-formula is of the form: $(x_1 \vee \neg x_2 \vee x_3) \wedge (x_1 \vee x_2 \vee x_3) \wedge (x_1 \vee \neg x_2 \vee \neg x_3)$, where x_1, x_2, x_3 are literals, and the sub-expressions $(x_1 \vee \neg x_2 \vee x_3)$, $(x_1 \vee x_2 \vee x_3)$, etc., are called *clauses*.

Thus, as 3SAT problem is defined as,

$$3SAT = \{\phi \mid \phi \text{ is a satisfiable 3cnf-formula}\}. \tag{14.5}$$

Theorem 14.1 *The SAT (Satisfiability) problem is in* NP, *i.e.,*

$$3SAT \in \mathsf{NTIME}(n^2).$$

Proof The proof idea is as follows: On input ϕ,

1. Check if the formula is in 3cnf,
2. For each variable, non-deterministically substitute it with 0 or 1,
3. Test if the assignment satisfies ϕ.

We know that NP is,

$$\mathsf{NP} = \bigcup_{k \in \mathbb{N}} \mathsf{NTIME}(n^k).$$

Let the set of variables be $\{x_1, x_2, \ldots, x_n\}$. We will use the following rule for encoding the positive and negative variables:

Literal	Encoding
x_i	$\bar{i}\#1$
$\neg x_i$	$\bar{i}\#0$

where $\bar{i}$ is encoding for x_i, #1 for positive sign, and #0 for negative sign. Thus, encoding for $(x_1 \vee \neg x_2) \wedge (\neg x_3 \vee x_4)$ is 1#1 $\vee$ 10#0 $\wedge$ 11#0 $\vee$ 100#1. The input to the machine is encoded list of variables appearing in the formula, followed with encoding of the formula itself. Thus, input to TM, as per above format is:

$$1\#10\#11\#100\ \#\#\ 1\#1 \vee 10\#0 \wedge 11\#0 \vee 100\#1,$$

which is called an instance of the SAT problem. With alphabet set as $\Sigma = \{0, 1, \wedge, \vee, \#\}$, the language L_{SAT} is:

$$L_{SAT} = \{w \mid w \in \Sigma^*, \text{ and } w \text{ is in standard form as } CNF\}. \tag{14.6}$$

A two-tape NDTM M that solves a SAT problem can be described as follows. The M employs "guess and check" strategy. The guessing generates nondeterministically, a truth assignment. The configurations corresponding to the computation initiated with the input string $w = (x_1 \vee \neg x_2) \wedge (\neg x_3 \vee x_4)$ are demonstrated in the following, to test the satisfiability of a general CNF expression. The initial configuration of TM M is:

Tape-2: BB
Tape-1: B1#10#11#100 ## 1#1 $\vee$ 10#0 $\wedge$ 11#0 $\vee$ 100#1B

1. If input on Tape-1 is not in standard format of CNF, computation halts and input is rejected.
2. The encoding of the first variable on tape-1 is copied on tape-2. This is followed with # and nondeterministically writing 0 or 1. This is repeated for the remaining variables. After these variables ## is written. If t is truth assignment, then for the variable x_i its value is $t(x_i)$. Now, we have the following on the tapes:

   Tape-2: $B1\#t(x_1)\#\#10\#t(x_2)\#\#11\#t(x_3)\#\#100\#t(x_4)B$
   Tape-1: B1#10#11#100 ## 1#1 $\vee$ 10#0 $\wedge$ 11#0 $\vee$ 100#1B

3. The head on tape-2 is repositioned at the beginning of the tape, and on tape-1 it is moved past ## to the first variable in the formula.
   Note: Generating of truth assignment on tape-2 is the only instance of nondeterminism for M. The remainder of the computation checks whether the formula is satisfied by the nondeterministically selected truth assignment.

4. Next, when encoding of x_i is scanned on tape-1, the truth assignment for this variable is found on tape-2. Subsequent action of the machine is determined by the result of comparing value of the Boolean variable following x_i on tape-1 (0 for x_i negative and 1 for positive x_i) with the $t(x_i)$ on tape-2.
5. If the above do not match, current literal is not satisfied by the truth assignment. If the symbol following the literal on tape-1 is $\wedge$ or B, every literal in the current clause has been examined and has failed. (A clause is disjunctive expression of atoms: $x_1 \vee \cdots \vee x_n$). In this case, the truth assignment does not satisfy the formula, and M halts in a non-accepting state.
6. If "$\vee$" is read at tape-1, the tape heads are positioned to examine the next literal in the clause (go to step 4).
7. If the values match, the literal and current clause are satisfied by the truth assignment. The head on tape-1 moves to right to the next $\vee$ or B. If a B is encountered, the computation halts and accept the input. Otherwise, the next clause is processed by returning to step 4.

Since the solution using NDTM is in P, the SAT is NP.
This proves the Theorem. □

In the above discussion, the matching procedure in step 4 determines the rate of growth of time complexity of computation. In the *worst case* (deterministic TM), the matching requires computing the variables on tape-1 with each of the variables on Tape-2 to discover the match. This is done in time $O(k.2^n)$, where n is number of variables, and k is number of literals in the input.

Corollary 14.1 $SAT \in \mathsf{P}$ *if and only if* $\mathsf{P} = \mathsf{NP}$.

14.4 Cook–Levin Theorem

The Cook–Levin theorem is the central theorem in NP-completeness theory; this was the first theorem to demonstrate the existence of an NP-complete problem, namely, *satisfiability*. It was provided by Stephen Cook (1971) and, independently, by Leonid Levin (1973). Interestingly, it was the subject of lectures, in Russia, for some years before. They independently gave examples of combinatorial NP-complete problems whose definition seems to have nothing to do with Turing machines [9, 14]. Soon after, Karp showed that NP-completeness occurs widely and many problems of practical interest are NP-complete. To date, thousands of computational problems in a variety of disciplines have been found to be NP-complete.

Theorem 14.2 (Cook–Levin Theorem). SAT *is* NP-*complete.*

Proof The proof has two stages: (1) show that $SAT \in$ NP and (2) show that every language A in NP is polynomial-time reducible to SAT. Together, these two will show that SAT is NP-complete [9].

Theorem 14.1 above has already shown that SAT is NP.

To prove stage 2, we construct a polynomial time reduction for every $A \in$ NP to SAT. The reduction will turn a string $w \in A$ into a 3-cnf formula ϕ such that $w \in A$ iff $\phi \in$ 3-cnf, i.e., satisfying the conditions shown in Fig. 14.1a: for $w \in A$ there is $f(w) \in 3SAT$, and Fig. 14.1b: for $u \notin A$ there is $f(u) \notin 3SAT$.

The ϕ simulates the $NDTM$ for language A on input w. If machine accepts, ϕ has a satisfying assignment, that corresponds to accepting computation, otherwise No.

Let us assume that N is a non-deterministic TM that decides language A in polynomial time n^k, where $|w| = n$ and k is some integer. But, there is a question. How do we know that N actually exists?

We give a polynomial-time reduction from A to $3SAT$. The reduction converts a string w into a $3cnf$ formula ϕ such that $w \in A$ iff $\phi \in 3SAT$. For $A \in$ NP, let N be a nondeterministic TM that decides A in time n^k. The approach used shall be: use ϕ to simulate NDTM N on w.

Let $L(N) \in \mathsf{NTIME}(n^k)$. We construct a tableau for NDTM N on w which is a $n^k \times n^k$ matrix whose rows are configurations of some computation history of N on w (see Fig. 14.3). A tableau is accepting if the last row of the tableau has an accept state. Thus, NDTM N accepts w iff there is an accepting tableau for N on w.

Given w, we will construct a $3cnf$ formula ϕ with $O(|w|^{2k})$ clauses, describing logical constraints that accepting tableau for N on w the $3cnf$ formula ϕ will be satisfiable iff there is an accepting tableau for N on w.

For construction of tableau, the variables of formula ϕ will encode a tableau as follows. Let $C = Q \cup \Gamma \cup \{\#\}$, which is a constant sized set, such that each cell of the tableau contains a symbol from C, defined as: $cell[i, j]$, which represents a symbol in the cell at row i and column j, we can say that it is jth symbol in the ith configuration. For every $i \times j$ $(1 \le i, j \le n^k)$ and for every $s \in C$, we make a Boolean variable $x_{i,j,s}$ in ϕ. The total number of variables is $|C|n^{2k}$, which is $O(n^{2k})$.

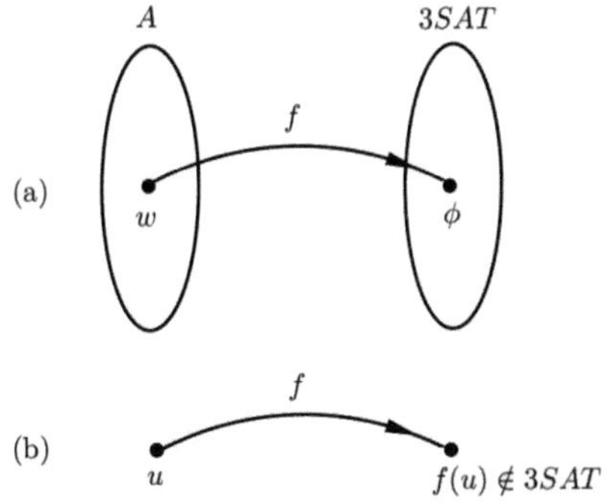

Fig. 14.1 Reduction f turns a string w into a 3-cnf formula

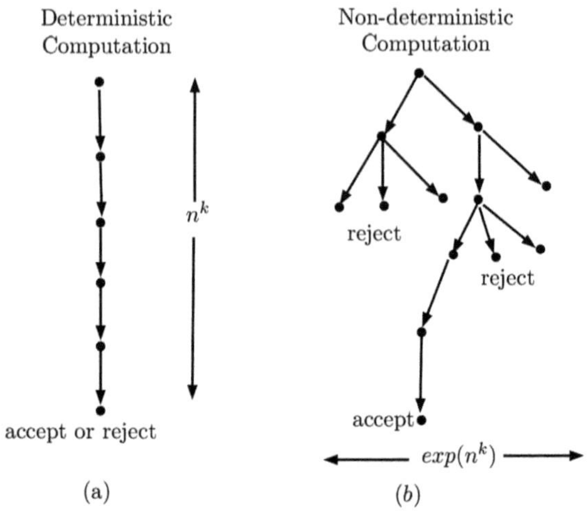

Fig. 14.2 **a** Computation of deterministic TM, **b** Computations of non-deterministic TM

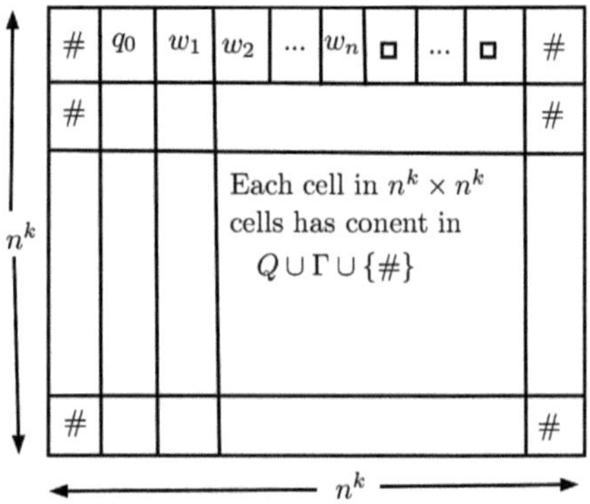

Fig. 14.3 Tableau for N on w as a $n^k \times n^k$ matrix

We will enforce the condition: for all i, j, s

$$x_{i,j,s} = 1 \Leftrightarrow cell[i, j] = s.$$

The idea is to construct ϕ such that every satisfying assignment to the variables $x_{i,j,s}$ corresponds to an accepting tableau for N on w (i.e., an assignment to all $cell[i, j]$'s of the tableau). The formula ϕ will be the logical AND of four CNF formulas,

$$\phi = \phi_{\text{cell}} \wedge \phi_{\text{start}} \wedge \phi_{\text{accept}} \wedge \phi_{\text{move}},$$

as follows:

ϕ_{cell}: for all i, j, there is a unique $s \in C$ with $x_{i,j,s} = 1$,
ϕ_{start}: first row of the table is equal to start configuration of TM N on w,
ϕ_{accept}: the last row of the table is equal to accept state,
ϕ_{move}: every row is a configuration that yields the configuration on next row.

$$\phi_{\text{start}} = X_{1,1,\#} \wedge X_{1,2,q_0} \wedge \\ X_{1,3,w_1} \wedge X_{1,4,w_2} \wedge \ldots \wedge X_{1,n+2,w_n} \wedge \\ X_{1,n+3,\square} \wedge \ldots \wedge X_{1,n^k-1,\square} \wedge X_{1,n^k,\#}.$$

The above has $O(n^k)$ clauses. The $\phi_{acccept}$ is equal to last row of the table, expressed by,

$$\phi_{\text{accept}} = \bigvee_{1 \le j \le n^k} X_{n^k, j, q_{\text{accept}}}.$$

Now the question is, how can we convert ϕ_{accept} into a $3cnf$ formula? Can we write the clause $(a_1 \vee a_2 \vee \ldots \vee a_t)$ as $(a_1 \vee a_2 \vee z_1) \wedge (\neg z_1 \vee a_3 \vee z_2) \wedge \ldots \wedge (\neg z_{t-3} \vee a_{t-1} \vee a_t)$, where z_i are new variables? This produces $O(t)$ new $3cnf$ clauses, and the new formula is SAT iff the old one is SAT.

ϕ_{cell}: for all i, j, there is a unique $s \in C$ with $x_{i,j,s} = 1$, such that,

$$\phi_{cell} = \bigwedge_{1 \le i,j \le n^k} \left[\left(\bigvee_{s \in C} X_{i,j,s} \right) \wedge \left(\bigwedge_{s,t \in C, s \ne t} (\neg X_{i,j,s} \vee \neg X_{i,j,t}) \right) \right]. \tag{14.7}$$

In the above, at least one $X_{i,j,s}$ is set to 1 in $X_{i,j,s}$ and at most one $X_{i,j,s}$ is set to 1 in, $(\neg X_{i,j,s} \vee \neg X_{i,j,t})$.

The ϕ_{cell} makes total $O(n^{2k})$ $3cnf$ clauses.

ϕ_{move}: Every row is a configuration that yields the configuration on the next row.

The question is: if one row yields the next row, how many cells can be different between the two rows? The answer is, at most three cells, as shown in Fig. 14.4. It shows that configuration has changed from first row to next row, state has changed from q_1 to q_2, symbol b at head position has been replaced by c, and head has moved to left. Note that, there are total three cells which have changed, and this is maximum.

ϕ_{move}: Every row is a configuration that yields the configuration on the next row. We note from Fig. 14.5 that every 2×3 window of cells is not legal (inconsistent with the transition function of N).

Now we sketch the proof using strong induction on i. The first row is a configuration. If it did not yield the 2nd row, there is a 2×3 illegal window on 1st and 2nd rows. Assume that rows 1, ..., L are all configurations that yield the next row, and that every window is legal. If row $L + 1$ did not yield row $L + 2$, then there is a 2×3 window along those two rows which is illegal.

Let the (i, j) window of a tableau is the tuple $(a_1, \ldots, a_6) \in C^6$, such that: cells $(i, j) = a_1$, $(i, j + 1) = a_2$, ..., $(i + 3, j + 3) = a_6$.

Fig. 14.4 Cells different between two rows

#	b	a	a	q_1	b	c	b	#
#	b	a	q_2	a	c	c	b	#

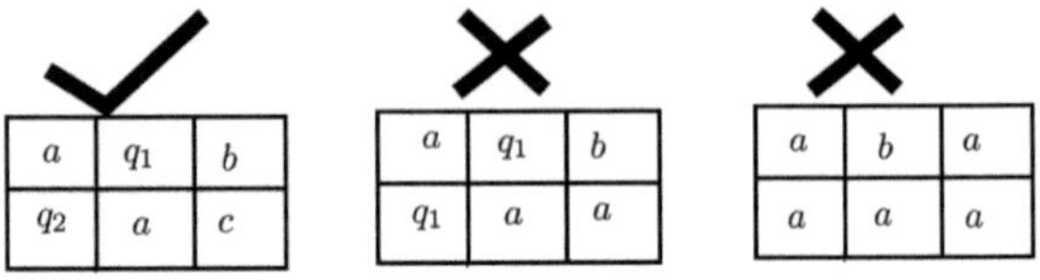

Fig. 14.5 All windows of 2×3 are not valid

We express ϕ_{move} as follows.

$$\phi_{\text{move}} : \bigwedge_{\substack{1 \le i \le n^k - 1 \\ 1 \le j \le n^k - 2}} \text{(the (i,j) window is legal)}$$

We can say that the (i, j) window is legal =

$$\bigwedge_{\substack{a_1, \ldots, a_6 \\ \text{is a legal window}}} (X_{i,j,a_1} \wedge X_{i,j+1,a_2} \wedge X_{i,j+2,a_3} \wedge X_{i+1,j,a_4} \wedge X_{i+1,j+1,a_5} \wedge X_{i+1,j+2,a_6})$$

$$\equiv \bigwedge_{\substack{a_1, \ldots, a_6 \\ \text{is NOT a legal window}}} (\bar{X}_{i,j,a_1} \vee \bar{X}_{i,j+1,a_2} \vee \bar{X}_{i,j+2,a_3} \vee \bar{X}_{i+1,j,a_4} \vee \bar{X}_{i+1,j+1,a_5} \vee \bar{X}_{i+1,j+2,a_6})$$

$$\phi_{\text{move}} = \bigwedge_{1 \le i, j \le n^k} \text{(the } (i, j) \text{ window is ``legal''}$$

$$\equiv \bigwedge_{\substack{(a_1, \ldots, a_6 \\ \text{IS NOT ``legal'')}}} (\bar{X}_{i,j,a_1} \vee \bar{X}_{i,j+1,a_2} \vee \bar{X}_{i,j+2,a_3} \vee \bar{X}_{i+1,j,a_4} \vee \bar{X}_{i+1,j+1,a_5} \vee \bar{X}_{i+1,j+2,a_6})$$

From above CNF, there are total $n^k.n^k = n^{2k}$ clauses, with worst case time complexity of $O(n^{2k})$.

Our goal was to prove that every A in NP has a polynomial time reduction to $3SAT$. For every $A \in N$, we know that A is decided by some nondeterministic n^k time Turing machine N. We adopted a generic method to reduce N and a string w to a $3cnf$ formula ϕ of $O(|w|^{2k})$ clauses such that satisfying assignments to the variables of ϕ directly correspond to accepting computation histories of N on w.

Thus, for any nondeterministic TM M that runs in some polynomial time $p(n)$, we can devise an algorithm that takes an input $|w| = n$, the running time is $O(p^2(n))$ on a multitape DTM. This proves that every language A in NP is polynomial-time reducible to SAT. □

14.5 NP-Completeness

Certain combinatorial problems, such as *traveling salesman problem* (TSP) and theorem proving in propositional logic, have long been recognized for their computational intractability, for which no algorithm has been found that can be guaranteed to solve it in time, bounded by the polynomial of the length of the input. These problems, together with a wide variety of other combinatorial problems, form the class NP-*complete* problems, no member of these is known to have a polynomial time algorithm, but if any one of these problems does have a polynomial algorithm, then they all have. If one knows that the problem he wishes to solve is NP-complete, and thus unlikely to have any polynomial time algorithm, he may better concentrate on more hopeful alternative approaches. For example, may look for algorithm that is exponential in time in the worst case but may work quicker on most practical problems, say, the *simplex method.*

Some of the examples of NP-complete problems are: a restricted form of satisfiability, Chromatic number, Exact cover, and Max-cut. A useful restatement of simple Max-cut problem is *Minimum edge deletion Bipartite Graph* [10].

Definition 14.3 (NP-*complete*) A language B is NP-complete if it satisfies two-conditions: (1) $B \in \mathsf{NP}$, (2) Every $A \in \mathsf{NP}$ is polynomial time reducible to B, i.e.,

$$B \in \mathsf{NP} \text{ and } \forall A : A \in \mathsf{NP} \text{ and } A \leq_P B \Rightarrow B \in \mathsf{NP}\text{-complete}.$$

Fig. 14.6 shows the relations between P, NP, NP-complete, and NP-hard problems: (a) for $\mathsf{P} \neq \mathsf{NP}$ and (b) for $\mathsf{P} = \mathsf{NP}$. The NP-hard therefore means "at least as hard as any NP-problem," although it might, in fact, be harder.

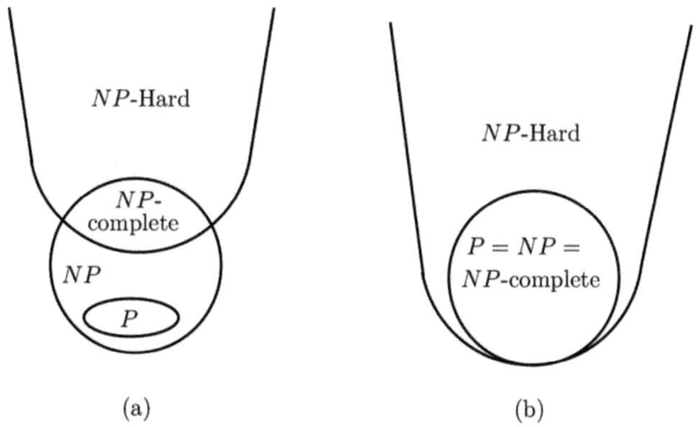

Fig. 14.6 P, NP, NP-complete, and NP-hard classes of problems: **a** $P \neq NP$, **b** $P = NP$

Definition 14.4 (NP-*Hard*) A language Q is *NP-hard* if every $L \in NP$ is polynomially reducible to Q, i.e.,

$$\forall L : L \in NP \wedge L \leq_P Q \Rightarrow Q \in NP - hard.$$

□

The NP-hard problem that is also NP is called NP-complete. All currently known NP-hard (NPH) problems have been proved to be NPC.

Among the NP-hard problems, one of *automating resolution* is NP-hard. It is a proof search problem for a given proof system, that asks, given a tautology, to find an approximately shortest proof of it. The computational complexity of such problems is of fundamental importance for automated theorem proving. In particular, among the proof systems for propositional logic, the *resolution* needs special attention as the implementations of satisfiability solvers are based on it [6].

The proof search problem for resolution is solvable in polynomial time if there is an algorithm that, given a contradictory CNF formula F as input that outputs a resolution refutation of F in time polynomial in $r + s$, where r is the size of F , and s is the length of the shortest resolution refutation of F. In simple terms, we can say that resolution is automatizable. However, the concept of automatizability applies not only to resolution but to any refutation or proof system, and one can ask for automating algorithms that run in quasi-polynomial time, subexponential time, etc. It has been shown that resolution is not automatizable unless P = NP [2].

Definition 14.5 (Co-NP) Co-NP is complement of NP, therefore, Co-NP is set of all the complements of all the NP problems. □

Theorem 14.3 (NP-complete Theorem) *If B is* NP-*Complete and $B \in P$, then* P = NP.

Proof If B is NP-Complete then every problem in NP is polynomially reducible to B. Since $B \in P$, therefore, every NP problem is polynomially reducible to B, which is P. Hence, every NP is P, i.e. P = NP. □

The logic of above theorem is also graphically presented in Fig. 14.6b.

Once we get NP-Complete, other NP problems can be reduced to it. However, establishing first NP-Complete problem is difficult.

Theorem 14.4 *If $B \in$* NP-*Complete and $B \leq_P C$ for $C \in$* NP, *then $C \in$* NP-*Complete.*

Proof We must show that every $A \in$ NP is polynomially reducible to C. Because B is NP-Complete, therefore, every $A \in$ NP is polynomially reducible to B (as per property of NP-Complete). And B in turn is polynomially reducible to C (given).

Because the property of polynomial is closed under the composition, we conclude that every $A \in NP$ is polynomially reducible to C. Therefore C is NP-Complete. □

The examples of NP-Complete (NPC) problems are: 3-SAT, *Hamiltonian path problem, subset construction problem*. All the NPC problems are verifiable in polynomial time, i.e., given a certificate of a solution, one could verify that the certificate is correct in polynomial time. The NPC problems are either of the two types, *decision problems* and *optimization problems*. A decision problem is, solving the problem by giving an answer "YES" or "NO", while *optimization problem* is, solving the problem by finding the optimal solution. Examples are: SHORTEST-PATH is an optimization problem, where given G, u, v, find a path from u to v with the fewest edges. But, PATH is a decision problem, i.e., given G, u, v, and k, whether there exist a path from u to v consisting of at most k edges.

There is also a class called P-complete in the complexity hierarchy [20].

Definition 14.6 (P-*complete*) A problem B is called P-complete iff the following holds: B solved in polynomial deterministic time iff the class of nondeterministic polynomial time languages is the same as deterministic polynomial time languages (i.e., $\mathsf{P} = \mathsf{NP}$). □

It is clear that the concept of P-complete holds only if $\mathsf{P} = \mathsf{NP}$.

More commonly known problems that are NPC are decision problems. Decision is easier than optimization problems—if there is an algorithm for an optimization problem, the algorithm can be used to solve the corresponding decision problem. For example, *Shortest-path* for the *Path*. Also, if optimization is easy, its corresponding decision is also easy. Or in another way, if one provides an evidence that decision problem is hard, then the corresponding optimization problem is also hard.

It has been shown that to determine whether the class of languages accepted by nondeterministic Turing machines operating in polynomial time was the same as that accepted by deterministic polynomial time-bounded Turing machines, was as hard as to decide if there was a deterministic polynomial algorithm for satisfiability problem. This problem of equivalence of two classes of problems is a long-standing open problem from complexity theory. However, intuitively it seems that the two classes are not the same. Hence, there may not be a polynomial algorithm for the satisfiability problem. Consequently, there may not be a polynomial algorithm for the other NP-complete problems like, traveling-salesman problem, maximum clique of a graph, minimal coloring of graphs, etc. However, no formal proof exists so far for the above to be true [19].

14.6 NP-Complete Problems

There are over 3000 known NPC problems [17]. No NPC problem has been found to have a polynomial solution. Further, if a problem is proved to be NPC, it is a good evidence for its intractability (hardness). So, one should not waste time on trying to find efficient algorithm for it, instead, focus on designing an approximate algorithm or try a solution for special case of the problem.

Following are some commonly referred NP-complete problems [11].

14.6.1 Knapsack Problem

It is a well-known combinatorial problem that finds its application in capital budgeting problems, loading problems, and solution of large optimization problems. A simplified version is called $0/1$ knapsack problem, stated as: Given a positive integer M and multiset $Q = \{(p_1, c_1), ..., (p_n, c_n)\}$ consisting of n pairs of positive integers, maximize sum $\sum \delta_i p_i$ subject to the constraints $\sum \delta_i c_i \leq M$ and $\delta_i = 0$ or 1. The (p_i, c_i) may be interpreted as the profit and weight associated with the ith object, which can be put into a knapsack[4] whose total weight capacity is M [12].

14.6.2 Traveling Salesman Problem

The traveling salesman problem (TSP) is one of the simplest and combinatorial problems. Given a list of n cities, and a matrix giving the distance between each pair of cities, the traveling salesman problem is to determine if you can visit all n cities and return to the starting city covering a total distance l or less. We focus on the decision version of the problem (Does a tour of length l or less exist?) and not the closely related optimization problem (What is the minimal length tour?). The traveling salesman problem is of considerable theoretical importance as it is representative of the large class of NP-complete problems.

The problem TSP is in the class NPC. Given a *certificate* of a sequence of vertices in the tour, a verifying algorithm can check whether each vertex appears once only in the tour, sums up the cost, and checks whether at most l in polynomial time. The TSP is defined as,

$$
\begin{aligned}
TSP = \{< G, c, l >: \\
& G = (V, E) \text{ is a complete graph,} \\
& c \text{ is a function from } V \times V \rightarrow Z, l \in Z, \text{ and} \\
& G \text{ has a travelling salesman tour with cost at most } l\}.
\end{aligned}
$$

Here Z is a set of integers.

[4] A soldier's or hiker's bag with shoulder straps, carried on the back.

14.6.3 Hamiltonian Path Problem

The Hamiltonian path problem and the Hamiltonian cycle problem are problems of determining whether a *Hamiltonian path* (a path in an undirected graph that visits each vertex exactly once) or a *Hamiltonian cycle* (returns back to the same vertex after traverse) exists in a given graph. Both problems are NP-complete.

The Existence of a *Hamiltonian Path* means whether a given graph G contains a path that visits every node exactly once? The Hamiltonian cycle problem is a special case of the traveling salesman problem, obtained by setting the distance between two cities equal to one if they are adjacent and two otherwise, and verifying that the total distance traveled is equal to n (if so, the route is a Hamiltonian circuit; if there is no Hamiltonian circuit then the shortest route will be longer than n).

14.6.4 Subset-Sum Problem

Given a (multi) set S of n positive integers and an integer target value u, the subset sum problem is to decide if there is a subset of S that sums up to u. The subset sum is a special case of the *knapsack problem*, and it is one of Karp's original NP-complete problems. The subset sum has a variety of applications, including: power indices, scheduling, set-based queries in databases, and various graph problems with cardinality constraints [13].

14.6.5 Clique Problem

It is Karp's 21 NP-complete problems. A Clique $G' = (V', E)$ is defined for an undirected graph $G = (V, E)$, such that $V' \subseteq V$, and each pair of V' is connected by an edge in E. That is, a clique is a *complete*[5] subgraph of G. A clique of size k has k number of vertices.

$$CLIQUE = \{\langle G, k\rangle : G \text{ is a graph with a cliquee of size } k\}.$$

Optimization problem in clique is: for a graph G, find the maximum clique; and the decision problem is: whether a clique of given size k exists in a given graph?

Some of the applications of clique are to model *social cliques*, groups of people who all know each other, etc. They are also used to model social networks and have adapted the social science terminology to graph theory.

As other examples, clique-finding algorithms have been used in chemistry to find chemicals that match a target structure and to model molecular docking and the binding sites of chemical reactions.

[5] In a complete graph, every vertex is connected with every other vertex.

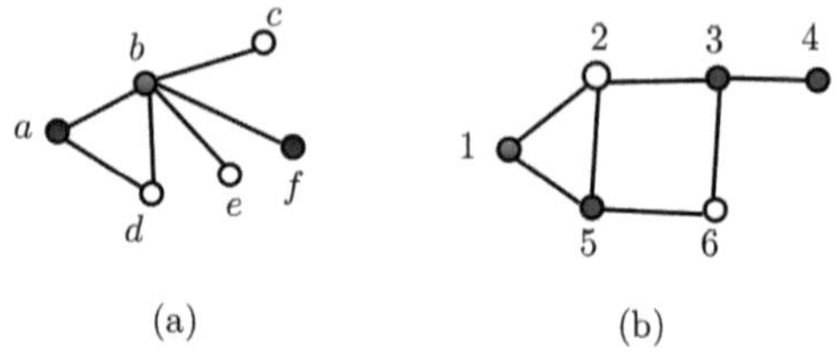

Fig. 14.7 Graphs with vertex cover: (a) $V' = \{a, b, f\}$, (b) $V' = \{1, 3, 4, 5\}$

14.6.6 Dominating Set Problem

In a graph $G = (V, E)$ a set of nodes $D \subseteq V$ is a *dominating set* if every node in $V \backslash D$ has a neighbor in D. A dominating set D is *connected* if the subgraph of G induced by D is connected.

There are many problems that are related to dominating sets, for example, *edge dominating sets*, *edge covers*, and *vertex covers*.

A set of edges $D \subseteq E$ is an edge dominating set if for each edge $(u, v) \in E \backslash D$ there is an edge $e \in D$ incident to u or v or both. Edge dominating sets are closely related to matching: a maximal matching is an edge dominating set.

A set of edges $C \subseteq E$ is an *edge cover* if for each node $v \in V$ there is an edge $e \in C$ with $v \in e$. An edge cover exists if and only if there are no isolated nodes.

Dominating sets have applications in wireless sensor networks. In such networks, we can interpret $G = (V, E)$ as a redundancy graph: an edge $(u, v) \in E$ indicates that the sensor nodes u and v are so close to each other such that they are pairwise redundant; in other words, whenever device u is active, device v can be asleep and vice versa. Hence, if D is a dominating set, then all other devices $V \backslash D$ can be asleep to conserve energy.

14.6.7 Vertex-Cover Problem

A vertex cover (sometimes node cover) of a graph is a set of vertices that includes at least one endpoint of every edge of the graph. The problem of finding a minimum vertex cover is a classical optimization problem. In its decision version, vertex-cover problem was one of Karp's 21 NP-complete problems.

Formally, a vertex cover V' of an undirected graph $G = (V, E)$ is a subset V' of V such that $(u, v) \in E \Rightarrow u \in V'$ or $v \in V'$, i.e., from the set of vertices V' every edge has atleast one endpoint in the vertex cover V'. Such a set is said to *cover* the edges of G. A typical example is shown in Fig. 14.7.

Vertex-cover optimization serves as a model for many real-world problems. For example, a city police is interested to install closed circuit TVs to cover all its streets, such that if a camera is installed at a junction of some streets (node), it will cover all streets connecting to this junction (due to 360 °C view angle of the camera!). To solve this problem, we need to select the nodes/junctions such that all the streets (edges) are covered. This problem solution is solving the vertex-cover problem.

14.6.8 Independent-Set Problem

For a graph $G = (V, E)$, a set of nodes $I \subseteq V$ is an *independent set* if no two nodes $u, v \in E$ are adjacent in the set I. Hence, for an edge $(u, v) \in E$, for $u \in I$, there is $v \notin I$. Such a graph G is interpreted as a *conflict* graph: an edge $(u, v) \in E$ indicates that the activities of u and v conflict with each other, but in set I there is no conflict.

As an example, if G is a wireless network, an edge (u, v) may indicate that the radio transmission of device u interferes with device v. In such a setting, an independent set I is a conflict-free set of activities: all devices in I can be active simultaneously. Usually, we are interested in finding large independent sets.

An independent set I is maximal if it cannot be extended, that is, $I \cup \{v\}$ is not an independent set for any $v \in V \backslash I$. In a centralized setting, a maximal independent set is easy to find by using a greedy algorithm, but it is a difficult problem from the perspective of distributed local algorithms. Finding a maximum independent set is a classical NP-hard optimization problem [21].

14.6.9 Graph Coloring Problem

The problem of *k-coloring* of a graph $G = (V, E)$ is an assignment of one of k distinct colors to each vertex $v \in V$ in the graph so that no two adjacent vertices are given the same color. The *chromatic number* of a graph is the smallest integer k, such that the graph can be k-colored.

The graph coloring problems can model a collection of scheduling tasks, such as examination scheduling, class scheduling, register allocation in a translated assembly language program during compilation, etc. Graph coloring is also related to other combinatorial problems, e.g., finding the maximum independent set in a graph. The problem of coloring a graph is NP-hard, even when it is restricted to graph of small chromatic number $k = 3$.

14.7 Solving SAT Problems

Given a language L, a verifier V is an algorithm that accepts a pair $\langle x, y\rangle$, where x is input and y is a witness.[6] The verifier (algorithm) has the following properties: (1) The algorithm always halts, (2) If $x \in L$ then there is a witness y such that the

---

[6] Also called *certificate*.

algorithm accepts $\langle x, y\rangle$. If $x \notin L$ then for all witnesses y, the algorithm rejects $\langle x, y\rangle$. Hence, the language of verifier is,

$$L_V = \{\langle x, y\rangle : x \in L, \text{ the } y \text{ is witness and } V(x, y) = 1\}. \tag{14.8}$$

The verier algorithm V is a Turing machine with input string, which is a pair (x, y).

Theorem 14.5 $L \in \mathsf{NP} \Leftrightarrow$ *if there exists a polynomial-time Turing machine V (a verifier), such that:*

$$L = \{x \mid \exists y \text{ (witness) } |y| = poly(|x|) \text{ and } V(x, y) \text{ accepts}\}.$$

Proof (1) If $L = \{x : \exists y\ |y| = poly(|x|)$ and $V(x, y)$ accepts$\}$, then $L \in NP$ because we can guess y and then run V.

(2) If $L \in \mathsf{NP}$ then $L = \{x : \exists y\ |y| = poly(|x|)$ and $V(x, y)$ accepts$\}$.

Let N be a non-deterministic poly-time TM that decides L and define $V(x, y)$ to accept if y is an accepting computation history of N on x. □

At present, all known algorithms for NP-complete problems require time that is *superpolynomial* of the size of input $|w| = n$, it is not known whether there exist any faster algorithms. Since there is no proven existence of deterministic polynomial algorithms for NP problems, some heuristic techniques are commonly adopted for such problems. The following techniques, which results in substantially faster algorithms, are often applied to solve computational problems that are in class NP:

- *Approximation*: Instead of searching for an optimal solution, search is carried out for a solution that is at most a factor from an optimal one.
- *Randomization*: Use randomness to get a faster average running time, even letting the algorithm to fail with some small probability [18].
- *Restriction*: By restricting the structure of the input (e.g., to planar graphs rather than non-planar), faster algorithms are usually possible.
- *Parameterization*: It is possible to obtain faster algorithms if certain parameters of the input are fixed [4].
- *Heuristic*: An algorithm that works “reasonably well” in many cases, but for which there is no proof that it is both always fast and always produces a good result [7].

One example of a heuristic algorithm is a *suboptimal* $O(n \log n)$ greedy coloring algorithm used for graph coloring during the register allocation phase of some compilers—a technique called graph-coloring global register allocation. Each vertex is a variable, edges are drawn between variables that are being used at the same time, and colors indicate the register assigned to each variable. Because most RISC (Reduced Instruction Set Computing) machines have a fairly large number of general-purpose registers, even a heuristic approach is effective for this application.

14.8 Counting Problems

The algorithms that count a number of alternate accepting paths of nondeterministic polynomial-time Turing machines (NTM) and discover their distinctive computational behavior were first studied by Valiant [22]. These algorithms belong to the complexity class #P—often viewed as counting analog of NP, and contains the problems such as #SAT, where objective is to compute the number of satisfying assignments of Boolean formula. The functions counting the certificates of NP-hard problems are often #P-hard, and hence are very hard to compute. It has been shown that the whole polynomial hierarchy can be reduced to #P. We call these algorithms as functions because instead of returning True/False, they return the count of number of paths of computation that leads to acceptance.

The list of functions exhibiting this "hard-to-count, easy-to-decode" behavior has been expanding. Such counting functions arise naturally in a variety of fields. Examples include the *permanent*[7] of an integer matrix, number of independent sets, cliques or vertex covers of a graph or the number of connected subgraphs in a network, number of spanning trees of a graph, or the number of matching of a graph [3].

It is possible to apply reductions between the counting functions. The proof of hardness of a counting problem #P typically involves showing that whole polynomial hierarchy can be reduced to problems in #P. Two types of reductions are common, (i) Cook and (ii) Karp.

Definition 14.7 The *Cook reduction* from function f to g means f can be computed in polynomial time by a deterministic TM with output (transducer) that uses oracle calls to g. □

Definition 14.8 The *Karp reduction* from f to g is a special case of polynomial time many-to-one reduction, with the additional property that the value of f on an instance x equals exactly to the value of g on an instance $h(x)$, which can be constructed in polynomila time, i.e., $f(x) = g(h(x))$. □

One of the standard ways to define counting classes, including the fundamental counting cass #P is by means of counting functions applied on the paths of appropriate TMs.

---

[7] The permanent of a square matrix is a function of the matrix similar to the determinant. The permanent is a polynomial in the entries of the matrix. E.g., the permanent of an $n \times n$ matrix $A = (a_{i,j})$ is defined as

$$\text{perm}(A) = \sum_{\sigma \in S_n} \prod_{i=1}^{n} a_i, \sigma(i).$$

The S_n is symmetric group, over all the permutations of number $1, 2, ..., n$. The sum extends to all the elements of the symmetric group. For example, $perm \begin{pmatrix} a & b \\ c & d \end{pmatrix} = ad + bc$.

Counting accepting paths

The obvious approach to define the complexity class #P, and the probelms in that, is through NTMs, where function value is given by the number of accepting computation paths, representing different solutions of corresponding NP problems:

$$\#\mathsf{P} = \{acc_M : \Sigma^* \to \mathbb{N} \mid M \text{ is a } NTM\}, \tag{14.9}$$

where $acc_M(x)$ is number of accepting paths of M on input x.

Counting "gap" between accepting and rejecting paths

This class is called TotP (for total number of computation paths for NTM). The definition subtracts "1" from the number of computation in order to allow for functions in the class to take zero values as well:

$$\mathsf{TotP} = \{tot_M : \Sigma^* \to \mathbb{N} \mid M \text{ is a } NTM\}, \tag{14.10}$$

where $tot_M(x) = \#(\text{all computation paths of } M \text{ on input } x) - 1$.

Table 14.1 provides a listing of some counting problems and their definitions.

14.9 Summary

A problem is in NP-complete if it is in NP and every problem in NP can be reduced into this problem.

A Boolean expression u in CNF (Conjunctive Normal Form), and output is True, if there is an assignment that satisfies u, else it is False. This expression is called SAT problem. For this, the Complexity in P is unknown, while in NP is Yes. Thus,

$$SAT = \{\langle\phi\rangle : \phi \text{ is satisfiable Boolean formula}\}.$$

The Cook–Levin theorem links the complexity of SAT problem to complexity of all the problems in NP. The SAT is NP-complete (NPC) problem. The Hamiltonian path problem and subset sum problems are NPC.

It can be proved using the Cook–Levin theorem that SAT is NP-Complete.

There are over 3000 known NP-Complete problems. If there is a polynomial solution to one of them, then all the NP-complete (NPC) problems will have polynomial solution.

Some of the popular NPC problems are: Knapsack problem, Traveling salesman problem (TSP), Hamiltonian path problem, subset-sum problem, etc.

All the NPC problems carry much significance as they have number of important applications, for example solving the problem of power distribution network in a

Table 14.1 Definitions of some counting problems

Problem	Definition
$\#SAT$	Given a formula ϕ in conjunctive normal form (CNF), count the number of satisfying assignments of ϕ
$\#2SAT$	Given a formula in CNF, where every clause contains two literals, count the number of satisfying assignments of ϕ
$\#DNF$	Given a formula ϕ in DNF (disjunctive normal form), count the satisfying assignments of ϕ
$\#HORNSAT$	Given a formula ϕ in CNF, where every clause contains at most one positive literal, count the satisfying assignments of ϕ
$\#NFA$	Given the encoding of an NFA and 1^m, count the number of words of length m accepted by M, i.e., $\|L(M) \cap \Sigma^m\|$
$\#PM$	Given the graph G, count the number of perfect matchings of G
$\#IS$	Given the graph G, count the number of independent sets of G
$\#BIS$	Given a bipartite graph G, count the number of independent sets of G
$(0, 1)$-$PERMANENT$	Given an $(n \times n)$ matrix A with entries $A_{ij} \in \{0, 1\}$, compute the permanent of A, i.e., $perm(A) = \sigma_{\sigma \in S_n} \prod_{i=1}^{n} a_i, \sigma(i)$

VLSI (very largescale integration) is nothing but solving TSP, which is NPC. Hence, there are abundant research efforts being put to find out efficient/near-polynomial solutions to these problems.

The NPC is subset of NP-hard problems, the latter are the hardest known class of problems. The NPC problems when solved using NTM provide polynomial complexity. For example, for Hamiltonian path problem (NPC), a NTM returns True if there is a path in the graph that connects all the vertices, without any loop. But, how many such paths exist, is an important problem, and it is called *counting* problem, represented by #P.

The counting problems are applied for SAT, called $\#SAT$, $\#PM$ (number of perfect matchings in a graph), and similar to this are many variants, some of them are defined in Table 14.1. Before such paths can be counted, reduction can be carried out, either through *Cook* reduction or *Karp* reduction.

Self Review Questions

1. Why the SAT problem, which is NP-*Complete* in time, is linear in space?
2. How the class NP can be defined using TM?
3. How the class NP can be defined formally?
4. How the decision version of TSP is different from its optimization version?
5. How the P-complete is different from NP-complete?
6. What is Cook–Levin theorem?
7. Give names of any two NP-hard problems.
8. What is condition for P = NP?
9. If $A \leq_P B$, and $B \in$ NP, then what is class of problem A?
10. If $A \leq_P B \leq_P C$, and $A \in$ NP, then what is class of C?
11. What is counting problem?
12. Define #P, $\#SAT$, and $\#2SAT$.
13. Why there is no problem such as #NP?
14. Is SAT more hard or $\#SAT$?

Exercises

A. Concepts based problems

Note: The $*$ marked exercises are provided with solutions at the end of this book.

1. Show the relations between various complexity classes, P, NP, NP-complete, and NP-hard using set theory graphs, when P = NP.
2. Define an undirected version of Hamiltonian path problem, given that G is an undirected graph, and G has a Hamiltonian path:

$$UHAMPATH = \{\langle G \rangle\} \tag{14.11}$$

   Prove that $UHAMPATH$ is NP-complete.
3. Give logical description of algorithms that compute the following:

   a. $\#2SAT$
   b. $\#SAT$
   c. $\#DNF$

4. Give an algorithm that solves 2SAT in polynomial time.

B. Analysis-based Problems

5. Is it possible that like the concept of NP-complete, there exists a concept of P-complete? Justify your answer for yes or no?

6. From the relations of complexity classes shown in Fig. 14.6a, it is clear that $\mathsf{P} \subseteq \mathsf{NP}$. How we justify the same in:

   a. Fig. 13.4 (Sect. 13.10.1), and
   b. Fig. 14.2?

7. Compute the permanent of matrix: $perm \begin{pmatrix} a & b & c \\ d & e & f \\ g & h & i \end{pmatrix}$
8. Consider the following problem: $UNSAT = \{\varphi$ a formula in $CNF \mid \varphi$ is not satisfiable$\}$. Show that $\overline{UNSAT} = SAT$, and, since SAT is in NP, the $UNSAT$ is in *co*-NP.

C. Proof-based Problems

9. Show that SAT is NP-Complete, without using the proof given in this chapter,
10. A *clique* in an undirected graph $G = (V, E)$ is its subgraph G' such that any two nodes of the subgraph are connected. A k-clique (or k-CLIQUE) is subgraph where every node is connected with k-nodes. Show that the following holds for k-clique:

    a. $3\ CLIQUE \in P$
    b. If $|V| = n$, then $\lfloor n/2 \rfloor\ CLIQUE \in NP$.

11. Prove that CLIQUE is NP-complete.
12. Prove that TSP (traveling salesman problem) is NP-complete.
13. Prove the following statement: $SAT \in \mathsf{P}$ *if and only if* $\mathsf{P} = \mathsf{NP}$.

D. Multiple choice Questions

14. The problems 2-SAT and 3-SAT are in the following category:

    (A) 2-SAT in P and 3-SAT is in NP-complete.
    (B) both are in P.
    (C) both are in NP-complete.
    (D) None of these.

15. * If A be a problem in class NP, then which one of the following is TRUE?

    (A) A may be undecidable.
    (B) If A is in NP-hard, then it is NP-complete.
    (C) No polynomial time algorithm exists for A.
    (D) If A is in P then $\mathsf{P} = \mathsf{NP}$.

16. Let A_1, A_2, A_3, A_4 be the four problems, with following conditions: A_1 is in NP-complete, $A_3 \leq_P A_1$ and $A_1 \leq_P A_2$. Also, A_3 and A_2 are not known to be in NP. Which of the following is true?

    (A) A_3 is NP-hard.
    (B) A_3 is NP-complete.

(C) A_2 is NP-complete.
(D) A_2 is NP-hard.

E. Advanced Knowledge Assessment Problems

17. Given a new computational problem, demonstrate that it is NP-complete by reducing a known NP-complete problem to it. Explain the reduction and the reasoning behind your choice of the problem to reduce from.
18. Investigate the complexity of the Boolean Satisfiability Problem (SAT) under various restrictions, such as $3SAT$, $kSAT$ (where each clause has exactly k literals), or Planar SAT (where variables and clauses are restricted to a planar graph). Determine the NP-completeness status of these variants.
19. Compare and contrast the complexity of the Hamiltonian Circuit Problem and the Traveling Salesman Problem. Prove that one is NP-complete by reducing it from the other.
20. Investigate the relationship between parallel computing models like NC and NP-completeness. Explore whether there are problems that are NC-equivalent but not known to be in P.

References

1. Agrawal M, Kayal N, Saxena N (2004) PRIMES is in P. Ann Math 2004:781–93
2. Atserias A, Müller M (2020) Automating resolution is NP-hard. J ACM (JACM) 67(5):1–17
3. Bakali E, Chalki A, Göbel A, Pagourtzis A, Zachos S (2022) Guest column: a panorama of counting problems the decision version of which is in P^3. ACM SIGACT News 53(3):46–68
4. Blažej V, Choudhary P, Knop D, Křišťan JM, Suchý O, Valla T (2023) Polynomial kernels for tracking shortest paths. Inf Process Lett 179:106315
5. Chowdhary KR (2015) Fundamentals of discrete mathematical structures. PHI Learning Pvt. Ltd., Chapter 5, pp 84–106
6. Chowdhary KR (2020) First order predicate logic. In: Fundamentals of artificial intelligence. Springer, New Delhi. https://doi.org/10.1007/978-81-322-3972-7_3
7. Chowdhary KR (2020) Heuristic search. In: Fundamentals of artificial intelligence. Springer India, New Delhi. https://doi.org/10.1007/978-81-322-3972-7_9
8. Chowdhary KR (2020) Automated planning. In: Fundamentals of artificial intelligence. Springer, New Delhi. https://doi.org/10.1007/978-81-322-3972-7_15
9. Cook SA (1971) The complexity of theorem-proving procedures. In: Proceedings of the third annual ACM symposium on theory of computing, pp 151–158
10. Garey MR, Johnson DS, Stockmeyer L (1974) Some simplified NP-complete problems. In: Proceedings of the sixth annual ACM symposium on theory of computing, pp 47–63
11. Garey MR, Johnson DS (1979) Computers and interactability: a guide to the theory of NP-completeness. Freeman, San Francisco, LA
12. Ibarra OH, Kim CE (1975) Fast approximation algorithms for the knapsack and sum of subset problems. J ACM (JACM) 22(4):463–468
13. Koiliaris K, Xu C (2019) Faster pseudopolynomial time algorithms for subset sum. ACM Trans Algorithms (TALG) 15(3):1–20

14. Levin L (1973) Universal search problems. Probl Inf Transm (in Russian) 9(3):115–116. Translated into English by Trakhtenbrot BA (1984) A survey of Russian approaches to perebor (brute-force searches) algorithms. Ann Hist Comput 6(4):384–400. https://doi.org/10.1109/MAHC.1984.10036. S2CID 950581. Translation see appendix
15. Loui MC (1996) Computational complexity theory. ACM Comput Surv (CSUR) 28(1):47–49
16. Malik S, Zhang L (2009) Boolean satisfiability from theoretical hardness to practical success. Commun ACM 52(8):76–82
17. http://orion.towson.edu/~mzimand/athcomp/List_of_NP-complete_problems.pdf. Accessed 15 Mar 2023
18. Purohit R (2012) Program verification through random testing, PhD thesis: Software Verification through Model Driven Approach, pp 47–61. JNV University, Jodhpur, India
19. Sahni S (1974) Computationally related problems. SIAM J Comput 3(4):262–279
20. Sahni S, Gonzalez T (1976) P-complete approximation problems. J ACM 23(3):555–565. https://doi.org/10.1145/321958.321975
21. Suomela J (2013) Survey of local algorithms. ACM Comput Surv (CSUR) 45(2):1–40
22. Valiant LG (1979) The complexity of computing the permanent. Theor Comput Sci 8(2):189–201

Chapter 15
Solutions

Solutions of Chapter 1

11 For the sets $|A| = m$, and $|B| = n$, find the maximum number of functions that can be defined from A to B.

Ans. A function is a mapping $f : A \rightarrow B$, and an instance of that is (a_i, b_j). Total such pairs are $|m| \times |n|$, and the number of functions that can be constructed are equal to number of subsets of the $\{a_i, b_j\}$. This is equal to $2^{|m|\times|n|}$, which is the maximum number of functions which can be defined. These functions also include the partial functions.

12 Which of the following functions are computable?

1. A function, which inverts every bit of an infinite stream of bits.
2. $S = \{x \mid x \notin x\}$
3. $f(x) = \begin{cases} x, & \text{if } odd(x); \\ x = x - 1, & \text{otherwise.} \end{cases}$
4. $f : x \rightarrow succ(x)$.

Ans. 3, 4 are computable.

28 If x is composite integer, then show that there is at least one prime p that divides x, and $p \leq \sqrt{x}$.

Proof Let p be a prime dividing x. If p^2 divides x then $p \leq \sqrt{x}$. If p^2 does not divide x then there is a second prime q such that pq divides x. Changing the notation, if necessary, we may suppose that $p < q$. Then $p^2 < pq < x$, and so $p < \sqrt{x}$. Thus, we conclude that $p \leq \sqrt{x}$.

K. R. Chowdhary, *Theory of Computation*,
https://doi.org/10.1007/978-981-97-6234-7_15

34 If $f : A \rightarrow B$, and $g : B \rightarrow C$, then prove the following:

1. If f and g are both *bijections* then $g \circ f$ is also *bijections*.
2. If f and g have inverses then $(g \circ f)^{-1} = f^{-1} \circ g^{-1}$.
3. If $f \circ g$ is *injection* then g is *injection*.
4. If $f \circ g$ is *surjection* then f is *surjection*.

Ans: (a) The f and g both bijections, show that they are both injections and surjections. Therefore, the functions $g \circ f$ as well as $f \circ g$ are bijections.
(b) A function is invertible if it is bijective. Since f and g both have inverses, so they are bijective. Hence, inverse of their composition is equal to composition of their inverses.
(c) $f \circ g$ is injective only when f is injective and g is injective.
(d) $f \circ g$ is surjective means that every $c \in C$ is image of some $a \in A$. Let us imagine that f is not surjective. Then there exists some $b \in B$ that is not an image of any element of A. But, in that case, g $(B \rightarrow C)$ is not a function as per functions definition, because every element of B has no image in C. So, the latter is not possible. So f is a surjection.

36 Show that the set of rational numbers is countable.

Proof For the apparent solution, we may try to list all rational numbers like this:

$$\begin{array}{ccccc} \frac{1}{1} & \frac{1}{2} & \frac{1}{3} & \frac{1}{4} & \dots \infty \\ \frac{2}{1} & \frac{2}{2} & \frac{2}{3} & \frac{2}{4} & \dots \infty \\ \frac{3}{1} & \frac{3}{2} & \frac{3}{3} & \frac{3}{4} & \dots \infty \\ \dots & \dots & \dots & \dots & \dots \infty \end{array}$$

We note that there are many infinite series; hence, the above set appears uncountable! However, with little intuition, we can sequence the above rational numbers as shown in Fig. 15.1.

Thus, we are able to produce an exhaustive list of rational numbers, whose elements can be easily paired with the elements of set $\mathbb{N}$. This proves that rational numbers are regular set [1]. □

Solutions of Chapter 2

2 Describe in simple words the languages corresponding to each of the below given regular expressions.

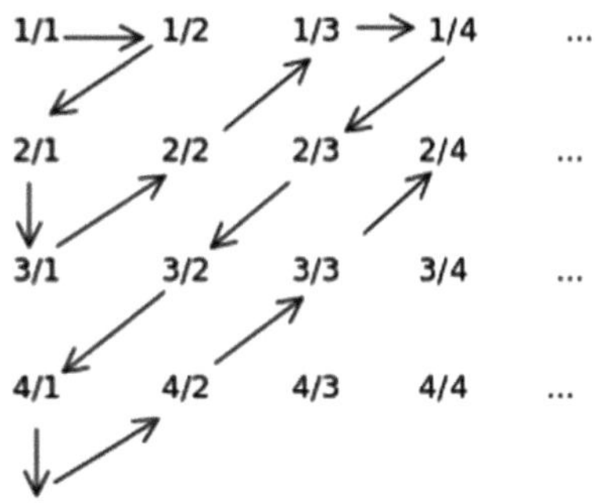

Fig. 15.1 An approach to exhaustingly list the rational numbers

(i) $(1+0)^*$
(ii) $(01)^*(10)^*$
(iii) $(0+1)^*(0+1)^+$
(iv) $((1+0)^2)^*(\varepsilon+1)^*$

Ans.

(i) $(1+0)^*$: All possible strings on 0 and 1. It is also equal to Σ^*.
(ii) $(01)^*(10)^*$: All strings on $\Sigma = \{0, 1\}$ of even length, including ε-string. The strings consists pairs of 01 and/or 10.
(iii) $(0+1)^*(0+1)^+$: Same as Σ^*, except that ε is not in the strings.
(iv) $((1+0)^2)^*(\varepsilon+1)^*$: All strings 00, 01, 10, 11, terminated with 1s, zero or more times.

9 Which of the following statements about regular expressions are True/False? Justify. (Note: R, S, T are regular expressions.)

1. $R(S+T) = RS+RT$: True
2. $(R+S)^* = (R^*S^*)^*$: False
3. $(R+S)^* = (R^*+S^*)$: False
4. $(RS+R)^*RS = (R+S)^*$: False
5. $(RS+R)^*R = R(SR+R)^*$: False
6. $S(RS+S)^*R = R+S(R+S)^*$: False
7. $(R+S)^*S = (R^*S)^*$: False

10 Consider the language Σ^*, where $\Sigma = \{a, b\}$. How many words this language has of length 2, of length 3, of length n?

Ans. 2^2, 2^3, 2^n, respectively.

19 Derive expressions for count of FA that can be constructed using following number of states: 3, 4, and 5. Thus, derive a general expression for count of finite automata, using n number of states. Note that there can be only one start state, and final states can be one or more, or may not be present.

Ans. We consider first FA of three states 0, 1, 2. Following is the table of possible arrangement of states:

Serial number	Start state	Final states	Non-final states
1.	0	1	2
2.	0	2	1
3.	0	1, 2	–
4.	0	–	1, 2
5.	1	0	2
6.	1	2	0
7.	1	0, 2	–
8.	1	–	0, 2
9.	2	0	1
10.	2	1	0
11.	2	0, 1	–
12.	2	–	0, 1

Similar way, if we list the configurations of states for $|Q| = 4$, we get total $(8 + 8 + 8 + 8 =)$ 32 different combinations of states, and for $|Q| = 5$ this figure is $16 \times 5 = 80$. Thus, for $|Q| = n$, by intuition, different combinations of possible states' set is of size $n \times 2^{(n-1)}$.

If size of alphabet $|\Sigma| = m$, and state set $|Q| = n$, then maximum number of different FAs that are possible, are: $n \times 2^{(n-1)} \times 2^{(n \times m)}$.

Connecting edges (transitions) to these states for alphabet Σ is straightforward: we need to have all possible transitions equal to $Q \times \Sigma$ for each FA, hence, it is left as an exercise.

24 Show that there cannot be a DFA of less than four states that can recognize the language,

$$\{w \in \{a, b\}^* \mid w \text{ contains even number of } a\text{'s and } b\text{'s}\}.$$

Ans. Even a's and even bs make a minimum length of string as four. Thus, there are a minimum of four transitions in the FA, and correspondingly, the states are also four.

29 Let A be the subset of binary strings of the language accepted by FA shown in Fig. 2.11. What is the size of set A if for every $w \in A$, its 1st, 4th, and 7th bits are 1?

(A) 2 (B) 4 (C) 5 (D) 7

Ans. We will follow an exhaustive approach here. Since bits S_1, S_4, S_7 are fixed as 1, our choice is for remaining 4 bits, $S_2S_3S_5S_6$, which can be in range 0000 to 1111. Thus, all possible strings with this restriction are:

1. 1001001
2. 1001011
3. 1001101
4. 1001111
5. 1011001
6. 1011011
7. 1011101
8. 1011111
9. 1101001
10. 1101011
11. 1101101
12. 1101111
13. 1111001
14. 1111011
15. 1111101
16. 1111111

Out of the above, strings S.no. 1, 2, 3, 4, 5, 9, 13 can be verified to be accepted by the FA shown in Fig. 2.11. Hence, correct choice of answer is D.

33 The DFA shown in Fig. 2.13 accepts the set of all strings over {0, 1} that,

(A) end with 00 (B) contain the substring 00.
(C) begin either with 0 or 1 (D) end with 0

Ans. All A, B, C, D are correct.

35 The regular expression 1^*1^* is equal to which of the following? (select one or more choices):

(A) $(1 + \varepsilon)^*$ (B) $\varepsilon 1^*$
(C) 1^* (D) $(11)^*$

Ans: 1^*1^* generates even as well as odd strings of 1, including the ε-string. The choice D is not possible, as it generates strings of even length only. The choice C generates all strings of 1s including ε-string. Similar is case with choice A and B. Hence, the correct choices are A, B, C.

Solutions of Chapter 3

1 Construct an NFA that accepts the strings based on the regular expression $(01 + 001 + 010)^*$.

Ans. The NFA is shown in Fig. 15.2.

5 For each of the following regular expressions draw the transition diagrams for corresponding NFAs.

a. $(0 + 1)^*01011(0 + 1)^*$
b. $(0 + 1)^*(011 + 0101)(0 + 1)^*$

Ans. The transition diagrams are shown in Fig. 15.3a and b, respectively.

7 Construct an NFA-ε for the language consisting of zero or more a's followed by zero or more b's followed by zero or more c's.

Ans. NFA is shown in Fig. 15.4.

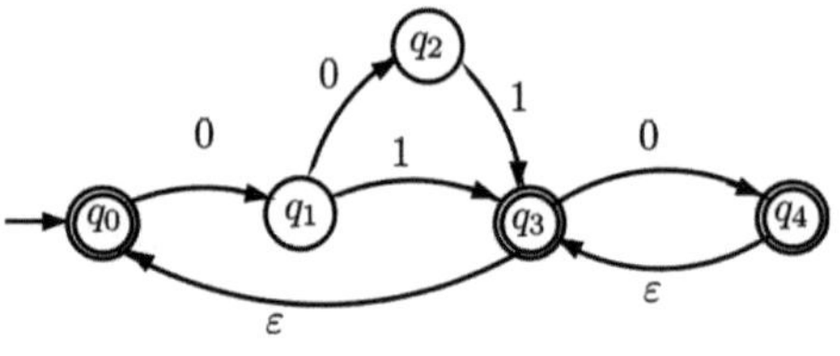

Fig. 15.2 Regular expression to NFA

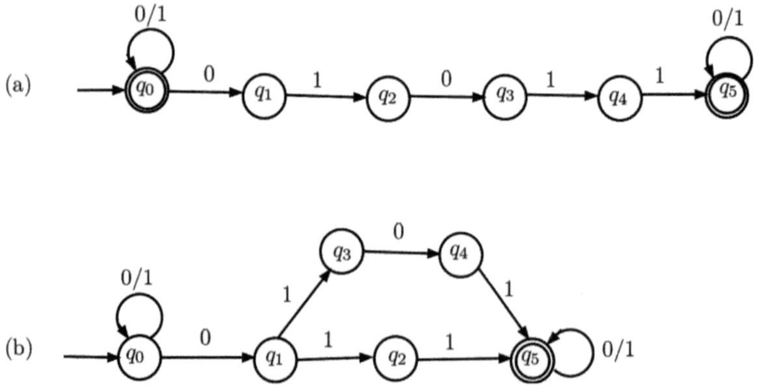

Fig. 15.3 Regular expression to NFA

Fig. 15.4 An NFA-ε

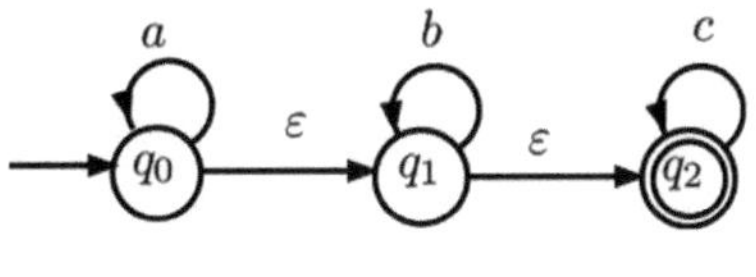

13 Consider an NFA having four states corresponding to regular expression: (01 + 011 + 0111)*. Obtain an equivalent DFA using subset construction method.

Ans. The NFA and equivalent DFA are shown in Figs. 15.5 and 15.6, respectively.

16 A DFA can be inverted by changing final states to non-final states and vice-versa. How you will invert an NFA?

Ans. There cannot be any standard Algorithm due to nondeterminism of an NFA.

19 Construct a Moore Machine which can count the number of occurrences of substring 111 in the input string. The input alphabet is $\Sigma = \{0, 1\}$.

We associate an output with each state in the Moore Machine as follows. Let us associate 1 to the state confirming the completion of substring 111 in the input (i.e., state q_3), and 0 to rest of all the states. The desired Moore Machine for this is shown in Fig. 15.7.

Fig. 15.5 An NFA-ε

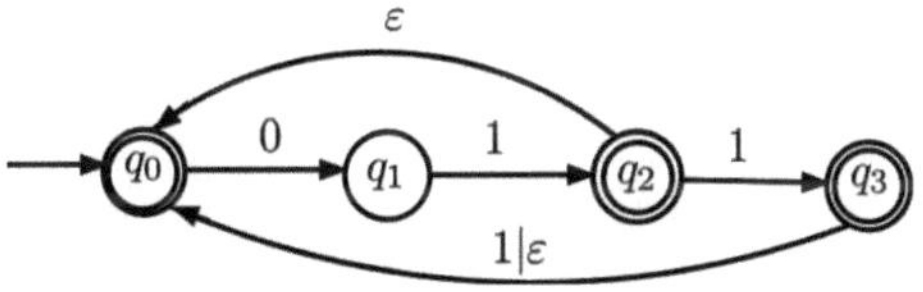

Fig. 15.6 Equivalent DFA of NFA-ε in Fig. 15.5

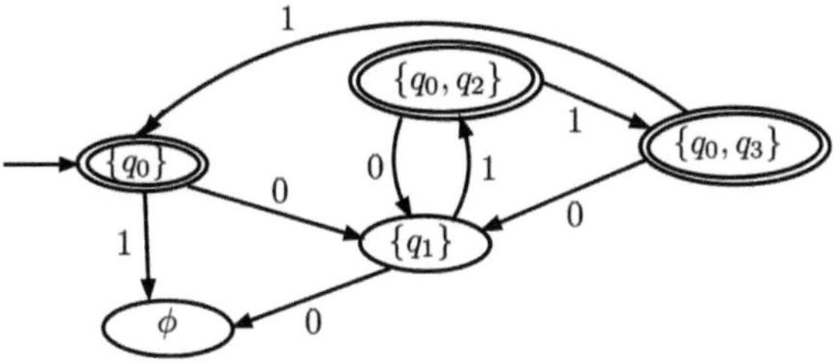

Fig. 15.7 Moore machine as "111" pattern counter

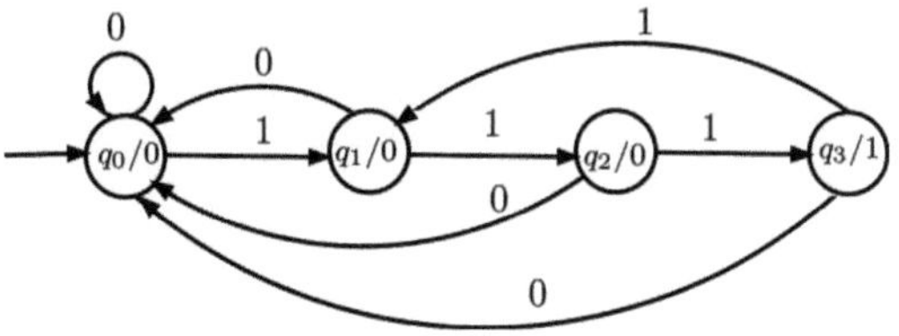

Table 15.1 Transition table for Fig. 15.7

Current state	Output $\lambda(q)$	Next state for input = 0	Next state for input = 1
q_0	0	q_0	q_1
q_1	0	q_0	q_2
q_2	0	q_0	q_3
q_3	1	q_0	q_1

The Transition Table 15.1 for the output and for mapping function λ are determined from transition diagram. Considering an input $w = 01110111$, the output sequence is 000010001. Two appearance of 1s in the output shows two occurrences of substring 111 in input x.

26 Consider the NFA M shown in Fig. 3.28 (shown here as Fig. 15.8). Let the language accepted by M be L. Let L' be the language accepted by an NFA M' obtained by interchanging the accepting and non-accepting states of M. Which of the following statements is true?

(A) $L' = \{0, 1\}^* - L$ (B) $L' = \{0, 1\}^*$ (C) $L' \subseteq L$ (D) $L_1 = L$

Ans. We note that the automaton in Fig. 15.9 is obtained by complementing all the states in automaton shown in Fig. 15.8. The original FA accepts all the strings of $\{0, 1\}$. Its complement will also accept strings over $(0 + 1)^*$. Hence, correct answer is B.

27 Map the NFA (P to S), shown in Fig. 15.10, with the regular expressions (A to D):

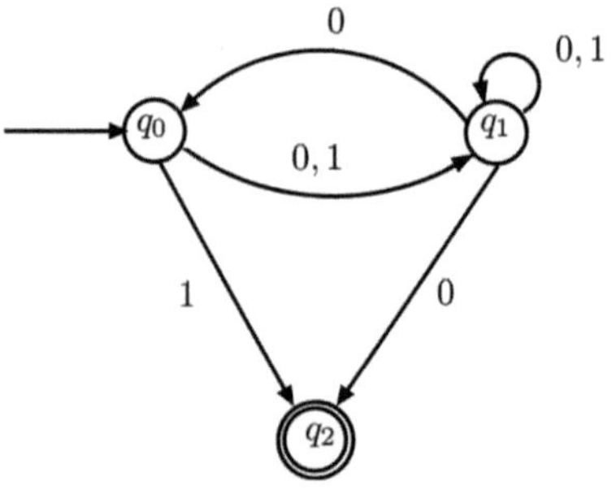

Fig. 15.8 NFA M

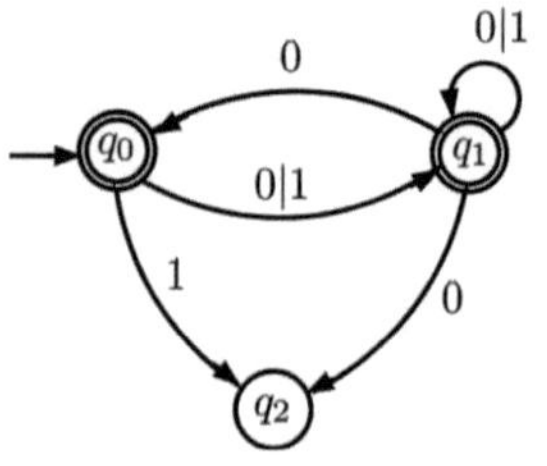

Fig. 15.9 Complement of NFA M in Fig. 15.8

A. $\varepsilon + 0(01^*1 + 00)^*01^*$
B. $\varepsilon + 0(10^*1 + 10)^*10^*$
C. $\varepsilon + 0(10^*1 + 00)^*0$
D. $\varepsilon + 0(10^*1 + 10)^*1$

Ans. The mappings are as follows:
$A = P, r_A = 001^*101^*$
$B = S, r_B = 010^*110^*$
$C = Q, r_C = 10^*10$
$D = R, r_D = 010^*110^*$

Solutions of Chapter 4

3 What is difference between NFA homomorphism and DFA homomorphism?

Ans. Every DFA is an NFA also. In DFA for each $a \in Sigma$, there is one transition from current state. A non-minimized DFA may have a corresponding DFA /NFA homomorphism. But, for a minimum DFA its homomorphism is a DFA only.An NFA's homomorphism is an NFA as well as DFA.

7 Find the minimal automaton by merging the states of the automaton shown in Fig. 15.11a.

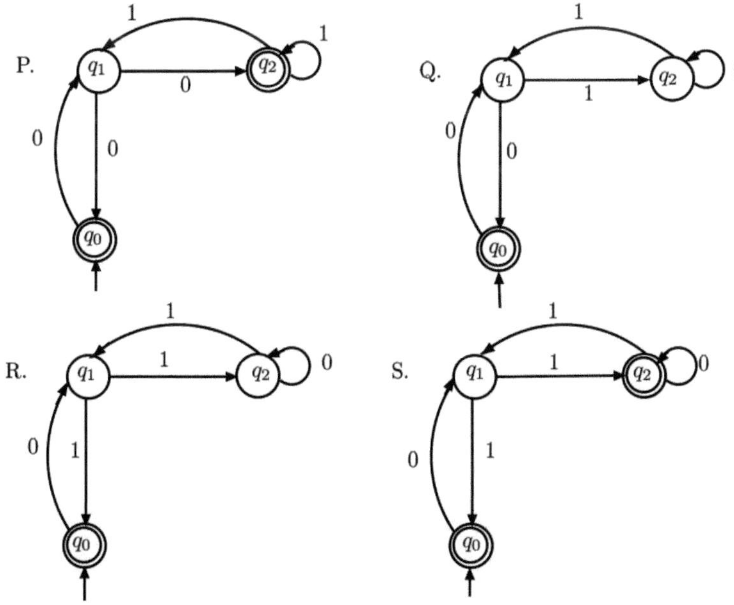

Fig. 15.10 NFAs

Ans. *Case I.* The merging of states in Fig. 15.11a corresponds to a homomorphism $h : M_1 \mapsto M_2$ as $h(q_0) = A$, $h(q_1) = h(q_3) = B$, $h(q_2) = h(q_4) = C$. The homomorphism obtained is a DFA-homomorphsim because initial and final automaton are DFAs.

The reduced automaton for M_1 (Fig. 15.11a) is shown as M_2 in Fig. 15.11b. *Case II.* In the automaton of Fig. 15.11a, we could have an alternate merging scenario: q_1, q_2 are merged, q_3, q_4 are merged, which would result to automaton shown in Fig. 15.12, i.e., $h(q_0) = A'$, $h(q_1) = h(q_2) = B'$, and $h(q_3) = h(q_4) = C'$, which is an NFA-*homomorphism.*

12 Is it possible that you get two different homomorphisms for a given DFA? Justify for Yes/No.

Ans. Yes. If the given DFA is not minimum, one homomorphism is NFA and other is minimum DFA. However, if the DFA is minimum, there is only one homomorphism, which is the current DFA itself.

13 Write a C program for minimization of 5-state DFA, with $\Sigma = \{a, b\}$.

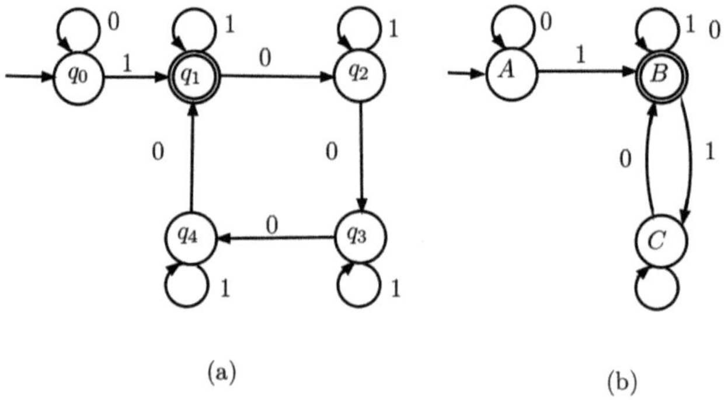

Fig. 15.11 **a** Finite automaton M_1, **b** Reduced automaton M_2

Fig. 15.12 Alternate reduced automaton for Fig. 15.11a

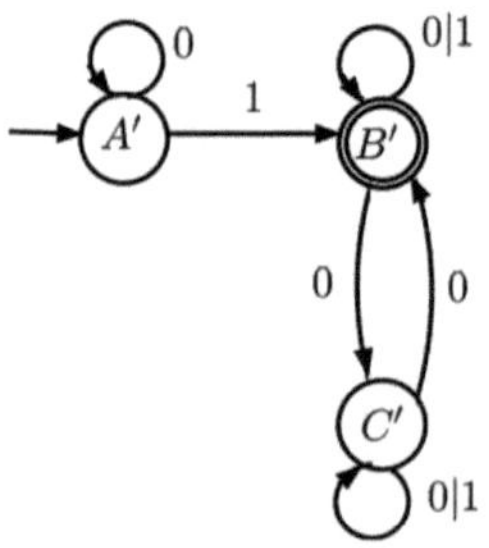

Ans. *Solution Hint.* Assume that DFA is given as a table or 2-dimensional array, where first column is of states 0–4, second column is of transitions from each state for input a, and third column is of transitions for each state for input b. Using this table as input, the C programs can fill the table of table-filling algorithm, which is nothing but the transition table of minimized DFA.

15 For the alphabet $\Sigma = \{a, b\}$, find out the equivalent classes for $L = \Sigma^* a \Sigma$.

Ans. $\Sigma^* aa$, $\Sigma^* ab$, $\Sigma^* ba + a$, $\Sigma^* bb + b + \varepsilon$.

17 How will you determine if a given DFA is minimum?

Ans. Construct a table using Table-filling Algorithm, if no entry (cell) of this table remains empty, then the DFA is already minimum, else it is not.

18 Find out the minimum DFA using table-filling (partition) method for the DFA shown in Fig. 15.13.

Ans. Following the relation of state distinguishability (Lemma 4.2 in Sect. 4.6) and Table-filling Algorithm (4.3 in Sect. 4.10), we partition the state space, and find out that every state in the Automaton shown in Fig. 15.13 is distinguishable with every other state, as shown in Fig. 15.14. This shows that automaton in Fig. 15.13 is minimum and cannot be further reduced. □

20 Find the equivalent reduced automaton for the one shown in Fig. 15.15.

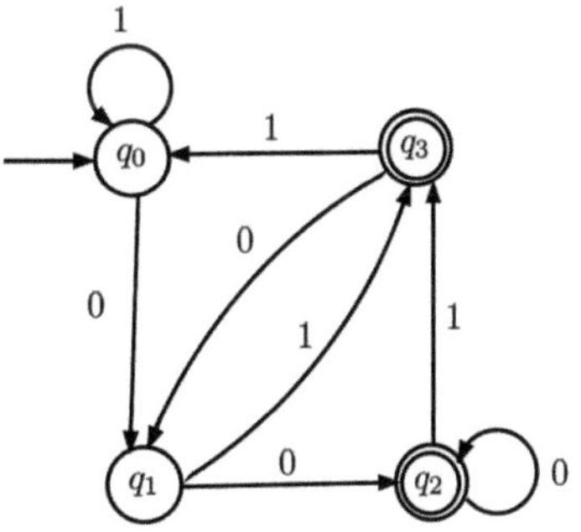

Fig. 15.13 An automaton M for $\Sigma^* 0 \Sigma$

q_1	×		
q_2	×	×	
q_3	×	×	×
	q_0	q_1	q_2

Fig. 15.14 Partition table for DFA in Fig. 15.13

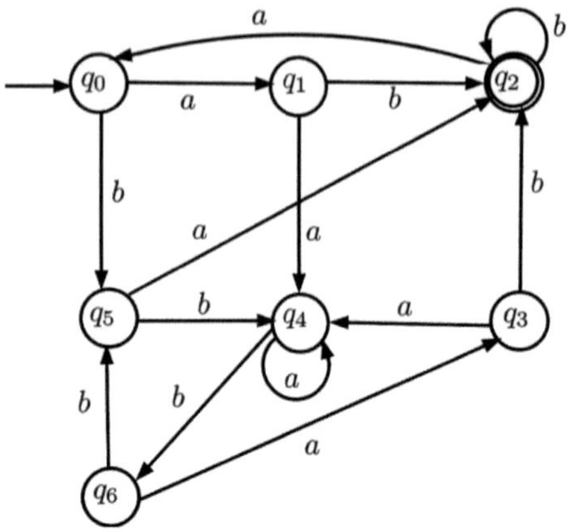

Fig. 15.15 Deterministic finite automaton

Ans. The initial partition for Fig. 15.15 is $(F, Q - F) = (\{q_2\}, \{q_0, q_1, q_3, q_4, q_5, q_6\})$. We split[1] these blocks according to Eq. 4.6 (Sect. 4.7) as follows:

1. Splitting (refinement of equivalence classes) $\{q_0, q_1, q_3, q_4, q_5, q_6\}$ with respect to (q_2, b) results to $\{q_1, q_6\}$, $\{q_0, q_3, q_4, q_5, q_6\}$.
2. Splitting $\{q_0, q_3, q_4, q_5\}$ with respect to $(\{q_1, q_6\}, a)$ results to $\{q_0, q_3\}$ and $\{q_4, q_5\}$.
3. Splitting $\{q_4, q_5\}$ with respect to (q_2, a) results to $\{q_4\}$ and $\{q_5\}$.

   The resulting minimized DFA is shown in Fig. 15.16.

24 What conclusions you draw from the following implications? Are these implications valid?

$\delta^*(p, u) \in F \Rightarrow \delta^*(q, u) \in F$, therefore,
$\delta^*(p, v) \notin F \Rightarrow \delta^*(q, v) \notin F$

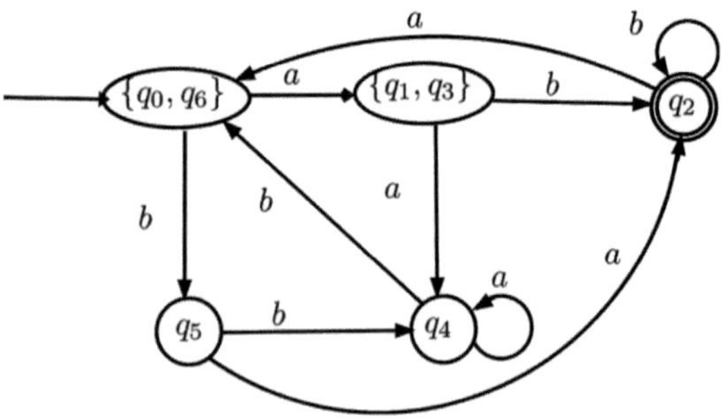

Fig. 15.16 Minimized finite automaton of Fig. 15.15

[1] The splitting process is refinement of the partition, see Algorithm 4.2 in Sect. 4.9.1.

Ans. The implication: $\delta^*(p, u) \in F \Rightarrow \delta^*(q, u) \in F$ is for any arbitrary string u. This means the states p and q are indistinguishable with each other for whatever is the input provided to these states. Hence, if any other string v is not accepted at p, it will not be accepted at q also. Accordingly, the statement:

$$\delta^*(p, u) \in F \Rightarrow \delta^*(q, u) \in F \models \delta^*(p, v) \notin F \Rightarrow \delta^*(q, v) \notin F.$$

is valid statement.

25 Show using concept of finite index of regular languages:

1. $\{a^n b^n \mid n \geq 0\}$ is not regular language,
2. $\{w \mid w \in (a + b)^* b(a + b)\}$ is regular language.

Ans. For $k \geq 0$, consider the set $\{\varepsilon, a, aa, ..., a^k\}$ of strings made of k number of a's. It is easy to see that there are distinguishable strings $x_0 \dots x_k$ with respect to language $\{a^n b^n \mid n \geq 0\}$. Note that, the value to k can be arbitrarily large, hence there cannot be DFA for $\{a^n b^n \mid n \geq 0\}$, and hence this is not a regular language.

On the other hand, for the language $L = \{w \mid w \in (a + b)^* b(a + b)\}$, the strings $x = abba$ and $y = ba$ are not distinguishable with respect to L. This is because for $z = a$, $xz = abbaa \notin L$, and also $yz = baa \notin L$. Thus, L is regular.

26 The minimized version of the FA shown in Fig. 15.17 has following number of states:

(A) 1 (B) 2 (C) 3 (D) 4

Ans. Since the state q_3 is unreachable, it can be removed. No further state can be removed. So, the answer is C.

Solutions of Chapter 5

6 Find the regular expression for the automaton shown in Fig. 15.18 using *state removal method*.

Fig. 15.17 FA with $\Sigma = \{a, b\}$

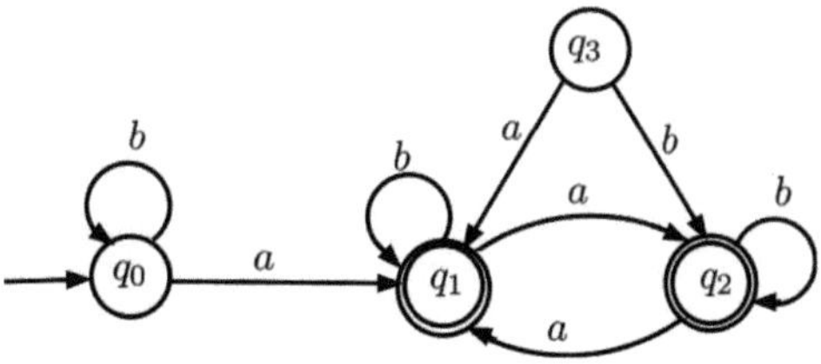

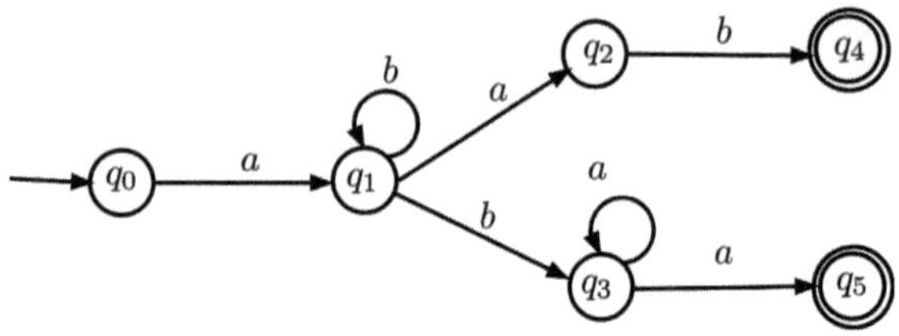

Fig. 15.18 A finite automaton

The reduction steps discussed above make use of rules discussed in Lemma 5.1. The resultant regular expression is $ab^*(ab + ba^*a)$.

The reduction steps for the finite automation, to obtain the regular expression, after conversion of FA into GNFA, are shown in Fig. 15.19.

7 Find the regular expression for DFA shown in Fig. 15.20, using Brozozowski's method.

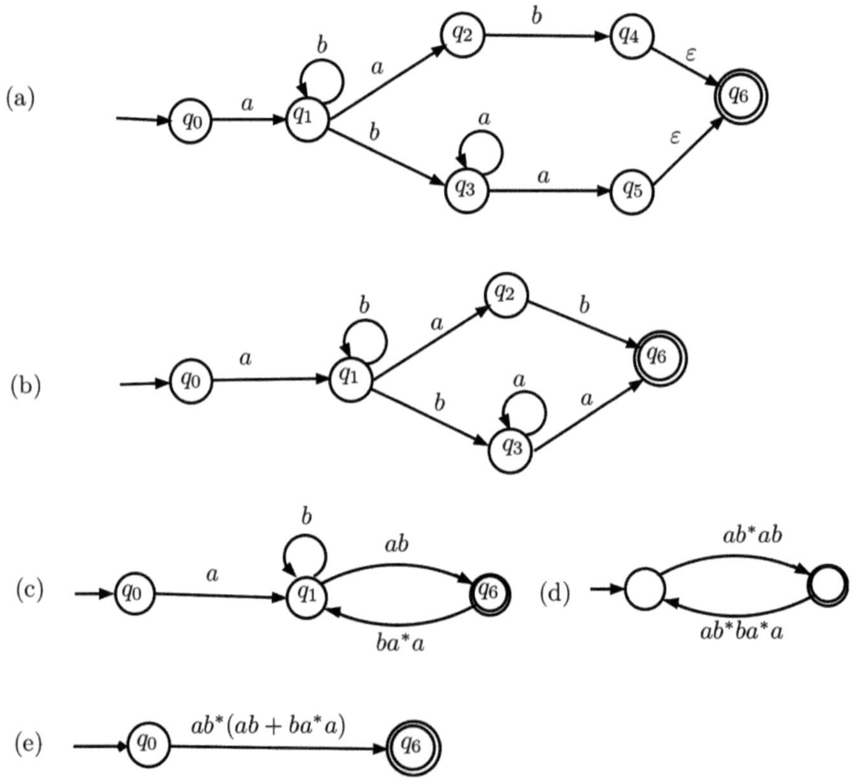

Fig. 15.19 Steps (a)–(e) are for construction of regular expression from a finite automaton

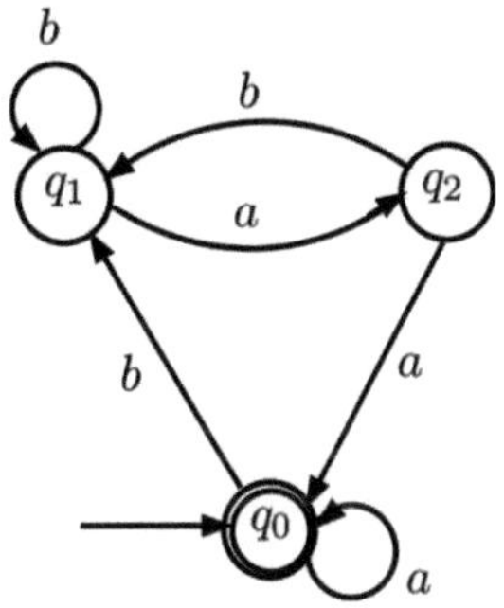

Fig. 15.20 DFA

We create the following set of equations to find the regular expression.

$$
\begin{aligned}
q_0 &= aq_0 + bq_1 + \varepsilon \\
q_1 &= bq_1 + aq_2 \\
q_2 &= aq_0 + bq_1
\end{aligned}
$$

Now, solve the equations:

$$
\begin{aligned}
q_1 &= bq_1 + a(aq_0 + bq_1) \\
&= bq_1 + aaq_0 + abq_1 \\
&= (b + ab)q_1 + aaq_0 \\
&= (b + ab)^*aaq_0.
\end{aligned}
$$

$$
\begin{aligned}
q_0 &= aq_0 + bq_1 + \varepsilon \\
&= aq_0 + (bq_1 + \varepsilon) \\
&= a^*(bq_1 + \varepsilon) \\
&= a^*bq_1 + a^* \\
&= a^*b(b + ab)^*aaq_0 + a^* \\
&= (a^*b(b + ab)^*aa)^*a^*.
\end{aligned}
$$

Hence, $(a^*b(b + ab)^*aa)^*a^*$ is regular expression for the FA shown in Fig. 15.20, and verify that it works.

16 For $L = \{a, b\}^*abb\{a, b\}^*$, find out the $\approx_L$–classes.

Ans. Following are the different $\approx_L$ classes for L:

$$[\varepsilon]_L, [a]_L, [ab]_L, \text{ and } [abb]_L.$$

This is because:

$$\begin{aligned}[\varepsilon]_L =&[b]_L,\\ [a]_L =&[aa]_L = [aba]_L,\\ [ab]_L =&[abab] = [abaab], \text{ and}\\ [abb]_L =&[abba]_L = [abbb]_L.\end{aligned}$$

From the above $\approx_L$ classes, we obtain *canonical automaton* for L, shown in Fig. 15.21.

17 Given the language L denoted by regular expression $((a^*b + \varepsilon)a)^*$, compute the regular expression that denotes $\overline{L}$.

Ans. (Hint: Translate this expression into an NFA, then convert into a DFA, then complement the DFA, and then obtain regular expression using GNFA).

24 Using Pumping Lemma show that $L = \{a^{n^2} \mid n \text{ is integer, and } n \geq 1\}$ is not regular.

Ans. For n to be integer and $n \geq 1$, L consists all the strings whose length is perfect square. That is, $L = \{a^1, a^2, a^9, ...\}$. To begin with, we assume that L is regular. Let there be a string $w \in L$, where $w = xyz = a^{n^2}$, where n is integer in pumping lemma, indicating the number of states. Using the pumping lemma a^{n^2} can be written as xyz, where $1 \leq |y| \leq n$, and $xy^kz \in L$ for $k \geq 0$. Now, we try to prepare as a strategy that $|xy^kz|$ is not a perfect square.

For this we want to represent a^{n^2} in the form of xy^kz, and try to show that when original expression is represented as xy^kz it fails to satisfy the criteria of a^{n^2}.

Since $|y|$ must be greater or equal to 1, let $|y| = m \geq 1$. Since we have assumed that w is perfect square, let there is some integer n, for which $|w| = n^2 = |xz| + |y| = (n^2 - m) + m$.

Now, let $k = 2$. Hence, xy^2z should be in L. Therefore,

$$|xy^2z| = |xz| + |y^2| = (n^2 - m) + 2m = n^2 + m.$$

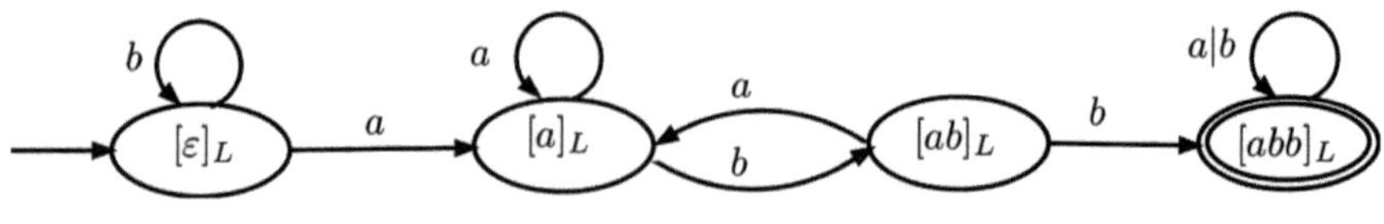

Fig. 15.21 Automaton for regular expression $\{a, b\}^*abb\{a, b\}^*$

This m can be at the most n, which happens when all the states are in y. Hence, $n^2 + m \leq n^2 + n$. Therefore,

$$n^2 < |xy^2z| \leq n^2 + n < n^2 + 2n + 1 = (n + 1)^2.$$

This indicates that the length of xy^2z lies between n^2 and $(n + 1)^2$, hence, the length is not a perfect square. This shows that $xy^2z \notin L$. Since this is in contradiction to our assumption, the L is not regular.

27 Show that language of binary numbers divisible by 3 is regular.

Ans. Consider the language of binary numbers, which are divisible by 3. We want to show that it is regular. Given w, the empty string, 00 (or 11), 01 and 10 are distinguished extensions resulting in three classes corresponding to numbers that give remainders 0, 1, and 2 when it is divided by 3. We note that there is no distinguishing extension any more (i.e., no other string exists, which produces some other remainders). Hence, the minimal automaton accepting this binary language would have three states corresponding to these three equivalence classes.

29 For $\Sigma = \{a, b\}$ and given that $a^n b^n$ is not regular, show that a language $L = \{w \mid w \text{ has equal number of} a\text{'s and} b\text{'s}\}$, is not regular.

Ans. According to its definition, the language L is $\{\varepsilon, ab, ba, aabb, bbaa, abba, abab, baba, baab, aaabbb, ...\}$. We note that the language defined by the expression $a^n b^n$ is a subset of language $\mathscr{L}(a^*b^*)$ as well as subset of L. Therefore,

$$\mathscr{L}(a^n b^n) \subseteq \mathscr{L}(a^*b^*) \cup L. \tag{15.1}$$

The expression a^*b^* constructs the strings as follows: any number of a's (including nulls) followed by any number of b's (including nulls). Language L consists of strings with equal number of a's and b's in any order. Therefore, the strings common in these are only the set of strings in which there is n number of a's followed by n number of b's, where $n \in \mathbb{N}$. This is because strings in L that are not in a^*b^* are outside the intersection set. This set consists of strings that are ordered on $a...ab...b$ restricted to equal numbers of as and bs, due to the set L. The intersection set is nothing but $a^n b^n$ only. Hence,

$$\mathscr{L}(a^n b^n) = \mathscr{L}(a^*b^*) \cap L. \tag{15.2}$$

If L is regular, the intersection of language $\mathscr{L}(a^*b^*)$ and L, i.e. $\mathscr{L}(a^n b^n)$ should be regular as per Theorem 5.6 (Sect. 5.3.2). Since $a^n b^n$ is not a regular expression, hence out of a^*b^* and L, out of them or both are not regular. Since a^*b^* is regular, therefore only possibility is that L is not regular. This proves that L is not regular.

32 Are the class of regular languages closed under the operation of infinite union? Prove or disapprove it.

Ans. From Theorem 5.5 (Sect. 5.3.1), the infinite union of regular languages will be recognized by corresponding infinite of automata, which in turn will have infinite number of states. Due to infinite number of states, the latter is not a FA, and hence the language is not regular.

35 Show that the set $R = \{a^n b^n \mid n \geq 0\}$ is non-regular using MN-theorem.

Ans. The Myhill-Nerode theorem can be used to show whether R is regular or non-regular by determining number of $\approx_R$-equivalence classes. If $k \neq m$, then $a^k \not\approx_R a^m$, since $a^k b^k \in R$ but $a^m b^k \notin R$. Therefore, there are infinitely many $\approx_R$-classes, at least one for each a^k, $k \geq 0$. By the Myhill-Nerode theorem, R is not regular.

37 Show that $L = \{ww \mid w \in \{0, 1\}^*\}$ is not regular}.

Ans. Take any distinct pair $i, j \geq 0$. We take $0^i 1 \approx_L 0^j 1 (i \neq j)$. We note that $0^i 1 0^i 1 \in L$, but $0^j 1 0^i 1 \notin L$. Hence, $\approx_L$ has an infinite index. Thus L is not regular as per Myhill-Nerode theorem part-

Solutions of Chapter 6

3 Is the following grammar regular? Justify. If it is regular, find out its regular expression.

$A \rightarrow B0$
$B \rightarrow A1$
$C \rightarrow 0.$

Ans. Yes. Regular expression is: 0(10)* as well (10)*0

4 Construct the grammar for balancing brackets, i.e., for (), (())), ()()(), ...

Ans. $S \rightarrow (S)S \mid \varepsilon$

17 Find out the context-free grammars for each of the languages given below:

(a) $L_1 = \{a^{3i} b^i \mid i \geq 1\}$

All the sentences have three number of a's and that follows with one b. Accordingly, the grammar productions are:

$$S \rightarrow a^3 Sb \mid \varepsilon$$

(b) $L_2 = \{a^i b^j \mid i \geq j \geq 0\}$

The number of a's that precedes to b's in every sentence are greater than number of b's.

$$S \rightarrow AaSb \mid \varepsilon$$

$$A \rightarrow aA \mid \varepsilon$$

(c) $L_3 = \{w \mid w \in \{a, b\}^* \wedge \#a(w) = 2\#b(w)\}$

There can be three ways for this: $w \in \{(aab) \cup (aba) \cup (baa)\}^*$. Therefore, the productions are:

$$S \rightarrow aabS \mid \varepsilon$$
$$S \rightarrow abaS \mid \varepsilon$$
$$S \rightarrow baaS \mid \varepsilon$$

20 Derive various arithmetic expressions $a * (a + a)a - a$ using CFG $G = (V, \Sigma, S, P)$, where,

$V = \{E\}$, (E stands for expression)
$\Sigma = \{+, -, *, /, (,), a\}$
$S = E$, and

P is:

1. $E \rightarrow E + E$
2. $E \rightarrow E - E$
3. $E \rightarrow E/E$
4. $E \rightarrow E * E$
5. $E \rightarrow (E)$
6. $E \rightarrow a$.

Having above grammar, we can obtain various derivation of expression using this grammar.

A string of symbols in the form of expression "$a * (a + a)/a - a$," can be generated by using CFG G as given in Table 15.2.

First, the table shows that original expression "$a * (a + a)/a - a$" is a syntactically correct expression because we have been able to generate it using the production rules given in the grammar. Second, it shows associativity between various symbols and the order of their computation. For example, in step 1, the value of first E (in $E - E$) is computed as multiplication of $E * E$. This indicates the precedence of multiplication over the subtraction. In the move from step 3 to 4, it shows that the first symbol E in step 3 is computed as E/E.

Table 15.2 Derivation steps for expression $a * (a + a)/a - a$

Steps:				
1	E	$\Rightarrow$	$E - E$	By rule 2
2		$\Rightarrow$	$E * E - E$	By rule 4
3		$\Rightarrow$	$a * E - E$	By rule 6
4		$\Rightarrow$	$a * E/E - E$	By rule 3
5		$\Rightarrow$	$a * (E)/E - E$	By rule 5
6		$\Rightarrow$	$a * (E + E)/E - E$	By rule 1
7		$\Rightarrow$	$a * (a + E)/E - E$	By rule 6
8		$\Rightarrow$	$a * (a + a)/E - E$	By rule 6
9		$\Rightarrow$	$a * (a + a)/a - E$	By rule 6
10		$\Rightarrow$	$a * (a + a)/a - a$	By rule 6

Applying other rules of grammar G are able to generate the given expression, and many other expressions corresponding to four arithmetic operators and parentheses.

29 Show that following CFGs are ambiguous.

1. $S \rightarrow abb \mid bb \mid aS \mid a$
2. $S \rightarrow SaSaS \mid b$

Ans. The part (a) can be parsed in two ways:

$S \Rightarrow abb$ and $S \Rightarrow aS \Rightarrow abb$, which shows two parses for the string abb.

The strings in part (b) can also be parsed in two ways. Consider following parses:
$S \Rightarrow SaSaS \Rightarrow Sa$ **SaSaS** $aS \Rightarrow babababab$
and $S \Rightarrow SaSaS \Rightarrow$ **SaSaS** $aSaS \Rightarrow babababab$
The bold-faced characters show the position of substitution. Accordingly, the grammars are ambiguous.

35 Given the regular languages A, B, a *Cartesian product language* is defined as: $A \times B = \{xy \mid x \in A$ and $y \in B$, and $|x| = |y|\}$. Show $A \times B$ is context-free language.

Ans. Since regular languages A and B have grammars $A \rightarrow aC|a$, and $B \rightarrow bD|b$, the product $A \times B$ will have grammar like $E \rightarrow \alpha$, where $\alpha = aCbD$, which is a production in CFG. Every string in $A \times B$ will be generated using productions like this.

36 Show that the language $L = \{w \in \{a, b\}^* \mid \#a(w) = \#b(w)\}$ is an unambiguous context-free language. Here $\#a(w)$ stands for number of a's in w.

Ans. The strings $\#a(w) = \#b(w)$ can be recognized by PDA, which pushes a's and pops them when b's are encountered. Hence, the language is CFL.

37 If L_1 and L_2 are context-free languages, then show that $L_1 \cup L_2$, L_1L_2, and L_1^* are also context-free languages.

Ans. See Theorem 6.2 in Sect. 6.5

39 Show that CFLs are not closed on intersection.

Ans. For the purpose of intersection of context-free languages, consider two CFLs and corresponding CFGs as follows:

$L_1 = \{a^n b^n c^m \mid m, n \geq 0\}$, and Grammar $G_1 : S \rightarrow AC, A \rightarrow aAb \mid \varepsilon, C \rightarrow cC \mid \varepsilon$.

$L_2 = \{a^n b^m c^m \mid m, n \geq 0\}$, and Grammar $G_2 : S \rightarrow AB, A \rightarrow aA \mid \varepsilon, B \rightarrow bBc \mid \varepsilon$.

The intersection of L_1, L_2 is,

$$L_1 \cap L_2 = \{a^n b^n c^n \mid n \geq 0\}.$$

which is not a CFL.

Since one example is sufficient to contradict the assumption of CFLs as closed on intersection, it is enough to show that they are not closed under intersection.

40 Consider following productions of a precedence grammar:

$$\begin{aligned}
S &\rightarrow A \\
A &\rightarrow A + B \mid B \\
B &\rightarrow B * C \mid C \\
C &\rightarrow (A) \mid \varepsilon
\end{aligned} \tag{15.3}$$

Find out the complete matrix of precedence relations for this grammar

Table 15.3 Nonterminals and their LTC/RTC

Nonterminal	LTC	RTC
C	(ε	) ε
B	($\varepsilon *$	) $\varepsilon *$
A	($\varepsilon * +$	) $\varepsilon * +$
S	($\varepsilon * +$	) $\varepsilon * +$

Table 15.4 Precedence relations of grammar in Eq. 15.3

	(	ε	$*$	$+$	)
)			$\gtrdot$	$\gtrdot$	$\gtrdot$
ε			$\gtrdot$	$\gtrdot$	$\gtrdot$
$*$	$\lessdot$	$\lessdot$	$\gtrdot$	$\gtrdot$	$\gtrdot$
$+$	$\lessdot$	$\lessdot$	$\lessdot$	$\gtrdot$	$\gtrdot$
(	$\lessdot$	$\lessdot$	$\lessdot$	$\lessdot$	$\doteq$

Ans. In this grammar, $\Sigma = \{+, *, (,), \varepsilon\}$ and $V = \{S, A, B, C\}$. If $C \Rightarrow z$, then the leftmost terminal of z must be "(" or "ε". If $B \Rightarrow z$, the leftmost terminal of z must be "(", "ε", or "$*$". If we continue in the same manner, we arrive at Table 15.3, which shows the possible left and rightmost terminal characters (LTC and RTC) of the derivations of each nonterminal.

Let us find out now the precedence relations. The Production $C \rightarrow (A)$ is in the category of rule (1)[2], because this production is like $A \rightarrow xaBby$, which say that precedence operator is "$\doteq$", hence the relation ($\doteq$) holds in grammar G.

Because $A \rightarrow A + B$ and $*$ is RTC of derivation of A, hence the precedence relations $* \gtrdot +$ holds as per rule (2).

Because, $C \rightarrow (A)$ and "(" is a LTC of derivation of A, the precedence relation ($\lessdot$) holds true as per rule (3).

Table 15.4 shows the complete matrix of precedence relations.

42 Match the entries (a–d) to those one right side (1–4):

Ans. The argument "a.", i.e., number of formal parameters agrees to the actual parameters in a function, has representation as $\{a^n b^m c^n d^m \mid n \geq 1, m \geq 1\}$.

The argument "b.", i.e., arithmetic expressions with matched pairs of parenthesis, has representation as $X \rightarrow XbX \mid XcX \mid dXf \mid g$.

The argument "c.", i.e., Palindromes, has representation as $S \rightarrow bSb \mid cSc \mid \varepsilon$.

[2] See Sect. 6.10 for precedence rules.

Finally, the argument "d.", identifiers are declared before their use, has representation as $L_2 = \{wcw \mid w \in (a \mid b)^*\}$.

Hence, the correct matching is D.

44 If P is language p^*q^* and $Q = \{p^nq^n \mid n \geq 0\}$, which of the following is always regular language?

(A) $P - Q$ (B) $P \cap Q$ (C) $\Sigma^* - Q$ (D) $\Sigma^* - P$

Ans. Since P is regular, its complement $\Sigma^* - P$ is also regular. Hence, the answer is D.

We note that P is regular language, and Q is CFL.
A is false because it consists all the strings which are not p^nq^n.
B is false because intersection of regular language and CFL is not regular.
C is false because complement of CFL is not regular.

Solutions of Chapter 7

1 Remove the useless symbols and productions from the following grammar:

$$S \rightarrow aS \mid A \mid B,$$
$$A \rightarrow a, \quad C \rightarrow bb, \quad B \rightarrow aBa.$$

Ans. Let us first identify the productions that can lead to terminal string. These are,

$$A \rightarrow a, \quad C \rightarrow bb, \quad S \rightarrow A.$$

Since variable B does not lead to terminal string, it can be removed along with its production. Similarly, the variable C and its production can be removed. The simplified grammar is,

$$S \rightarrow aS \mid A, A \rightarrow a.$$

□

2 Convert the CFG $G = (V, \Sigma, S, P)$, with productions given below, into Chomsky normal form.

$S \rightarrow aA \mid bB$
$A \rightarrow aaA \mid b$
$B \rightarrow bbB \mid a$
$\Sigma = \{a, b\}$
$V = \{S, A, B\}$
S is start symbol.

Ans. First considering productions of the form $A \to a$, these are two only. Hence,

$$P' = \{A \to b, B \to a\}.$$

Next consider the productions of the form $A \to X_1 X_2 \ldots X_n$, where $X_i \in (\Sigma \cup V)$ and $n \geq 2$. These are,

$$\begin{aligned}&S \to aA\\&S \to bB\\&A \to aaA\\&B \to bbB\end{aligned}$$

Convert these to the form $A \to C_1 C_2 \ldots C_n$. Hence, the above are transformed as,

$$\begin{aligned}&S \to C_1 A,\ C_1 \to a\\&S \to C_2 B,\ C_2 \to b\\&A \to C_3 C_4 A,\ C_3 \to a,\ C_4 \to a\\&B \to C_5 C_6 B,\ C_5 \to b,\ C_6 \to b\end{aligned}$$

Note that, to make it efficient, we could have written $A \to C_1 C_1 A$, where C_1 is already defined. Therefore, instead of C_5, C_6 we could have used C_2, as the production $C_2 \to b$ is already defined.

Add these productions to P'.

Now, pickup the productions of the form $A \to C_1 C_2 \ldots C_n$ in and convert them to the form $A \to C_1 D_1$, $D_1 \to C_2 D_2$, etc. These productions in P' are:

$$\begin{aligned}&A \to C_3 C_4 A\\&B \to C_5 C_6 B\end{aligned}$$

Convert these productions into the form given below, and add them into P'.

$$\begin{aligned}&A \to C_3 D_1\\&D_1 \to C_4 A\\&B \to C_5 D_2\\&D_2 \to C_6 B\end{aligned}$$

Add rest of productions also into P'. The final P' and V' are,

$$\begin{aligned}P' = \{&A \to b,\ B \to a,\ S \to C_1 A,\ C_1 \to a,\ S \to C_2 B,\\&C_2 \to b,\ A \to C_3 D_1,\ D_1 \to C_4 A,\ C_3 \to a,\\&C_4 \to a,\ B \to C_5 D_2,\ D_2 \to C_6 B,\ C_5 \to b,\ C_6 \to b\}.\end{aligned}$$

$$V = \{S, A, B, C_1, C_2, C_3, C_4, C_5, C_6, D_1, D_2\}.$$

A CNF grammar, equal to the original given grammar is, therefore

$G' = (V', \Sigma, S, P')$.

6 Given the CFG $G = (V, \Sigma, S, P)$, where $V = \{A_1, A_2, A_3\}$, $\Sigma = \{a, b\}$, $S = A_1$, and P is:

$A_1 \rightarrow A_2A_3$
$A_2 \rightarrow A_3A_1|b$
$A_3 \rightarrow A_1A_2|a.$

Convert this CFG into Greibach Normal form.

Step 1: *Ordering rule*: We note that the order rule is violated only in the rule, $A_3 \rightarrow A_1A_2$, hence only this production, is to be changed, as follows:

$$A_3 \rightarrow A_3A_1A_3A_2 \mid a,$$

where in $A_3 \rightarrow A_1A_2$, the A is substituted by A_2A_3, and A_2 is substituted by A_3A_1, hence $A_3A_1A_3A_2$.

Step 2: Eliminate left recursion in $A_3 \rightarrow A_3A_1A_3A_2$:

$$\begin{aligned} A_3 &\rightarrow aA_4 \mid a, \\ A_4 &\rightarrow A_1A_3A_2A_4 \mid A_1A_3A_2. \end{aligned}$$

Now, the A_4 rule violates the order-rule.

Step 3: Violation in A_4 is corrected as follows:

$$\begin{aligned} A_4 &\rightarrow A_1A_3A_2 \\ &\Rightarrow A_2A_3A_3A_2 \\ &\Rightarrow A_3A_1A_3A_3A_2 \mid bA_3A_3A_2 \\ &\rightarrow aA_4A_1A_3A_3A_2 \mid bA_3A_3A_2 \mid a \end{aligned}$$

The final rule set is GNF, as given below:

$$\begin{aligned} A_1 &\rightarrow bA_3 \mid aA_1A_3 \\ A_2 &\rightarrow aA_1 \mid b \\ A_3 &\rightarrow aA_4 \mid a \\ A_4 &\rightarrow aA_4A_1A_3A_3A_2 \mid bA_3A_3A_2 \mid a. \end{aligned}$$

6 Write an algorithm for construction of dependency graph shown in Fig. 7.1 (Sect. 7.2.3).

Ans. With original grammar $G = (V, \Sigma, S, P)$ and new grammar $G' = (V', \Sigma, S, P')$, we initialize $V' = \phi$, $P' = \phi$. As a next step, we update the V' and P' as,

$$P' = P' \cup \{A_i \rightarrow ab\},$$
$$V' = V' \cup \{A_i\}.$$

An algorithm, which iteratively computes V' and P', is given as algorithm 15.1. The algorithm continues as long as there remain variables $A_j \in V$ having production like $A_j \rightarrow X_1 X_2 \dots X_n \in P$, where $X_i \in (\Sigma \cup V')$. These are added in V' and P', respectively, in every iteration.

Algorithm 15.1 Construction of an equivalent simplified grammar

$V' = \{A_i \mid A_i \rightarrow u, u \in \Sigma^*\}$
$V = V - \{A_i\}$
$P' = \{A_i \rightarrow u\}$
$P = P - \{A_i \rightarrow u\}$
while there exist $A_j \rightarrow X_1 X_2 \dots X_n \in P$, where $X_{(i=1,n)} \in (\Sigma \cup V')$ **do**
    $V' = V' \cup \{A_j\}$
    $P' = P' \cup \{A_j \rightarrow X_1 X_2 \dots X_n\}$
    $V = V - \{A_j\}$
    $P = P - \{A_j \rightarrow X_1 X_2 \dots X_n\}$
end while

The non-terminals and productions, which have not formed the part of *variable dependency graph*, get eliminated from the grammar G'. Since this grammar has fewer variables and rules (may be terminals also), the grammar is simpler. The eliminated variables are *useless variables*, and the eliminated productions are called *useless productions*.

22 Linear-time algorithm for CFG to find out all symbols that would appear in some sentential form.

Ans. Consider some symbol $X_i \in \Sigma$, for which we want to determine whether or not X_i appears in some sentential form $\alpha \in (V \cup \Sigma)^*$. For X_i to appear in some sentential form α, it suffices to know whether or not X_i appears in some variable[3]. Construct a graph with vertices $V \cup \{X_i\}$. If there is a production rule $A \rightarrow \alpha$, where α contains terminal, say, a, then add an edge $A \rightarrow a$; If there is a production rule $A \rightarrow \beta$, where β contains variable B, then add an edge $A \rightarrow B$. It is easy to check that a can appear in variable A if and only if there

[3] X_i is in a variable A if there is a production $A \rightarrow \alpha X_i \beta$.

is a path from A to a in the graph. If we proceed in similar manner, we shall reach to root of the tree, that is S. We note that both the construction and reachability test can be done in linear time, with respect to the number of symbols ($\Sigma \cup V$).

24 Give algorithm to decide the following: "Is $L(G)$ finite, for a given $CFG\ G$?

Ans. Convert G to Greibach normal form (without useless symbols), that is, all productions are of the form $A \rightarrow a\gamma$, where $\gamma \in V^*$. Build a directed graph with vertices V (i.e., variables), and add an edge $A \rightarrow B$ if B appears in γ. $L(G)$ is finite if and only if the graph does not contain cycles.

Solutions of Chapter 8

2 How the stack store is useful in recognition of CFLs? Give a general explanation.

Ans. The context-free languages have certain structure. For example, the corresponding grammar has a production $A \rightarrow bcA|a$, and let the input string be $bcbcbca$. The stack has initially, the start symbol A. Due to this grammar, the top symbol A is popped and bcA, with top symbol bc and A below these. The bc are popped, compared with input, and tape head is advanced. Next, A is replaced by bc. This process is replaced for the input substring $bcbcbc$. Next, the stack top A is popped, and replaced by a. Now, the top of stack matches with input a.

At this stage, input is read completely, and stack is also empty. Hence, input is recognized.

4 What are the conditions for a PDA to be a deterministic?

Ans. For a PDA,

$$M = (Q, \Sigma, \Gamma, \delta, q_0, F, Z_0) \tag{15.4}$$

to be deterministic, following conditions need to be fulfilled:

1. $|\delta(q, a, Z)| \leq 1$; i.e., the choice of next state is one state only, where $a \in \Sigma$, or $a = \varepsilon$, and $Z \in \Gamma$.
2. For all $a \in \Sigma$, if $\delta(q, a, Z)$ does not produce non-null move then $\delta(q, \varepsilon, Z) = \phi$. That is, there are moves for all $a \in \Sigma$, then ε-move does not exist. The latter is called $\delta(q, \varepsilon, Z) = \phi$.

14 Explain the significance of stack operations shown in Fig. 8.4 (Sect. 8.4.3).

Ans. Going deep in γ in Fig. 8.4, while still processing only x in the input, may mean transitions through number of states between times t_i and t_j shown in this figure. Though there is equal amount of advancing of read head, in both the cases, i.e., stack penetrates into γ vs not, but during the time we penetrate into γ, there are certain computations carried out. Whereas these computations do not occur when γ part of the string is not touched (see Eq. 8.13). Hence, if Eq. (8.13) holds true, it is not guaranteed that Eq. (8.12) will also hold true.

17 Construct a Pushdown automata that accepts the language:

$$\{a^i b^j c^k \mid i, j, k \geq 0 \text{ and } i = j, \text{ or } j = k\}.$$

Ans. (Hint: Think the solution as NPDA, which non-deterministically branches from start state after reading a to solve either $a^n b^n c^m$ or $a^n b^m c^m$, each having final state. If either of the sequence reaches to final state, the input is accepted.)

20 The following grammars generate the same language, however, they have many different characteristics. List these characteristics.

(1) $S \rightarrow aAc, \ A \rightarrow bAb, \ A \rightarrow b.$
(2) $S \rightarrow aAc, \ A \rightarrow Abb, \ A \rightarrow b.$

Ans. The first grammar generates all the strings $w = auc$, where $|u| \geq 3, u = b^{2n+1}$, and $n \geq 0$. We note that grammar (2) generates exactly the same strings. Since each grammar generates exactly one type of trees, hence these grammars are unambiguous. The grammar (1) is not LR(k) for any value of k, since given the partial string ab^m there is no information by which we can replace any b by A, hence the parsing must wait until the c has been read from the input. For example, consider the derivation

$$S \Leftarrow aAc \Leftarrow abAbc \Leftarrow abbbc = ab^3c$$

now, given the substring ab^3, a LR(k) parser, for $k = 1$, or 2 or any other value, cannot make out that it is 2nd b that is to be replaced by A. It is only when we see the letter c, we are able to say that it is 2nd b form left/right to be replaced by A. But, the grammar (2) is LR(0) and also a bounded context-free language. The sentential forms of grammars (1) and (2) are $\{ab^{2n+1}c\}$, $\{aAb^{2n}c\}$, respectively. For parsing, we must reduce the substring ab to aA, a substring Abb to A, and the substring aAc to S. Thus, the LR(k) is definitely a property of the grammar, and not of the language only. The distinction of grammar is important when syntax and semantics both are considered—the first is characteristic of grammar, while the latter is of the language.

23 Show that the grammar $G = (V, \Sigma, S, P)$ is not LL(k), where tuples are defined as follows:

$S \rightarrow A \mid B$
$A \rightarrow aAb \mid ab$
$B \rightarrow aBc \mid ac$

Ans. For every k, we can find leftmost derivation of the form,

$$S \Rightarrow^* S \Rightarrow A \Rightarrow^* a^k b^k$$

and

$$S \Rightarrow^* S \Rightarrow B \Rightarrow^* a^k c^k$$

where $a^k b^k : k = a^k c^k : k = a^k$, but $A \neq B$. Hence, the proof as per the Definition 8.9 (Sect. 8.10.1).

25 Let $G = (\{S\}, \{a, b\}, S, P)$ be a context-free grammar where the rule set P is: $S \rightarrow aSb \mid SS \mid \varepsilon$,

Which of the following statements is true?

(A) There exist $u, v \in L(G)$ such that $uv \notin L(G)$
(B) There exists a DPDA that accepts $L(G)$
(C) We can find a DFA that accepts $L(G)$
(D) G is not an ambiguous grammar

[Hint: Because *a*s and *b*s are always equal in every string, it can be recognized by a PDA. Answer is B]

Solutions of Chapter 9

23 Show that the function $inv(w)$ (inversion), where $w \in \{a, b\}^*$, is Turing computable.

(Hint: For input say, *ababb*, construct output as $XXXXXbbaba$, then move last symbol, i.e., "a" in place of last "X" and write "B" in place of last symbol; repeat this process till all the alphabet are shifted to left).

24a Construct a TM that recognizes a binary strings having equal number of 0's and 1's

On each pass to right, a 0 and a 1 are changed to X, then the head goes to the left most position of the string. We assume that left most symbol is B, i.e., machine configuration at begin is $Bq_0\alpha B$, where string α has equal number of 1's and 0's. The machine accepts α when the whole input has been converted to Xs.

The transition table below shows the transitions to accept the input.

State	0	1	X	B
q_0	(q_1, X, R)	(q_2, X, R)	(q_0, X, R)	(q_4, B, L)
q_1	$(q_1, 0, R)$	(q_3, X, L)	(q_1, X, R)	
q_2	(q_3, X, L)	$(q_2, 1, R)$	(q_2, X, R)	
q_3	$(q_3, 0, L)$	$(q_3, 1, L)$	(q_3, X, L)	(q_0, B, R)

The above transitions are also shown in the transition graph in Fig. 15.22.

24b Construct a TM for the language $\{ww^R \mid w \in \{0, 1\}^*\}$.

Naturally, the language strings are even palindromes. Fig. 15.23 shows the transition diagram for above Turing machine. The transition table can be easily constructed using this diagram. The grammar for this language is $S \to 0S0 \mid 1S1 \mid \varepsilon$.

The Fig. 15.24 is TM for odd Palindrome language, i.e., $\{w \mid w = u(0+1)u^R$, and $u \in \{0, 1\}^*\}$. The grammar for this language is $S \to 0S0 \mid 1S1 \mid 0 \mid 1$.

24c Constrict a TM to recognize the language $\{w\#w \mid w \in \{0, 1\}^*\}$.

The solution idea is simple – we mark every time the matching symbols pair 1-1 or 0-0, in two w's.

The Fig. 15.25 shows the transition diagram.

24d Construct a TM that multiplies two positive integers that are given in unary notation.

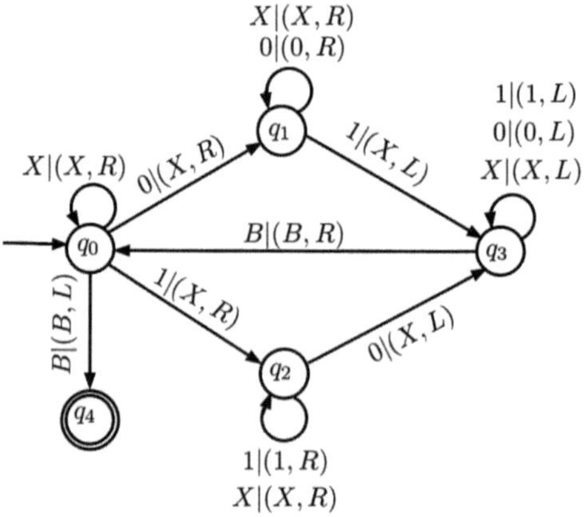

Fig. 15.22 TM for $L = \{w \mid w$ has equal number of 0's, and 1's

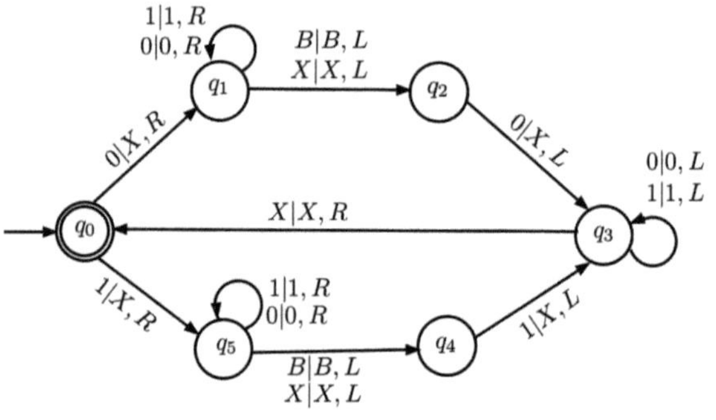

Fig. 15.23 TM for $L = \{ww^R \mid w \in \{0, 1\}^*\}$

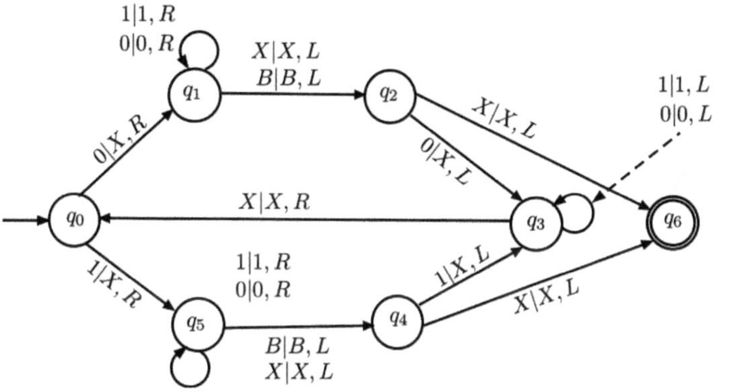

Fig. 15.24 TM for $L = \{w \mid w = w^R \in \{0, 1\}^*\}$, and w is an odd Palindrome

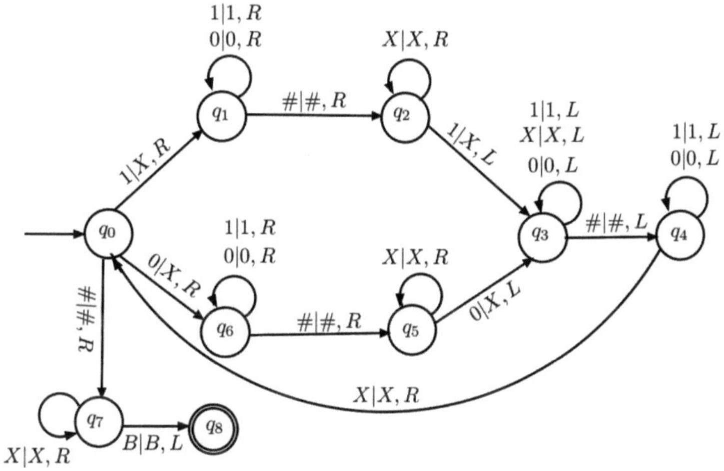

Fig. 15.25 TM for $L = \{w\#w \mid w \in \{0, 1\}^*\}$

Let the configuration on the tape before and after the solution in as shown in Fig. 15.26. Considering it as a basic TM model, let the numbers to be multiplied are x and y, and their product is xy. Assume that x and y are represented by their weights, i.e., $w(x)$, $w(y)$, respectively. Fig. 15.26 shows for x, y as 3, 3 in unary format.

The steps for multiplying x and y can be as follows.

1. Write a zero after y.
2. Replace each 1 in x by X, and for each such replacement copy y at the right of original $y0\alpha$. Here α is xy constructed so far, initially, null.
3. When all x's contents are X's, the result of $x \times y$ is available as $\alpha = xy$.

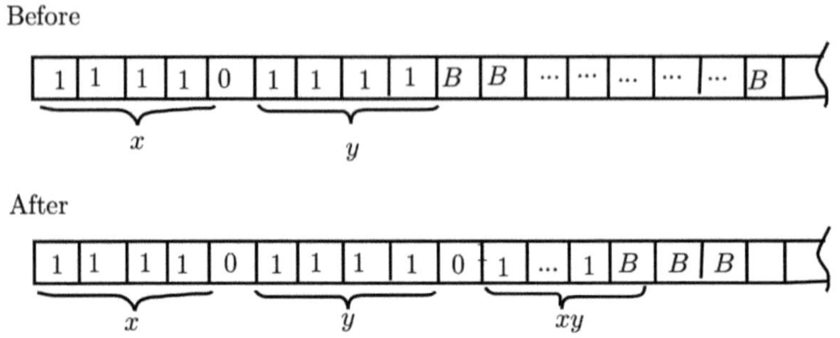

Fig. 15.26 Turing machine to multiply two integers

Solutions of Chapter 10

5 Two-tape TM to recognize language $L = \{ww^R \mid w \in \{a, b\}^*\}$.
While the original string w is on tape 1, perform the following steps:

1. Copy string w on tape 2.
2. Move head 1 to extreme left (rewind), and maintain the head 2 at right.
3. Aligns both heads on opposite, i.e., head 1 to extreme left, head 2 to extreme right.
4. Compare tape 1 and 2, by moving heads in opposite directions (i.e., head 1 to R, and head 2 to L).
5. Accept when done.

The transition diagram in Fig. 15.27 also shows this sequence of steps. The transition $X|S, S$ in tape-2 either stands for $a|a, S$ or for $b|b, S$, which means when tape 1'rewinds', the tape-2 remains stationary, without changing the symbol at the current head position. Similarly, in the "align", when tape-1 head takes a R move, the head of tape-2 remains stationary and the symbol at that position remains unchanged. Note that the above two-tape TM also accepts the odd palindrome language $\{w = w^R \mid w \in \{a, b\}^*\}$.

Time complexity of this TM is total number of transitions in copy, rewind, compare, and align operations. For $|w| = n$, following are the count of transitions:

Align: 1 transition
Copy: n transitions
Align: 1 transition
Rewind: n transitions

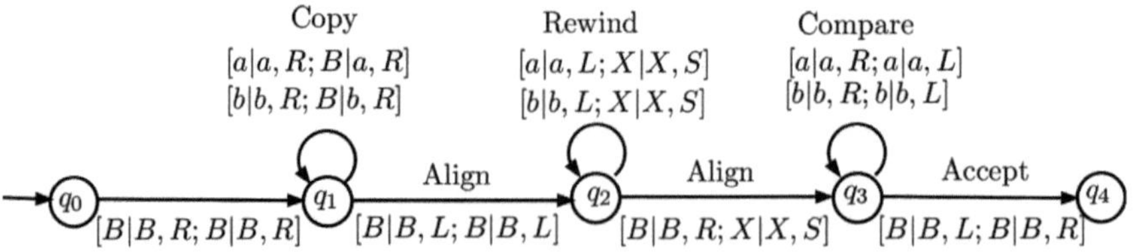

Fig. 15.27 Two-tape TM to recognize language $L = \{ww^R \mid w \in \{a, b\}^*\}$

Align: 1 transition
Compare: n transitions
Align: 1 transition.

Thus, the total transitions are $3n + 4$, and time complexity is $O(n)$. This is a case of polynomial complexity (i.e., P).

7 Construct a 2-tape TM to recognize the language $L = \{ww \mid w \in \{a, b\}^*\}$.

In Fig. 15.28, $X \in \{a, b\}$ represents the symbol on tape-1, and $Y \in \{a, b\}$ represents the symbol on tape 2. In a transition, when same symbol X is shown in both tapes 1 and 2, like in $[X|X, R;\ B|X, R]$, all X are either a or b. Similar is the case with $[X|X, R;\ X|X, R]$ transition at q_4. Initially, the string ww is on tape-1. Following are the steps by TM to recognize the language ww:

1. *Copy:* Copy tape 1 to tape-2; on completion of this both R/W heads are at right most positions of tape 1 and tape 2. This is done by loop in state q_1.
2. *Align:* Move both heads left – head 1 for 2 steps and head 2 for 1 step in every iteration in the loop formed of states q_2, q_3 so that when head 2 has covered half distance on tape 2, the head 1 is to its extreme left.
3. *Align:* ($q_2 \rightarrow q_4$) Move both heads right, each one step. Due to this, Head-1 moves to first symbol of first w of ww, and head-2 moves to 1st symbol of second w.
4. *Compare:* Comparing the two w of input ww in state q_4.
5. Accept in state q_5 when done. □

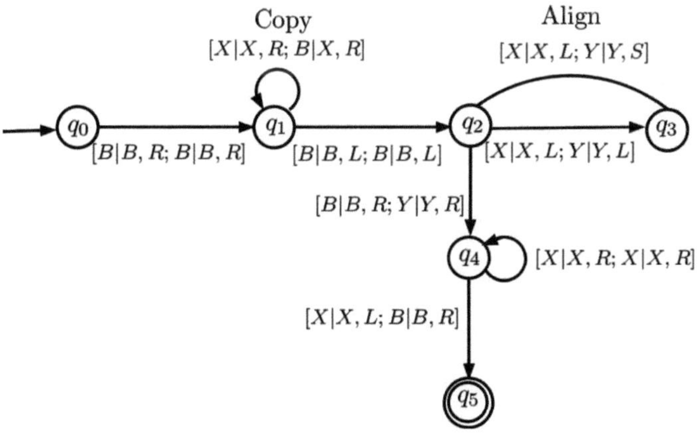

Fig. 15.28 Two-tape TM to recognize $L = \{ww \mid w \in \{a, b\}^*\}$

Solutions of Chapter 11

6 Generate the language for the following matrix grammar:

$G = (V, \Sigma, S, M)$, where $S = S_0$, $\Sigma = \{a, b, c\}$, and $M = \{[S_0 \to S_0 S_1], [S_0 \to aS_0b, S_1 \to cS_1], [S_0 \to ab, S_1 \to c]\}$.

The grammar generates the language $\{a^n b^n c^n \mid n \geq 1\}$.

Note that, in each derivation, the first matrix ($[S_0 \to S_0 S_1]$) has to be applied exactly once. Otherwise, nonterminals cannot be eliminated. We have the following derivation using this matrix grammar.

$$\begin{aligned} S &\Rightarrow S_0 S_1 \\ &\Rightarrow aS_0bS_1 \\ &\Rightarrow aabbS_1 \\ &\Rightarrow aabbcS_1 \\ &\Rightarrow aabbcc \\ &\Rightarrow a^2b^2c^2 \end{aligned}$$

15 Prove that Halting problem is solvable for linear bounded automata.

Proof Our argument here will be based upon the number of possible configurations for an LBA M. Let's assume M has one track (this is allowed because one can use additional tape symbols to simulate tracks as we did with Turing machines), l instructions ($|Q| = l$), an alphabet Γ of tape symbols, and an input tape which holds $|w| = n$ characters. The M has same configuration as a Turing machine and consists of the followings:

1. an instruction (current state),
2. the tape head's position, and
3. the content of the tape.

For example, $w_i q_i w_j$, where current instruction[4] is q_i, head position is first symbol of w_j, and content of tape is $w_i w_j$. We now ask: how many different configurations can there be? It is not too difficult to find out. With $\Gamma \cup V| = m$, symbols and a tape which is $|w| = n$ squares long, we can have only m^n different tapes. The tape head can be on any of the n squares and, we can be executing any of the l instructions. Thus possible different configurations for the LBA M are only,

[4] A state in TM or any automata is in fact an instruction. As the machine runs and goes through the transitions to different states, it moves from instruction to instruction. Effect of executing instructions is changing memory (tape) contents.

Possible patterns of strings × no. of head positions in the strings × number of states
$= m^n \times n \times l$

Let us return to a technique we used to prove the pumping lemma for finite automata. We observe that if the LBA enters the same configuration twice then it will do this again and again, indicating that it is stuck in a loop! The theorem follows from this statement. We only need to simulate and observe the LBA for $n \times m^n \times l$ steps.

If M has not halted within $m^n * n * l$ steps, it must be in a repeating configuration, and therefore looping. We can therefore decide after this number of steps whether or not the input string will be accepted or rejected. The halting problem is solvable for linear bounded automata, as the following is decidable:

$$Halt_{LBA} = \{< M, w >| \; M \text{ is an LBA and } M \text{ halts on } w.\}$$

As linear-bounded automata are recognizers for context-sensitive languages, and every context-sensitive language must be *recursive*. Since, we are able to distinguish the presence of loop (which in TM we cannot !), the halting problem is solvable for LBA.

20 Grammar for the language $\{a^p \mid p \text{ is prime}\}$.

The grammar for primes is as given below:

(1) $S \to SC$ S(1, 2)
(2) $S \to AA$ S(3)
(3) $A \to B$ S(4) (F5)
(4) $C \to D$ S(3) F(7)
(5) $C \to C$ S(6)
(6) $B \to A$ S(6) F(3)
(7) $B \to A$ S(7) F(8)
(8) $D \to A$ S(9) F(10)
(9) $D \to C$ S(9) F(3)
(10) $A \to a$ S(10)

After applying the rule $S \to AA$, the intermediate string is of the form A^2C^{p-2}. For an intermediate string of the form A^nC^{p-n}, the grammar, beginning with rule $A \to B$, tests to see if $p - n$ is a multiple of n. If n does divide $p - n$, the rule $C \to C$ will eventually fail and the grammar will stop without having produced a terminal string. If n does not divide $p - n$, the rule $C \to D$ will fail, rule $D \to A$ will increment n by 1, and $n + 1$ will be tested. If rule $D \to A$ fails, then $n = p$, so that p is a prime, and rule $A \to a$ converts A's to terminal symbols.

24 Ans. A

25 Ans. B

26 Ans. D

27 Ans. D

Solutions of Chapter 12

11 Show that Turing Machine as language enumerator.

The steps of enumerator are as follows:

1. Such machines produce the exhaustive list of string of the language, progressively longer and longer.
2. Enumeration has no input, and its computation continues indefinitely if the language is infinite.
3. For enumeration, a TM of tape $k \geq 2$ is used, tape-1 is output tape, which would hold all the generated strings, separated by #, and other tapes are working tapes.
4. Output tape-1 has: $B\#u_1\#u_2\# \ldots \#u_i\# \ldots$, where $u_i \in L$.
5. Tape head-1 has two types of moves: R, S. Others heads may move R, L, S.

17 Prove that intersection of R and RE languages is RE.

Proof The proof is as follows.

1. Let L_1 and L_2 be languages recognized by Turing machines M_1 and M_2, respectively.
2. Let a new Turing machine M' runs the intersection $L_1 \cap L_2$. The M' simply executes M_1 and M_2 one after the other on the same input w: It first simulates M_1 on w. If M_1 halts by accepting it, M' clears the tape, copies the input word w on the tape and starts simulating M_2. If M_2 also accepts w then M' accepts.
3. Clearly, M' recognizes $L_1 \cap L_2$, and if M_1 and M_2 halt on all inputs then also M' halts on all inputs.

If any of M_1 or M_2 loops, M' also loops, since latter simulates M_1 and M_2. This shows that language of M' is RE. □

19 Show that decidable languages are closed under the operations of *union* and *intersection*.

(a) *Closed on Union*. Let there be two decidable languages L_1 and L_2. Since they are decidable, let L_1 has decider M_1 (Turing machine) and L_2 has decider M_2, such that $L_1 = L(M_1)$ and $L_2 = L(M_2)$. We can prove that the union of these languages, $L_3 = L_1 \cup L_2$, is decidable by showing how we can build a decider M_3 for L_3 using the deciders for L_1 and L_2.

We would build decider for L_3 using a two-tape Turing machine which accepts any string in $L_1 \cup L_2$ as follows. We call tape of M_1 as tape-1 and tape of M_2 as tape-2.

1. Input string w is on tape-1.
2. *copy* input string w from tape-1 to tape-2, so that both tapes now contain w.
3. *run* M_1 on tape-1; if M_1 accepts w, then M_3 accepts; if M_1 rejects w then go to step-4.
4. *run* M_2 on tape-2; if M_2 accepts w, then M_3 accepts; if M_2 rejects w then M_3 rejects.

Since both M_1 and M_2 are deciders (i.e., they always halt) then M_3 is also a decider, it will never loop but halt. Since every multitape TM has an equivalent single tape TM, so we can manipulate the definition above and make it a single tape TM.
(b) *Closed on Intersection*. The intersection is done similarly, but the machine M_3 is defined as follows:

1. Input string w is on tape-1.
2. *copy* input string w to tape 2.
3. *run* M_1 on tape-1; if M_1 accepts w, then go to step-4; if M_1 rejects w then M_3 rejects.
4. *run* M_2 on tape-2: if M_2 accepts w, then M_3 accepts; if M_2 rejects w then M_3 rejects.

25 Show that the diagonal language L_d is recursively enumerable.

Proof We construct an acceptor Turing machine D for the diagonal language L_d that works as follows. On input w_i, D simulates M_i on w_i, and accepts w_i if and only if M_i accepts w_i. So, language of D, $L(D) = L_d$. This shows that L_d is recursively enumerable. □

26 Show that *Universality* of a language of CFG is undecidable. A language is universal if $L = \Sigma^*$.

Proof It appears that we will be able to find a string that a CFG G can generate as well as that G cannot generate. One way for doing this is to generate all strings of G in lexicographic order and then keep checking them through parsing, with increasing length, let time for checking every string is a finite amount of time. Note that this does not have a definite stopping criterion. As we get to longer and longer, strings of a given length n increase exponentially (2^n). Therefore, it cannot be mapped one-to-one with the countable integers $\mathbb{N}$. This shows universality of language $L = \Sigma^*$ is undecidable.

27 Answer (A): I is true because a grammar can be determined as CFG by its structure. II is true because the intersection of two regular languages can be infinite only when both of them are infinite. And, infinity of a language can be decided by having length of accepted string more than count of the number of states.

28 Answer (B)

32 There is a table comprising of all rows as the characteristic vectors $\langle w_{i,j} \rangle$, where $(i, 1)$, ..., (i, j), ... is characteristic vector of ith language. And, corresponding to all these rows, there is one column representing the characteristic vector of all the Turing machines $\langle T_i \rangle$, then "a characteristic vector constructed by complementing the diagonal vector of $\langle w_{i,j} \rangle$ cannot be characteristic vector of any language". Prove this statement.
Ans. This is diagonalization theorem, and the complement is the diagonal language $\overline{L_d}$, which is not a recursively enumerable language. See Theorem 12.20 (Sect. 12.11.2).

Solutions of Chapter 13

11 Find out the membership of a language that is decided in time $t(n) = 7.5n^2 + 100n \log n$.

If a language L is decided in time $t(n) = 7.5n^2 + 100n \log n$, then as per the definition of DTIME, $L \in \mathsf{DTIME}[7.5n^2 + 100n \log n]$. But, there is a constant c so that $cn^2 > 7.5n^2 + 100n \log n$ for all but finitely many inputs. Hence, we can write, $L \in \mathsf{DTIME}[cn^2]$. But, by linear speedup theorem, if there is k-tape Turing machine $(k > 1)$ that decides L in cn^2 time, then there is another k-tape Turing machine, that decides L in n^2 time. so, $L \in \mathsf{DTIME}[n^2]$.

21 If $A \leq_T B$ and B is a regular language, does that imply that A is a regular language?

The answer is NO. For example, define the languages $A = \{0^n 1^n \mid n \geq 0\}$ and $B = \{1\}$, both over the alphabet $\Sigma = \{0, 1\}$. Define the function $f : \Sigma^* \rightarrow \Sigma^*$ as

$$f(w) = \begin{cases} 1 & \text{if } w \in A, \\ 0 & \text{if } w \notin A. \end{cases} \tag{15.5}$$

We note that A is a context-free language, so it is also Turing-decidable. Thus, f is a computable function. Also, $w \in A$ if and only if $f(w) = 1$, which is true if and only if $f(w) \in B$. Hence, $A \leq_T B$. Language A is nonregular, but B is regular since it is finite.

22 Show that $\mathsf{NL} \subseteq \mathsf{P}$.

Proof Let L be a NL, and M be a non-deterministic log-space Turing machine that recognizes L. As shown in expression 13.19 there are $2^{O(s(n))} = n^{O(1)}$ possible configurations for computing $M(x)$, with input $|x| = n$. We show the transitions through a directed graph where vertices are the configurations, and edges are transitions between states determined by the δ. Since the number of configurations is a polynomial function of n, the vertices are also a polynomial function of length of input as well as number of states. Hence, in polynomial time (of n), we can do a depth-first search to see whether there is a path from the initial configuration that ultimately leads to acceptance. This describes a polynomial-time algorithm for deciding L. This proves the theorem.

Solutions of Chapter 14

15 If A be a problem in class NP, then which one of the following is TRUE?
(A) A may be undecidable.
(B) If A is in NP-hard, then it is NP-complete.
(C) There is no polynomial time algorithm for A
(D) If A is in P, then P = NP

Ans. Fig. 14.6 (Sect. 14.5) shows the relation between various standard complexity classes. Since problem A is decidable, so option "A" is false. Option "B" implies that every NP-hard problem is also NP-complete, which is false.

As per Fig. 14.6, every problem of type P is also NP, but not the reverse. So, choice "C" is false. From the same figure, it is clear that the answer is choice "D".

Reference

1. Kenneth K, John R (1965) Algebraic theory of machines. I. Prime decomposition theorem for finite semigroups and machines. Trans Am Math Soci 116:450–464

Index

K. R. Chowdhary, *Theory of Computation*,
https://doi.org/10.1007/978-981-97-6234-7

MIX
Papier aus verantwortungsvollen Quellen
Paper from responsible sources
FSC® C105338

If you have any concerns about our products,
you can contact us on
ProductSafety@springernature.com

In case Publisher is established outside the EU,
the EU authorized representative is:
Springer Nature Customer Service Center GmbH
Europaplatz 3, 69115 Heidelberg, Germany

Printed by Libri Plureos GmbH
in Hamburg, Germany